HEDGEFUNDS

ADVANCES IN FINANCIAL ENGINEERING
Edited by Andrew W. Lo

Lev Dynkin, Anthony Gould, Hay Hyman, Vadim Konstantionvsky, and Bruce Phelps, *Quantitative Management of Bond Portfolios*

Andrew W. Lo, *Hedge Funds: An Analytic Perspective*

For my mother, Julia Yao Lo

Contents

5   Hedge Fund Beta Replication   121

6   A New Measure of Active Investment Management   168

7   Hedge Funds and Systemic Risk   198

8   An Integrated Hedge Fund Investment Process   217

9   Practical Considerations   237

Figures

Color Plates

Acknowledgments

This monograph grew out of a research program on hedge funds that I embarked upon almost a decade ago, and a number of the chapters have been drawn from papers I co-authored with a number of my former students. Where appropriate, I have excerpted and, in some cases, modified passages to suit the current context and composition without detailed citations and quotation marks so as to preserve continuity. However, I wish to acknowledge those sources explicitly here: Section 2.3 is excerpted from Getmansky, Lo, and Mei (2004), Chapter 3 is excerpted from Getmansky, Lo, and Makarov (2004), Chapter 4 is excerpted from Lo, Petrov, and Wierzbicki (2003), Chapter 5 is excerpted from Hasanhodzic and Lo (2007), Chapter 6 is excerpted from Lo (2007), Chapter 7 is excerpted from Chan et al. (2006), Section 9.3 is excerpted from Lo (2004), Section 9.4 is excerpted from Getmansky, Lo, and Mei (2004), Chapter 10 is excerpted from Khandani and Lo (2007), and Chapter 11 is excerpted from Healy and Lo (2009). I thank Nicholas Chan, Mila Getmansky, Shane Haas, Jasmina Hasanhodzic, Alex Healy, Amir Khandani, Igor Makarov, Shauna Mei, Constantin Petrov, and Martin Wierzbicki for allowing me to incorporate those papers in this volume, and for their collaboration over the years. I am particularly indebted to Jasmina Hasanhodzic for updating many of the tables and figures in this volume. Despite the fact that I have been a faculty member at MIT for two decades, I am continually amazed by the quality of students with whom I have had the pleasure and privilege of working.

In fact, I cannot think of a more conducive environment for conducting the kind of research described in this volume than MIT and the Laboratory for Financial Engineering, and I am grateful to this wonderful institution as well as to my colleagues—especially Dimitris Bertsimas, John Cox, Jerry Hausman, the late Franco Modigliani, Whitney Newey, Jun Pan, Tommy Poggio, Steve Ross, Paul Samuelson, Tom Stoker, and Jiang Wang—from whom I learn new things every day. I must also include in this category Bob Merton; although he is no longer at MIT, his wisdom permeates the Sloan School to this day, and my intellectual debt to him has only deepened during the countless lunches to which he has treated me over the years.

I thank Gifford Fong, Mark Kritzman, and the CFA Institute for starting me down the path of writing this monograph through a Research Foundation grant, which led to *The Dynamics of the Hedge Fund Industry*, a precursor to this volume. I am also grateful to Peter Dougherty at Princeton University Press for his enthusiasm in publishing this manuscript and his guidance and friendship over the years, and to Seth Ditchik who took over as editor after Peter was kicked upstairs. And I thank Lucy Day Werts Hobor for shepherding this project through the production process, Carol Dean for copy-editing the manuscript, and Dr. Richard Comfort for preparing the index.

I am also grateful to AlphaSimplex Group, LLC, its investors, and a number of business colleagues for providing a live laboratory for studying and implementing quantitative investment processes. While I had no doubt that academic research could contribute significantly to the business of investment management, I did not expect the business of investment management to yield so many new and interesting academic insights. I have written elsewhere that the hedge fund industry is the Galapagos Islands of the economy because of the remarkable speed and clarity with which evolution occurs in that business, and because of this fact, I believe that a new theory of economic dynamics will eventually emerge from the study of hedge funds. I am grateful to Arnout Eikeboom, Doyne Farmer, Gifford Fong, Jacob Goldfield, Charles Harris, Jim Hodge, Steve Solomon, Jonathan Spring, Andre Stern, Donald Sussman, and Phil Vasan for developing my understanding of the business world.

Finally, I wish to thank my family—Nancy, Derek, and Wesley—for their patience and support during the past few years as I juggled, sometimes imperfectly, the various projects that I undertook, and Barbara Jansen, Svetlana Sussman, and Sara Salem for organizing my life and leveraging my time so effectively. And this book is dedicated to my mother, Julia Yao Lo, who has been a constant source of encouragement and inspiration for me; she is the main reason I ended up in my current profession rather than as an inmate on Riker's Island.

HEDGEFUNDS

1
Introduction

One of the fastest growing sectors of the financial services industry is the *hedge fund* or *alternative-investments* sector, currently estimated at more than $1 trillion in assets worldwide. One of the main reasons for such interest is the performance characteristics of hedge funds—often known as "high-octane" investments: Many hedge funds have yielded double-digit returns for their investors and, in many cases, in a fashion that seems uncorrelated with general market swings and with relatively low volatility. Most hedge funds accomplish this by maintaining both long and short positions in securities—hence the term "hedge" fund—which, in principle, gives investors an opportunity to profit from both positive and negative information while at the same time providing some degree of "market neutrality" because of the simultaneous long and short positions. Long the province of foundations, family offices, and high-net-worth investors, alternative investments are now attracting major institutional investors such as large state and corporate pension funds, insurance companies, and university endowments, and efforts are underway to make hedge fund investments available to individual investors through more traditional mutual fund investment vehicles.

However, many institutional investors are not yet convinced that alternative investments comprise a distinct *asset class*, i.e., a collection of investments with a reasonably homogeneous set of characteristics that are stable over time. Unlike equities, fixed income instruments, and real estate—asset classes each defined by a common set of legal, institutional, and statistical properties—alternative investments is a mongrel categorization that includes private equity, risk arbitrage, commodity futures, convertible bond arbitrage, emerging-market equities, statistical arbitrage, foreign currency speculation, and many other strategies, securities, and styles. Therefore, the need for a set of portfolio analytics and risk management protocols specifically designed for alternative investments has never been more pressing.

Part of the gap between institutional investors and hedge fund managers is due to differences in investment mandate, regulatory oversight, and business culture between the two groups, yielding very different perspectives on what a good investment process should look like. For example, a typical hedge fund manager's perspective can be characterized by the following statements:

- The manager is the best judge of the appropriate risk/reward trade-off of the portfolio and should be given broad discretion in making investment decisions.
- Trading strategies are highly proprietary and therefore must be jealously guarded lest they be reverse-engineered and copied by others.
- Return is the ultimate and, in most cases, the only objective.
- Risk management is not central to the success of a hedge fund.
- Regulatory constraints and compliance issues are generally a drag on performance; the whole point of a hedge fund is to avoid these issues.
- There is little intellectual property involved in the fund; the general partner *is* the fund.[1]

Contrast these statements with the following characterization of a typical institutional investor:

- As fiduciaries, institutions need to understand the investment process before committing to it.
- Institutions must fully understand the risk exposures of each manager and, on occasion, may have to circumscribe the manager's strategies to be consistent with the institution's overall investment objectives and constraints.
- Performance is not measured solely by return but also includes other factors such as risk adjustments, tracking error relative to a benchmark, and peer group comparisons.
- Risk management and risk transparency are essential.
- Institutions operate in a highly regulated environment and must comply with a number of federal and state laws governing the rights, responsibilities, and liabilities of pension plan sponsors and other fiduciaries.
- Institutions desire structure, stability, and consistency in a well-defined investment process that is institutionalized—not dependent on any single individual.

---

[1] Of course, many experts in intellectual property law would certainly classify trading strategies, algorithms, and their software manifestations as intellectual property which, in some cases, are patentable. However, most hedge fund managers today (and, therefore, most investors) have not elected to protect such intellectual property through patents but have chosen instead to keep them as "trade secrets," purposely limiting access to these ideas even within their own organizations. As a result, the departure of key personnel from a hedge fund often causes the demise of the fund.

Now, of course, these are rather broad-brush caricatures of the two groups, made extreme for clarity, but they do capture the essence of the existing gulf between hedge fund managers and institutional investors. However, despite these differences, hedge fund managers and institutional investors clearly have much to gain from a better understanding of each other's perspectives, and they do share the common goal of generating superior investment performance for their clients. One of the purposes of this monograph is to help create more common ground between hedge fund managers and investors through new quantitative models and methods for gauging the risks and rewards of alternative investments.

This might seem to be more straightforward a task than it is because of the enormous body of literature on investments and quantitative portfolio management. However, several recent empirical studies have cast some doubt on the applicability of standard methods for assessing the risks and returns of hedge funds, concluding that they can often be quite misleading. For example, Asness, Krail, and Liew (2001) show that in some cases where hedge funds purport to be market neutral (namely, funds with relatively small market betas), including both contemporaneous and lagged market returns as regressors and summing the coefficients yields significantly higher market exposure. Getmansky, Lo, and Makarov (2004) argue that this is due to significant serial correlation in the returns of certain hedge funds, which is likely the result of illiquidity and smoothed returns. Such correlation can yield substantial biases in the variances, betas, Sharpe ratios, and other performance statistics. For example, in deriving statistical estimators for Sharpe ratios of a sample of mutual funds and hedge funds, Lo (2002) shows that the correct method for computing annual Sharpe ratios based on monthly means and standard deviations can yield point estimates that differ from the naive Sharpe ratio estimator by as much as 70%.

These empirical facts suggest that hedge funds and other alternative investments have unique properties, requiring new tools to properly characterize their risks and expected returns. In this monograph, we describe some of these unique properties and propose several new quantitative measures for modeling them.

One of the justifications for the unusually rich fee structures that characterize hedge fund investments is the fact that these funds employ active strategies involving highly skilled portfolio managers. Moreover, it is common wisdom that the most talented managers are first drawn to the hedge fund industry because the absence of regulatory constraints enables them to make the most of their investment acumen. With the freedom to trade as much or as little as they like on any given day, to go long or short any number of securities and with varying degrees of leverage, and to change investment strategies at a moment's notice, hedge fund managers enjoy enormous flexibility and discretion in pursuing performance. But dynamic investment strategies imply dynamic risk exposures, and while modern financial economics has much to say about the risk of *static* investments—the market beta is sufficient in this case—there is currently no single measure of the risks of a dynamic investment strategy.[2]

These challenges have important implications for both managers and investors since both parties seek to manage the risk/reward trade-offs of their investments. Consider, for example, the now-standard approach to constructing an optimal portfolio in the mean-variance sense:

$$\max_{\{\omega_i\}} E[U(W_1)] \tag{1.1}$$

$$\text{subject to} \qquad W_1 = W_0(1 + R_p), \tag{1.2a}$$

$$R_p \equiv \sum_{i=1}^{n} \omega_i R_i, \qquad 1 = \sum_{i=1}^{n} \omega_i, \tag{1.2b}$$

where R_i is the return of security i between this period and the next, W_1 is the individual's next period's wealth (which is determined by the product of $\{R_i\}$ and the portfolio weights $\{\omega_i\}$), and $U(\cdot)$ is the individual's utility function. By assuming that $U(\cdot)$ is quadratic or by assuming that individual security returns R_i are normally distributed random variables, it can be shown that maximizing the individual's expected utility is tantamount to constructing a mean-variance optimal portfolio ω^*.[3]

It is one of the great lessons of modern finance that mean-variance optimization yields benefits through diversification, the ability to lower volatility for a given level of expected return by combining securities that are not perfectly correlated. But what if the securities are hedge funds, and what if their correlations change over time, as hedge funds tend to do (Section 1.2)?[4] Table 1.1 shows that for the two-asset case with fixed means of 5% and 30%, respectively, and fixed standard deviations of 20% and 30%, respectively, as the correlation ρ between the two assets varies from -90% to 90%, the optimal portfolio weights—and the properties of the optimal portfolio—change dramatically. For example, with a -30% correlation between the two funds, the optimal portfolio holds 38.6% in the first fund and 61.4% in the second, yielding a Sharpe ratio of 1.01. But if the correlation changes to 10%, the optimal weights change to 5.2% in the first fund and 94.8% in the second, despite the fact that the Sharpe ratio of the new

---

[2] For this reason, hedge fund track records are often summarized with multiple statistics, e.g., mean, standard deviation, Sharpe ratio, market beta, Sortino ratio, maximum drawdown, and worst month.

[3] See, for example, Ingersoll (1987).

[4] Several authors have considered mean-variance optimization techniques for determining hedge fund allocations, with varying degrees of success and skepticism. See, in particular, Amenc and Martinelli (2002), Amin and Kat (2003c), Terhaar, Staub, and Singer (2003), and Cremers, Kritzman, and Page (2004).

Table 1.1.

Mean-Variance Optimal Portfolios for the Two-Asset Case*

ρ	$E[R^*]$	$SD[R^*]$	*Sharpe*	ω_1^*	ω_2^*
-90	15.5	5.5	2.36	58.1	41.9
-80	16.0	8.0	1.70	55.9	44.1
-70	16.7	10.0	1.41	53.4	46.6
-60	17.4	11.9	1.25	50.5	49.5
-50	18.2	13.8	1.14	47.2	52.8
-40	19.2	15.7	1.06	43.3	56.7
-30	20.3	17.7	1.01	38.6	61.4
-20	21.8	19.9	0.97	32.9	67.1
-10	23.5	22.3	0.94	25.9	74.1
0	25.8	25.1	0.93	17.0	83.0
10	28.7	28.6	0.92	5.2	94.8
20	32.7	32.9	0.92	-10.9	110.9
30	38.6	38.8	0.93	-34.4	134.4
40	48.0	47.7	0.95	-71.9	171.9
50	65.3	63.2	0.99	-141.2	241.2
60	108.1	99.6	1.06	-312.2	412.2
70	387.7	329.9	1.17	-1430.8	1530.8
80[†]	-208.0	-154.0	1.37	952.2	-852.2
90[†]	-76.8	-42.9	1.85	427.1	-327.1

* Mean-variance optimal portfolio weights for the two-asset case $(\mu_1, \sigma_1) = (5\%, 20\%)$, $(\mu_2, \sigma_2) = (30\%, 30\%)$, and $R_f = 2.5\%$, with fixed means and variances, and correlations ranging from -90% to 90%.

[†] These correlations imply non-positive-definite covariance matrices for the two assets.

portfolio, 0.92, is virtually identical to the previous portfolio's Sharpe ratio. The mean-variance-efficient frontiers are plotted in Figure 1.1 for various correlations between the two funds, and it is apparent that the optimal portfolio depends heavily on the correlation structure of the underlying assets. Because of the dynamic nature of hedge fund strategies, their correlations are particularly unstable over time and over varying market conditions, as we shall see in Section 1.2, and swings from -30% to 30% are not unusual.

Table 1.1 shows that as the correlation between the two assets increases, the optimal weight for asset 1 eventually becomes negative, which makes intuitive sense from a hedging perspective even if it is unrealistic for hedge fund investments and other assets that cannot be shorted. Note that for correlations of 80% and greater, the optimization approach does not yield a well-defined solution because a mean-variance-efficient tangency portfolio does not exist for the parameter values we hypothesized for the two assets. However, numerical

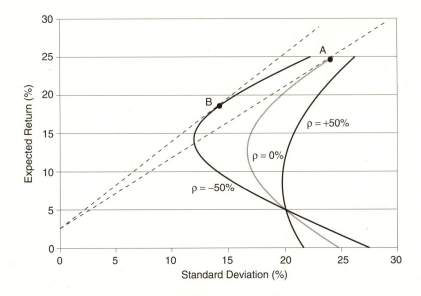

Figure 1.1. *Mean-variance efficient frontiers for the two-asset case. Parameters* $(\mu_1, \sigma_1) =$ *(5%, 20%),* $(\mu_2, \sigma_2) = (30\%, 30\%)$, *and correlation* $\rho = -50\%, 0\%, 50\%$.

optimization procedures may still yield a specific portfolio for this case (e.g., a portfolio on the lower branch of the mean-variance parabola) even if it is not optimal. This example underscores the importance of modeling means, standard deviations, and correlations in a consistent manner when accounting for changes in market conditions and statistical regimes; otherwise, degenerate or nonsensical "solutions" may arise.

To illustrate the challenges and opportunities in modeling the risk exposures of hedge funds, we provide three extended examples in this chapter. In Section 1.1, we present a hypothetical hedge fund strategy that yields remarkable returns with seemingly little risk; yet a closer examination reveals a different story. In Section 1.2, we show that correlations and market beta are sometimes incomplete measures of risk exposure for hedge funds, and that such measures can change over time, in some cases quite rapidly and without warning. And in Section 1.3, we describe one of the most prominent empirical features of the returns of many hedge funds—large positive serial correlation—and argue that serial correlation can be a very useful proxy for liquidity risk. These examples will provide an introduction to the more involved quantitative analysis in Chapters 3–8 and serve as motivation for an analytical approach to alternative investments. We conclude by presenting a brief review of the burgeoning hedge fund literature in Section 1.4.

Table 1.2.

Capital Decimation Partners, L. P., Performance Summary (January 1992 to
December 1999)*

	S&P 500	*CDP*
Monthly mean	1.4%	3.6%
Monthly SD	3.6%	5.8%
Minimum month	−8.9%	−18.3%
Maximum month	14.0%	27.0%
Annual Sharpe ratio	1.39	2.15
No. of negative months	36	6
Correlation to S&P 500	100%	61%
Growth of $1 since inception	$4	$26

* Performance summary of a simulated short-put-option strategy consisting of short-selling out-of-the-money S&P 500 put options with strikes approximately 7% out of the money and with maturities less than or equal to 3 months.

1.1 Tail Risk

Consider the 8-year track record of a hypothetical hedge fund, Capital Decimation Partners, LP. (CDP), summarized in Table 1.2. This track record was obtained by applying a specific investment strategy, to be revealed below, to actual market prices from January 1992 to December 1999. Before discussing the particular strategy that generated these results, consider its overall performance: an average monthly return of 3.6% versus 1.4% for the S&P 500 during the same period; a total return of 2,560% over the 8-year period versus 367% for the S&P 500; a Sharpe ratio of 2.15 versus 1.39 for the S&P 500; and only 6 negative monthly returns out of 96 versus 36 out of 96 for the S&P 500. In fact, the monthly performance history—displayed in Table 1.3—shows that, as with many other hedge funds, the worst months for this fund were August and September of 1998. Yet October and November of 1998 were the fund's two best months, and for 1998 as a whole the fund was up 87.3% versus 24.5% for the S&P 500! By all accounts, this is an enormously successful hedge fund with a track record that would be the envy of most managers.[5] What is its secret?

The investment strategy summarized in Tables 1.2 and 1.3 consists of shorting out-of-the-money S&P 500 put options on each monthly expiration date for maturities less than or equal to 3 months and with strikes approximately 7% out of the money. According to Lo (2001), the number of contracts sold each month is determined by the combination of: 丬) Chicago Board, Options Exchange

---

[5] In fact, as a mental exercise to check your own risk preferences, take a hard look at the monthly returns in Table 1.3 and ask yourself whether you would invest in such a fund.

Table 1.3.
Capital Decimation Partners, L.P., Monthly Performance History (January 1992 to December 1999)*

Month	1992		1993		1994		1995		1996		1997		1998		1999	
	SPX	CDP	SPX	CDP	SPX	CDP	SPX	CDP	SPX	CDP	SPX	CDP	SPX	CDP	SPX	CDP
Jan	8.2	8.1	-1.2	1.8	1.8	2.3	1.3	3.7	-0.7	1.0	3.6	4.4	1.6	15.3	5.5	10.1
Feb	-1.8	4.8	-0.4	1.0	-1.5	0.7	3.9	0.7	5.9	1.2	3.3	6.0	7.6	11.7	-0.3	16.6
Mar	0.0	2.3	3.7	3.6	0.7	2.2	2.7	1.9	-1.0	0.6	-2.2	3.0	6.3	6.7	4.8	10.0
Apr	1.2	3.4	-0.3	1.6	-5.3	-0.1	2.6	2.4	0.6	3.0	-2.3	2.8	2.1	3.5	1.5	7.2
May	-1.4	1.4	-0.7	1.3	2.0	5.5	2.1	1.6	3.7	4.0	8.3	5.7	-1.2	5.8	0.9	7.2
Jun	-1.6	0.6	-0.5	1.7	0.8	1.5	5.0	1.8	-0.3	2.0	8.3	4.9	-0.7	3.9	0.9	8.6
Jul	3.0	2.0	0.5	1.9	-0.9	0.4	1.5	1.6	-4.2	0.3	1.8	5.5	7.8	7.5	5.7	6.1
Aug	-0.2	1.8	2.3	1.4	2.1	2.9	1.0	1.2	4.1	3.2	-1.6	2.6	-8.9	-18.3	-5.8	-3.1
Sep	1.9	2.1	0.6	0.8	1.6	0.8	4.3	1.3	3.3	3.4	5.5	11.5	-5.7	-16.2	-0.1	8.3
Oct	-2.6	-3.0	2.3	3.0	-1.3	0.9	0.3	1.1	3.5	2.2	-0.7	5.6	3.6	27.0	-6.6	-10.7
Nov	3.6	8.5	-1.5	0.6	-0.7	2.7	2.6	1.4	3.8	3.0	2.0	4.6	10.1	22.8	14.0	14.5
Dec	3.4	1.3	0.8	2.9	-0.6	10.0	2.7	1.5	1.5	2.0	-1.7	6.7	1.3	4.3	-0.1	2.4
Year	14.0	38.2	5.7	23.7	-1.6	33.6	34.3	22.1	21.5	28.9	26.4	84.8	24.5	87.3	20.6	105.7

* Monthly returns of a simulated short-put-option strategy consisting of short-selling out-of-the-money S&P 500 (SPX) put options with strikes approximately 7% out of the money and with maturities less than or equal to 3 months.

Date	Index	Action	Qty	Strike	Price	Expiry	Amount	Margin			Return
19 Jun 1992	403.67	Expired	340	385	$0.000	Jun 92	$0	$51,000			
	403.67	Mark to Market	2,200	380	$1.125	Jul 92	$7,866,210	$27,500	$12,223,475	$7,363,539	0.6%
						Total Margin	$7,866,210				
17 Jul 1992	415.62	Expired	2,200	380	$0.000	Jul 92	$0	$247,500			
	415.62	New	2,700	385	$1.813	Sep 92	$8,075,835		$12,470,975	$7,512,636	2.0%
						Total Margin	$8,075,835				
21 Aug 1992	414.85	Mark to Market	2,700	385	$1.000	Sep 92	$8,471,925	$219,375	$12,690,350	$7,644,789	1.8%
						Total Margin	$8,471,925				
18 Sep 1992	422.92	Expired	2,700	385	$0.000	Sep 92	$0	$270,000			
	422.92	New	2,370	400	$5.375	Dec 92	$8,328,891		$12,960,350	$7,807,440	2.1%
						Total Margin	$8,328,891				
16 Oct 1992	411.73	Mark to Market	2,370	400	$7.000	Dec 92	$10,197,992	-$385,125			
	411.73	Liquidate	2,370	400	$7.000	Dec 92	$0	$0			
	411.73	New	1,761	400	$7.000	Dec 92	$7,577,494.95		$12,575,225	$7,575,437	-3.0%
						Total Margin	$7,577,495				
20 Nov 1992	426.65	Mark to Market	1,761	400	$0.938	Dec 92	$6,411,801	$1,067,606			
	426.65	New	496	400	$0.938	Dec 92	$1,805,936		$13,642,831	$8,218,573	8.5%
						Total Margin	$8,217,737				
18 Dec 1992	441.20	Expired	1,873	400	$0.000	Dec 92	$0	$175,594	$13,818,425	$8,324,352	1.3%

1992 Total Return: 38.2%

* Simulated positions and profit/loss statement for 1992 for a trading strategy that consists of shorting out-of-the-money put options on the S&P 500 once a month.

Table 1.5.
Capital Decimation Partners II, L.P., Weekly Positions in XYZ*

Week t	P_t ($)	Position (no. of shares)	Value ($)	Financing ($)
0	40.000	7,057	282,281	−296,974
1	39.875	7,240	288,712	−304,585
2	40.250	5,850	235,456	−248,918
3	36.500	33,013	1,204,981	−1,240,629
4	36.875	27,128	1,000,356	−1,024,865
5	36.500	31,510	1,150,101	−1,185,809
6	37.000	24,320	899,841	−920,981
7	39.875	5,843	232,970	−185,111
8	39.875	5,621	224,153	−176,479
9	40.125	4,762	191,062	−142,159
10	39.500	6,280	248,065	−202,280
11	41.250	2,441	100,711	−44,138
12	40.625	3,230	131,205	−76,202
13	39.875	4,572	182,300	−129,796
14	39.375	5,690	224,035	−173,947
15	39.625	4,774	189,170	−137,834
16	39.750	4,267	169,609	−117,814
17	39.250	5,333	209,312	−159,768
18	39.500	4,447	175,657	−124,940
19	39.750	3,692	146,777	−95,073
20	39.750	3,510	139,526	−87,917
21	39.875	3,106	123,832	−71,872
22	39.625	3,392	134,408	−83,296
23	39.875	2,783	110,986	−59,109
24	40.000	2,445	97,782	−45,617
25	40.125	2,140	85,870	−33,445

* Simulated weekly positions in XYZ for a particular trading strategy over a 6-month period.

Shorting deep out-of-the-money puts is a well-known artifice employed by unscrupulous hedge fund managers to build an impressive track record quickly, and most sophisticated investors are able to avoid such chicanery. However, imagine an investor presented with a position report such as Table 1.5, but for 500 securities, not just 1, as well as a corresponding track record that is likely to be even more impressive than that of Capital Decimation Partners, L.P.[8] Without additional analysis that explicitly accounts for the dynamic aspects of the trading

[8] A portfolio of options is worth more than an option on the portfolio, hence shorting 500 puts on the individual stocks that constitute the SPX yields substantially higher premiums than shorting puts on the index.

strategy described in Table 1.5, it is difficult for an investor to fully appreciate the risks inherent in such a fund.

In particular, static methods such as traditional mean-variance analysis cannot capture the risks of dynamic trading strategies such as those of Capital Decimation Partners (note the impressive Sharpe ratio in Table 1.2). In the case of the strategy of shorting out-of the-money put options on the S&P 500, returns are positive most of the time and losses are infrequent, but when they occur, they are extreme. This is a very specific type of risk signature that is not well summarized by static measures such as standard deviation. In fact, the estimated standard deviations of such strategies tend to be rather low, hence a naive application of mean-variance analysis such as risk budgeting—an increasingly popular method used by institutions to make allocations based on risk units—can lead to unusually large allocations to funds like Capital Decimation Partners. The fact that total position transparency does not imply risk transparency is further cause for concern.

This is not to say that the risks of shorting out-of-the-money puts are inappropriate for all investors—indeed, the thriving catastrophe reinsurance industry makes a market in precisely this type of risk, often called *tail risk*. However, such insurers do so with full knowledge of the loss profile and probabilities for each type of catastrophe, and they set their capital reserves and risk budgets accordingly. The same should hold true for institutional investors in hedge funds, but the standard tools and lexicon of the industry currently provide only an incomplete characterization of such risks. The need for a new set of dynamic risk analytics specifically targeted for hedge fund investments is clear.

1.2 Nonlinear Risks

One of the most compelling reasons for investing in hedge funds is that their returns seem relatively uncorrelated with market indexes such as the S&P 500, and modern portfolio theory has convinced even the most hardened skeptic of the benefits of diversification. For example, Table 1.6 reports the correlation matrix for the returns of the Credit Suisse/Tremont (CS/Tremont) hedge fund–indexes, where each index represents a particular hedge fund *style* such as currencies, emerging markets, relative value and so on. The last four rows report the correlations of all these hedge fund indexes with the returns of more traditional investments: the S&P 500 and indexes for small-cap equities, long-term government bonds, and long-term corporate bonds. These correlations show that many hedge fund styles have low or, in some cases, negative correlation with broad-based market indexes and also exhibit a great deal of heterogeneity, ranging from −71.9% (between Long/Short Equity and Dedicated Shortsellers) to 92.9% (between Event Driven and Distressed).

Table 1.6.

Correlation Matrix for CS/Tremont Hedge Fund Index Returns (January 1994 to July 2007)*

Index	Hedge Fund Index	Convertible Arbitrage	Dedicated Short Bias	Emerging Markets	Equity Market Neutral	Event Driven	Fixed Income Arbitrage	Global Macro	Long/Short Equity
Hedge Fund Index	100.0	41.1	-48.8	65.2	33.3	67.4	44.2	85.4	79.3
Convertible Arbitrage	41.1	100.0	-25.7	30.1	33.9	56.5	53.7	29.1	28.7
Dedicated Short Bias	-48.8	-25.7	100.0	-54.5	-31.8	-62.6	-9.9	-13.5	-71.9
Emerging Markets	65.2	30.1	-54.5	100.0	22.1	67.2	27.1	41.5	59.7
Equity Market Neutral	33.3	33.9	-31.8	22.1	100.0	35.1	13.1	21.9	34.8
Event Driven	67.4	56.5	-62.6	67.2	35.1	100.0	38.3	37.9	66.7
Fixed Income Arbitrage	44.2	53.7	-9.9	27.1	13.1	38.3	100.0	44.2	21.7
Global Macro	85.4	29.1	-13.5	41.5	21.9	37.9	44.2	100.0	43.0
Long/Short Equity	79.3	28.7	-71.9	59.7	34.8	66.7	21.7	43.0	100.0
Managed Futures	16.1	-11.2	8.6	-6.9	12.4	-11.3	-3.9	24.7	3.4
Multi-Strategy	23.0	39.8	-12.3	2.6	23.1	24.6	30.2	14.3	22.1
Event Driven Multi-Strategy	68.6	56.4	-54.0	66.7	32.0	93.5	40.8	41.9	64.5
Distressed	58.6	49.5	-62.0	58.9	33.4	92.9	32.2	31.4	59.0
Risk Arbitrage	39.8	40.2	-49.8	42.2	30.7	66.0	15.0	13.9	51.3
Large Company Stocks	48.6	14.1	-75.6	48.2	36.5	56.1	3.4	23.5	59.2
Small Company Stocks	57.7	27.6	-78.4	54.9	24.2	65.4	12.4	23.3	76.4
Long-Term Corporate Bonds	18.4	7.6	-0.9	1.4	7.2	5.6	11.9	23.7	10.6
Long-Term Government Bonds	11.7	2.7	10.9	-8.9	4.4	-8.1	8.3	21.4	2.4

Table 1.6.
(*continued*)

Index	Managed Futures	Multi-Strategy	Event Driven Multi-Strategy	Distressed	Risk Arbitrage	Large Stocks	Small Stocks	Long-Term Corporate Bonds	Long-Term Government Bonds
Hedge Fund Index	16.1	23.0	68.6	58.6	39.8	48.6	57.7	18.4	11.7
Convertible Arbitrage	-11.2	39.8	56.4	49.5	40.2	14.1	27.6	7.6	2.7
Dedicated Short Bias	8.6	-12.3	-54.0	-62.0	-49.8	-75.6	-78.4	-0.9	10.9
Emerging Markets	-6.9	2.6	66.7	58.9	42.2	48.2	54.9	1.4	-8.9
Equity Market Neutral	12.4	23.1	32.0	33.4	30.7	36.5	24.2	7.2	4.4
Event Driven	-11.3	24.6	93.5	92.9	66.0	56.1	65.4	5.6	-8.1
Fixed Income Arbitrage	-3.9	30.2	40.8	32.2	15.0	3.4	12.4	11.9	8.3
Global Macro	24.7	14.3	41.9	31.4	13.9	23.5	23.3	23.7	21.4
Long/Short Equity	3.4	22.1	64.5	59.0	51.3	59.2	76.4	10.6	2.4
Managed Futures	100.0	6.8	-12.7	-8.0	-13.7	-13.8	-10.6	18.1	24.0
Multi-Strategy	6.8	100.0	28.7	17.0	12.0	10.2	24.0	2.8	-1.8
Event Driven Multi-Strategy	-12.7	28.7	100.0	74.3	63.0	48.9	62.0	1.6	-9.8
Distressed	-8.0	17.0	74.3	100.0	55.0	54.8	59.9	9.3	-4.7
Risk Arbitrage	-13.7	12.0	63.0	55.0	100.0	44.5	56.7	1.8	-8.9
Large Company Stocks	-13.8	10.2	48.9	54.8	44.5	100.0	61.2	8.0	-5.1
Small Company Stocks	-10.6	24.0	62.0	59.9	56.7	61.2	100.0	-0.1	-14.0
Long-Term Corporate Bonds	18.1	2.8	1.6	9.3	1.8	8.0	-0.1	100.0	94.3
Long-Term Government Bonds	24.0	-1.8	-9.8	-4.7	-8.9	-5.1	-14.0	94.3	100.0

* All values are percentages and are based on monthly data. Multi-Strategy index data are for the period from April 1994 to July 2007, while the data for Large Company Stocks, Small Company Stocks, Long-Term Corporate Bonds, and Long-Term Government Bonds are for the period from January 1994 to December 2006.

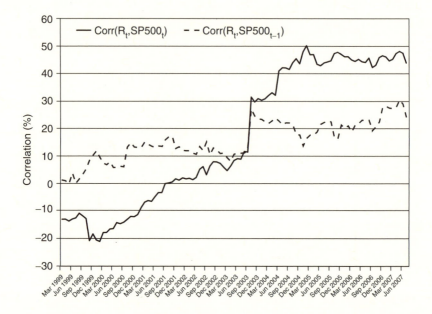

Figure 1.2. *Sixty-month rolling correlations between CS/Tremont Multi-Strategy index returns and the contemporaneous and lagged returns of the S&P 500 (March 1999 to July 2007). Under the null hypothesis of no correlation, the approximate standard error of the correlation coefficient is $1/\sqrt{60} = 13\%$; hence the differences between the beginning-of-sample and end-of-sample correlations are statistically significant at the 1% level.*

However, correlations can change over time. For example, consider a rolling 60-month correlation between the CS/Tremont Multi-Strategy index and the S&P 500 from March 1999 to July 2007, plotted in Figure 1.2. At the start of the sample in March 1999, the correlation is −13.0%, drops to −17.8% a year later, and increases to 30.3% by January 2004. Although such changes in rolling correlation estimates are partly attributable to estimation errors,[9] in this case another possible explanation for the positive trend in correlation is the enormous inflow of capital into Multi-strategy funds and Funds of Funds over the past 5 years. As assets under management increase, it becomes progressively more difficult for fund managers to implement strategies that are truly uncorrelated with broad-based market indexes like the S&P 500. Moreover, Figure 1.2 shows that the correlation between the Multi-Strategy index return and the lagged S&P 500 return has also increased in the past year, indicating an increase in the illiquidity exposure

---

[9] Under the null hypothesis of no correlation, the approximate standard error of the correlation coefficient is $1/\sqrt{60} = 13\%$.

Table 1.7.

Correlation Matrix for Seven CS/Tremont Hedge Fund Index Returns (April 1994 to July 2007)*

	Hedge Fund Index	Convertible Arbitrage	Emerging Markets	Equity Market Neutral	Distressed	Long/Short Equity	Multi-Strategy
April 1994 to December 1999							
Hedge Fund Index	100.0	52.8	65.5	38.3	58.1	70.9	8.8
Convertible Arbitrage	52.8	100.0	45.7	31.3	62.1	37.9	29.5
Emerging Markets	65.5	45.7	100.0	26.8	60.1	59.2	-11.7
Equity Market Neutral	38.3	31.3	26.8	100.0	48.0	44.9	17.4
Distressed	58.1	62.1	60.1	48.0	100.0	64.3	1.5
Long/Short Equity	70.9	37.9	59.2	44.9	64.3	100.0	4.4
Multi-Strategy	8.8	29.5	-11.7	17.4	1.5	4.4	100.0
January 2000 to July 2007							
Hedge Fund Index	100.0	23.7	74.2	11.8	57.3	97.0	60.5
Convertible Arbitrage	23.7	100.0	3.0	39.2	32.7	16.9	57.7
Emerging Markets	74.2	3.0	100.0	18.9	52.8	72.5	45.4
Equity Market Neutral	11.8	39.2	18.9	100.0	0.8	9.0	36.9
Distressed	57.3	32.7	52.8	0.8	100.0	47.9	53.5
Long/Short Equity	97.0	16.9	72.5	9.0	47.9	100.0	56.1
Multi-Strategy	60.5	57.7	45.4	36.9	53.5	56.1	100.0
Difference Between Two Correlation Matrices							
Hedge Fund Index	0.0	29.0	-8.7	26.5	0.8	-26.1	-51.7
Convertible Arbitrage	29.0	0.0	42.7	-7.9	29.4	21.0	-28.2
Emerging Markets	-8.7	42.7	0.0	7.9	7.2	-13.4	-57.1
Equity Market Neutral	26.5	-7.9	7.9	0.0	47.2	36.0	-19.4
Distressed	0.8	29.4	7.2	47.2	0.0	16.4	-52.0
Long/Short Equity	-26.1	21.0	-13.4	36.0	16.4	0.0	-51.7
Multi-Strategy	-51.7	-28.2	-57.1	-19.4	-52.0	-51.7	0.0

* All values are percentages and are based on monthly data.

of this investment style (Getmansky, Lo, and Makarov, 2004, and Chapter 3). This is also consistent with large inflows of capital into the hedge fund sector.

Correlations between hedge fund style categories can also shift over time, as Table 1.7 illustrates. Over the sample period from April 1994 to July 2007, the correlation between the Convertible Arbitrage and Emerging Market indexes is 30.1%, but Table 1.7 shows that during the first half of the sample (April 1994 to December 1999) this correlation is 45.7% and during the second half (January 2000 to July 2007) it is 3.0%. The third panel in Table 1.7, which reports the difference of the correlation matrices from the two subperiods, suggests that hedge fund–index correlations are not very stable over time.

A graph of the 60-month rolling correlation between the Convertible Arbitrage and the Emerging Market indexes from January 1999 to July 2007 provides a clue as to the source of this nonstationarity: Figure 1.3 shows a sharp drop in the correlation during the month of September 2003. This is the first month for which the August 1998 data point—the start of the Long Term Capital Management (LTCM) event—is not included in the 60-month rolling window. During this period, the default in Russian government debt triggered a global "flight to quality" that apparently changed many correlations from zero to one over the course of just a few days, and Table 1.8 shows that in August 1998 the returns for the Convertible Arbitrage and Emerging Market indexes were −4.64% and −23.03, respectively. In fact, 10 out of the 13 style category indexes yielded negative returns in August 1998, many of which were extreme outliers relative to the entire sample period; hence rolling windows containing this month can yield dramatically different correlations than those without it.

In the physical and natural sciences, sudden changes from low correlation to high correlation are examples of *phase-locking behavior*, situations in which otherwise uncorrelated actions suddenly become synchronized.[10] The fact that market conditions can create phase-locking behavior is certainly not new—market crashes have been with us since the beginning of organized financial markets—but prior to 1998, few hedge fund investors and managers incorporated this possibility into their investment processes in any systematic fashion.

One way to capture phase-locking effects is to estimate a risk model for returns in which such events are explicitly allowed. For example, suppose returns are generated by the following two-factor model:

$$R_{it} = \alpha_i + \beta_i \Lambda_t + I_t Z_t + \epsilon_{it} \tag{1.3}$$

---

[10] One of the most striking examples of phase-locking behavior is the automatic synchronization of the flickering of Southeast Asian fireflies. See Strogatz (1994) for a description of this remarkable phenomenon as well as an excellent review of phase-locking behavior in biological systems.

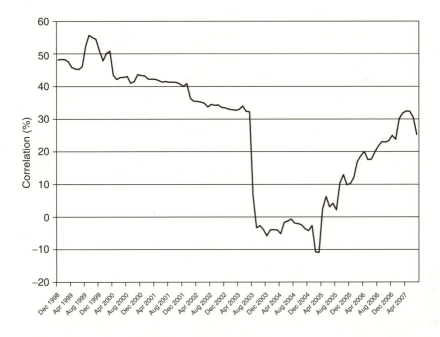

Figure 1.3. *Sixty-month rolling correlations between CS/Tremont Convertible Arbitrage and Emerging Market index returns (January 1999 to July 2007). The sharp decline in September 2003 is due to the fact that this is the first month in which the August 1998 observation is dropped from the 60-month rolling window.*

Assume that Λ_t, I_t, Z_t, and ϵ_{it} are mutually independently and identically distributed (IID) with the following moments:

$$
\begin{aligned}
\mathrm{E}[\Lambda_t] &= \mu_\lambda, & \mathrm{Var}[\Lambda_t] &= \sigma_\lambda^2, \\
\mathrm{E}[Z_t] &= 0, & \mathrm{Var}[Z_t] &= \sigma_z^2, \\
\mathrm{E}[\epsilon_{it}] &= 0, & \mathrm{Var}[\epsilon_{it}] &= \sigma_{\epsilon_i}^2,
\end{aligned}
\tag{1.4}
$$

and let the phase-locking event indicator I_t be defined by

$$
I_t = \begin{cases} 1 & \text{with probability } p, \\ 0 & \text{with probability } 1 - p. \end{cases}
\tag{1.5}
$$

According to (1.3), expected returns are the sum of three components: the fund's alpha, α_i a "market" component Λ_t, to which each fund has its own individual sensitivity β_i, and a phase-locking component that is identical across all funds at all times, taking only one of two possible values, either 0 (with probability p) or Z_t (with probability $1 - p$). If we assume that p is small, say 0.001, then most of the time the expected returns of fund i are determined by $\alpha_i + \beta_i \Lambda_t$, but every

Table 1.8.

CS/Tremont Hedge Fund Index and Market Index Returns (August 1998 to October 1998)*

	August 1998 (%)	September 1998 (%)	October 1998 (%)
Index			
Aggregate index	−7.55	−2.31	−4.57
Convertible Arbitrage	−4.64	−3.23	−4.68
Dedicated Shortseller	22.71	−4.98	−8.69
Emerging Markets	−23.03	−7.40	1.68
Equity Market Neutral	−0.85	0.95	2.48
Event Driven	−11.77	−2.96	0.66
Distressed	−12.45	−1.43	0.89
Event Driven Multi-Strategy	−11.52	−4.74	0.26
Risk Arbitrage	−6.15	−0.65	2.41
Fixed Income Arbitrage	−1.46	−3.74	−6.96
Global Macro	−4.84	−5.12	−11.55
Long/Short Equity	−11.43	3.47	1.74
Managed Futures	9.95	6.87	1.21
Multi-Strategy	1.15	0.57	−4.76
Ibbotson S&P 500	−14.46	6.41	8.13
Ibbotson Small Cap	−20.10	3.69	3.56
Ibbotson LT Corporate Bonds	0.89	4.13	−1.90
Ibbotson LT Government Bonds	4.65	3.95	−2.18

*Monthly returns of CS/Tremont hedge fund indexes and Ibbotson stock and bond indexes.
Source: AlphaSimplex Group.

once in a while an additional term Z_t appears. If the volatility σ_z of Z_t is much larger than the volatilities of the market factor Λ_t and the idiosyncratic risk ϵ_{it}, then the common factor Z_t will dominate the expected returns of all stocks when $I_t = 1$, i.e., phase-locking behavior occurs.

More formally, consider the *conditional correlation coefficient* of two funds i and j, defined as the ratio of the conditional covariance divided by the square root of the product of the conditional variances, conditioned on $I_t = 0$:

$$\text{Corr}[R_{it}, R_{jt} \mid I_t = 0] = \frac{\beta_i \beta_j \sigma_\lambda^2}{\sqrt{\beta_i^2 \sigma_\lambda^2 + \sigma_{\epsilon_i}^2} \sqrt{\beta_j^2 \sigma_\lambda^2 + \sigma_{\epsilon_j}^2}} \qquad (1.6)$$

$$\approx 0 \qquad \text{for } \beta_i \approx \beta_j \approx 0, \qquad (1.7)$$

where we assume $\beta_i \approx \beta_j \approx 0$ to capture the market neutral characteristic that many hedge fund investors desire. Now consider the conditional correlation conditioned on $I_t = 1$:

$$\text{Corr}[R_{it}, R_{jt} \mid I_t = 1] = \frac{\beta_i \beta_j \sigma_\lambda^2 + \sigma_z^2}{\sqrt{\beta_i^2 \sigma_\lambda^2 + \sigma_z^2 + \sigma_{\epsilon_i}^2} \sqrt{\beta_j^2 \sigma_\lambda^2 + \sigma_z^2 + \sigma_{\epsilon_j}^2}} \tag{1.8}$$

$$\approx \frac{1}{\sqrt{1 + \sigma_{\epsilon_i}^2/\sigma_z^2} \sqrt{1 + \sigma_{\epsilon_j}^2/\sigma_z^2}} \quad \text{for } \beta_i \approx \beta_j \approx 0. \tag{1.9}$$

If σ_z^2 is large relative to $\sigma_{\epsilon_i}^2$ and $\sigma_{\epsilon_j}^2$, i.e., if the variability of the catastrophe component dominates the variability of the residuals of both funds—a plausible condition that follows from the very definition of a catastrophe—then (1.9) will be approximately equal to 1! When phase locking occurs, the correlation between two funds i and j—close to 0 during normal times—can become arbitrarily close to 1.

An insidious feature of (1.3) is the fact that it implies a very small value for the *unconditional correlation*, which is the quantity most readily estimated and the most commonly used in risk reports, Value-at-Risk calculations, and portfolio decisions. To see why, recall that the unconditional correlation coefficient is simply the unconditional covariance divided by the product of the square roots of the unconditional variances:

$$\text{Corr}[R_{it}, R_{jt}] \equiv \frac{\text{Cov}[R_{it}, R_{jt}]}{\sqrt{\text{Var}[R_{it}]\text{Var}[R_{jt}]}}, \tag{1.10}$$

$$\text{Cov}[R_{it}, R_{jt}] = \beta_i \beta_j \sigma_\lambda^2 + \text{Var}[I_t Z_t] = \beta_i \beta_j \sigma_\lambda^2 + p\sigma_z^2, \tag{1.11}$$

$$\text{Var}[R_{it}] = \beta_i^2 \sigma_\lambda^2 + \text{Var}[I_t Z_t] + \sigma_{\epsilon_i}^2 = \beta_i^2 \sigma_\lambda^2 + p\sigma_z^2 + \sigma_{\epsilon_i}^2. \tag{1.12}$$

Combining these expressions yields the unconditional correlation coefficient under (1.3):

$$\text{Corr}[R_{it}, R_{jt}] = \frac{\beta_i \beta_j \sigma_\lambda^2 + p\sigma_z^2}{\sqrt{\beta_i^2 \sigma_\lambda^2 + p\sigma_z^2 + \sigma_{\epsilon_i}^2} \sqrt{\beta_j^2 \sigma_\lambda^2 + p\sigma_z^2 + \sigma_{\epsilon_j}^2}} \tag{1.13}$$

$$\approx \frac{p}{\sqrt{p + \sigma_{\epsilon_i}^2/\sigma_z^2} \sqrt{p + \sigma_{\epsilon_j}^2/\sigma_z^2}} \quad \text{for } \beta_i \approx \beta_j \approx 0. \tag{1.14}$$

If we let $p = 0.001$ and assume that the variability of the phase-locking component is 10 times the variability of the residuals ϵ_i and ϵ_j, this implies an unconditional correlation of:

$$\text{Corr}[R_{it}, R_{jt}] \approx \frac{p}{\sqrt{p+0.1}\sqrt{p+0.1}} = \frac{0.001}{0.101} = 0.0099,$$

or less than 1%. As the variance σ_z^2 of the phase-locking component increases, the unconditional correlation (1.14) also increases, so that eventually the existence of Z_t will have an impact. However, to achieve an unconditional correlation coefficient of, say, 10%, σ_z^2 would have to be about 100 times larger than σ_ϵ^2. Without the benefit of an explicit risk model such as (1.3), it is virtually impossible to detect the existence of a phase-locking component from standard correlation coefficients.

Hedge fund returns exhibit other nonlinearities that are not captured by linear methods such as correlation coefficients and linear factor models. An example of a simple nonlinearity is an asymmetric sensitivity to the S&P 500, i.e., different beta coefficients for down markets versus up markets. Specifically, consider the following regression:

$$R_{it} = \alpha_i + \beta_i^+ \Lambda_t^+ + \beta_i^- \Lambda_t^- + \epsilon_{it}, \tag{1.15}$$

where

$$\Lambda_t^+ = \begin{cases} \Lambda_t & \text{if } \Lambda_t > 0, \\ 0 & \text{otherwise}, \end{cases} \qquad \Lambda_t^- = \begin{cases} \Lambda_t & \text{if } \Lambda_t \leq 0, \\ 0 & \text{otherwise}, \end{cases} \tag{1.16}$$

and Λ_t is the return on the S&P 500 index. Since $\Lambda_t = \Lambda_t^+ + \Lambda_t^-$, the standard linear model in which fund i's market betas are identical in up and down markets is a special case of the more general specification (1.15), the case where $\beta_i^+ = \beta_i^-$. However, the estimates reported in Table 1.9 for the hedge fund–index returns in Table 1.6 show that beta asymmetries can be quite pronounced for certain hedge fund styles. For example, the Distressed index has an up-market beta of 0.08—seemingly market neutral—however, its down-market beta is 0.41! For the Managed Futures index, the asymmetries are even more pronounced: The coefficients are of opposite sign, with a beta of 0.14 in up markets and a beta of −0.34 in down markets. These asymmetries are to be expected for certain nonlinear investment strategies, particularly those that have optionlike characteristics such as the short-put strategy of Capital Decimation Partners (Section 1.1). Such nonlinearities can yield even greater diversification benefits than more traditional asset classes—for example, Managed Futures seems to provide S&P 500 downside protection with little exposure on the upside—but investors must first be aware of the specific nonlinearities to take advantage of them.

Table 1.9.

Regressions of Monthly CS/Tremont Hedge Fund Index Returns on the S&P 500 Index Return and on Positive and Negative S&P 500 Index Returns (January 1994 to July 2007)*

Category	α	$t(\alpha)$	β	$t(\beta)$	Adj. R^2 (%)	R^2 (%)	p-val (F) (%)	α	$t(\alpha)$	β^+	$t(\beta^+)$	β^-	$t(\beta^-)$	Adj. R^2 (%)	R^2 (%)	p-val (F) (%)
Hedge Fund	0.66	4.34	0.26	7.12	23.5	23.9	0.0	0.94	3.77	0.18	2.58	0.35	4.87	23.9	24.9	0.0
Convertible Arbitrage	0.68	6.49	0.05	1.90	1.6	2.2	5.9	0.73	4.20	0.03	0.71	0.06	1.27	1.0	2.3	15.9
Dedicated Short Bias	0.79	3.10	-0.90	-14.69	57.0	57.3	0.0	0.50	1.20	-0.82	-7.05	-0.99	-8.24	56.9	57.5	0.0
Emerging Markets	0.39	1.21	0.53	6.86	22.1	22.6	0.0	1.29	2.47	0.26	1.84	0.81	5.41	23.9	24.8	0.0
Equity Market Neutral	0.73	11.93	0.07	5.00	12.9	13.4	0.0	0.64	6.29	0.10	3.67	0.04	1.53	13.1	14.2	0.0
Event Driven	0.77	7.29	0.22	8.52	30.6	31.1	0.0	1.26	7.53	0.07	1.56	0.37	7.69	35.7	36.5	0.0
Fixed Income Arbitrage	0.51	5.94	0.01	0.60	-0.4	0.2	54.7	0.72	5.21	-0.05	-1.36	0.08	2.01	1.4	2.6	12.1
Global Macro	0.95	4.00	0.18	3.08	5.0	5.6	0.2	1.13	2.87	0.12	1.14	0.23	2.06	4.6	5.7	0.9
Long/Short Equity	0.62	3.35	0.42	9.38	35.0	35.4	0.0	0.82	2.71	0.36	4.24	0.48	5.53	34.8	35.6	0.0
Managed Futures	0.66	2.40	-0.09	-1.39	0.6	1.2	16.6	-0.15	-0.32	0.14	1.17	-0.34	-2.66	3.1	4.2	3.1
Event Driven Multi-Strategy	0.73	6.04	0.20	6.97	22.7	23.2	0.0	1.20	6.16	0.06	1.21	0.35	6.26	26.4	27.3	0.0
Distressed	0.87	7.26	0.24	8.35	29.8	30.2	0.0	1.42	7.50	0.08	1.47	0.41	7.60	34.9	35.7	0.0
Risk Arbitrage	0.52	6.07	0.13	6.26	19.1	19.6	0.0	0.71	5.10	0.07	1.85	0.19	4.73	20.1	21.1	0.0
Multi-Strategy	0.77	7.74	0.03	1.44	0.7	1.3	15.3	0.83	5.08	0.02	0.38	0.05	1.13	0.2	1.4	32.5

* Multi-Strategy index is for the period from April 1994 to July 2007.

These empirical results suggest the need for a more sophisticated analysis of hedge fund returns, one that accounts for asymmetries in factor exposures, phase-locking behavior, jump risk, nonstationarities, and other nonlinearities that are endemic to high-performance active investment strategies. In particular, nonlinear risk models must be developed for the various types of securities that hedge funds trade (e.g., equities, fixed income instruments, foreign exchange, commodities, and derivatives), and for each type of security, the risk model should include the following general groups of factors:

- Price factors
- Sectors
- Investment style
- Volatilities
- Credit
- Liquidity
- Macroeconomic factors
- Sentiment
- Nonlinear interactions

The last category involves dependencies between the previous groups of factors, some of which are nonlinear in nature. For example, credit factors may become more highly correlated with market factors during economic downturns, and virtually uncorrelated at other times. Often difficult to detect empirically, these types of dependencies are more readily captured through economic intuition and practical experience and should not be overlooked when constructing a risk model.

Finally, although the common factors listed above may serve as a useful starting point for developing a quantitative model of hedge fund risk exposures, it should be emphasized that a certain degree of customization will be required. To see why, consider the following list of key components of a typical long/short equity hedge fund:

- Investment style (value, growth, etc.)
- Fundamental analysis (earnings, analyst forecasts, accounting data)
- Factor exposures (S&P 500, industries, sectors, characteristics)
- Portfolio optimization (mean-variance analysis, market neutrality)
- Stock loan considerations (hard-to-borrow securities, short "squeezes")
- Execution costs (price impact, commissions, borrowing rate, short rebate)
- Benchmarks and tracking error (T-bill rate vs. S&P 500).

Then compare them with a similar list for a typical fixed income hedge fund:

- Yield-curve models (equilibrium vs. arbitrage models)
- Prepayment models (for mortgage-backed securities)
- Optionality (call, convertible, and put features)
- Credit risk (defaults, rating changes, etc.)

- Inflationary pressures, central bank activity
- Other macroeconomic factors and events.

The degree of overlap is astonishingly small. While these differences are also present among traditional institutional asset managers, they do not have nearly the latitude that hedge fund managers do in their investment activities, hence the differences are not as consequential for traditional managers. Therefore, the number of unique hedge fund–risk models may have to match the number of hedge fund styles that exist in practice.

1.3 Illiquidity and Serial Correlation

In addition to the dynamic and nonlinear risk exposures described in Sections 1.1 and 1.2, many hedge funds exhibit a third characteristic that differentiates them from more traditional investments: credit and liquidity risk. Although liquidity and credit are separate sources of risk exposures for hedge funds and their investors—one type of risk can exist without the other—they have been inextricably intertwined in the minds of most investors because of the problems encountered by Long Term Capital Management and many other fixed income relative-value hedge funds in August and September of 1998. Because many hedge funds rely on leverage, the size of the positions are often considerably larger than the amount of collateral posted to support these positions. Leverage has the effect of a magnifying glass, expanding small profit opportunities into larger ones but also expanding small losses into larger losses. And when adverse changes in market prices reduce the market value of collateral, credit is withdrawn quickly, and the subsequent forced liquidation of large positions over short periods of time can lead to widespread financial panic, as in the aftermath of the default of Russian government debt in August 1998.[11] Along with the many benefits of an integrated global financial system is the associated cost that a financial crisis in one country can be more easily transmitted to several others.

The basic mechanisms driving liquidity and credit are familiar to most hedge fund managers and investors, and there has been much progress in the recent literature in modeling both credit and liquidity risk.[12] However, the complex network of creditor/obligor relationships, revolving credit agreements, and other

---

[11] Note that in the case of Capital Decimation Partners in Section 1.1, the fund's consecutive returns of −18.3% and −16.2% in August and September 1998 would have made it virtually impossible for the fund to continue without a massive injection of capital. In all likelihood, it would have closed down along with many other hedge funds during those fateful months, never to realize the extraordinary returns that it would have earned had it been able to withstand the losses in August and September (Table 1.3).

[12] See, for example, Bookstaber (1999, 2000) and Kao (1999), and their citations.

financial interconnections is largely unmapped. Perhaps some of the newly developed techniques in the mathematical theory of networks will allow us to construct systemic measures for liquidity and credit exposures and the robustness of the global financial system to idiosyncratic shocks. The "small-world" networks considered by Watts and Strogatz (1998) and Watts (1999) seem to be particularly promising starting points.

A more immediate method for gauging the liquidity risk exposure of a given hedge fund is to examine the autocorrelation coefficients ρ_k of the fund's monthly returns, where $\rho_k \equiv \text{Cov}[R_t, R_{t-k}]/\text{Var}[R_t]$ is the kth-order autocorrelation of $\{R_t\}$,[13] which measures the degree of correlation between month t's return and month $t+k$'s return. To see why autocorrelations may be useful indicators of liquidity exposure, recall that one of the earliest financial asset-pricing models is the Martingale model, in which asset returns are serially uncorrelated ($\rho_k = 0$ for all $k \neq 0$). Indeed, the title of Samuelson's (1965) seminal paper—"Proof That Properly Anticipated Prices Fluctuate Randomly"—provides a succinct summary of the motivation of the Martingale property: In an informationally efficient market, price changes must be unforecastable if they are properly anticipated, i.e., if they fully incorporate the expectations and information of all market participants.

This extreme version of market efficiency is now recognized as an idealization that is unlikely to hold in practice.[14] In particular, market frictions such as transaction costs, borrowing constraints, costs of gathering and processing information, and institutional restrictions on short sales and other trading practices do exist, and they all contribute to the possibility of serial correlation in asset returns that cannot easily be "arbitraged" away precisely because of the presence of these frictions. From this perspective, the degree of serial correlation in an asset's returns can be viewed as a proxy for the magnitude of the frictions, and illiquidity is one of most common forms of such frictions. For example, it is well known that the historical returns to residential real estate investments are considerably more highly autocorrelated than, say, the returns to S&P 500 indexes during the same sample period. Similarly, the returns to the S&P 500 futures exhibit less serial correlation than those of the index itself. In both examples, the more liquid instrument exhibits less serial correlation, and the economic rationale is a modified version of Samuelson's (1965) argument—predictability in asset returns is exploited and eliminated only to the extent allowed by market frictions. Despite the fact that the returns to residential real estate are highly predictable, it is impossible to take full advantage of such predictability because of the high

---

[13] The kth-order autocorrelation of a time series $\{R_t\}$ is defined as the correlation coefficient between R_t and R_{t-k}, which is simply the covariance between R_t and R_{t-k} divided by the square root of the product of the variances of R_t and R_{t-k}. But since the variances of R_t and R_{t-k} are the same under the assumption of stationarity, the denominator of the autocorrelation is simply the variance of R_t.

[14] See, for example, Farmer and Lo (2000), Lo (2004), and the discussion in Section 9.3.

transaction costs associated with real estate transactions, the inability to short-sell properties, and other frictions.[15]

A closely related phenomenon that buttresses this interpretation of serial correlation in hedge fund returns is the "nonsynchronous trading" effect, in which the autocorrelation is induced in a security's returns because those returns are computed with closing prices that are not necessarily established at the same time each day (see, for example, Campbell, Lo, and MacKinlay, 1997, Chapter 3). In contrast to earlier studies of nonsynchronous trading in exchange-traded equity markets—which were unable to generate empirical levels of serial correlation purely from non-trading (e.g., Lo and MacKinlay, 1988, 1990a, and Kadlec and Patterson, 1999)—Getmansky, Lo, and Makarov (2004) show that for hedge funds, significantly higher levels of serial correlation can be explained by the combination of illiquidity and "performance smoothing," of which nonsynchronous trading is a special case. However, even when prices are synchronously measured (as they are for most hedge funds, since portfolios are "marked to market" at month end), there are several other channels by which illiquidity exposure can induce serial correlation in the reported returns of hedge funds, including naïve methods for valuing illiquid securities like linear extrapolation or "matrix pricing" heuristics, as well as deliberate "performance smoothing." We explore these possibilities in more depth in Chapter 3.

To obtain a summary measure of the overall statistical significance of the autocorrelations, Ljung and Box (1978) propose the following statistic:

$$Q = T(T+2) \sum_{k=1}^{p} \hat{\rho}_k^2/(T-k), \qquad (1.17)$$

which is asymptotically χ_p^2 under the null hypothesis of no autocorrelation.[16] By forming the sum of squared autocorrelations, the statistic Q reflects the absolute magnitudes of the $\hat{\rho}_k$'s irrespective of their signs, hence funds with large positive or negative autocorrelation coefficients exhibit large Q-statistics.

To illustrate the potential value of autocorrelations and the Q-statistic for measuring liquidity risk, we estimate these quantities with monthly historical total returns of the 10 largest (as of February 11, 2001) mutual funds from various start dates through June 2000, and 12 hedge funds from various inception dates to January 2001. Monthly total returns for the mutual funds were obtained from the University of Chicago's Center for Research in Securities Prices. The 12 hedge funds were selected from the Altvest database to yield a diverse range of annual Sharpe ratios (from 1 to 5) computed in the standard way ($\sqrt{12}\, \widehat{SR}$, where

---

[15] These frictions have led to the creation of real-estate investment trusts (REITs), and the returns to these securities—which are considerably more liquid than the underlying assets on which they are based—exhibit much less serial correlation.

[16] See Kendall, Stuart, and Ord (1983, Section 50.13) for details.

$\widehat{SR}$ is the Sharpe ratio estimator applied to monthly returns), with the additional requirement that the funds have a minimum 5-year history of returns. The names of the hedge funds have been omitted to maintain their privacy, and we will refer to them only by their stated investment styles, e.g., Relative Value, Risk Arbitrage.

Table 1.10 reports the means, standard deviations, $\hat{\rho}_1$ to $\hat{\rho}_6$, and the p-values of the Q-statistic using the first six autocorrelations for the sample of mutual funds and hedge funds. The first subpanel shows that the 10 mutual funds have very little serial correlation in returns, with first-order autocorrelations ranging from -3.99% to 12.37% and with p-values of the corresponding Q-statistics ranging from 10.95% to 80.96%, implying that none of the Q-statistics is significant at the 5% level.[17] The lack of serial correlation in these 10 mutual fund returns is not surprising. Because of their sheer size, these funds consist primarily of highly liquid securities and, as a result, there is little discretion in valuing such portfolios. Moreover, many of the SEC regulations that govern the mutual fund industry (e.g., detailed prospectuses, daily net asset value calculations, and quarterly filings) were enacted specifically to guard against arbitrary marks, price manipulation, and other unsavory investment practices.

The results for the 12 hedge funds are considerably different. In sharp contrast to the mutual fund sample, the hedge fund sample displays substantial serial correlation, with first-order autocorrelation coefficients that range from -20.17% to 49.01%, with 8 out of 12 funds that have Q-statistics with p-values less than 5%, and with 10 out of 12 funds with p-values less than 10%. The only two funds with p-values that are not significant at the 5% or 10% level are the Risk Arbitrage A and Risk Arbitrage B funds, which have p-values of 74.10% and 93.42%, respectively. This is consistent with the notion of serial correlation as a proxy for liquidity risk because among the various types of funds in this sample, risk arbitrage is likely to be the most liquid, since by definition such funds invest in securities that are exchange-traded and where trading volume is typically heavier than usual because of the impending merger events on which risk arbitrage is based.

Of course, there are several other aspects of liquidity that are not captured by serial correlation, and certain types of trading strategies can generate serial

[17] The p-value of a statistic is defined as the smallest level of significance for which the null hypothesis can be rejected based on the statistic's value. For example, a p-value of 16.73% for the Q-statistic of Washington Mutual Investors implies that the null hypothesis of no serial correlation can be rejected only at the 16.73% significance level—at any smaller level of significance, say 5%, the null hypothesis cannot be rejected. Therefore, smaller p-values indicate stronger evidence against the null hypothesis, and larger p-values indicate stronger evidence in favor of the null hypothesis. p-values are often reported instead of test statistics because they are easier to interpret (to interpret a test statistic, one must compare it to the critical values of the appropriate distribution; this comparison is performed in computing the p-value). See, for example, Bickel and Doksum (1977, Section 5.2.B) for further discussion of p-values and their interpretation.

Table 1.10.

Autocorrelations of Mutual Fund and Hedge Fund Returns*

	Start Date	T	$\hat{\mu}$ (%)	$\hat{\sigma}$ (%)	$\hat{\rho}_1$ (%)	$\hat{\rho}_2$ (%)	$\hat{\rho}_3$ (%)	$\hat{\rho}_4$ (%)	$\hat{\rho}_5$ (%)	$\hat{\rho}_6$ (%)	p-value of Q_6 (%)
Mutual funds											
Vanguard 500 Index	Oct 1976	286	1.30	4.27	-3.99	-6.60	-4.94	-6.38	10.14	-3.63	31.85
Fidelity Magellan	Jan 1967	402	1.73	6.23	12.37	-2.31	-0.35	0.65	7.13	3.14	17.81
Investment Company of America	Jan 1963	450	1.17	4.01	1.84	-3.23	-4.48	-1.61	6.25	-5.60	55.88
Janus	Mar 1970	364	1.52	4.75	10.49	-0.04	-3.74	-8.16	2.12	-0.60	30.32
Fidelity Contrafund	May 1967	397	1.29	4.97	7.37	-2.46	-6.81	-3.88	2.73	-4.47	42.32
Washington Mutual Investors	Jan 1963	450	1.13	4.09	-0.10	-7.22	-2.64	0.65	11.55	-2.61	16.73
Janus Worldwide	Jan 1992	102	1.81	4.36	11.37	3.43	-3.82	-15.42	-21.36	-10.33	10.95
Fidelity Growth and Income	Jan 1986	174	1.54	4.13	5.09	-1.60	-8.20	-15.58	2.10	-7.29	30.91
American Century Ultra	Dec 1981	223	1.72	7.11	2.32	3.35	1.36	-3.65	-7.92	-5.98	80.96
Growth Fund of America	July 1964	431	1.18	5.35	8.52	-2.65	-4.11	-3.17	3.43	0.34	52.45
Hedge funds											
Convertible/Option Arbitrage	May 1992	104	1.63	0.97	42.59	28.97	21.35	2.91	-5.89	-9.72	0.00
Relative Value	Dec 1992	97	0.66	0.21	25.90	19.23	-2.13	-16.39	-6.24	1.36	3.32
Mortgage–Backed Securities	Jan 1993	96	1.33	0.79	42.04	22.11	16.73	22.58	6.58	-1.96	0.00
High Yield Debt	Jun 1994	79	1.30	0.87	33.73	21.84	13.13	-0.84	13.84	4.00	1.11
Risk Arbitrage A	Jul 1993	90	1.06	0.69	-4.85	-10.80	6.92	-8.52	9.92	3.06	74.10
Long/Short Equities	Jul 1989	138	1.18	0.83	-20.17	24.62	8.74	11.23	13.53	16.94	0.05
Multi-Strategy A	Jan 1995	72	1.08	0.75	48.88	23.38	3.35	0.79	-2.31	-12.82	0.06
Risk Arbitrage B	Nov 1994	74	0.90	0.77	-4.87	2.45	-8.29	-5.70	0.60	9.81	93.42
Convertible Arbitrage A	Sep 1992	100	1.38	1.60	33.75	30.76	7.88	-9.40	3.64	-4.36	0.06
Convertible Arbitrage B	Jul 1994	78	0.78	0.62	32.36	9.73	-4.46	6.50	-6.33	-10.55	8.56
Multi-Strategy B	Jun 1989	139	1.34	1.63	49.01	24.60	10.60	8.85	7.81	7.45	0.00
Fund of Funds	Oct 1994	75	1.68	2.29	29.67	21.15	0.89	-0.90	-12.38	3.01	6.75

* Means, standard deviations, and autocorrelation coefficients for monthly total returns of mutual funds and hedge funds from various start dates through June 2000 for the mutual fund sample and various start dates through December 2000 for the hedge fund sample. "$\hat{\rho}_k$" denotes the kth autocorrelation coefficient, and "p-value of Q_6" denotes the significance level of the Ljung–Box (1978) Q-statistic $T(T+2)\sum_{k=1}^{6}\rho_k^2/(T-k)$, which is asymptotically χ_6^2 under the null hypothesis of no serial correlation. Data is monthly with various sample periods.

Source: AlphaSimplex Group.

correlation even though they invest in highly liquid instruments. In particular, conditioning variables such as investment style, the types of securities traded, and other aspects of the market environment should be taken into account, perhaps through the kind of risk model proposed in Section 1.2. However, as a first cut for measuring and comparing the liquidity exposures of various hedge fund investments, autocorrelation coefficients and Q-statistics provide a great deal of insight and information in a convenient manner. A more detailed analysis of serial correlation in hedge fund returns is presented by Getmansky, Lo, and Makarov (2004) and summarized in Chapter 3.

1.4 Literature Review

The explosive growth of the hedge fund sector over the past several years has generated a rich literature both in academia and among practitioners, including a number of books, newsletters, and trade magazines; several hundred published articles and an entire journal dedicated solely to this industry (the *Journal of Alternative Investments*). Thanks to the availability of hedge fund–returns data from sources such as Altvest, CISDM, HedgeFund.net, HFR, and Lipper TASS, a number of empirical studies have highlighted the unique risk/reward profiles of hedge fund investments. For example, Ackermann, McEnally, and Ravenscraft (1999), Fung and Hsieh (1999, 2000, 2001), Liang (1999, 2000, 2001), Agarwal and Naik (2000b,c), Edwards and Caglayan (2001), Kao (2002), and Amin and Kat (2003a) provide comprehensive empirical studies of historical hedge fund performance using various hedge fund databases. Brown, Goetzmann, and Park (2000, 2001a,b), Fung and Hsieh (1997a,b), Brown, Goetzmann, and Ibbotson (1999), Agarwal and Naik (2000a,d), Brown and Goetzmann (2003), and Lochoff (2002) present more detailed performance attribution and style analysis for hedge funds.

Several recent empirical studies have challenged the lack of correlation between hedge fund returns and market indexes, arguing that the standard methods of assessing their risks and rewards may be misleading. For example, Asness, Krail, and Liew (2001) show that in several cases where hedge funds purport to be market neutral (i.e., funds with relatively small market betas), including both contemporaneous and lagged market returns as regressors and summing the coefficients yields significantly higher market exposure. Moreover, in deriving statistical estimators for Sharpe ratios of a sample of mutual funds and hedge funds, Lo (2002) proposes a better method for computing annual Sharpe ratios based on monthly means and standard deviations, yielding point estimates that differ from the naive Sharpe ratio estimator by as much as 70% in his empirical application. Getmansky, Lo, and Makarov (2004) focus directly on the unusual degree of serial correlation in hedge fund returns and argue that illiquidity exposure and smoothed returns are the most common sources of such serial correlation. They also propose methods for estimating the degree of return smoothing and adjusting performance statistics like the Sharpe ratio to account for serial correlation.

The persistence of hedge fund performance over various time intervals has also been studied by several authors. Such persistence may be indirectly linked to serial correlation; e.g., persistence in performance usually implies positively autocorrelated returns. Agarwal and Naik (2000c) examine the persistence of hedge fund performance over quarterly, half-yearly, and yearly intervals by examining the series of wins and losses for two, three, and more consecutive time periods. Using net-of-fee returns, they find that persistence is highest at the quarterly horizon and decreases when moving to the yearly horizon. The authors also find that performance persistence, whenever present, is unrelated to the type of hedge fund strategy. Brown, Goetzmann, Ibbotson, and Ross (1992), Ackermann, McEnally, and Ravenscraft (1999), and Baquero, Horst, and Verbeek (2004) show that survivorship bias—the fact that most hedge fund databases do not contain funds that were unsuccessful and went out of business—can affect the first and second moments and cross-moments of returns and generate spurious persistence in performance when there is dispersion of risk among the population of managers. However, using annual returns of both defunct and currently operating offshore hedge funds between 1989 and 1995, Brown, Goetzmann, and Ibbotson (1999) find virtually no evidence of performance persistence in raw returns or risk-adjusted returns, even after breaking funds down according to their returns-based style classifications.

Fund flows in the hedge fund industry have been considered by Agarwal, Daniel, and Naik (2004) and Getmansky (2004), with the expected conclusion that funds with higher returns tend to receive higher net inflows and funds with poor performance suffer withdrawals and eventually liquidation, much like the case with mutual funds and private equity.[18] Agarwal, Daniel, and Naik (2004), Goetzmann, Ingersoll, and Ross (2003), and Getmansky (2004) all find decreasing returns to scale among their samples of hedge funds, implying that an optimal amount of assets under management exists for each fund and mirroring similar findings for the mutual fund industry by Pérold and Salomon (1991) and the private equity industry by Kaplan and Schoar (2004). Hedge fund survival rates have been studied by Brown, Goetzmann, and Ibbotson (1999), Fung and Hsieh (2000), Liang (2000, 2001), Bares, Gibson, and Gyger (2003), Brown, Goetzmann, and Park (2001b), Gregoriou (2002), and Amin and Kat (2003b). Baquero, Horst, and Verbeek (2004) estimate liquidation probabilities of hedge funds and find that they are greatly dependent on past performance.

The survival rates of hedge funds have been estimated by Brown, Goetzmann, and Ibbotson (1999), Fung and Hsieh (2000), Liang (2000, 2001), Brown,

---

[18] See, for example, Ippolito (1992), Chevalier and Ellison (1997), Goetzmann and Peles (1997), Gruber (1996), Sirri and Tufano (1998), Zheng (1999), and Berk and Green (2004) for studies on mutual fund flows, and Kaplan and Schoar (2004) for private-equity fund flows.

Goetzmann, and Park (2001a,b), Gregoriou (2002), Amin and Kat (2003b), Bares, Gibson, and Gyger (2003), and Getmansky, Lo, and Mei (2004). Brown, Goetzmann, and Park (2001b) show that the probability of liquidation increases with increasing risk and that funds with negative returns for two consecutive years have a higher risk of 'shutting down. Liang (2000) finds that the annual hedge fund attrition rate is 8.3% for the 1994–1998 sample period using Lipper TASS data, and Baquero, Horst, and Verbeek (2004) find a slightly higher rate of 8.6% for the 1994–2000 sample period. Baquero, Horst, and Verbeek (2004) also find that surviving funds outperform nonsurviving funds by approximately 2.1% per year, which is similar to the findings of Fung and Hsieh (2000, 2002b) and Liang (2000), and that investment style, size, and past performance are significant factors in explaining survival rates. Many of these patterns are also documented by Liang (2000), Boyson (2002), and Getmansky, Lo, and Mei (2004). In particular, Getmansky, Lo, and Mei (2004) find that attrition rates in the Lipper TASS database from 1994 to 2004 differ significantly across investment styles, from a low of 5.2% per year on average for convertible arbitrage funds to a high of 14.4% per year on average for managed futures funds. They also relate a number of factors to these attrition rates, including past performance, volatility, and investment style, and document differences in illiquidity risk between active and liquidated funds. In analyzing the life cycle of hedge funds, Getmansky (2004) finds that the liquidation probabilities of individual hedge funds depend on fund-specific characteristics such as past returns, asset flows, age, and assets under management, as well as category-specific variables such as competition and favorable positioning within the industry.

Brown, Goetzmann, and Park (2001b) find that the half-life of Lipper TASS hedge funds is exactly 30 months, while Brooks and Kat (2002) estimate that approximately 30% of new hedge funds do not make it past 36 months because of poor performance. In Amin and Kat's (2003b) study, 40% of their hedge funds do not make it to the fifth year. Howell (2001) observed that the probability of hedge funds failing in their first year was 7.4%, only to increase to 20.3% in their second year. Poor-performing younger funds drop out of databases at a faster rate than older funds (Getmansky, 2004; Jen, Heasman, and Boyatt, 2001), presumably because younger funds are more likely to take additional risks to obtain a good performance that they can use to attract new investors, whereas older funds that have survived already have track records with which to attract and retain capital.

A number of case studies of hedge fund liquidations have been published recently, no doubt spurred by the most well-known liquidation in the hedge fund industry to date: Long Term Capital Management. The literature on LTCM is vast, spanning a number of books, journal articles, and news stories; a representative sample includes Greenspan (1998), McDonough (1998), Pérold (1999), the President's Working Group on Financial Markets (1999), and MacKenzie (2003). Ineichen (2001) has compiled a list of selected hedge funds and analyzed the reasons for their liquidation. Kramer (2001) focuses on fraud, providing detailed accounts of six of history's most egregious cases. Although it is virtually impossible to obtain hard data on the frequency of fraud among liquidated hedge funds,[19] in a study of more than 100 hedge funds liquidated during the past two decades, Feffer and Kundro (2003) conclude that "half of all failures could be attributed to operational risk alone," of which fraud is one example. In fact, they observe that, "The most common operational issues related to hedge fund losses have been misrepresentation of fund investments, misappropriation of investor funds, unauthorized trading, and inadequate resources" (Feffer and Kundro, 2003, p. 5). The last of these issues is, of course, not related to fraud, but Feffer and Kundro (2003, Figure 2) report that only 6% of their sample involved inadequate resources, whereas 41% involved misrepresentation of investments, 30% misappropriation of funds, and 14% unauthorized trading. These results suggest that operational issues are indeed an important factor in hedge fund liquidations and deserve considerable attention from investors and managers alike.

Collectively, these studies show that the dynamics of hedge funds are quite different from those of more traditional investments, and the remaining chapters provide more detailed support for this claim.

---

[19] The lack of transparency and the unregulated status of most hedge funds are significant barriers to any systematic data collection effort, hence it is difficult to draw inferences about industry norms.

2
Basic Properties of Hedge Fund Returns

It is clear from Chapter 1 that hedge funds exhibit unique and dynamic characteristics that bear further study. Fortunately, the returns of many individual hedge funds are now available through a number of commercial databases such as Altvest, CISDM, HedgeFund.net, HFR, and Lipper TASS. For the empirical analysis in this book, we use two main sources: (1) a set of aggregate hedge fund–index returns from CS/Tremont, and (2) the Lipper TASS database of hedge funds, which consists of monthly returns and accompanying information for 7,924 individual hedge funds (as of September 2007) from February 1977 to August 2007.[1]

The CS/Tremont indexes are asset-weighted indexes of funds with a minimum of $10 million of assets under management (AUM), a minimum 1-year track record, and current audited financial statements. An aggregate index is computed from this universe, and 10 subindexes based on investment style are also computed using a similar method. Indexes are computed and rebalanced on a monthly frequency, and the universe of funds is redefined on a quarterly basis.

The Lipper TASS database consists of monthly returns, assets under management, and other fund-specific information for 7,924 individual funds from February 1977 to August 2007. The database is divided into two parts: *Live funds* and *Graveyard funds*. Hedge funds that are in the Live database are considered to be active as of August 31, 2007.[2] As of September 2007, the combined database

---

[1] For further information about these data see http://www.hedgeindex.com (CS/Tremont indexes) and http://www.lipperweb.com (Lipper TASS). We also use data from Altvest, the University of Chicago's Center for Research in Security Prices, and Yahoo!Finance.

[2] Once a hedge fund decides not to report its performance, is liquidated, is closed to new investment, restructured, or merged with other hedge funds, the fund is transferred into the Graveyard database. A hedge fund can be listed in the Graveyard database only after being listed in the Live database. Because the Lipper TASS database fully represents returns and asset information for live and dead funds, the

of both live and dead hedge funds contained 7,924 funds with at least one monthly return observation. Out of these 7,924 funds, 4,266 are in the Live database and 3,658 in the Graveyard database. The earliest data available for a fund in either database is February 1977. Lipper TASS started tracking dead funds in 1994, hence it has been only since 1994 that Lipper TASS has transferred funds from the Live database to the Graveyard database. Funds dropped from the Live database prior to 1994 are not included in the Graveyard database, which may yield a certain degree of survivorship bias.[3]

The majority of the 7,924 funds reported U.S. dollar returns net of management and incentive fees on a monthly basis,[4] and we eliminated 1,735 funds that reported in currencies other than the U.S. dollar, leaving 6,189 funds in the Combined database (3,088 in the Live database and 3,101 in the Graveyard database). We then eliminated 57 funds that reported only gross returns, leaving 6,132 funds in the Combined database (3,068 in the Live database and 3,064 in the Graveyard database). We also eliminated funds reporting returns on a quarterly, not monthly, basis, leaving 6,107 funds in the Combined database (3,065 in the Live database and 3,042 in the Graveyard database). Finally, we dropped funds that did not report assets under management or reported only partial assets under management, leaving a final sample of 5,617 hedge funds in the Combined database, which consists of 2,701 funds in the Live database and 2,916 funds in the Graveyard database. For the empirical analysis in Section 3.1, we impose an additional filter that requires funds to have at least 5 years of nonmissing returns. This obviously creates additional survivorship bias in the remaining sample of funds, but since the main objective is to estimate measures of illiquidity exposure

---

effects of survivorship bias are minimized. However, the database is subject to *back-fill bias*—when a fund decides to be included in the database, Lipper TASS adds the fund to the Live database and includes all available prior performance of the fund. Hedge funds do not need to meet any specific requirements to be included in the Lipper TASS database. Because of reporting delays and time lags in contacting hedge funds, some Graveyard funds can be incorrectly listed in the Live database for a period of time. However, Lipper TASS has adopted a policy of transferring funds from the Live database to the Graveyard database if they do not report over an 8- to 10-month period.

[3] For studies attempting to quantify the degree and impact of survivorship bias, see Baquero, Horst, and Verbeek (2004), Brown, Goetzmann, Ibbotson, and Ross (1992), Brown, Goetzmann, and Ibbotson (1999), Brown, Goetzmann, and Park (2001a), Carpenter and Lynch (1999), Fung and Hsieh (1997b, 2000), Horst, Nijman, and Verbeek (2001), Hendricks, Patel, and Zeckhauser (1997), and Schneeweis and Spurgin (1996).

[4] Lipper TASS defines returns as the change in net-asset value during the month (assuming the reinvestment of any distributions on the reinvestment date used by the fund) divided by the net-asset value at the beginning of the month, net of management fees, incentive fees, and other fund expenses. Therefore, these reported returns should approximate the returns realized by investors. Lipper TASS also converts all foreign currency–denominated returns to U.S. dollar returns using the appropriate exchange rates.

Table 2.1.

Number of Funds in the Lipper TASS Hedge Fund Live, Graveyard, and Combined
Databases (February 1977 to August 2007)

		Number of Lipper TASS Funds		
Category	*Definition*	*Live*	*Graveyard*	*Combined*
1	Convertible Arbitrage	75	101	176
2	Dedicated Short Bias	17	20	37
3	Emerging Markets	175	174	349
4	Equity Market Neutral	149	182	331
5	Event Driven	257	247	504
6	Fixed Income Arbitrage	134	125	259
7	Global Macro	111	178	289
8	Long/Short Equity Hedge	771	947	1718
9	Managed Futures	173	356	529
10	Multi-Strategy	135	95	230
11	Fund of Funds	704	491	1195
	Total	2701	2916	5617

and not to make inferences about overall performance, this filter may not be as
problematic.[5]

Lipper TASS also classifies funds into one of 11 different investment styles,
listed in Table 2.1 and described in the Appendix, of which 10 correspond exactly
to the CS/Tremont subindex definitions.[6] Table 2.1 also reports the number of
funds in each category for the Live, Graveyard, and Combined databases, and it
is apparent from these figures that the representation of investment styles is not
evenly distributed but is concentrated among four categories: Long/Short Equity
(1,718), Fund of Funds (1,195), Managed Futures (529), and Event Driven (504).
Together, these four categories account for 70.3% of the funds in the Combined
database. Figure 2.1 shows that the relative proportions of the Live and Graveyard
databases are roughly comparable, with the exception of two categories: Funds
of Funds (26% in the Live database and 18% in the Graveyard database) and
Managed Futures (6% in the Live database and 12% in the Graveyard database).
This reflects the current trend in the industry toward Funds of Funds, and the
somewhat slower growth of Managed Futures funds.

In Section 2.1 we present some summary statistics for the CS/Tremont indexes,
and Section 2.2 contains similar statistics for the Lipper TASS database. Using
the Lipper TASS Graveyard database, Section 2.3 reports a variety of attrition

---

[5] See the references in footnote 3.

[6] This is no coincidence—the CS/Tremont indexes were created by Tremont Capital Management in
partnership with Credit Suisse. TASS was subsequently sold to Lipper.

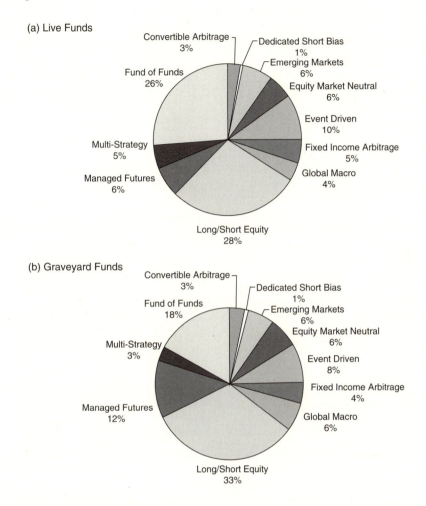

Figure 2.1. *Breakdown of Lipper TASS Live funds and Graveyard funds by category.*

rates for Lipper TASS hedge funds, stratified by investment style, by assets under management, and over time.

2.1 CS/Tremont Indexes

In Section 1.2, we considered the correlation properties of the CS/Tremont hedge fund indexes. Table 2.2 reports summary statistics for the monthly returns of the CS/Tremont indexes from January 1994 to July 2007. Also included for purposes

Table 2.2.

Summary Statistics for Monthly CS/Tremont Hedge Fund Index Returns and Various Hedge Fund Risk Factors*

	Sample Size	Annual Mean (%)	Annual S.D. (%)	Correlation With S&P 500 (%)	Min	Median	Max	Skew	Kurt	ρ_1	ρ_2	ρ_3	p-value of Ljung–Box Q-Statistic
Hedge Fund	163	10.87	7.52	48.9	−7.55	0.85	8.53	0.08	5.52	12.1	3.4	−1.4	42.2
Convertible Arbitrage	163	8.71	4.56	14.8	−4.68	1.03	3.57	−1.36	6.32	56.3	37.8	14.1	0.0
Dedicated Short Bias	163	−0.60	16.75	−75.7	−8.69	−0.41	22.71	0.83	5.08	11.9	−4.7	−3.8	35.1
Emerging Markets	163	10.59	15.66	47.6	−23.03	1.56	16.42	−0.73	8.03	29.0	1.9	−1.0	0.9
Equity Market Neutral	163	9.61	2.83	36.7	−1.15	0.79	3.26	0.34	3.46	29.5	17.6	10.1	0.0
Event Driven	163	11.68	5.47	55.7	−11.77	1.07	3.68	−3.44	27.76	32.8	14.2	2.1	0.6
Fixed Income Arbitrage	163	6.20	3.65	4.8	−6.96	0.72	2.05	−3.00	18.80	37.7	5.9	0.8	0.1
Global Macro	163	13.39	10.52	23.6	−11.55	1.17	10.60	0.03	6.25	5.7	3.7	8.6	1.6
Long/Short Equity	163	12.09	9.86	59.5	−11.44	0.91	13.01	0.20	7.07	16.7	5.0	−5.6	1.5
Managed Futures	160	6.90	11.91	−10.9	−9.35	0.37	9.95	0.01	3.23	5.5	−12.6	−7.8	23.1
Multi-Strategy	163	9.62	4.24	11.4	−4.76	0.85	3.61	−1.21	6.32	4.2	5.5	12.2	75.5
Event Driven Multi-Strategy	163	11.03	5.93	48.1	−11.52	0.93	4.66	−2.49	19.49	31.5	15.5	4.8	1.4
Distressed	163	13.09	6.14	55.0	−12.45	1.21	4.10	−2.96	22.81	28.5	12.9	1.0	1.3
Risk Arbitrage	163	7.63	4.07	44.2	−6.15	0.58	3.81	−1.17	9.48	25.5	−2.6	−9.9	1.2
S&P 500	163	11.22	14.09	100.00	−14.46	1.34	9.78	−0.60	3.80	−0.6	−3.0	4.9	75.4
Banks	156	18.57	11.15	58.49	−17.47	1.71	10.70	−1.19	9.93	27.7	8.9	4.2	6.4
LIBOR	163	0.13	0.72	−0.09	−0.94	0.01	0.63	−0.80	7.53	52.4	35.7	31.3	0.0
USD	163	−1.07	7.28	4.66	−5.35	−0.12	5.58	0.03	3.02	8.7	−3.3	4.9	45.1
Oil	163	17.04	30.16	−5.00	−21.63	1.54	36.40	0.18	3.90	−5.2	−14.9	9.6	1.2
Gold	163	4.73	12.97	−4.26	−9.31	−0.12	16.85	0.89	4.98	−9.3	−12.4	17.0	11.7
Lehman bond	163	5.99	3.98	3.15	−2.71	0.49	3.50	0.00	2.94	20.8	−6.4	6.7	7.7
Large minus small cap	163	−2.10	11.98	1.69	−14.60	−0.31	9.81	−0.24	4.61	2.0	3.0	5.2	25.5
Value minus growth	163	1.13	15.19	−44.58	−15.74	−0.04	15.50	0.07	6.07	3.0	7.4	1.7	38.0
Credit spread	163	4.03	1.36	−7.47	2.09	3.44	8.24	1.02	3.13	94.5	88.6	84.1	0.0
Term spread	163	1.47	1.18	−12.03	−0.40	1.19	3.97	0.50	1.99	97.0	93.3	89.9	0.0
VIX	163	0.08	4.03	−70.28	−15.38	−0.05	22.06	0.67	8.67	−7.4	−20.6	−11.5	6.7

* Data goes from January 1994 to July 2007 for all hedge fund indexes and risk factors, except for the Multi-Strategy index (April 1994 to July 2007) and Banks risk factor (January 1994 to December 2006).

Table 2.3.

Definitions of Aggregate Measures of Market Conditions and Risk Factors

Variable	Definition
S&P 500	Monthly return of the S&P 500 index including dividends
Banks	Monthly return of equal-weighted portfolio of bank stocks in CRSP (SIC codes 6000–6199 and 6710)
LIBOR	Monthly first difference in U.S. dollar 6-month London interbank offer rate
USD	Monthly return on U.S. Dollar Spot Index
Oil	Monthly return on NYMEX crude-oil front-month futures contract
Gold	Monthly return on gold spot price index
Lehman bond	Monthly return on Dow Jones/Lehman Bond Index
Large cap minus small cap	Monthly return difference between Dow Jones large-cap and small-cap indexes
Value minus growth	Monthly return difference between Dow Jones value and growth indexes
Credit spread	Beginning-of-month difference between KDP High Yield Daily Index and U.S. 10-year yield
Term spread	Beginning-of-month 10-year U.S. dollar swap rate minus 6-month U.S. dollar LIBOR
VIX	Monthly first difference in the VIX implied volatility index

of comparison are summary statistics for a number of aggregate measures of market conditions, and their definitions are given in Table 2.3.

Table 2.2 shows that there is considerable heterogeneity in the historical risk and return characteristics of the various categories of hedge fund investment styles. For example, the annualized mean return ranges from −0.60% for Dedicated Shortsellers to 13.39% for Global Macro, and the annualized volatility ranges from 2.83% for Equity Market Neutral to 15.66% for Emerging Markets. Correlations of the hedge fund indexes with the S&P 500 are generally low, with the largest correlation at 59.5% for Long/Short Equity and the lowest correlation at −75.7% for Dedicated Shortsellers—as investors have discovered, hedge funds offer greater diversification benefits than many traditional asset classes. However, these correlations can vary over time, as illustrated in Section 1.2.

Despite their heterogeneity, several indexes do share a common characteristic: negative skewness. Convertible Arbitrage, Emerging Markets, Event Driven, Distressed, Event Driven Multi-Strategy, Risk Arbitrage, Fixed Income Arbitrage, and Multi-Strategy all have skewness coefficients less than zero, in some cases substantially so. This property is an indication of tail risk exposure, as in the case of Capital Decimation Partners (Section 1.1) and is consistent with the nature of the investment strategies employed by funds in those categories. For example, Fixed Income Arbitrage strategies are known to generate fairly consistent profits, with occasional losses that may be extreme, hence a skewness coefficient of −3.00 is not surprising. A more direct measure of tail risk or "fat tails" is kurtosis—the normal distribution has a kurtosis of 3.00, so values greater than this represent fatter tails than the normal. Not surprisingly, the two categories with the most negative skewness—Event Driven (−3.44) and Fixed Income Arbitrage (−3.00)—also have the largest kurtosis, 27.76 and 18.80, respectively.

Several indexes also exhibit a high degree of positive serial correlation as measured by the first three autocorrelation coefficients $\hat{\rho}_1$, $\hat{\rho}_2$, and $\hat{\rho}_3$ and the Ljung–Box Q-statistic. In comparison to the S&P 500, which has a first-order autocorrelation coefficient of −0.6%, the autocorrelations of the hedge fund indexes are very high, with values of 56.3% for Convertible Arbitrage, 37.7% for Fixed Income Arbitrage, and 32.8% for Event Driven. As we discussed in Section 1.3, serial correlation can be a symptom of illiquidity risk exposure, and we shall focus on this issue in more detail in Chapter 3.

Table 2.4 illustrates an important characteristic of hedge fund returns— their remarkably diverse correlation patterns. Although certain indexes are quite highly correlated (e.g., Event Driven and Distressed), others exhibit strong negative correlation (e.g., Event Driven and Dedicated Shortseller), implying potentially significant diversification benefits.

2.2 Lipper TASS Data

To develop a sense of the dynamics of the Lipper TASS database, in Table 2.5 we report annual frequency counts of the funds in the database at the start of each year, funds entering during the year, funds exiting during the year, and funds entering and exiting within the year. The table shows that despite the start date of February 1977, the database is relatively sparsely populated until the 1990s, with the largest increase in new funds in 2004 and the largest number of funds exiting the database in 2006. The attrition rates reported in Table 2.5 are defined as the ratio of funds exiting in a given year to the number of existing funds at the start of the year. Lipper TASS began tracking fund exits starting only in 1994, hence attrition rates cannot be computed for prior years. For the unfiltered sample of all funds, the average attrition rate from 1994 to 1999 is 7.18%, which is very similar to the 8.54% attrition rate obtained by Liang (2001) for the same period.

Table 2.6 contains basic summary statistics for the funds in the Lipper TASS Live, Graveyard, and Combined databases. Not surprisingly, there is a great deal of variation in mean returns and volatilities both across and within categories and databases. For example, the 257 Event Driven funds in the Live database

Table 2.4.

Correlation Matrix for CS/Tremont Hedge Fund Index Returns (January 1994 to July 2007)*

	Hedge Fund	Convertible Arbitrage	Dedicated Short Bias	Emerging Markets	Equity Market Neutral	Event Driven	Fixed Income Arbitrage
Hedge Fund	100.0						
Convertible Arbitrage	41.1	100.0					
Dedicated Short Bias	−48.8	−25.7	100.0				
Emerging Markets	65.2	30.1	−54.5	100.0			
Equity Market Neutral	33.3	33.9	−31.8	22.1	100.0		
Event Driven	67.4	56.5	−62.6	67.2	35.1	100.0	
Fixed Income Arbitrage	44.2	53.7	−9.9	27.1	13.1	38.3	100.0
Global Macro	85.4	29.1	−13.5	41.5	21.9	37.9	44.2
Long/Short Equity	79.3	28.7	−71.9	59.7	34.8	66.7	21.7
Managed Futures	16.1	−11.2	8.6	−6.9	12.4	−11.3	−3.9
Multi-Strategy	23.0	39.8	−12.3	2.6	23.1	24.6	30.2
Event Driven Multi-Strategy	68.6	56.4	−54.0	66.7	32.0	93.5	40.8
Distressed	58.6	49.5	−62.0	58.9	33.4	92.9	32.2
Risk Arbitrage	39.8	40.2	−49.8	42.2	30.7	66.0	15.0

Table 2.4.

(*continued*)

	Global Macro	Long/Short Equity	Managed Futures	Multi-Strategy	Event Driven Multi-Strategy	Distressed	Risk Arbitrage
Hedge Fund							
Convertible Arbitrage							
Dedicated Short Bias							
Emerging Markets							
Equity Market Neutral							
Event Driven							
Fixed Income Arbitrage							
Global Macro	100.0						
Long/Short Equity	43.0	100.0					
Managed Futures	24.7	3.4	100.0				
Multi-Strategy	14.3	22.1	6.8	100.0			
Event Driven Multi-Strategy	41.9	64.5	−12.7	28.7	100.0		
Distressed	31.4	59.0	−8.0	17.0	74.3	100.0	
Risk Arbitrage	13.9	51.3	−13.7	12.0	63.0	55.0	100.0

* All values are percentages and are based on monthly data.

have an average mean return of 13.06% and an average standard deviation of 6.72%, but in the Graveyard database the 247 Event Driven funds have an average mean return of 9.83% and a much higher average standard deviation of 9.29%. Not surprisingly, average volatilities in the Graveyard database are uniformly higher than those in the Live database because the higher-volatility funds are more likely to be eliminated.[7]

Average serial correlations also vary considerably across categories in the Combined database, but six categories stand out: Convertible Arbitrage (31.3%), Fund of Funds (15.9%), Event Driven (17.7%), Emerging Markets (12.0%), Fixed Income Arbitrage (15.3%), and Multi-Strategy (11.5%). Given the descriptions of these categories provided by Lipper TASS (Appendix A.1) and common wisdom about the nature of the strategies involved—these categories include some of the most illiquid securities traded—serial correlation seems to be a reasonable proxy for illiquidity and smoothed returns (Lo, 2001; Getmansky, Lo, and Makarov, 2004; and Chapter 3). Alternatively, equities and futures are among the most liquid securities in which hedge funds invest, and it is not surprising, that the average first-order serial correlations for Equity Market Neutral, Long/Short Equity, and Managed Futures are 3.2%, 5.9%, and 0.1%, respectively. Dedicated Shortseller funds also have a low average first-order autocorrelation, 1.6%, which is consistent with the high degree of liquidity that often characterizes shortsellers (by definition, the ability to short a security implies a certain degree of liquidity).

These summary statistics suggest that illiquidity and smoothed returns may be important attributes for hedge fund returns that can be captured to some degree by serial correlation and the time-series model of smoothing in Chapter 3.

Finally, Table 2.7 reports the year-end assets under management for funds in each of the 11 Lipper TASS categories for the Combined database from 1977 to 2007, and the relative proportions are plotted in plate 1. Table 2.7 shows that the total assets in the Lipper TASS Combined database is approximately $654 billion, which is a significant percentage—though not nearly exhaustive—of the estimated $1 trillion in the hedge fund industry today.[8] The two dominant categories in the most recent year are Long/Short Equity ($168.5 billion) and Fund of Funds ($146.6 billion), but Figure 2.2 shows that the relative proportions can change significantly over time (see Getmansky, 2004, for a more detailed analysis of fund flows in the hedge fund industry).

---

[7] This effect works at both ends of the return distribution—funds that are wildly successful are also more likely to leave the database since they have less of a need to advertise their performance. That the Graveyard database also contains successful funds is supported by the fact that in some categories, the average mean return in the Graveyard database is the same as or higher than in the Live database, e.g., Convertible Arbitrage, Equity Market Neutral, and Dedicated Shortseller.

[8] Of course, part of the $654 billion is Graveyard funds, hence the proportion of current hedge fund assets represented by the Lipper TASS database is less.

Table 2.5a.

Annual Frequency Counts of Entries into and Exits out of the Lipper TASS Hedge Fund Combined Database (February 1977 to August 2007)*

Year	Existing Funds	New Entries	New Exits	Intra Year Entry and Exit	Total Funds	Attrition Rate (%)
1977	0	2	0	0	2	–
1978	2	1	0	0	3	–
1979	3	1	0	0	4	–
1980	4	2	0	0	6	–
1981	6	1	0	0	7	–
1982	7	3	0	0	10	–
1983	10	4	0	0	14	–
1984	14	8	0	0	22	–
1985	22	5	0	0	27	–
1986	27	15	0	0	42	–
1987	42	22	0	0	64	–
1988	64	12	0	0	76	–
1989	76	37	0	0	113	–
1990	113	62	0	0	175	–
1991	175	58	0	0	233	–
1992	233	99	0	0	332	–
1993	332	205	0	0	537	–
1994	537	229	7	14	759	1.3
1995	759	269	51	8	977	6.7
1996	977	301	100	10	1,178	10.2
1997	1,178	341	93	7	1,426	7.9
1998	1,426	309	120	12	1,615	8.4
1999	1,615	408	164	16	1,859	10.2
2000	1,859	388	199	11	2,048	10.7
2001	2,048	415	244	6	2,219	11.9
2002	2,219	443	243	11	2,419	11.0
2003	2,419	522	230	15	2,711	9.5
2004	2,711	526	295	16	2,942	10.9
2005	2,942	422	413	18	2,951	14.0
2006	2,951	232	471	11	2,712	16.0
2007	2,712	118	129	2	2,701	4.8

* Table produced using filtered data, without the minimum-sample-size filter imposed on each fund.

2.3 Attrition Rates

Since the collapse of LTCM in 1998, it has become clear that hedge fund liquidations can have major consequences for the global financial system. In this

Table 2.5b.
Annual Frequency Counts of Entries into and Exits out of the Lipper TASS Hedge Fund
Combined Database (February 1977 to August 2007)*

Year	Existing Funds	New Entries	New Exits	Intra Year Entry and Exit	Total Funds	Attrition Rate (%)
1977	0	4	0	0	4	–
1978	4	2	0	0	6	–
1979	6	2	0	0	8	–
1980	8	4	0	0	12	–
1981	12	3	0	0	15	–
1982	15	6	0	0	21	–
1983	21	9	0	0	30	–
1984	30	15	0	0	45	–
1985	45	8	0	0	53	–
1986	53	23	0	0	76	–
1987	76	33	0	0	109	–
1988	109	34	0	0	143	–
1989	143	46	0	0	189	–
1990	189	116	0	0	305	–
1991	305	112	0	0	417	–
1992	417	161	0	0	578	–
1993	578	260	0	0	838	–
1994	838	273	19	2	1,092	2.3
1995	1,092	314	69	1	1,337	6.3
1996	1,337	352	124	5	1,565	9.3
1997	1,565	384	107	6	1,842	6.8
1998	1,842	383	169	9	2,056	9.2
1999	2,056	469	189	5	2,336	9.2
2000	2,336	490	228	6	2,598	9.8
2001	2,598	644	244	4	2,998	9.4
2002	2,998	684	280	7	3,402	9.3
2003	3,402	819	267	9	3,954	7.8
2004	3,954	926	342	11	4,538	8.6
2005	4,538	727	522	17	4,743	11.5
2006	4,743	433	673	9	4,503	14.2
2007	4,503	96	333	1	4,266	7.4

* The Lipper TASS Graveyard database did not exist prior to 1994; hence attrition rates are available
only from 1994 to 2007. Table produced using unfiltered data.

section, we provide a brief review of the hedge fund attrition rates documented in
Getmansky, Lo, and Mei (2004).

Because of the voluntary nature of inclusion in the Lipper TASS database,
Graveyard funds do not consist solely of liquidations. Lipper TASS gives one

of seven distinct reasons for each fund assigned to the Graveyard database, summarized in Table 2.8. It may seem reasonable to confine our attention to the Graveyard funds categorized as liquidated (status code 1) or perhaps to drop the funds that are closed to new investment (status code 4) from our sample. However, because our purpose is to develop a broader perspective on the dynamics of the hedge fund industry, we argue that using the entire Graveyard database may be more informative. For example, by eliminating Graveyard funds that are closed to new investors, we create a downward bias in the performance statistics of the remaining funds. Because we do not have detailed information about each of these funds, we cannot easily determine how any particular selection criterion will affect the statistical properties of the remainder. Therefore, we choose to include the entire set of Graveyard funds in our analysis but caution readers to keep in mind the composition of this sample when interpreting our empirical results.

For concreteness, Table 2.9 reports frequency counts for Graveyard funds in each status code and style category, as well as assets under management at the time of transfer to the Graveyard database.[9] These counts show that 2,644 of the 2,916 Graveyard funds, or 91%, fall into the first three categories, categories that can plausibly be considered liquidations, and within each of these three categories, the relative frequencies across style categories are roughly comparable, with Long/Short Equity being the most numerous and Dedicated Shortseller being the least numerous. Of the remaining 272 funds with status codes 4–9, only status code 4—funds that are closed to new investors—is distinctly different in character from the other status codes. There are only 6 funds in this category, and these funds are all likely to be "success stories," providing some counterbalance to the many liquidations in the Graveyard sample. Of course, this is not to say that 6 out of 2,916 is a reasonable estimate of the success rate in the hedge fund industry because we have not included any of the Live funds in this calculation. Nevertheless, these 6 funds in the Graveyard sample do underscore the fact that hedge fund data are subject to a variety of biases that do not always point in the same direction, and we prefer to leave them in so as to reflect these biases as they occur naturally rather than to create new biases of our own. For the remainder of this chapter, we shall refer to all funds in the Lipper TASS Graveyard database as liquidations for expositional simplicity.

Figure 2.2 provides a visual comparison of average means, standard deviations, Sharpe ratios, and first-order autocorrelation coefficients ρ_1 in the Live and Graveyard databases. (Table 2.6 contains basic summary statistics for the funds in the Lipper TASS Live, Graveyard, and Combined databases.) Not surprisingly, there is a great deal of variation in mean returns and volatilities both across and within categories and databases. For example, the 75 Convertible Arbitrage funds in the Live database have an average mean return of 8.80% and an average

---

[9] Of the 2,916 funds in the Graveyard database, 80 funds did not have status codes assigned; hence we coded them as 9 (unknown).

Table 2.6.

Means and Standard Deviations of Basic Summary Statistics for Hedge Funds in the Lipper TASS Hedge Fund Live, Graveyard, and Combined Databases (February 1977 to August 2007)*

Category	Sample Size	Annualized Mean (%) Mean	SD	Annualized SD (%) Mean	SD	ρ_1 (%) Mean	SD	Annualized Sharpe Ratio Mean	SD	Annualized Adjusted Sharpe Ratio Mean	SD	Ljung-Box Q_{12} p-Value (%) Mean	SD
Live Funds													
Convertible Arbitrage	75	8.80	4.96	6.22	7.04	38.8	20.7	2.66	3.82	1.50	1.59	12.9	23.5
Dedicated Short Bias	17	−1.58	6.71	19.70	10.40	0.1	13.7	−0.18	0.43	−0.23	0.58	55.4	31.1
Emerging Markets	175	20.31	21.69	16.45	13.25	12.7	18.5	1.80	1.76	1.93	2.19	36.4	30.7
Equity Market Neutral	149	7.82	9.48	6.46	4.84	3.0	23.1	1.85	1.98	1.98	1.55	45.5	34.0
Event Driven	257	13.06	11.13	6.72	4.74	20.7	19.1	3.15	6.18	2.54	3.78	31.3	31.6
Fixed Income Arbitrage	134	8.13	7.59	5.29	3.35	16.0	25.8	2.52	4.23	2.27	2.26	42.3	34.8
Global Macro	111	10.51	10.36	12.25	7.31	3.2	18.3	0.97	0.88	1.21	1.16	44.6	28.7
Long/Short Equity Hedge	771	14.90	10.73	13.68	8.41	8.1	18.7	1.26	1.01	1.32	0.89	39.8	30.9
Managed Futures	173	11.71	17.12	18.26	10.97	3.5	17.9	0.82	0.98	0.85	0.61	43.5	31.5
Multi-Strategy	135	12.74	14.52	8.54	11.17	15.1	22.9	2.58	3.37	2.40	3.35	34.6	32.1
Fund of Funds	704	10.23	7.76	6.08	4.30	17.8	18.4	2.12	1.70	2.04	1.63	35.3	28.4
All Funds	2701	12.36	11.99	10.21	8.79	12.9	20.8	1.85	2.74	1.76	1.99	37.5	31.0
All Except Fund of Funds	1997	13.12	13.08	11.67	9.49	11.2	21.3	1.76	3.01	1.66	2.09	38.3	31.9
Graveyard Funds													
Convertible Arbitrage	101	6.65	6.49	6.32	5.21	25.7	25.4	1.83	4.28	1.55	2.62	27.9	32.0
Dedicated Short Bias	20	3.30	10.33	24.69	18.62	−2.9	17.2	0.36	0.87	0.20	0.41	50.8	30.4
Emerging Markets	174	5.71	31.94	25.35	20.37	11.4	19.4	0.60	1.26	0.73	1.42	45.8	31.0
Equity Market Neutral	182	7.33	21.66	9.49	10.84	3.4	24.1	0.85	1.34	0.82	1.23	41.5	30.1

Event Driven	247	9.83	12.29	9.29	9.59	14.6	22.9	1.78	3.25	1.46	1.81	34.3	31.9
Fixed Income Arbitrage	125	6.20	13.06	6.93	6.69	14.5	23.5	2.54	5.13	2.22	4.62	43.0	34.0
Global Macro	178	7.78	43.65	16.86	18.75	0.6	22.8	0.41	1.00	0.47	1.06	47.2	31.9
Long/Short Equity Hedge	947	9.84	19.96	18.37	15.18	4.0	22.0	−0.08	22.74	0.78	1.18	43.8	30.4
Managed Futures	356	4.87	25.56	19.53	19.59	−1.6	18.7	0.30	1.28	0.36	1.13	47.6	29.9
Multi-Strategy	95	5.12	18.93	11.97	15.23	6.2	26.0	1.22	3.46	1.43	4.29	45.0	34.3
Fund of Funds	491	5.36	9.83	9.63	9.48	13.2	21.6	1.10	1.58	1.07	1.24	40.9	31.3
All Funds	2916	7.49	21.65	14.97	15.46	7.2	22.9	0.68	13.13	0.92	1.82	42.6	31.4
All Except Fund of Funds	2425	7.92	23.30	16.05	16.19	6.0	23.0	0.59	14.39	0.89	1.92	42.9	31.4
Combined Funds													
Convertible Arbitrage	176	7.57	5.97	6.27	6.04	31.3	24.3	2.19	4.10	1.53	2.22	21.4	29.5
Dedicated Short Bias	37	1.06	9.07	22.40	15.41	1.6	15.6	0.11	0.75	0.00	0.53	53.0	30.4
Emerging Markets	349	13.03	28.21	20.89	17.72	12.0	18.9	1.21	1.64	1.33	1.94	41.1	31.2
Equity Market Neutral	331	7.55	17.25	8.13	8.79	3.2	23.6	1.30	1.73	1.34	1.50	43.3	31.9
Event Driven	504	11.48	11.81	7.98	7.62	17.7	21.2	2.47	5.00	2.03	3.06	32.7	31.8
Fixed Income Arbitrage	259	7.20	10.61	6.08	5.29	15.3	24.7	2.53	4.67	2.25	3.58	42.6	34.4
Global Macro	289	8.83	34.84	15.09	15.54	1.6	21.2	0.63	0.99	0.76	1.15	46.1	30.6
Long/Short Equity Hedge	1718	12.11	16.66	16.27	12.81	5.9	20.7	0.53	16.86	1.03	1.09	41.9	30.7
Managed Futures	529	7.10	23.35	19.11	17.25	0.1	18.5	0.47	1.21	0.52	1.01	46.2	30.5
Multi-Strategy	230	9.60	16.87	9.96	13.08	11.5	24.5	2.03	3.46	2.02	3.76	38.6	33.3
Fund of Funds	1195	8.23	8.99	7.54	7.13	15.9	19.9	1.70	1.72	1.65	1.56	37.5	29.7
All Funds	5617	9.83	17.84	12.68	12.92	10.0	22.1	1.25	9.64	1.33	1.95	40.0	31.3
All Except Fund of Funds	4422	10.26	19.53	14.07	13.75	8.4	22.4	1.12	10.83	1.25	2.04	40.8	31.7

* These columns contain means and standard deviations of p-values for the Ljung–Box Q-statistic for each fund using the first 11 autocorrelations of returns.

Table 2.7.

Assets under Management at Year End for Funds in Each of the 11 Categories in the Lipper TASS Combined Hedge Fund Database (1977 to 2007)*

Year	Convert Arbitrage	Dedicated Short Bias	Emerging Markets	Equity Market Neutral	Event Driven	Fixed Income Arbitrage	Global Macro	Long/Short Equity	Managed Futures	Multi-Strategy	Fund of Funds	Total
1977					2.0				5.4			7.4
1978					3.7				18.0			21.7
1979					6.0				44.3			50.3
1980					12.0				55.0			67.0
1981					19.4				62.3			81.7
1982					27.7	13.5			72.1		65.7	179.1
1983					59.3	20.4		6.4	62.4		96.7	245.2
1984					112.2	21.7	5.7	12.9	60.2		126.3	339.1
1985					163.2	16.5	4.2	45.8	112.9		212.3	554.9
1986					239.2	63.2	70.6	115.6	209.6		256.2	954.4
1987					271.3	94.4	84.3	228.8	582.9	1,830.0	396.1	3,487.8
1988	3.8				621.8	92.4	167.9	405.1	843.0	1,813.7	708.4	4,656.1
1989	54.2		133.8	41.8	769.1	135.0	343.4	924.3	926.2	2,120.9	850.3	6,299.0
1990	82.8	63.4	202.8	38.5	684.2	268.2	782.5	1,544.2	1,122.3	2,581.0	1,127.2	8,497.1
1991	196.0	57.3	478.5	61.0	1,105.4	582.1	1,533.1	2,817.1	1,373.3	3,157.9	1,884.7	13,246.5
1992	417.7	61.5	968.1	115.2	1,810.4	821.1	5,036.4	4,824.9	1,508.1	3,895.5	2,782.9	22,241.9
1993	917.5	79.3	2,952.5	338.6	3,215.0	1,516.5	13,626.6	8,345.1	2,646.8	5,483.3	6,243.1	45,364.2
1994	914.6	160.4	5,154.9	527.5	4,192.0	2,107.5	11,341.5	10,645.5	3,141.1	4,572.0	6,884.7	49,641.6
1995	973.9	171.5	5,229.8	751.2	5,349.1	3,155.3	12,599.3	13,782.7	2,897.4	6,605.2	9,898.2	61,413.4
1996	1,634.1	253.8	7,431.5	1,577.4	7,578.9	5,321.2	15,856.9	18,895.9	2,833.4	7,523.8	13,395.4	82,302.5
1997	3,154.7	428.1	12,123.3	3,214.6	12,066.5	9,306.7	24,960.7	28,531.4	2,273.7	10,686.2	20,742.3	127,488.2
1998	3,693.0	622.3	6,935.1	5,407.6	16,353.7	8,955.3	22,979.7	31,028.1	3,689.2	9,980.5	22,172.2	131,816.5
1999	4,292.0	691.5	9,003.7	8,142.9	18,716.2	7,936.3	16,118.8	49,537.7	4,314.8	11,396.4	25,943.3	156,093.5
2000	5,849.5	928.7	7,325.1	11,809.6	24,515.9	7,677.8	5,743.4	66,909.9	4,265.8	11,324.8	30,961.0	177,311.7
2001	14,698.5	914.0	7,369.5	16,748.1	31,908.0	10,243.2	4,351.1	70,907.3	5,999.3	15,220.2	40,694.9	219,053.9
2002	17,830.7	520.4	9,276.7	17,511.2	34,093.0	15,528.3	6,090.3	66,612.0	8,894.0	17,048.8	51,109.0	244,514.4
2003	24,093.8	360.9	18,412.9	19,444.5	48,820.2	20,236.3	14,667.8	80,901.4	17,025.6	26,598.6	76,751.7	347,313.7
2004	27,170.0	329.3	28,116.2	21,717.0	71,209.0	29,282.7	21,207.2	103,535.7	23,720.1	37,720.4	115,384.1	479,391.6
2005	16,678.0	353.6	38,820.8	20,067.6	86,698.6	31,021.8	22,965.2	126,980.6	24,797.1	45,440.8	124,325.4	538,149.6
2006	18,966.6	664.2	52,089.7	22,572.5	94,952.7	31,678.0	30,113.8	153,131.4	29,661.6	47,612.0	139,596.3	621,038.8
2007	9,717.4	566.8	58,449.2	22,766.8	92,379.0	33,723.6	31,413.9	168,535.0	29,142.4	60,522.2	146,626.9	653,843.2

* Values are in millions of U.S. dollars.

Table 2.8.

Lipper TASS Status Codes for Funds in the Graveyard Database

Status Code	Definition
1	Fund liquidated
2	Fund no longer reporting
3	Unable to contact fund
4	Fund closed to new investment
5	Fund has merged into another entity
7	Fund dormant
9	Unknown*

* Of the 2,916 funds in the Graveyard database, 80 did not have status codes assigned, hence we coded them as 9's ("Unknown").

standard deviation of 6.22%, but in the Graveyard database, the 101 Convertible Arbitrage funds have an average mean return of 6.65% and an average standard deviation of 6.32%. As expected, average volatilities in the Graveyard database are uniformly higher than those in the Live database because the higher-volatility funds are more likely to be eliminated. This effect operates at both ends of the return distribution—funds that are wildly successful are also more likely to leave the database since they have less motivation to advertise their performance. That the Graveyard database also contains successful funds is supported by the fact that in some categories the average mean return in the Graveyard database is the same as or higher than in the Live database, e.g., Convertible Arbitrage, Equity Market Neutral, and Dedicated Shortseller.

Figure 2.3 displays a histogram of year-to-date returns at the time of liquidation. The fact that the distribution is skewed to the left is consistent with the conventional wisdom that performance is a major factor in determining the fate of a hedge fund. However, note that there is nontrivial weight in the right half of the distribution, suggesting that recent performance is not the only relevant factor.

Finally, Figure 2.4 provides a summary of two key characteristics of the Graveyard funds: the age distribution of funds at the time of liquidation, and the distribution of their assets under management. The median age of Graveyard funds is 36 months; hence half of all liquidated funds never reached their fourth anniversary. The mode of the distribution is 23 months. The median assets under management for funds in the Graveyard database is $10.5 million, not an uncommon size for a typical startup hedge fund.

To develop a sense of the dynamics of the Lipper TASS database and the birth and death rates of hedge funds over the past decade,[10] in Table 2.10 we report annual frequency counts for the funds in the database at the start of each year,

---

[10] Recall that Lipper TASS launched its Graveyard database in 1994; hence this is the beginning of the sample for Table 2.10.

Table 2.9.

Frequency Counts and Assets under Management of Funds in the Lipper TASS Graveyard Database by Category and Graveyard Inclusion Code*

Code	All Funds	Convertible Arbitrage	Dedicated Short Bias	Emerging Markets	Equity Market Neutral	Event Driven	Fixed Income Arbitrage	Global Macro	Long/Short Equity Hedge	Managed Futures	Multi-Strategy	Fund of Funds
Frequency Count												
1	1,290	48	11	82	104	93	50	71	382	198	50	201
2	847	32	4	51	35	85	37	49	321	58	27	148
3	507	12	2	21	30	46	23	39	179	40	11	104
4	6	0	0	0	0	1	2	0	2	0	0	1
5	80	4	1	4	5	12	6	6	21	12	3	6
7	2	0	0	0	0	1	0	0	1	0	0	0
9	184	5	2	16	8	9	7	13	41	48	4	31
Total	2,916	101	20	174	182	247	125	178	947	356	95	491
Assets under Management†												
1	47,134	3,596	100	2,379	2,581	4,974	3,733	10,377	9,345	1,726	2,768	5,554
2	83,302	10,985	339	1,939	1,704	20,081	3,455	2,220	24,770	1,489	1,190	15,130
3	44,790	600	61	4,224	1,750	3,165	1,492	552	10,625	814	331	21,176
4	462	0	0	0	0	100	33	0	223	0	0	106
5	4,247	38	31	124	131	969	498	1,775	497	67	97	21
7	8	0	0	0	0	6	0	0	2	0	0	0
9	15,215	137	18	1,818	126	5,534	488	115	2,496	1,790	111	2,582
Total	195,157	15,356	549	10,485	6,293	34,830	9,699	15,039	47,958	5,886	4,497	44,568

* All values are in millions of U.S. dollars.
† Assets under management are at the time of transfer into the Graveyard database.

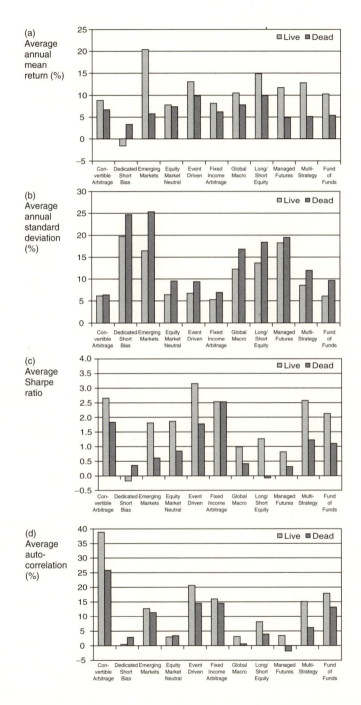

Figure 2.2. *Comparison of average means, standard deviations, Sharpe ratios, and first-order autocorrelation coefficients for categories of funds in the Lipper TASS Live and Graveyard databases (January 1994 to August 2007).*

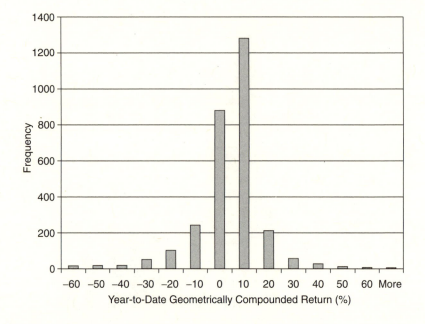

Figure 2.3. *Histogram of year-to-date return at the time of liquidation of hedge funds in the Lipper TASS Graveyard database (January 1994 to August 2007).*

funds entering the Live database during the year, funds exiting during the year and moving to the Graveyard database, and funds entering and exiting within the year. The panel labelled "All Funds" contains frequency counts for all funds, and the remaining 11 panels contain the same statistics for each category. Also included in Table 2.10 are attrition rates, defined as the ratio of funds exiting in a given year to the number of existing funds at the start of the year, and the performance of the category as measured by the annual compound return of the CS/Tremont index for that category.

For the filtered sample of all funds in the Lipper TASS database, and over the sample period from 1994 to 2006, the average attrition rate is 9.9%.[11] This is similar to the 8.5% attrition rate obtained by Liang (2001) for the 1994–1999

---

[11] We do not include 2007 in this average because Lipper TASS typically waits 8 to 10 months before moving a nonreporting fund from the Live to the Graveyard database. Therefore, the attrition rate is severely downward-biased for 2007 since the year is not yet complete, and many nonreporting funds in the Live database have not yet been classified as Graveyard funds. Hedge funds often go through an "incubation period" where managers trade with limited resources to develop a track record. If successful, the manager will provide the return stream to a database vendor like Lipper TASS, and the vendor usually enters the entire track record into the database, providing the fund with an "instant history." According to Fung and Hsieh (2000), the average incubation period—from a fund's inception to its entry into the Lipper TASS database—is 1 year.

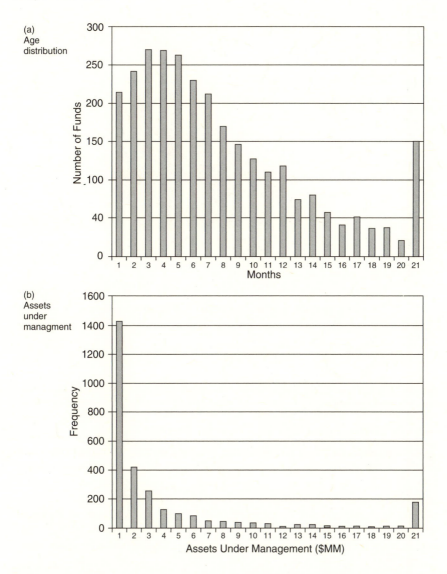

Figure 2.4. *Histograms of age distribution and assets under management at the time of liquidation for funds in the Lipper TASS Graveyard database (January 1994 to August 2007).*

sample period. The aggregate attrition rate rises in 1998, partly because of LTCM's demise and the dislocation caused by its aftermath. The attrition rate increases to a peak of 11.9% in 2001, mostly because of the Long/Short Equity category—presumably a result of the bursting of the technology bubble.

Table 2.10a.
Attrition Rates for All Hedge Funds in the Lipper TASS Hedge Fund Database within Each Style Category (January 1994 to August 2007, filtered data).

All Funds

Year	Existing Funds	New Entries	New Exits	Intrayear Entry and Exit	Total Funds	Attrition Rate (%)	Index Return (%)
1994	537	229	7	14	759	1.3	−4.4
1995	759	269	51	8	977	6.7	21.7
1996	977	301	100	10	1,178	10.2	22.2
1997	1,178	341	93	7	1,426	7.9	25.9
1998	1,426	309	120	12	1,615	8.4	−0.4
1999	1,615	408	164	16	1,859	10.2	23.4
2000	1,859	388	199	11	2,048	10.7	4.8
2001	2,048	415	244	6	2,219	11.9	4.4
2002	2,219	443	243	11	2,419	11.0	3.0
2003	2,419	522	230	15	2,711	9.5	15.4
2004	2,711	526	295	16	2,942	10.9	9.6
2005	2,942	422	413	18	2,951	14.0	7.6
2006	2,951	232	471	11	2,712	16.0	13.9
2007	2,712	118	129	2	2,701	4.8	8.7

Long/Short Equity Hedge

Year	Existing Funds	New Entries	New Exits	Intrayear Entry and Exit	Total Funds	Attrition Rate (%)	Index Return (%)
1994	126	46	0	2	172	0.0	−8.1
1995	172	64	6	0	230	3.5	23.0
1996	230	104	13	1	321	5.7	17.1
1997	321	115	23	2	413	7.2	21.5
1998	413	108	27	3	494	6.5	17.2
1999	494	154	36	9	612	7.3	47.2
2000	612	176	53	6	735	8.7	2.1
2001	735	147	98	2	784	13.3	−3.7
2002	784	127	102	6	809	13.0	−1.6
2003	809	139	97	5	851	12.0	17.3
2004	851	140	105	5	886	12.3	11.6
2005	886	135	138	5	883	15.6	9.7
2006	883	61	148	5	796	16.8	14.4
2007	796	25	50	0	771	6.3	9.0

Equity Market Neutral

Year	Existing Funds	New Entries	New Exits	Intrayear Entry and Exit	Total Funds	Attrition Rate (%)	Index Return (%)
1994	10	6	0	0	16	0.0	−2.0
1995	16	9	1	0	24	6.3	11.0
1996	24	7	0	0	31	0.0	16.6
1997	31	14	0	0	45	0.0	14.8
1998	45	28	1	2	72	2.2	13.3
1999	72	36	12	2	96	16.7	15.3
2000	96	17	13	0	100	13.5	15.0
2001	100	37	6	0	131	6.0	9.3
2002	131	31	17	2	145	13.0	7.4
2003	145	33	22	2	156	15.2	7.1
2004	156	39	35	2	160	22.4	6.5
2005	160	25	24	0	161	15.0	6.1
2006	161	14	26	1	149	16.1	11.2
2007	149	14	14	0	149	9.4	5.6

Convertible Arbitrage

Year	Existing Funds	New Entries	New Exits	Intrayear Entry and Exit	Total Funds	Attrition Rate (%)	Index Return (%)
1994	17	10	0	0	27	0.0	−8.1
1995	27	9	2	1	34	7.4	16.6
1996	34	11	4	0	41	11.8	17.9
1997	41	6	3	0	44	7.3	14.5
1998	44	11	5	0	50	11.4	−4.4
1999	50	9	2	0	57	4.0	16.0
2000	57	12	1	0	68	1.8	25.6
2001	68	30	10	0	88	14.7	14.6
2002	88	27	2	0	113	2.3	4.0
2003	113	17	10	0	120	8.8	12.9
2004	120	7	19	0	108	15.8	2.0
2005	108	6	23	0	91	21.3	−2.5
2006	91	2	17	0	76	18.7	14.3
2007	76	1	2	0	75	2.6	4.0

Table 2.10a.

(continued)

Event Driven

Year	Existing Funds	New Entries	New Exits	Intrayear Entry and Exit	Total Funds	Attrition Rate (%)	Index Return (%)
1994	48	15	0	0	63	0.0	0.7
1995	63	26	0	0	89	0.0	18.3
1996	89	26	3	0	112	3.4	23.1
1997	112	29	1	0	140	0.9	20.0
1998	140	25	4	1	161	2.9	-4.9
1999	161	25	17	0	169	10.6	22.3
2000	169	43	13	0	199	7.7	7.3
2001	199	34	17	3	216	8.5	11.5
2002	216	51	25	2	242	11.6	0.2
2003	242	54	21	1	275	8.7	20.0
2004	275	50	31	0	294	11.3	14.5
2005	294	33	34	3	293	11.6	9.0
2006	293	24	64	1	253	21.8	15.7
2007	253	9	5	0	257	2.0	11.9

Dedicated Short Bias

Year	Existing Funds	New Entries	New Exits	Intrayear Entry and Exit	Total Funds	Attrition Rate (%)	Index Return (%)
1994	5	2	0	0	7	0.0	14.9
1995	7	1	1	1	7	14.3	-7.4
1996	7	4	1	0	10	14.3	-5.5
1997	10	4	0	0	14	0.0	0.4
1998	14	1	0	0	15	0.0	-6.0
1999	15	5	1	0	19	6.7	-14.2
2000	19	4	0	0	23	0.0	15.8
2001	23	1	7	0	17	30.4	-3.6
2002	17	1	1	0	17	5.9	18.1
2003	17	5	1	0	21	5.9	-32.6
2004	21	0	4	0	17	19.0	-7.7
2005	17	2	2	0	17	11.8	17.0
2006	17	0	1	0	16	5.9	-6.6
2007	16	1	0	0	17	0.0	4.8

Managed Futures

Year	Existing Funds	New Entries	New Exits	Intrayear Entry and Exit	Total Funds	Attrition Rate (%)	Index Return (%)
1994	134	41	4	8	171	3.0	12.0
1995	171	35	18	2	188	10.5	-7.1
1996	188	32	41	3	179	21.8	12.0
1997	179	30	28	2	181	15.6	3.1
1998	181	20	23	0	178	12.7	20.6
1999	178	35	34	2	179	19.1	-4.7
2000	179	17	26	0	170	14.5	4.2
2001	170	21	20	0	171	11.8	1.9
2002	171	15	29	0	157	17.0	18.3
2003	157	31	13	2	175	8.3	14.1
2004	175	43	15	2	203	8.6	6.0
2005	203	35	37	1	201	18.2	-0.1
2006	201	11	35	1	177	17.4	8.1
2007	177	6	10	0	173	5.6	2.2

Fixed Income Arbitrage

Year	Existing Funds	New Entries	New Exits	Intrayear Entry and Exit	Total Funds	Attrition Rate (%)	Index Return (%)
1994	14	16	0	0	30	0.0	0.3
1995	30	10	2	1	38	6.7	12.5
1996	38	15	2	1	51	5.3	15.9
1997	51	14	3	2	62	5.9	9.3
1998	62	14	13	0	63	21.0	-8.2
1999	63	9	9	1	63	14.3	12.1
2000	63	8	8	0	63	12.7	6.3
2001	63	18	5	1	76	7.9	8.0
2002	76	20	7	0	89	9.2	5.8
2003	89	31	7	0	113	7.9	8.0
2004	113	35	6	0	142	5.3	6.9
2005	142	22	24	2	140	16.9	0.6
2006	140	14	24	0	130	17.1	8.7
2007	130	11	7	0	134	5.4	1.7

Table 2.10a.
(continued)

Multi-Strategy

Year	Existing Funds	New Entries	New Exits	Intrayear Entry and Exit	Total Funds	Attrition Rate (%)	Index Return (%)
1994	14	5	2	2	17	14.3	–
1995	17	10	1	0	26	5.9	11.9
1996	26	13	1	0	38	3.8	14.1
1997	38	9	7	0	40	18.4	18.3
1998	40	9	3	1	46	7.5	7.7
1999	46	12	1	1	57	2.2	9.4
2000	57	15	1	1	71	1.8	11.2
2001	71	14	1	0	84	1.4	5.5
2002	84	17	5	0	96	6.0	6.3
2003	96	26	12	3	110	12.5	15.0
2004	110	21	13	2	118	11.8	7.5
2005	118	27	20	1	125	16.9	7.5
2006	125	21	16	0	130	12.8	14.5
2007	130	7	2	0	135	1.5	8.1

Global Macro

Year	Existing Funds	New Entries	New Exits	Intrayear Entry and Exit	Total Funds	Attrition Rate (%)	Index Return (%)
1994	40	14	1	1	53	2.5	–5.7
1995	53	17	7	0	63	13.2	30.7
1996	63	11	12	4	62	19.0	25.6
1997	62	18	7	0	73	11.3	37.1
1998	73	14	3	2	84	4.1	–3.6
1999	84	17	17	1	84	20.2	5.8
2000	84	10	28	0	66	33.3	11.7
2001	66	12	12	0	66	18.2	18.4
2002	66	33	5	0	94	7.6	14.7
2003	94	23	7	1	110	7.4	18.0
2004	110	24	10	0	124	9.1	8.5
2005	124	23	24	0	123	19.4	9.2
2006	123	15	29	0	109	23.6	13.5
2007	109	9	7	0	111	6.4	9.0

Emerging Markets

Year	Existing Funds	New Entries	New Exits	Intrayear Entry and Exit	Total Funds	Attrition Rate (%)	Index Return (%)
1994	32	26	0	0	58	0.0	12.5
1995	58	30	2	0	86	3.4	–16.9
1996	86	23	4	0	105	4.7	34.5
1997	105	45	6	0	144	5.7	26.6
1998	144	27	24	3	147	16.7	–37.7
1999	147	29	13	0	163	8.8	44.8
2000	163	20	26	3	157	16.0	–5.5
2001	157	4	24	0	137	15.3	5.8
2002	137	8	11	0	134	8.0	7.4
2003	134	21	12	0	143	9.0	28.8
2004	143	19	9	0	153	6.3	12.5
2005	153	26	8	1	171	5.2	17.4
2006	171	23	14	0	180	8.2	20.5
2007	180	9	14	0	175	7.8	12.1

Fund of Funds

Year	Existing Funds	New Entries	New Exits	Intrayear Entry and Exit	Total Funds	Attrition Rate (%)	Index Return (%)
1994	97	48	0	1	145	0.0	–
1995	145	58	11	3	192	7.6	–
1996	192	55	19	1	228	9.9	–
1997	228	57	15	1	270	6.6	–
1998	270	52	17	0	305	6.3	–
1999	305	77	22	0	360	7.2	–
2000	360	66	30	1	396	8.3	–
2001	396	97	44	0	449	11.1	–
2002	449	113	39	1	523	8.7	–
2003	523	142	28	1	637	5.4	–
2004	637	148	48	5	737	7.5	–
2005	737	88	79	5	746	10.7	–
2006	746	47	97	3	696	13.0	–
2007	696	26	18	2	704	2.6	–

*Index returns are annual compound returns of the CS/Tremont hedge fund indexes. Attrition rates for 2007 are severely downward-biased because Lipper TASS typically waits 8–10 months before moving a nonreporting fund from the Live database to the Graveyard database; therefore, as of August 2007, many nonreporting funds in the Live database have not yet been moved to the Graveyard database.

Table 2.10b.

Attrition Rates for All Hedge Funds in the Lipper TASS Hedge Fund Database within Each Style Category (January 1994 to August 2007, unfiltered data).

Year	Existing Funds	New Entries	New Exits	Intrayear Entry and Exit	Total Funds	Attrition Rate (%)	Index Return (%)
			All Funds				
1994	838	273	19	2	1,092	2.3	−4.4
1995	1,092	314	69	1	1,337	6.3	21.7
1996	1,337	352	124	5	1,565	9.3	22.2
1997	1,565	384	107	6	1,842	6.8	25.9
1998	1,842	383	169	9	2,056	9.2	−0.4
1999	2,056	469	189	5	2,336	9.2	23.4
2000	2,336	490	228	6	2,598	9.8	4.8
2001	2,598	644	244	4	2,998	9.4	4.4
2002	2,998	684	280	7	3,402	9.3	3.0
2003	3,402	819	267	9	3,954	7.8	15.4
2004	3,954	926	342	11	4,538	8.6	9.6
2005	4,538	727	522	17	4,743	11.5	7.6
2006	4,743	433	673	9	4,503	14.2	13.9
2007	4,503	96	333	1	4,266	7.4	8.7
			Long/Short Equity Hedge				
1994	198	58	3	0	253	1.5	−8.1
1995	253	80	9	0	324	3.6	23.0
1996	324	121	21	0	424	6.5	17.1
1997	424	130	22	3	532	5.2	21.5
1998	532	132	31	2	633	5.8	17.2
1999	633	178	47	3	764	7.4	47.2
2000	764	224	56	4	932	7.3	2.1
2001	932	225	99	2	1058	10.6	−3.7
2002	1,058	179	118	4	1119	11.2	−1.6
2003	1,119	212	110	3	1221	9.8	17.3
2004	1,221	252	136	4	1337	11.1	11.6
2005	1,337	221	166	4	1392	12.4	9.7
2006	1,392	143	207	3	1328	14.9	14.4
2007	1,328	24	119	0	1233	9.0	9.0

Year	Existing Funds	New Entries	New Exits	Intrayear Entry and Exit	Total Funds	Attrition Rate (%)	Index Return (%)
			Equity Market Neutral				
1994	14	9	1	0	22	7.1	−2.0
1995	22	10	1	0	31	4.5	11.0
1996	31	12	0	0	43	0.0	16.6
1997	43	16	0	0	59	0.0	14.8
1998	59	31	2	1	88	3.4	13.3
1999	88	41	10	1	119	11.4	15.3
2000	119	19	17	0	121	14.3	15.0
2001	121	57	7	1	171	5.8	9.3
2002	171	62	17	0	216	9.9	7.4
2003	216	54	28	1	242	13.0	7.1
2004	242	48	37	0	253	15.3	6.5
2005	253	48	37	1	264	14.6	6.1
2006	264	17	41	0	240	15.5	11.2
2007	240	7	37	0	210	15.4	5.6
			Convertible Arbitrage				
1994	27	13	0	0	40	0.0	−8.1
1995	40	9	0	0	49	0.0	16.6
1996	49	13	8	0	54	16.3	17.9
1997	54	9	3	0	60	5.6	14.5
1998	60	15	6	0	69	10.0	−4.4
1999	69	11	3	0	77	4.3	16.0
2000	77	15	0	0	92	0.0	25.6
2001	92	29	8	0	113	8.7	14.6
2002	113	28	4	0	137	3.5	4.0
2003	137	17	11	0	143	8.0	12.9
2004	143	10	14	0	139	9.8	2.0
2005	139	12	34	0	117	24.5	−2.5
2006	117	4	18	0	103	15.4	14.3
2007	103	2	9	0	96	8.7	4.0

Table 2.10b.
(*continued*)

Managed Futures

Year	Existing Funds	New Entries	New Exits	Intrayear Entry and Exit	Total Funds	Attrition Rate (%)	Index Return (%)
1994	194	55	8	1	241	4.1	12.0
1995	241	40	26	0	255	10.8	-7.1
1996	255	47	51	1	251	20.0	12.0
1997	251	38	35	1	254	13.9	3.1
1998	254	26	40	0	240	15.7	20.6
1999	240	39	44	0	235	18.3	-4.7
2000	235	19	34	0	220	14.5	4.2
2001	220	24	21	0	223	9.5	1.9
2002	223	24	37	0	210	16.6	18.3
2003	210	42	19	1	233	9.0	14.1
2004	233	67	20	1	280	8.6	6.0
2005	280	42	41	0	281	14.6	-0.1
2006	281	23	46	3	258	16.4	8.1
2007	258	4	28	1	234	10.9	2.2

Fixed Income Arbitrage

Year	Existing Funds	New Entries	New Exits	Intrayear Entry and Exit	Total Funds	Attrition Rate (%)	Index Return (%)
1994	23	16	0	0	39	0.0	0.3
1995	39	12	5	0	46	12.8	12.5
1996	46	16	4	0	58	8.7	15.9
1997	58	16	3	1	71	5.2	9.3
1998	71	15	14	0	72	19.7	-8.2
1999	72	13	8	0	77	11.1	12.1
2000	77	14	11	0	80	14.3	6.3
2001	80	23	6	0	97	7.5	8.0
2002	97	29	7	0	119	7.2	5.8
2003	119	57	6	0	170	5.0	8.0
2004	170	53	10	0	213	5.9	6.9
2005	213	31	29	1	215	13.6	0.6
2006	215	22	41	0	196	19.1	8.7
2007	196	7	10	0	193	5.1	1.7

Event Driven

Year	Existing Funds	New Entries	New Exits	Intrayear Entry and Exit	Total Funds	Attrition Rate (%)	Index Return (%)
1994	66	17	0	0	83	0.0	0.7
1995	83	26	0	0	109	0.0	18.3
1996	109	30	2	0	137	1.8	23.1
1997	137	30	2	0	165	1.5	20.0
1998	165	29	4	1	190	2.4	-4.9
1999	190	34	16	0	208	8.4	22.3
2000	208	44	15	0	237	7.2	7.3
2001	237	51	17	2	271	7.2	11.5
2002	271	64	28	2	307	10.3	0.2
2003	307	64	25	1	346	8.1	20.0
2004	346	61	28	0	379	8.1	14.5
2005	379	43	36	2	386	9.5	9.0
2006	386	35	69	1	352	17.9	15.7
2007	352	2	20	0	334	5.7	11.9

Dedicated Short Bias

Year	Existing Funds	New Entries	New Exits	Intrayear Entry and Exit	Total Funds	Attrition Rate (%)	Index Return (%)
1994	11	3	0	0	14	0.0	14.9
1995	14	0	1	0	13	7.1	-7.4
1996	13	3	1	0	15	7.7	-5.5
1997	15	3	1	0	17	6.7	0.4
1998	17	1	0	0	18	0.0	-6.0
1999	18	5	1	0	22	5.6	-14.2
2000	22	3	0	0	25	0.0	15.8
2001	25	1	7	0	19	28.0	-3.6
2002	19	1	1	0	19	5.3	18.1
2003	19	4	0	0	23	0.0	-32.6
2004	23	1	4	0	20	17.4	-7.7
2005	20	2	1	0	21	5.0	17.0
2006	21	0	3	0	18	14.3	-6.6
2007	18	1	0	0	19	0.0	4.8

Table 2.10b.
(continued)

Multi-Strategy

Year	Existing Funds	New Entries	New Exits	Intrayear Entry and Exit	Total Funds	Attrition Rate (%)	Index Return (%)
1994	25	6	3	1	28	12.0	–
1995	28	12	7	0	33	25.0	11.9
1996	33	15	1	0	47	3.0	14.1
1997	47	16	3	0	60	6.4	18.3
1998	60	13	5	1	68	8.3	7.7
1999	68	14	2	0	80	2.9	9.4
2000	80	17	2	0	95	2.5	11.2
2001	95	20	2	0	113	2.1	5.5
2002	113	29	5	0	137	4.4	6.3
2003	137	32	12	2	157	8.8	15.0
2004	157	32	13	2	176	8.3	7.5
2005	176	42	25	1	193	14.2	7.5
2006	193	31	26	0	198	13.5	14.5
2007	198	14	13	0	199	6.6	8.1

Global Macro

Year	Existing Funds	New Entries	New Exits	Intrayear Entry and Exit	Total Funds	Attrition Rate (%)	Index Return (%)
1994	56	12	3	0	65	5.4	-5.7
1995	65	21	6	0	80	9.2	30.7
1996	80	14	16	4	78	20.0	25.6
1997	78	20	7	1	91	9.0	37.1
1998	91	20	8	2	103	8.8	-3.6
1999	103	15	15	1	103	14.6	5.8
2000	103	18	32	0	89	31.1	11.7
2001	89	18	13	0	94	14.6	18.4
2002	94	38	7	0	125	7.4	14.7
2003	125	41	10	1	156	8.0	18.0
2004	156	37	10	0	183	6.4	8.5
2005	183	43	29	1	197	15.8	9.2
2006	197	22	39	0	180	19.8	13.5
2007	180	14	13	0	174	7.2	9.0

Emerging Markets

Year	Existing Funds	New Entries	New Exits	Intrayear Entry and Exit	Total Funds	Attrition Rate (%)	Index Return (%)
1994	50	25	0	0	75	0.0	12.5
1995	75	34	0	0	109	0.0	-16.9
1996	109	26	5	0	130	4.6	34.5
1997	130	43	8	0	165	6.2	26.6
1998	165	27	30	2	162	18.2	-37.7
1999	162	31	13	0	180	8.0	44.8
2000	180	22	26	1	176	14.4	-5.5
2001	176	6	28	0	154	15.9	5.8
2002	154	14	14	0	154	9.1	7.4
2003	154	24	12	1	166	7.8	28.8
2004	166	39	9	0	196	5.4	12.5
2005	196	50	9	0	237	4.6	17.4
2006	237	35	26	0	246	11.0	20.5
2007	246	4	19	0	231	7.7	12.1

Fund of Funds

Year	Existing Funds	New Entries	New Exits	Intrayear Entry and Exit	Total Funds	Attrition Rate (%)	Index Return (%)
1994	174	59	1	1	232	0.6	–
1995	232	70	14	1	288	6.0	–
1996	288	55	15	0	328	5.2	–
1997	328	63	23	0	368	7.0	–
1998	368	74	29	0	413	7.9	–
1999	413	88	30	0	471	7.3	–
2000	471	95	35	1	531	7.4	–
2001	531	190	36	0	685	6.8	–
2002	685	216	42	0	859	6.1	–
2003	859	272	34	0	1097	4.0	–
2004	1,097	326	61	3	1362	5.6	–
2005	1,362	193	115	8	1440	8.4	–
2006	1,440	101	157	1	1384	10.9	–
2007	1,384	24	65	0	1343	4.7	–

* Index returns are annual compound returns of the CS/Tremont hedge fund indexes. Attrition rates for 2007 are severely downward-biased because Lipper TASS typically waits 8–10 months before moving a nonreporting fund from the Live database to the Graveyard database; therefore, as of August 2007, many nonreporting funds in the Live database have not yet been moved to the Graveyard database.

Table 2.11.

Decomposition of Attrition Rates by Category for All Hedge Funds in the Lipper TASS Hedge Fund Database (January 1994 to August 2007), Corresponding CS/Tremont Hedge Fund Index Returns, and Assets under Management

Year	All Funds	Convert Arb	Ded Short	Emerging Mkts	Equity Market Neutral	Event Driven	Fixed Income Arbitrage	Global Macro	Long/Short Equity	Managed Futures	Multi-Strategy	Fund of Funds
				Total Attrition Rates and Components by Category (%)								
1994	1.3	0.0	0.0	0.0	0.0	0.0	0.0	0.2	0.0	0.7	0.4	0.0
1995	6.7	0.3	0.1	0.3	0.1	0.0	0.3	0.9	0.8	2.4	0.1	1.4
1996	10.2	0.4	0.1	0.4	0.0	0.3	0.2	1.2	1.3	4.2	0.1	1.9
1997	7.9	0.3	0.0	0.5	0.0	0.1	0.3	0.6	2.0	2.4	0.6	1.3
1998	8.4	0.4	0.0	1.7	0.1	0.3	0.9	0.2	1.9	1.6	0.2	1.2
1999	10.2	0.1	0.1	0.8	0.7	1.1	0.6	1.1	2.2	2.1	0.1	1.4
2000	10.7	0.1	0.0	1.4	0.7	0.7	0.4	1.5	2.9	1.4	0.1	1.6
2001	11.9	0.5	0.3	1.2	0.3	0.8	0.2	0.6	4.8	1.0	0.0	2.1
2002	11.0	0.1	0.0	0.5	0.8	1.1	0.2	0.2	4.6	1.3	0.2	1.8
2003	9.5	0.4	0.0	0.5	0.9	0.9	0.3	0.3	4.0	0.5	0.5	1.2
2004	10.9	0.7	0.1	0.3	1.3	1.1	0.2	0.4	3.9	0.6	0.5	1.8
2005	14.0	0.8	0.1	0.3	0.8	1.2	0.8	0.8	4.7	1.3	0.7	2.7
2006	16.0	0.6	0.0	0.5	0.9	2.2	0.8	1.0	5.0	1.2	0.5	3.3
2007	4.8	0.1	0.0	0.5	0.5	0.2	0.3	0.3	1.8	0.4	0.1	0.7
Mean	9.9	0.3	0.1	0.6	0.5	0.7	0.4	0.7	2.9	1.6	0.3	1.7
S.D.	3.5	0.2	0.1	0.5	0.4	0.6	0.3	0.4	1.7	1.0	0.2	0.8
				Total Returns of CS/Tremont Hedge Fund Indexes by Category (%)								
1994	-4.4	-8.1	14.9	12.5	-2.0	0.7	0.3	-5.7	-8.1	12.0	—	—
1995	21.7	16.6	-7.4	-16.9	11.0	18.3	12.5	30.7	23.0	-7.1	11.9	—
1996	22.2	17.9	-5.5	34.5	16.6	23.1	15.9	25.6	17.1	12.0	14.1	—
1997	25.9	14.5	0.4	26.6	14.8	20.0	9.3	37.1	21.5	3.1	18.3	—
1998	-0.4	-4.4	-6.0	-37.7	13.3	-4.9	-8.2	-3.6	17.2	20.6	7.7	—
1999	23.4	16.0	-14.2	44.8	15.3	22.3	12.1	5.8	47.2	-4.7	9.4	—
2000	4.8	25.6	15.8	-5.5	15.0	7.3	6.3	11.7	2.1	4.2	11.2	—

2001	4.4	14.6	−3.6	5.8	9.3	11.5	8.0	18.4	−3.7	1.9	5.5	—
2002	3.0	4.0	18.1	7.4	7.4	0.2	5.8	14.7	−1.6	18.3	6.3	—
2003	15.4	12.9	−32.6	28.8	7.1	20.0	8.0	18.0	17.3	14.1	15.0	—
2004	9.6	2.0	−7.7	12.5	6.5	14.5	6.9	8.5	11.6	6.0	7.5	—
2005	7.6	−2.5	17.0	17.4	6.1	9.0	0.6	9.2	9.7	−0.1	7.5	—
2006	13.9	14.3	−6.6	20.5	11.2	15.7	8.7	13.5	14.4	8.1	14.5	—
2007	8.7	4.0	4.8	12.1	5.6	11.9	1.7	9.0	9.0	2.2	8.1	—
Mean	11.3	9.5	−1.3	11.6	10.1	12.1	6.6	14.1	12.9	6.8	10.7	
S.D.	9.9	10.2	14.6	22.1	5.2	9.1	6.2	12.3	14.3	8.4	4.1	

Total Assets Under Management ($ millions) and Percentage Breakdown by Category (%)

Year												
1994	49,642	1.8	0.3	10.4	1.1	8.4	4.2	22.8	21.4	6.3	9.2	13.9
1995	61,413	1.6	0.3	8.5	1.2	8.7	5.1	20.5	22.4	4.7	10.8	16.1
1996	82,303	2.0	0.3	9.0	1.9	9.2	6.5	19.3	23.0	3.4	9.1	16.3
1997	127,488	2.5	0.3	9.5	2.5	9.5	7.3	19.6	22.4	1.8	8.4	16.3
1998	131,817	2.8	0.5	5.3	4.1	12.4	6.8	17.4	23.5	2.8	7.6	16.8
1999	156,093	2.7	0.4	5.8	5.2	12.0	5.1	10.3	31.7	2.8	7.3	16.6
2000	177,312	3.3	0.5	4.1	6.7	13.8	4.3	3.2	37.7	2.4	6.4	17.5
2001	219,054	6.7	0.4	3.4	7.6	14.6	4.7	2.0	32.4	2.7	6.9	18.6
2002	244,514	7.3	0.2	3.8	7.2	13.9	6.4	2.5	27.2	3.6	7.0	20.9
2003	347,314	6.9	0.1	5.3	5.6	14.1	5.8	4.2	23.3	4.9	7.7	22.1
2004	479,392	5.7	0.1	5.9	4.5	14.9	6.1	4.4	21.6	4.9	7.9	24.1
2005	538,150	3.1	0.1	7.2	3.7	16.1	5.8	4.3	23.6	4.6	8.4	23.1
2006	621,039	3.1	0.1	8.4	3.6	15.3	5.1	4.8	24.7	4.8	7.7	22.5
2007	653,843	1.5	0.1	8.9	3.5	14.1	5.2	4.8	25.8	4.5	9.3	22.4
Mean	248,887	3.8	0.3	6.7	4.2	12.5	5.6	10.4	25.8	3.8	8.0	18.8
S.D.	189,445	2.1	0.2	2.3	2.2	2.7	1.0	8.1	5.1	1.3	1.2	3.3

* Attrition rates for 2007 are severely downward-biased because Lipper TASS typically waits 8–10 months before moving a nonreporting fund from the Live database to the Graveyard database; therefore, as of August 2007, many nonreporting in the Live database have not yet been moved to the Graveyard database. Consequently the reported means and standard deviations in all three panels are computed over the 1994–2006 period.

Although 9.9% is the average attrition rate for the entire Lipper TASS database, there is considerable variation in average attrition rates across categories. Averaging the annual attrition rates from 1994 to 2006 within each category yields the following:

Convertible Arbitrage	9.6%	Global Macro	14.5%
Dedicated Shortseller	8.8%	Long/Short Equity	9.4%
Emerging Markets	8.3%	Managed Futures	13.7%
Equity Market Neutral	9.7%	Multi-Strategy	8.9%
Event Driven	7.6%	Fund of Funds	7.9%
Fixed Income Arbitrage	10.0%		

These averages illustrate the different risks involved in each of the 11 investment styles. At 7.6%, Event Driven enjoys the lowest average attrition rate, which is not surprising since this category has one of the lowest average return volatilities of 7.98% (Table 2.6). The highest average attrition rate is 14.5% for Global Macro, which is also consistent with the 15.09% average volatility of this category, one of the highest among all 11 categories.

Within each category, the year-to-year attrition rates exhibit different patterns, partly attributable to the relative performance of the categories. For example, Emerging Markets experienced a 16.7% attrition rate in 1998, no doubt because of the turmoil in emerging markets in 1997 and 1998, which is reflected in the -37.7% return in the CS/Tremont Emerging Markets Index for 1998. The opposite pattern is also present—during periods of unusually good performance, attrition rates decline, as in the case of Long/Short Equity from 1995 to 2000 where the attrition rates were 3.5%, 5.7%, 7.2%, 6.5%, 7.3%, and 8.7%, respectively. Of course, in the 3 years following the bursting of the technology bubble—2001 to 2003—the attrition rates for Long/Short Equity shot up to 13.3%, 13.0%, and 12.0%, respectively. These patterns are consistent with the basic economic of the hedge fund industry: Good performance begets more assets under management, greater business leverage, and staying power; poor performance leads to the Graveyard database.

To develop a better sense of the relative magnitudes of attrition across categories, Table 2.11 and plate 2a provide a decomposition by category where the attrition rates in each category are renormalized so that when they are summed across categories in a given year, the result equals the aggregate attrition rate for that year. From these renormalized figures, it is apparent that there is an increase in the proportion of the total attrition rate due to Long/Short Equity funds beginning in 2001. In fact, Table 2.11 shows that of the total attrition rates of 11.9%, 11.0%, and 9.5% in the years 2001 to 2003, the Long/Short Equity category was responsible for 4.8, 4.6, and 4.0 percentage points of those totals, respectively. Despite the fact that the average attrition rate for the Long/Short Equity category is only 9.4% from 1994 to 2006, the funds in this category are more numerous, hence they contribute more to the aggregate attrition rate. Plate 2b provides a measure of the impact of these attrition rates on the industry by plotting the total assets under management of funds in the Lipper TASS database along with the relative proportions in each category. Long/Short Equity funds are indeed a significant fraction of the industry, hence the increase in their attrition rates in recent years may be cause for some concern. Chan, Getmansky, Haas, and Lo (2005) provide a more detailed analysis of hedge fund liquidation probabilities using logit analysis and find that a number of factors influence the likelihood of a hedge fund's liquidation, including past performance, assets under management, fund flows, and age. Given these factors, their estimates imply that the average liquidation probability for all funds in 2004—given the market conditions at the end of 2004— is greater than 11%, which is higher than the historical unconditional attrition rate of 9.9%.

3

Serial Correlation, Smoothed Returns, and Illiquidity

It is apparent from the basic empirical properties outlined in Chapter 2 that one of the most significant characteristics of hedge fund returns is serial correlation. This is somewhat surprising because serial correlation is often (though incorrectly) associated with market inefficiencies, implying a violation of the Random Walk Hypothesis and the presence of predictability in returns. This seems inconsistent with the popular belief that the hedge fund industry attracts the best and the brightest fund managers in the financial services sector. In particular, if a fund manager's returns are predictable, the implication is that the manager's investment policy is not optimal; if his returns next month can be reliably forecasted to be positive, he should increase his positions this month to take advantage of this forecast, and vice versa for the opposite forecast. By taking advantage of such predictability the fund manager eventually eliminates it, along the lines of Samuelson's (1965) original "proof that properly anticipated prices fluctuate randomly." Given the outsize financial incentives of hedge fund managers to produce profitable investment strategies, the existence of significant unexploited sources of predictability seems unlikely.

However, Getmansky, Lo, and Makarov (2004) argue that in most cases, serial correlation in hedge fund returns is not due to unexploited profit opportunities but is more likely the result of illiquid securities contained in the fund, i.e., securities that are not actively traded and for which market prices are not always readily available. In such cases, the reported returns of funds containing illiquid securities appear to be smoother than *true* economic returns—returns that fully reflect all available market information concerning those securities—and this in turn imparts a downward bias on the estimated return variance and yields a positive serial return correlation. The prospect of a spurious serial correlation and biased sample moments in reported returns is not new. Such effects have been derived and empirically documented extensively in the literature on *nonsynchronous trading*, which refers to security prices recorded at different times but which are erroneously treated as if they were recorded simultaneously.[1] However, this literature has focused exclusively on equity market microstructure effects as the sources of nonsynchronicity—closing prices that are set at different times or prices that are "stale"—where the temporal displacement is on the order of minutes, hours, or, in extreme cases, several days.[2] In the context of hedge funds, we model serial correlation as the outcome of illiquidity exposure, and while nonsynchronous trading may be one symptom or by-product of illiquidity, it is not the only aspect of illiquidity that affects hedge fund returns. Even if prices were sampled synchronously, they may still yield highly serially correlated returns if the securities are not actively traded.[3] Therefore, although this formal econometric model of illiquidity is similar to those in the nonsynchronous trading literature, the motivation is considerably broader—linear extrapolation of prices for thinly traded securities, the use of smoothed broker-dealer quotes, trading restrictions arising from control positions and other regulatory requirements, and in some cases deliberate performance-smoothing behavior—and the corresponding interpretations of the parameter estimates must be modified accordingly.

Regardless of the particular mechanism by which hedge fund returns are smoothed and serial correlation is induced, the common theme and underlying driver is illiquidity exposure, and although we argue that the sources of serial correlation are spurious for most hedge funds, nevertheless the economic impact of serial correlation can be quite real. For example, spurious serial correlation yields misleading performance statistics such as volatility, Sharpe ratio, correlation, and market beta estimates, statistics commonly used by investors to determine whether or not they will invest in a fund, how much capital to allocate to a fund, what

---

[1] For example, the daily prices of financial securities quoted in the *Wall Street Journal* are usually closing prices, prices at which the last transaction in each of the securities occurred on the previous business day. If the last transaction in security A occurs at 2:00 p.m. and the last transaction in security B occurs at 4:00 p.m., then included in B's closing price is information not available when A's closing price was set. This can create spurious serial correlation in asset returns since economywide shocks are reflected first in the prices of the most frequently traded securities, with less frequently traded stocks responding with a lag. Even when there is no statistical relation between securities A and B, their reported returns appear to be serially correlated and cross-correlated simply because we have mistakenly assumed that they are measured simultaneously. One of the first to recognize the potential impact of nonsynchronous price quotes was Fisher (1966). Since then more explicit models of nontrading have been developed by Atchison, Butler, and Simonds (1987), Dimson (1979), Cohen et al. (1983a,b), Shanken (1987), Cohen et al. (1978, 1979, 1986), Kadlec and Patterson (1999), Lo and MacKinlay (1988, 1990a), and Scholes and Williams (1977). See Campbell, Lo, and MacKinlay (1997, Chapter 3) for a more detailed review of this literature.

[2] For such application, Lo and MacKinlay (1988, 1990a) and Kadlec and Patterson (1999) show that nonsynchronous trading cannot explain all of the serial correlation in weekly returns of equal- and value-weighted portfolios of U.S. equities during the past three decades.

[3] In fact, for most hedge funds, returns are computed on a monthly basis, hence the pricing or "mark-to-market" of a fund's securities typically occurs synchronously on the last day of the month.

kinds of risk exposures they are bearing, and when to redeem their investments. Moreover, spurious serial correlation can lead to wealth transfers between new, existing, and departing investors in much the same way that using stale prices for individual securities to compute mutual fund net-asset values can lead to wealth transfers between buy-and-hold investors and day traders (see, for example, Boudoukh et al., 2002).

In Section 3.1 we present an explicit econometric model of smoothed returns, and in Section 3.2 we discuss its implications for common performance statistics such as the mean, standard deviation, and Sharpe ratio. We find that the induced serial correlation and impact on the Sharpe ratio can be quite significant even for mild forms of smoothing, and we provide several specific smoothing profiles to develop further intuition.

3.1 An Econometric Model of Smoothed Returns

There are several potential explanations for serial correlation in financial asset returns, e.g., time-varying expected returns, time-varying leverage, and incentive fees with high-water marks. However, after considering each of these alternatives in detail, Getmansky, Lo, and Makarov (2004) conclude that the most plausible explanation in the context of hedge funds is illiquidity and smoothed returns. Although these are two distinct phenomena, it is important to consider illiquidity and smoothed returns in tandem because one facilitates the other—for actively traded securities, both theory and empirical evidence suggest that in the absence of transaction costs and other market frictions, returns are unlikely to be very smooth.

As discussed above, nonsynchronous trading is a plausible source of serial correlation in hedge fund returns. In contrast to the studies by Lo and MacKinlay (1988, 1990a) and Kadlec and Patterson (1999), in which they conclude that it is difficult to generate serial correlations in weekly U.S. equity portfolio returns much greater than 10%–15% through nonsynchronous trading effects alone, we argue that in the context of hedge funds, significantly higher levels of serial correlation can be explained by the combination of illiquidity and smoothed returns, of which nonsynchronous trading is a special case. To see why, note that the empirical analysis in the nonsynchronous-trading literature is devoted exclusively to exchange-traded equity returns, not hedge fund returns, hence their conclusions may not be relevant in this context. For example, Lo and MacKinlay (1990a) argue that securities would have to go without trading for several days on average to induce serial correlations of 30%, and they dismiss such nontrading intervals as unrealistic for most exchange-traded U.S. equity issues. However, such nontrading intervals are considerably more realistic for the types of securities held by many hedge funds, e.g., emerging-market debt, real estate, restricted securities, control positions in publicly traded companies, asset-backed securities, and other exotic OTC derivatives. Therefore, nonsynchronous trading of this magnitude is likely to be an explanation for the serial correlation observed in hedge fund returns.

But even when prices are synchronously measured—as they are for many funds that mark their portfolios to market at the end of the month to strike a net-asset value at which investors can buy into or cash out of the fund—there are several other channels by which illiquidity exposure can induce serial correlation in the reported returns of hedge funds. Apart from the nonsynchronous trading effect, naive methods for determining the fair market value or *marks* for illiquid securities can yield serially correlated returns. For example, one approach to valuing illiquid securities is to extrapolate linearly from the most recent transaction price (which, in the case of emerging-market debt, might be several months ago), which yields a price path that is a straight line, or at best a series of straight lines. Returns computed from such marks are smoother, exhibiting lower volatility and higher serial correlation than true economic returns, i.e., returns computed from mark-to-market prices where the market is sufficiently active to allow all available information to be impounded in the price of the security. Of course, for securities that are more easily traded and with deeper markets, mark-to-market prices are more readily available, extrapolated marks are not necessary, and serial correlation is therefore less of an issue. But for securities that are thinly traded, or not traded at all for extended periods of time, marking them to market is often an expensive and time-consuming procedure that cannot easily be performed frequently.[4] Therefore, we argue in this monograph that serial correlation may serve as a proxy for a fund's liquidity exposure.

Even if a hedge fund manager does not make use of any form of linear extrapolation to mark the securities in his portfolio, he may still be subject to smoothed returns if he obtains marks from broker-dealers that engage in such extrapolation. For example, consider the case of a conscientious hedge fund manager attempting to obtain the most accurate mark for his portfolio at month end by getting bid/offer quotes from three independent broker-dealers for every security in his portfolio and then marking each security at the average of the three quote midpoints. By averaging the quote midpoints, the manager is inadvertently downward-biasing price volatility, and if any of the broker-dealers employ linear extrapolation in formulating their quotes (and many do, through sheer necessity because they have little else to go on for the most illiquid securities) or if they fail to update their quotes because of light volume, serial correlation will also be induced in reported returns.

Finally, a more prosaic channel by which serial correlation may arise in the reported returns of hedge funds is through *performance smoothing*, the

---

[4] Liang (2003) presents a sobering analysis of the accuracy of hedge fund returns that underscores the challenges of marking a portfolio to market.

unsavory practice of reporting only part of the gains in months when a fund has positive returns so as to partially offset potential future losses and thereby reduce volatility and improve risk-adjusted performance measures such as the Sharpe ratio. For funds containing liquid securities that can be easily marked to market, performance smoothing is more difficult and, as a result, less of a concern. Indeed, it is only for portfolios of illiquid securities that managers and brokers have any discretion in marking their positions. Such practices are generally prohibited by various securities laws and accounting principles, and great care must be exercised in interpreting smoothed returns as deliberate attempts to manipulate performance statistics. After all, as discussed above, there are many other sources of serial correlation in the presence of illiquidity, none of which is motivated by deceit. Nevertheless, managers do have certain degrees of freedom in valuing illiquid securities—e.g., discretionary accruals for unregistered private placements and venture capital investments—and Chandar and Bricker (2002) conclude that managers of certain closed-end mutual funds do use accounting discretion to manage fund returns around a passive benchmark. Therefore, the possibility of deliberate performance smoothing in the less regulated hedge fund industry must be kept in mind in interpreting any empirical analysis of smoothed returns.

To quantify the impact of all these possible sources of serial correlation, denote by R_t the true economic return of a hedge fund in period t and let R_t satisfy the following linear single-factor model:

$$R_t = \mu + \beta \Lambda_t + \epsilon_t, \qquad \mathrm{E}[\Lambda_t] = \mathrm{E}[\epsilon_t] = 0, \qquad \epsilon_t, \ \Lambda_t \sim \mathrm{IID}, \qquad (3.1\mathrm{a})$$

$$\mathrm{Var}[R_t] \equiv \sigma^2. \tag{3.1b}$$

True returns represent the flow of information that would determine the equilibrium value of the fund's securities in a frictionless market. However, true economic returns are not observed. Instead, let R_t^o denote the reported or observed return in period t and let

$$R_t^o = \theta_0 R_t + \theta_1 R_{t-1} + \cdots + \theta_k R_{t-k}, \tag{3.2}$$

$$\theta_j \in [0, 1], \qquad j = 0, \ldots, k, \tag{3.3}$$

$$1 = \theta_0 + \theta_1 + \cdots + \theta_k, \tag{3.4}$$

which is a weighted average of the fund's true returns over the most recent $(k + 1)$ periods, including the current period.

This averaging process captures the essence of smoothed returns in several respects. From the perspective of illiquidity-driven smoothing, (3.2) is consistent with several models in the nonsynchronous-trading literature. For example, Cohen et al. (1986, Chapter 6.1) propose a similar weighted-average model for observed returns.[5] Alternatively, (3.2) can be viewed as the outcome of marking portfolios to simple linear extrapolations of acquisition prices when market prices are unavailable, or mark-to-model returns where the pricing model is slowly varying through time. And of course, (3.2) also captures the intentional smoothing of performance.

The constraint (3.4) that the weights sum to 1 implies that the information driving the fund's performance in period t will eventually be fully reflected in observed returns, but this process could take up to $(k+1)$ periods from the time the information is generated.[6] This is a sensible restriction in the current context of hedge funds for several reasons. Even the most illiquid securities eventually trade, and when that occurs, all of the cumulative information affecting that security is fully impounded into its transaction price. Therefore the parameter k should be selected to match the kind of illiquidity of the fund, e.g., a fund comprised mostly of exchange-traded U.S. equities requires a much lower value of k than a private equity fund. Alternatively, in the case of intentional smoothing of performance, the necessity for periodic external audits of fund performance imposes a finite limit on the extent to which deliberate smoothing can persist.[7]

---

[5] In particular, their specification for observed returns is

$$r_{j,t}^{o} = \sum_{l=0}^{N} (\gamma_{j,t-l,l} r_{j,t-l} + \theta_{j,t-l}),$$

where $r_{j,t-l}$ is the true but unobserved return for security j in period $t-l$, the coefficients $\{\gamma_{j,t-l,l}\}$ are assumed to sum to 1, and $\theta_{j,t-l}$ are random variables meant to capture "bid/ask bounce." The authors motivate their specification of nonsynchronous trading in the following way (p. 116): "Alternatively stated, the $\gamma_{j,t,0}, \gamma_{j,t,1}, \ldots, \gamma_{j,t,N}$ comprise a delay distribution that shows how the true return generated in period t impacts on the returns actually observed during t and the next N periods." In other words, the essential feature of nonsynchronous trading is the fact that information generated at date t may not be fully impounded into prices until several periods later.

[6] In Lo and MacKinlay's (1990a) model of nonsynchronous trading, they propose a stochastic nontrading horizon so that observed returns are an infinite-order moving average of past true returns, where the coefficients are stochastic. In that framework, the waiting time for information to become fully impounded into future returns may be arbitrarily long (but with increasingly remote probability).

[7] In fact, if a fund allows investors to invest and withdraw capital only at prespecified intervals, imposing lockups in between, and external audits are conducted at these same prespecified intervals, then it may be argued that performance smoothing is irrelevant. For example, no investor should be disadvantaged by investing in a fund that offers annual liquidity and engages in annual external audits with which the fund's net-asset value is determined by a disinterested third party for purposes of redemptions and new investments. However, there are at least two additional concerns that remain—historical track records are still affected by smoothed returns, and estimates of a fund's liquidity exposure are also affected—both of which are important factors in a typical hedge fund investor's overall investment process. Moreover, there is the additional concern of whether third-party auditors are truly objective and free of all conflicts of interest.

3.2 Implications for Performance Statistics

Given the smoothing mechanism outlined in Section 3.1, we have the following implications for the statistical properties of observed returns.

Proposition 3.2.1. *(Getmansky, Lo, and Makarov, 2004). Under (3.2)–(3.4), the statistical properties of observed returns are characterized by*

$$E[R_t^o] = \mu, \tag{3.5}$$

$$\text{Var}[R_t^o] = c_\sigma^2 \, \sigma^2 \leq \sigma^2, \tag{3.6}$$

$$\text{SR}^o \equiv \frac{E[R_t^o]}{\sqrt{\text{Var}[R_t^o]}} = c_s \, \text{SR} \geq \text{SR} \equiv \frac{E[R_t]}{\sqrt{\text{Var}[R_t]}}, \tag{3.7}$$

$$\beta_m^o \equiv \frac{\text{Cov}[R_t^o, \Lambda_{t-m}]}{\text{Var}[\Lambda_{t-m}]} = \begin{cases} c_{\beta,m}\, \beta & \text{if } 0 \leq m \leq k, \\ 0 & \text{if } m > k, \end{cases} \tag{3.8}$$

$$\text{Cov}[R_t^o, R_{t-m}^o] = \begin{cases} \left(\sum_{j=0}^{k-m} \theta_j \theta_{j+m} \right) \sigma^2 & \text{if } 0 \leq m \leq k, \\ 0 & \text{if } m > k, \end{cases} \tag{3.9}$$

$$\text{Corr}[R_t^o, R_{t-m}^o] = \frac{\text{Cov}[R_t^o, R_{t-m}^o]}{\text{Var}[R_t^o]} = \begin{cases} \dfrac{\sum_{j=0}^{k-m} \theta_j \theta_{j+m}}{\sum_{j=0}^{k} \theta_j^2} & \text{if } 0 \leq m \leq k, \\ 0 & \text{if } m > k, \end{cases} \tag{3.10}$$

where

$$c_\mu \equiv \theta_0 + \theta_1 + \cdots + \theta_k, \tag{3.11}$$

$$c_\sigma^2 \equiv \theta_0^2 + \theta_1^2 + \cdots + \theta_k^2, \tag{3.12}$$

$$c_s \equiv 1/\sqrt{\theta_0^2 + \cdots + \theta_k^2}, \tag{3.13}$$

$$c_{\beta,m} \equiv \theta_m. \tag{3.14}$$

Proposition 3.2.1 shows that smoothed returns of the form (3.2)–(3.4) do not affect the expected value of R_t^o but reduce its variance, hence boosting the Sharpe ratio of observed returns by a factor of c_s. From (3.8), we see that smoothing also affects β_0^o, the contemporaneous market beta of observed returns, biasing it toward 0 or "market neutrality," and induces correlation between current observed returns and lagged market returns up to lag k. This provides a formal interpretation of the empirical analysis of Asness, Krail, and Liew (2001) in which many hedge funds were found to have significant lagged market exposure despite relatively low contemporaneous market betas.

Smoothed returns also exhibit positive serial correlation up to order k according to (3.10), and the magnitude of the effect is determined by the pattern of weights $\{\theta_j\}$. If, for example, the weights are disproportionately centered on a small number of lags, relatively little serial correlation will be induced. However, if the weights are evenly distributed among many lags, this will result in higher serial correlation. A useful summary statistic for measuring the concentration of weights is

$$\xi \equiv \sum_{j=0}^{k} \theta_j^2 \in [0, 1], \tag{3.15}$$

which is simply the denominator of (3.10). This measure is well known in the industrial organization literature as the *Herfindahl index*, a measure of the concentration of firms in a given industry, where θ_j represents the market share of firm j. Because $\theta_j \in [0, 1]$, ξ is also confined to the unit interval and is minimized when all the θ_j's are identical, which implies a value of $1/(k+1)$ for ξ, and is maximized when one coefficient is 1 and the rest are 0, in which case $\xi = 1$. In the context of smoothed returns, a lower value of ξ implies more smoothing, and the upper bound of 1 implies no smoothing, hence we shall refer to ξ as a *smoothing index*.

In the special case of equal weights, $\theta_j = 1/(k+1)$ for $j = 0, \ldots, k$, the serial correlation of observed returns takes on a particularly simple form:

$$\text{Corr}[R_t^o, R_{t-m}^o] = 1 - \frac{m}{k+1}, \qquad 1 \leq m \leq k, \tag{3.16}$$

which declines linearly in the lag m. This can yield substantial correlations even when k is small—e.g., if $k = 2$ so that smoothing takes place over only a current quarter (i.e., this month and the previous 2 months), the first-order autocorrelation of monthly observed returns is 66.7%.

To develop a sense for just how much observed returns can differ from true returns under the smoothed-return mechanism (3.2)–(3.4), denote by $\Delta(T)$ the difference between the cumulative observed and true returns over T holding periods, where we assume that $T > k$:

$$\Delta(T) \equiv \left(R_1^o + R_2^o + \cdots + R_T^o \right) - (R_1 + R_2 + \cdots + R_T) \tag{3.17}$$

$$= \sum_{j=0}^{k-1} (R_{-j} - R_{T-j}) \left(1 - \sum_{i=0}^{j} \theta_i \right). \tag{3.18}$$

Then we have the following proposition.

Proposition 3.2.2. *(Getmansky, Lo, and Makarov, 2004). Under (3.2)–(3.4) and for $T > k$,*

$$E[\Delta(T)] = 0, \tag{3.19}$$

$$\text{Var}[\Delta(T)] = 2\sigma^2 \sum_{j=0}^{k-1} \left(1 - \sum_{l=0}^{j} \theta_l\right)^2 = 2\sigma^2 \zeta, \tag{3.20}$$

$$\zeta \equiv \sum_{j=0}^{k-1} \left(1 - \sum_{l=0}^{j} \theta_l\right)^2 \leq k. \tag{3.21}$$

Proposition 3.2.2 shows that the cumulative difference between observed and true returns has 0 expected value, and its variance is bounded above by $2k\sigma^2$.

To develop further intuition for the impact of smoothed returns on observed returns, Getmansky, Lo, and Makarov (2004) consider the following three specific sets of weights $\{\theta_j\}$ or smoothing profiles:[8]

$$\theta_j = \frac{1}{k+1} \quad \text{(straight-line)}, \tag{3.22a}$$

$$\theta_j = \frac{k+1-j}{(k+1)(k+2)/2} \quad \text{(sum-of-years)}, \tag{3.22b}$$

$$\theta_j = \frac{\delta^j(1-\delta)}{1-\delta^{k+1}}, \quad \delta \in (0, 1) \quad \text{(geometric)}. \tag{3.22c}$$

The straight-line profile weights each return equally. In contrast, the sum-of-years and geometric profiles weight the current return the most heavily and then have monotonically declining weights for lagged returns, with the sum-of-years weights declining linearly and the geometric weights declining more rapidly (Figure 3.1).

More detailed information about the three smoothing profiles is contained in Table 3.1. The first panel reports the smoothing coefficients $\{\theta_j\}$, constants $c_{\beta,0}$, c_σ, c_s, and ζ, and the first three autocorrelations of observed returns for the straight-line profile for $k = 0, 1, \ldots, 5$. Consider the case where $k = 2$. Despite the relatively short smoothing period of 3 months, the effects are dramatic: Smoothing reduces the market beta by 67%, increases the Sharpe ratio by 73%, and induces first- and second-order serial correlations of 67% and 33%, respectively, in observed returns. Moreover, the variance of the cumulative discrepancy between observed and true returns $2\sigma^2\zeta$ is only slightly larger than the variance of monthly

---

[8] Students of accounting will recognize these profiles as commonly used methods for computing depreciation. The motivation for these depreciation schedules is not entirely without relevance in the smoothed-return context.

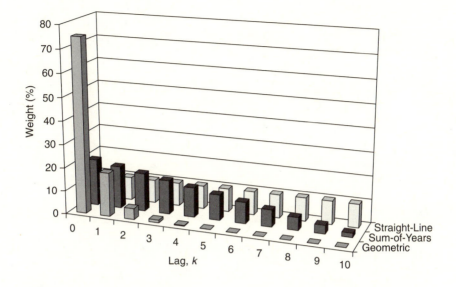

Figure 3.1. *Straight-line, sum-of-years, and geometric smoothing profiles for k = 10.*

true returns σ^2, suggesting that it may be difficult to detect these types of smoothed returns even over time.

As k increases, the effects become more pronounced—for $k = 5$, the market beta is reduced by 83%, the Sharpe ratio is increased by 145%, and the first three autocorrelation coefficients are 83%, 67%, and 50%, respectively. However, in this extreme case, the variance of the discrepancy between true and observed returns is approximately 3 times the monthly variance of true returns, in which case it may be easier to identify smoothing from realized returns.

The sum-of-years profile is similar to, although somewhat less extreme than, the straight-line profile for the same values of k because more weight is placed on the current return. For example, even in the extreme case of $k = 5$, the sum-of-years profile reduces the market beta by 71%, increases the Sharpe ratio by 120%, induces autocorrelations of 77%, 55%, and 35%, respectively, in the first three lags, and has a discrepancy variance that is approximately 1.6 times the monthly variance of true returns.

The last two panels in Table 3.1 contain results for the geometric smoothing profile for two values of δ, 0.25 and 0.50. For $\delta = 0.25$, the geometric profile places more weight on the current return than the other two smoothing profiles for all values of k; hence the effects tend to be less dramatic. Even in the extreme case of $k = 5$, 75% of current true returns are incorporated into observed returns, the market beta is reduced by only 25%, the Sharpe ratio is increased by only 29%, the first three autocorrelations are 25%, 6%, and 1% respectively, and the discrepancy variance is approximately 13% of the monthly variance of true

Table 3.1.

Implications of Smoothing Profiles for Performance Statistics*

k	θ_0 (%)	θ_1 (%)	θ_2 (%)	θ_3 (%)	θ_4 (%)	θ_5 (%)	c_β	c_σ	c_s	ρ_1^0 (%)	ρ_2^0 (%)	ρ_3^0 (%)	ρ_4^0 (%)	ρ_5^0 (%)	ζ (%)
				Straight-line Smoothing											
0	100.0	—	—	—	—	—	1.00	1.00	1.00	0.0	0.0	0.0	0.0	0.0	—
1	50.0	50.0	—	—	—	—	0.50	0.71	1.41	50.0	0.0	0.0	0.0	0.0	25.0
2	33.3	33.3	33.3	—	—	—	0.33	0.58	1.73	66.7	33.3	0.0	0.0	0.0	55.6
3	25.0	25.0	25.0	25.0	—	—	0.25	0.50	2.00	75.0	50.0	25.0	0.0	0.0	87.5
4	20.0	20.0	20.0	20.0	20.0	—	0.20	0.45	2.24	80.0	60.0	40.0	20.0	0.0	120.0
5	16.7	16.7	16.7	16.7	16.7	16.7	0.17	0.41	2.45	83.3	66.7	50.0	33.3	16.7	152.8
				Sum-of-Years Smoothing											
0	100.0	—	—	—	—	—	1.00	1.00	1.00	0.0	0.0	0.0	0.0	0.0	—
1	66.7	33.3	—	—	—	—	0.67	0.75	1.34	40.0	0.0	0.0	0.0	0.0	11.1
2	50.0	33.3	16.7	—	—	—	0.50	0.62	1.60	57.1	21.4	0.0	0.0	0.0	27.8
3	40.0	30.0	20.0	10.0	—	—	0.40	0.55	1.83	66.7	36.7	13.3	0.0	0.0	46.0
4	33.3	26.7	20.0	13.3	6.7	—	0.33	0.49	2.02	72.7	47.3	25.5	9.1	0.0	64.9
5	28.6	23.8	19.0	14.3	9.5	4.8	0.29	0.45	2.20	76.9	54.9	35.2	18.7	6.6	84.1
				Geometric Smoothing ($\delta = 0.25$)											
0	100.0	—	—	—	—	—	1.00	1.00	1.00	0.0	0.0	0.0	0.0	0.0	—
1	80.0	20.0	—	—	—	—	0.80	0.82	1.21	23.5	0.0	0.0	0.0	0.0	4.0
2	76.2	19.0	4.8	—	—	—	0.76	0.79	1.27	24.9	5.9	0.0	0.0	0.0	5.9
3	75.3	18.8	4.7	1.2	—	—	0.75	0.78	1.29	25.0	6.2	1.5	0.0	0.0	6.5
4	75.1	18.8	4.7	1.2	0.3	—	0.75	0.78	1.29	25.0	6.2	1.6	0.4	0.0	6.6
5	75.0	18.8	4.7	1.2	0.3	0.1	0.75	0.77	1.29	25.0	6.2	1.6	0.4	0.1	6.7
				Geometric Smoothing ($\delta = 0.50$)											
0	100.0	—	—	—	—	—	1.00	1.00	1.00	0.0	0.0	0.0	0.0	0.0	—
1	66.7	33.3	—	—	—	—	0.67	0.75	1.34	40.0	0.0	0.0	0.0	0.0	11.1
2	57.1	28.6	14.3	—	—	—	0.57	0.65	1.53	47.6	19.0	0.0	0.0	0.0	20.4
3	53.3	26.7	13.3	6.7	—	—	0.53	0.61	1.63	49.4	23.5	9.4	0.0	0.0	26.2
4	51.6	25.8	12.9	6.5	3.2	—	0.52	0.60	1.68	49.9	24.6	11.7	4.7	0.0	29.6
5	50.8	25.4	12.7	6.3	3.2	1.6	0.51	0.59	1.71	50.0	24.9	12.3	5.9	2.3	31.4

*Implications of three different smoothing profiles for observed betas, standard deviations, Sharpe ratios, and serial correlation coefficients for a fund with IID true returns. Straight-line smoothing is given by $\theta_j = 1/(k+1)$; sum-of-years smoothing is given by $\theta_j = (k+1-j)/[(k+1)(k+2)/2]$; geometric smoothing is given by $\theta_j = \delta^j(1-\delta)/(1-\delta^{k+1})$. c_β, c_σ, and c_s denote multipliers associated with the beta, standard deviation, and Sharpe ratio of observed returns, respectively, ρ_j^o denotes the jth autocorrelation coefficient of observed returns, and ζ is proportional to the variance of the discrepancy between true and observed multiperiod returns.

returns. As δ increases, less weight is placed on the current observation, and the effects on performance statistics become more significant. When $\delta = 0.50$ and $k = 5$, geometric smoothing reduces the market beta by 49%, increases the Sharpe ratio by 71%, induces autocorrelations of 50%, 25%, and 12%, respectively, for the first three lags, and yields a discrepancy variance that is approximately 63% of the monthly variance of true returns.

The results in Table 3.1 show that a rich set of biases can be generated by even simple smoothing profiles, and even the most casual empirical observation suggests that smoothed returns may be an important source of serial correlation in hedge fund returns. To address this issue directly, in Sections 3.3 and 3.4 we propose methods for estimating the smoothing profile and adjusting performance statistics accordingly.

3.3 Estimation of Smoothing Profiles

Although the parameters of the three smoothing profiles (3.22) in Section 3.2 can all be easily estimated from the sample moments of fund returns (e.g., means, variances, and autocorrelations), we want to estimate more general forms of smoothing. Therefore, in this section we propose two estimation procedures— maximum likelihood and linear regression—that place fewer restrictions on a fund's smoothing profile than the three examples (3.22). We start by reviewing the steps for maximum-likelihood estimation of an MA(k) process slightly modified to accommodate this context and constraints. To that end, define the de-meaned observed returns process X_t as

$$X_t = R_t^o - \mu \tag{3.23}$$

and observe that (3.2)–(3.4) imply the following properties for X_t:

$$X_t = \theta_0 \eta_t + \theta_1 \eta_{t-1} + \cdots + \theta_k \eta_{t-k}, \tag{3.24}$$

$$1 = \theta_0 + \theta_1 + \cdots + \theta_k, \tag{3.25}$$

$$\eta_k \sim \mathcal{N}(0, \sigma_\eta^2), \tag{3.26}$$

where, for purposes of estimation, we have added the parametric assumption (3.26) that η_k is normally distributed. From (3.24), it is apparent that X_t is a moving-average process of order k, or MA(k). For a given set of observations $\mathbf{X} \equiv [\, X_1 \; \cdots \; X_T \,]'$, the likelihood function is well known to be

$$\mathcal{L}(\boldsymbol{\theta}, \sigma_\eta) = (2\pi)^{-T/2} (\det \Gamma)^{-1/2} \exp(-\tfrac{1}{2} \mathbf{X}' \Gamma^{-1} \mathbf{X}), \qquad \Gamma \equiv \mathrm{E}[\mathbf{X}\mathbf{X}'], \tag{3.27}$$

where $\boldsymbol{\theta} \equiv [\theta_0 \; \cdots \; \theta_k]'$ and the covariance matrix Γ is a function of the parameters $\boldsymbol{\theta}$ and σ_η. It can be shown that for any constant κ,

$$\mathcal{L}(\kappa\boldsymbol{\theta}, \sigma_\eta/\kappa) = \mathcal{L}(\boldsymbol{\theta}, \sigma_\eta), \tag{3.28}$$

and therefore an additional identification condition is required. The most common identification condition imposed in the time-series literature is the normalization $\theta_0 \equiv 1$. However, in this context, the condition (3.25) that the MA coefficients sum to 1 is imposed—an economic restriction that smoothing takes place over only the most recent $(k+1)$ periods—and this is sufficient to identify the parameters $\boldsymbol{\theta}$ and σ_η. The likelihood function (3.27) may then be evaluated and maximized via the "innovations algorithm" of Brockwell and Davis (1991, Chapter 8.3),[9] and the properties of the estimator are given by the following proposition.

Proposition 3.3.1. *(Getmansky, Lo, and Makarov, 2004). Under the specification (3.24)–(3.26), X_t is invertible on the set $\{\boldsymbol{\theta} : \theta_0 + \theta_1 + \theta_2 = 1, \; \theta_1 < 1/2, \; \theta_1 < 1 - 2\theta_2\}$ and the maximum likelihood estimator $\hat{\boldsymbol{\theta}}$ satisfies the following properties:*

$$1 = \hat{\theta}_0 + \hat{\theta}_1 + \hat{\theta}_2, \tag{3.29}$$

$$\sqrt{T}\left(\begin{bmatrix} \hat{\theta}_1 \\ \hat{\theta}_2 \end{bmatrix} - \begin{bmatrix} \theta_1 \\ \theta_2 \end{bmatrix}\right) \overset{a}{\sim} \mathcal{N}(0, \mathbf{V}_\theta), \tag{3.30}$$

$$\mathbf{V}_\theta =$$
$$\begin{bmatrix} -(-1+\theta_1)(-1+2\theta_1)(-1+\theta_1+2\theta_2) & -\theta_2(-1+2\theta_1)(-1+\theta_1+2\theta_2) \\ -\theta_2(-1+2\theta_1)(-1+\theta_1+2\theta_2) & (-1+\theta_1-2(-1+\theta_2)\theta_2)(-1+\theta_1+2\theta_2) \end{bmatrix}. \tag{3.31}$$

By applying the above procedure to observed de-meaned returns, we may obtain estimates of the smoothing profile $\hat{\boldsymbol{\theta}}$ for each fund.[10] Because of the scaling property (3.28) of the MA(k) likelihood function, a simple procedure for obtaining estimates of the smoothing model with the normalization (3.25) is to transform estimates $(\breve{\boldsymbol{\theta}}, \breve{\sigma})$ from standard MA(k) estimation packages such as SAS or RATS by dividing each $\breve{\theta}_i$ by $1 + \breve{\theta}_1 + \cdots + \breve{\theta}_k$ and multiplying $\breve{\sigma}$ by the same factor. The likelihood function remains unchanged, but the transformed smoothing coefficients now satisfy (3.25).

---

[9] See Getmansky, Lo, and Makarov (2004) for further details.

[10] Recall from Proposition 3.2.1 that the smoothing process (3.2)–(3.4) does not affect the expected return, i.e., the sample mean of observed returns is a consistent estimator of the true expected return. Therefore, we may use $R_t^o - \hat{\mu}$ in place of X_t in the estimation process without altering any of the asymptotic properties of the maximum-likelihood estimator.

Now suppose that we are willing to impose additional structure upon the return-generating process for true returns, i.e., a linear single-factor model (3.1). In that case, a simpler method for estimating the smoothing profile is available. By substituting (3.1) into (3.2), we can re-express observed returns as

$$R_t^o = \mu + \beta \left(\theta_0 \Lambda_t + \theta_1 \Lambda_{t-1} + \cdots + \theta_k \Lambda_{t-k} \right) + u_t, \tag{3.32}$$

$$u_t = \theta_0 \epsilon_t + \theta_1 \epsilon_{t-1} + \cdots + \theta_k \epsilon_{t-k}. \tag{3.33}$$

Suppose we estimate the following linear regression of observed returns on contemporaneous and lagged market returns:

$$R_t^o = \mu + \gamma_0 \Lambda_t + \gamma_1 \Lambda_{t-1} + \cdots + \gamma_k \Lambda_{t-k} + u_t, \tag{3.34}$$

as in Asness, Krail, and Liew (2001). Using the normalization (3.4) from the smoothing model, we can readily obtain estimators for β and $\{\theta_j\}$:

$$\hat{\beta} = \hat{\gamma}_0 + \hat{\gamma}_1 + \cdots + \hat{\gamma}_k, \qquad \hat{\theta}_j = \hat{\gamma}_j / \hat{\beta}. \tag{3.35}$$

Moreover, a specification check for (3.32)–(3.33) can be performed by testing the following set of equalities:

$$\beta = \frac{\gamma_0}{\theta_0} = \frac{\gamma_1}{\theta_1} = \cdots = \frac{\gamma_k}{\theta_k}. \tag{3.36}$$

Because of serial correlation in u_t, ordinary least-squares estimates (3.35) are not efficient and the usual standard errors are incorrect, but the estimates are still consistent and may be a useful first approximation for identifying smoothing in hedge fund returns.[11]

There is yet another variation of the linear single-factor model that may help to disentangle the effects of illiquidity from return smoothing. Suppose that a fund's true economic returns R_t satisfies

$$R_t = \mu + \beta \Lambda_t + \epsilon_t, \quad \epsilon_t \sim \text{IID}(0, \sigma_\epsilon^2), \tag{3.37}$$

but instead of assuming that the common factor Λ_t is IID as in (3.1), let Λ_t be serially correlated. While this alternative may seem to be a minor variation of the smoothing model (3.2)–(3.4), the difference in interpretation is significant. A serially correlated Λ_t captures the fact that a fund's returns may be autocorrelated because of an illiquid common factor, even in the absence of any smoothing process such as (3.2)–(3.4). Of course, this still begs the question of what the

---

[11] To obtain efficient estimates of the smoothing coefficients, a procedure like the maximum-likelihood estimator in Section 3.3 must be used.

ultimate source of serial correlation in the common factor might be, but by combining (3.37) with the smoothing process (3.2)–(3.4), it may be possible to distinguish between *systematic smoothing* versus *idiosyncratic smoothing*, the former attributable to the asset class and the latter resulting from fund-specific characteristics.

To see why the combination of (3.37) and (3.2)–(3.4) may have different implications for observed returns, suppose for the moment that there is no smoothing; i.e., $\theta_0 = 1$ and $\theta_k = 0$ for $k > 0$ in (3.2)–(3.4). Then observed returns are simply given by

$$R_t^o = \mu + \beta \Lambda_t + \epsilon_t, \qquad \epsilon_t \sim \text{IID}(0, \sigma_\epsilon^2), \tag{3.38}$$

where R_t^o is now serially correlated solely through Λ_t. This specification implies that the ratios of observed-return autocovariances will be identical across all funds with the same common factor:

$$\frac{\text{Cov}[R_t^o, R_{t-k}^o]}{\text{Cov}[R_t^o, R_{t-l}^o]} = \frac{\beta \, \text{Cov}[\Lambda_t, \Lambda_{t-k}]}{\beta \, \text{Cov}[\Lambda_t, \Lambda_{t-l}]} = \frac{\text{Cov}[\Lambda_t, \Lambda_{t-k}]}{\text{Cov}[\Lambda_t, \Lambda_{t-l}]}. \tag{3.39}$$

Moreover, (3.37) implies that in the regression equation (3.34), the coefficients of the lagged factor returns are zero and the error term is not serially correlated.

More generally, consider the combination of a serially correlated common factor (3.37) and smoothed returns (3.2)–(3.4). This more general econometric model of observed returns implies that the appropriate specification of the regression equation is

$$R_t^o = \mu + \gamma_0 \Lambda_t + \gamma_1 \Lambda_{t-1} + \cdots + \gamma_k \Lambda_{t-k} + u_t, \tag{3.40}$$

$$u_t = \theta_0 \epsilon_t + \theta_1 \epsilon_{t-1} + \cdots + \theta_k \epsilon_{t-k}, \qquad \epsilon_t \sim \text{IID}(0, \sigma_\epsilon^2), \tag{3.41}$$

$$1 = \theta_0 + \theta_1 + \cdots + \theta_k. \tag{3.42}$$

To the extent that serial correlation in R_t^o can be explained mainly by the common factor, the lagged coefficient estimates of (3.40) are statistically insignificant, the residuals are serially uncorrelated, and the ratios of autocovariance coefficients are roughly constant across funds with the same common factor. To the extent that the smoothing process (3.2)–(3.4) is responsible for serial correlation in R_t^o, the lagged coefficient estimates of (3.40) are significant, the residuals are serially correlated, and the ratios $\hat{\gamma}_j / \hat{\theta}_j$ are roughly the same for all $j \geq 0$ and are a consistent estimate of the factor loading or beta of the fund's true economic returns with respect to the factor Λ_t.

Perhaps the most difficult challenge in estimating (3.40)–(3.42) is to correctly identify the common factor Λ_t. Unlike a simple market model regression meant to estimate the sensitivity of a fund's returns to a broad-based market index, the ability to distinguish between the effects of systematic illiquidity and idiosyncratic return smoothing via (3.40) relies heavily on correct specification of the common factor. Using a common factor in (3.40) that is highly serially correlated but not the appropriate factor for a given fund may yield misleading estimates for the degree of smoothing in that fund's observed returns. Therefore, the common factor Λ_t must be selected or constructed carefully to match the specific risk exposures of the fund, and the parameter estimates of (3.40) must be interpreted cautiously and with several specific alternative hypotheses at hand.[12]

The choice between maximum-likelihood and linear regression analysis depends primarily on the plausibility of the assumptions required by each approach. Maximum-likelihood estimation has a number of attractive statistical properties like consistency and asymptotic normality under certain regularity conditions, but it may not perform well in small samples or when the underlying distribution of true returns is not normal, as hypothesized.[13] Moreover, even if normality is satisfied and a sufficient sample size is available, the proposed smoothing model (3.2)–(3.4) simply may not apply to some of the funds in this sample. Therefore, Getmansky, Lo, and Makarov (2004) have proposed several "specification checks" to assess the validity of the maximum-likelihood estimation procedure. On the other hand, linear regression analysis is not without its own limitations, the most significant being the assumption of a linear factor model for the return-generating process. While such models are the basis of the most popular financial paradigms—the Capital Asset Pricing Model (CAPM) and the Arbitrage Pricing Theory (APT)—they clearly do not apply as readily to hedge fund returns, as the examples in Chapter 1 have shown. Therefore, both estimation procedures have advantages and disadvantages that must be weighed against each other on a case-by-case basis. For practical purposes, it may be best to use both techniques and compare the two sets of results as a final robustness check.

3.4 Smoothing-Adjusted Sharpe Ratios

One of the main implications of smoothed returns is that Sharpe ratios are biased upward, in some cases substantially (Proposition 3.2.1).[14] The mechanism

---

[12] See Getmansky, Lo, and Makarov (2004, Section 6.4) for an empirical example that highlights the pitfalls and opportunities of the common factor specification (3.40)–(3.42).

[13] In fact, there is substantial evidence that financial asset returns are not normally distributed but characterized by skewness, leptokurtosis, and other non-Gaussian properties (see, for example, Lo and MacKinlay, 1999). Given the dynamic nature of hedge fund strategies, it would be even less plausible for their returns to be normally distributed.

[14] There are a number of other concerns regarding the use and interpretation of Sharpe ratios in the context of hedge funds. See Agarwal and Naik (2000a, 2004), Goetzmann et al. (2002), Lo (2001), Sharpe (1994), Spurgin (2001), and Weisman (2002) for examples where Sharpe ratios can be

by which this bias occurs is through the reduction in volatility because of the smoothing process, but an additional bias occurs when monthly Sharpe ratios are annualized by multiplying by $\sqrt{12}$. If monthly returns are independently and identically distributed, this is the correct procedure, but Lo (2002) shows that for non-IID returns an alternative procedure must be used, one that accounts for serial correlation in returns in a very specific manner.[15] Specifically, denote by $R_t(q)$ the following q-period return:

$$R_t(q) \equiv R_t + R_{t-1} + \cdots + R_{t-q+1}, \tag{3.43}$$

where the effects of compounding are ignored for computational convenience.[16] For IID returns, the variance of $R_t(q)$ is directly proportional to q, hence the Sharpe ratio satisfies the simple relation

$$SR(q) = \frac{E[R_t(q)] - R_f(q)}{\sqrt{\text{Var}[R_t(q)]}} = \frac{q(\mu - R_f)}{\sqrt{q}\,\sigma} = \sqrt{q}\,SR. \tag{3.44}$$

Using Hansen's (1982) generalized method of moments (GMM) estimator, Lo (2002) derives the asymptotic distribution of $\widehat{SR}(q)$ as

$$\sqrt{T}\,(\widehat{SR}(q) - \sqrt{q}\,SR) \overset{a}{\sim} \mathcal{N}(0,\ V_{\text{IID}}(q)), \qquad V_{\text{IID}}(q) = q\,V_{\text{IID}} = q\,(1 + \tfrac{1}{2}SR^2). \tag{3.45}$$

For non-IID returns, the relation between SR and $SR(q)$ is somewhat more involved because the variance of $R_t(q)$ is not just the sum of the variances of component returns but also includes all the covariances. Specifically, under the assumption that returns $\{R_t\}$ are stationary,

$$\text{Var}[R_t(q)] = \sum_{i=0}^{q-1}\sum_{j=0}^{q-1} \text{Cov}[R_{t-i}, R_{t-j}] = q\sigma^2 + 2\sigma^2 \sum_{k=1}^{q-1}(q-k)\rho_k, \tag{3.46}$$

---

misleading indicators of the true risk-adjusted performance of hedge fund strategies, and for alternate methods of constructing optimal portfolios of hedge funds.

[15] See also Jobson and Korkie (1981), who were perhaps the first to derive rigorous statistical properties of performance measures such as the Sharpe ratio and the Treynor measure.

[16] The exact expression is, of course,

$$R_t(q) \equiv \prod_{j=0}^{q-1}(1 + R_{t-j}) - 1.$$

For most (but not all) applications, (3.43) is an excellent approximation. Alternatively, if R_t is defined to be the continuously compounded return (i.e., $R_t \equiv \log(P_t/P_{t-1})$, where P_t is the price or net asset value at time t), then (3.43) is exact.

where $\rho_k \equiv \text{Cov}[R_t, R_{t-k}]/\text{Var}[R_t]$. This yields the following relation between SR and SR(q):

$$\text{SR}(q) = \eta(q)\,\text{SR}, \qquad \eta(q) \equiv \frac{q}{\sqrt{q + 2\sum_{k=1}^{q-1}(q-k)\rho_k}}. \qquad (3.47)$$

Note that (3.47) reduces to (3.44) if the autocorrelations $\{\rho_k\}$ are zero, as in the case of IID returns. However, for non-IID returns the adjustment factor for time-aggregated Sharpe ratios is generally not $\sqrt{q}$ but a function of the first $(q-1)$ autocorrelations of returns, which is readily estimated from the sample autocorrelations of returns; hence

$$\widehat{\text{SR}}(q) = \hat{\eta}(q)\,\widehat{\text{SR}}, \qquad \hat{\eta}(q) \equiv \frac{q}{\sqrt{q + 2\sum_{k=1}^{q-1}(q-k)\hat{\rho}_k}}, \qquad (3.48)$$

where $\hat{\rho}_k$ is the sample kth-order autocorrelation coefficient.

Lo (2002) also derives the asymptotic distribution of (3.48) under fairly general assumptions for the returns process (stationarity and ergodicity) using the generalized method of moments. However, in the context of hedge fund returns, the usual asymptotic approximations may not be satisfactory because of the small sample sizes that characterize hedge fund data—a 5-year track record, which amounts to only 60 monthly observations, is considered quite a long history in this fast-paced industry. Therefore, Getmansky, Lo, and Makarov (2004) derive an alternate asymptotic distribution using the continuous-record asymptotics of Richardson and Stock (1989). Specifically, as the sample size T increases without bound, let q grow as well so that the ratio converges to some finite limit between 0 and 1:

$$\lim_{q,T\to\infty} q/T = \tau \in (0, 1). \qquad (3.49)$$

This condition is meant to provide an asymptotic approximation that may be more accurate for small-sample situations, i.e., situations where q is a significant fraction of T. For example, in the case of a fund with a 5-year track record, computing an annual Sharpe ratio with monthly data corresponds to a value of 0.20 for the ratio q/T.

Now as q increases without bound, SR(q) also tends to infinity; hence we must renormalize it to obtain a well-defined asymptotic sampling theory. In particular, observe that

$$\text{SR}(q) = \frac{E[R_t(q)] - R_f(q)}{\sqrt{\text{Var}[R_t(q)]}} = \frac{q(\mu - R_f)}{\sqrt{\text{Var}[R_t(q)]}}, \qquad (3.50)$$

$$\frac{\text{SR}(q)}{\sqrt{q}} = \frac{\mu - R_f}{\sqrt{\text{Var}[R_t(q)]/q}}, \qquad (3.51)$$

$$\lim_{q\to\infty} \frac{\text{SR}(q)}{\sqrt{q}} = \frac{\mu - R_f}{\bar{\sigma}}, \qquad (3.52)$$

where $\bar{\sigma}$ can be viewed as a kind of long-run average return standard deviation, which is generally not identical to the unconditional standard deviation σ of monthly returns except in the IID case. To estimate $\bar{\sigma}$, we can either follow Lo (2002) and use sample autocorrelations as in (3.48) or estimate $\bar{\sigma}$ directly accordingly to Newey and West (1987):

$$\hat{\bar{\sigma}}_{NW}^2 \equiv \frac{1}{T} \sum_1^T (R_t - \hat{\mu})^2 + \frac{2}{T} \sum_{j=1}^m \left(1 - \frac{j}{m+1}\right) \sum_{t=j+1}^T (R_t - \hat{\mu})(R_{t-j} - \hat{\mu}),$$

(3.53)

where $\hat{\mu}$ is the sample mean of $\{R_t\}$. For this estimator of $\bar{\sigma}$, we have the following asymptotic result.

Proposition 3.4.1. *(Getmansky, Lo, and Makarov, 2004). As m and T increase without bound so that $m/T \to \lambda \in (0, 1)$, $\hat{\bar{\sigma}}_{NW}^2$ converges weakly to the following functional $f(W)$ of standard Brownian motion on $[0, 1]$:*[17]

$$f(W) \equiv \frac{2\bar{\sigma}^2}{\lambda} \left(\int_0^1 W(r)\left[W(r) - W(\min(r + \lambda, 1))\right] dr \right.$$

$$\left. - W(1) \int_0^\lambda (\lambda - r)\left(W(1 - r) - W(r)\right) dr + \frac{\lambda(1 - \lambda^2/3)}{2} W^2(1) \right). \quad (3.54)$$

From (3.54), a straightforward computation yields the following expectations:

$$E[\hat{\bar{\sigma}}_{NW}^2] = 1 - \lambda + \frac{\lambda^2}{3}, \qquad E[1/\hat{\bar{\sigma}}_{NW}] \approx \sqrt{\frac{1 + \lambda}{1 - \lambda + \lambda^2/3}}. \quad (3.55)$$

Hence the following bias-corrected estimator for the Sharpe ratio is proposed for small samples:

$$\widehat{SR}(q) = \frac{\sqrt{q}(\hat{\mu} - R_f)}{\hat{\bar{\sigma}}_{NW}} \sqrt{\frac{1 - \lambda + \lambda^3/2}{1 + \lambda}}, \quad (3.56)$$

and its asymptotic distribution is given by the following proposition.

Proposition 3.4.2. *(Getmansky, Lo, and Makarov, 2004). As m, q, and T increase without bound so that $m/T \to \lambda \in (0, 1)$ and $q/T \to \tau \in (0, 1)$, the Sharpe ratio*

---

[17] See Billingsley (1968) for the definition of weak convergence and related results.

estimator $\widehat{SR}(q)$ *converges weakly to the following random variable:*

$$\widehat{SR}(q) \Rightarrow \left(\frac{SR(q)}{f(W)} + \frac{\sqrt{\tau} W(1)}{f(W)} \right) \sqrt{\frac{1 - \lambda + \lambda^3/2}{1 + \lambda}}, \tag{3.57}$$

where $f(W)$ is given by (3.54), $SR(q)$ is given by (3.50), and $W(\cdot)$ is standard Brownian motion defined on $[0, 1]$.

Monte Carlo simulations show that the second term of (3.57) does not account for much bias when $\tau \in (0, \frac{1}{2}]$ and that (3.57) is an excellent approximation to the small-sample distributions of Sharpe ratios for non-IID returns.[18]

3.5 Empirical Analysis of Smoothing and Illiquidity

Using the method of maximum likelihood, Getmansky, Lo, and Makarov (2004) estimate the smoothing model (3.2)–(3.4) by estimating an MA(2) process for observed returns assuming normally distributed errors, with the additional constraint that the MA coefficients sum to 1,[19] and we apply the same procedure to our updated and enlarged sample of funds in the Lipper TASS Combined Hedge Fund database from February 1977 to August 2004. For purposes of estimating (3.2), we impose an additional filter on our data, eliminating funds with less than 5 years of nonmissing monthly returns. This leaves a sample of 1,840 funds for which we estimate the MA(2) smoothing model. The maximum-likelihood estimation procedure did not converge for three of these funds, indicating some sort of misspecification or data errors, hence we have results for 1,837 funds.[20] Table 3.2 contains summary statistics for maximum-likelihood estimate of the smoothing parameters $(\theta_0, \theta_1, \theta_2)$ and smoothing index ξ, and Table 3.3 presents maximum-likelihood estimates of the smoothing model for the 50 most illiquid funds of the 1,837 funds as ranked by $\hat{\theta}_0$.

Table 3.2 shows that three categories seem to exhibit smaller average values of $\hat{\theta}_0$ than the rest—Convertible Arbitrage (0.719), Event Driven (0.786), and Fixed Income Arbitrage (0.775). Consider, in particular, the Convertible Arbitrage

---

[18] Getmansky, Lo, and Makarov (2004) have tabulated the percentiles of the distribution of (3.57) by Monte Carlo simulation for an extensive combination of values of q, τ, and λ and have offered to provide them to interested readers upon request.

[19] However, we do not impose the constraints that $\theta_i \in [0, 1]$ so as to obtain an indication of potential misspecification, i.e., estimates that fall outside the unit interval. See Getmansky, Lo, and Makarov (2004, Section 5.3) for additional specification tests of their smoothing model.

[20] The reference numbers for the funds that did not yield maximum-likelihood estimates are 1018, 1405, and 4201.

Table 3.2.

Means and Standard Deviations of Maximum-Likelihood Estimates of MA(2) Smoothing Process $R_t^o = \theta_0 R_t + \theta_1 R_{t-1} + \theta_2 R_{t-2}$.*

Category	Number of Funds	MA(2) Coefficient Estimates						ξ		Test Statistic $z(\theta_0)$ for H: $\theta_0 = 1$
		θ_0		θ_1		θ_3				
		Mean	SD	Mean	SD	Mean	SD	Mean	SD	
Convertible Arbitrage	76	0.719	0.161	0.201	0.148	0.080	0.101	0.621	0.327	15.558
Dedicated Short Bias	16	1.070	0.484	0.045	0.166	−0.115	0.331	1.508	2.254	−0.579
Emerging Markets	136	0.836	0.145	0.146	0.098	0.018	0.106	0.762	0.285	13.179
Equity Market Neutral	65	0.891	0.203	0.047	0.189	0.062	0.138	0.895	0.396	4.326
Event Driven	183	0.786	0.143	0.158	0.105	0.056	0.102	0.687	0.235	20.307
Fixed Income Arbitrage	65	0.775	0.169	0.147	0.104	0.078	0.120	0.682	0.272	10.714
Global Macro	88	0.999	0.202	0.047	0.161	−0.047	0.147	1.090	0.501	0.036
Long/Short Equity	532	0.880	0.179	0.092	0.125	0.028	0.142	0.851	0.398	15.453
Managed Futures	230	1.112	0.266	−0.032	0.193	−0.080	0.162	1.379	0.942	−6.406
Multi-Strategy	47	0.805	0.157	0.113	0.128	0.082	0.076	0.713	0.270	8.503
Fund of Funds	396	0.874	0.638	0.102	0.378	0.024	0.292	0.409	10.917	3.931
All	1,837	0.890	0.357	0.092	0.223	0.017	0.188	1.014	5.096	

*This process was subject to the normalization $1 = \theta_0 + \theta_1 + \theta_2$, where $\xi \equiv \theta_0^2 + \theta_1^2 + \theta_2^2$. Data are for 1,837 hedge funds in the Lipper TASS Combined database with at least 5 years of returns history during the period from February 1977 to August 2004.

category, which has a mean of 0.719 for $\hat{\theta}_0$. This is, of course, the average across all 79 funds in this category, but if it were the point estimate of a given fund, it would imply that only 71.9% of the fund's true current monthly return would be reported, with the remaining 28.1% distributed over the next 2 months (recall the constraint that $\hat{\theta}_0 + \hat{\theta}_1 + \hat{\theta}_2 = 1$). The estimates 0.201 and 0.080 for $\hat{\theta}_1$ and $\hat{\theta}_2$ imply that, on average, the current reported return also includes 20% of last month's true return and 8% of the true return 2 months ago.[21]

To develop a more formal statistical sense of the significance of these average values of $\hat{\theta}_0$, we can compute a z-statistic for the null hypothesis that the expected value of $\hat{\theta}_0$ is 1 by dividing the difference between 1 and each mean by its corresponding standard error, which can be approximated by the cross-sectional standard deviation divided by the square root of the number of funds in the average, assuming that the $\hat{\theta}_0$'s are cross-sectionally independently and identically distributed.[22] Under the null hypothesis of no smoothing, the z-statistic is asymptotically standard normal. These z-statistics are reported in the last column of Table 3.2 and confirm the intuition that the categories with the lowest average $\hat{\theta}_0$'s are significantly different from 1 (recall that the 99% critical value for a standard normal distribution is 2.33). Overall, the summary statistics in Table 3.2 are broadly consistent with common intuition about the nature of the strategies and securities involved in these fund categories, which contain the most illiquid securities and therefore have the most potential for smoothed returns and serial correlation.

Table 3.3 contains the smoothing parameter estimates for the top 50 funds ranked in order of increasing $\hat{\theta}_0$, which provides a more direct view of illiquidity and smoothed returns. In contrast to the averages in Table 3.2, the parameter estimates of θ_0 among these 50 funds range from 0.456 to 0.579, implying that only one-half to two-thirds of the current month's true returns are reflected in observed returns. The asymptotic standard errors are generally quite small, ranging from 0.029 to 0.069; hence the smoothing parameters seem to be estimated reasonably precisely.

The funds in Table 3.3 fall mainly into five categories: Fund of Funds (15), Convertible Arbitrage (8), Long/Short Equity (8), Fixed Income Arbitrage (7), and Event Driven (6). Together, these five categories account for 44 of the 50 funds in Table 3.3. A more complete summary of the distribution of smoothing parameter estimates across the different fund categories is provided in Figure 3.2, which contains a graph of the smoothing coefficients $\hat{\theta}_0$ by category, where 9 out of the 1,837 funds have been omitted, because their $\hat{\theta}_0$'s were larger than 2.0, so as to preserve the resolution of the graph.

---

[21] The averages do not always sum to 1 exactly because of rounding errors.

[22] The IID assumption is almost surely violated in the cross section (after all, the categories are supposed to group funds by certain common characteristics), but the relative rankings of the z-statistics across categories may still contain useful information.

Table 3.3.

First 50 Funds in a Ranked List of 1,837 Hedge Funds in the Lipper TASS Hedge Fund Combined Database (February 1977 to August 2004)*

Code	Category	Start	End	T	θ_0	$SE(\theta_0)$	θ_1	$SE(\theta_1)$	θ_2	$SE(\theta_2)$	x
1463	Equity Market Neutral	Jan 1995	Aug 2004	116	0.456	0.029	0.324	0.022	0.220	0.026	0.361
34563	Equity Market Neutral	Jan 1995	Aug 2004	116	0.456	0.029	0.330	0.022	0.214	0.026	0.363
4346	Event Driven	Jan 1995	Nov 2000	71	0.468	0.041	0.336	0.029	0.196	0.037	0.370
180	Long/Short Equity	Jun 1989	Aug 1996	87	0.480	0.040	0.343	0.027	0.177	0.036	0.379
1201	Convertible Arbitrage	Sep 1994	Aug 2004	120	0.485	0.036	0.368	0.022	0.147	0.033	0.392
4273	Fixed Income Arbitrage	Jan 1995	Jun 2001	78	0.495	0.033	0.187	0.034	0.318	0.029	0.381
518	Fixed Income Arbitrage	Dec 1993	May 2000	78	0.506	0.032	0.144	0.035	0.350	0.028	0.399
971	Convertible Arbitrage	Sep 1994	Dec 2000	76	0.512	0.037	0.172	0.037	0.316	0.032	0.391
1997	Convertible Arbitrage	Jan 1998	Jan 2004	73	0.512	0.046	0.268	0.037	0.220	0.039	0.383
2142	Emerging Markets	Aug 1998	Aug 2004	73	0.513	0.049	0.300	0.035	0.187	0.042	0.388
1204	Convertible Arbitrage	Oct 1995	Aug 2004	107	0.516	0.043	0.336	0.027	0.148	0.038	0.401
4529	Event Driven	Jan 1999	Aug 2004	68	0.518	0.050	0.288	0.038	0.195	0.044	0.389
1234	Fund of Funds	Oct 1994	Mar 2001	78	0.526	0.059	0.442	0.020	0.032	0.056	0.473
1657	Long/Short Equity	Oct 1995	Aug 2004	107	0.528	0.046	0.352	0.027	0.120	0.041	0.417
4146	Convertible Arbitrage	Jun 1997	Aug 2004	87	0.532	0.050	0.321	0.033	0.146	0.044	0.408
1696	Fund of Funds	Jan 1995	Jan 2000	61	0.532	0.066	0.403	0.030	0.065	0.060	0.450
4459	Fund of Funds	Jul 1999	Aug 2004	62	0.534	0.061	0.336	0.038	0.129	0.054	0.415
3721	Long/Short Equity	Nov 1998	Aug 2004	70	0.536	0.055	0.302	0.038	0.162	0.048	0.405
1584	Fund of Funds	Jan 1996	Jan 2004	97	0.537	0.044	0.252	0.035	0.212	0.037	0.396
2315	Long/Short Equity	Feb 1999	Aug 2004	67	0.541	0.058	0.298	0.040	0.161	0.050	0.407
1827	Fixed Income Arbitrage	Oct 1996	Dec 2003	87	0.541	0.046	0.226	0.039	0.232	0.038	0.398
2209	Fund of Funds	Apr 1997	Jan 2004	82	0.542	0.050	0.268	0.038	0.189	0.043	0.402
4153	Event Driven	Mar 1999	Jul 2004	65	0.543	0.063	0.356	0.035	0.101	0.056	0.432
2774	Equity Market Neutral	Jan 1995	Jun 2000	66	0.544	0.056	0.266	0.043	0.190	0.048	0.403
4209	Fund of Funds	Mar 1999	Aug 2004	66	0.544	0.069	0.445	0.022	0.011	0.066	0.494

120	Fixed Income Arbitrage	Oct 1998	Jul 1982	196	0.545	0.031	0.238	0.026	0.218	0.027	0.401
4080	Fund of Funds	Jul 2004	Jan 1999	67	0.549	0.064	0.354	0.036	0.097	0.056	0.436
1907	Fund of Funds	Aug 2004	Sep 1997	84	0.550	0.048	0.222	0.041	0.229	0.040	0.404
3148	Convertible Arbitrage	Aug 2004	Mar 1999	66	0.551	0.060	0.285	0.042	0.163	0.051	0.412
3149	Convertible Arbitrage	Aug 2004	Feb 1999	67	0.554	0.060	0.288	0.042	0.158	0.051	0.415
2396	Long/Short Equity	Aug 2004	Nov 1997	82	0.554	0.047	0.192	0.043	0.254	0.040	0.409
1659	Fund of Funds	Sep 2003	Jan 1997	81	0.554	0.055	0.295	0.038	0.150	0.047	0.417
1920	Fixed Income Arbitrage	Nov 2002	Nov 1997	61	0.555	0.067	0.336	0.040	0.110	0.058	0.432
2286	Long/Short Equity	Aug 2004	Feb 1998	79	0.555	0.051	0.226	0.042	0.218	0.043	0.407
4739	Multi-Strategy	Aug 2004	Aug 1999	61	0.557	0.060	0.241	0.048	0.201	0.050	0.409
33846	Fund of Funds	Aug 2004	Jan 1998	80	0.558	0.055	0.266	0.040	0.175	0.046	0.413
3225	Fund of Funds	Jul 2004	Jan 1999	67	0.559	0.053	0.185	0.048	0.257	0.044	0.412
34189	Fund of Funds	Jul 2004	Jan 1999	67	0.559	0.062	0.290	0.043	0.151	0.053	0.419
2997	Fund of Funds	Aug 2004	Jun 1999	63	0.559	0.060	0.238	0.048	0.203	0.050	0.411
33876	Event Driven	Aug 2004	Dec 1997	81	0.563	0.064	0.400	0.028	0.038	0.058	0.478
2755	Long/Short Equity	Jun 2004	Mar 1992	148	0.565	0.046	0.359	0.024	0.076	0.041	0.454
3114	Event Driven	Aug 2004	Dec 1991	153	0.567	0.044	0.326	0.027	0.107	0.038	0.439
415	Convertible Arbitrage	Aug 1996	Jul 1988	98	0.567	0.054	0.307	0.035	0.125	0.046	0.432
4007	Fixed Income Arbitrage	Aug 2004	Mar 1999	66	0.568	0.059	0.224	0.048	0.207	0.049	0.416
33845	Fund of Funds	Aug 2004	Jan 1998	80	0.569	0.058	0.279	0.041	0.152	0.049	0.424
4006	Fixed Income Arbitrage	Aug 2004	Mar 1999	66	0.569	0.060	0.225	0.048	0.207	0.050	0.417
1633	Event Driven	Jan 1999	Apr 1993	70	0.571	0.065	0.312	0.041	0.118	0.056	0.437
1471	Long/Short Equity	Aug 2004	Oct 1996	95	0.575	0.048	0.177	0.043	0.248	0.039	0.424
35997	Fund of Funds	Jul 2004	Oct 1995	106	0.576	0.049	0.238	0.038	0.187	0.041	0.423
37321	Multi-Strategy	Aug 2004	Oct 1994	119	0.579	0.048	0.249	0.036	0.172	0.040	0.427

* Funds have at least 5 years of returns history and are ranked in increasing order of the estimated smoothing parameter $\hat{\theta}_0$ of the MA(2) smoothing process $R_t^o = \theta_0 R_t + \theta_1 R_{t-1} + \theta_2 R_{t-2}$, subject to the normalization $1 = \theta_0 + \theta_1 + \theta_2$, and estimated via maximum likelihood.

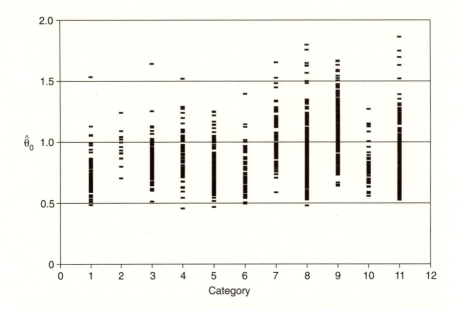

Figure 3.2. *Estimated smoothing coefficients $\hat{\theta}_0$ in the interval [0, 2] for 1,837 funds in the Lipper TASS hedge fund database with at least 5 years of returns (February 1977 to August 2004). Of the 1,837 funds in the sample, ordered by categories 1 to 11, only 9 funds yielded $\hat{\theta}_0$'s greater than 2 and have been omitted to preserve the resolution of the graph. Category definitions: $1 = Convertible \; Arbitrage$; $2 = Dedicated \; Short \; Bias$; $3 = Emerging \; Markets$; $4 = Equity \; Market \; Neutral$; $5 = Event \; Driven$; $6 = Fixed-Income \; Arbitrage$; $7 = Global \; Macro$; $8 = Long/Short \; Equity$; $9 = Managed \; Futures$; $10 = Multi-Strategy$; $11 = Fund \; of \; Funds$.*

Figure 3.2 shows that although there is considerable variation within each category, nevertheless some clear differences between categories emerge. For example, categories 1, 3, 5, 6, and 10 (Convertible Arbitrage, Emerging Markets, Event Driven, Fixed Income Arbitrage, and Multi-Strategy, respectively) have clearly discernible concentrations of $\hat{\theta}_0$'s that are lower than 1 and lower than those of the other categories, suggesting more illiquid funds and more smoothed returns. On the other hand, categories 2, 7, and 9 (Dedicated Shortseller, Global Macro, and Managed Futures, respectively) have concentrations that are at or above 1, suggesting just the opposite—more liquidity and less return smoothing.

To develop further intuition for the smoothing model (3.2)–(3.4) and the possible interpretations of the smoothing-parameter estimates, we reproduce the analysis in Getmansky, Lo, and Makarov (2004), where they apply the same estimation procedure to the returns of the Ibbotson stock and bond indexes, the Merrill Lynch Convertible Securities Index,[23] the CS/Tremont hedge fund indexes, and two mutual funds: the highly liquid Vanguard 500 Index Fund and the considerably less liquid American Express Extra Income Fund.[24] Table 3.4 contains summary statistics, market betas (where the market return is taken to be the S&P 500 total return), contemporaneous and lagged market betas as in Asness, Krail, and Liew (2001), and smoothing-coefficient estimates for these index and mutual fund returns.[25]

Consistent with our interpretation of $\hat{\theta}_0$ as an indicator of liquidity, the returns of the most liquid portfolios in the first panel of Table 3.4—the Ibbotson Large Company Index, the Vanguard 500 Index Fund (which is virtually identical to the Ibbotson Large Company Index, except for sample period and tracking error), and the Ibbotson Long-Term Government Bond Index—have smoothing-parameter estimates near unity: 0.92 for the Ibbotson Large Company Index, 1.12 for the Vanguard 500 Index Fund, and 0.92 for the Ibbotson Long-Term Government Bond Index. The first-order autocorrelation coefficients and lagged market betas also confirm their lack of serial correlation; 9.8% first-order autocorrelation for the Ibbotson Large Company Index, -2.3% for the Vanguard 500 Index Fund, and 6.7% for the Ibbotson Long-Term Government Bond Index, and lagged market betas that are statistically indistinguishable from 0. However, the values of $\hat{\theta}_0$ of the less liquid portfolios are less than 1.00: 0.82 for the Ibbotson Small Company Index, 0.84 for the Ibbotson Long-Term Corporate Bond Index, 0.82 for the Merrill Lynch Convertible Securities Index, and 0.67 for the American Express Extra Income Fund, and their first-order serial correlation coefficients are 15.6%, 15.6%, 6.4%, and 35.4%, respectively, which, with the exception of that for the

---

[23] This is described by Merrill Lynch as a "market value-weighted index that tracks the daily price only, income and total return performance of corporate convertible securities, including U.S. domestic bonds, Eurobonds, preferred stocks and Liquid Yield Option Notes."

[24] As of January 31, 2003, the net assets of the Vanguard 500 Index Fund (ticker symbol: VFINX) and the AXP Extra Income Fund (ticker symbol: INEAX) are given by http://finance.yahoo.com/ as $59.7 billion and $1.5 billion, respectively, and the descriptions of the two funds are as follows:

The Vanguard 500 Index Fund seeks investment results that correspond with the price and yield performance of the S&P 500 Index. The fund employs a passive management strategy designed to track the performance of the S&P 500 Index, which is dominated by the stocks of large U.S. companies. It attempts to replicate the target index by investing all or substantially all of its assets in the stocks that make up the index.

AXP Extra Income Fund seeks high current income; capital appreciation is secondary. The fund ordinarily invests in long-term high-yielding, lower-rated corporate bonds. These bonds may be issued by U.S. and foreign companies and governments. The fund may invest in other instruments such as: money market securities, convertible securities, preferred stocks, derivatives (such as futures, options and forward contracts), and common stocks.

[25] Market betas were obtained by regressing returns on a constant and the total return of the S&P 500, and contemporaneous and lagged market betas were obtained by regressing returns on a constant, the contemporaneous total return of the S&P 500, and the first two lags.

Table 3.4.

Summary Statistics and Smoothing-Parameter Estimates for Various Indexes and Mutual Funds*

Series	Period	T	Mean (%)	SD (%)	$\hat{\rho}_1$ (%)	$\hat{\rho}_2$ (%)	$\hat{\rho}_3$ (%)	Market Model $\hat{\beta}$	$SE(\hat{\beta})$	R^2 (%)
Ibbotson Small Company	Jan 1926–Dec 2001	912	1.35	8.63	15.6	1.7	−10.6	1.27	0.03	66.9
Ibbotson Long-Term Government Bonds	Jan 1926–Dec 2001	912	0.46	2.22	6.7	0.3	−8.3	0.07	0.01	2.8
Ibbotson Long-Term Corporate Bonds	Jan 1926–Dec 2001	912	0.49	1.96	15.6	0.3	−6.0	0.08	0.01	5.2
Ibbotson Large Company	Jan 1926–Dec 2001	912	1.03	5.57	9.8	−3.2	−10.7	1.00	0.00	100.0
Merrill Lynch Convertibles Index	Jan 1994–Oct 2002	168	0.99	3.43	6.4	12.0	5.1	0.59	0.05	48.6
AXP Extra Income Fund (INEAX)	Jan 1984–Dec 2001	216	0.67	2.04	35.4	13.1	2.5	0.21	0.03	20.7
Vanguard 500 Index Trust (VFINX)	Sep 1976–Dec 2001	304	1.16	4.36	−2.3	−6.8	−3.2	1.00	0.00	100.0
CS/Tremont Indexes:										
Aggregate Hedge Fund Index	Jan 1994–Oct 2002	106	0.87	2.58	11.2	4.1	−0.4	0.31	0.05	24.9
Convertible Arbitrage	Jan 1994–Oct 2002	106	0.81	1.40	56.6	42.6	15.6	0.03	0.03	1.1
Dedicated Short Bias	Jan 1994–Oct 2002	106	0.22	5.29	7.8	−6.3	−5.0	−0.94	0.08	58.6
Emerging Markets	Jan 1994–Oct 2002	106	0.54	5.38	29.4	1.2	−2.1	0.62	0.11	24.0
Equity Market Neutral	Jan 1994–Oct 2002	106	0.89	0.92	29.4	18.1	8.4	0.10	0.02	21.1
Event Driven	Jan 1994–Oct 2002	106	0.83	1.81	34.8	14.7	3.8	0.23	0.04	30.2
Fixed Income Arbitrage	Jan 1994–Oct 2002	106	0.55	1.18	39.6	10.8	5.4	0.02	0.03	0.7
Global Macro	Jan 1994–Oct 2002	106	1.17	3.69	5.6	4.6	8.3	0.24	0.09	7.5
Long/Short	Jan 1994–Oct 2002	106	0.98	3.34	15.9	5.9	−4.6	0.48	0.06	36.7
Managed Futures	Jan 1994–Oct 2002	106	0.55	3.44	3.2	−6.3	0.7	−0.12	0.08	2.5

Table 3.4.
(continued)

| | | | | | Contemporaneous and Lagged Market Model | | | | R^2 |
Series	Period	T	$\hat{\beta}_0$	SE($\hat{\beta}_0$)	$\hat{\beta}_1$	SE($\hat{\beta}_1$)	$\hat{\beta}_2$	SE($\hat{\beta}_2$)	(%)
Ibbotson Small Company	Jan 1926–Dec 2001	912	1.25	0.03	0.16	0.03	0.03	0.03	68.0
Ibbotson Long-Term Government Bonds	Jan 1926–Dec 2001	912	0.07	0.01	−0.03	0.01	−0.02	0.01	3.6
Ibbotson Long-Term Corporate Bonds	Jan 1926–Dec 2001	912	0.08	0.01	−0.01	0.01	−0.01	0.01	5.3
Ibbotson Large Company	Jan 1926–Dec 2001	912	1.00	0.00	0.00	0.00	0.00	0.00	100.0
Merrill Lynch Convertibles Index	Jan 1994–Oct 2002	168	0.60	0.05	0.15	0.05	0.07	0.04	52.2
AXP Extra Income Fund (INEAX)	Jan 1984–Dec 2001	216	0.21	0.03	0.12	0.03	0.04	0.03	28.7
Vanguard 500 Index Trust (VFINX)	Sep 1976–Dec 2001	304	1.00	0.00	0.00	0.00	0.00	0.00	100.0
CS/Tremont Indexes:									
Aggregate Hedge Fund Index	Jan 1994–Oct 2002	106	0.32	0.05	0.06	0.05	0.16	0.05	32.1
Convertible Arbitrage	Jan 1994–Oct 2002	106	0.04	0.03	0.09	0.03	0.06	0.03	12.0
Dedicated Short Bias	Jan 1994–Oct 2002	106	−0.93	0.08	−0.06	0.08	0.08	0.08	59.3
Emerging Markets	Jan 1994–Oct 2002	106	0.63	0.11	0.19	0.11	0.03	0.12	26.2
Equity Market Neutral	Jan 1994–Oct 2002	106	0.10	0.02	0.02	0.02	0.00	0.02	22.1
Event Driven	Jan 1994–Oct 2002	106	0.23	0.03	0.11	0.03	0.04	0.03	38.2
Fixed Income Arbitrage	Jan 1994–Oct 2002	106	0.03	0.03	0.05	0.03	0.09	0.03	12.9
Global Macro	Jan 1994–Oct 2002	106	0.26	0.09	−0.01	0.09	0.23	0.09	14.1
Long/Short	Jan 1994–Oct 2002	106	0.49	0.06	0.06	0.06	0.15	0.06	40.7
Managed Futures	Jan 1994–Oct 2002	106	−0.13	0.08	−0.17	0.08	0.02	0.08	7.8

Table 3.4.
(continued)

Series	Period	T	$\hat\theta_0$	$SE(\hat\theta_0)$	$\hat\theta_1$	$SE(\hat\theta_1)$	$\hat\theta_2$	$SE(\hat\theta_2)$	ξ
Ibbotson Small Company	Jan 1926–Dec 2001	912	0.82	0.03	0.13	0.02	0.04	0.03	0.69
Ibbotson Long-Term Government Bonds	Jan 1926–Dec 2001	912	0.92	0.05	0.06	0.03	0.01	0.03	0.86
Ibbotson Long-Term Corporate Bonds	Jan 1926–Dec 2001	912	0.84	0.04	0.14	0.02	0.02	0.03	0.73
Ibbotson Large Company	Jan 1926–Dec 2001	912	0.92	0.05	0.09	0.03	-0.01	0.03	0.85
Merrill Lynch Convertibles Index	Jan 1994–Oct 2002	168	0.82	0.07	0.02	0.06	0.16	0.05	0.70
AXP Extra Income Fund (INEAX)	Jan 1984–Dec 2001	216	0.67	0.03	0.24	0.03	0.09	0.04	0.51
Vanguard 500 Index Trust (VFINX)	Sep 1976–Dec 2001	304	1.12	0.17	-0.03	0.07	-0.09	0.07	1.26
CS/Tremont Indexes:									
Aggregate Hedge Fund Index	Jan 1994–Oct 2002	106	0.86	0.12	0.09	0.08	0.04	0.08	0.76
Convertible Arbitrage	Jan 1994–Oct 2002	106	0.49	0.01	0.26	0.03	0.25	0.03	0.37
Dedicated Short Bias	Jan 1994–Oct 2002	106	0.99	0.20	0.08	0.09	-0.07	0.10	0.99
Emerging Markets	Jan 1994–Oct 2002	106	0.75	0.08	0.24	0.05	0.01	0.07	0.62
Equity Market Neutral	Jan 1994–Oct 2002	106	0.71	0.06	0.18	0.05	0.12	0.06	0.54
Event Driven	Jan 1994–Oct 2002	106	0.68	0.05	0.23	0.05	0.09	0.06	0.52
Fixed Income Arbitrage	Jan 1994–Oct 2002	106	0.63	0.04	0.28	0.04	0.08	0.05	0.49
Global Macro	Jan 1994–Oct 2002	106	0.91	0.14	0.04	0.08	0.05	0.08	0.84
Long/Short	Jan 1994–Oct 2002	106	0.82	0.10	0.13	0.07	0.06	0.07	0.68
Managed Futures	Jan 1994–Oct 2002	106	1.04	0.23	0.04	0.10	-0.08	0.11	1.08

*Summary statistics and maximum-likelihood estimates of MA(2) smoothing process $R_t^o = \theta_0 R_t + \theta_1 R_{t-1} + \theta_2 R_{t-2}$, $\xi \equiv \theta_0^2 + \theta_1^2 + \theta_2^2$, subject to the normalization $1 = \theta_0 + \theta_1 + \theta_2$, for the returns of various indexes and two mutual funds, the Vanguard 500 Index Trust (which tracks the S&P 500 index) and the AXP Extra Income Fund (which focuses on high current income and invests in long-term, high-yielding, lower-rated corporate bonds). Total returns of the S&P 500 index are used for both market models.

Merrill Lynch Convertible Securities Index, are considerably higher than those of the more liquid portfolios.[26] Also, the lagged market betas are statistically significant at the 5% level for the Ibbotson Small Company Index (*t*-statistic for $\hat{\beta}_1$: 5.41), the Ibbotson Long-Term Government Bond Index (*t*-statistic for $\hat{\beta}_1$: −2.30), the Merrill Lynch Convertible Securities Index (*t*-statistic for $\hat{\beta}_1$: 3.33), and the AXP Extra Income Fund (*t*-statistic for $\hat{\beta}_1$: 4.64).

The results for the CS/Tremont hedge fund indexes in the second panel in Table 3.4 are also consistent with the empirical results in Tables 3.2 and 3.3— indexes corresponding to hedge fund strategies involving less liquid securities tend to have lower $\hat{\theta}_0$'s. For example, the smoothing-parameter estimates $\hat{\theta}_0$ of the Convertible Arbitrage, Emerging Markets, and Fixed Income Arbitrage indexes are 0.49, 0.75, and 0.63, respectively, and the first-order serial correlation coefficients of 56.6%, 29.4%, and 39.6%, respectively. In contrast, the smoothing-parameter estimates of the more liquid hedge fund strategies such as Dedicated Short Bias and Managed Futures are 0.99 and 1.04, respectively, with first-order serial correlation coefficients of 7.8% and 3.2%, respectively.

While these findings are generally consistent with the results in Tables 3.2 and 3.3, it should be noted that the process of aggregation can change the statistical behavior of any time series. For example, Granger (1980, 1988) observes that the aggregation of a large number of stationary autoregressive processes can yield a time series that exhibits long-term memory, characterized by serial correlation coefficients that decay very slowly (hyperbolically, as opposed to geometrically as in the case of a stationary ARMA process). Therefore, while it is true that the aggregation of a collection of illiquid funds generally yields an index with smoothed returns,[27] the reverse need not be true—smoothed index returns need not imply that all of the funds comprising the index are illiquid. The latter inference can be made only with the benefit of additional information—essentially identification restrictions—about the statistical relations among the funds in the index (namely, covariances and possibly other higher-order comoments), or the existence of common factors driving fund returns.

It is interesting to note that the first lagged market beta $\hat{\beta}_1$ for the CS/Tremont indexes is statistically significant at the 5% level in only three cases (Convertible Arbitrage, Event Driven, and Managed Futures), but that the second lagged beta $\hat{\beta}_2$ is significant in five cases (the overall index, Convertible Arbitrage, Fixed

---

[26] However, note that the second-order autocorrelation of the Merrill Lynch Convertible Securities Index is 12.0%, which is second only to the AXP Extra Income Fund in absolute magnitude, two orders of magnitude larger than the second-order autocorrelation of the Ibbotson bond indexes and one order of magnitude larger than the Ibbotson stock indexes.

[27] It is, of course, possible that the smoothing coefficients of some funds may exactly offset those of other funds so as to reduce the degree of smoothing in an aggregate index. However, such a possibility is extremely remote and pathological if each of the component funds exhibits a high degree of smoothing.

Income Arbitrage, Global Macro, and Long/Short). Obviously, the S&P 500 index is likely to be inappropriate for certain styles (e.g., Emerging Markets), and these somewhat inconsistent results suggest that using a lagged market beta adjustment may not completely account for the impact of illiquidity and smoothed returns.

Overall, the patterns in Table 3.4 confirm our interpretation of smoothing coefficients and serial correlation as proxies for liquidity and suggest that there may be broader applications of this model of smoothed returns to other investment strategies and asset classes.

To illustrate the potential impact of serial correlation on performance statistics such as Sharpe ratios, we apply the serial correlation–adjusted Sharpe ratio estimator (3.48) in Section 3.4 to the mutual fund and hedge fund returns data in Table 1.10. Table 3.5 shows that the 10 mutual funds have very little serial correlation in returns, with p-values of Q-statistics ranging from 13.2% to 80.2%. Indeed, the largest absolute level of autocorrelation among the 10 mutual funds is the 12.4% first-order autocorrelation of the Fidelity Magellan Fund. Using a risk-free rate R_f of 5%/12 per month, the monthly Sharpe ratios of these 10 funds range from 0.14 (Growth Fund of America) to 0.32 (Janus Worldwide), with robust standard errors of 0.05 and 0.11, respectively. Because of the lack of serial correlation in the monthly returns of these mutual funds, there is little difference between the IID estimator for the annual Sharpe ratio $\sqrt{q}\,\widehat{\text{SR}}$ and the robust estimator $\widehat{\text{SR}}(12)$ that accounts for serial correlation. For example, even in the case of the Fidelity Magellan Fund, which has the highest first-order autocorrelation among the 10 mutual funds, the difference between $\sqrt{q}\,\widehat{\text{SR}} = 0.73$ and $\widehat{\text{SR}}(12) = 0.66$ is not substantial (and certainly not statistically significant). Note that the robust estimator is marginally lower than the IID estimator, indicating the presence of positive serial correlation in the monthly returns of the Magellan Fund. In contrast, for Washington Mutual Investors, the IID estimate of the annual Sharpe ratio is $\sqrt{q}\,\widehat{\text{SR}} = 0.60$, but the robust estimate $\widehat{\text{SR}}(12) = 0.65$ is larger because of negative serial correlation in the fund's monthly returns (recall that negative serial correlation implies that the variance of the sum of 12 monthly returns is less than 12 times the variance of monthly returns).

The robust standard errors $\text{SE}_3(12)$ with $m = 3$ for $\widehat{\text{SR}}(12)$ range from 0.17 (Janus) to 0.47 (Fidelity Growth and Income) and take on similar values when $m = 6$, which indicates that the robust estimator is reasonably well behaved for this data set. The magnitudes of the standard errors yield 95% confidence intervals for annual Sharpe ratios that do not contain 0 for any of the 10 mutual funds. For example, the 95% confidence interval for the Vanguard 500 Index is $0.85 \pm (1.96 \times 0.26)$, which is [0.33, 1.36]. These results indicate Sharpe ratios for the 10 mutual funds that are statistically different from zero at the 95% confidence level.

The results for the 12 hedge funds are different in several respects. The mean returns are higher, and the standard deviations are lower, implying much higher Sharpe ratio estimates for hedge funds than for mutual funds. The monthly Sharpe ratio estimates $\widehat{\text{SR}}$ range from 0.60 (Convertible Arbitrage A and B Funds) to

Table 3.5.

Raw and Adjusted Sharpe Ratios for Mutual Funds and Hedge Funds*

	Start Date	T	$\hat{\mu}$ (%)	$\hat{\sigma}$ (%)	$\hat{\rho}_1$ (%)	$\hat{\rho}_2$ (%)	$\hat{\rho}_3$ (%)	p-value of Q_{11} (%)	Monthly $\widehat{SR}$	SE_3	$\sqrt{12}\,\widehat{SR}$	$\widehat{SR}(12)$	Annual $SE_3(12)$	$SE_6(12)$
Mutual funds														
Vanguard 500 Index	Jan 1976	286	1.30	4.27	−4.0	−6.6	−4.9	64.5	0.21	0.06	**0.72**	**0.85**	0.26	0.25
Fidelity Magellan	Jan 1967	402	1.73	6.23	12.4	−2.3	−0.4	28.6	0.21	0.06	**0.73**	**0.66**	0.20	0.21
Investment Company of America	Jan 1963	450	1.17	4.01	1.8	−3.2	−4.5	80.2	0.19	0.05	**0.65**	**0.71**	0.22	0.22
Janus	Mar 1970	364	1.52	4.75	10.5	−0.0	−3.7	58.1	0.23	0.06	**0.81**	**0.80**	0.17	0.17
Fidelity Contrafund	May 1967	397	1.29	4.97	7.4	−2.5	−6.8	58.2	0.18	0.05	**0.61**	**0.67**	0.23	0.23
Washington Mutual Investors	Jan 1963	450	1.13	4.09	−0.1	−7.2	−2.6	22.8	0.17	0.05	**0.60**	**0.65**	0.20	0.20
Janus Worldwide	Jan 1992	102	1.81	4.36	11.4	3.4	−3.8	13.2	0.32	0.11	**1.12**	**1.29**	0.46	0.37
Fidelity Growth and Income	Jan 1986	174	1.54	4.13	5.1	−1.6	−8.2	60.9	0.27	0.09	**0.95**	**1.18**	0.47	0.40
American Century Ultra	Dec 1981	223	1.72	7.11	2.3	3.4	1.4	54.5	0.18	0.07	**0.64**	**0.71**	0.27	0.25
Growth Fund of America	Jul 1964	431	1.18	5.35	8.5	−2.7	−4.1	45.4	0.14	0.05	**0.50**	**0.49**	0.19	0.20
Hedge funds														
Convertible/Option Arbitrage	May 1992	104	1.63	0.97	42.6	29.0	21.4	0.0	1.26	0.28	**4.35**	**2.99**	1.04	1.11
Relative Value	Dec 1992	97	0.66	0.21	25.9	19.2	−2.1	4.5	1.17	0.17	**4.06**	**3.38**	1.16	1.07
Mortgage-Backed Securities	Jan 1993	96	1.33	0.79	42.0	22.1	16.7	0.1	1.16	0.24	**4.03**	**2.44**	0.53	0.54
High Yield Debt	Jun 1994	79	1.30	0.87	33.7	21.8	13.1	5.2	1.02	0.27	**3.54**	**2.25**	0.74	0.72
Risk Arbitrage A	Jul 1993	90	1.06	0.69	−4.9	−10.8	6.9	30.6	0.94	0.20	**3.25**	**3.83**	0.87	0.85
Long/Short Equities	Jul 1989	138	1.18	0.83	−20.2	24.6	8.7	0.1	0.92	0.06	**3.19**	**2.32**	0.35	0.37
Multi-Strategy A	Jan 1995	72	1.08	0.75	48.9	23.4	3.3	0.3	0.89	0.40	**3.09**	**2.18**	1.14	1.19
Risk Arbitrage B	Nov 1994	74	0.90	0.77	−4.9	2.5	−8.3	96.1	0.63	0.14	**2.17**	**2.47**	0.79	0.77
Convertible Arbitrage A	Sep 1992	100	1.38	1.60	33.8	30.8	7.9	0.8	0.60	0.18	**2.08**	**1.43**	0.44	0.45
Convertible Arbitrage B	Jul 1994	78	0.78	0.62	32.4	9.7	−4.5	23.4	0.60	0.18	**2.06**	**1.67**	0.68	0.62
Multi-Strategy B	Jun 1989	139	1.34	1.63	49.0	24.6	10.6	0.0	0.57	0.16	**1.96**	**1.17**	0.25	0.25
Fund of Funds	Oct 1994	75	1.68	2.29	29.7	21.1	0.9	23.4	0.56	0.19	**1.93**	**1.39**	0.67	0.70

*Monthly and annual Sharpe ratio estimates for a sample of mutual funds and hedge funds based on monthly total returns from various start dates through June 2000 for the mutual fund sample and various start dates through December 2000 for the hedge fund sample. $\hat{\rho}_k$ denotes the kth autocorrelation coefficient, and Q_{11} denotes the Ljung–Box (1978) Q-statistic $T(T+2)\sum_{k=1}^{11}\hat{\rho}_k^2/(T-k)$, which is asymptotically χ_{11}^2 under the null hypothesis of no serial correlation. $\widehat{SR}$ denotes the usual Sharpe ratio estimator $(\hat{\mu}-R_f)/\hat{\sigma}$ based on monthly data, where R_f is assumed to be 5.0%/12 per month, and $\widehat{SR}(12)$ denotes the annual Sharpe ratio estimator which takes into account serial correlation in monthly returns. All standard errors are based on GMM estimators using Newey and West's (1987) procedure with truncation lag $m=3$ for entries in the "SE_3" and "$SE_3(12)$" columns, and $m=6$ for entries in the "$SE_6(12)$" column.

1.26 (Convertible/Option Arbitrage Fund), in contrast to the range of 0.14–0.32 for the 10 mutual funds. However, the serial correlation in hedge fund returns is also much higher. For example, the first-order autocorrelation coefficient ranges from -20.2% to 49.0% among the 12 hedge funds, whereas the highest first-order autocorrelation is 12.4% among the 10 mutual funds. The p-values provide a more complete summary of the presence of serial correlation—all but 4 of the 12 hedge funds have p-values less than 5% and several have p-values less than 1%.

The impact of serial correlation on the annual Sharpe ratios of hedge funds is dramatic. When the IID estimator $\sqrt{12}\,\widehat{SR}$ is used for the annual Sharpe ratio, the Convertible/Option Arbitrage Fund has a Sharpe ratio estimate of 4.35, but when serial correlation is properly taken into account by $\widehat{SR}(12)$, the estimate drops to 2.99, implying that the IID estimator overstates the annual Sharpe ratio by 45%. The annual Sharpe ratio estimate for the Mortgage-Backed Securities Fund drops to 2.44 from 4.03 when serial correlation is taken into account, implying an overstatement of 65%. However, the annual Sharpe ratio estimate of the Risk Arbitrage A Fund *increases* to 3.83 from 3.25 because of negative serial correlation in its monthly returns.

The sharp differences between the annual IID and robust Sharpe ratio estimates underscore the importance of correctly accounting for serial correlation in analyzing the performance of hedge funds. Naively estimating the annual Sharpe ratios by multiplying $\widehat{SR}$ by $\sqrt{12}$ yields the rank ordering given in Table 3.5, but once serial correlation is taken into account, the rank ordering changes to 3, 2, 5, 7, 1, 6, 8, 4, 10, 9, 12, 11.

The robust standard errors for the annual robust Sharpe ratio estimates of the 12 hedge funds range from 0.25 to 1.14 which, although larger than those in the mutual fund sample, nevertheless imply 95% confidence intervals that generally do not include 0. For example, even in the case of the Multi-Strategy B Fund which has the lowest robust Sharpe ratio estimate of 1.17, its 95% confidence interval is $1.17 \pm 1.96 \times 0.25$, which is [0.68, 1.66]. This is also consistent with previous studies documenting the fact that hedge funds do seem to exhibit statistically significant excess returns.[28] The similarity of the standard errors between the $m = 3$ and $m = 6$ cases for the hedge fund sample indicate that the robust estimator is also well behaved in this case despite the presence of significant serial correlation in monthly returns.

The empirical examples in this section illustrate the potential impact that serial correlation can have on performance measures such as the Sharpe ratio, and the importance of properly accounting for departures from the standard IID framework. In particular, robust Sharpe ratio estimators contain significant additional information about the risk/reward trade-offs for hedge funds and should be used in place of more traditional measures.

---

[28] See, for example, Ackermann, McEnally, and Ravenscraft (1999), Brown, Goetzmann, and Ibbotson (1999), Brown, Goetzmann, and Park (2001a), Fung and Hsieh (1997a,b, 2000), and Liang (1999, 2000, 2001).

4

Optimal Liquidity

It should be apparent from Chapter 3 that liquidity is an important risk factor for hedge funds. Many studies—in both academic journals and more applied forums—have made considerable progress in defining liquidity, measuring the cost of immediacy and price impact, deriving optimal portfolio rules in the presence of transaction costs, investigating the relationship between liquidity and arbitrage, and estimating liquidity risk premia in the context of various partial and general equilibrium asset-pricing models.[1] However, relatively little attention has been paid to the more practical problem of integrating liquidity directly into the portfolio construction process.[2]

---

[1] See, for example, Acharya and Pedersen (2002), Aiyagari and Gertler (1991), Atkinson and Wilmott (1995), Amihud and Mendelson (1986b), Bertsimas and Lo (1998), Boyle and Vorst (1992), Chordia, Roll, and Subrahmanyam (2000, 2001, 2002), Chordia, Subrahmanyam, and Anshuman (2001), Cohen et al. (1981), Constantinides (1986), Davis and Norman (1991), Dumas and Luciano (1991), Epps (1976), Garman and Ohlson (1981), Gromb and Vayanos (2002), Grossman and Laroque (1990), Grossman and Vila (1992), Heaton and Lucas (1994, 1995), Hodges and Neuberger (1989), Holmstrom and Tirole (2001), Huang (2003), Litzenberger and Rolfo (1984), Leland (1985), Liu and Longstaff (2000), Lo, Mamaysky, and Wang (2004), Magill and Constantinides (1976), Morton and Pliska (1995), Pastor and Stambaugh (2003), Sadka (2003), Shleifer and Vishny (1997), Tuckman and Vila (1992), Vayanos (1998), Vayanos and Vila (1995), and Willard and Dybvig (1999).

[2] Of course, many studies have considered the practical significance of trading costs or "slippage" in investment management, e.g., Arnott and Wagner (1990), Bertsimas and Lo (1998), Bodurtha and Quinn (1990), Brinson, Hood, and Beebower (1986), Brinson, Singer, and Beebower (1991), Chan and Lakonishok (1993, 1995), Collins and Fabozzi (1991), Cuneo and Wagner (1975), Gammill and Pérold (1989), Hasbrouck and Schwartz (1988), Keim and Madhavan (1997), Leinweber (1993, 1994), Loeb (1983), Pérold (1988), Schwartz and Whitcomb (1988), Stoll (1993), Treynor (1981), Wagner and Banks (1992), Wagner and Edwards (1993), and the papers in Sherrerd (1993). None of these studies focuses squarely on the quantitative trade-off between expected return, risk, and liquidity. However, Michaud (1989) observes that standard mean-variance portfolio optimization does not take liquidity

In this chapter, we present the results of Lo, Petrov, and Wierzbicki (2003) in which they model liquidity using simple measures such as trading volume and percentage bid/offer spreads and then introduce these measures into the standard mean-variance portfolio optimization process to yield optimal mean-variance-liquidity portfolios. They begin by proposing several measures of the liquidity ℓ_i of an individual security, from which they define the liquidity ℓ_p of a portfolio $\omega_p \equiv [\omega_{p1} \; \omega_{p2} \; \cdots \; \omega_{pn}]'$ as the weighted average $\sum_i \ell_i \omega_{pi}$ of the individual securities' liquidities. Using these liquidity measures, they construct three types of *liquidity-optimized* portfolios: (1) a mean-variance-efficient portfolio subject to a liquidity filter requiring that each security in the portfolio have a minimum level of liquidity ℓ_o; (2) a mean-variance-efficient portfolio subject to a constraint that the portfolio have a minimum level of liquidity ℓ_o; and (3) a mean-variance-liquidity-efficient portfolio where the optimization problem has three terms in its objective function: mean, variance, and liquidity. Using three different definitions of liquidity—turnover, percentage bid/offer spread, and a nonlinear function of market capitalization and trade size—they show empirically that liquidity-optimized portfolios have some very attractive properties and that even simple forms of liquidity optimization can yield significant benefits in terms of reducing a portfolio's liquidity risk exposure without sacrificing a great deal of expected return per unit risk.

In Section 4.1, we describe their simple measures of liquidity and propose an additional measure that is particularly relevant for hedge fund investments—the first-order serial correlation coefficient. Using these liquidity measures, we define the three types of liquidity-optimized portfolios in Section 4.2 and then review some empirical examples of liquidity-optimized portfolios in Section 4.3. We discuss extensions and open issues in Section 4.4.

4.1 Liquidity Metrics

The natural starting point of any attempt to integrate liquidity into the portfolio optimization process is to develop a quantitative measure of liquidity, i.e., a liquidity metric. Liquidity is a multifaceted concept involving at least three distinct attributes of the trading process—price, time, and size—hence a liquid security is one that can be traded quickly, with little price impact, and in large quantities. Therefore, we are unlikely to find a single statistic that summarizes all of these attributes. To represent these distinct features, Lo, Petrov, and Wierzbicki (2003)

---

into account, and proposes liquidity constraints and quadratic penalty functions in a mean-variance framework in Michaud (1998, Chapter 12).

start with the following five quantities on which their liquidity metrics are based:

$$\text{Trading volume} \equiv \text{total number of shares traded at time } t, \quad (4.1)$$

$$\text{Logarithm of trading volume} \equiv \log(\text{trading volume}), \quad (4.2)$$

$$\text{Turnover} \equiv \frac{\text{trading volume}}{\text{shares outstanding}}, \quad (4.3)$$

$$\text{Percentage bid/ask spread} \equiv \frac{\text{ask} - \text{bid}}{(\text{ask} + \text{bid})/2}, \quad (4.4)$$

$$\text{Loeb price impact function} \equiv f(\text{trade size, market cap}), \quad (4.5)$$

where the first three variables measure the amount of trading and the last two measure the cost.[3]

Perhaps the most common measure of the liquidity of a security is its trading volume. It is almost tautological to say that a security is more liquid if it is traded more frequently and in greater quantities. Both trading volume and turnover capture this aspect of liquidity, and because these two variables are so highly correlated (see, for example, Lo and Wang, 2000), we will use only one of the three measures of trading activity (4.1)–(4.3) in our empirical analysis. Given Lo and Wang's (2000) motivation for turnover in the context of modern asset-pricing models such as the Capital Asset Pricing Model and the Arbitrage Pricing Theory, we shall adopt turnover (4.3) as our measure of trading activity.

Another popular measure of the liquidity of a security is the cost of transacting in it, either as buyer or seller; hence the bid/ask spread is the natural candidate. Smaller bid/ask spreads imply lower costs of trading, whereas larger bid/ask spreads are partly attributable to a liquidity premium demanded by market makers for making markets in illiquid securities.[4]

Market capitalization—the market value of total outstanding equity—has also been proposed as an important proxy for liquidity. Larger amounts of outstanding equity tend to be traded more frequently and at a lower cost because there is a larger market for the stock. Of course, even a large amount of outstanding equity can be distributed among a small number of major shareholders, yielding little liquidity for the stock, but this seems to be the exception rather than the rule. We adopt the specification proposed by Loeb (1983) in which he provides estimates

---

[3] The third dimension of liquidity—time to completion of a purchase or sale—is obviously missing from this list, but only because of lack of data. With access to time-stamped orders of a large institutional trading desk, time-based measures of liquidity can easily be constructed as well.

[4] See, for, example, Amihud and Mendelson (1986a, 1986b), Glosten and Milgrom (1985), Lo, Mamaysky, and Wang (2004), Tiniç (1972), and Vayanos (1998).

of the percentage round-trip total trading cost including (1) the market maker's spread, (2) the price concession, and (3) the brokerage commission. The total trading cost is an array with nine capitalization categories and nine block sizes (Loeb, 1983, Table II). This matrix provides a good approximation for liquidity, but to account for the continuous nature of market capitalization and block sizes beyond his original specification, we interpolate and extrapolate Loeb's table using a two-dimensional spline.[5]

Plate 3 is a graphical representation of our parametrization of Loeb's specification, and our Matlab source code is provided in Appendix A.2. To minimize the impact of ad hoc extrapolation procedures such as the one we use to extend Loeb (1983) (see footnote 5 below), Lo, Petrov, and Wierzbicki (2003) used a fixed block size of $250,000 in all their calculations involving Loeb's liquidity metric, and for this size the extrapolation/capping of the trading cost is used rather infrequently.

However, Lo, Petrov, and Wierzbicki (2003) developed these liquidity measures primarily for equity portfolios, not hedge fund investments. In particular, measures such as market capitalization and bid/ask spreads do not have any obvious analogues for ownership interests in private partnerships. Therefore, we require a different liquidity metric for hedge fund investments, and the analysis in Chapter 3 yields a natural alternative: the first-order serial correlation coefficient.

Liquidity Metrics for Individual Securities

To construct liquidity metrics, we begin by computing (4.1)–(4.5) with daily data and then aggregating the daily measures to yield monthly quantities. The monthly trading volume is defined as the sum of the daily trading volume for all the days in the month, and the monthly log volume is simply the natural logarithm of the monthly trading volume. Monthly turnover is defined as the sum of the daily turnover for all the days in the month (see Lo and Wang, 2000, for further discussion). The monthly bid/ask spread measure is defined as a mean of

---

[5] Loeb's original matrix does not allow for a block sizes in excess of 5% of a stock's total market capitalization which, in our sample, would imply a maximum block size of 5% × $2.84 million = $0.142 million, a relatively small number. To relax this restriction, we extrapolate the total cost function to allow for block sizes of up to 20% of market capitalization, where the extrapolation is performed linearly by fixing the capitalization level and using the last two available data points along the block-size dimension. The maximum total cost is capped at 50%, an arbitrary large number. For example, for the $0–$10 million capitalization sector (see Table II in Loeb, 1983) and block sizes of $5,000, $25,000, and $250,000 the total spread/price costs are 17.3%, 27.3%, and 43.8%, respectively. The cost at the next block size of $500,000 is computed as

$$\min\left[50\%, \; 43.8\% + (500{,}000 - 250{,}000) \times (43.8\% - 27.3\%)/(50{,}000 - 25{,}000)\right] = 50\%.$$

the daily bid/ask spreads for all the days in the month. And finally, the average monthly Loeb price impact measure is defined as a mean of the corresponding daily measures for all days in the month.

Having defined monthly counterparts to the daily variables (4.1)–(4.5), we renormalize the five monthly measures to yield quantities that are of comparable scale. Let $\tilde{\ell}_{it}$ represent one of our five liquidity variables for security i in month t. Then the corresponding *liquidity metric* ℓ_{it} is defined as

$$\ell_{it} \equiv \frac{\tilde{\ell}_{it} - \min_{k,\tau} \tilde{\ell}_{k\tau}}{\max_{k,\tau} \tilde{\ell}_{k\tau} - \min_{k,\tau} \tilde{\ell}_{k\tau}}, \tag{4.6}$$

where the maximum and minimum in (4.6) are computed over all stocks k and all dates τ in the sample so that each of the five normalized measures—which we now refer to as a *liquidity metric* to distinguish it from the unnormalized variable— takes on values strictly between 0 and 1. Therefore, if the turnover-based liquidity metric for a given security is 0.50 in a particular month, this implies that the level of turnover exceeds the minimum turnover by 50% of the difference between the maximum and minimum turnovers for all securities and across all months in our sample. Note that for consistency we use the *reciprocal* of the monthly bid/ask spread measure in defining ℓ_{it} for bid/ask spreads so that larger numerical values imply more liquidity, as do the other four measures.

For hedge fund investments, we propose the following liquidity metric in month t:

$$\hat{\rho}_{1t} = \frac{\sum_{k=2}^{T}(R_{t-k} - \hat{\mu}_t)(R_{t-k-1} - \hat{\mu}_t)}{\sum_{k=1}^{T}(R_{t-k} - \hat{\mu}_t)^2}, \qquad \hat{\mu}_t \equiv \frac{1}{T}\sum_{k=1}^{T}R_{t-k}, \tag{4.7}$$

which is a T-month rolling-window estimate of the first-order autocorrelation of $\{R_t\}$ using returns from months $t-1$ to $t-T-1$.

Liquidity Metrics for Portfolios

Now consider a portfolio p of securities defined by the vector of portfolio weights $\boldsymbol{\omega}_p \equiv [\omega_{p1} \ \omega_{p2} \ \cdots \ \omega_{pn}]'$, where $\boldsymbol{\omega}_p'\iota = 1$ and $\iota \equiv [1 \ \cdots \ 1]'$. Assume for the moment that this is a long-only portfolio so that $\boldsymbol{\omega}_p \geq 0$. Then a natural definition of the liquidity ℓ_{pt} of this portfolio is simply

$$\ell_{pt} \equiv \sum_{i=1}^{n}\omega_{pi}\ell_{it}, \tag{4.8}$$

which is a weighted average of the liquidities of the securities in the portfolio.

For portfolios that allow short positions, (4.8) is not appropriate because short positions in illiquid securities may cancel out long positions in equally illiquid securities, yielding a very misleading picture of the overall liquidity of the portfolio. To address this concern, we propose the following definition for the liquidity metric of a portfolio with short positions, along the lines of Lo and Wang's (2000) definition of portfolio turnover:

$$\ell_{pt} \equiv \sum_{i=1}^{n} \frac{|\omega_{pi}|}{\sum_{j=1}^{n} |\omega_{pj}|} \ell_{it}. \tag{4.9}$$

In the absence of short positions, (4.9) reduces to (4.8), but when short positions are present, their liquidity metrics are given positive weight as with the long positions, and then all the weights are renormalized by the sum of the absolute values of the weights.

Qualifications

Although the liquidity metrics described above are convenient definitions for purposes of mean-variance portfolio optimization, they have a number of limitations that should be kept in mind. First, (4.8) implicitly assumes that there are no interactions or cross-effects in liquidity among securities, which need not be the case. For example, two securities in the same industry might have similar liquidity metrics individually but may become somewhat more difficult to trade when combined in a portfolio because they are considered close substitutes by investors. This assumption can be relaxed by specifying a more complex *liquidity matrix* in which ℓ_{it} are the diagonal entries but where interaction terms ℓ_{ijt} are specified in the off-diagonal entries. In that case, the liquidity metric for the portfolio p is simply the quadratic form

$$\ell_{pt} \equiv \sum_{i=1}^{n} \sum_{j=1}^{n} \omega_{pi} \omega_{pj} \ell_{ijt}. \tag{4.10}$$

The off-diagonal liquidity metrics are likely to involve subtleties of the market microstructure of securities in the portfolio as well as more fundamental economic links among the securities; hence for our current purposes, we assume that they are zero.

For the hedge fund liquidity measure $\hat{\rho}_{1t}$, the portfolio measure (4.10) is still incorrect because correlation is not a linear quadratic operator. In particular, if we denote by $\mathbf{R}_t \equiv [R_{1t} \ \cdots \ R_{nt}]'$ the vector of month-t returns for n hedge funds and by $\boldsymbol{\omega}_p \equiv [\omega_{p1} \ \cdots \ \omega_{pt}]'$ a portfolio P of these funds, then the serial correlation coefficient of the portfolio return R_{pt} is given by

$$\rho_{p1} = \frac{\text{Cov}[R_{pt}, R_{pt-1}]}{\text{Var}[R_{pt}]} = \frac{\omega' \Gamma_1 \omega}{\omega' \Gamma_0 \omega}, \tag{4.11a}$$

$$\text{where} \quad \Gamma_i \equiv E[(\mathbf{R}_t - \mu)(\mathbf{R}_{t-i} - \mu)'], \qquad \mu \equiv E[\mathbf{R}_t]. \tag{4.11b}$$

Note that Γ_i is the ith order autocovariance matrix of the vector time series $\{\mathbf{R}_t\}$ and need not be symmetric except when $i = 0$, in which case Γ_0 reduces to the covariance matrix of $\{\mathbf{R}_t\}$. Even in the absence of any cross-autocorrelation between funds, (4.11) does not reduce to either (4.8) or (4.10). To see why, denote the ith order autocorrelation matrix by Υ_i; hence

$$\Upsilon_i = \mathbf{D}^{-1/2} \Gamma_i \mathbf{D}^{-1/2}, \qquad \mathbf{D} = \text{diag}(\sigma_1^2, \dots, \sigma_n^2), \tag{4.12}$$

where $\mathbf{D}$ is a diagonal matrix with the variances of the funds along the diagonal. Then (4.11) may be rewritten in terms of the autocorrelation matrix Υ_1 as

$$\rho_{p1} = \frac{\omega' \mathbf{D}^{1/2} \mathbf{D}^{-1/2} \Gamma_1 \mathbf{D}^{-1/2} \mathbf{D}^{1/2} \omega}{\omega' \mathbf{D}^{1/2} \mathbf{D}^{-1/2} \Gamma_0 \mathbf{D}^{-1/2} \mathbf{D}^{1/2} \omega} = \frac{\tilde{\omega}' \Upsilon_1 \tilde{\omega}}{\tilde{\omega}' \Upsilon_0 \tilde{\omega}}, \qquad \tilde{\omega} \equiv \mathbf{D}^{1/2} \omega. \tag{4.13}$$

Even if Υ_1 were diagonal, (4.13) would not simplify to (4.8) but would reduce instead to

$$\rho_{p1} = \frac{\sum_{i=1}^{n} \tilde{\omega}^2 \rho_{i1}}{\sum_{j=1}^{n} \tilde{\omega}_j^2} = \sum_{i=1}^{n} \delta_i \rho_{i1}, \qquad \delta_i \equiv \frac{\sigma_i^2}{\sum_{j=1}^{n} \omega_j^2 \sigma_j^2} \omega_i^2. \tag{4.14}$$

If, in addition to being mutually uncorrelated at all leads and lags, all n funds also have equal variances, then (4.14) will become

$$\rho_{p1} = \sum_{i=1}^{n} \delta_i \rho_{i1}, \qquad \delta_i \equiv \frac{\omega_i^2}{\sum_{j=1}^{n} \omega_j^2}, \tag{4.15}$$

which is related to (4.8) in a nonlinear fashion.

Second, because (4.8) is a function only of the portfolio weights and not of the dollar value of the portfolio, ℓ_{pt} is scale-independent. While this also holds true for mean-variance analysis as a whole, the very nature of liquidity is dependent on scale to some degree. Consider the case where IBM comprises 10% of two portfolios p and q. According to (4.8), the contribution of IBM to the liquidity of the overall portfolio would be the same in these two cases: 10% times the liquidity metric of IBM. However, suppose that the dollar value of portfolio p is $100,000 and the dollar value of portfolio q is $100 million. Is a $10,000 position in IBM identical to a \$10 million position in terms of liquidity? At issue is the fact that, except for Loeb's measure of price impact, the liquidity metrics defined by the variables (4.1)–(4.4) and (4.7) are not functions of trade size, hence are scale-independent. Of course, this is easily remedied by reparametrizing the liquidity metric ℓ_{it} so that it varies with trade size, much like Loeb's price impact function, but this creates at least three additional challenges: (1) There is little empirical evidence to determine the appropriate functional specification;[6] (2) trade size may not be the only variable that affects liquidity; and (3) making ℓ_{it} a function of trade size complicates the portfolio optimization problem considerably, rendering virtually all of the standard mean-variance results scale-dependent. For these reasons, we shall continue to assume scale independence for ℓ_{it} throughout this study (even for Loeb's price impact function, for which we fix the trade size at \$250,000) and leave the more challenging case for future research.

More generally, the liquidity variables (4.1)–(4.5) and (4.7) are rather simple proxies for liquidity and do not represent liquidity premia derived from dynamic equilibrium models of trading behavior,[7] nor is (4.7) meant to be a portfolio serial correlation coefficient. Therefore, these variables may not be stable through time and over very different market regimes. However, given their role in influencing the price, time, and size of transactions in equity markets, the liquidity metrics defined by (4.1)–(4.5) and (4.7) are likely to be highly correlated with equilibrium liquidity premia under most circumstances and should serve as reasonable local approximations to the liquidity of a portfolio.

Finally, because our liquidity metrics are ad hoc and not the by-product of expected utility maximization, they have no objective interpretation and must be calibrated to suit each individual application. Of course, we might simply assert that liquidity is a sufficiently distinct characteristic of a financial security that investors will exhibit specific preferences along this dimension, much as for a security's mean and variance. However, unlike mean and variance, it is difficult to identify plausible preference rankings for securities of varying liquidity levels. Moreover, there are approximation theorems that derive mean-variance preferences from expected utility theory (see, for example, Levy and Markowitz, 1979), and corresponding results for our liquidity metrics have yet to be developed.

Nevertheless, liquidity is now recognized to be such a significant factor in investment management that, despite the qualifications described above, there

---

[6] However, see Bertsimas and Lo (1998), Chan and Lakonishok (1993, 1995), Hausman, Lo, and MacKinlay (1992), Kraus and Stoll (1972), Lillo, Farmer, and Mantegna (2003), and Loeb (1983) for various approximations in a number of contexts.

[7] This literature is vast and overlaps with the literature on financial asset-pricing models with transactions costs. Some of the more relevant examples include Amihud and Mendelson (1986b), Bagehot (1971), Constantinides (1986), Demsetz (1968), Gromb and Vayanos (2002), Lo, Mamaysky, and Wang (2004), Tiniç (1972), Vayanos (1998), and Vayanos and Vila (1999). For a more complete list of citations, see the references contained in Lo, Mamaysky, and Wang (2004).

is considerable practical value in incorporating even ad hoc measures of liquidity into standard mean-variance portfolio theory. We turn to this challenge in Section 4.2.

4.2 Liquidity-Optimized Portfolios

Armed with quantitative liquidity metrics $\{\ell_{it}\}$ for individual securities and portfolios, we can now incorporate liquidity directly into the portfolio construction process. There are at least three methods for doing this: (1) imposing a liquidity filter for securities to be included in a portfolio optimization program; (2) constraining the portfolio optimization program to yield a mean-variance-efficient portfolio with a minimum level of liquidity; and (3) adding the liquidity metric to the mean-variance objective function directly. We describe each of these methods in more detail in this section and refer to portfolios obtained from these procedures as *mean-variance-liquidity* (MVL) *optimal* portfolios.[8]

Liquidity Filters

In this formulation, the portfolio optimization process is applied only to securities with liquidity metrics greater than some threshold level ℓ_o. Denote by U the universe of all securities to be considered in the portfolio optimization process and let U_o denote the subset of securities in U for which $\ell_{it} \geq \ell_o$:

$$U_o \equiv \{\, i \in U : \ell_{it} \geq \ell_o \,\}. \qquad (4.16)$$

The standard mean-variance optimization process can now be applied to the securities in U_o to yield mean-variance-efficient liquidity-filtered portfolios:

$$\min_{\{\omega\}} \ \tfrac{1}{2}\omega'\mathbf{\Sigma}_o\,\omega \qquad (4.17a)$$

$$\text{subject to } \mu_p = \omega'\mu_o, \qquad (4.17b)$$

$$1 = \omega'\iota, \qquad (4.17c)$$

---

[8] For expositional convenience, all of the tables and graphs in this section use standard deviations in place of variances as risk measures. Nevertheless, we shall continue to refer to graphs of efficient frontiers as "mean-variance-liquidity efficient frontiers" despite the fact that standard deviation is the x-axis, not variance. We follow this convention because the objective function on which the efficient frontiers are based are mean-variance objective functions and because "mean–standard deviation–liquidity" is simply too cumbersome a phrase to use more than once.

where μ_o is the vector of expected returns of securities in U_o and Σ_o is the return covariance matrix of securities in U_o, and as μ_p is varied, the set of ω_p^* that solve (4.17) yields the ℓ_o-liquidity-filtered mean-variance-efficient frontier.

Liquidity Constraints

An alternative to imposing a liquidity filter is to impose an additional constraint in the mean-variance optimization problem:

$$\min_{\{\omega\}} \ \tfrac{1}{2}\omega'\Sigma\,\omega \tag{4.18a}$$

$$\text{subject to } \mu_p = \omega'\mu, \tag{4.18b}$$

$$\ell_o = \begin{cases} \omega'\ell_t & \text{if } \omega \geq 0, \\ \sum_{i=1}^{n} \dfrac{|\omega_{pi}|}{\sum_{j=1}^{n} |\omega_{pj}|}\, \ell_{it} & \text{otherwise,} \end{cases} \tag{4.18c}$$

$$1 = \omega'\iota, \tag{4.18d}$$

where μ is the vector of expected returns of securities in the unconstrained universe U, Σ is the return covariance matrix of securities in U, and $\ell_t \equiv [\ell_{1t} \ \cdots \ \ell_{nt}]'$ is the vector of liquidity metrics for securities in U, and as μ_p is varied, the set of ω_p^* that solve (4.18) yields the ℓ_o-liquidity-constrained mean-variance-efficient frontier. Note that the liquidity constraint (4.18c) is in two parts, depending on whether ω is long-only or long-short. For simplicity, a nonnegativity restriction is imposed on ω in the empirical example so that the constraint reduces to $\ell_p = \omega'\ell_t$.

Mean-Variance-Liquidity Objective Function

Perhaps the most direct method of incorporating liquidity into the mean-variance portfolio optimization process is to include the liquidity metric in the objective function:[9]

$$\max_{\{\omega\}} \ \omega'\mu \ - \ \frac{\lambda}{2}\,\omega'\Sigma\omega + \phi\,\omega'\ell_t \tag{4.19a}$$

$$\text{subject to } 1 = \omega'\iota, \qquad 0 \leq \omega, \tag{4.19b}$$

where λ is the risk tolerance parameter, ϕ determines the weight placed on liquidity, and ω is constrained to be nonnegative so as to simplify the expression for the liquidity of the portfolio.

[9] See, for example, Michaud (1998, Chapter 12).

4.3 Empirical Examples

To illustrate the practical relevance of liquidity metrics for investment management, we consider two empirical examples: Lo, Petrov, and Wierzbicki's (2003) liquidity-optimized portfolios of 50 randomly selected U.S. stocks, and liquidity-optimized portfolios of the 13 CS/Tremont hedge fund indexes.

Liquidity-Optimized Portfolios of 50 Stocks

Lo, Petrov, and Wierzbicki (2003) construct the three types of liquidity-optimized portfolios described in Section 4.2 using historical data for 50 U.S. stocks selected from the University of Chicago's Center for Research in Securities Prices (CRSP) and the New York Stock Exchange's Trades and Quotes (TAQ) database for the sample period from January 2, 1997, to December 31, 2001. These 50 stocks were drawn randomly from 10 market capitalization brackets, based on December 31, 1996, closing prices, so as to yield a representative portfolio with sufficiently diverse liquidity characteristics (see Lo, Petrov, and Wierzbicki, 2003, for details on their sampling procedure). Lo, Petrov, and Wierzbicki (2003) compute correlation matrices for turnover, volume, Loeb's metric, and the bid/ask spread and conclude that the correlations between the various liquidity measures are generally consistent with each other but are not all perfectly correlated; hence each measure seems to capture certain aspects of liquidity not reflected in the others. The single exception is volume and turnover, which are extremely highly correlated, and so they eliminate volume and log volume from consideration and confine their attention to turnover, bid/ask spreads, and Loeb's metric in their empirical analysis.

To compute mean-variance-liquidity frontiers, they require estimates of the expected return μ and covariance matrix Σ of the 50 stocks in their sample. Using daily returns data from January 2, 1997, to December 31, 2001, they compute the following standard estimators:

$$\hat{\mu} = \frac{1}{T} \sum_{t=1}^{T} \mathbf{R}_t, \tag{4.20a}$$

$$\widehat{\Sigma} = \frac{1}{T-1} \sum_{t=1}^{T} (\mathbf{R}_t - \hat{\mu})(\mathbf{R}_t - \hat{\mu})', \tag{4.20b}$$

where $\mathbf{R}_t \equiv [R_{1t} \ \cdots \ R_{50t}]'$ is the vector of date-t returns of the 50 stocks in our sample. They convert these estimates to a monthly frequency by multiplying by 21, the number of trading days per month. Liquidity-optimized portfolios may then be constructed with these estimates and any one of the liquidity metrics defined in Section 4.1. To underscore the fact that liquidity can vary considerably from

Table 4.1.

Significant Months during the Sample Period*

Month	*Event*
December 1996	Beginning of sample
August 1998	Russian default/LTCM
October 1998	Aftermath of LTCM's demise
March 2000	First peak of the S&P 500
July 2000	Second peak of the S&P 500
April 2001	First bottom of the S&P 500
September 2001	9/11 terrorist attacks, second bottom of the S&P 500
December 2001	End of sample

* The sample period is December 1996 to December 2001, for which liquidity-optimized portfolios are constructed.

one month to the next, they construct liquidity-optimized portfolios for eight particular months, listed in Table 4.1, which include the start and end of the sample as controls as well as months that contain significant liquidity events such as the default of Russian government debt in August 1998 and the terrorist attacks of September 11, 2001. Lo, Petrov, and Wierzbicki (2003) construct liquidity-filtered, liquidity-constrained, and mean-variance-liquidity optimized portfolios for their data, but to conserve space we will present only a small subset of their results here, the liquidity-constrained portfolio results.

Table 4.2 summarizes the characteristics of liquidity-constrained portfolios using monthly normalized turnover as the liquidity metric. The results in Table 4.2 show that initial levels of liquidity constraints have little impact on performance. In fact, for every month in Table 4.1, imposing a liquidity constraint of 2.29 has virtually no impact on the Sharpe ratio, and in some months (e.g., March 2000) the threshold can be increased well beyond 2.29 without any loss in performance for the tangency portfolio.

To fully appreciate the impact of adding a liquidity dimension to traditional mean-variance analysis, a three-dimensional graphical representation of the mean-variance-liquidity surface is necessary. Plate 4 shows liquidity-constrained mean-variance-liquidity-efficient frontiers for each of the months in Table 4.1. At the "ground level" of each of the three-dimensional coordinate cubes in Plate 4, we have the familiar expected-return and standard deviation axes. The liquidity threshold ℓ_o of (4.16) is measured along the vertical axis. In the plane of ground level, the liquidity level is zero; hence the efficient frontier is the standard Markowitz mean-variance-efficient frontier, and this frontier is identical across all the months in their sample since estimated mean $\hat{\mu}$ and covariance matrix $\hat{\Sigma}$ are based on the entire sample of daily data from January 2, 1997, to December 31, 2001, and do not vary over time. However, as the liquidity metric is used to constrain the portfolios in constructing the mean-variance-efficient frontier, the

Table 4.2.

Monthly Means and Standard Deviations of Tangency and Minimum-Variance Portfolios of Liquidity-Constrained Mean-Variance-Liquidity Efficient Frontiers for 50 Randomly Selected Stocks*

	Liquidity Threshold	Tangency		Minimum Variance		
		Mean	SD	Mean	SD	Sharpe
Dec 1996	0.00	4.13	5.72	1.53	3.37	0.65
Dec 1996	2.29	4.13	5.72	1.53	3.39	0.65
Dec 1996	4.57	4.99	7.36	1.69	4.15	0.62
Dec 1996	6.86	5.71	9.53	1.98	5.69	0.55
Dec 1996	9.15	5.78	11.18	2.26	7.66	0.48
Dec 1996	11.43	5.65	13.03	2.61	9.88	0.40
Dec 1996	13.72	5.28	14.86	2.83	12.39	0.33
Aug 1998	0.00	4.13	5.72	1.53	3.37	0.65
Aug 1998	2.29	4.13	5.72	1.53	3.38	0.65
Aug 1998	4.57	4.81	6.93	1.76	4.09	0.63
Aug 1998	6.86	5.90	9.44	2.14	5.57	0.58
Aug 1998	9.15	6.11	10.97	2.60	7.56	0.52
Aug 1998	11.43	6.12	12.69	3.16	9.84	0.45
Aug 1998	13.72	6.13	14.95	3.81	12.38	0.38
Oct 1998	0.00	4.13	5.72	1.53	3.37	0.65
Oct 1998	2.29	4.13	5.72	1.53	3.37	0.65
Oct 1998	4.57	4.13	5.72	1.55	3.42	0.65
Oct 1998	6.86	4.46	6.33	1.66	3.75	0.64
Oct 1998	9.15	4.98	7.42	1.76	4.33	0.61
Oct 1998	11.43	5.52	8.69	1.90	5.09	0.59
Oct 1998	13.72	5.62	9.38	2.02	5.98	0.55
Oct 1998	16.00	5.66	10.10	2.25	6.98	0.52
Oct 1998	18.29	5.63	10.85	2.45	8.03	0.48
Oct 1998	20.58	5.56	11.67	2.65	9.13	0.44
Oct 1998	22.86	5.51	12.62	2.84	10.27	0.40
Oct 1998	25.15	5.37	13.51	3.02	11.46	0.37
Oct 1998	27.44	4.96	13.97	3.17	12.70	0.32
Mar 2000	0.00	4.13	5.72	1.53	3.37	0.65
Mar 2000	2.29	4.13	5.72	1.53	3.37	0.65
Mar 2000	4.57	4.13	5.72	1.53	3.37	0.65
Mar 2000	6.86	4.13	5.72	1.73	3.48	0.65
Mar 2000	9.15	4.12	5.70	1.97	3.82	0.65
Mar 2000	11.43	4.54	6.41	2.24	4.33	0.64
Mar 2000	13.72	5.06	7.38	2.52	4.98	0.63
Mar 2000	16.00	5.61	8.47	2.79	5.73	0.61
Mar 2000	18.29	5.77	9.04	3.06	6.55	0.59
Mar 2000	20.58	5.87	9.64	3.33	7.43	0.57
Mar 2000	22.86	5.93	10.26	3.60	8.35	0.54
Mar 2000	25.15	5.96	10.95	3.87	9.31	0.51
Mar 2000	27.44	5.98	11.74	4.14	10.29	0.47
Mar 2000	29.72	6.00	12.64	4.42	11.31	0.44
Mar 2000	32.01	6.01	13.62	4.67	12.36	0.41
Mar 2000	34.29	6.01	14.74	4.84	13.44	0.38
Mar 2000	36.58	6.03	16.08	4.84	14.66	0.35

Table 4.2.
(continued)

	Liquidity Threshold	Tangency		Minimum Variance		Sharpe
		Mean	SD	Mean	SD	
Mar 2000	38.87	6.03	17.61	4.86	16.08	0.32
Mar 2000	41.15	6.00	19.33	4.85	17.70	0.29
Mar 2000	43.44	5.83	20.85	4.76	19.45	0.26
Jul 2000	0.00	4.13	5.72	1.53	3.37	0.65
Jul 2000	2.29	4.13	5.72	1.53	3.37	0.65
Jul 2000	4.57	4.12	5.70	1.73	3.62	0.65
Jul 2000	6.86	4.96	7.23	1.97	4.42	0.63
Jul 2000	9.15	5.92	9.38	2.33	5.61	0.59
Jul 2000	11.43	6.14	10.61	2.70	7.06	0.54
Jul 2000	13.72	6.17	11.78	3.09	8.67	0.49
Jul 2000	16.00	6.24	13.25	3.50	10.37	0.44
Jul 2000	18.29	6.36	15.08	3.91	12.15	0.39
Jul 2000	20.58	6.51	17.26	4.32	14.00	0.35
Apr 2001	0.00	4.13	5.72	1.53	3.37	0.65
Apr 2001	2.29	4.13	5.72	1.53	3.37	0.65
Apr 2001	4.57	4.16	5.77	1.63	3.66	0.65
Apr 2001	6.86	5.33	7.95	1.69	4.45	0.61
Apr 2001	9.15	5.90	9.53	1.94	5.59	0.57
Apr 2001	11.43	5.92	10.45	2.09	6.95	0.53
Apr 2001	13.72	5.80	11.48	2.31	8.48	0.47
Apr 2001	16.00	5.55	12.63	2.55	10.10	0.40
Apr 2001	18.29	5.28	14.19	2.78	11.80	0.34
Sep 2001	0.00	4.13	5.72	1.53	3.37	0.65
Sep 2001	2.29	4.13	5.72	1.53	3.37	0.65
Sep 2001	4.57	4.13	5.72	1.79	3.65	0.65
Sep 2001	6.86	4.63	6.57	2.10	4.42	0.64
Sep 2001	9.15	5.49	8.23	2.50	5.52	0.61
Sep 2001	11.43	6.05	9.65	2.92	6.86	0.58
Sep 2001	13.72	6.34	10.87	3.40	8.36	0.54
Sep 2001	16.00	6.44	11.99	4.04	10.01	0.50
Sep 2001	18.29	6.55	13.48	4.75	11.83	0.45
Dec 2001	0.00	4.13	5.72	1.53	3.37	0.65
Dec 2001	2.29	4.13	5.72	1.53	3.37	0.65
Dec 2001	4.57	4.11	5.70	1.67	3.64	0.65
Dec 2001	6.86	4.96	7.19	1.91	4.52	0.63
Dec 2001	9.15	5.88	9.14	2.33	5.81	0.59
Dec 2001	11.43	6.35	10.68	2.87	7.35	0.55
Dec 2001	13.72	6.55	12.02	3.47	9.06	0.51
Dec 2001	16.00	6.69	13.49	4.24	10.97	0.46
Dec 2001	18.29	6.80	15.13	5.07	13.11	0.42

*There are 5 stocks from each of 10 market capitalization brackets, and the data are based on a monthly normalized turnover liquidity metric for the months of December 1996, August 1998, October 1998, March 2000, July 2000, April 2001, September 2001, and December 2001. Expected returns and covariances of the 50 individual securities are estimated with daily returns data from January 2, 1997, to December 31, 2001, and do not vary from month to month.

risk/reward profile of the frontier changes, as depicted by the color of the surface. By construction, the liquidity of a constrained portfolio is always equal to the liquidity threshold ℓ_o, and since the normalization of all liquidity metrics is performed cross-sectionally as well as through time, the color and the height of the frontiers at different dates have the same meaning and can be compared to one another.

In the upper left subplot in Plate 4, which contains the MVL frontier for December 1996, the period when the distribution of average turnover was at its historically low mean and standard deviation, the saillike surface is rather flat and has relatively little surface area. The infeasibility of the constrained portfolio optimization problem at higher liquidity thresholds is responsible for the tattered edges of the surface starting at the fourth liquidity level (note that the size of the liquidity increments is identical across all months and that the axes all have the same scale). At the highest levels of liquidity, only the most liquid segments of the MVL frontier appear in Plate 4. Because of the generally positive correlation between liquidity and market capitalization, and the fact that the large-cap stocks in the sample have modest expected returns and volatilities as compared to the smaller-cap stocks, at higher liquidity threshold levels, portfolios on the MVL frontier consist mostly of defensive large-cap equities.

In the upper right subplot in Plate 4 (August 1998), liquidity conditions have improved—the MVL frontier rises up from the ground-level plane almost vertically, and up to the third liquidity threshold the shape of the frontier remains almost unaffected by the liquidity constraint. In the left second-row subplot in Plate 4 we observe a dramatic increase in liquidity—the MVL frontier is twice as tall as the December 1996 frontier, and the level of liquidity at which the surface starts bending to the right is significantly higher than in previous subplots. In the right second-row subplot in Plate 4, corresponding to the first peak in the S&P 500 (March 2000), the MVL frontier is at its tallest and it is apparent that the liquidity constraint is irrelevant up to a very high-liquidity threshold.

The third and fourth rows in Plate 4 tell a very different story. The shape and height of the MVL frontier change dramatically starting with the left third-row subplot for July 2000 (the second peak of the S&P 500) and moving clockwise to April 2001 (the first bottom of the S&P 500), September 2001 (the terrorist attacks on 9/11), and December 2001 (the last month of the sample). In the face of the bear market of 2000–2001, liquidity conditions have clearly deteriorated, and Plate 4 provides a detailed road map of the dynamics of this trend.

An alternative to describing the evolution of the MVL surface is to select a small number of characteristic points on this surface and plot their trajectories in mean–standard deviation–liquidity space through time. For any mean-variance-efficient frontier, the most relevant point is, of course, the tangency portfolio. In Figure 4.1, the *trajectories* of the tangency portfolio are plotted for various levels of the liquidity constraint and over time. Each point along the trajectory

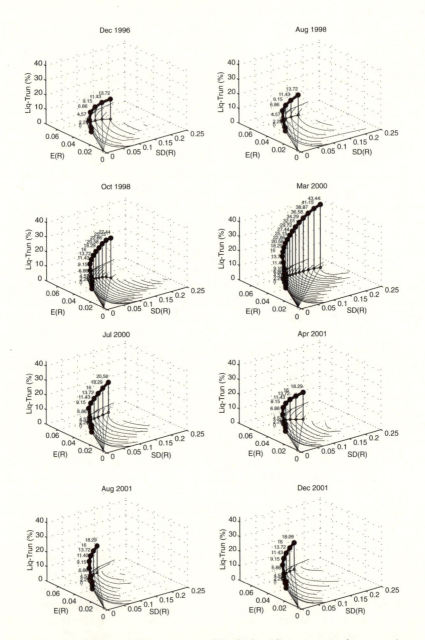

Figure 4.1. Trajectories of the tangency portfolio for liquidity-constrained mean-variance-liquidity efficient frontiers for 50 randomly selected stocks (5 from each of 10 market capitalization brackets), based on a monthly normalized turnover liquidity metric for the months of December 1996, August 1998, October 1998, March 2000, July 2000, April 2001, September 2001, and December 2001. Expected returns and covariances of the 50 individual securities are estimated with daily returns data from January 2, 1997, to December 31, 2001, and do not vary from month to month.

corresponds to the tangency portfolio of the efficient frontier for a given liquidity threshold ℓ_o. The numerical value of the threshold (in percent) is displayed next to the tangency point, and the position of each point is projected onto the ground-level plane for visual clarity. In addition, two sets of lines are drawn on the ground-level plane: a straight line connecting the riskless portfolio to each tangency portfolio (whose slope is the Sharpe ratio of the tangency portfolio) and curved lines which are MVL frontiers for various levels of the liquidity filter. For each subplot, the trajectory of the tangency point starts at the same location on the ground-level plane.

In the absence of any liquidity effects, the trajectory of the tangency portfolio would be vertical and its projection onto the ground-level plane would coincide with its starting point, but because the liquidity constraint does have an impact on the mean-variance combinations that are feasible, Figure 4.1 shows that for successively higher liquidity constraints, the risk/reward profile of the efficient frontier—as measured by the tangency portfolio—worsens, but at different rates for different months. In particular, as the threshold increases, the trajectory of the tangency portfolio moves eastward and away from the viewer. The ground-level projection of the tangency trajectory moves initially in the east/northeast direction but always yielding less desirable Sharpe ratios. In some cases, as the liquidity threshold increases, the ground-level projection of the tangency portfolio turns southeast, yielding tangency portfolios with higher volatility and lower expected return but with higher levels of liquidity. At some point, when it becomes impossible for any of the 50 randomly selected securities to satisfy the liquidity constraint, the trajectory terminates. The dynamics of the trajectory of the tangency portfolio is a qualitative alternative to assessing the impact of liquidity on the characteristics of a mean-variance optimal portfolio.

Figure 4.2 summarizes the trajectories in Figure 4.1 by plotting the Sharpe ratio as a function of the liquidity threshold for each of the months in Table 4.1. This two-dimensional representation of a three-dimensional object is a simple way to highlight the trade-off between liquidity and investment performance. The liquidity-constrained trajectories in Figure 4.2 are all concave, and each trajectory is comprised of three distinct segments. The first segment—beginning at the left boundary of the graph—is parallel to the liquidity axis, indicating that liquidity constraints have no effect on the tangency portfolio's Sharpe ratio. The second segment is decreasing and concave, implying Sharpe ratios that decline at increasingly faster rates as the liquidity threshold is increased. The third segment is decreasing but linear, implying Sharpe ratios that decline with increasing liquidity thresholds but at a constant rate.

Intuitively, an optimal mean-variance-liquidity portfolio—one that balances all three characteristics in some fashion—should be located somewhere along the second segments of the Sharpe ratio curves in Figure 4.2. It is along these segments that marginal increases in the liquidity threshold yield increasingly

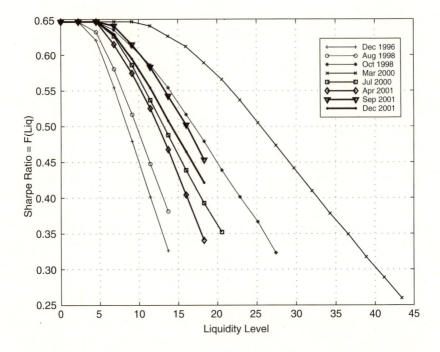

Figure 4.2. *Sharpe ratio trajectories of tangency portfolios of liquidity-constrained mean-variance-liquidity efficient frontiers for 50 randomly selected stocks (5 from each of 10 market capitalization brackets), based on a monthly normalized turnover liquidity metric, as a function of the liquidity threshold, for the months of December 1996, August 1998, October 1998, March 2000, July 2000, April 2001, September 2001, and December 2001. Expected returns and covariances of the 50 individual securities are estimated with daily returns data from January 2, 1997, to December 31, 2001, and do not vary from month to month. Thicker lines are used to represent trajectories from more recent months.*

higher costs in terms of poorer Sharpe ratios; hence there should be some liquidity threshold along this segment that balances an investor's preference for liquidity and the risk/reward profile of the tangency portfolio. Of course, turning this heuristic argument into a formal procedure for constructing MVL-optimal portfolios requires the specification of preferences for mean, variance, and liquidity, which is precisely the approach developed in the optimization problem (4.19) in Section 4.2.

Liquidity-Optimized Portfolios of Hedge Fund Indexes

The mean-variance-liquidity optimization framework in Section 4.2 can also be applied to hedge fund returns, and as an illustration of this approach, we consider forming a portfolio of the 13 CS/Tremont hedge fund indexes considered in Section 2.1. Using monthly data from January 1994 to February 2004, we estimate the means, variances, and covariances of the 13 index return series and then construct liquidity-filtered and liquidity-constrained portfolios as described in Section 4.2 using the first-order autocorrelation coefficient $\hat{\rho}_1$ as well as the *p*-value of the Ljung–Box Q-statistic (1.17) with three autocorrelation coefficients (Section 1.3).

Table 4.3 reports summary statistics for the tangency and minimum-variance portfolios corresponding to liquidity-filtered and liquidity-constrained mean-variance-liquidity efficient frontiers for different liquidity thresholds and for the two different liquidity metrics, $\hat{\rho}_1$ and Q. When no liquidity restrictions are imposed, the optimal portfolio yields a Sharpe ratio of 3.37, considerably higher than the Sharpe ratios in Table 4.2 but not unusual for a portfolio of hedge fund indexes (recall the power of diversification and the fact that hedge funds often yield higher Sharpe ratios than individual stocks because of the nature of their investment strategies and risk exposures). As liquidity restrictions become more severe, the performance of the tangency portfolio decays, but as in Table 4.2, the decay is remarkably mild for liquidity-constrained portfolios, with the Sharpe ratio declining only by 0.37 to 3.00 for a constraint of 36.26% for the portfolio's $\hat{\rho}_1$. Not surprisingly, the performance of liquidity-filtered portfolios declines more rapidly and discontinuously because filtering eliminates certain indexes altogether, whereas constraints change the weightings of the indexes but allow all of them to be included in the portfolio. These results suggest that a potentially significant amount of liquidity risk in portfolios of hedge funds may be reduced through mean-variance-liquidity optimization.

To see how the portfolio weights change as a function of the liquidity threshold, Figure 4.3 depicts the tangency portfolio weights for four liquidity thresholds. It is clear from these graphs that liquidity constraints do have an impact on portfolio weights, with some indexes having zero weight at certain liquidity thresholds, and that as the liquidity thresholds change, the weights can change significantly as well.

Plate 5 contains plots of the corresponding three-dimensional mean-variance-liquidity efficient frontiers, and Figure 4.4 shows the trajectories of the tangency portfolio as the liquidity threshold varies. The steepness of the surfaces and trajectories in Plate 5 and Figure 4.4 respectively, confirms the patterns in Table 4.3—there is relatively little performance loss in imposing mild liquidity constraints on hedge fund portfolios. The two-dimensional mean-variance frontiers in Plate 6 and the summary graph of the Sharpe ratios of the tangency portfolios in Figure 4.5 provide a more detailed view of this phenomenon. As liquidity thresholds increase, it is clear that the slopes of the tangent lines to the efficient frontiers of the liquidity-constrained portfolios in the right column do not decline a great deal.

Table 4.3.

Monthly Means and Standard Deviations of Tangency and Minimum-Variance Portfolios of Liquidity-Filtered and Liquidity-Constrained Mean-Variance-Liquidity Efficient Frontiers for 13 CS/Tremont Hedge Fund Indexes (January 1994 to February 2004)*

Liquidity Level	Tangency Portfolio		MinVar Portfolio		Sharpe
	E[R]	SD[R]	E[R]	SD[R]	
ρ_1 Measure of Liquidity-Filtered Portfolios					
−2.61	9.18	2.13	8.23	1.98	3.37
0.38	9.12	2.18	8.16	2.02	3.26
3.37	9.12	2.18	8.16	2.02	3.26
6.36	9.16	2.20	8.18	2.03	3.26
9.35	9.16	2.20	8.18	2.03	3.26
12.34	9.55	2.58	8.77	2.43	2.93
15.33	9.55	2.58	8.77	2.43	2.93
18.32	9.55	2.58	8.77	2.43	2.93
21.31	9.55	2.58	8.77	2.43	2.93
24.30	9.55	2.58	8.77	2.43	2.93
27.29	9.78	2.67	8.97	2.51	2.91
30.28	9.79	4.21	7.97	3.69	1.85
ρ_1 Measure of Liquidity-Constrained Portfolios					
−2.61	9.18	2.13	8.23	1.98	3.37
0.38	9.18	2.13	8.23	1.98	3.37
3.37	9.18	2.13	8.23	1.98	3.37
6.36	9.18	2.13	8.23	1.98	3.37
9.35	9.18	2.13	8.23	1.98	3.37
12.34	9.18	2.13	8.23	1.98	3.37
15.33	9.18	2.13	8.23	1.98	3.37
18.32	9.18	2.13	8.26	1.98	3.37
21.31	9.17	2.13	8.25	1.98	3.37
24.30	9.19	2.14	8.27	1.98	3.36
27.29	9.18	2.16	8.23	1.99	3.33
30.28	9.27	2.23	8.16	2.03	3.26
33.27	9.35	2.33	8.31	2.14	3.15
36.26	9.57	2.53	8.50	2.33	3.00
39.25	9.74	2.76	8.73	2.58	2.81
42.24	9.86	3.03	8.91	2.89	2.60
45.23	9.99	3.38	9.11	3.25	2.36
48.22	—	—	—	—	—
51.21	—	—	—	—	—
54.20	—	—	—	—	—
Q-Statistic Measure of Liquidity-Filtered Portfolios					
1.30	9.18	2.13	8.23	1.98	3.37
3.03	9.60	2.49	8.85	2.35	3.05
4.77	9.55	2.58	8.77	2.43	2.93

Table 4.3.
(continued)

Liquidity Level	Tangency Portfolio		MinVar Portfolio		Sharpe
	E[R]	SD[R]	E[R]	SD[R]	
Q-Statistic Measure of Liquidity-Filtered Portfolios (*contd.*)					
6.50	9.55	2.58	8.77	2.43	2.93
8.23	9.55	2.58	8.77	2.43	2.93
9.97	9.55	2.58	8.77	2.43	2.93
11.70	9.78	2.67	8.97	2.51	2.91
13.44	9.74	2.62	8.93	2.52	2.95
15.17	9.74	2.62	8.93	2.52	2.95
Q-Statistic Measure of Liquidity-Constrained Portfolios					
1.30	9.18	2.13	8.23	1.98	3.37
3.03	9.18	2.13	8.23	1.98	3.37
4.77	9.18	2.13	8.23	1.98	3.37
6.50	9.18	2.13	8.23	1.98	3.37
8.23	9.18	2.13	8.23	1.98	3.37
9.97	9.16	2.13	8.25	1.98	3.36
11.70	9.18	2.13	8.26	1.98	3.37
13.44	9.17	2.13	8.25	1.98	3.36
15.17	9.29	2.17	8.30	2.01	3.35
16.91	9.30	2.19	8.32	2.04	3.33
18.64	9.35	2.23	8.38	2.08	3.29
20.38	9.44	2.29	8.48	2.12	3.25
22.11	9.48	2.34	8.55	2.17	3.20
23.85	9.52	2.39	8.61	2.23	3.15
25.58	9.56	2.45	8.70	2.30	3.09
27.31	9.65	2.52	8.78	2.37	3.03
29.05	9.66	2.58	8.87	2.45	2.97
30.78	9.74	2.66	8.95	2.53	2.91
32.52	9.77	2.74	9.05	2.62	2.84
34.25	9.80	2.82	9.15	2.71	2.77

*Two liquidity metrics are used, the first-order serial correlation coefficient ρ_1 and the Ljung–Box (1978) Q-statistic using the first three autocorrelation coefficients.

4.4 Summary and Extensions

Because the integration of liquidity directly into portfolio management processes has not become standard practice, many aspects of our analysis can be improved upon and extended. Our liquidity metrics are clearly simplistic and not based on any equilibrium considerations, and our definition of portfolio liquidity as the weighted average of individual securities' liquidity measures may not be the best

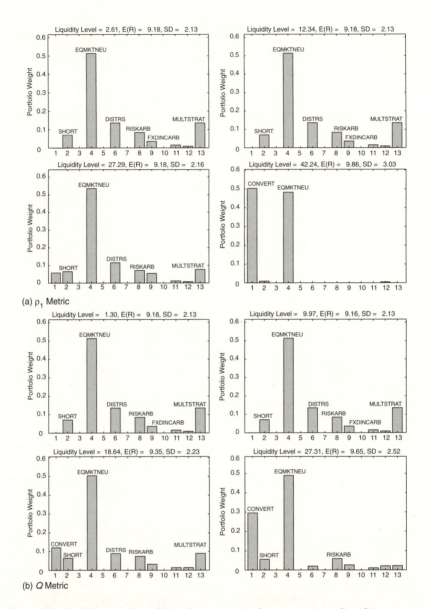

Figure 4.3. *Portfolio weights of liquidity-constrained mean-variance-liquidity tangency portfolios of 13 CS/Tremont hedge fund indexes (January 1994 to February 2004). Four levels of liquidity constraints are depicted using two liquidity metrics: the first-order serial correlation coefficient ρ_1 and the Ljung–Box Q-statistic using the first three autocorrelation coefficients. SHORT = Dedicated Shortseller; EQMKTNEU = Equity Market Neutral; DISTRS = Distressed; RISKARB = Risk Arbitrage; FXDINCARB = Fixed Income Arbitrage; MULTSTRAT = Multi-Strategy; CONVERT = Convertible Arbitrage.*

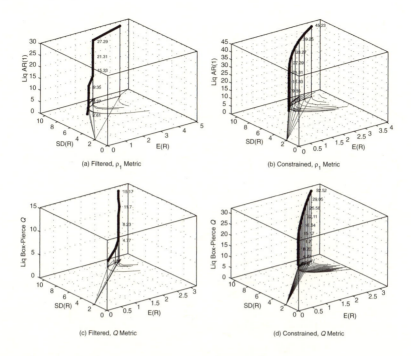

Figure 4.4. *Trajectories of the tangency portfolios of filtered and constrained mean-variance-liquidity efficient frontiers of 13 CS/Tremont hedge fund indexes (January 1994 to February 2004). The two liquidity metrics are the first-order serial correlation coefficient ρ_1, and the Ljung–Box Q-statistic using the first three autocorrelation coefficients.*

definition in all contexts. Better methods of measuring liquidity will obviously lead to better MVL portfolios.[10] The dynamics of liquidity should also be modeled explicitly, in which case static mean-variance optimization may no longer be appropriate but should be replaced by dynamic optimization methods such as stochastic dynamic programming. In fact, Chapters 7 and 10 underscore the impact that liquidity shocks can have on the hedge fund industry, and in Chapter 11, we propose one novel approach to reduce a hedge fund portfolio's exposures even in the face of the most extreme form of illiquidity—a gate that prevents an investor from redeeming his investment. Preferences for liquidity must be investigated in more detail: Do such preferences exist, and if so, are they stable and how should they best be parametrized? Finally, estimation error has been ignored in the portfolio construction process, and just as sampling variation affects mean and covariance matrix estimators, liquidity estimators are also subject to sampling

[10] See, for example, Chordia, Roll, and Subrahmanyam (2000, 2001, 2002), Getmansky, Lo, and Makarov (2003), Glosten and Harris (1988), Lillo, Farmer, and Mantegna (2003), Lo, Mamaysky, and Wang (2004), Pastor and Stambaugh (2003), and Sadka (2003) for alternate measures of liquidity.

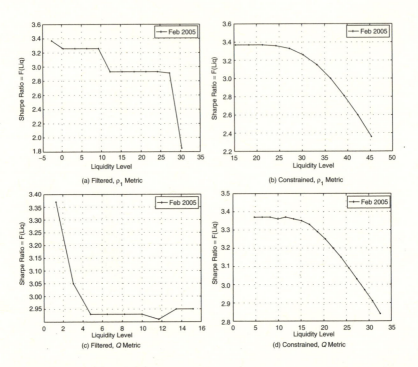

Figure 4.5. *Filtered and constrained Sharpe ratio trajectories of tangency portfolios for filtered and constrained mean-variance-liquidity efficient frontiers for 13 CSFB/Tremont hedge fund indexes (January 1994 to February 2004). The two liquidity metrics are the first-order serial correlation coefficient ρ_1 and the Ljung–Box Q-statistic using the first three autocorrelation coefficients.*

variation and this may have significant impact on the empirical properties of MVL portfolios.[11] This is especially relevant for hedge fund applications because of their higher volatility, shorter samples, and dynamic risk exposures, all of which increase estimation error.

---

[11] See, for example, Jobson and Korkie (1980, 1981), Klein and Bawa (1976, 1977), and Michaud (1998).

5

Hedge Fund Beta Replication

As institutional investors take a more active interest in alternative investments, a significant gap has emerged between the culture and expectations of these investors and hedge fund managers. Pension plan sponsors typically require transparency from their managers and impose a number of restrictions in their investment mandates because of regulatory requirements such as ERISA rules; hedge fund managers rarely provide position-level transparency and bristle at any restrictions on their investment process because restrictions often hurt performance. Plan sponsors require a certain degree of liquidity in their assets to meet their pension obligations and also desire significant capacity because of their limited resources in managing large pools of assets; hedge fund managers routinely impose lockups of 1–3 years, and the most successful managers have the least capacity to offer, in many cases returning investors' capital once they make their personal fortunes. And as fiduciaries, plan sponsors are hypersensitive to the outsized fees that hedge funds charge and are concerned about misaligned incentives induced by performance fees; hedge fund managers argue that their fees are fair compensation for their unique investment acumen, and at least for now, the market seems to agree.

This cultural gap raises the natural question of whether it is possible to obtain hedge fund–like returns without investing in hedge funds. In short, can hedge fund returns be "cloned"?

In this chapter, we provide one answer to this challenge by constructing "linear clones" of individual hedge funds in the Lipper TASS hedge fund database. These are passive portfolios of common risk factors like the S&P 500 and the U.S. Dollar indexes, with portfolio weights estimated by regressing individual hedge fund returns on the risk factors. If a hedge fund generates part of its expected return and risk profile from certain common risk factors, then it may be possible to design a low-cost passive portfolio—not an active dynamic trading strategy— that captures some of that fund's risk/reward characteristics by taking on just those risk exposures. For example, if a particular long/short equity hedge fund is 40% long-growth stocks, it may be possible to create a passive portfolio that has similar characteristics, e.g., a long-only position in a passive growth portfolio coupled with a 60% short position in stock index futures.

The magnitude of hedge fund alpha that can be captured by a linear clone depends, of course, on how much of a fund's expected return is driven by common risk factors versus manager-specific alpha. This can be measured empirically. While portable alpha strategies have become fashionable lately among institutions, our research suggests that for certain classes of hedge fund strategies, portable beta may be an even more important source of untapped expected returns and diversification. In particular, in contrast to previous studies employing more complex factor-based models of hedge fund returns, we use six factors that correspond to basic sources of risk and, consequently, of expected return: the stock market, the bond market, currencies, commodities, credit, and volatility. These factors are also chosen because, with the exception of volatility, each of them is tradable via liquid exchange-traded securities such as futures or forward contracts.

Using standard regression analysis, we decompose the expected returns of a sample of 2,097 individual hedge funds from the Lipper TASS hedge fund Live database into factor-based risk premia and manager-specific alpha, and we find that for certain hedge fund–style categories, a significant fraction of the funds' expected returns are due to risk premia. For example, in the category of Convertible Arbitrage funds, the average percentage contribution of the U.S. Dollar Index risk premium, averaged across all funds in this category, is 67%. While estimates of manager-specific alpha are also quite significant in most cases, these results suggest that at least a portion of a hedge fund's expected return can be obtained by bearing factor risks.

To explore this possibility, we construct linear clones using five of the six factors (we omit volatility because the market for volatility swaps and futures is still developing) and compare their performance to that of the original funds. For certain categories such as Equity Market Neutral, Global Macro, Long/Short Equity Hedge, Managed Futures, Multi-Strategy, and Fund of Funds, linear clones have comparable performance to their fund counterparts, but for other categories such as Event Driven and Emerging Markets, clones do not perform nearly as well. However, in all cases, linear clones are more liquid (as measured by their serial correlation coefficients), more transparent and scalable (by construction), and have correlations to a broad array of market indexes that are similar to those of the hedge funds on which they are based. For these reasons, we conclude that hedge fund replication, at least for certain types of funds, is both possible and, in some cases, worthy of serious consideration.

We begin in Section 5.1 with a brief review of the literature on hedge fund replication, and in Section 5.2 we provide two simple examples that motivate this endeavor. In Section 5.3 we present a linear regression analysis of hedge fund returns from the Lipper TASS hedge fund Live database, with which we decompose the funds' expected returns into risk premia and manager-specific alpha. These results suggest that for certain hedge fund styles, linear clones may yield reasonably compelling investment performance, and we explore this possibility directly in Section 5.4. We conclude in Section 5.5.

5.1 Literature Review

In a series of recent papers, Kat and Palaro (2005, 2006a,b) argue that sophisticated dynamic trading strategies involving liquid futures contracts can replicate many of the statistical properties of hedge fund returns. More generally, Bertsimas, Kogan, and Lo (2001) have shown that securities with very general payoff functions (like hedge funds and complex derivatives) can be synthetically replicated to an arbitrary degree of accuracy by dynamic trading strategies—called *epsilon-arbitrage strategies*—involving more liquid instruments. While these results are encouraging for the hedge fund replication problem, the replicating strategies are quite involved and not easily implemented by a typical institutional investor. Indeed, some of the derivatives-based replication strategies may be more complex than the hedge fund strategies they are intended to replicate, defeating the very purpose of replication.[1]

The motivation for our study comes instead from Sharpe's (1992) asset-class factor models in which he proposes to decompose a mutual fund's return into two distinct components: asset-class factors such as large-cap stocks, growth stocks, and intermediate government bonds, which he interprets as "style," and an uncorrelated residual that he interprets as "selection." This approach was applied by Fung and Hsieh (1997a) to hedge funds, but where the factors were derived statistically from a principal components analysis of the covariance matrix of their sample of 409 hedge funds and commodity trading advisors (CTAs). While such factors may yield high in-sample R^2's, they suffer from significant overfitting bias and also lack economic interpretation, which is one of the primary motivations for Sharpe's (1992) decomposition. Several authors have estimated factor models for hedge funds using more easily interpretable factors such as fund characteristics and indexes (Schneeweis and Spurgin, 1998; Liang, 1999; Edwards and Caglayan, 2001; Capocci and Hubner, 2004; Hill, Mueller, and Balasubramanian, 2004) and the returns to certain options-based strategies and other basic portfolios (Fung and Hsieh, 2001, 2004; Agarwal and Naik 2000a,b, 2004).

---

[1] Nevertheless, derivatives-based replication strategies may serve a different purpose that is not vitiated by complexity: risk attribution, with the ultimate objective of portfolio risk management. Even if an underlying hedge fund strategy is simpler than its derivatives-based replication strategy, the replication strategy may still be useful in measuring the overall risk exposures of the hedge fund and designing a hedging policy for a portfolio of hedge fund investments.

However, the most direct application of Sharpe's (1992) analysis to hedge funds is by Ennis and Sebastian (2003). They provide a thorough style analysis of the HFR Fund of Funds index and conclude that funds of funds are not market neutral and although they do exhibit some market-timing abilities, "the performance of hedge funds has not been good enough to warrant their inclusion in balanced portfolios. The high cost of investing in funds of funds contributes to this result" (Ennis and Sebastian, 2003, p. 111). This conclusion is the starting point for our study of linear clones.

5.2 Two Examples

Before turning to an empirical analysis of individual hedge fund returns, we provide two concrete examples that span the extremes of the hedge fund replication problem. For one hedge fund strategy, we show that replication can be accomplished easily, and for another strategy, we find replication to be almost impossible using linear models.

Capital Decimation Partners

The first example is a hypothetical strategy proposed by Lo (2001) and described in Section 1.1 called Capital Decimation Partners, which yields an enviable track record that many investors would associate with a successful hedge fund: a 43.1% annualized mean return and 20% annualized volatility, implying a Sharpe ratio of 2.15,[2] and with only 6 negative months over the 96-month simulation period from January 1992 to December 1999 (Table 1.2). A closer inspection of this strategy's monthly returns in Table 1.3 yields few surprises for the seasoned hedge fund investor—the most challenging period for CDP was the summer of 1998 during the LTCM crisis, when the strategy suffered losses of −18.3% and −16.2% in August and September, respectively. But those investors courageous enough to maintain their CDP investment during this period were rewarded with returns of 27.0% in October and 22.8% in November. Overall, 1998 was the second-best year for CDP, with an annual return of 87.3%.

Section 1.1 reveals that this strategy consists of shorting puts on the S&P 500 that are 7% out of the money. Given the relatively infrequent nature of 7% losses, CDP's risk/reward profile can seem very attractive in comparison to

---

[2] As a matter of convention, throughout this book we define the Sharpe ratio as the ratio of the monthly average return to the monthly standard deviation, then annualized by multiplying by the square root of 12. In the original definition of the Sharpe ratio, the numerator is the *excess* return of the fund, in excess of the risk-free rate. Given the time variation in this rate over the sample period, we use the total return so as to allow readers to select their own benchmarks.

more traditional investments, but there is nothing unusual or unique about CDP. Investors willing to take on tail risk—the risk of rare but severe events—will be paid well for this service (consider how much individuals are willing to pay each month for their homeowner's, auto mobile, health, and life insurance policies). CDP involves few proprietary elements and can be implemented by most investors; hence this is one example of a hedge fund–like strategy that can easily be cloned.

Capital Multiplication Partners

Consider now the case of Capital Multiplication Partners (CMP), a hypothetical fund based on a dynamic asset-allocation strategy between the S&P 500 and 1-month U.S. Treasury bills, where the fund manager can correctly forecast which of the two assets will do better in each month and invests the fund's assets in the higher-yielding asset at the start of the month.[3] Therefore, the monthly return of this perfect market-timing strategy is simply the larger of the monthly returns of the S&P 500 and T-bills. The source of this strategy's alpha is clear: Merton (1981) observes that perfect market timing is equivalent to a long-only investment in the S&P 500 plus a put option on the S&P 500 with a strike price equal to the T-bill return. Therefore, the economic value of perfect market timing is equal to the sum of monthly put-option premia over the life of the strategy. And there is little doubt that such a strategy contains significant alpha: A $1 investment in CMP in January 1926 grows to $23,143,205,448 by December 2004! Table 5.1 provides a more detailed performance summary of CMP that confirms its remarkable characteristics—CMP's Sharpe ratio of 2.50 exceeds that of Warren Buffett's Berkshire Hathaway, arguably the most successful pooled investment vehicle of all time![4]

It should be obvious to even the most naive investor that CMP is a fantasy because no one can time the market perfectly. Therefore, attempting to replicate such a strategy with exchange-traded instruments seems hopeless. But suppose we try to replicate it anyway—how close can we come? In particular, suppose we attempt to relate CMP's monthly returns to the monthly returns of the S&P 500 by fitting a simple linear regression (Figure 5.1). The optionlike nature of CMP's perfect market-timing strategy is apparent in the scatter of points in Figure 5.1, and visually it is obvious that the linear regression does not capture the essence of this inherently nonlinear strategy. However, the formal measure of how well the linear regression fits the data, $\overline{R}^2$, is 70.3% in this case, which suggests a very strong linear relationship indeed. But when the estimated linear regression is used

[3] This example was first proposed by Bob Merton in his 15.415 Finance Theory class at the MIT Sloan School of Management.

[4] During the period from November 1976 to December 2004, the annualized mean and standard deviation of Berkshire Hathaway's Series A shares were 29.0% and 26.1%, respectively, for a Sharpe ratio of 1.12 using 0% for the risk-free benchmark return.

Table 5.1.

Capital Multiplication Partners, L.P., and Clone Performance Summary (January 1926 to December 2004)

	S&P 500	T-Bill	CMP	Clone
Monthly mean	1.0%	0.3%	2.6%	0.7%
Monthly SD	5.5%	0.3%	3.6%	3.0%
Minimum month	−29.7%	−0.1%	−0.1%	−16.3%
Maximum month	42.6%	1.4%	42.6%	23.4%
Annual Sharpe ratio	0.63	4.12	2.50	0.79
No. of negative months	360	12	10	340
Correlation to S&P 500	100%	−2%	84%	100%
Growth of $1 since inception	$3,098	$18	$2.3 × 10^{10}	$429

*Performance summary of a simulated monthly perfect market-timing strategy for the S&P 500, 1-month U.S. Treasury bills, and a passive linear clone.

to construct a fixed portfolio of the S&P 500 and 1-month T-bills, the results are not nearly as attractive as CMP's returns, as Table 5.1 shows.

This example underscores the difficulty in replicating certain strategies with genuine alpha using linear clones and cautions against using $\overline{R}^2$ as the only metric of success. Despite the high $\overline{R}^2$ achieved by the linear regression of CMP's returns on the market index, the actual performance of the linear clone falls far short of the strategy because a linear model can never capture the optionlike payoff structure of the perfect market timer.

5.3 Linear Regression Analysis

To explore the full range of possibilities for replicating hedge fund returns illustrated by the two extremes of CDP and CMP, we investigate the characteristics of a sample of individual hedge funds drawn from the Lipper TASS hedge fund database. The database is divided into two parts: Live funds and Graveyard funds. Hedge funds in the Live database are considered to be active as of the end of our sample period, August 2007.[5] We confine our attention to funds in the Live

---

[5] Once a hedge fund decides not to report its performance, is liquidated, is closed to new investment, restructured, or merged with other hedge funds, the fund is transferred into the Graveyard database. A hedge fund can be listed in the Graveyard database only after being listed in the Live database. Because the Lipper TASS database fully represents returns and asset information for live and dead funds, the effects of suvivorship bias are minimized. However, the database is subject to *back-fill bias*—when a fund decides to be included in the database, Lipper TASS adds the fund to the Live database and includes all available prior performance of the fund. Hedge funds do not need to meet any specific requirements to be included in the Lipper TASS database. Because of reporting delays and time lags in contacting hedge funds, some Graveyard funds can be incorrectly listed in the Live database for

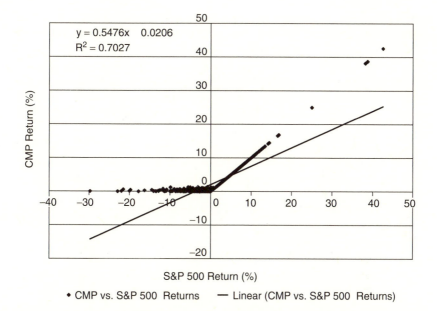

Figure 5.1. *Regression of CMP returns on S&P 500 returns (January 1926 to December 2004). Scatterplot of simulated monthly returns of a perfect market-timing strategy for the S&P 500 and 1-month U.S. Treasury bills, against monthly returns of the S&P 500.*

database since we wish to focus on the most current set of risk exposures in the hedge fund industry, and we acknowledge that the Live database suffers from survivorship bias (see the references in footnote 3 on page 35).

However, the importance of such a bias for our application is tempered by two considerations. First, many successful funds leave the sample as well as the poor performers, reducing the upward bias in expected returns. In particular, Fung and Hsieh (2000) estimate the magnitude of survivorship bias to be 3.00% per year, and Liang's (2000) estimate is 2.24% per year. Second, the focus of our study is on the *relative* performance of hedge funds versus that of relatively passive portfolios of liquid securities, and as long as our cloning process is not selectively applied to a peculiar subset of funds in the Lipper TASS database, any survivorship bias should impact both funds and clones identically, leaving their relative performances unaffected.

Of course, other biases plague the Lipper TASS database, such as backfill bias (including funds with return histories that start before the date of inclusion),[6]

---

a period of time. However, Lipper TASS has adopted a policy of transferring funds from the Live database to the Graveyard database if they do not report over an 8- to 10-month period.

[6] See footnote 2 on page 34.

selection bias (inclusion in the database is voluntary—hence only funds seeking new investors are included),[7] and other potential biases imparted by the process by which Lipper TASS decides which funds to include and which to omit (part of this process is qualitative). As with survivorship bias, the hope is that the impact of these additional biases will be similar for clones and for funds, leaving relative comparisons unaffected. Unfortunately, there is little to be done about such biases other than to acknowledge their existence and to interpret the outcome of our empirical analysis with an extra measure of caution.

Although the Lipper TASS hedge fund Live database starts in February 1977, we limit our analysis to the sample period from February 1986 to August 2007 because this is the timespan for which we have complete data for all of the risk factors. Of these funds, we drop those that (1) do not report net-of-fee returns;[8] (2) report returns in currencies other than the U.S. dollar;[9] (3) report returns less frequently than monthly; (4) do not provide assets under management or only provide estimates; and (5) have fewer than 36 monthly returns. These filters yield a final sample of 2,097 funds.

Summary Statistics

Lipper TASS classifies funds into one of 11 different investment styles, listed in Table 5.2 and described in the Appendix, of which 10 correspond exactly to the CS/Tremont subindex definitions.[10] Table 5.2 also reports the number of funds in each category for our sample, as well as summary statistics for the individual funds and for the equal-weighted portfolio of funds in each of the categories. The category counts show that the funds are not evenly distributed across investment styles but are concentrated among five categories: Long/Short Equity Hedge (602), Fund of Funds (591), Event Driven (217), Managed Futures (127), and Emerging Markets (118). Together, these five categories account for 79% of the 2,097 funds in our sample. The performance summary statistics in Table 5.2 underscore the reason for the growing interest in hedge funds in recent years—double-digit cross-sectional average returns for most categories with average volatility lower than that of the S&P 500, implying average annualized

---

[7] We are not aware of any studies focusing on this type of bias, but the impact of selection on statistical inference has been explored in some detail by several authors. See, for example, Leamer (1978) and the citations within.

[8] Lipper TASS defines returns as the change in net-asset value during the month (assuming the reinvestment of any distributions on the reinvestment date used by the fund) divided by the net-asset value at the beginning of the month, net of management fees, incentive fees, and other fund expenses. Therefore, these reported returns should approximate the returns realized by investors.

[9] Lipper TASS converts all foreign currency–denominated returns to U.S. dollar returns using the appropriate exchange rates.

[10] See footnote 6 on page 36.

Table 5.2.

Summary Statistics for Lipper TASS Live Hedge Funds Included in the Sample (February 1986 to August 2007)

Category	Sample Size	Annualized Mean (%)		Annualized SD (%)		Annualized Sharpe Ratio		ρ_1(%)		Ljung–Box Q_{12} p-Value (%)		Annualized Performance of Equal-Weighted Portfolio of Funds		
		Mean	SD	Mean	SD	Mean	SD	Mean	SD	Mean	SD	Mean (%)	SD(%)	Sharpe
Convertible Arbitrage	66	7.79	5.44	5.83	5.01	2.36	3.59	42.7	15.7	6.3	14.0	10.13	4.37	2.32
Dedicated Short Bias	14	−1.19	7.62	20.84	10.95	−0.19	0.50	5.8	10.1	50.6	24.6	−3.04	25.15	−0.12
Emerging Markets	118	19.63	13.19	15.61	11.52	1.68	1.14	13.0	14.5	38.6	30.3	19.29	16.25	1.19
Equity Market Neutral	103	8.12	6.35	6.51	5.33	1.82	1.46	4.1	24.1	42.0	33.5	10.55	3.18	3.32
Event Driven	217	12.00	5.85	6.67	5.08	2.71	4.23	21.2	15.8	29.8	29.8	13.20	6.13	2.15
Fixed Income Arbitrage	90	7.72	4.31	5.32	3.61	3.21	8.19	15.4	22.9	37.7	32.6	8.64	3.66	2.36
Global Macro	81	9.61	7.22	11.15	5.32	0.97	0.75	8.2	17.2	43.3	30.2	15.91	10.76	1.48
Long/Short Equity Hedge	602	13.82	8.28	13.25	7.91	1.24	0.76	9.1	16.9	39.8	30.1	16.80	8.25	2.04
Managed Futures	127	10.15	6.85	17.76	9.57	0.70	0.65	5.9	16.2	33.8	28.1	13.91	15.58	0.89
Multi-Strategy	88	11.39	8.20	8.47	9.01	2.01	1.66	18.2	20.4	25.9	28.5	18.65	11.10	1.68
Fund of Funds	591	9.97	4.71	6.06	3.72	2.03	1.33	19.5	14.4	29.9	28.7	11.24	5.40	2.08
All Funds	2097	11.55	7.72	9.81	7.89	1.77	2.55	14.7	18.4	34.1	30.2	13.96	5.98	2.33

Sharpe ratios ranging from a low of -0.19 for Dedicated Short Bias funds to a high of 3.21 for Fixed Income Arbitrage funds.

Another feature of the data highlighted by Table 5.2 is the large positive average return autocorrelations for funds in Convertible Arbitrage (42.7%), Emerging Markets (13.0%), Event Driven (21.2%), Fixed Income Arbitrage (15.4%), Multi-Strategy (18.2%), and Fund of Funds (19.5%) categories. Lo (2001) and Getmansky, Lo, and Makarov (2004) have shown that such high serial correlation in hedge fund returns is likely to be an indication of illiquidity exposure. There is, of course, nothing inappropriate about hedge funds taking on liquidity risk—indeed, this is a legitimate and often lucrative source of expected return—as long as investors are aware of such risks and not misled by the siren call of attractive Sharpe ratios.[11] But illiquidity exposure is typically accompanied by capacity limits, and we shall return to this issue when we compare the properties of hedge funds to those of more liquid alternatives such as linear clones.

Factor Model Specification

To determine the explanatory power of common risk factors for hedge funds, we perform a time-series regression for each of the 2,097 hedge funds in our sample, regressing the hedge fund's monthly returns on the following six factors: (1) USD: the U.S. Dollar Index return; (2) BOND: the return on the Lehman Corporate AA Intermediate Bond Index; (3) CREDIT: the spread between the Lehman BAA Corporate Bond Index and the Lehman Treasury Index; (4) SP500: the S&P 500 total return; (5) CMDTY: the Goldman Sachs Commodity Index (GSCI) total return; and (6) DVIX: the first difference of the end-of-month value of the CBOE Volatility Index (VIX). These six factors are selected for two reasons: They provide a reasonably broad cross section of risk exposures for a typical hedge fund (stocks, bonds, currencies, commodities, credit, and volatility), and each of the factor returns can be realized through relatively liquid instruments so that the returns of linear clones may be achievable in practice. In particular, there are forward contracts for each of the component currencies of the U.S. Dollar Index, and there are futures contracts for the stock and bond indexes and for the components of the commodity index. Futures contracts on the VIX Index were introduced by the CBOE in March 2004 and are not as liquid as the other index futures, but the OTC market for variance and volatility swaps is growing rapidly.

The linear regression model provides a simple but useful decomposition of a hedge fund's return R_{it} into several components:

$$R_{it} = \alpha_i + \beta_{i1}\text{RiskFactor}_{1t} + \cdots + \beta_{iK}\text{RiskFactor}_{Kt} + \epsilon_{it}. \qquad (5.1)$$

---

[11] It is no coincidence that the categories with the highest degree of average positive serial correlation are also the categories with the highest average Sharpe ratios. Smooth return series, by definition, have higher Sharpe ratios than more volatile return series with the same mean.

From this decomposition, we have the following characterization of the fund's expected return and variance:

$$E[R_{it}] = \alpha_i + \beta_{i1}E[\text{RiskFactor}_{1t}] + \cdots + \beta_{iK}E[\text{RiskFactor}_{Kt}], \quad (5.2)$$

$$Var[R_{it}] = \beta_{i1}^2 Var[\text{RiskFactor}_{1t}] + \cdots + \beta_{iK}^2 Var[\text{RiskFactor}_{Kt}]$$

$$+ \text{Covariances} + Var[\epsilon_{it}], \quad (5.3)$$

where "Covariances" is the sum of all pairwise covariances between RiskFactor_{pt} and RiskFactor_{qt} weighted by the product of their respective beta coefficients $\beta_{ip}\beta_{iq}$.

This characterization implies that there are two distinct sources of a hedge fund's expected return: (1) beta exposures β_{ik} multiplied by the risk premia associated with those exposures $E[\text{RiskFactor}_{kt}]$, and (2) manager-specific alpha α_i. By manager-specific we do not mean to imply that a hedge fund's unique source of alpha is without risk—we are simply distinguishing this source of expected return from those that have clearly identifiable risk factors associated with them. In particular, it may well be the case that α_i arises from risk factors other than the six we have proposed, and a more refined version of (5.1)—one that reflects the particular investment style of the manager—may yield a better-performing linear clone.

From (5.3) we see that a hedge fund's variance has three distinct sources: the variances of the risk factors multiplied by the squared beta coefficients, the variance of the residual ϵ_{it} (which may be related to the specific economic sources of α_i), and the weighted covariances among the factors. This decomposition highlights the fact that a hedge fund can have several sources of risk, each of which should yield some risk premium (i.e., risk-based alpha), otherwise investors would not be willing to bear such risk. By taking on exposure to multiple risk factors, a hedge fund can generate attractive expected returns from the investor's perspective (see, for example, Capital Decimation Partners in Section 1.1).[12]

Factor Exposures

Table 5.3 presents summary statistics for the beta coefficients or factor exposures in (5.1) estimated for each of the 2,097 hedge funds by ordinary least squares and grouped by category. In particular, for each category we report the minimum,

---

[12] Litterman (2005) calls such risk exposures "exotic betas" and argues that "[t]he adjective 'exotic' distinguishes it from market beta, the only beta which deserves to get paid a risk premium." We disagree—there are several well-established economic models that illustrate the possibility of multiple sources of systematic risk, each of which commands a positive risk premium, e.g., Merton (1973) and Ross (1976). We believe that hedge funds are practical illustrations of these multifactor models of expected returns.

median, mean, and maximum beta coefficient for each of the six factors and the intercept, across all regressions in that category. For example, the upper left block of entries labelled "Intercept" presents summary statistics for the intercepts from the individual hedge fund regressions within each category, and the "Mean" column shows that the average manager-specific alpha is positive for all categories, ranging from 0.37% per month for Managed Futures funds to 1.26% per month for Emerging Markets funds. This suggests that managers in the sample are, on average, indeed contributing value above and beyond the risk premia associated with the six factors we have chosen in (5.1). We shall return to this important issue in Section 5.3.

The panel in Table 5.3 with the heading R_{SP500} provides summary statistics for the beta coefficients corresponding to the S&P 500 return factor, and the entries in the "Mean" column are broadly consistent with each of the category definitions. For example, funds in the Dedicated Short Bias category have an average S&P 500 beta of -1.08, which is consistent with their short-selling mandate. On the other hand, Equity Market Neutral funds have an average S&P 500 beta of 0.03, confirming their market neutral status. And Long/Short Equity hedge funds, which are mandated to provide partially hedged equity market exposure, have an average S&P 500 beta of 0.42.

The remaining panels in Table 5.3 show that risk exposures do vary considerably across categories. This is more easily seen in Plate 7 which plots the mean beta coefficients for all six factors, category by category. From Plate 7, we see that Convertible Arbitrage funds have three main exposures (long credit, long bonds, and long volatility), whereas Emerging Markets funds have four somewhat different exposures (long stocks, short USD, long credit, and long commodities). The category with the smallest overall risk exposures is Equity Market Neutral, and not surprisingly, this category exhibits one of the lowest average mean returns, 8.12%.

The lower right panel in Table 5.3 contains a summary of the explanatory power of (5.1) as measured by the $\overline{R}^2$ statistic of the regression (5.1). The mean $\overline{R}^2$'s range from a low of 8.4% for Equity Market Neutral (as expected, given this category's small average factor exposures to all six factors) to a high of 46.5% for Dedicated Short Bias (which is also expected given this category's large negative exposure to the S&P 500).

To provide further intuition for the relation between $\overline{R}^2$ and fund characteristics, we regress $\overline{R}^2$ on several fund characteristics and find that lower $\overline{R}^2$ funds are those with higher Sharpe ratios, higher management fees, and higher incentive fees. This accords well with the intuition that funds providing greater diversification benefits (i.e., lower $\overline{R}^2$'s) command higher fees in equilibrium. See Lo and Hasanhodzic (2006) for further details.

Table 5.3.

Summary Statistics for Multivariate Linear Regressions of Monthly Returns of Hedge Funds in the Lipper TASS Live Database (February 1986 to August 2007)*

Category	Sample Size	Statistic	Intercept					R_{SP500}				
			Min	Med	Mean	Max	SD	Min	Med	Mean	Max	SD
Convertible Arbitrage	66	beta	−0.32	0.58	0.59	1.53	0.33	−0.29	0.00	−0.01	0.50	0.11
		t-stat	−1.32	3.31	5.44	57.62	8.76	−3.00	0.08	0.08	3.57	1.18
Dedicated Short Bias	14	beta	−0.17	0.58	0.69	2.26	0.52	−1.74	−1.13	−1.08	−0.50	0.34
		t-stat	−0.19	1.36	1.27	2.53	0.68	−12.88	−4.80	−5.87	−0.78	3.53
Emerging Markets	118	beta	−0.64	0.99	1.26	6.11	0.98	−0.49	0.30	0.40	2.16	0.42
		t-stat	−0.97	2.49	2.92	10.57	2.07	−2.38	2.01	1.88	6.02	1.61
Equity Market Neutral	103	beta	−0.42	0.59	0.68	2.14	0.43	−1.11	0.01	0.03	1.05	0.28
		t-stat	−0.76	2.66	3.64	17.26	3.43	−3.90	0.10	0.47	4.25	1.87
Event Driven	217	beta	−0.22	0.87	0.93	3.02	0.43	−0.56	0.09	0.13	1.05	0.20
		t-stat	−0.72	4.25	5.34	105.56	7.57	−3.51	1.15	1.36	14.77	1.90
Fixed Income Arbitrage	90	beta	−0.22	0.60	0.66	2.02	0.39	−0.34	0.02	0.00	0.31	0.11
		t-stat	−0.41	3.63	5.15	53.91	6.98	−2.38	0.27	0.11	3.33	1.15
Global Macro	81	beta	−1.23	0.56	0.52	2.40	0.69	−0.50	0.10	0.29	2.35	0.49
		t-stat	−2.10	1.24	1.37	8.39	1.68	−3.47	0.80	0.90	5.68	1.72
Long/Short Equity Hedge	602	beta	−1.83	0.76	0.84	5.15	0.66	−1.10	0.35	0.42	3.95	0.48
		t-stat	−2.11	1.98	2.07	11.33	1.50	−24.85	2.01	2.28	20.86	2.65
Managed Futures	127	beta	−4.50	0.44	0.37	3.26	0.91	−1.24	0.06	0.17	3.43	0.56
		t-stat	−2.30	0.84	0.92	8.86	1.66	−2.44	0.39	0.51	10.08	1.45
Multi-Strategy	88	beta	−0.78	0.74	0.79	4.17	0.56	−0.94	0.08	0.17	1.59	0.34
		t-stat	−0.94	3.44	4.07	11.75	3.09	−2.38	1.32	1.46	6.85	1.71
Fund of Funds	591	beta	−3.12	0.45	0.48	4.74	0.41	−0.78	0.16	0.22	1.72	0.24
		t-stat	−3.19	2.59	3.03	15.41	2.38	−2.96	2.04	2.33	27.18	2.12

Table 5.3.
(continued)

Category	Sample Size	Statistic	R_{LB}					R_{USD}				
			Min	Med	Mean	Max	SD	Min	Med	Mean	Max	SD
Convertible Arbitrage	66	beta	−0.17	0.18	0.22	1.21	0.23	−0.70	−0.03	−0.07	0.63	0.25
		t-stat	−0.88	1.44	1.43	4.48	1.21	−2.23	−0.23	−0.07	3.65	1.33
Dedicated Short Bias	14	beta	−1.50	−0.03	0.04	0.85	0.61	−0.46	0.06	0.27	1.11	0.54
		t-stat	−1.72	−0.06	0.07	1.41	1.03	−1.30	0.23	0.38	1.75	0.94
Emerging Markets	118	beta	−3.67	−0.03	−0.03	2.24	0.66	−2.19	−0.37	−0.41	2.16	0.64
		t-stat	−2.70	−0.06	0.11	3.41	1.18	−6.62	−1.03	−1.07	2.25	1.34
Equity Market Neutral	103	beta	−1.43	−0.01	−0.01	1.75	0.41	−2.49	0.00	−0.06	1.25	0.43
		t-stat	−3.75	−0.12	−0.01	3.20	1.24	−4.19	−0.01	−0.09	3.71	1.39
Event Driven	217	beta	−1.99	0.04	0.02	1.34	0.36	−2.02	−0.09	−0.17	0.52	0.37
		t-stat	−3.64	0.26	0.26	4.61	1.26	−4.10	−0.51	−0.43	3.74	1.40
Fixed Income Arbitrage	90	beta	−0.89	0.07	0.16	1.81	0.39	−1.28	0.03	0.03	0.76	0.33
		t-stat	−3.75	0.60	0.73	4.08	1.47	−3.82	0.33	0.37	4.18	1.55
Global Macro	81	beta	−3.95	0.10	0.08	1.74	0.73	−2.68	−0.12	−0.21	1.35	0.81
		t-stat	−3.74	0.23	0.35	7.38	1.61	−7.69	−0.49	−0.64	3.57	1.86
Long/Short Equity Hedge	602	beta	−3.79	−0.01	−0.01	3.04	0.55	−5.96	−0.09	−0.17	2.35	0.72
		t-stat	−2.46	−0.03	0.01	3.44	1.04	−4.50	−0.28	−0.32	4.05	1.29
Managed Futures	127	beta	−1.43	0.50	0.54	2.49	0.68	−3.81	−0.25	−0.34	1.68	0.73
		t-stat	−1.63	1.04	1.12	6.48	1.31	−5.10	−0.63	−0.60	1.99	1.08
Multi-Strategy	88	beta	−1.89	0.07	0.02	2.39	0.55	−4.93	−0.01	−0.20	0.87	0.76
		t-stat	−2.84	0.41	0.44	4.68	1.43	−3.97	−0.07	−0.08	3.27	1.49
Fund of Funds	591	beta	−2.16	0.03	0.05	1.82	0.29	−3.43	−0.14	−0.19	0.80	0.35
		t-stat	−2.63	0.23	0.37	12.29	1.21	−5.65	−0.89	−0.81	3.37	1.23

Table 5.3.
(continued)

Category	Sample Size	Statistic	R_{CS}					ΔVIX				
			Min	Med	Mean	Max	SD	Min	Med	Mean	Max	SD
Convertible Arbitrage	66	beta	0.00	0.44	0.59	2.72	0.56	−0.23	0.05	0.05	0.23	0.07
		t-stat	0.04	3.49	3.46	8.34	1.80	−1.66	0.70	0.74	3.54	0.90
Dedicated Short Bias	14	beta	−0.84	−0.08	−0.02	1.42	0.68	−0.23	0.04	0.07	0.66	0.25
		t-stat	−2.14	−0.19	−0.07	2.96	1.38	−1.77	0.18	0.10	1.26	0.97
Emerging Markets	118	beta	−0.50	0.38	0.50	2.82	0.56	−1.38	0.03	0.06	1.90	0.31
		t-stat	−1.97	1.32	1.28	4.71	1.29	−3.36	0.20	0.22	2.64	1.22
Equity Market Neutral	103	beta	−1.55	0.03	0.03	1.12	0.35	−1.10	−0.02	−0.02	0.64	0.22
		t-stat	−3.81	0.10	−0.12	3.00	1.53	−4.81	−0.24	−0.14	3.02	1.51
Event Driven	217	beta	−1.46	0.25	0.32	2.51	0.43	−0.57	0.01	0.00	0.75	0.16
		t-stat	−4.35	1.43	1.82	11.65	2.07	−7.01	0.14	0.01	3.27	1.36
Fixed Income Arbitrage	90	beta	−1.24	0.17	0.27	1.50	0.43	−0.49	0.03	0.05	0.66	0.19
		t-stat	−3.03	1.13	1.55	12.98	2.22	−3.21	0.39	0.81	5.64	2.05
Global Macro	81	beta	−0.91	0.16	0.15	1.53	0.47	−0.86	0.04	0.08	0.90	0.28
		t-stat	−2.77	0.26	0.40	4.13	1.24	−3.42	0.33	0.28	2.68	1.19
Long/Short Equity Hedge	602	beta	−2.35	0.17	0.21	4.38	0.61	−1.66	0.05	0.04	2.29	0.32
		t-stat	−4.78	0.54	0.59	4.89	1.36	−4.82	0.30	0.26	3.95	1.27
Managed Futures	127	beta	−3.95	−0.29	−0.33	1.53	0.64	−0.86	0.09	0.11	0.95	0.29
		t-stat	−2.89	−0.67	−0.62	2.56	1.02	−2.92	0.44	0.55	3.00	1.20
Multi-Strategy	88	beta	−1.23	0.17	0.25	3.12	0.54	−0.85	0.04	0.04	0.86	0.22
		t-stat	−2.03	1.20	1.54	6.11	1.99	−3.44	0.49	0.68	4.43	1.55
Fund of Funds	591	beta	−1.80	0.16	0.18	1.51	0.29	−0.86	0.06	0.07	0.64	0.12
		t-stat	−3.60	1.17	1.23	6.43	1.43	−2.20	0.92	0.92	4.92	1.11

Table 5.3.
(continued)

Category	Sample Size	Statistic	R_{GSCI} Min	Med	Mean	Max	SD	Statistic	Significance (%) Min	Med	Mean	Max	SD
Convertible Arbitrage	66	beta	−0.04	0.01	0.02	0.10	0.03	Adj. R^2	−5.8	17.6	16.8	64.4	13.3
		t-stat	−1.53	0.63	0.52	1.70	0.74	$p(F)$	0.0	0.3	9.1	89.8	20.2
Dedicated Short Bias	14	beta	−0.29	−0.08	−0.07	0.17	0.11	Adj. R^2	14.3	47.6	46.5	79.9	17.7
		t-stat	−1.95	−0.93	−0.78	1.50	1.04	$p(F)$	0.0	0.0	0.5	6.2	1.6
Emerging Markets	118	beta	−0.15	0.07	0.08	0.38	0.09	Adj. R^2	−0.8	17.3	20.7	67.9	14.2
		t-stat	−2.07	1.02	0.99	2.93	0.97	$p(F)$	0.0	0.1	4.8	51.0	11.4
Equity Market Neutral	103	beta	−0.11	0.01	0.02	0.28	0.06	Adj. R^2	−9.2	7.1	8.4	47.2	10.6
		t-stat	−2.66	0.46	0.44	2.63	1.17	$p(F)$	0.0	7.5	23.1	96.6	28.2
Event Driven	217	beta	−0.20	0.02	0.02	0.29	0.05	Adj. R^2	−7.6	18.6	20.2	70.0	16.1
		t-stat	−2.63	0.74	0.74	4.98	1.13	$p(F)$	0.0	0.2	9.4	95.1	19.1
Fixed Income Arbitrage	90	beta	−0.05	0.01	0.01	0.10	0.03	Adj. R^2	−13.5	8.3	12.4	77.3	16.1
		t-stat	−1.76	0.21	0.36	2.59	1.06	$p(F)$	0.0	5.8	22.2	97.1	28.5
Global Macro	81	beta	−0.08	0.04	0.08	0.53	0.14	Adj. R^2	−10.9	7.9	16.0	61.5	18.9
		t-stat	−1.34	0.77	0.98	6.16	1.49	$p(F)$	0.0	3.8	19.0	87.7	25.1
Long/Short Equity Hedge	602	beta	−0.33	0.06	0.08	0.83	0.11	Adj. R^2	−12.9	18.4	21.8	92.7	18.0
		t-stat	−2.59	1.18	1.15	6.75	1.28	$p(F)$	0.0	0.1	10.0	99.7	20.1
Managed Futures	127	beta	−0.31	0.08	0.12	0.72	0.15	Adj. R^2	−5.5	8.5	11.6	45.0	10.7
		t-stat	−1.83	1.19	1.29	5.74	1.24	$p(F)$	0.0	1.7	11.2	76.7	18.5
Multi-Strategy	88	beta	−0.06	0.03	0.07	0.78	0.14	Adj. R^2	−4.5	17.5	18.8	67.8	16.7
		t-stat	−0.83	1.23	1.33	8.36	1.35	$p(F)$	0.0	0.2	13.3	93.4	25.2
Fund of Funds	591	beta	−0.17	0.04	0.05	0.60	0.05	Adj. R^2	−10.2	22.9	25.3	93.6	16.4
		t-stat	−3.03	1.72	1.66	5.72	1.02	$p(F)$	0.0	0.1	3.9	98.4	11.5

* The six factors are the S&P 500 total return, the Lehman Corporate AA Intermediate Bond Index return, the U.S. Dollar Index return, the spread between the Lehman U.S. Aggregate Long Credit BAA Bond Index and the Lehman Treasury Long Index, the first difference of the CBOE Volatility Index (VIX), and the Goldman Sachs Commodity Index (GSCI) total return.

Table 5.4.

Decomposition of the Total Mean Returns of 2,097 Hedge Funds in the Lipper TASS Live Database (February 1986 to August 2007)*

Category	Sample Size	Avgerage E[R]	Average of Percentage Contribution of Factors to Total Expected Return (%)						
			CREDIT	USD	SP500	BOND	DVIX	CMDTY	ALPHA
Convertible Arbitrage	66	9.4	6.3	4.9	−0.1	12.1	−0.6	1.9	75.5
Dedicated Short Bias	14	−1.2	4.6	−0.9	141.3	61.0	−0.5	30.6	−136.1
Emerging Markets	118	19.8	0.4	3.6	17.4	−0.8	−0.1	5.1	74.3
Equity Market Neutral	103	9.1	0.2	0.6	24.9	−5.0	−0.7	17.0	62.9
Event Driven	217	13.6	1.1	3.5	10.3	2.8	−0.2	2.0	80.6
Fixed Income Arbitrage	90	9.4	0.9	3.4	−2.2	10.1	0.0	1.3	86.6
Global Macro	81	11.7	−0.5	12.8	38.3	10.7	2.1	10.2	26.3
Long/Short Equity Hedge	602	15.3	0.4	2.0	37.1	1.8	0.1	6.0	52.5
Managed Futures	127	11.9	−0.2	−1.8	−2.2	35.1	1.0	15.2	52.9
Multi-Strategy	88	12.8	−0.6	4.3	10.7	4.4	−0.3	4.8	76.8
Fund of Funds	591	9.5	0.9	8.4	41.7	−1.6	−0.3	7.3	43.7
All Funds	2097	12.4	0.7	4.4	28.3	4.0	0.0	6.9	55.6

* Values are based on percentage contributions from six factors and manager-specific alpha.

Expected-Return Decomposition

Using the parameter estimates of (5.1) for the individual hedge funds in our sample, we can now reformulate the question of whether or not a hedge fund strategy can be cloned as a question about how much of a hedge fund's expected return is due to risk premia from identifiable factors. If it is a significant portion and the relationship is primarily linear, then a passive portfolio with just these risk exposures—created by means of liquid instruments such as index futures, forwards, and other marketable securities—may be a reasonable alternative to a less liquid and opaque investment in the fund.

Table 5.4 summarizes the results of the expected-return decomposition (5.2) for the sample of 2,097 funds grouped according to their style categories and for all funds. Each row in Table 5.4 contains the average total mean return of funds in a given category and averages of the percentage contributions of each of the six factors and the manager-specific alpha to that average total mean return.[13] Note that the average percentage contributions add up to 100% when summed across all six factors and the manager-specific alpha because this decomposition sums to 100% for each fund, and when this decomposition is averaged across all funds, the sum is preserved.

The first-row entries indicate that the most significant contributors to the average total mean return of −1.2% for Dedicated Short Bias funds are SP500

---

[13] Throughout this article, all statistics except for those related to the first-order autocorrelation have been annualized to facilitate interpretation and comparison.

(141.3%), BOND (61.0%), and CMDTY (30.6%), and the average contribution of manager-specific alpha is -136.1%. This implies that, on average, Dedicated Short Bias funds earn more than all of their mean returns from the risk premia associated with the six factor exposures and that the average contribution of other sources of alpha is negative! Of course, this does not mean that Dedicated Short Bias managers are not adding value—the results in Table 5.4 are averages across all funds in the sample, hence the positive manager-specific alphas of successful managers are dampened and, in some cases, outweighed by the negative manager-specific alphas of the unsuccessful ones.

Table 5.4 shows considerable variation in the importance of manager-specific alpha for the other categories. More than 86% of the average total return of Fixed Income Arbitrage funds is due to manager-specific alpha, but for Global Macro the manager-specific alpha accounts for 26.3%. For the entire sample of 2,097 funds, 55.6% of the average total return is attributable to manager-specific alpha, implying that, on average, the remaining 44.4% is due to the risk premia from the six factors. These results suggest that for certain types of hedge fund strategies, a multifactor portfolio may yield some of the same benefits but in a transparent, scalable, lower-cost vehicle.

5.4 Linear Clones

The multivariate regression results in Section 5.3 suggest that linear clones may be able to replicate some of the risk exposures of hedge funds, and in this section we investigate this possibility directly by considering two types of clones. The first type consists of *fixed-weight* portfolios, where we use the entire sample of a given fund's returns to estimate a set of portfolio weights for the instruments corresponding to the factors used in the linear regression. These portfolio weights are fixed through time for each fund, hence the term "fixed-weight."[14] But because this approach involves a certain degree of "look-ahead" bias—we use the entire history of a fund's returns to construct the portfolio weights applied each period to compute the clone portfolio return—we also construct a second type of linear clone based on *rolling-window regressions*.

---

[14] In Hasanhodzic and Lo (2006), the term "buy-and-hold" was used to describe this type of clone. Although this is consistent with the passive nature of the clone portfolio, it is not strictly accurate because a portfolio with fixed weights requires periodic rebalancing to maintain these fixed weights. Moreover, if a clone is to be implemented via futures and forward contracts as we propose, then even in the absence of portfolio rebalancings, some trading will be necessary as maturing contracts are "rolled" into those of the next maturity date. For these reasons, we now refer to clone portfolios with constant portfolio weights over time as fixed-weight clones.

Fixed-Weight Versus Rolling-Window Clones

To construct a fixed-weight linear clone for fund i, we begin by regressing the fund's returns $\{R_{it}\}$ on five of the six factors we considered in Section 5.3 (we drop the DVIX factor because its returns are not as easily realized with liquid instruments), where we omit the intercept and constrain the beta coefficients to sum to 1:

$$R_{it} = \beta_{i1}\text{SP500}_t + \beta_{i2}\text{BOND}_t + \beta_{i3}\text{USD}_t$$
$$+ \beta_{i4}\text{CREDIT}_t + \beta_{i5}\text{CMDTY}_t + \epsilon_{it}, \quad t = 1, \ldots, T \quad (5.4a)$$

$$\text{subject to } 1 = \beta_{i1} + \cdots + \beta_{i5}. \quad (5.4b)$$

This is the same technique proposed by Sharpe (1992) for conducting "style analysis," however, our motivation is quite different. We omit the intercept because our objective is to estimate a weighted average of the factors that best replicates the fund's returns, and omitting the constant term forces the least-squares algorithm to use the factor means to fit the mean of the fund, an important feature of replicating hedge fund expected returns with factor risk premia. And we constrain the beta coefficients to sum to 1 to yield a portfolio interpretation for the weights. Note that we do not constrain the regression coefficients to be nonnegative as Sharpe (1992) does, because unlike Sharpe's original application to long-only mutual funds, in our context all five factors correspond to instruments that can be short-sold, and we do expect to be short-selling each of these instruments on occasion to achieve the kind of risk exposures hedge funds typically exhibit. For example, clones of Dedicated Short Bias funds will undoubtedly require shorting the SP500 factor.

The estimated regression coefficients $\{\beta_{ik}^*\}$ are then used as portfolio weights for the five factors, hence the portfolio returns are equivalent to the fitted values R_{it}^* of the regression equation. However, we implement an additional renormalization so that the resulting portfolio return $\widehat{R}_{it}$ has the same sample volatility as the original fund's return series:

$$R_{it}^* \equiv \beta_{i1}^*\text{SP500}_t + \beta_{i2}^*\text{BOND}_t + \beta_{i3}^*\text{USD}_t$$
$$+ \beta_{i4}^*\text{CREDIT}_t + \beta_{i5}^*\text{CMDTY}_t, \quad (5.5)$$

$$\widehat{R}_{it} \equiv \gamma_i R_{it}^*, \quad \gamma_i \equiv \frac{\sqrt{\sum_{t=1}^{T}(R_{it} - \overline{R}_i)^2/(T-1)}}{\sqrt{\sum_{t=1}^{T}(R_{it}^* - \overline{R}_i^*)^2/(T-1)}}, \quad (5.6)$$

$$\overline{R}_i \equiv \frac{1}{T}\sum_{t=1}^{T} R_{it}, \quad \overline{R}_i^* \equiv \frac{1}{T}\sum_{t=1}^{T} R_{it}^*. \quad (5.7)$$

The motivation for this renormalization is to create a fair comparison between the clone portfolio and the fund by equalizing their volatilities. Renormalizing (5.5) is equivalent to changing the leverage of the clone portfolio since the sum of the renormalized betas $\gamma_i \sum_k \beta_{ik}^*$ will equal the renormalization factor γ_i, not 1. If γ_i exceeds 1, then positive leverage is required, and if less than 1, the portfolio is not fully invested in the five factors. A more complete expression of the portfolio weights of clone i may be obtained by introducing an additional asset that represents leverage (i.e., borrowing and lending), in which case the portfolio weights of the five factors and this additional asset must sum to 1:

$$1 = \gamma_i(\beta_{i1}^* + \cdots + \beta_{i5}^*) + \delta_i. \qquad (5.8)$$

The clone return is then given by

$$\widehat{R}_{it} = \gamma_i(\beta_{i1}^* \, \mathrm{SP500}_t + \cdots + \beta_{i5}^* \, \mathrm{CMDTY}_t) + \delta_i \, R_l, \qquad (5.9)$$

where R_l is the borrowing/lending rate. Since this rate depends on many factors such as the credit quality of the respective counterparties, the riskiness of the instruments and portfolio strategy, the size of the transaction, and general market conditions, we do not attempt to assume a particular value for R_l but simply point out its existence.[15]

As discussed above, fixed-weight linear clones are affected by look-ahead bias because the entire histories of fund and factor returns are used to construct the clones' portfolio weights and renormalization factors. To address this issue, we present an alternate method of constructing linear clones using a rolling window for estimating the regression coefficients and renormalization factors. Rolling-window estimators can also address the ubiquitous issue of nonstationarity that affects most financial time-series studies; time-varying means, volatilities, and general market conditions can be captured to some degree by using rolling windows.

To construct a rolling-window linear clone, for each month t we use a 24-month rolling window from months $t - 24$ to $t - 1$ to estimate the same regression (5.4a)

---

[15] However, it should be kept in mind that the futures and forward contracts corresponding to the five factors in (5.5) have sizable amounts of leverage built into the contracts themselves, so that for reasonable values of γ_i, we can rewrite (5.9) as

$$\widehat{R}_{it} = \beta_{i1}^* \, (\gamma_i \mathrm{SP500}_t) + \cdots + \beta_{i5}^* \, (\gamma_i \mathrm{CMDTY}_t) + \delta_i \, R_l \qquad (5.10)$$

$$= \beta_{i1}^* \, \mathrm{SP500}_t^* + \cdots + \beta_{i5}^* \, \mathrm{CMDTY}_t^*, \qquad (5.11)$$

where we have redefined five new instruments in (5.11) that can achieve γ_i times the leverage of the original instruments in (5.9) at no additional cost. Since the coefficients $\{\beta_{ik}^*\}$ sum to 1 by construction, there is no need for any additional borrowing or lending because each redefined instrument is already leveraged by the factor γ_i; hence $\delta_i \equiv 0$ in (5.11).

as before:[16]

$$R_{it-k} = \beta_{it1}\text{SP500}_{t-k} + \beta_{it2}\text{BOND}_{t-k} + \beta_{it3}\text{USD}_{t-k} + \beta_{it4}\text{CREDIT}_{t-k}$$

$$+ \beta_{it5}\text{CMDTY}_{t-k} + \epsilon_{it-k}, \quad k = 1, \ldots, 24 \tag{5.12a}$$

$$\text{subject to } 1 = \beta_{it1} + \cdots + \beta_{it5}, \tag{5.12b}$$

but now the coefficients are indexed by both i and t since we repeat this process each month for every fund i. The parameter estimates are then used in the same manner as in the fixed-weight case to construct clone returns $\widehat{R}_{it}$:

$$R_{it}^* \equiv \beta_{it1}^*\text{SP500}_t + \beta_{it2}^*\text{BOND}_t + \beta_{it3}^*\text{USD}_t$$

$$+ \beta_{it4}^*\text{CREDIT}_t + \beta_{it5}^*\text{CMDTY}_t, \tag{5.13}$$

$$\widehat{R}_{it} \equiv \gamma_{it} R_{it}^*, \quad \gamma_{it} \equiv \frac{\sqrt{\sum_{k=1}^{24}(R_{it-k} - \overline{R}_{it})^2/23}}{\sqrt{\sum_{k=1}^{24}(R_{it-k}^* - \overline{R}_{it}^*)^2/23}}, \tag{5.14}$$

$$\overline{R}_{it} \equiv \frac{1}{24}\sum_{k=1}^{24}R_{it-k}, \quad \overline{R}_{it}^* \equiv \frac{1}{24}\sum_{k=1}^{24}R_{it-k}^*, \tag{5.15}$$

where the renormalization factors γ_{it} are now indexed by time t to reflect the fact that they are also computed within the rolling window. This implies that for any given clone i, the volatility of its returns over the entire history will no longer be identical to the volatility of its matching fund because the renormalization process is applied only to rolling windows, not to the entire history of returns. However, as long as volatilities do not shift dramatically over time, the rolling-window renormalization process should yield clones with similar volatilities.

Although rolling-window clones may seem more practically relevant because they avoid the most obvious forms of look-ahead bias, they have drawbacks as well. For example, the rolling-window estimation procedure generates more frequent rebalancing needs for the clone portfolio, which is counter to the passive spirit of the cloning endeavor. Moreover, rolling-window estimators are typically subject to greater estimation error because of the smaller sample size. This implies that at least part of the rebalancing of rolling-window clones is unnecessary. The

---

[16] If there are missing observations within this 24-month window, we extend the window backward in time until we obtain 24 data points for our regression. Our choice of 24 months for the rolling window was a compromise between the desire to capture nonstationarities in the data and the need for a sufficient number of observations to estimate the parameters of the clone. We did not try other window lengths because we wished to reduce the impact of "back-test bias" or overfitting on our empirical results.

amount of rebalancing can, of course, be controlled by adjusting the length of the rolling window—a longer window implies more stable weights, but stability implies less flexibility in capturing potential nonstationarities in the data.

Ultimately, the choice between fixed-weight and rolling-window clones depends on the nature of the application, the time-series properties of the strategies being cloned, and the specific goals and constraints of the investor. A passive investor with little expertise in trading and risk management may well prefer the fixed-weight clone, whereas a more active investor with trading capabilities and a desire to implement dynamic asset-allocation policies prefers the rolling-window clone. For these reasons, we present results for both types of clones in this sections.

Performance Results

Table 5.5 presents a comparison between the performance of fixed-weight and rolling-window linear clones and the original funds from which the clones are derived.[17] The results are striking—for several categories, the average mean returns of the clones are only slightly lower than those of their fund counterparts, and in some categories, the clones do better. For example, the average mean return of the Equity Market Neutral fixed-weight clones is 8.89%, and the corresponding figure for the funds is 9.14%. For Long/Short Equity Hedge funds, the average mean returns for fixed-weight clones and funds are 14.69% and 15.28%, respectively. And in the Multi-Strategy category, the average mean returns for fixed-weight clones and funds are 11.01% and 12.85%, respectively.

In two cases, the average mean returns of the fixed-weight clones are higher than those of the funds: Global Macro (15.42% vs. 11.72%) and Managed Futures (23.60% vs. 11.90%). However, these differences are not necessarily statistically significant because of the variability in the mean returns of funds and clones within their own categories. Even in the case of Managed Futures, the difference in the average mean return between fixed-weight clones and funds—more than 10 percentage points—is not significant because of the large fluctuations in the average mean returns of the Managed Futures fixed-weight clones and their corresponding funds (e.g., one standard deviation of the average mean of the Managed Futures fixed-weight clones is 12.87% according to Table 5.5, and one standard deviation of the average mean of the corresponding sample of funds is 7.90% according to Table 5.2). Nevertheless, these results suggest that for certain categories the performance of fixed-weight clones may be comparable to that of their corresponding funds.

---

[17] Note that each type of clone has its own set of matching results for the funds. This is because the first 24 months of each fund's history are used to calibrate the initial estimates of the rolling-window clones; hence they are not included in the rolling-window data set from which fund and clone performance statistics are computed.

Table 5.5.

Performance Comparison of Fixed-Weight and Rolling-Window Linear Clones of Hedge Funds in the Lipper TASS Live Database and Their Corresponding Funds (February 1986 to August 2007)

| Category | Sample Size | Fixed-Weight Linear Clones | | | | | | | | | |
| | | Annual Mean Return (%) | | Annual SD (%) | | Annual Sharpe | | ρ(%) | | p-value (Q₁₂) (%) | |
		Mean	SD	Mean	SD	Mean	SD	Mean	SD	Mean	SD
Funds											
Convertible Arbitrage	66	9.42	4.80	5.93	4.69	2.46	3.22	43.3	14.5	5.2	11.8
Dedicated Short Bias	14	−1.23	7.64	22.67	9.24	−0.15	0.48	3.1	9.7	42.6	32.6
Emerging Markets	118	19.80	12.15	17.81	13.32	1.54	1.03	17.0	11.9	30.7	29.2
Equity Market Neutral	103	9.14	4.94	7.15	5.51	1.72	1.20	4.0	21.7	37.7	32.4
Event Driven	217	13.58	5.75	7.27	5.09	2.63	4.12	23.7	15.2	24.8	30.1
Fixed Income Arbitrage	90	9.38	4.16	5.58	3.52	2.78	4.33	18.6	21.7	38.4	33.3
Global Macro	81	11.72	7.43	12.54	6.90	1.01	0.56	5.0	12.7	42.3	28.8
Long/Short Equity Hedge	602	15.28	7.63	14.56	8.13	1.22	0.61	11.4	14.2	34.7	30.6
Managed Futures	127	11.90	7.90	18.59	9.86	0.77	0.67	3.5	10.9	39.7	32.8
Multi-Strategy	88	12.85	8.26	9.17	9.41	1.99	1.11	20.5	18.2	23.8	28.2
Fund of Funds	591	9.52	4.29	6.35	4.08	1.85	0.99	21.3	13.8	29.7	27.3
All Funds	2,097	12.44	7.46	10.65	8.48	1.68	1.95	16.3	16.9	31.6	30.1
All Except Fund of Funds	1,506	13.59	8.10	12.33	9.13	1.61	2.21	14.4	17.6	32.4	31.1
Linear Clones											
Convertible Arbitrage	66	6.00	2.38	5.93	4.69	1.28	0.50	12.9	9.0	50.2	22.4
Dedicated Short Bias	14	−7.34	10.15	22.67	9.24	−0.46	0.62	0.0	5.6	62.4	29.4
Emerging Markets	118	14.63	9.64	17.81	13.32	1.08	0.56	1.3	7.9	58.7	27.8
Equity Market Neutral	103	8.89	6.80	7.15	5.51	1.36	0.63	2.8	8.9	48.8	25.9
Event Driven	217	9.40	5.91	7.27	5.09	1.43	0.44	5.2	9.2	54.6	25.2
Fixed Income Arbitrage	90	7.10	4.47	5.58	3.52	1.41	0.53	8.9	8.0	58.0	27.0
Global Macro	81	15.42	9.48	12.54	6.90	1.28	0.62	3.3	9.1	47.1	25.0
Long/Short Equity Hedge	602	14.69	9.50	14.56	8.13	1.14	0.51	−0.1	8.8	56.5	26.9
Managed Futures	127	23.60	12.87	18.59	9.86	1.33	0.46	3.8	8.4	45.8	27.1
Multi-Strategy	88	11.01	10.76	9.17	9.41	1.43	0.53	2.1	8.0	58.8	23.0
Fund of Funds	591	9.18	5.90	6.35	4.08	1.54	0.39	1.7	9.0	55.4	26.6
All Funds	2,097	11.97	9.26	10.65	8.48	1.32	0.53	2.4	9.2	54.7	26.5
All Except Fund of Funds	1,506	13.06	10.08	12.33	9.13	1.24	0.56	2.7	9.3	54.5	26.5

Table 5.5.

(continued)

		24-Month Rolling-Window Linear Clones									
	Sample	Annual Mean Return (%)		Annual SD (%)		Annual Sharpe		ρ_1 (%)		p-value (Q_6) (%)	
Category	Size	Mean	SD	Mean	SD	Mean	SD	Mean	SD	Mean	SD
Funds											
Convertible Arbitrage	66	7.79	5.44	5.83	5.01	2.36	3.59	42.7	15.7	6.3	14.0
Dedicated Short Bias	14	-1.19	7.62	20.84	10.95	-0.19	0.50	5.8	10.1	50.6	24.6
Emerging Markets	118	19.63	13.19	15.61	11.52	1.68	1.14	13.0	14.5	38.6	30.3
Equity Market Neutral	103	8.12	6.35	6.51	5.33	1.82	1.46	4.1	24.1	42.0	33.5
Event Driven	217	12.00	5.85	6.67	5.08	2.71	4.23	21.2	15.8	29.8	29.8
Fixed Income Arbitrage	90	7.72	4.31	5.32	3.61	3.21	8.19	15.4	22.9	37.7	32.6
Global Macro	81	9.61	7.22	11.15	5.32	0.97	0.75	8.2	17.2	43.3	30.2
Long/Short Equity Hedge	602	13.82	8.28	13.25	7.91	1.24	0.76	9.1	16.9	39.8	30.1
Managed Futures	127	10.15	6.85	17.76	9.57	0.70	0.65	5.9	16.2	33.8	28.1
Multi-Strategy	88	11.39	8.20	8.47	9.01	2.01	1.66	18.2	20.4	25.9	28.5
Fund of Funds	591	9.97	4.71	6.06	3.72	2.03	1.33	19.5	14.4	29.9	28.7
All Funds	2,097	11.55	7.72	9.81	7.89	1.77	2.55	14.7	18.4	34.1	30.2
All Except Fund of Funds	1,506	12.18	8.54	11.28	8.58	1.66	2.88	12.9	19.4	35.8	30.6
Linear Clones											
Convertible Arbitrage	66	2.68	3.94	6.00	6.00	0.68	0.62	4.3	9.6	55.1	32.2
Dedicated Short Bias	14	-3.37	14.15	23.44	13.14	-0.44	0.76	-3.4	12.6	51.8	24.4
Emerging Markets	118	7.26	9.04	19.23	15.68	0.68	0.62	8.4	11.4	43.3	28.7
Equity Market Neutral	103	4.55	5.91	6.94	5.75	0.74	0.79	4.3	13.2	51.7	29.5
Event Driven	217	7.40	4.93	6.75	5.23	1.23	0.59	5.4	12.7	50.0	26.0
Fixed Income Arbitrage	90	3.47	4.03	5.23	3.74	0.80	0.69	6.2	13.3	51.9	30.7
Global Macro	81	12.46	10.85	12.45	7.14	1.06	0.79	6.1	14.5	43.7	27.2
Long/Short Equity Hedge	602	11.30	8.95	14.28	8.77	0.95	0.59	1.8	14.0	44.2	28.9
Managed Futures	127	16.88	12.73	19.05	10.26	0.97	0.66	7.2	9.6	42.3	26.2
Multi-Strategy	88	7.74	8.19	8.84	9.18	1.05	0.65	3.8	13.6	43.5	30.2
Fund of Funds	591	6.99	5.41	6.16	4.49	1.25	0.52	0.9	11.4	54.1	28.4
All Funds	2,097	8.65	8.44	10.53	9.16	1.02	0.65	3.2	12.8	48.5	28.8
All Except Fund of Funds	1,506	9.30	9.29	12.25	9.92	0.93	0.67	4.2	13.2	46.2	28.7

On the other hand, at 9.40% the average performance of the Event Driven fixed-weight clones is considerably lower than the 13.58% average for the funds. While also not statistically significant, this gap is understandable given the idiosyncratic and opportunistic nature of most Event Driven strategies. Moreover, a significant source of the profitability of Event Driven strategies is the illiquidity premium that managers earn by providing capital in times of distress. This illiquidity premium is clearly missing from a clone portfolio of liquid securities; hence we should expect a sizable performance gap in this case. The same can be said for the Emerging Markets fixed-weight clones (14.63%) versus their fund counterparts (19.80%).

The results for the rolling-window clones are broadly consistent with those of the fixed-weight clones, though the average performance of the rolling-window clones is typically lower than that of their fixed-weight counterparts. For example, the average mean returns of the rolling-window clones for all categories except Global Macro and Managed Futures are lower than those of their fixed-weight versions, in some cases by a factor of 2 or 3. Part of these differences can be explained by the different sample periods on which rolling-window clones are based—observe that the average mean returns of the underlying funds are lower in the rolling-window sample than in the fixed-weight sample for all categories except Dedicated Short Bias and Fund of Funds. But the more likely source of the performance difference between the rolling-window and the fixed-weight clones is the combined effects of look-ahead bias for the fixed-weight clones and the increased estimation errors implicit in the rolling-window clones.

Given these two effects, the performance of the rolling-window clones is all the more remarkable in categories such as Dedicated Short Bias (−3.37% average mean return vs. −1.19% average mean return for the corresponding sample of funds), Equity Market Neutral (4.55% clones vs. 8.12% funds), Global Macro (12.46% clones vs. 9.61% funds), Long/Short Equity Hedge (11.30% clones vs. 13.82% funds), and Managed Futures (16.88% clones vs. 10.15% funds). In the case of Dedicated Short Bias funds, it is not surprising that rolling-window clones are able to outperform their fixed-weight counterparts—the rolling-window feature provides additional flexibility for capturing time-varying expected returns (such as the bull market of the 1980s and 1990s) that a fixed-weight strategy simply cannot. And in the case of Managed Futures, like the fixed-weight clones, the rolling-window clones exhibit considerable cross-sectional variation in their mean returns; hence the superior performance of clones in this case may not be statistically significant.

Nevertheless, like the fixed-weight clones, rolling-window clones also fall short substantially in the categories of Emerging Markets (7.26% clones vs. 19.63% funds), Event Driven (7.40% clones vs. 12.00% funds), and Fixed Income Arbitrage (3.47% vs. 7.72%). Funds in these categories earn part of their expected returns from bearing illiquidity risk, which is clearly absent from the clone portfolios constructed with the five factors employed. Therefore, we should expect clones to underperform their fund counterparts in these categories.

Another metric of comparison between clones and funds is the average Sharpe ratio, which adjusts for the volatilities of the respective strategies. Of course, given our renormalization process (5.7), the standard deviations of the fixed-weight clones are identical to those of their fund counterparts, so a comparison of Sharpe ratios reduces to a comparison of mean returns in this case. However, the average Sharpe ratio of a category is not the same as the ratio of that category's average mean return to its average volatility, so the Sharpe ratio statistics in Table 5.5 and Figure 5.2 do provide some incremental information. Moreover, for the rolling-window clones, there may be some differences in volatilities depending on the time-series properties of the underlying funds, which makes Sharpe ratio comparisons more informative.

The average Sharpe ratio of the fixed-weight sample of Convertible Arbitrage funds is 2.46, which is almost twice the average Sharpe ratio of 1.28 for the fixed-weight clones, a significant risk-adjusted performance gap. Noticeable gaps also exist for Event Driven, Emerging Markets, and Fixed Income Arbitrage clones versus funds (recall that funds in these categories are likely to earn illiquidity risk premia not available to the corresponding clones). And for Global Macro and Managed Futures, the average Sharpe ratios of the fixed-weight clones are, in fact, higher than those of the funds in these categories.

The gaps between the average Sharpe ratios of rolling-window clones and those of the underlying funds tend to be more substantial—for the two reasons cited above—but with some notable exceptions. On average, rolling-window clones in the Global Macro and Managed Futures categories do better than their fund counterparts on a risk-adjusted basis, with average Sharpe ratios of 1.06 and 0.97, respectively, as compared to average Sharpe ratios of 0.97 and 0.70, respectively, for the corresponding sample of funds.

Liquidity

Table 5.5 provides another comparison worth noting: the average first-order autocorrelation coefficients of clones and funds. The first-order autocorrelation ρ_1 is the correlation between a fund's current return and the previous month's return, and Lo (2001, 2002) and Getmansky, Lo, and Makarov (2004) observe that positive values for ρ_1 in hedge fund returns is a proxy for illiquidity risk. Table 5.5 and Figure 5.3 show that the clones have much lower average autocorrelations than their fund counterparts, with the exception of Managed Futures, for which both clones and funds have very low average autocorrelations. For example, the average autocorrelation of Convertible Arbitrage funds in the fixed-weight sample is 43.3%, and the corresponding average values for Convertible Arbitrage fixed-weight and rolling-window clones are only 12.9% and 4.3%, respectively. The average autocorrelation of Fund of Funds is 21.3% in the fixed-weight sample, and the corresponding values for the fixed-weight and rolling-window clones are only 1.7% and 0.9%, respectively.

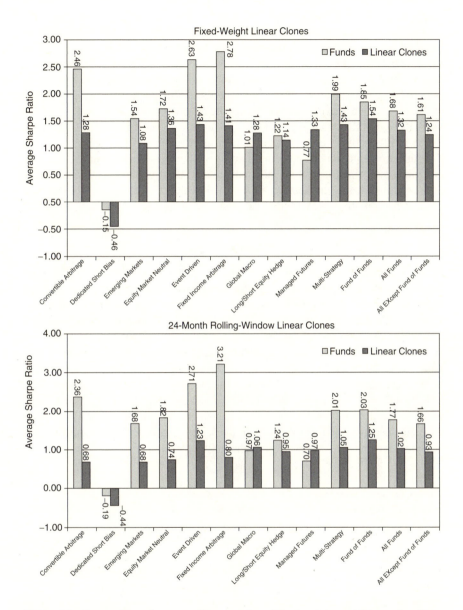

Figure 5.2. *Comparison of average Sharpe ratios of fixed-weight and 24-month rolling-window linear clones and their corresponding funds in the Lipper TASS Live database (February 1986 to August 2007).*

The last two columns of each of the two subpanels in Table 5.5 provide a more formal measure of the statistical significance of autocorrelation in the monthly returns of clones and funds, the Ljung–Box Q-statistic, based on the first 12 autocorrelation coefficients in the fixed-weight case and on the first 6 autocorrelation coefficients in the rolling-window case.[18] Smaller p-values indicate more statistically significant autocorrelations, and for every single category, the average p-value of the funds is lower than that of the clones. These results confirm our intuition that, by construction, clones are more liquid than their corresponding funds, highlighting another potential advantage of clone portfolios over direct investments in hedge funds. However, this advantage comes at a cost; as we saw in Section 5.4, the performance gap between clones and funds is particularly large for those categories with the highest levels of illiquidity exposure.

Leverage Ratios

Another consideration in evaluating the practical significance of fixed-weight linear clones is the magnitude of the renormalization factors γ_i. As discussed in Section 5.4, these factors represent adjustments in the clone portfolios' leverage so as to yield comparable levels of volatility. If the magnitudes are too large, this may render the cloning process impractical for the typical investor, who may not have sufficient credit to support such leverage. The summary statistics in the left panel in Table 5.6 for the renormalization factors $\{\gamma_i\}$ suggest that this is not likely to be a concern—the average γ_i across all funds in the fixed-weight sample is 1.97, and the median value is 1.74, implying that the typical amount of additional leverage required to yield fixed-weight clones of comparable volatility is 74%–97%, on average, which is far less than the leverage afforded by standard futures contracts such as the S&P 500.[19] For the individual categories, the average value

---

[18] Ljung and Box (1978) propose the following statistic to gauge the significance of the first m autocorrelation coefficients of a time series with T observations:

$$Q \;=\; T(T+2)\sum_{k=1}^{m}\hat{\rho}_k^2/(T-k), \tag{5.16}$$

which is asymptotically χ_m^2 under the null hypothesis of no autocorrelation. By forming the sum of squared autocorrelations, the statistic Q reflects the absolute magnitudes of the $\hat{\rho}_k$'s irrespective of their signs, hence funds with large positive or negative autocorrelation coefficients exhibit large Q-statistics.

[19] As of July 28, 2006, the initial margin requirement of the S&P 500 futures contract that trades on the Chicago Mercantile Exchange is $19,688, with a maintenance margin requirement of $15,750. Given the contract value of $250 times the S&P 500 Index and the settlement price of $1284.30 on July 28, 2006, for the September 2006 contract, the initial and maintenance margin requirements are 6.1% and 4.9% of the contract value, respectively, implying leverage ratios of 16.3 and 20.4, respectively. See http://www.cme.com for further details.

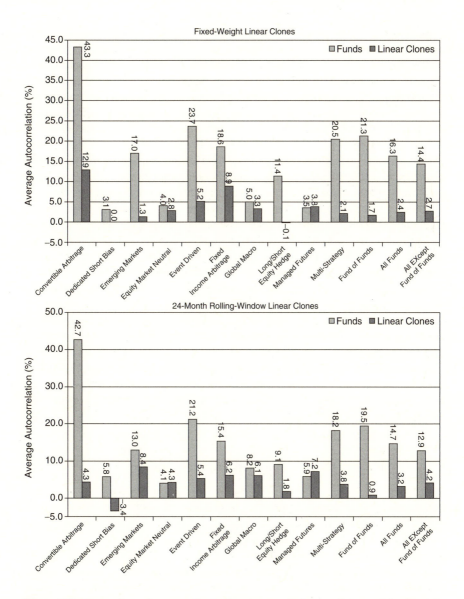

Figure 5.3. *Comparison of average first-order autocorrelation coefficients of fixed-weight and 24-month rolling-window linear clones and their corresponding funds in the Lipper TASS Live database (February 1986 to August 2007).*

of γ_i for fixed-weight clones varies from a low of 1.54 for Dedicated Short Bias and 1.61 for Fund of Funds to a high of 2.82 for Managed Futures. This accords well with our intuition that Fund of Funds is lower in volatility because of its diversified investment profile, and Managed Futures is higher in volatility given the leverage already incorporated into the futures contracts traded by commodity trading advisors (CTAs) and commodity pool operators (CPOs). In fact, outside the Managed Futures category, even the maximum values for γ_i are relatively mild—ranging from 2.97 for Dedicated Short Bias to 8.38 for Long/Short Equity Hedge—and the maximum value of 21.08 for Managed Futures is also reasonably conservative for that category (see footnote 19 on page 148).

Developing intuition for the leverage ratios for the rolling-window clones is slightly more challenging because they vary over time for each clone, so the right panel in Table 5.6 reports the cross-sectional means and standard deviations of the time-series means, standard deviations, first-order autocorrelations, and Q-statistic p-values of each clone i's $\{\gamma_{it}\}$. For example, the value 1.53 is the mean across all rolling-window clones of the time-series mean leverage ratio of each clone, and the value 0.44 is the cross-sectional standard deviation, across all rolling-window clones, of those time-series means. Table 5.6 shows that the average time-series mean leverage ratios for rolling-window clones are somewhat lower than those for their fixed-weight counterparts but roughly comparable, ranging from a low of 1.31 for Fund of Funds to a high of 1.94 for Managed Futures, with the standard deviations of the time-series means, ranging from 0.31 for Fund of Funds to 0.52 for Fixed Income Arbitrage. However, none of these leverage ratios fall outside the realm of practical possibility for the five instruments implicit in the cloning process.

Equal-Weighted Clone Portfolios

The results in Table 5.5 suggest that clone portfolios consisting primarily of futures and forward contracts, properly leveraged, can yield comparable volatility levels and some of the same risk exposures as certain types of hedge fund strategies. But these impressions are based on averages of the 2,097 funds in the sample and their corresponding clones, not on specific realizable portfolios. To address this issue, in this section we report the characteristics of equal-weighted portfolios of all fixed-weight and rolling-window clones and compare them to the characteristics of equal-weighted portfolios of the corresponding funds. By including all clones and funds in each of their respective portfolios, we avoid the potential selection biases that can arise from picking a particular subset of clones, e.g., those with particularly high $\overline{R}^2$'s or statistically significant factor exposures.

Figure 5.4 plots the cumulative returns of the equal-weighted portfolios of fixed-weight and rolling-window clones, as well as the equal-weighted portfolios of their respective funds and the S&P 500. The top panel shows that the

Table 5.6.

Summary Statistics for Renormalization Factors γ_i of Fixed-Weight and 24-Month Rolling-Window Clones of Hedge Funds in the Lipper TASS Live Database (February 1986 to August 2007)

| Category | Sample Size | Fixed-Weight Linear Clone Renormalization Factor | | | | | 24-Month Rolling-Window Linear Clone Renormalization Factor* | | | | | | | |
| | | Min | Median | Mean | Max | SD | TS-Mean | | TS-SD | | ρ_1 | | p-value (Q_6) | |
							Mean	SD	Mean	SD	Mean	SD	Mean	SD
All Funds	2097	0.11	1.74	1.97	21.08	0.94	1.53	0.44	0.31	0.26	79.47	16.11	2.76	11.44
Convertible Arbitrage	66	0.25	1.65	1.73	3.59	0.56	1.45	0.37	0.32	0.17	86.93	10.08	0.83	6.71
Dedicated Short Bias	14	1.12	1.42	1.54	2.97	0.45	1.44	0.51	0.22	0.19	79.68	16.76	2.97	10.07
Emerging Markets	118	0.95	1.87	1.98	4.45	0.69	1.59	0.39	0.37	0.36	81.75	12.10	0.78	3.77
Equity Market Neutral	103	0.49	2.09	2.28	5.92	0.94	1.77	0.51	0.37	0.26	75.92	18.04	3.08	10.68
Event Driven	217	0.11	1.58	1.72	8.32	0.73	1.33	0.34	0.25	0.18	80.11	17.55	3.92	15.18
Fixed Income Arbitrage	90	0.16	1.95	2.12	5.06	0.97	1.43	0.52	0.34	0.23	76.34	19.32	5.27	17.72
Global Macro	81	1.18	2.17	2.52	6.30	1.11	1.85	0.52	0.41	0.34	75.50	15.41	3.39	12.03
Long/Short Equity Hedge	602	0.96	1.87	2.13	8.38	0.90	1.66	0.41	0.35	0.27	79.80	15.42	2.45	10.74
Managed Futures	127	1.38	2.57	2.82	21.08	1.84	1.94	0.43	0.48	0.34	77.43	17.36	4.74	15.10
Multi-Strategy	88	0.68	1.77	1.88	3.82	0.61	1.45	0.44	0.31	0.22	80.58	16.46	3.10	12.85
Fund of Funds	591	0.43	1.47	1.61	7.46	0.58	1.31	0.31	0.21	0.20	79.52	16.03	2.27	9.46

* TS = Time series.

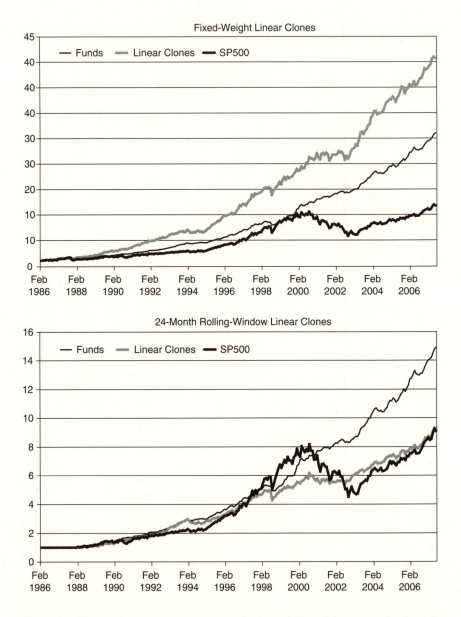

Figure 5.4. *Cumulative returns of equal-weighted portfolios of funds and fixed-weight and 24-month rolling-window linear clones and of the S&P 500 Index (February 1986 to August 2007).*

equal-weighted portfolio of all fixed-weight clones outperforms both the equal-weighted portfolio of corresponding funds and the S&P 500 over the sample period. However, the bottom panel shows that the performance of the equal-weighted portfolio of 24-month rolling-window clones is not quite as impressive, underperforming both the funds portfolio and the S&P 500. However, the clones portfolio underperforms the S&P 500 only slightly, and apparently with less volatility, as visual inspection suggests.

Tables 5.7 and 5.8 and Figure 5.5 provide a more detailed performance comparison of the portfolios of clones and funds. In particular, Figure 5.5, which plots the Sharpe ratios of the equal-weighted portfolios of the two types of clones and their corresponding funds for all funds and category by category, shows that for some categories the fixed-weight clone portfolios underperform the fund portfolios, e.g., Dedicated Short Bias (−0.24 for the clone portfolio vs. 0.00 for the fund portfolio), Emerging Markets (0.88 clones vs. 1.27 funds), Equity Market Neutral (2.08 clones vs. 3.72 funds), Fixed Income Arbitrage (1.80 clones vs. 3.19 funds), and Multi-Strategy (1.23 clones vs. 1.43 funds). However, in other categories, the fixed-weight clone portfolios have comparable performance and, in some cases, superior performance, e.g., Managed Futures, where the fixed-weight clone portfolio exhibits a Sharpe ratio of 1.90 versus 0.98 for the corresponding fund portfolio. When all clones are used to construct an equal-weighted portfolio, Table 5.7 reports an annualized mean return of 17.75% with an annualized standard deviation of 9.87% over the sample period, implying a Sharpe ratio of 1.80. The annualized mean and standard deviation for an equal-weighted portfolio of all funds are 15.39% and 7.41%, respectively, yielding a Sharpe ratio of 2.08.

The lower panel in Figure 5.5 provides a comparison of the Sharpe ratios of the rolling-window clone portfolios with those of their fund counterparts, exhibiting patterns similar to those of the fixed-weight fund and clone portfolios. The rolling-window clone portfolios underperform in some categories but yield comparable performance in others, and superior performance in the categories of Dedicated Short Bias (−0.09 clones vs. −0.12 funds) and Managed Futures (0.90 clones vs. 0.89 funds). For the equal-weighted portfolio of all rolling-window clones, the average return is 11.62% with a standard deviation of 8.21%, yielding a Sharpe ratio of 1.42; by comparison, the equal-weighted portfolio of all funds has a 13.96% average return with a standard deviation of 5.98%, yielding a Sharpe ratio of 2.33.

Tables 5.7 and 5.8 also report skewness, kurtosis, and autocorrelation coefficients for the two types of clone portfolios, which gives a more detailed characterization of the risks of the return streams. For some of the categories, the differences in these measures between clones and funds are quite striking. For example, according to Table 5.7, the portfolio of Fixed Income Arbitrage funds in the fixed-weight case exhibits a skewness coefficient of −6, a kurtosis coefficient of 63, and a first-order autocorrelation coefficient of 23%, implying

Table 5.7.

Performance Comparison of Equal-Weighted Portfolios of All Fixed-Weight Linear Clones versus Funds in the Lipper TASS Live Database (February 1986 to August 2007)

Statistic	All Funds Funds	All Funds Clones	Convertible Arb Funds	Convertible Arb Clones	Dedicated Short Bias Funds	Dedicated Short Bias Clones	Emerging Markets Funds	Emerging Markets Clones	Equity Market Neutral Funds	Equity Market Neutral Clones	Event Driven Funds	Event Driven Clones
Annual Compound Return	16.21	18.70	12.40	7.21	−2.52	−8.24	20.96	14.93	13.99	13.89	15.12	12.65
Annualized Mean	15.39	17.75	11.83	7.08	0.09	−5.75	20.50	15.60	13.23	13.28	14.92	12.42
Annualized SD	7.41	9.87	4.05	4.54	23.14	23.94	16.12	17.76	3.56	6.39	11.09	9.38
Annualized Sharpe	2.08	1.80	2.92	1.56	0.00	−0.24	1.27	0.88	3.72	2.08	1.34	1.32
Skewness	0	0	0	−1	0	1	−1	−1	0	0	−8	−2
Kurtosis	12	4	6	8	4	5	8	6	6	4	107	17
ρ_1 (≥ **20% highlighted**)	12	−3	**42**	9	12	−5	**36**	−5	1	−14	16	8
ρ_2 (≥ **20% highlighted**)	−2	1	14	4	−1	−6	6	−4	1	1	−2	−4
ρ_3 (≥ **20% highlighted**)	−5	−1	0	1	−3	7	−5	6	15	11	−14	−6
Correlations To Various Market Indexes (≥ **50% highlighted**, ≤ **−25% highlighted**):												
S&P 500 Index	**62**	**84**	33	**59**	**−72**	**−95**	49	**90**	32	**61**	**56**	**90**
MSCI World Index	**56**	**69**	29	**51**	**−68**	**−85**	**54**	**82**	25	50	47	**70**
Russell 1000 Index	**63**	**84**	34	**59**	**−75**	**−95**	49	**90**	33	**61**	**57**	**89**
Russell 2000 Index	**68**	**66**	43	**55**	**−81**	**−73**	**52**	**74**	26	40	**64**	**76**
NASDAQ 100 Stock Index	**53**	**66**	31	49	**−80**	**−78**	42	**75**	26	47	43	**70**
BBA LIBOR USD 3-Month	−14	**−35**	−17	**−27**	9	5	−7	−13	−13	**−27**	3	−19
DJ Lehman Bond Comp GLBL	8	42	3	29	−3	−5	−5	19	17	46	−13	13
U.S. Treasury N/B (GT10)	−9	**−40**	6	−16	−2	−9	14	−2	−16	**−54**	12	−10
U.S. Treasury N/B (GT2)	1	**−32**	5	−14	−10	−16	17	4	−10	**−41**	19	−2
U.S. Treasury N/B (GT30)	−11	**−39**	3	−18	3	−4	10	−4	−15	**−54**	12	−12
Gold (Spot $/oz)	3	−6	2	12	−2	4	3	6	−9	−3	−5	−11
U.S. Dollar Spot Index	7	−2	7	−3	−7	8	6	−13	−4	8	16	13
Generic 1st NYMEX Crude Future	−11	−5	−6	−8	11	13	−6	−12	−5	1	−16	−8
Implied Call Volatility												

Table 5.7.
(continued)

Statistic	All Funds		Convertible Arb		Dedicated Short Bias		Emerging Markets		Equity Market Neutral		Event Driven	
	Funds	Clones	Funds	Clones	Funds	Clones	Funds	Clones	Funds	Clones	Funds	Clones
Six Risk Factors:												
CREDIT	11	7	46	66	−29	−34	37	50	−1	5	26	32
USD	−13	−11	−3	−15	14	34	−17	−39	3	9	−2	−3
BOND	12	50	8	37	−2	5	−5	13	17	62	−3	24
SP500	62	84	33	59	−72	−95	48	90	32	61	56	90
DVIX	−42	−48	−25	−49	52	64	−35	−64	−12	−41	−63	−59
CMDTY	9	27	3	13	0	−3	1	18	11	35	2	7
CSFB/Tremont Indexes:												
All Funds	82	54	45	46	−55	−42	58	49	44	50	63	56
Convertible Arbitrage	47	24	76	36	−17	−9	35	20	30	24	55	29
Dedicated Short Bias	−68	−65	−45	−55	89	77	−57	−77	−29	−43	−72	−70
Emerging Markets	72	43	42	43	−57	−51	92	55	21	29	64	49
Equity Market Neutral	47	37	32	23	−27	−37	30	39	35	34	37	35
Event Driven	78	56	62	59	−57	−56	69	63	36	38	90	63
Fixed Income Arbitrage	32	15	36	27	−4	1	23	9	25	14	35	18
Global Macro	52	32	25	25	−17	−11	31	17	34	41	30	31
Long/Short Equity Hedge	84	61	39	50	−80	−60	58	65	42	46	68	61
Managed Futures	18	5	−11	−7	12	12	−8	−6	9	14	−11	−3
Multi-Strategy	31	18	30	23	−7	−9	4	16	29	12	26	20

Table 5.7.
(continued)

Statistic	Fixed Income Arbitrage		Global Macro		Long/Short Equity Hedge		Managed Futures		Multi-Strategy		Fund of Funds	
	Funds	Clones	Funds	Clones	Funds	Clones	Funds	Clones	Funds	Clones	Funds	Clones
Annual Compound Return	11.14	8.07	18.88	24.06	18.37	18.37	16.25	35.94	18.26	16.60	12.34	15.58
Annualized Mean	10.66	7.88	18.13	22.32	17.54	17.90	16.50	32.53	17.71	16.36	11.87	14.89
Annualized SD	3.34	4.38	12.20	10.81	10.38	13.53	16.76	17.12	12.35	13.26	6.11	8.07
Annualized Sharpe	3.19	1.80	1.49	2.07	1.69	1.32	0.98	1.90	1.43	1.23	1.94	1.85
Skewness	-6	0	2	0	-2	-1	1	0	-3	-1	0	0
Kurtosis	63	5	12	4	15	6	6	3	43	15	8	5
ρ_1 (≥ 20% highlighted)	23	2	-6	1	16	-7	6	10	1	9	19	1
ρ_2 (≥ 20% highlighted)	18	8	-15	4	-3	-3	-14	-5	-8	1	6	5
ρ_3 (≥ 20% highlighted)	5	4	3	9	-5	3	-14	2	13	-7	-5	-1
Correlations To Various Market Indexes (≥ 50% highlighted, ≤ -25% highlighted):												
S&P 500 Index	-3	7	10	51	77	94	-2	12	40	79	57	82
MSCI World Index	-6	0	6	38	65	78	0	9	32	60	55	64
Russell 1000 Index	-3	7	9	50	79	94	-3	12	41	78	58	82
Russell 2000 Index	3	12	9	35	89	76	-6	0	47	66	63	66
NASDAQ 100 Stock Index	2	5	9	36	73	77	-8	2	34	59	49	63
BBA LIBOR USD 3-Month	-7	-30	-9	-46	-11	-18	-12	-47	3	-18	-18	-34
DJ Lehman Bond Comp GLBL	5	42	14	62	1	19	25	80	-9	16	8	36
U.S. Treasury N/B (GT10)	-3	-47	-7	-62	-1	-14	-28	-87	9	-17	-12	-35
U.S. Treasury N/B (GT2)	2	-41	-7	-57	8	-5	-22	-82	13	-8	-4	-27
U.S. Treasury N/B (GT30)	-4	-48	-7	-60	-6	-16	-25	-80	10	-17	-14	-34
Gold (Spot $/oz)	1	9	13	0	-7	-7	14	3	3	-10	8	-10
U.S. Dollar Spot Index	12	14	-12	-7	13	4	-14	-23	11	11	13	6
Generic 1st NYMEX Crude Future	2	4	-14	1	-11	-9	-3	13	-8	-8	-6	-4
Implied Call Volatility												

Table 5.7.
(continued)

Statistic	Fixed Income Arbitrage		Global Macro		Long/Short Equity Hedge		Managed Futures		Multi-Strategy		Fund of Funds	
	Funds	Clones	Funds	Clones	Funds	Clones	Funds	Clones	Funds	Clones	Funds	Clones
Six Risk Factors:												
CREDIT	25	29	5	−9	20	25	−24	**−55**	23	21	6	12
USD	18	25	−11	−7	−9	−15	−10	−9	2	3	−9	0
BOND	12	**61**	9	**71**	7	25	22	**89**	−2	27	15	47
SP500	−3	7	11	**51**	**77**	**94**	−1	12	40	**79**	**57**	**82**
DVIX	24	−10	5	−21	**−54**	**−59**	12	7	**−42**	**−48**	**−31**	**−48**
CMDTY	7	21	21	35	6	23	10	37	11	18	12	24
CSFB/Tremont Indexes:												
All Funds	34	28	**55**	44	**73**	**54**	25	13	**72**	**53**	**89**	**56**
Convertible Arbitrage	45	33	28	28	36	20	2	6	**59**	26	**52**	27
Dedicated Short Bias	4	−1	−23	**−34**	**−79**	**−73**	9	12	**−62**	**−62**	**−61**	**−62**
Emerging Markets	18	6	23	22	**64**	49	−5	−12	**63**	45	**73**	42
Equity Market Neutral	−4	1	27	23	43	39	18	11	39	33	45	37
Event Driven	22	19	36	36	**73**	**59**	−7	−8	**79**	**57**	**78**	**56**
Fixed Income Arbitrage	**76**	31	17	22	18	10	9	8	39	17	38	18
Global Macro	41	33	**52**	34	37	27	35	22	41	30	**61**	35
Long/Short Equity Hedge	10	12	37	41	**90**	**65**	6	7	**74**	**59**	**85**	**60**
Managed Futures	−6	11	42	20	0	0	**85**	35	2	6	18	7
Multi-Strategy	33	23	31	22	27	16	12	2	39	22	34	19

Table 5.8.

Performance Comparison of Equal-Weighted Portfolios of All 24-Month Rolling-Window Linear Clones versus Funds in the Lipper TASS Live Database (February 1986 to August 2007)

Statistic	All Funds		Convertible Arb		Dedicated Short Bias		Emerging Markets		Equity Market Neutral		Event Driven	
	Funds	Clones	Funds	Clones	Funds	Clones	Funds	Clones	Funds	Clones	Funds	Clones
Annual Compound Return	14.69	11.89	10.51	5.16	−6.00	−6.76	19.50	6.83	11.02	6.92	13.81	8.89
Annualized Mean	13.96	11.62	10.13	5.17	−3.04	−2.78	19.29	9.42	10.55	6.86	13.20	8.89
Annualized SD	5.98	8.21	4.37	5.07	25.15	29.56	16.25	22.08	3.18	5.46	6.13	8.32
Annualized Sharpe	2.33	1.42	2.32	1.02	−0.12	−0.09	1.19	0.43	3.32	1.26	2.15	1.07
Skewness	1	−1	0	−1	0	1	−1	−2	1	0	−1	0
Kurtosis	6	7	7	5	4	8	10	20	5	5	13	7
ρ_1(≥ 20% **highlighted**)	13	−6	**42**	7	12	−2	**31**	7	0	−8	**39**	−4
ρ_2(≥ 20% **highlighted**)	−1	−2	13	4	−1	−9	6	1	7	−3	6	−11
ρ_3(≥ 20% **highlighted**)	−6	10	−2	0	−5	17	−1	5	13	−2	3	−3
Correlations To Various Market Indexes (≥ 50% **highlighted**, ≤ −25% **highlighted**):												
S&P 500 Index	**52**	**64**	36	**59**	**−72**	**−87**	**51**	**78**	27	41	**52**	**65**
MSCI World Index	45	49	33	48	**−69**	**−77**	**54**	**70**	27	36	50	**53**
Russell 1000 Index	**53**	**64**	37	**59**	**−75**	**−87**	**52**	**79**	28	42	**54**	**65**
Russell 2000 Index	**60**	47	47	47	**−83**	**−64**	**53**	**61**	31	31	**64**	**51**
NASDAQ 100 Stock Index	46	**51**	34	45	**−83**	**−74**	43	**65**	29	30	43	48
BBA LIBOR USD 3-Month	−18	−16	−22	−14	11	−5	−7	−2	−1	−21	−7	−10
DJ Lehman Bond Comp GLBL	10	25	1	14	−2	2	−10	1	7	29	2	10
U.S. Treasury N/B (GT10)	−12	−23	7	−6	−3	−15	15	10	−2	**−33**	4	−7
U.S. Treasury N/B (GT2)	−6	−15	5	1	−11	−23	17	17	4	−20	9	4
U.S. Treasury N/B (GT30)	−15	−24	5	−10	2	−10	10	4	−3	**−33**	0	−9
Gold (Spot $/oz)	7	2	7	5	−3	4	9	4	−3	1	−6	−10
U.S. Dollar Spot Index	10	4	7	7	−5	2	16	3	−3	13	9	13
Generic 1st NYMEX Crude	−13	−5	−9	−8	12	18	−4	−9	−4	4	−16	−3
Future Implied Call Volatility												

Table 5.8.
(continued)

Statistic	All Funds		Convertible Arb		Dedicated Short Bias		Emerging Markets		Equity Market Neutral		Event Driven	
	Funds	Clones	Funds	Clones	Funds	Clones	Funds	Clones	Funds	Clones	Funds	Clones
Six Risk Factors:												
CREDIT	20	23	52	57	-32	-38	39	49	4	16	33	32
USD	-7	-8	-8	-6	14	25	-16	-20	-9	11	0	6
BOND	16	32	7	22	-2	8	-4	2	4	41	5	16
SP500	52	65	36	59	-72	-87	51	78	26	42	52	65
DVIX	-29	-46	-27	-42	53	61	-40	-61	-12	-25	-46	-44
CMDTY	14	24	4	15	0	-5	8	7	17	28	-3	2
CSFB/Tremont Indexes:												
All Funds	84	53	41	43	-58	-39	62	48	30	35	63	54
Convertible Arbitrage	46	30	74	28	-14	-9	36	23	25	26	56	31
Dedicated Short Bias	-67	-66	-50	-53	86	68	-57	-70	-33	-41	-71	-62
Emerging Markets	71	48	41	38	-55	-47	90	54	18	27	63	45
Equity Market Neutral	46	38	33	24	-23	-37	29	28	38	22	38	32
Event Driven	78	61	64	52	-54	-50	71	66	34	36	90	61
Fixed Income Arbitrage	32	21	30	21	-4	-6	28	18	22	18	35	25
Global Macro	55	30	18	27	-20	-12	36	21	12	24	30	35
Long/Short Equity Hedge	83	58	40	43	-81	-51	59	57	40	37	68	54
Managed Futures	21	0	-10	-3	11	19	-13	-21	10	8	-12	-3
Multi-Strategy	31	11	28	17	-7	-9	4	3	23	10	28	16

Table 5.8.
(continued)

Statistic	Fixed Income Arbitrage		Global Macro		Long/Short Equity Hedge		Managed Futures		Multi-Strategy		Fund of Funds	
	Funds	Clones	Funds	Clones	Funds	Clones	Funds	Clones	Funds	Clones	Funds	Clones
Annual Compound Return	8.92	4.14	16.49	15.09	17.77	12.81	13.51	15.62	19.65	15.99	11.68	12.18
Annualized Mean	8.64	4.13	15.91	15.18	16.80	12.79	13.91	16.17	18.65	15.73	11.24	11.78
Annualized SD	3.66	3.75	10.76	14.83	8.25	11.57	15.58	17.93	11.10	12.89	5.40	6.79
Annualized Sharpe	2.36	1.10	1.48	1.02	2.04	1.11	0.89	0.90	1.68	1.22	2.08	1.73
Skewness	-8	-1	1	2	0	-1	1	0	3	1	0	-1
Kurtosis	**81**	7	10	14	4	7	6	4	**20**	7	5	7
ρ_1($\geq$ **20% highlighted**)	18	-8	14	-2	16	-16	2	12	12	17	16	-3
ρ_2($\geq$ **20% highlighted**)	8	-13	-10	-7	4	0	-16	-6	0	-5	6	4
ρ_3($\geq$ **20% highlighted**)	-5	0	-8	3	-2	9	-11	2	12	8	-6	13
Correlations To Various Market Indexes ($\geq$ **50% highlighted**, $\leq$ **-25% highlighted**):												
S&P 500 Index	-9	11	6	14	**70**	**85**	-2	-10	12	21	**50**	**65**
MSCI World Index	-11	5	-3	10	**63**	**68**	-6	-15	12	11	**50**	**50**
Russell 1000 Index	-9	11	6	13	**73**	**84**	-4	-10	14	21	**52**	**65**
Russell 2000 Index	2	20	4	1	**87**	**63**	-6	-9	23	14	**59**	47
NASDAQ 100 Stock Index	0	6	0	3	**71**	**67**	-9	-9	14	15	46	**50**
BBA LIBOR USD 3-Month	-8	-15	-17	-22	-13	-12	-12	-13	-6	-7	-23	-18
DJ Lehman Bond Comp GLBL	5	15	14	36	6	17	20	31	-1	7	13	28
U.S. Treasury N/B (GT10)	-3	-15	-19	**-36**	-1	-13	**-28**	**-38**	-6	-9	-14	**-28**
U.S. Treasury N/B (GT2)	3	-13	-21	**-36**	5	-2	-24	**-35**	-1	-2	-8	-19
U.S. Treasury N/B (GT30)	-6	-17	-16	**-34**	-6	-15	**-25**	**-34**	-7	-9	-16	**-28**
Gold (Spot $/oz)	4	11	11	10	0	-5	13	14	9	0	9	-3
U.S. Dollar Spot Index	13	14	-1	-10	11	5	-6	-6	20	10	12	8
Generic 1st NYMEX Crude Future	1	-3	-9	-2	-14	-10	-4	12	-3	-6	-8	-7
Implied Call Volatility												

Table 5.8.
(continued)

Statistic	Fixed Income Arbitrage		Global Macro		Long/Short Equity Hedge		Managed Futures		Multi-Strategy		Fund of Funds	
	Funds	Clones	Funds	Clones	Funds	Clones	Funds	Clones	Funds	Clones	Funds	Clones
Six Risk Factors:												
CREDIT	24	38	−3	−9	32	29	−21	−25	5	12	18	19
USD	19	11	−5	−13	−9	−11	−3	−8	15	18	−6	0
BOND	13	34	21	38	8	20	23	37	7	16	19	39
SP500	−9	11	7	14	69	85	−2	−10	13	21	50	65
DVIX	26	−25	6	−6	−45	−56	14	7	−14	−18	−25	−47
CMDTY	5	10	18	20	12	17	11	25	11	22	13	21
CSFB/Tremont Indexes:												
All Funds	32	27	56	36	73	52	27	9	70	41	90	53
Convertible Arbitrage	46	32	23	23	36	24	1	11	48	24	49	31
Dedicated Short Bias	7	−19	−17	−23	−79	−71	8	0	−45	−45	−61	−61
Emerging Markets	14	18	31	22	63	50	−2	1	55	26	73	45
Equity Market Neutral	−9	10	23	19	40	39	17	14	31	26	46	35
Event Driven	22	32	35	31	73	59	−5	3	62	39	78	58
Fixed Income Arbitrage	78	22	18	22	19	15	8	5	33	21	38	25
Global Macro	40	22	57	34	37	27	36	11	49	28	64	34
Long/Short Equity Hedge	9	19	33	26	90	59	7	9	57	38	86	54
Managed Futures	−8	8	47	26	0	−5	85	34	6	4	18	−5
Multi-Strategy	38	14	22	8	27	12	11	0	25	16	32	8

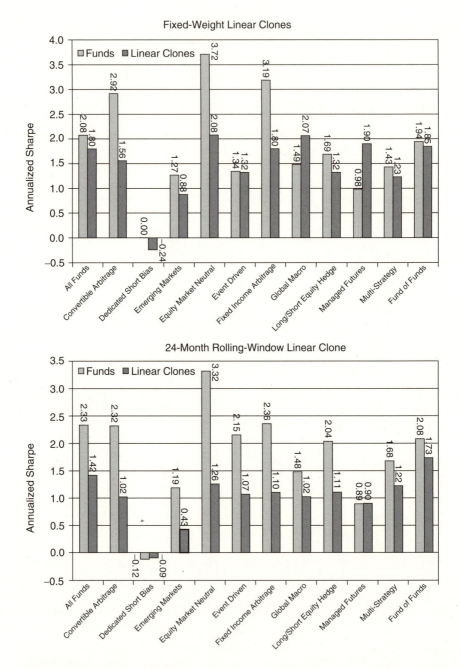

Figure 5.5. *Comparison of Sharpe ratios of equal-weighted portfolios of funds versus fixed-weight and 24-month rolling-window linear clones of hedge funds in the Lipper TASS Live database (February 1986 to August 2007).*

a negatively skewed return distribution with fat tails and significant illiquidity exposure. In contrast, the portfolio of Fixed Income Arbitrage fixed-weight clones has a skewness of 0, a kurtosis of 5, and a first-order autocorrelation of 2%, and the portfolio of Fixed Income Arbitrage rolling-window clones has similar characteristics, which is consistent with the fact that the clone portfolios are comprised of highly liquid securities. Other examples of this difference in liquidity exposure include the portfolios of funds in the Convertible Arbitrage, Emerging Markets, Event Driven, Fixed Income Arbitrage, and Fund of Funds categories, all of which exhibit significant positive first-order autocorrelation coefficients (42%, 36%, 16%, 23%, and 19%, respectively) in contrast to those of their fixed-weight clone counterparts (9%, −5%, 8%, 2%, and 1%, respectively). Similarly, the first-order autocorrelations of the portfolios of funds in these five categories using the rolling-window sample (42%, 31%, 39%, 18%, and 16%, respectively) are all larger than those of their rolling-window clone counterparts (7%, 7%, −4%, −8%, and −3%).

While the statistical properties of clone portfolios may seem more attractive, it should be kept in mind that some of these characteristics are related to performance. In particular, one source of negative skewness and positive kurtosis is the kind of option-based strategies associated with Capital Decimation Partners (Section 1.1), which is a legitimate source of expected return. And liquidity exposure is another source of expected return, as in the case of Fixed Income Arbitrage where one common theme is to purchase illiquid bonds and short-sell more liquid bonds with matching nominal cash flows. By reducing exposure to these risk factors through clones, we should expect a corresponding reduction in expected return. For example, in the case of Fixed Income Arbitrage, Table 5.7 reports that the portfolio of funds yields an average return of 10.66% with a standard deviation of 3.34% for a Sharpe ratio of 3.19, as compared to the fixed-weight portfolio of clones' average return of 7.88% with a standard deviation of 4.38% for a Sharpe ratio of 1.80.

In addition to its expected return and volatility, a portfolio's correlation with major market indexes is another important characteristic that concerns hedge fund investors because of the diversification benefits that alternative investments have traditionally provided. Tables 5.7 and 5.8 show that the fixed-weight and rolling-window clone portfolios exhibit correlations that are similar to those of their matching portfolios of funds for a variety of stock, bond, currency, commodity, and hedge fund indexes.[20] For example, the portfolio of Convertible Arbitrage funds in the fixed-weight sample has a 33% correlation to the S&P 500, a −17% correlation to 3-month LIBOR, a 7% correlation to the U.S. Dollar Index, and a

---

[20] Except for the SP500 and DVIX factors, the index returns used to compute the correlations in Tables 5.7 and 5.8 are derived solely from the indexes themselves in the usual way ($Return_t \equiv (Index_t - Index_{t-1})/Index_t$), with no accounting for any distributions. The SP500 factor does include dividends, and the DVIX factor is the first difference of the month-end VIX index.

76% correlation to the CS/Tremont Convertible Arbitrage index. In comparison, the portfolio of Convertible Arbitrage fixed-weight clones has a 59% correlation to the S&P 500, a −27% correlation to 3-month LIBOR, a −3% correlation to the U.S. Dollar Index, and a 36% correlation to the CS/Tremont Convertible Arbitrage index.

However, some differences do exist. The equal-weighted portfolios of funds tend to have a higher correlation with the corresponding CS/Tremont hedge fund index of the same category than the equal-weighted portfolios of both types of clones. For example, the correlation between the portfolio of funds and the CS/Tremont hedge fund index in the fixed-weight sample is 82%, and the corresponding correlation for the portfolio of fixed-weight clones with the same index is 54%, and the same correlations for the rolling-window case are 84% and 53%, respectively. This pattern is repeated in every single category for both types of clones and is not unexpected given that the CS/Tremont indexes are constructed from the funds themselves. On the other hand, the portfolios of clones are sometimes more highly correlated with certain indexes than those of their fund counterparts because of how the clones are constructed. For example, the correlation of the portfolio of Equity Market Neutral fixed-weight clones with the BOND factor is 62%, whereas the correlation of the portfolio of corresponding Equity Market Neutral funds is only 17%. This difference is likely a result of the fact that the BOND factor is one of the five factors used to construct clone returns, so the correlations of clone portfolios to these factors are typically larger in absolute value than those of the corresponding fund portfolios.

A summary of the differences in correlation properties between funds and clones is provided by Table 5.9. The first column in each of the two subpanels labelled "% Same Sign" contains the percentage of the 28 market index correlations in Tables 5.7 and 5.8, respectively, for which the fund correlation and the clone correlation are of the same sign. The next two columns of each subpanel contain the mean and standard deviation of the absolute differences in fund and clone correlation across the 28 market index correlations. These results show remarkable agreement in sign for both fixed-weight and rolling-window clones, ranging from 62% to 97%, and mean absolute differences ranging from 9% to 23%. And even for the largest mean absolute difference of 23% (fixed-weight clones in the Global Macro category), 90% of the correlations exhibit the same sign in this category.

Overall, the results in Tables 5.7–5.9 show that the correlations of clone portfolios are generally comparable in sign and magnitude to those of the fund portfolios, implying that portfolios of clones can provide some of the same diversification benefits as their hedge fund counterparts.

5.5 Summary and Extensions

A portion of every hedge fund's expected return is risk premia—compensation to investors for bearing certain risks. One of the most important benefits of hedge

Table 5.9.

Comparison of Signs and Absolute Differences of Correlations of Funds and Clones to 30 Market Indexes (February 1986 to August 2007)*

	Fixed-Weight Linear Clones			Rolling-Window Linear Clones		
Category	% Same Sign	Mean $\|\rho_f - \rho_c\|$	SD $\|\rho_f - \rho_c\|$	% Same Sign	Mean $\|\rho_f - \rho_c\|$	SD $\|\rho_f - \rho_c\|$
All Funds	90	18	10	97	12	8
Convertible Arbitrage	86	15	10	93	10	9
Dedicated Short Bias	83	9	7	79	11	6
Emerging Markets	83	19	12	93	12	9
Equity Market Neutral	90	17	13	83	12	10
Event Driven	79	16	11	93	9	6
Fixed Income Arbitrage	69	16	16	62	15	12
Global Macro	90	23	19	93	10	7
Long/Short Equity Hedge	93	11	6	93	10	7
Managed Futures	76	21	21	90	9	10
Multi-Strategy	76	18	12	97	9	9
Fund of Funds	93	18	9	90	14	10

* Fixed-weight and 24-month rolling-window linear clones are constructed from hedge funds in the Lipper TASS Live Database.

fund investments is the nontraditional types of risks they encompass, such as tail risk, liquidity risk, and credit risk. Most investors would do well to take on small amounts of such risks if they are not already doing so because these factors usually yield attractive risk premia and many of these risks are not highly correlated with those of traditional long-only investments. Although hedge funds with talented managers are always likely to outperform passive fixed-weight portfolios, the challenges of manager selection and monitoring, the lack of transparency, the limited capacity of such managers, and the high fees may tip the scales for the institutional investor in favor of clone portfolios. In such circumstances, portable beta may be a reasonable alternative to portable alpha.

Our empirical findings suggest that the possibility of cloning hedge fund returns is real. For certain hedge fund categories, the average performance of clones is comparable—on both a raw return and a risk-adjusted basis—to that of their hedge fund counterparts. For other categories, like Event Driven and Emerging Markets, clones are less successful.

The differences in the performance of clones across hedge fund categories raise an important philosophical issue: What is the source of the clones' value-added? One possible interpretation is that the cloning process reverse-engineers a hedge fund's proprietary trading strategy, thereby profiting from the fund's intellectual property. Two assumptions underlie this interpretation, both of which are rather unlikely: (1) It is possible to reverse-engineer a hedge fund's strategy using a linear regression of its monthly returns on a small number of market index returns, and (2) all hedge funds possess intellectual property worth reverse-engineering. Given the active nature and complexity of most hedge fund strategies, it is hard to imagine reverse-engineering them by regressing their monthly returns on five factors. However, if such strategies have risk factors in common, it is not hard to imagine identifying them by averaging a reasonable cross section of time-series regressions of monthly returns on those risk factors. As for whether all hedge funds have intellectual property worth reverse-engineering, we have purposely included *all* the Lipper TASS hedge funds in our sample—not just the successful ones— and it is unlikely that all of the 2,097 funds possess significant manager-specific alpha. In fact, for our purposes, the main attraction of this sample of hedge funds is the funds' beta exposures.

Our interpretation of the clones' value-added is less devious: By analyzing the monthly returns of a large cross section of hedge funds (some of which have genuine manager-specific alpha and others that do not), it is possible to identify common risk factors from which those funds earn part, but not necessarily all, of their expected returns. By taking similar risk exposures, it should be possible to earn similar risk premia from those exposures; hence at least part of the hedge funds' expected returns can be attained, but in a lower-cost, transparent, scalable, and liquid manner.

As encouraging as our empirical results may seem, a number of qualifications should be kept in mind. First, we observed a significant performance difference between fixed-weight and rolling-window clones, and this gap must be weighed carefully in any practical implementation of the cloning process. The fixed-weight approach yields a better historical performance and lower turnover but is subject to look-ahead bias and so the performance may not be achievable out of sample. The rolling-window approach yields a less attractive historical performance, but the simulated performance may be more attainable, and the flexibility of rolling-window estimators may be critical for capturing nonstationarities such as time-varying means, volatilities, and regime changes. The costs and benefits of each approach must be evaluated on a case-by-case basis with the specific objectives and constraints of the investor in mind.

Second, despite the promising properties of linear clones in several style categories, it is well known that certain hedge fund strategies contain inherent nonlinearities that cannot be captured by linear models (see, for example, Capital Multiplication Partners). Therefore, more sophisticated nonlinear methods— including nonlinear regression, regime-switching processes, stochastic volatility models, and Kat and Palaro's (2005) copula-based algorithm—may yield significant benefits in terms of performance and goodness-of-fit. However, there is an important trade-off between the goodness-of-fit and complexity of the replication process, and this trade-off varies from one investor to the next. As more sophisticated replication methods are used, the resulting clone becomes less passive, requiring more trading and risk management expertise and eventually becoming as dynamic and complex as the hedge fund strategy itself.

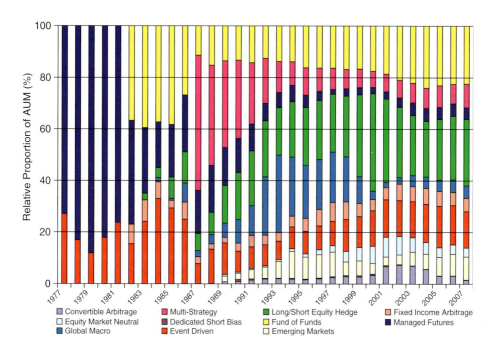

Plate 1. Relative proportions of assets under management at year-end in the 11 categories of the Lipper TASS hedge fund combined database (1977 to 2007)

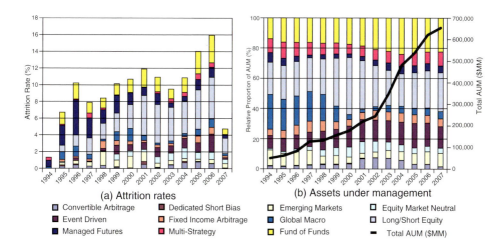

Plate 2. Attrition rates and total assets under management for funds in the Lipper TASS Live and Graveyard databases (January 1994 to August 2007). The data for 2007 is incomplete, and attrition rates for this year are severely downward-biased because of an 8- to 10-month lag in transferring nonreporting funds from the Live database to the Graveyard database

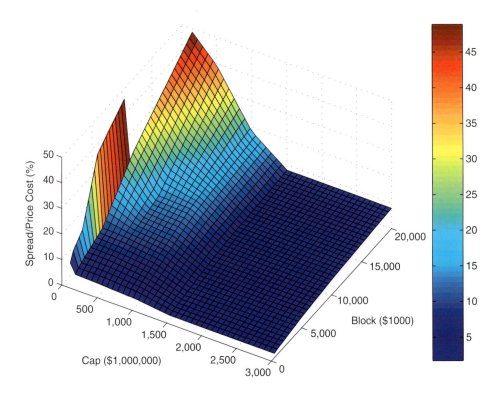

Plate 3. Loeb's (1983) price impact function gives the percentage total cost as a function of block size and market capitalization, with spline interpolation and linear extrapolation

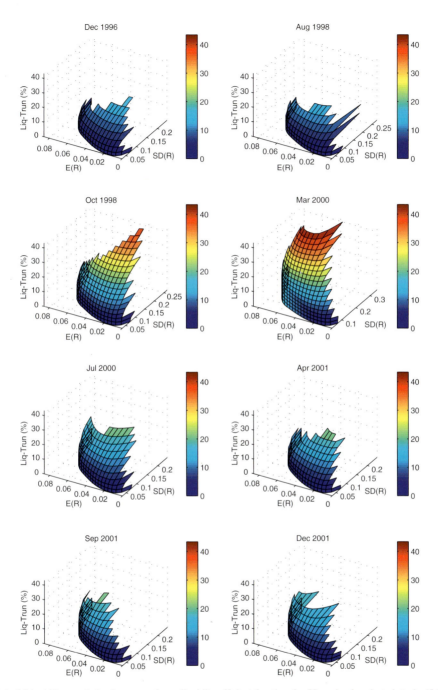

Plate 4. Liquidity-constrained mean-variance-liquidity efficient frontiers for 50 randomly selected stocks (5 from each of 10 market capitalization brackets), based on a monthly normalized turnover liquidity metric for the months of December 1996, August 1998, October 1998, March 2000, July 2000, April 2001, September 2001, and December 2001. Expected returns and covariances of the 50 individual securities are estimated with daily returns data from January 2, 1997, to December 31, 2001, and do not vary from month to month. Color strips to the right of each figure provide the correspondence between liquidity levels and the spectrum. Source: Lo, Petrov, and Wierzbicki (2003)

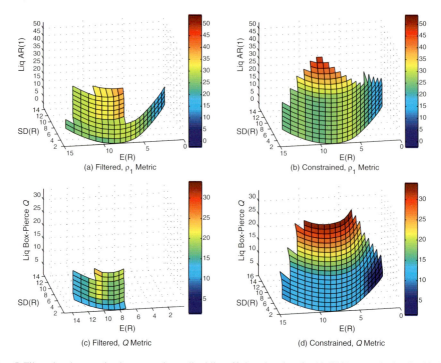

Plate 5. Filtered and constrained mean-variance-liquidity efficient frontiers for 13 CS/Tremont hedge fund indexes (January 1994 to February 2004). The two liquidity metrics are the first-order serial correlation coefficient ρ_1 and the Ljung–Box Q-statistic using the first three autocorrelation coefficients

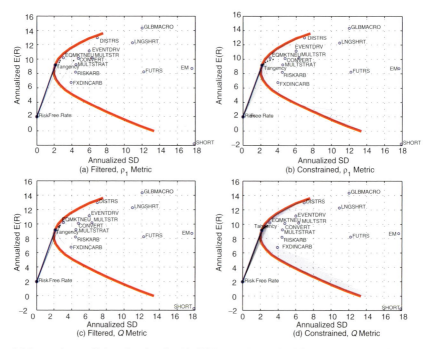

Plate 6. Mean-variance efficient frontiers for 13 CS/Tremont hedge fund indexes (January 1994 to February 2004). Data for various levels of liquidity constraints and filters are depicted using two liquidity metrics: the first-order serial correlation coefficient ρ_1 and the Ljung–Box Q-statistic using the first three autocorrelation coefficients

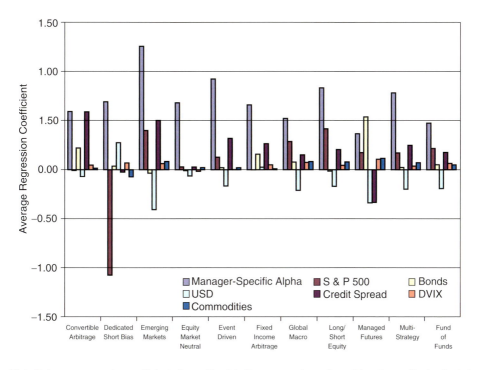

Plate 7. Average regression coefficients for multivariate linear regressions of monthly returns of hedge funds in the Lipper TASS Live database (February 1986 to August 2007). The six factors are the S&P 500 total return, the Lehman Corporate AA Intermediate Bond Index return, the U.S. Dollar Index return, the spread between the Lehman U.S. Aggregate Long Credit BAA Bond Index and the Lehman Treasury Long Index, the first difference of the CBOE Volatility Index (VIX), and the Goldman Sachs Commodity Index (GSCI) total return

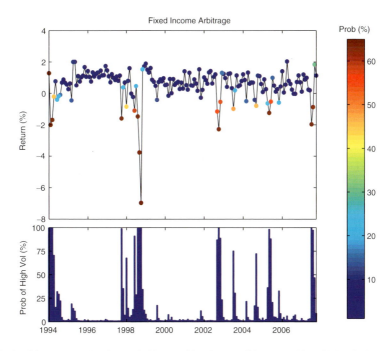

Plate 8. Monthly returns and regime-switching model estimates of the probability of being in the high-volatility state for CS/Tremont Fixed-Income Arbitrage hedge fund index (January 1994 to October 2007)

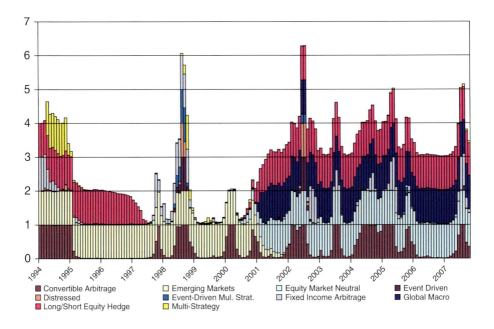

Plate 9. Aggregate hedge fund risk indicator: Sum of monthly regime-switching model estimates of the probability of being in the low-mean state for 11 CS/Tremont hedge fund indexes (January 1994 to October 2007)

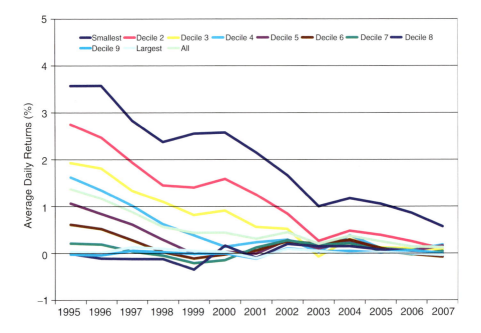

Plate 10. Year-by-year average daily returns of Lo and MacKinlay's (1990c) contrarian trading strategy applied to all U.S. common stocks (CRSP share codes 10 and 11) with share prices above $5 and below $2,000, and market-capitalization deciles (January 3, 1995, to August 31, 2007)

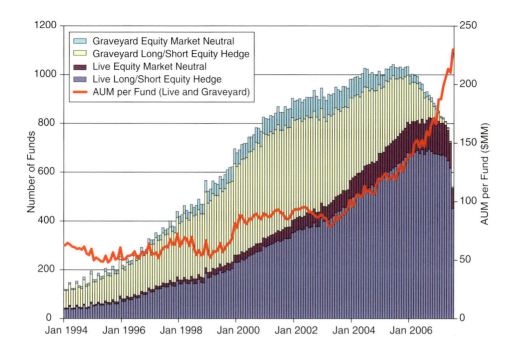

Plate 11. Number of funds and average assets under management per fund in the Lipper TASS Long/Short Equity hedge and Equity Market Neutral categories (January 1994 to July 2007)

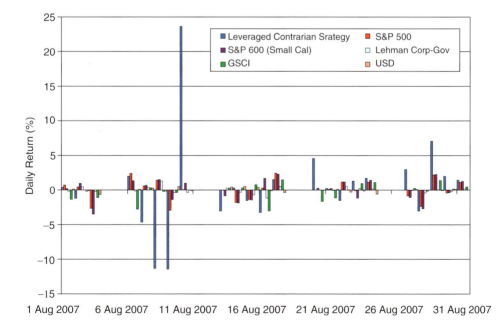

Plate 12. Leveraged daily returns of Lo and MacKinlay's (1990c) contrarian trading strategy in August 2007. The contrarian trading strategy is applied to all U.S. common stocks (CRSP share codes 10 and 11) with share prices above $5 and below $2,000, and market-capitalization deciles, from Monday July 30, 2007, to Friday August 31, 2007, with 8:1 leverage or a return multiplier of 4

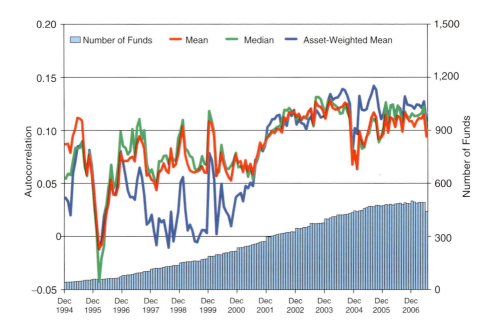

Plate 13. Mean, median, and asset-weighted mean 60-month rolling autocorrelations of funds in the Lipper TASS Live and Graveyard databases in the Long/Short Equity hedge and Equity Market Neutral categories (December 1994 to June 2007)

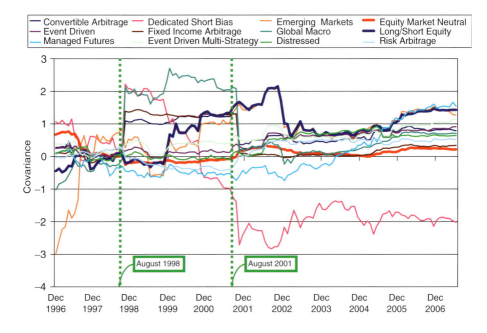

Plate 14. Thirty-six-month rolling-window pairwise covariances between the CS/Tremont Multi-Strategy index and other CS/Tremont sector indexes (December 1996 to June 2007)

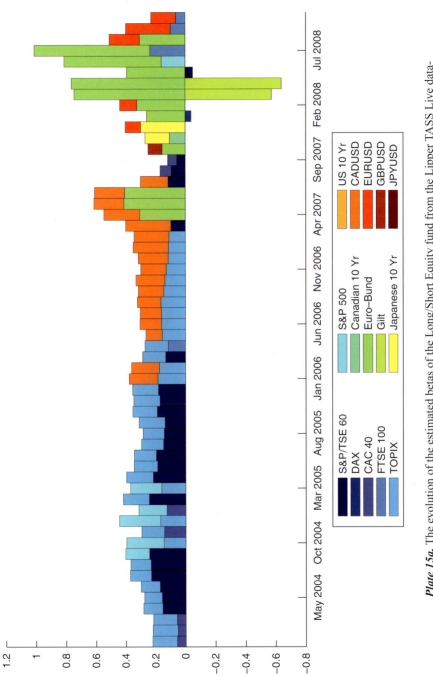

Plate 15a. The evolution of the estimated betas of the Long/Short Equity fund from the Lipper TASS Live database with the largest factor turnover (1.14 factors per month).

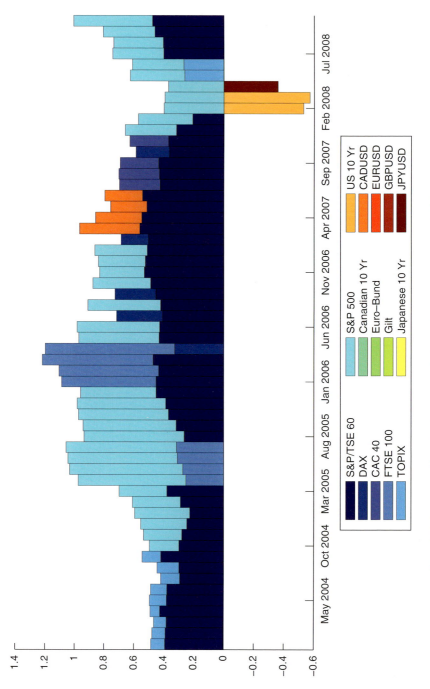

Plate 15b. The Long/Short Equity fund with the median factor turnover (0.727 factors per month).

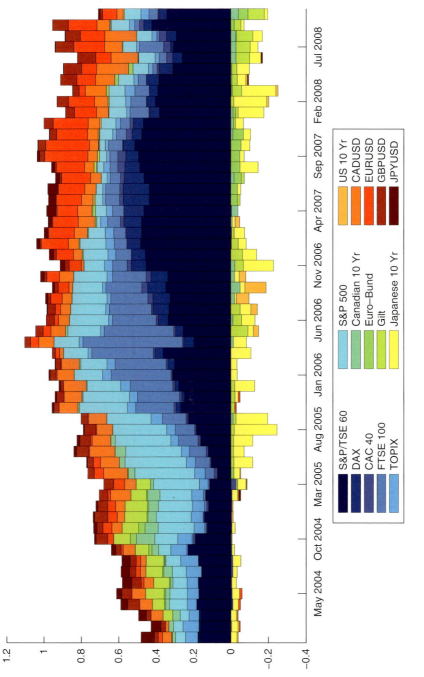

Plate 15c. An equal-weighted portfolio of the forty-seven Long/Short Equity funds in our sample.

Annual Returns

Year	S&P/TSE 60 Futures	DAX Futures	CAC 40 Futures	FTSE 100 Futures	TOPIX Futures	S&P 500 Futures	Canadian 10 Yr Futures	Euro-Bund Futures	Long Gilt Futures	Japanese 10 Yr Futures	US 10 Yr Futures	CAD Forwards	EUR Forwards	GBP Forwards	JPY Forwards
2000	3.4%	-10.5%	-3.9%	-14.9%	-24.3%	-15.1%	6.2%	5.3%	4.8%	4.4%	9.9%	-4.3%	-9.1%	-7.9%	-15.8%
2001	-17.2%	-28.5%	-25.2%	-18.2%	-19.7%	-15.9%	1.7%	-0.6%	-1.9%	4.6%	3.4%	-5.7%	-5.2%	-1.5%	-16.4%
2002	-15.7%	-47.0%	-37.1%	-25.6%	-16.7%	-23.6%	8.1%	8.4%	6.9%	5.0%	15.2%	1.7%	19.7%	13.1%	8.8%
2003	22.2%	32.5%	15.3%	13.5%	27.2%	28.7%	3.4%	2.4%	-1.7%	-0.8%	2.3%	24.0%	21.0%	13.6%	9.0%
2004	11.5%	4.4%	7.1%	5.9%	11.3%	9.2%	5.8%	7.9%	2.4%	3.2%	4.0%	8.8%	8.5%	10.3%	3.2%
2005	23.3%	24.2%	24.1%	15.2%	44.9%	1.4%	3.5%	4.2%	2.8%	0.6%	-0.7%	2.8%	-13.6%	-9.0%	-15.9%
2006	15.1%	18.5%	17.3%	9.1%	3.3%	10.1%	0.2%	-3.8%	-4.8%	0.2%	-1.7%	-1.3%	9.1%	13.4%	-5.7%
2007	6.9%	17.4%	0.2%	1.5%	-12.4%	-0.1%	1.3%	-2.2%	0.3%	3.4%	6.6%	16.7%	9.2%	1.8%	1.6%
2008	-28.9%	-43.5%	-41.5%	-33.6%	-43.7%	-39.6%	6.6%	7.8%	4.3%	1.8%	12.4%	-19.9%	-11.7%	-20.7%	14.4%

Annual Volatilities

Year	S&P/TSE 60 Futures	DAX Futures	CAC 40 Futures	FTSE 100 Futures	TOPIX Futures	S&P 500 Futures	Canadian 10 Yr Futures	Euro-Bund Futures	Long Gilt Futures	Japanese 10 Yr Futures	US 10 Yr Futures	CAD Forwards	EUR Forwards	GBP Forwards	JPY Forwards
2000	28.7%	23.6%	23.8%	20.1%	23.8%	22.8%	5.4%	4.7%	5.7%	3.5%	5.5%	5.3%	12.1%	8.8%	10.6%
2001	20.7%	28.9%	26.9%	20.9%	26.8%	21.8%	6.9%	4.9%	5.2%	3.4%	7.3%	5.7%	11.4%	8.3%	10.1%
2002	18.2%	37.6%	34.6%	27.6%	24.2%	26.4%	6.1%	5.1%	4.8%	2.9%	7.0%	6.2%	9.0%	6.8%	10.3%
2003	11.2%	31.3%	25.5%	19.4%	22.3%	16.4%	6.0%	6.2%	5.7%	4.7%	7.7%	9.0%	10.0%	8.0%	8.4%
2004	12.3%	15.7%	13.8%	10.0%	17.5%	11.0%	5.7%	4.1%	4.3%	3.7%	6.3%	8.8%	10.7%	10.3%	10.1%
2005	11.3%	11.8%	10.8%	8.5%	13.7%	10.1%	4.2%	3.8%	4.1%	2.9%	4.5%	7.9%	9.0%	8.3%	8.7%
2006	13.8%	15.3%	14.6%	12.4%	18.9%	9.7%	3.9%	3.8%	3.7%	3.6%	3.8%	7.2%	7.4%	7.8%	8.2%
2007	15.4%	14.9%	16.9%	16.9%	20.6%	15.6%	4.7%	4.2%	4.4%	3.4%	5.2%	9.3%	6.1%	7.0%	9.2%
2008	40.4%	39.0%	39.5%	37.3%	50.2%	41.6%	7.0%	6.8%	7.5%	6.0%	9.7%	15.9%	13.0%	13.1%	14.6%

Ratios of Annual Returns to Annual Volatilities

Year	S&P/TSE 60 Futures	DAX Futures	CAC 40 Futures	FTSE 100 Futures	TOPIX Futures	S&P 500 Futures	Canadian 10 Yr Futures	Euro-Bund Futures	Long Gilt Futures	Japanese 10 Yr Futures	US 10 Yr Futures	CAD Forwards	EUR Forwards	GBP Forwards	JPY Forwards
2000	0.12	-0.44	-0.16	-0.74	-1.02	-0.66	1.15	1.12	0.84	1.25	1.80	-0.82	-0.75	-0.90	-1.48
2001	-0.83	-0.99	-0.94	-0.87	-0.74	-0.73	0.24	-0.12	-0.37	1.35	0.46	-1.01	-0.45	-0.18	-1.62
2002	-0.86	-1.25	-1.07	-0.93	-0.69	-0.90	1.33	1.66	1.44	1.72	2.17	0.27	2.19	1.92	0.85
2003	1.99	1.04	0.60	0.70	1.22	1.75	0.57	0.39	-0.29	-0.17	0.30	2.67	2.09	1.70	1.08
2004	0.94	0.28	0.52	0.59	0.64	0.84	1.02	1.95	0.57	0.85	0.64	1.01	0.80	1.00	0.32
2005	2.05	2.05	2.23	1.78	3.28	0.14	0.82	1.10	0.68	0.21	-0.15	0.35	-1.51	-1.07	-1.83
2006	1.09	1.21	1.19	0.73	0.18	1.04	0.06	-0.99	-1.28	0.07	-0.43	-0.18	1.22	1.72	-0.69
2007	0.45	1.17	0.01	0.09	-0.60	0.00	0.27	-0.52	0.07	1.01	1.26	1.79	1.51	0.26	0.17
2008	-0.72	-1.12	-1.05	-0.90	-0.87	-0.95	0.94	1.14	0.57	0.30	1.27	-1.25	-0.91	-1.58	0.99

Plate 16. Annual returns, volatilities, and ratios of the fifteen hedging factors. Note that the 2008 returns do not include December.

Third, the replicating factors we proposed are only a small subset of the many liquid instruments available to the institutional investor. By expanding the universe of factors to include options and other derivative securities and customizing the set of factors to each hedge fund category (and perhaps to each fund), it should be possible to achieve additional improvements in performance, including the ability to capture tail risk and other nonlinearities, in a fixed-weight portfolio. In fact, Haugh and Lo (2001) show that a judiciously constructed fixed-weight portfolio of simple put and call options can yield an excellent approximation to certain dynamic trading strategies, and this approach can be adopted in our context to create better clones.

Finally, we have not incorporated any transaction costs or other frictions into our performance analysis of clone portfolios, which clearly have an impact on performance. More passive clones are less costly to implement, but they may not capture as many risk exposures and nonlinearities as the more sophisticated versions. However, by construction, clones have a significant cost advantage over a traditional fund of funds investment, not only because of the extra layer of fees that funds of funds typically charge but also because of the clone portfolio's more efficient use of capital as a result of the cross-netting of margin requirements and incentive fees. For example, consider a fund of funds with equal allocations to two managers, each of which charges a 2% management fee and a 20% incentive fee, and suppose that in a given year one manager generates a 25% return and the other manager loses 5%. Assuming a 1% management fee and a 10% incentive fee for the fund of funds, and no loss carryforwards for the underlying funds from previous years, this scenario yields a net return of only 4.05% for the fund of funds investors. In this case, the fees paid by the investors amount to a stunning 59.5% of the net profits generated by the underlying hedge funds.

Of course, a number of implementation issues remain to be resolved before hedge fund clones become a reality, e.g., the estimation methods for computing clone portfolio weights, the implications of the implied leverage required by the renormalization process, the optimal rebalancing interval, the types of strategies to be cloned, and the best method for combining clones into a single portfolio. We are cautiously optimistic that the promise of our initial findings will provide sufficient motivation to take on these practical challenges. Moreover, the same technology used for hedge-fund beta replication can also be deployed for risk reduction and hedging purposes, as we shall see in Chapter 11.

6

A New Measure of Active Investment Management

With the growing popularity of hedge funds and other absolute-return investment strategies, there is a widening gap between the performance metrics of traditional investment management and alternatives. While alpha, beta, volatility, tracking error, the Sharpe ratio, and the information ratio have become the standard tools for gauging the value-added of long-only portfolio managers, they have not had as much impact among investors of absolute-return strategies. Part of this gap is no doubt cultural in origin; the growth of the mutual fund industry was accelerated by the broad acceptance of portfolio theory and the benefits of diversification. This in turn led to the push for indexation and benchmark-based performance attribution, from which many of the current performance measures emerged.

However, another possible reason for the lack of impact of traditional performance measures for alternative investments is the fact that such measures are static and do not capture the dynamic and predictive nature of active investment strategies. Specifically, measures such as alpha, beta, tracking error, and the information ratio are all functions of parameters of the portfolio-return and benchmark-return distributions at a single point in time, e.g., expected returns, covariances, and variances. None of these measures involves the relation between returns at *multiple points in time*, yet such multipoint statistics are often the central focus of active investment strategies. For example, the most admired portfolio managers of our time are revered for their ability to foresee certain market trends well in advance of the public, to detect mispriced securities and exploit them ahead of the market, or to enter or exit certain investments before others recognize the opportunities. In every case, these investment skills involve forecasts or predictions, yet the standard performance measures listed above do not depend explicitly on the forecast power of the portfolio manager.

In this chapter, using an insight that first appeared in Grinblatt and Titman (1989, 1993), we propose a new measure of the economic value of active management—an active/passive (AP) decomposition—that takes into account forecast power explicitly. It is a simple decomposition of the expected return of a portfolio into two components: one that depends only on the average values of portfolio weights and asset returns and another that depends on the correlation between portfolio weights and returns. It is this latter component that directly measures the value of active management—the portfolio weights of a successful manager are generally positively correlated with returns, yielding a positive contribution to the portfolio's expected return. This correlation is directly affected by the manager's forecasting abilities because portfolio weights are functions of the manager's prior information. Therefore, the correlation between portfolio weights and returns at date t is a measure of the predictive power of the information used by the manager to select date-t portfolio weights. In short, it is a measure of the manager's asset-timing ability.

Of course, it is possible to generate positive expected returns without any variability in portfolio weights: A buy-and-hold strategy in assets with positive risk premia such as the S&P 500 will yield a positive expected return. In this case, the active component described above contributes nothing to the portfolio's expected return; hence the portfolio can be said to be passive. This is a novel definition of passive and active investing and has little to do with the standard definitions involving deviations from a benchmark portfolio. We show that a more natural definition for a passive portfolio is one where the portfolio weights are uncorrelated with returns. If weights have no forecast power, then active management is adding no value and the only source of expected return is risk premia, which can usually be generated by a buy-and-hold portfolio.

The AP decomposition is a simple consequence of the definition of covariance and is trivial for active managers to implement. In fact, position-level information is not necessary—only average portfolio weights and individual-asset average returns are needed to perform the decomposition. Moreover, because the decomposition is based on an identity, the empirical version holds exactly, allowing us to attribute realized or ex-post performance accurately and exhaustively to active and passive components.

Finally, when asset returns are assumed to satisfy a linear K-factor model such as the Capital Asset Pricing Model, the Arbitrage Pricing Theory, or any other linear pricing model, the AP decomposition yields several additional insights. In particular, a portfolio's expected return can be decomposed into three distinct components when returns exhibit a linear factor structure: security selection, factor-timing ability, and risk premia. The first two components may be interpreted as the result of active management, and the last component is passive. This decomposition provides one explanation for the seemingly persistent differences between long-only and alternative investments—the long-only constraint imposes a limit on the amount of factor timing that can be accomplished, and this limit may be a severe handicap in environments where factor risk premia change sign, i.e., periods of time-varying expected returns. A factor-based AP decomposition also addresses a recent concern of many institutional investors—that they are paying hedge funds for alpha but are getting beta instead. The relevant question is whether the beta exposure is time-varying or fixed—if it is the former, then it may be considered a genuine source of active value, but if it is the latter, it may be possible to achieve the same exposures in a more passive manner.

We begin in Section 6.1 with a brief review of the performance attribution literature and present the main results of the chapter in Section 6.2. We provide several analytical examples in Section 6.3 and then show how to implement the decomposition in Section 6.4. Section 6.5 contains a detailed empirical example of an AP decomposition applied to a statistical arbitrage strategy using daily data for NASDAQ size deciles from January 2, 1990, to December 29, 1995. We conclude in Section 6.6 with some extensions and qualifications.

6.1 Literature Review

The origins of performance attribution can be traced back to the Capital Asset Pricing Model of Sharpe (1964) and Lintner (1965), who derived a linear relation between the excess return of an investment and its systematic risk or market beta, i.e., the security market line:

$$R_{pt} - R_f = \beta_p(R_{mt} - R_f) + \epsilon_{pt}, \quad \mathrm{E}[\epsilon_t | R_{mt}] = 0. \tag{6.1}$$

Departures from this linear relation were generically termed *alpha*,

$$R_{pt} - R_f = \alpha_p + \beta_p(R_{mt} - R_f) + \epsilon_{pt}, \tag{6.2}$$

and Treynor (1965), Sharpe (1966), and Jensen (1968, 1969) applied this measure to gauge the economic value-added of mutual fund managers. Since then, a variety of related measures have been proposed, including

$$\frac{\mathrm{E}[R_{pt}] - R_f}{\sigma_p} = \text{Sharpe ratio}, \tag{6.3}$$

$$\frac{\mathrm{E}[R_{pt}] - R_f}{\beta_p} = \text{Treynor ratio}, \tag{6.4}$$

$$\frac{\alpha_p}{\sigma(\epsilon_{pt})} = \text{information ratio}, \tag{6.5}$$

where σ_p and $\sigma(\epsilon_{pt})$ denote the standard deviations of R_{pt} and the residual ϵ_{pt} in (6.2), respectively. Graham and Harvey (1997) and Modigliani and Modigliani (1997) have derived risk-adjusted transformations of these basic measures, and

Sharpe (1992) has proposed a constrained-regression framework for performing style analysis.

All these measures are essentially static in nature because they are based on characteristics of the marginal distributions of returns at a single date t, e.g., means, variances, and contemporaneous covariances of the portfolio and market returns.[1] Even Sharpe's (1992) regression-based decomposition—which is a conditional measure by construction—is static because the conditioning information is contemporaneous with portfolio returns at date t. None of these measures captures the time-series dependence between dates t and $t + 1$, which should be the central focus of any forecasting measure of investment skill.

In contrast to these static measures, Treynor and Mazuy (1966) were among the first to propose a dynamic measure of active management. To pick up market-timing skills, Treynor and Mazuy (1966) augmented the linear framework of (6.1) with a quadratic term $(R_{mt} - R_f)^2$. Formally, this is still a contemporaneous regression; hence its parameters do not involve any time-series properties, but the motivation—to detect asymmetries in up and down markets—is distinctly dynamic.

In a recent comment on the fundamental indexation approach of Arnott, Hsu, and Moore (2005), Treynor (2005) focuses on the covariance between portfolio weights and returns but only in the specific context of explaining the potential improvements of fundamental indexation over market-capitalization weights. The AP decomposition described in this chapter provides a considerably more general framework for thinking about the benefits and costs of any indexation algorithm.

A more explicit measure of market-timing skill is given by Merton (1981), Henriksson and Merton (1981), and Henriksson (1984), who showed that perfect market timing is equivalent to a buy-and-hold investment in the market that is fully protected by put options on the market with a riskless-rate strike. Imperfect market-timing skill may then be modeled as a partially insured investment in the market. Although this measure may also seem like a static one because it involves parameters at a single point in time of the multivariate distribution of market returns and corresponding put-option prices, it is in fact dynamic because of the multiperiod nature of options prices.[2] In other words, the dynamics of market timing have been compressed into the put-option price, which is then used as the "numeraire" for market-timing skill in Merton's (1981) framework.

---

[1] Of course, data spanning many dates are used to estimate these parameters, but the parameters themselves are single-point statistics, as opposed to multipoint statistics such as autocorrelations. Moreover, the estimates for the standard performance metrics are almost always computed under the assumption that the data are independently and identically distributed, which rules out any non-random-walk behavior, the starting point of any active investment strategy.

[2] In particular, one of the option-pricing parameters is the maturity date, which renders the option price a multipoint statistic.

Finally, Grinold and Kahn (2000, Chapter 17) describe a bottoms-up approach to performance attribution within a linear factor model framework in which benchmark timing is a component. Although they do not focus explicitly on the covariance between portfolio weights and returns, it is implicit in their time-series expression of "active benchmark timing return,"[3] and in a footnote they acknowledge that the same type of decomposition can be applied to individual securities.[4]

However, the most relevant study for our approach is by Grinblatt and Titman (1993), in which they observe that the covariance between portfolio weights and returns should be positive for an informed investor, who can "profit from these changing expected returns by tilting his portfolio weights over time in favor of assets with expected returns that have increased, and away from assets with expected returns that have decreased." Rather than using the covariance to decompose expected returns, they propose the following "Portfolio Change Measure" to measure performance:[5]

$$\text{Portfolio Change Measure} = \sum_j \sum_t \left[R_{jt}(\omega_{jt} - \omega_{jt-k}) \right] / T.$$

Although this measure does not capture the same information as the covariance between weights and returns, they were clearly aware of the possibility of decomposing expected returns using this covariance.[6]

The measure of active management proposed in Section 6.2 is a more direct version of these last two notions of market timing, in which each portfolio weight is viewed as a bet on the future return of a given asset, and bets that yield positive profits over time, i.e., asset-timing ability, are indications of investment skill. Moreover, we show that a portfolio's total expected return is completely determined by the sum of these bets and the passive returns from each asset's expected returns weighted by its average portfolio weight, hence there are no other sources of expected return other than these two.

6.2 The AP Decomposition

Consider a portfolio P invested in n securities indexed by $i = 1, \ldots, n$ and defined by its weights $\{\omega_{it}\}$ in those securities at date t. Denote by R_{pt} the portfolio's

---

[3] Equation 17.27 of Grinold and Kahn (2000, p. 504) is proportional to the covariance between factor betas and returns and is the sample counterpart to (6.17b) below.

[4] See footnote 9 of Grinold and Kahn (2000, p. 504). We thank Lisa Goldberg for this citation.

[5] See Grinblatt and Titman (1993, p. 51), equation (4b).

[6] Part of the motivation for this less direct performance measure is to relate it to the "Event Study Measure" from the prior literature by Cornell (1979) and Copeland and Mayers (1982). See also Grinblatt and Titman (1989) for additional theoretical motivation for their measure.

return between dates $t - 1$ and t, which is given by

$$R_{pt} = \sum_{i=1}^{n} \omega_{it} R_{it}, \tag{6.6}$$

where R_{it} is the date-t return of security i. Assuming that the means, variances, and covariances of individual securities' returns are well-defined, the main result of the chapter follows almost immediately from the definition of expected return and is presented in Section 6.2. This very general result implies a new way of defining passive and active investing, which is described in Section 6.2. And by imposing additional structure on asset returns—a linear factor structure, in particular—we show in Section 6.2 that our decomposition provides a new way of distinguishing between alpha and beta.

The General Result

We start with the following assumptions:

Assumption 6.2.1. *The returns $\{R_{it}\}$ for each security i forms a stationary and ergodic stochastic process with finite moments up to order 4.*

Assumption 6.2.2. *Date-t portfolio weights $\{\omega_{it}\}$ are stationary and ergodic stochastic processes that are functions of state variables $\mathbf{X}_{t-1}$.*

Assumption 6.2.1 is standard and implies that the means, variances, and covariances for all asset returns are well-defined and that estimators of these parameters have well-behaved limiting distributions with finite variances, which is useful for conducting statistical inferences.

Assumption 6.2.2 requires more discussion. Beginning with Markowitz (1952), much of the investments literature has assumed that portfolio weights are nonstochastic. The motivation for this starting point is the focus on portfolio optimization, in which the portfolio weights are the choice variables with respect to which a mean-variance objective function is optimized. From this perspective, the expected return of a portfolio is simply a weighted average of the expected returns of each component security weighted by the fraction of the portfolio devoted to that security.

But in practice portfolio weights are not fixed parameters—they represent decisions taken by a portfolio manager and, as such, depend on a number of inputs. Therefore, from an investor's perspective, the statistical properties of a portfolio's return are determined not just by the return distributions of the component securities but also by the characteristics of the portfolio weights. In fact, the investor in an active investment product pays dearly for the services of the portfolio manager and is paying largely for that manager's portfolio weights! Accordingly, unless a manager's portfolio weights depend on inputs that are nonstochastic and known to us, and we have complete knowledge of the functional relationship between inputs and weights, we must view portfolio weights as random variables. And if portfolio weights are random variables, it is not surprising that the stochastic relation between weights and returns can have significant implications for the properties of their product, which we shall demonstrate shortly in Proposition 6.2.1 below.

Assumption 6.2.2 provides a simple but important set of restrictions for the kind of randomness that a well-defined set of portfolio weights can exhibit. Perhaps the most important restriction is that the date-t weights $\{\omega_t\}$ can depend on information only *prior* to date t; otherwise unlimited arbitrage opportunities will abound. To see why, suppose that we remove this restriction. Then consider the following portfolio:

$$\omega_{it} = \frac{\max[0, R_{it}]}{\sum_{j=1}^{n} \max[0, R_{jt}]}, \quad R_{pt} = \sum_{i=1}^{n} \omega_{it} R_{it} \geq 0, \tag{6.7}$$

which places positive weight at date t on only those securities with a positive return at date t. This is clearly an arbitrage if the returns are not all degenerate. Assumption 6.2.2 eliminates such possibilities and is equivalent to ruling out look-ahead bias in the construction of portfolio weights.

Given these assumptions, we have the following general decomposition for a portfolio's expected returns.

Proposition 6.2.1. *Under Assumptions 6.2.1–6.2.2, the expected return of any portfolio P satisfies the following decomposition:*

$$E[R_{pt}] = \sum_{i=1}^{n} E[\omega_{it} R_{it}] = \sum_{i=1}^{n} (\text{Cov}[\omega_{it}, R_{it}] + E[\omega_{it}]E[R_{it}]) \tag{6.8}$$

$$= \sum_{i=1}^{n} \text{Cov}[\omega_{it}, R_{it}] + \sum_{i=1}^{n} E[\omega_{it}]E[R_{it}] \equiv \delta_p + \nu_p, \tag{6.9}$$

$$\text{where} \quad \delta_p \equiv \sum_{i=1}^{n} \text{Cov}[\omega_{it}, R_{it}] \quad \text{(active component)},$$

$$\nu_p \equiv \sum_{i=1}^{n} E[\omega_{it}]E[R_{it}] \quad \text{(passive component)},$$

$$\theta_p \equiv \frac{\delta_p}{\delta_p + \nu_p} \quad \text{(active ratio)}. \tag{6.10}$$

Proposition 6.2.1 is a simple decomposition of a portfolio's expected return into two components: the sum of the covariances between portfolio weights and returns and the sum of the products of expected portfolio weights and expected returns.

Although this active/passive decomposition follows trivially from the definition of covariance, it has some surprisingly useful implications for identifying the relative contributions of active and passive investment management.

The motivation for attributing the covariance terms δ_p in (6.10) to active management is that, by definition, active implies a conscious decision on the part of the portfolio manager to buy, sell, or avoid a security—summarized in the portfolio weights $\{\omega_{it}\}$—and the impact of these decisions on a portfolio's total expected return $E[R_{pt}]$ is captured by the covariances in (6.10). In particular, if a manager has positive weights when security returns are positive and negative weights when security returns are negative, on average, this implies positive covariances between portfolio weights and returns and has a positive impact on the portfolio's expected return. In effect, the covariance term captures the manager's timing ability, asset by asset, and while perfect timing of the sort described in (6.7) is not possible, imperfect timing certainly is (see Grinblatt and Titman, 1989, 1993 for further discussion).

However, there is another source of positive expected return that has nothing to do with asset timing: The manager may be holding passive long positions in securities with positive expected returns and passive short positions in securities with negative expected returns. For example, buy-and-hold investors in the S&P 500 should expect a positive expected return over time because of the equity risk premium. This passive source of expected return is captured by the second term ν_p in (6.10), which has no timing component whatsoever but involves only the first moments of the marginal distributions of returns and weights. Similarly, a dedicated short-seller whose sole investment mandate is to identify and short overvalued companies faces a significant challenge from the negative equity risk premium implicit in any passive short equity position.

The distinction between timing and risk premia is more obvious from a slightly modified version of (6.10):

$$E[R_{pt}] = \sum_{i=1}^{n} \sigma(\omega_{it})\sigma(R_{it})\mathrm{Corr}[\omega_{it}, R_{it}] + \sum_{i=1}^{n} E[\omega_{it}]E[R_{it}]. \tag{6.11}$$

If the portfolio weights $\{\omega_{it}\}$ are constant through time, it is difficult to argue that such a portfolio is being actively managed, and (6.11) supports this intuition: A constant portfolio implies zero variance for the portfolio weights, which implies no active component according to (6.11). Nevertheless, constant portfolios can still generate positive expected returns simply by holding securities with positive expected returns as captured by the passive component. But (6.11) shows that the larger the correlation between weights and returns and the larger the variances of returns and weights, the bigger the contribution from active management.

Alternatively, (6.11) implies that a negative correlation between weights and returns detracts from a portfolio's expected return, and higher return- and weight-volatility make this worse. This suggests one possible approach to improving the active component of a portfolio strategy: decreasing (increasing) the volatility of weights for those securities where the correlations between weights and returns are negative (positive).

The quantity θ_p defined in (6.10)—which we call the *active ratio*—provides a useful summary statistic for the degree to which a portfolio is actively managed. Unlike the traditional static measures of active performance such as the Sharpe and the information ratios (Section 6.1), θ_p is dynamic, unit-free, and independent of the choice of benchmark. The dynamic nature of θ_p is clear from the decomposition (6.11)—the time-series properties of returns affect θ_p directly, in contrast to static performance measures. The fact that θ_p is unit-free is obvious from a simple dimensional analysis of this ratio: Both the numerator and denominator are defined as returns per unit time; hence the ratio is invariant to any unit of measurement. In other words, if θ_p is estimated to be 28%, then this is the fraction of the portfolio's return due to active management irrespective of whether we estimate θ_p with daily, weekly, or monthly data. Contrast this with the information ratio—if an investment has an information ratio of 0.28, it matters a great deal whether this is a daily, monthly, or annual estimate. Finally, θ_p requires no benchmark for its definition, although it is certainly trivial to compute θ_p relative to a benchmark by simply applying (6.10) to the excess returns of a portfolio. However, one of the most important implications of (6.10) is that active investment management is not simply adding value in excess of a passive benchmark, which can be done passively by taking on nonbenchmark factor exposures in a multifactor world. We shall return to this issue in Section 6.2 when we impose a linear factor structure on asset returns.

A New Definition of Passive Investing

The AP decomposition (6.10) implies that constant portfolios have no active component. But what about portfolios with time-varying weights that are traditionally considered passive? For example, a value-weighted portfolio of all securities is clearly a passive portfolio, yet the portfolio weights change according to the market values of the component securities; hence $\sigma(\omega_{it})$ is generally positive for all securities in this case. Does this portfolio's expected return have a nonzero active component?

The answer is no, as long as the individual securities' returns are serially independent, i.e., as long as the Random Walk Hypothesis holds for all securities. To see why, let P_{it} and S_{it} denote the price and shares outstanding of asset i at date t, respectively, and observe that the value-weighted portfolio is given by

$$\omega_{it} = \frac{P_{it-1}S_{it-1}}{\sum_{j=1}^{n} P_{jt-1}S_{jt-1}} = \frac{P_{it-2}(1 + R_{it-1})S_{it-1}}{\sum_{j=1}^{n} P_{jt-2}(1 + R_{jt-1})S_{jt-1}}, \qquad (6.12)$$

which depends on returns at date $t - 1$. If returns are serially independent, then the correlations $\mathrm{Corr}[\omega_{it}, R_{it}]$ are all zero, hence the active component in (6.11) is zero despite the fact that the volatilities of the weights are nonzero.

If, on the other hand, returns are not serially independent, then it is possible for the AP decomposition to yield a nonzero active component to a buy-and-hold portfolio. This is a sensible outcome because the presence of serial correlation implies that past returns do contain forecast power for future returns; hence a portfolio strategy with weights that change as a function of past returns may benefit from (or be hurt by) such serial correlation.

This suggests a broader but more precise definition for a passive portfolio.

Definition 6.2.1. *A passive portfolio is any portfolio with weights ω_{it} that are uncorrelated with its corresponding returns R_{it} for all $i = 1, \ldots, n$.* [7]

Under this definition, a portfolio is passive if its weights do not contain any information related to future returns. Whether or not the portfolio is benchmarked is irrelevant. For example, consider a portfolio with a market beta of 1.00, achieved through S&P 500 futures contracts, that also happens to include a diversified buy-and-hold basket of commodities.[8] The expected return of such a portfolio is likely to exceed the S&P 500 because of the positive risk premium associated with the commodities component, but should the excess return be attributed to active management? With traditional performance measures, this portfolio is likely to exhibit positive alpha, but the AP decomposition will yield a very different conclusion.

The crucial characteristic of an active portfolio is the deliberate and successful use of information for forecasting returns—this is usually what we have in mind when we speak of investment skill. In the next section, we sharpen the distinction between alpha and other sources of expected return by assuming a linear factor structure for individual asset returns.

Alpha Versus Beta

To distinguish explicitly between alpha and beta, we have to impose additional structure on the return-generating processes for individual assets.

Assumption 6.2.3. *For each asset i, the return R_{it} satisfies a linear K-factor model:*[9]

$$R_{it} = \alpha_i + \beta_{i1}F_{1t} + \cdots + \beta_{iK}F_{Kt} + \epsilon_{it}, \tag{6.13}$$

$$0 = E[\epsilon_{it}|F_{1t}, \ldots, F_{Kt}], \tag{6.14}$$

where the factors F_{kt} are stationary and ergodic stochastic processes.

---

[7] We define constant-weight portfolios to be uncorrelated with returns since their covariances with returns are zero, even though in this case the correlation coefficient is undefined because the variance of the portfolio weight is zero.

[8] Commodities have historically exhibited very little correlation to the S&P 500, hence including a buy-and-hold portfolio of commodities is unlikely to affect the overall market beta of the portfolio.

[9] For notational simplicity, we omit the riskless rate R_f from this specification, but without any loss in generality, some readers may prefer to interpret both the asset return R_{it} and the factor returns F_{kt} as excess returns, in excess of R_f.

Although the linear K-factor structure is presented as an assumption, several authors have derived theories to support such a specification, including Merton's (1973) Intertemporal Capital Asset Pricing Model, Ross's (1976) Arbitrage Pricing Theory, and Lo and Wang's (2006) dynamic equilibrium model of returns and trading volume. However, in Assumption 6.2.3 we leave room for the presence of an intercept α_i, which most other equilibrium asset-pricing models rule out because the presence of nonzero α_i may create arbitrage opportunities.[10] Since the AP decomposition is considerably more general than any particular asset-pricing model or linear factor structure, for our purposes we remain agnostic about whether or not α_i is zero for all assets and merely leave it as a possibility within our framework.

Under Assumption 6.2.3, the return R_{pt} of an arbitrary portfolio of assets may be written as

$$R_{pt} = \sum_{i=1}^{n} \omega_{it} R_{it} \tag{6.15a}$$

$$= \sum_{i=1}^{n} \omega_{it} \alpha_i + \left(\sum_{i=1}^{n} \omega_{it} \beta_{i1} \right) F_{1t}$$

$$+ \cdots + \left(\sum_{i=1}^{n} \omega_{it} \beta_{iK} \right) F_{Kt} + \sum_{i=1}^{n} \omega_{it} \epsilon_{it} \tag{6.15b}$$

$$= \alpha_{pt} + \sum_{k=1}^{K} \beta_{pk,t} F_{kt} + \epsilon_{pt}, \tag{6.15c}$$

$$\text{where } \beta_{pk,t} \equiv \sum_{i=1}^{n} \omega_{it} \beta_{ik}, \quad \alpha_{pt} \equiv \sum_{i=1}^{n} \omega_{it} \alpha_i. \tag{6.15d}$$

Armed with this return decomposition, the corresponding AP decomposition for expected returns follows immediately.

Proposition 6.2.2. *Under Assumptions 6.2.1–6.2.3, the expected return of any portfolio P satisfies the following decomposition:*

$$\mathrm{E}[R_{pt}] = \sum_{i=1}^{n} \alpha_i \mathrm{E}[\omega_{it}] + \sum_{k=1}^{K} \mathrm{Cov}[\beta_{pk,t}, F_{kt}] + \sum_{k=1}^{K} \mathrm{E}[\beta_{pk,t}] \mathrm{E}[F_{kt}] \tag{6.16}$$

$$= \text{security selection} + \text{factor timing} + \text{risk premia},$$

---

[10] In particular, if the magnitudes of α_i are too large or there are too many assets with nonzero α_i, then it may be possible to construct a portfolio that has no factor risks and no idiosyncratic risk but a nonzero intercept, which implies arbitrage.

where

$$\text{security selection} \equiv \sum_{i=1}^{n} \alpha_i E[\omega_{it}], \tag{6.17a}$$

$$\text{Factor timing} \equiv \sum_{k=1}^{K} \text{Cov}[\beta_{pk,t}, F_{kt}], \tag{6.17b}$$

$$\text{Risk premia} \equiv \sum_{k=1}^{K} E[\beta_{pk,t}]E[F_{kt}], \tag{6.17c}$$

and

$$E[\beta_{pk,t}] = \sum_{i=1}^{n} \beta_{ik}E[\omega_{it}], \quad k = 1, \ldots, K, \tag{6.18a}$$

$$\text{Cov}[\beta_{pk,t}, F_{kt}] = \sum_{i=1}^{n} \beta_{ik}\text{Cov}[\omega_{it}, F_{kt}], \quad k = 1, \ldots, K. \tag{6.18b}$$

Proposition 6.2.2 provides a more refined decomposition than Proposition 6.2.1, thanks to the linear K-factor structure assumed in Assumption 6.2.3. Expected returns are now the sum of three components: a security-selection component (6.17a) that depends on the α_i's, a factor-timing component (6.17b) that depends on the covariance between the portfolio betas and factors, and a risk-premia component (6.17c) that represents the expected return from passive exposures to factor risks. The first two components can be viewed as active sources of expected return, with the third being the passive component as in Proposition 6.2.1.

This factor-based AP decomposition clarifies several issues surrounding the measurement of active management. The first is the well-known implication of any multifactor model that expected returns in excess of a benchmark need not be due to investment acumen but may simply be passive exposures to nonmarket risk factors (see, for example, Merton, 1973, and Ross, 1976). For example, if a portfolio with unit market beta has a passive credit factor beta of 0.5 (in other words, there is no time variation in this beta), then (6.17c) shows that this portfolio will yield half the risk premium of the credit factor in addition to the equity risk premium. Such an outperformance can be achieved purely through passive means.

A second issue that Proposition 6.2.2 resolves is the historical disparity between the expected returns of long-only investments and hedge funds. Some have argued that the distinction is due to the outsize rewards from hedge fund fee structures, which tend to draw the most talented portfolio managers from the long-only world along with their alpha sources. Whether or not this exodus of talent from mutual funds to hedge funds is real is debatable, but (6.16) provides another explanation that is at least as compelling: The long-only constraint is a severe handicap from the perspective of expected returns because it hampers a portfolio manager's ability to engage in factor timing. By allowing weights to be negative, a hedge fund manager can create negative factor betas for his portfolio, which will yield positive expected returns if the corresponding factor risk premia are negative. Long-only managers cannot do this easily if factor betas are largely positive; hence one source of positive expected return is unavailable to them. Therefore, we should not expect long-only managers to be able to generate the level of expected returns that unconstrained managers can produce.

A third issue on which Proposition 6.2.2 sheds significant light is the recent concern of many institutional investors that they are paying hedge funds for alpha but are getting beta instead. Proposition 6.2.2 shows how to assess the value-added of hedge funds that make directional bets: Check the covariances of their portfolio betas with the factors. If hedge funds possess factor-timing ability or "allocation alpha" (Leibowitz, 2005a,b), this should be viewed as legitimate alpha or active management. But if the beta exposures are being generated passively, i.e., not with covariances (6.17b) but with relatively stable weights in (6.17c), then there are cheaper alternatives such as the "beta grazers" in Leibowitz (2005a,b), the "swing assets" in Leibowitz and Bova (2005), or the futures-based hedge fund beta replication strategies described in Hasanhodzic and Lo (2006). This suggests the following definition of passive investing in the context of a linear K-factor model.

Definition 6.2.2. *A portfolio is said to have passive factor exposure to factor k if its portfolio beta $\beta_{pk,t}$ is uncorrelated with the factor F_{kt}.*

Note that Definition 6.2.2 leaves open the possibility that a portfolio is passive with respect to one factor but active with respect to another. This is particularly important for the hedge fund industry, which is extraordinarily heterogeneous and where highly specialized investment expertise can and should thrive.

Of course, passive beta exposures to nontraditional betas such as credit, liquidity, volatility, and yield-curve twists may be more difficult to generate and manage for a typical pension plan sponsor than S&P 500 beta, in which case higher management fees may be justifiable. But unless the manager is providing some form of active management—unique sources of α_i's or factor-timing ability— there should be downward pressure on the corresponding management fees, and incentive fees certainly cannot be justified.

One final insight provided by Proposition 6.2.2 is that investment expertise can manifest itself in two distinct formats: identifying untapped sources of expected return (the α_i's) and creating additional expected return through factor timing (the time-varying $\beta_{pk,t}$'s). Even if all the α_i's are zero, as some academic studies claim, there can still be substantial value-added from active management as long as risk premia vary over time and as functions of market conditions.

6.3 Some Analytical Examples

In this section we provide three examples of AP decomposition where active and passive components can be evaluated analytically. Section 6.3 contains a simple numerical example that highlights the basic computations involved in the decomposition. In Section 6.3, we consider mean-reversion and momentum strategies, and in Section 6.3 we provide an analysis of a stop-loss strategy.

A Numerical Example

Consider a portfolio of two assets, one yielding a monthly return that alternates between 1% and 2% (Asset 1) and the other yielding a fixed monthly return of 0.15% (Asset 2). Let the weights of this portfolio, called A1, be given by 75% in Asset 1 and 25% in Asset 2. The chart and table in Figure 6.1 illustrate the dynamics of this portfolio over a 12-month period, where the expected return of the portfolio is 1.16% per month, none of which is due to the active component. Therefore $\theta_p = 0\%$ in this case.

Now consider portfolio A2, which differs from A1 only in that the portfolio weight for Asset 1 alternates between 50% and 100% as asset 1's return alternates between 1% and 2% (see the chart in Figure 6.2). In this case, the total expected return is 1.29% per month, of which 0.13% is due to the positive correlation between the portfolio weight for Asset 1 and its return. This yields an active ratio θ_p of 9.71%. Note that this ratio does not depend on the sampling interval of the returns, in contrast to the 1.29% and 0.13%, both of which are monthly returns.

Finally, consider a third portfolio A3 which also has alternating weights for Asset 1 but in the direction exactly opposite Asset 1's returns: When the return is 1%, the portfolio weight is 100%, and when the return is 2%, the portfolio weight is 50%. This is obviously counterproductive, and Figure 6.3 confirms this intuition. Portfolio A3 loses 0.13% per month from its active component, and its active ratio $\theta_p = -12.05\%$.

Note that in all three cases the passive components are identical at 1.16% per month because the average weight for each asset is the same across all three portfolios. The only differences among A1, A2, and A3 are the dynamics of the portfolio weights, and these differences give rise to different values for the active component δ_p and the active ratio θ_p.

Mean Reversion and Momentum Strategies

Consider a simple asset-allocation example where one asset is the risk-free asset that yields R_f and the other is a risky asset with return R_t that satisfies a stationary

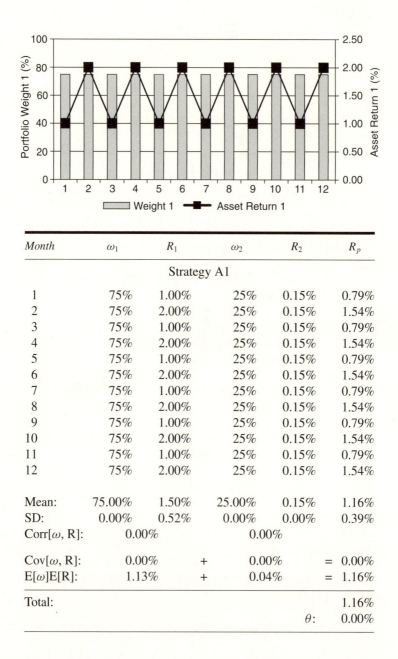

Month	ω_1	R_1	ω_2	R_2	R_p
			Strategy A1		
1	75%	1.00%	25%	0.15%	0.79%
2	75%	2.00%	25%	0.15%	1.54%
3	75%	1.00%	25%	0.15%	0.79%
4	75%	2.00%	25%	0.15%	1.54%
5	75%	1.00%	25%	0.15%	0.79%
6	75%	2.00%	25%	0.15%	1.54%
7	75%	1.00%	25%	0.15%	0.79%
8	75%	2.00%	25%	0.15%	1.54%
9	75%	1.00%	25%	0.15%	0.79%
10	75%	2.00%	25%	0.15%	1.54%
11	75%	1.00%	25%	0.15%	0.79%
12	75%	2.00%	25%	0.15%	1.54%
Mean:	75.00%	1.50%	25.00%	0.15%	1.16%
SD:	0.00%	0.52%	0.00%	0.00%	0.39%
Corr[ω, R]:	0.00%		0.00%		
Cov[ω, R]:	0.00%	+	0.00%	=	0.00%
E[ω]E[R]:	1.13%	+	0.04%	=	1.16%
Total:					1.16%
				θ:	0.00%

Figure 6.1. *The expected return of a constant portfolio does not contain any active component.*

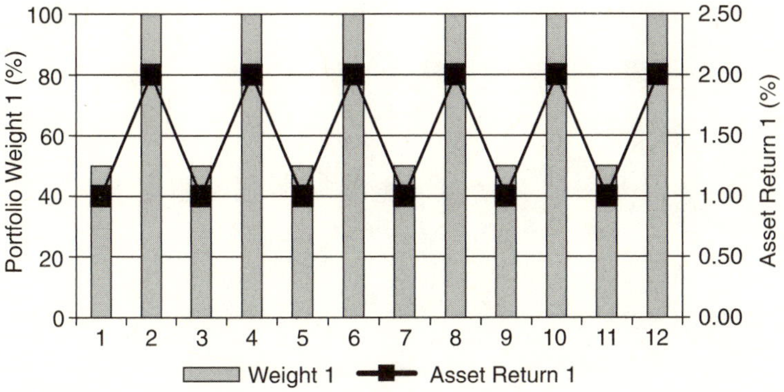

Month	ω_1	R_1	ω_2	R_2	R_p
			Strategy A2		
1	50%	1.00%	50%	0.15%	0.58%
2	100%	2.00%	0%	0.15%	2.00%
3	50%	1.00%	50%	0.15%	0.58%
4	100%	2.00%	0%	0.15%	2.00%
5	50%	1.00%	50%	0.15%	0.58%
6	100%	2.00%	0%	0.15%	2.00%
7	50%	1.00%	50%	0.15%	0.58%
8	100%	2.00%	0%	0.15%	2.00%
9	50%	1.00%	50%	0.15%	0.58%
10	100%	2.00%	0%	0.15%	2.00%
11	50%	1.00%	50%	0.15%	0.58%
12	100%	2.00%	0%	0.15%	2.00%
Mean:	75.00%	1.50%	25.00%	0.15%	1.29%
SD:	26.11%	0.52%	26.11%	0.00%	0.74%
Corr[ω, R]:	100.00%		0.00%		
Cov[ω, R]:	0.13%	+	0.00%	=	0.13%
E[ω]E[R]:	1.13%	+	0.04%	=	1.16%
Total:					1.29%
				θ:	9.71%

Figure 6.2. *The portfolio weights are positively correlated with returns, which adds value to the portfolio and yields a positive active component.*

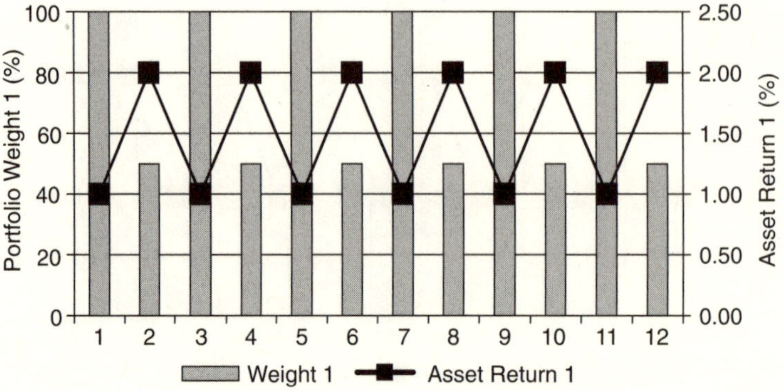

Month	ω_1	R_1	ω_2	R_2	R_p
			Strategy A3		
1	100%	1.00%	0%	0.15%	1.00%
2	50%	2.00%	50%	0.15%	1.08%
3	100%	1.00%	0%	0.15%	1.00%
4	50%	2.00%	50%	0.15%	1.08%
5	100%	1.00%	0%	0.15%	1.00%
6	50%	2.00%	50%	0.15%	1.08%
7	100%	1.00%	0%	0.15%	1.00%
8	50%	2.00%	50%	0.15%	1.08%
9	100%	1.00%	0%	0.15%	1.00%
10	50%	2.00%	50%	0.15%	1.08%
11	100%	1.00%	0%	0.15%	1.00%
12	50%	2.00%	50%	0.15%	1.08%
Mean:	75.00%	1.50%	25.00%	0.15%	1.04%
SD:	26.11%	0.52%	26.11%	0.00%	0.04%
Corr[ω, R]:	-100.00%		0.00%		
Cov[ω, R]:	-0.13%	+	0.00%	=	-0.13%
E[ω]E[R]:	1.13%	+	0.04%	=	1.16%
Total:					1.04%
				θ:	-12.05%

Figure 6.3. *The portfolio weights are negatively correlated with returns, which subtracts value from the portfolio and yields a negative active component.*

autoregressive process with one lag or AR(1):

$$R_t = \mu + \rho(R_{t-1} - \mu) + \epsilon_t, \quad \epsilon_t \text{ IID WN}(0, \sigma_\epsilon^2), \tag{6.19}$$

$$\omega_t = \gamma_1 + \gamma_2 R_{t-1}, \tag{6.20}$$

$$R_{pt} = \omega_t R_t + (1 - \omega_t) R_f. \tag{6.21}$$

The asset-allocation strategy (6.20) is a simple linear function of the last period's return plus a constant and covers two important cases: a mean-reversion strategy ($\gamma_2 < 0$) and a momentum strategy ($\gamma_2 > 0$). The expected return of this strategy can be easily derived as

$$\text{E}[R_{pt}] = \text{Cov}[\omega_t, R_t] + \text{E}[\omega_t]\text{E}[R_t] + (1 - \text{E}[\omega_t]) R_f, \tag{6.22a}$$

$$= \gamma_2 \rho \text{Var}[R_t] + (\gamma_1 + \gamma_2 \mu)\mu + (1 - \gamma_1 - \gamma_2 \mu)R_f. \tag{6.22b}$$

This expression shows that the passive component is a weighted average of the two assets using the expected values of the weights ω_t and $1 - \omega_t$. On the other hand, the active component is a function of γ_2, ρ, and the return variance of the risky asset. These three parameters represent the sum total of the information content in the strategy (6.20). If γ_2 is of the same sign as ρ, then the active component is positive—the strategy is a momentum strategy when returns exhibit momentum ($\rho > 0$) and a mean-reversion strategy when returns exhibit mean reversion ($\rho < 0$). If, on the other hand, γ_2 is of opposite sign to ρ, then the active component will subtract value because the strategy will be exactly out of phase with the risky asset. And as the variance of R_t increases, the active component becomes larger in absolute value, magnifying both positive and negative timing ability.

A Stop-Loss Policy

Suppose that a portfolio manager implements a stop-loss policy on an existing portfolio strategy with return R_t so that if the strategy's return falls below a threshold ζ at date $t - 1$, the entire portfolio will be invested in the risk-free asset at date t, and if the strategy's return is greater than or equal to ζ, the entire portfolio will be invested in the strategy. Assuming that the strategy's return-generating process is an AR(1), we can specify the dynamics R_{pt} of the combined portfolio-plus-stop-loss strategy as

$$R_t = \mu + \rho(R_{t-1} - \mu) + \epsilon_t, \quad \epsilon_t \text{ IID } \mathcal{N}(0, \sigma_\epsilon^2), \tag{6.23}$$

$$\omega_t = \begin{cases} 1 & \text{if } R_{t-1} > \zeta, \\ 0 & \text{if } R_{t-1} \leq \zeta, \end{cases} \tag{6.24}$$

$$R_{pt} = \omega_t R_t + (1 - \omega_t) R_f, \tag{6.25}$$

where we have assumed that ϵ_t is Gaussian so that we can solve for expected returns in a closed form. Under these specifications, the expected return of R_{pt} is given by

$$E[R_{pt}] = \text{Cov}[\omega_t, R_t] + E[\omega_t]E[R_t] + (1 - E[\omega_t])\, R_f$$

$$= \rho\sigma\phi\left(\frac{\alpha - \mu}{\sigma}\right) + \mu\left(1 - \Phi\left(\frac{\alpha - \mu}{\sigma}\right)\right)$$

$$+ R_f\, \Phi\left(\frac{\alpha - \mu}{\sigma}\right). \tag{6.26}$$

The first term in (6.26) is the active component, and the second two terms are the passive component. As long as $\rho > 0$, implying momentum for the risky asset, the active component increases the expected return of the portfolio. This result makes intuitive sense because the stop-loss policy (6.24) activates when past returns fall below ζ, and a lower past return implies lower future returns when $\rho \geq 0$. If, however, $\rho < 0$, then the stop-loss policy (6.24) becomes counterproductive because returns are mean-reverting; hence the time to switch to the riskless asset is after a very large positive return in the most recent past.

Table 6.1 provides a numerical illustration of the AP decomposition for various values of the two parameters ζ and ρ. When $\rho = -25\%$, the active component is negative regardless of the threshold ζ, although higher values of ζ make the active component more costly because more upside is eliminated by the stop-loss policy. When $\rho = 0$, the active component is 0 because returns follow a random walk in this case, and any portfolio strategy based on prior returns will be uncorrelated with current returns. And when ρ is positive, the active component becomes positive as well, and as predicted by (6.26), the larger the threshold and the larger the ρ, the more valuable the stop-loss and the larger the active ratio.

See Kaminski and Lo (2007) for a more detailed analysis of the performance of stop-loss policies.

6.4 Implementing the AP Decomposition

The AP decomposition in Section 6.2 is a simple function of means, variances, and covariances of portfolio weights and returns; hence its implementation is a straightforward exercise in estimating unconditional first and second moments. In fact, in Section 6.4 we show that the properly defined sample moments of portfolio weights and returns are related in exactly the same way as their population counterparts in (6.10); hence the decomposition must hold exactly as an identity when applied to the data. However, there is one subtlety in implementing (6.10)

Table 6.1.
Measures of the Value of a Stop-Loss Policy*

				Annualized			
		$E[R_{pt}]$	Active	Passive	Active (%)	$E[\omega_t]$	$1 - E[\omega_t]$
$\alpha(\%)$	$\rho(\%)$						
−1.0	−25	1.6%	−6.6%	8.1%	−423.1%	62.5%	37.5%
−0.5	−25	1.2%	−6.7%	8.0%	−547.6%	59.1%	40.9%
0.0	−25	0.9%	−6.8%	7.8%	−720.9%	55.7%	44.3%
0.5	−25	0.7%	−6.9%	7.6%	−962.5%	52.3%	47.7%
1.0	−25	0.5%	−6.9%	7.4%	−1,290.0%	48.8%	51.2%
−1.0	0	8.1%	0.0%	8.1%	0.0%	62.5%	37.5%
−0.5	0	8.0%	0.0%	8.0%	0.0%	59.1%	40.9%
0.0	0	7.8%	0.0%	7.8%	0.0%	55.7%	44.3%
0.5	0	7.6%	0.0%	7.6%	0.0%	52.3%	47.7%
1.0	0	7.4%	0.0%	7.4%	0.0%	48.8%	51.2%
−1.0	25	14.7%	6.6%	8.1%	44.7%	62.5%	37.5%
−0.5	25	14.7%	6.7%	8.0%	45.8%	59.1%	40.9%
0.0	25	14.6%	6.8%	7.8%	46.8%	55.7%	44.3%
0.5	25	14.5%	6.9%	7.6%	47.5%	52.3%	47.7%
1.0	25	14.3%	6.9%	7.4%	48.1%	48.8%	51.2%
−1.0	50	21.3%	13.1%	8.1%	61.8%	62.5%	37.5%
−0.5	50	21.4%	13.5%	8.0%	62.8%	59.1%	40.9%
0.0	50	21.5%	13.7%	7.8%	63.7%	55.7%	44.3%
0.5	50	21.4%	13.8%	7.6%	64.4%	52.3%	47.7%
1.0	50	21.3%	13.8%	7.4%	65.0%	48.8%	51.2%

*Data are for a portfolio with monthly returns that follow an AR(1) and monthly parameter values $R_f = 5\%/12$, $E[R_t] = 10\%/12$, and $Var[R_t] = (20\%)^2/12$.

that is not addressed by the population version, namely, selection of the sampling interval, and this is considered in Section 6.4.

Population Versus Sample Moments

Assumptions 6.2.1 and 6.2.2 are generally sufficient to ensure that the usual sample means, variances, and covariances of portfolio weights and returns will be well-behaved estimators for their population values (see, for example, White, 1984). Therefore, implementing the fundamental decomposition (6.10) involves nothing more challenging than estimating first and second moments. Moreover, the fact that sample moments are related to each other in the same way that population moments are related makes the application of (6.10) to the data almost trivial. For example, consider the sample covariance between portfolio weights and returns for asset i:

$$\frac{1}{T}\sum_{t=1}^{T}(\omega_{it}-\overline{\omega}_i)(R_{it}-\overline{R}_i) = \frac{1}{T}\sum_{t=1}^{T}\left(\omega_{it}R_{it}-\overline{\omega}_i R_{it}-\omega_{it}\overline{R}_i+\overline{\omega}_i\overline{R}_i\right) \quad (6.27\text{a})$$

$$= \frac{1}{T}\sum_{t=1}^{T}\omega_{it}R_{it} - \frac{\overline{\omega}_i}{T}\sum_{t=1}^{T}R_{it}$$

$$-\frac{\overline{R}_i}{T}\sum_{t=1}^{T}\omega_{it}+\overline{\omega}_i\overline{R}_i \quad (6.27\text{b})$$

$$= \frac{1}{T}\sum_{t=1}^{T}\omega_{it}R_{it} - \overline{\omega}_i\overline{R}_i. \quad (6.27\text{c})$$

Therefore,

$$\frac{1}{T}\sum_{t=1}^{T}\omega_{it}R_{it} = \frac{1}{T}\sum_{t=1}^{T}(\omega_{it}-\overline{\omega}_i)(R_{it}-\overline{R}_i)+\overline{\omega}_i\overline{R}_i, \quad (6.28)$$

which is the sample-moment counterpart to (6.10) for a single asset i. Repeated applications of (6.27) to the sample average of a portfolio will result in the sample version of (6.10); hence the AP decomposition must also hold in-sample. With properly defined first and second moments, (6.10) is an identity for sample moments as well as for population moments.

However, there is an even simpler approach to estimating the AP decomposition that eliminates the need for second moments altogether, and that is to infer the active component by subtracting the passive component from the total expected return:

$$\delta_p = \mathrm{E}[R_{pt}] - \nu_p. \quad (6.29)$$

Because the right side of (6.29) involves only first moments, the active component δ_p and the active ratio θ_p may be computed solely from the average weights and average returns of the portfolio; hence,

$$\hat{\delta}_p = \frac{1}{T}\sum_{t=1}^{T}R_{pt} - \sum_{i=1}^{n}\overline{\omega}_i\overline{R}_i, \quad (6.30)$$

$$\text{where } \overline{\omega}_i \equiv \frac{1}{T}\sum_{t=1}^{T}\omega_{it}, \quad \overline{R}_i \equiv \frac{1}{T}\sum_{t=1}^{T}R_{it},$$

$$\hat{\theta}_p = \frac{\hat{\delta}_p}{\frac{1}{T}\sum_{t=1}^{T}R_{pt}}. \quad (6.31)$$

In particular, it is not necessary for a manager to provide position-level transparency to give investors a clear sense of the value of his investment process. This is a particularly important characteristic of the fundamental decomposition (6.10) when applied to hedge fund strategies because of the secrecy surrounding such strategies. Few hedge fund managers should balk at divulging average weights and returns, unless of course the manager's average weights do not vary much over time, in which case the investors should reconsider paying hedge fund fees to such a manager.

GMM Estimation

The simplicity of the estimators (6.30) and (6.31) may suggest that statistical inference is not needed, but the issue of assessing the accuracy of these estimators still should be addressed. Fortunately, given Assumptions 6.2.1 and 6.2.2, it is possible to derive the asymptotic distributions of (6.30) and (6.31) under fairly general conditions. These results are summarized in the following proposition (see Appendix A.4 for the proof).

Proposition 6.4.1. *Under Assumptions 6.2.1 and 6.2.2, the active component δ_p and active ratio θ_p of any portfolio P may be estimated consistently by their sample counterparts (6.30) and (6.31), and both estimators are asymptotically normal with variances that may be consistently estimated via the generalized method of moments.*

The Sampling Interval

One important practical issue surrounding implementation of the AP decomposition is the choice of sampling interval for weights and returns. This obviously does not affect the population version of the decomposition but is of critical importance in practical applications. However, even for the population version, the relevance of the sampling interval can be understood in the context of time aggregation. Consider a portfolio strategy in which the weights $\{\omega_{it}(\mathbf{X}_{t-1})\}$ vary each period but we observe portfolio weights and returns only every q periods. If we now apply the AP decomposition to this subset of weights and returns, would we arrive at the same values for δ_p and ν_p appropriately scaled? The answer is no. To see why, we must first define the precise set of observables at each q-period interval and then ask whether these observables satisfy the same relation (6.10) as their one-period counterparts.

First, consider aggregating the portfolio return R_{pt} over q periods and ignore the effects of compounding for simplicity:

$$R_{pt} = \sum_{i=1}^{n} \omega_{it} R_{it}, \tag{6.32}$$

$$R_{p\tau}(q) = \sum_{t=(\tau-1)q+1}^{\tau q} R_{pt} = \sum_{t=(\tau-1)q+1}^{\tau q} \sum_{i=1}^{n} \omega_{it} R_{it} \tag{6.33}$$

$$= \sum_{i=1}^{n} \sum_{t=(\tau-1)q+1}^{\tau q} \omega_{it} R_{it}. \tag{6.34}$$

Then the expected value of the q-period portfolio return is given by

$$E[R_{p\tau}(q)] = \sum_{i=1}^{n} \sum_{t=(\tau-1)q+1}^{\tau q} E[\omega_{it} R_{it}] \tag{6.35}$$

$$= \sum_{i=1}^{n} q\, E[\omega_{it} R_{it}] \quad \text{(from stationarity)} \tag{6.36}$$

$$= \sum_{i=1}^{n} q\, \text{Cov}[\omega_{it}, R_{it}] + \sum_{i=1}^{n} q\, E[\omega_{it}]E[R_{it}]. \tag{6.37}$$

The equality (6.37) shows that (6.9) aggregates linearly over time, so that the q-period expected return of a portfolio is equal to the sum of q times the active component and q times the passive component.

However, the question we started with is whether (6.9) remains the same with q-period inputs, and (6.37) has q-period returns only on the left side. To address our original problem, let us rewrite the right side of (6.33) with q-period variables as well:

$$R_{p\tau}(q) = \sum_{i=1}^{n} \sum_{t=(\tau-1)q+1}^{\tau q} \omega_{it} \frac{R_{it}}{R_{i\tau}(q)} R_{i\tau}(q) \tag{6.38}$$

$$= \sum_{i=1}^{n} \omega_{i\tau}(q)\, R_{i\tau}(q),$$

$$\text{where } \omega_{i\tau}(q) \equiv \sum_{t=(\tau-1)q+1}^{\tau q} \omega_{it} \frac{R_{it}}{R_{i\tau}(q)}. \tag{6.39}$$

In (6.39) the q-period portfolio return $R_{p\tau}(q)$ is shown to be equal to the product of q-period asset returns $R_{i\tau}(q)$ and q-period weights $\omega_{i\tau}(q)$, however, note that these weights are not simply averages of ω_{it} over q periods but are return-weighted averages. In fact, the only set of q-period portfolio weights that, when multiplied by q-period asset returns yield the same q-period portfolio return as the time-aggregated portfolio return $R_{p\tau}(q)$ is the return-weighted average defined in (6.39).

Now we are prepared to answer the question we first posed regarding the effect of time aggregation on (6.9). Suppose we apply the decomposition to q-period weights and returns—will we arrive at a scaled version of the one-period decomposition? The q-period version is given by

$$E[R_{p\tau}(q)] = \sum_{i=1}^{n} E[\omega_{i\tau}(q) \, R_{i\tau}(q)] \tag{6.40}$$

$$= \sum_{i=1}^{n} \mathrm{Cov}[\omega_{i\tau}(q), R_{i\tau}(q)] + \sum_{i=1}^{n} E[\omega_{i\tau}(q)]E[R_{i\tau}(q)], \tag{6.41}$$

and from (6.41) it is easy to see that the q-period version does not reduce to q times the one-period version as in (6.39). In particular, the covariances of q-period weights and returns involve complex cross-products of one-period weights and returns within the q-period interval, and even the expected values of q-period weights involve comoments between weights and returns across the interval. In fact, much of the complexity of (6.41) is an artefact of the time aggregation and has little to do with the underlying investment process.

For this reason, it is critical that the sampling interval be at least as fine as the finest decision interval of the investment process (Figures 6.4a and 6.4b). If portfolio decisions are made on a weekly basis, then (6.10) must be implemented with data sampled at least once a week. If, on the other hand, the strategy employs daily information, then weekly data will not suffice (Figure 6.4c).

Sampling more finely than for the finest decision interval is always acceptable because an unchanged portfolio weight may always be viewed as an active decision to maintain a position, i.e., "let it ride." Although Warren Buffett changes his portfolio weights rather slowly over time, this is quite deliberate and not due to lethargy or inertia. However, one useful implication of this longer decision interval is that we are unlikely to be misled by applying our decomposition to the monthly returns and weights of his portfolio, whereas the same cannot be said for the legendary day trader Steven Cohen of SAC Capital.

Moreover, random shifts in portfolio weights in between decision intervals may add noise to the estimates (6.30) and (6.31) but do not affect the consistency of the estimators since, by definition, the noise is independent of returns (if they are correlated with returns, then they are considered part of the information in

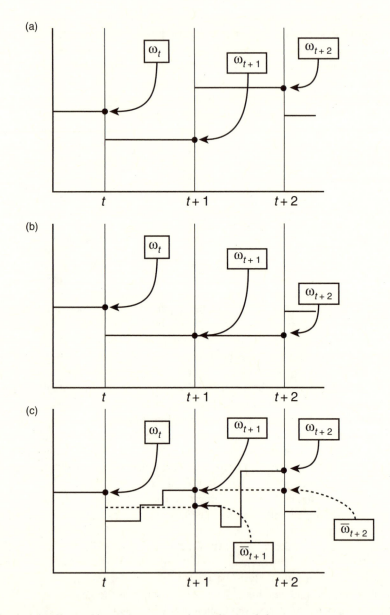

Figure 6.4. *All possible configurations of sampling and decision intervals. (a) matched sampling and decision intervals, (b) more frequent sampling intervals, (c) less frequent sampling intervals.*

portfolio weights and count toward the active component). Therefore, more finely sampled data are always preferred, but at a minimum the data must be sampled at least as finely as the investment decision interval, otherwise the AP decomposition may not accurately reflect the true active and passive contributions of the manager.

6.5 An Empirical Application

To develop a better understanding of the characteristics of the AP decomposition, we apply our framework to a specific market neutral equity trading strategy that, by construction, is particularly dynamic. The strategy, first proposed by Lo and MacKinlay (1990c), is an example of a *statistical arbitrage* program consisting of buying losers and selling winners in proportion to their under- or overperformance relative to the cross-section mean. Specifically, let

$$\omega_{it} = -\frac{1}{n}(R_{it-1} - \overline{R}_{t-1}), \quad \overline{R}_{t-1} \equiv \frac{1}{n}\sum_{i=1}^{n} R_{it-1}, \quad (6.42)$$

which implies that the weights sum to 0 at each date t; hence these are arbitrage portfolios. The fact that these weights are so directly tied to returns implies very active trading, and the fact that the weights sum to 0 implies very little market beta exposure. These two implications suggest that much of this portfolio's return is due to active management and that θ should be quite large.

Trading NASDAQ Size Deciles

We apply this strategy to the daily returns of the five smallest size-decile portfolios of all NASDAQ stocks, as constructed by the University of Chicago's Center for Research in Security Prices (CRSP) from January 2, 1990, to December 29, 1995.[11] Table 6.2 reports the cross-autocorrelations of these five decile returns, and the lead/lag pattern that emerges from this table—the fact that larger-decile returns today are more highly correlated with smaller-decile returns tomorrow than smaller-decile returns today are with larger-decile returns tomorrow— underscores the likely profitability of the contrarian strategy (6.42). Of course, trading NASDAQ size deciles is obviously unrealistic in practice, but our purpose is to illustrate the performance of the expected-return decomposition (6.10), not to derive an implementable trading strategy.

Figure 6.5 illustrates the remarkable performance of the contrarian strategy (6.42) over the 1990–1995 sample period, and Table 6.3 contains summary

[11] We selected this time period purposely because of the emergence of day-trading in the early 1990s, an important source of profitability for statistical arbitrage strategies.

Table 6.2.

First-Order Cross-Autocorrelation Matrix of the Daily Returns of the Five Smallest
CRSP-NASDAQ Size Deciles (January 2, 1990, to December 29, 1995)*

	R_{1t+1} (%)	R_{2t+1} (%)	R_{3t+1} (%)	R_{4t+1} (%)	R_{5t+1} (%)
R_{1t}	10.0	21.5	15.8	18.1	16.7
R_{2t}	23.4	15.4	20.2	19.7	15.8
R_{3t}	26.2	25.0	15.2	23.9	21.6
R_{4t}	25.4	27.0	24.3	18.2	18.7
R_{5t}	25.4	26.6	26.5	26.2	19.4

* Decile 1 is the smallest-capitalization decile.

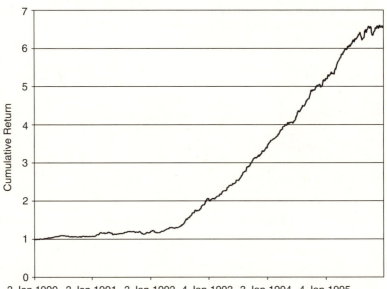

Figure 6.5. *Cumulative return of a daily mean-reversion strategy of Lo and MacKinlay (1990c) applied to the five smallest CRSP-NASDAQ size deciles (January 2, 1990, to December 29, 1995).*

statistics for the daily returns of the five deciles and the strategy. With an annualized average return of 31.4% and a standard deviation of 7.9%, this strategy's performance is considerably better than that of any of the five deciles, which is one indication that active management is playing a significant role in this case.

This intuition is confirmed by the AP decomposition of the strategy's expected return into active and risk-premia components in Table 6.4. On an annualized

Table 6.3.

Summary Statistics for the Daily Returns of the Five Smallest CRSP-NASDAQ Size Deciles and the Daily Returns of a Mean-Reversion Strategy of Lo and MacKinlay (1990c)*

	Decile1	*Decile 2*	*Decile 3*	*Decile 4*	*Decile 5*	R_{pt}
Mean × 250	27.4%	17.5%	14.0%	13.7%	12.8%	31.4%
SD × sqrt(250)	12.2%	9.8%	8.9%	9.1%	9.5%	7.9%
SR × sqrt(250)	2.25	1.78	1.58	1.50	1.35	3.95
Min	−2.9%	−2.7%	−2.7%	−3.3%	−3.5%	−2.2%
Median	0.1%	0.1%	0.1%	0.1%	0.1%	0.1%
Max	6.7%	3.6%	2.0%	2.1%	2.3%	2.4%
Skew	0.6	0.0	−0.5	−0.7	−0.9	−0.1
XSKurt	5.1	2.4	2.1	3.1	3.9	1.7
ρ_1	10.0%	15.4%	15.2%	18.2%	19.4%	4.7%
ρ_2	10.3%	7.7%	10.1%	13.9%	10.5%	0.9%
ρ_3	5.7%	4.2%	7.5%	9.2%	11.0%	7.5%

* This strategy was applied to the decile returns from January 2, 1990, to December 29, 1995. Decile 1 is the smallest-capitalization decile.

basis, the active component yields 32%, which exceeds the strategy's total expected return of 31.4%, implying an active ratio of 101.9% and a slightly negative risk-premia component. In this case, more than all of the strategy's expected return comes from active management, and the risk-premia component subtracts value. The explanation for this rather unusual phenomenon was provided by Lo and MacKinlay (1990c, Section 5.3.1), who observed that because the contrarian strategy holds losers and shorts winners, on average it buys the low-mean assets and shorts the high-mean assets. Therefore, the risk-premia component—which is the sum of average portfolio weights multiplied by average returns—consists of positive average weights for low-mean stocks and negative average weights for high-mean stocks for this strategy. Fortunately, the positive correlation between weights and returns is more than sufficient to compensate for the negative risk premia, as Table 6.4 confirms.

Daily Versus Monthly Transparency

To illustrate the importance of the sampling interval in the measurement of the active ratio, suppose we are given only the following monthly information for this daily strategy: month-end portfolio weights and the monthly returns of each of the five deciles. Table 6.5 shows that the strategy's expected return cannot be correctly computed from this information because much of the return comes from daily bets that are not captured by month-end portfolio weights. The decomposition of the incorrect expected return of −4.0% is reported in the lower panel of Table 6.4

Table 6.4.

GMM Estimates of the Active Ratio θ of the Daily and Monthly Returns of a
Mean-Reversion Strategy of Lo and MacKinlay (1990c)*

	Estimate	*SE*	*t-Stat*
Daily			
Portfolio mean × 250	31.4%	0.3%	91.00
Risk premia × 250	0.6%	3.5%	−0.17
Active component × 250	32.0%	3.5%	9.24
Active ratio	101.9%	0.3%	354.40
Monthly			
Portfolio mean × 12	−4.0%	1.0%	−3.98
Risk premia × 12	0.1%	4.0%	0.03
Active component × 12	−4.1%	4.1%	−1.01
Active ratio	102.6%	11.8%	8.66

* This strategy was applied to the five smallest CRSP-NASDAQ size-decile returns from January 2, 1990, to December 29, 1995. Daily estimates employ a truncation lag of 6 in computation of the Newey–West asymptotic standard errors, and monthly estimates employ a truncation lag of 3.

Table 6.5.

Summary Statistics for the Monthly Returns of the Five Smallest CRSP-NASDAQ
Size Deciles and the Monthly Returns of a Mean-Reversion Strategy of Lo and
MacKinlay (1990c)*

	Decile1	*Decile 2*	*Decile 3*	*Decile 4*	*Decile 5*	R_{pt}
Mean × 12	27.5%	17.4%	13.9%	13.7%	12.8%	−4.0%
SD × sqrt(12)	20.6%	17.7%	15.6%	15.0%	15.9%	8.8%
SR × sqrt(12)	1.34	0.98	0.89	0.91	0.80	−0.45
Min	−8.0%	−11.3%	−9.0%	−9.7%	−11.4%	−6.6%
Median	1.6%	1.0%	1.2%	1.0%	1.5%	−0.5%
Max	26.4%	21.5%	18.1%	16.8%	16.2%	9.7%
Skew	1.2	0.9	0.7	0.5	0.1	1.2
XSKurt	3.3	3.0	2.1	2.0	1.2	4.7
ρ_1	36.4%	43.7%	43.2%	41.4%	45.0%	8.2%
ρ_2	17.3%	16.6%	18.9%	10.1%	13.7%	15.7%
ρ_3	−5.6%	−2.7%	−3.1%	−7.8%	−7.0%	−3.2%

* This strategy was applied to the decile returns from January 1990 to December 1995. Decile 1 is the smallest-capitalization decile.

and also has no bearing on the daily strategy—the estimates imply that the active component yields −4.1%, which is clearly false. By observing only month-end weights and cumulative returns, we have no way of inferring the profitability of decisions made at a daily frequency.

6.6 Summary and Extensions

The investment management industry has developed a series of measures to gauge the performance of portfolio managers. Most of these measures are based on characteristics of the marginal distributions of asset and portfolio returns at a single point in time. Also, the typical statistical procedures used to estimate these characteristics implicitly assume that the data are independently and identically distributed, which eliminates any possibility of dynamic effects such as intertemporal correlations and forecast power.

In contrast to these static measures, the AP decomposition and active ratio— which are based on the definition of covariance—are multipoint statistics that capture the very essence of active management: time-series predictability. A successful portfolio manager is one whose decisions are more often right than wrong, but right and wrong have specific meanings in this context: positive correlation between portfolio weights and returns. Given that portfolio weights are functions of a manager's prior and proprietary information, positive correlation between weights and returns is a clear indication of forecast power and, consequently, active investment skills.

This definition of active management provides a natural dichotomy between active and passive investing. A passive portfolio has no forecast power and can therefore be implemented more easily than an active portfolio. This is a sensible generalization of the standard definition of a passive portfolio, i.e., a constant mix of liquid benchmarks.

If asset returns are assumed to satisfy a linear multifactor model, the AP decomposition shows that a portfolio's expected returns can be decomposed into three components: deviations from the linear factor model or alpha, positive correlation between portfolio betas and factor realizations or factor timing, and static factor exposures times risk premia. This decomposition provides a clear and simple framework for resolving the question of whether hedge fund investors are paying for alpha and getting beta from their investments. Moreover, the AP decomposition provides one explanation for the historical differences in performance between long-only and long/short portfolios: The long-only restriction severely limits a manager's factor-timing ability, which can be a substantial performance drag during periods where risk premia change sign.

Finally, because the AP decomposition is an identity in any given sample of data, it can be used to conduct detailed performance attributions, factor by factor and asset by asset. By separating the active and passive components of a portfolio, it should be possible to study and improve the performance of both.

7
Hedge Funds and Systemic Risk

The term "systemic risk" is commonly used to describe the possibility of a series of correlated defaults among financial institutions—typically banks—that occurs over a short period of time and is often caused by a single major event. A classic example is a banking panic in which large groups of depositors decide to withdraw their funds simultaneously, creating a run on bank assets that can ultimately lead to multiple bank failures. Banking panics were not uncommon in the United States during the nineteenth and early twentieth centuries, culminating in the 1930–1933 period with an average of 2,000 bank failures per year according to Mishkin (1997), which prompted the Glass–Steagall Act of 1933 and establishment of the Federal Deposit Insurance Corporation (FDIC) in 1934.

Although today banking panics are virtually nonexistent thanks to the FDIC and related central banking policies, systemic risk exposures have taken shape in other forms. In particular, the proliferation of hedge funds in recent years has indelibly altered the risk/reward landscape of financial investments. Unregulated and opaque investment partnerships that engage in a variety of active investment strategies, hedge funds have generally yielded double-digit returns historically but not without commensurate risks, and such risks are currently not widely appreciated or well understood. In particular, we argue that the risk/reward profile for most hedge funds differs in important ways from that for more traditional investments, and such differences may have potentially significant implications for systemic risk. This was underscored by the aftermath of the default of Russian government debt in August 1998, when Long Term Capital Management and many other fixed income hedge funds suffered catastrophic losses over the course of a few weeks, creating significant stress on the global financial system and several major financial institutions, i.e., creating systemic risk.

In this chapter, we consider the impact of hedge funds on systemic risk by examining the unique risk-and-return profiles of hedge funds—at both the individual-fund and the aggregate-industry levels—and proposing some new risk measures for hedge fund investments. Two major themes have emerged from August 1998: the importance of liquidity and leverage and the capriciousness of correlations among instruments and portfolios thought to be uncorrelated. The precise mechanism by which these two sets of issues posed systemic risks in 1998 is now well understood. The higher degree of leverage used by many hedge funds makes them more sensitive to swings in market prices. When adverse change in market prices reduces the market value of their collateral, they must either post additional collateral or face the forced liquidation of large positions over short periods of time, which can lead to widespread financial panic, as in the aftermath of the default of Russian government debt in August 1998. The more illiquid the portfolio, the larger the price impact of a forced liquidation, which erodes the fund's risk capital that much more quickly (see Chapter 10 for a recent case study that may have involved such a liquidation). Now if many funds face the same "death spiral" at a given point in time (i.e., if they become more highly correlated during times of distress) and if those funds are obligors of the a small number of major financial institutions, then a market event like that of August 1998 can cascade quickly into a global financial crisis. This is *systemic risk*.

Therefore, the two main themes of this study are illiquidity exposure and time-varying hedge fund correlations, both of which are intimately related to the dynamic nature of hedge fund investment strategies and their risk exposures. In particular, one of the justifications for the unusually rich fees that hedge funds charge is the fact that highly skilled hedge fund managers are engaged in active portfolio management. It is common wisdom that the most talented managers are first drawn to the hedge fund industry because the absence of regulatory constraints enables them to make the most of their investment acumen. With the freedom to trade as much or as little as they like on any given day, to go long or short any number of securities and with varying degrees of leverage, and to change investment strategies at a moment's notice, hedge fund managers enjoy enormous flexibility and discretion in pursuing investment returns. But dynamic investment strategies imply dynamic risk exposures, and while modern financial economics has much to say about the risk of *static* investments—the market beta is a sufficient statistic in this case—there is currently no single summary measure of the risks of a dynamic investment strategy.[1]

In Section 7.1, we turn to the issue of liquidity—one of the central aspects of systemic risk—and present several measures for gauging illiquidity exposure in hedge funds and other asset classes, which we apply to individual and index data. Since systemic risk is directly related to hedge fund failures, in Section 7.2 we investigate attrition rates of hedge funds in the Lipper TASS database and present a logit analysis that yields estimates of a fund's probability of liquidation as a function of various fund characteristics such as return history, assets under

---

[1] Accordingly, hedge fund track records are often summarized with multiple statistics, e.g., mean, standard deviation, Sharpe ratio, market beta, Sortino ratio, maximum drawdown, and worst month.

management, and recent fund flows. In Section 7.3, we present estimates of statistical regime-switching models for hedge fund indexes that capture certain nonlinearities unique to the hedge fund industry. We conclude in Section 7.4 by discussing the current industry outlook implied by the analytics and empirical results of this study. Our tentative inferences suggest that the hedge fund industry may be heading into a challenging period of lower expected returns and that systemic risk has been increasing steadily over the recent past. To address this growing concern, we put forward a modest proposal to establish a new entity patterned after the U.S. National Transportation Safety Board.

Our preliminary findings must be qualified by the acknowledgment that all of our measures of systemic risk are *indirect* and therefore open to debate and interpretation. The main reason for this less-than-satisfying state of affairs is the fact that hedge funds are currently not required to disclose any information about their risks and returns to the public, so empirical studies of the hedge fund industry are based on only very limited hedge fund data, provided voluntarily to Lipper TASS, which may or may not be representative of the industry as a whole. Even after February 1, 2006, when, in response to the U.S. Securities and Exchange Commission (SEC) Rule 203(b)(3)–2 (which was subsequently struck down by the U.S. Court of Appeals in June 2006) many hedge funds became registered investment advisers, the regular filings of these funds did not include critical information such as a fund's degree of leverage, the liquidity of a fund's portfolio, the identities of the fund's major creditors and obligors, and the specific terms under which the fund's investors have committed their capital. Without this kind of information for the majority of funds in the industry, it is virtually impossible to construct direct measures of systemic risk, even by regulatory authorities like the SEC. However, as the hedge fund industry grows, the number and severity of hedge fund failures will undoubtedly increase as well, eventually moving the industry toward greater transparency.

7.1 Measuring Illiquidity Risk

The different categories of hedge funds described in Section 7.2 suggest that hedge funds are likely to exhibit a heterogeneous array of risk exposures. However, a common theme surrounding systemic risk is credit and liquidity. Although they are separate sources of risk exposure for hedge funds and their investors—one type of risk can exist without the other—liquidity and credit have been inextricably intertwined in the minds of most investors because of the problems encountered in August and September of 1998 by Long Term Capital Management and many other fixed income relative-value hedge funds. Because many hedge funds rely on leverage, the sizes of the positions are often considerably larger than the amount of collateral posted to support these positions. Leverage has the effect of a magnifying glass, expanding small profit opportunities into larger ones but also expanding small losses into larger losses. And when adverse changes in market prices reduce the market value of collateral, credit is withdrawn quickly and the subsequent forced liquidation of large positions over short periods of time can lead to widespread financial panic, as in the aftermath of the default of Russian government debt in August 1998. Along with the many benefits of a truly global financial system is the cost that a financial crisis in one country can have dramatic repercussions in several others, i.e., contagion.

Getmansky, Lo, and Makarov (2004) address these issues in more detail by first examining other explanations of serial correlation in hedge fund returns that are unrelated to illiquidity and smoothing—in particular, time-varying expected returns, time-varying leverage, and incentive fees with high-water marks—and showing that none of them can account for the magnitudes of serial correlation in hedge fund returns (Chapters 1 and 3). They propose a specific econometric model of smoothed returns consistent with both illiquidity exposure and performance smoothing, and they estimate it using the historical returns of individual funds in the Lipper TASS hedge fund database. They find that funds with the most significant amount of smoothing tend to be the more illiquid (e.g., emerging market debt, fixed income arbitrage), and after correcting for the effects of smoothed returns, some of the most successful types of funds tend to have considerably less attractive performance characteristics.

However, for the purpose of developing a more highly aggregated measure to address systemic risk exposure, a simpler approach is to use serial correlation coefficients, as we proposed in Section 1.3 and in Chapter 3. Having established the relevance of serial correlation as a proxy for illiquidity in Chapters 1 and 3, we now turn to the measurement of illiquidity in the context of systemic risk. To that end, let $\rho_{1t,i}$ denote the first-order autocorrelation coefficient in month t for fund i using a rolling window of past returns. Then an aggregate measure of illiquidity ρ_t^* in the hedge fund sector may be obtained by a cross-sectional weighted average of these rolling autocorrelations, where the weights ω_{it} are simply the proportion of assets under management for fund i:

$$\rho_t^* \equiv \sum_{i=1}^{N_t} \omega_{it} \rho_{1t,i}, \tag{7.1}$$

$$\omega_{it} \equiv \frac{\text{AUM}_{it}}{\sum_{j=1}^{N_t} \text{AUM}_{jt}}, \tag{7.2}$$

where N_t is the number of funds in the sample in month t and AUM_{jt} is the assets under management for fund j in month t.

Figure 7.1 plots these weighted correlations from January 1980 to August 2004 using all funds in the Lipper TASS Combined database with at least 36

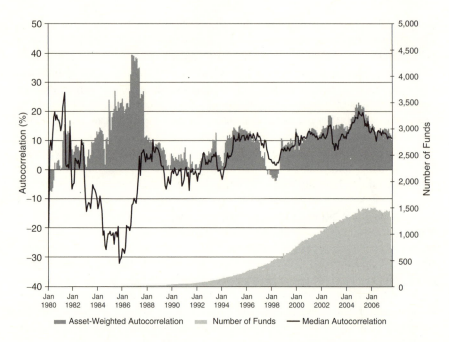

Figure 7.1. *Monthly cross-sectional median and weighted-mean first-order autocorrelation coefficients of individual hedge funds in the Lipper TASS combined hedge fund database with at least 36 consecutive trailing months of returns (January 1980 to August 2007).*

consecutive trailing months of nonmissing returns, along with the number of funds each month (at the bottom, measured by the right vertical axis) and the median correlation in the cross section.[2] The median correlation is quite different from the asset-weighted correlation in the earlier part of the sample, but as the number of funds increases over time, the behavior of the median becomes closer to that of ρ_t^*.

Figure 7.1 also shows considerable swings in ρ_t^* over time, with dynamics that seem to be related to liquidity events. In particular, consider the following events: Between November 1980 and July 1982, the S&P 500 dropped 23.8%; in October 1987, the S&P 500 fell by 21.8%; in 1990, the Japanese "bubble economy" burst; in August 1990, the Persian Gulf War began with Iraq's invasion of Kuwait, ending in January 1991 with Kuwait's liberation by coalition forces; in February 1994, the U.S. Federal Reserve started a tightening cycle that caught many hedge funds by surprise, causing significant dislocation in bond markets

---

[2] The number of funds in the early years is relatively low, reaching a level of 50 or more only in late 1987; therefore the weighted correlations before then may be somewhat less informative.

worldwide; the end of 1994 witnessed the start of the "tequila crisis" in Mexico; in August 1998, Russia defaulted on its government debt; and between August 2000 and September 2002, the S&P 500 fell by 46.3%. In each of these cases, the weighted autocorrelation rose in the aftermath, and in most cases abruptly. Of course, the fact that we are using a 36-month rolling window suggests that as outliers drop out of the window, correlations can shift dramatically. However, as a coarse measure of liquidity in the hedge fund sector, the weighted autocorrelation seems to be intuitively appealing and informative. Figure 7.1 shows that in the most recent past, the weighted autocorrelation is on the rise, implying that hedge funds are taking more illiquidity exposure. This is another indirect indicator of a rise in systemic risk in the hedge fund industry.

7.2 Hedge Fund Liquidations

Since the collapse of LTCM in 1998, it has become clear that hedge fund liquidations can be a significant source of systemic risk. In this section, we consider several measures of liquidation probabilities for hedge funds in the Lipper TASS database, including a review of hedge fund attrition rates documented in Getmansky, Lo, and Mei (2004) (see also Section 2.3) and a logit analysis of hedge fund liquidations in the Lipper TASS Graveyard database. By analyzing the factors driving hedge fund liquidations, we may develop a broader understanding of the likely triggers of systemic risk in this sector.

Because of the voluntary nature of inclusion in the Lipper TASS database, Graveyard funds do not consist solely of liquidations. Lipper TASS gives one of seven distinct reasons for each fund assigned to the Graveyard, ranging from liquidated (status code 1) to uknown (status code 9). It may seem reasonable to confine our attention to those Graveyard funds categorized as liquidated or perhaps to drop funds that are closed to new investment (status code 4) from our sample. However, because our purpose is to develop a broader perspective on the dynamics of the hedge fund industry, we argue that using the entire Graveyard database may be more informative. For example, by eliminating Graveyard funds that are closed to new investors, we create a downward bias in the performance statistics of the remaining funds. Because we do not have detailed information about each of these funds, we cannot easily determine how any particular selection criterion will affect the statistical properties of the remainder. Therefore, we choose to include the entire set of Graveyard funds in our analysis but caution readers to keep in mind the composition of this sample when interpreting our empirical results.

To estimate the influence of various hedge fund characteristics on the likelihood of liquidation, in this section we report the results of a logit analysis of liquidations in the Lipper TASS database. Logit can be viewed as a generalization of the linear regression model to situations where the dependent variable takes on only a

Table 7.1.

Definition of Explanatory Variables in Logit Analysis of Hedge Fund Liquidations in the Lipper TASS Database (January 1994 to August 2004)

Variable	*Definition*
AGE	Current age of the fund (in months)
ASSETS	Natural logarithm of current total assets under management
$ASSETS_{-1}$	Natural logarithm of total assets under management as of December 31 of the previous year
RETURN	Current year-to-date total return
$RETURN_{-1}$	Total return last year
$RETURN_{-2}$	Total return 2 years ago
FLOW	Fund's current year-to-date total dollar inflow divided by previous year's assets under management, where dollar inflow in month τ is defined as $FLOW_\tau \equiv AUM_\tau - AUM_{\tau-1}(1 + R_\tau)$ and AUM_τ is the total assets under management at the beginning of month τ, R_τ is the fund's net return for month τ, and year-to-date total dollar inflow is simply the cumulative sum of monthly inflows since January of the current year
$FLOW_{-1}$	Previous year's total dollar inflow divided by assets under management the year before
$FLOW_{-2}$	Total dollar inflow 2 years ago divided by assets under management the year before

finite number of discrete values (see, for example, Maddala, 1983, for details). To estimate the logit model of liquidation, we use a sample of 4,536 Lipper TASS Live and Graveyard funds from February 1977 to August 2004, of which 1,765 are in the Graveyard database and 2,771 are in the Live database. As discussed in Section 2.2, the Graveyard database was initiated only in January 1994; hence this is the start date of our sample for purposes of estimating the logit model of liquidation. For tractability, we focus on annual observations only, so the dependent variable Z_{it} indicates whether fund i is live or liquidated in year t.[3] Over the sample period from January 1994 to August 2004, we have 23,925 distinct observations for Z_{it}, and after filtering out funds that do not have at least 2 years of history, we are left with 12,895 observations.

Associated with each Z_{it} is the set of explanatory variables listed in Table 7.1. The motivation for AGE, ASSETS, and RETURN are well known—older

[3] Note that a fund cannot "die" more than once; hence liquidation occurs exactly once for each fund i in the Graveyard database. In particular, the time series observations of funds in the Graveyard database is always $\{0, 0, \ldots, 0, 1\}$. This suggests that a more appropriate statistical technique for modeling hedge fund liquidations is survival analysis, which we plan to pursue in a future study. However, for purposes of summarizing the impact of certain explanatory variables on the probability of hedge fund liquidations, logit analysis is a reasonable choice.

funds, funds with greater assets, and funds with better recent performance are all less likely to be liquidated; hence we expect negative coefficients for these explanatory variables (recall that a larger conditional mean for Z^* implies a higher probability that $Z_{it} = 1$ or liquidation). The FLOW variable is motivated by the well-known "return-chasing" phenomenon in which investors flock to funds that have shown good recent performance and leave funds that have underperformed (see, for example, Chevalier and Ellison, 1997; Sirri and Tufano, 1998; and Agarwal, Daniel, and Naik, 2004). Because assets under management is highly persistent—with a correlation of 94.3% between its contemporaneous and lagged values—we include only the lagged variable ASSETS$_{-1}$ in our logit analysis, yielding the following specification which we call Model 1:

$$Z_{it} = G(\beta_0 + \beta_1 \text{AGE}_{it} + \beta_2 \text{ASSETS}_{it-1}$$

$$+ \beta_3 \text{RETURN}_{it} + \beta_4 \text{RETURN}_{it-1} + \beta_5 \text{RETURN}_{it-2}$$

$$+ \beta_6 \text{FLOW}_{it} + \beta_7 \text{FLOW}_{it-1} + \beta_8 \text{FLOW}_{it-2} + \epsilon_{it}). \quad (7.3)$$

Table 7.2 contains maximum-likelihood estimates of (7.3) in the first three columns, with statistically significant parameters in bold. Note that most of the parameter estimates are highly significant. This is because of the unusually large sample size, which typically yields statistically significant estimates because of the small standard errors implied by large samples (recall that the standard errors of consistent and asymptotically normal estimators converge to 0 at a rate of $1/\sqrt{n}$, where n is the sample size). This suggests that we may wish to impose a higher threshold of statistical significance in this case, so as to provide a better balance between Type I and Type II errors.[4]

The negative signs of all the coefficients other than the constant term confirm our intuition that age, assets under management, cumulative return, and fund flows all have a negative impact on the probability of liquidation. The fact that RETURN$_{-2}$ is not statistically significant suggests that the most recent returns have the highest degree of relevance for hedge fund liquidations, a possible indication of the short-term performance-driven nature of the hedge fund industry. The R^2 of this regression is 29.3%, which implies a reasonable level of explanatory power for this simple specification.[5]

To address fixed effects associated with the calendar year and hedge fund style category, in Model 2 we include indicator variables for 10 out of 11 calendar years,

---

[4] See Leamer (1978) for further discussion of this phenomenon, known as "Lindley's Paradox."

[5] This R^2 is the adjusted generalized coefficient of determination proposed by Nagelkerke (1991), which renormalizes Cox and Snell's (1989) R^2 measure by its maximum (which is less than unity) so that it spans the entire unit interval. See Nagelkerke (1991) for further discussion.

Table 7.2.

Maximum Likelihood Estimates of a Logit Model for Hedge Fund Liquidations*

	Model 1			Model 2			Model 3			Model 4			Model 5		
	β	$SE(\beta)$	p-Value (%)	β	$SE(\beta)$	p-Value (%)	β	$SE(\beta)$	p-Value (%)	β	$SE(\beta)$	p-Value (%)	β	$SE(\beta)$	p-Value (%)
Sample Size	12,895			12,895			12,895			12,846			12,310		
R^2 (%)	29.3			34.2			34.2			34.5			35.4		
Constant	4.73	0.34	<0.01	2.31	0.41	<0.01	-5.62	0.18	<0.01	-5.67	0.18	<0.01	-7.04	0.26	<0.01
AGE	-0.03	0.00	<0.01	-0.03	0.00	<0.01	-1.62	0.07	<0.01	-1.66	0.07	<0.01	-2.08	0.10	<0.01
ASSETS$_{-1}$	-0.26	0.02	<0.01	-0.19	0.02	<0.01	-0.34	0.04	<0.01	-0.36	0.04	<0.01	-0.38	0.06	<0.01
RETURN	-2.81	0.19	<0.01	-2.86	0.20	<0.01	-0.67	0.05	<0.01	-0.67	0.05	<0.01	-0.61	0.06	<0.01
RETURN$_{-1}$	-1.39	0.16	<0.01	-1.40	0.17	<0.01	-0.36	0.04	<0.01	-0.36	0.04	<0.01	-0.44	0.06	<0.01
RETURN$_{-2}$	-0.04	0.09	67.5	-0.38	0.14	0.7	-0.12	0.04	0.7	-0.12	0.05	1.1	-0.17	0.07	1.3
FLOW	-0.63	0.08	<0.01	-0.49	0.07	<0.01	-32.72	4.91	<0.01	-33.27	5.04	<0.01	-32.93	6.74	<0.01
FLOW$_{-1}$	-0.13	0.04	0.0	-0.11	0.03	0.1	-7.53	2.33	0.1	-7.60	2.37	0.1	-19.26	4.71	<0.01
FLOW$_{-2}$	-0.09	0.02	<0.01	-0.11	0.02	<0.01	-1.74	0.36	<0.01	-1.64	0.36	<0.01	-1.83	0.51	0.0
I(1994)				0.79	0.38	3.9	0.79	0.38	3.9	0.82	0.39	3.4	1.01	0.54	5.9
I(1995)				1.24	0.27	<0.01	1.24	0.27	<0.01	1.18	0.28	<0.01	1.37	0.37	0.0
I(1996)				1.83	0.20	<0.01	1.83	0.20	<0.01	1.83	0.21	<0.01	1.92	0.28	<0.01
I(1997)				1.53	0.21	<0.01	1.53	0.21	<0.01	1.52	0.21	<0.01	2.03	0.27	<0.01
I(1998)				1.81	0.18	<0.01	1.81	0.18	<0.01	1.80	0.19	<0.01	2.29	0.24	<0.01
I(1999)				2.10	0.18	<0.01	2.10	0.18	<0.01	2.05	0.18	<0.01	2.25	0.24	<0.01
I(2000)				2.25	0.17	<0.01	2.25	0.17	<0.01	2.19	0.17	<0.01	2.08	0.24	<0.01
I(2001)				1.97	0.17	<0.01	1.97	0.17	<0.01	1.96	0.17	<0.01	1.80	0.25	<0.01
I(2002)				1.46	0.16	<0.01	1.46	0.16	<0.01	1.41	0.16	<0.01	1.50	0.22	<0.01
I(2003)				1.55	0.16	<0.01	1.55	0.16	<0.01	1.53	0.16	<0.01	1.71	0.22	<0.01
I(ConvertArb)				0.44	0.20	2.9	0.44	0.20	2.9	0.43	0.20	3.4	0.16	0.34	62.5
I(DedShort)				0.05	0.37	88.9	0.05	0.37	88.9	-0.03	0.39	94.3	0.20	0.49	68.0
I(EmrgMkt)				0.25	0.15	10.2	0.25	0.15	10.2	0.24	0.15	11.7	0.54	0.20	0.7
I(EqMktNeut)				0.12	0.20	54.7	0.12	0.20	54.7	0.15	0.20	46.7	0.53	0.25	3.4
I(EventDr)				0.33	0.15	3.0	0.33	0.15	3.0	0.31	0.15	4.7	-0.01	0.24	97.4
I(FixedInc)				0.50	0.19	1.1	0.50	0.19	1.1	0.45	0.20	2.3	0.33	0.30	26.8
I(GlobMac)				0.32	0.18	7.4	0.32	0.18	7.4	0.24	0.18	20.2	0.33	0.25	17.9
I(LongShortEq)				0.18	0.11	10.2	0.18	0.11	10.2	0.15	0.11	16.6	0.14	0.15	36.4
I(MgFut)				0.49	0.12	<0.01	0.49	0.12	<0.01	0.49	0.13	0.0	0.71	0.16	<0.01
I(MultiStrat)				0.17	0.25	49.4	0.17	0.25	49.4	0.18	0.25	48.5	0.85	0.29	0.3

* Based on annual observations of liquidation status from the Lipper TASS database for the sample period January 1994 to August 2004. The dependent variable Z takes on the value 1 in the year a hedge fund is liquidated and is 0 in all prior years.

and 10 out of 11 hedge fund categories, yielding the following specification:

$$Z_{it} = G\left(\beta_0 + \sum_{k=1}^{10} \zeta_k I(YEAR_{k,i,t}) + \sum_{k=1}^{10} \xi_k I(CAT_{k,i,t}) \right.$$

$$+ \beta_1 AGE_{it} + \beta_2 ASSETS_{it-1} + \beta_3 RETURN_{it}$$

$$+ \beta_4 RETURN_{it-1} + \beta_5 RETURN_{it-2} + \beta_6 FLOW_{it}$$

$$\left. + \beta_7 FLOW_{it-1} + \beta_8 FLOW_{it-2} + \epsilon_{it} \right), \tag{7.4}$$

where

$$I(YEAR_{k,i,t}) \equiv \begin{cases} 1 & \text{if } t = k, \\ 0 & \text{otherwise,} \end{cases} \tag{7.5a}$$

$$I(CAT_{k,i,t}) \equiv \begin{cases} 1 & \text{if fund } i \text{ is in category } k, \\ 0 & \text{otherwise.} \end{cases} \tag{7.5b}$$

The columns labelled "Model 2" in Table 7.2 contain the maximum-likelihood estimates of (7.4) for the same sample of funds as in Model 1. The coefficients for AGE, ASSETS, and RETURN exhibit the same qualitative properties as in Model 1, but the fixed-effect variables provide some additional explanatory power, yielding an R^2 of 34.2%. In particular, the coefficients for the 1999 and 2000 indicator variables are higher than those of the other year indicators, a manifestation of the impact of August 1998 and the collapse of LTCM and other fixed income relative-value hedge funds. The impact of LTCM can also be seen from the coefficients of the category indicators—at 0.50, Fixed Income Relative Value has the largest estimate among all 10 categories. Managed Futures has a comparable coefficient of 0.49, which is consistent with the higher volatility of such funds and the fact that this category exhibits the highest attrition rate, 14.4%, during the 1994–2003 sample period (see Getmansky, Lo, and Mei, 2004, for a more detailed discussion of hedge fund attrition rates). However, the fact that the Convertible Arbitrage and Event Driven categories are the next largest, with coefficients of 0.44 and 0.33, respectively, is somewhat surprising given their unusually low attrition rates of 5.2% and 5.4%, respectively (see Getmansky, Lo, and Mei, 2004). This suggests that the conditional probabilities produced by a logit analysis—which control for assets under management, fund flows, and performance—yields information not readily available from the unconditional frequency counts of simple attrition statistics. The remaining category indicators are statistically insignificant at the 5% level.

To facilitate comparisons across explanatory variables, we standardize each of the nonindicator explanatory variables by subtracting its mean, dividing by its standard deviation, and then re-estimating the parameters of (7.4) via maximum likelihood. This procedure yields estimates that are renormalized to standard deviation units of each explanatory variable and are contained in the columns labelled "Model 3" in Table 7.2. The renormalized estimates show that fund flows are an order of magnitude more important in determining the probability of liquidation than assets under management, returns, or age, with normalized coefficients of -32.72 and -7.53 for FLOW and FLOW$_{-1}$, respectively.

Finally, we re-estimate the logit model (7.4) for two subsets of funds using standardized explanatory variables. In Model 4, we omit Graveyard funds that have either merged with other funds or are closed to new investments (status codes 4 and 5), yielding a subsample of 12,846 observations. And in Model 5, we omit all Graveyard funds except those that have been liquidated (status code 1), yielding a subsample of 12,310 observations. The last two sets of columns in Table 7.2 show that the qualitative features of most of the estimates are unchanged, with the funds in Model 5 exhibiting somewhat higher sensitivity to the lagged FLOW variable. However, the fixed-effects category in Model 5 does differ in some ways from those in Models 2–4, with significant coefficients for Emerging Markets, Equity Market Neutral, and Multi-Strategy, as well as for Managed Futures. This suggests that there are significant differences between the full Graveyard sample and the subsample of funds with status code 1 and bears further study.

Because of the inherent nonlinearity of the logit model, the coefficients of the explanatory variables cannot be as easily interpreted as in the linear regression model. One way to remedy this situation is to compute the estimated probability of liquidation implied by the parameter estimates $\hat{\boldsymbol{\beta}}$ and specific values for the explanatory variables, which is readily accomplished by observing that

$$p_{it} \equiv \text{Prob}\,(Z_{it} = 1) \;\; = \;\; \text{Prob}\,(Z_{it}^{*} > 0) \tag{7.6a}$$

$$= \text{Prob}\,(\mathbf{X}_{it}'\boldsymbol{\beta} + \epsilon_{it} > 0) \;\; = \;\; \frac{\exp(\mathbf{X}_{it}'\boldsymbol{\beta})}{1 + \exp(\mathbf{X}_{it}'\boldsymbol{\beta})}, \tag{7.6b}$$

$$\hat{p}_{it} = \frac{\exp(\mathbf{X}_{it}'\hat{\boldsymbol{\beta}})}{1 + \exp(\mathbf{X}_{it}'\hat{\boldsymbol{\beta}})}\,. \tag{7.6c}$$

Table 7.3 reports year-by-year summary statistics for the estimated liquidation probabilities $\{\hat{p}_{it}\}$ of each fund in our sample, where each $\hat{p}_{it}$ is computed using values of the explanatory variables in year t. The left panel in Table 7.3 contains summary statistics for estimated liquidation probabilities from Model 1, and the right panel contains corresponding figures from Model 5. We have also stratified

Table 7.3.

Year-by-Year Summary Statistics for the Probability of Liquidation Implied by the Parameter Estimates of Two Specifications of a Logit Model for Hedge Fund Liquidations*

Model 1

	1994	1995	1996	1997	1998	1999	2000	2001	2002	2003	2004
					Live Funds						
Mean	4.19	5.47	5.84	5.04	6.32	5.17	5.59	6.84	8.92	7.11	11.04
SD	7.49	9.33	11.15	9.74	9.66	8.61	8.15	9.23	10.15	8.00	10.91
Min	0.01	0.01	0.00	0.00	0.00	0.00	0.00	0.00	0.00	0.00	0.00
10%	0.13	0.19	0.19	0.18	0.31	0.20	0.35	0.44	0.68	0.41	0.89
25%	0.43	0.51	0.52	0.56	0.99	0.79	1.10	1.39	2.05	1.45	2.66
50%	1.16	1.46	1.52	1.59	2.71	2.18	2.80	3.69	5.62	4.49	7.55
75%	4.21	6.03	5.11	4.83	7.20	5.55	6.54	8.39	12.01	10.22	16.31
90%	12.13	16.17	16.85	13.27	16.76	12.80	13.78	16.23	21.61	17.26	26.33
Max	52.49	58.30	72.97	90.06	77.63	87.06	75.83	92.36	79.02	92.44	79.96
Count	357	483	629	773	924	1,083	1,207	1,317	1,480	1,595	1,898
					Graveyard Funds						
Mean	36.59	32.85	31.89	39.75	30.64	27.68	22.78	28.17	25.22	21.55	17.01
SD	24.46	22.77	18.86	22.70	21.67	19.24	17.67	20.03	18.22	15.91	14.30
Min	4.91	2.50	1.05	0.25	0.00	0.53	0.22	0.98	0.13	0.02	0.25
10%	6.08	8.39	10.63	9.29	6.86	4.98	2.41	5.94	5.50	2.64	2.26
25%	22.06	16.28	17.47	21.81	12.13	12.84	9.14	12.07	10.58	8.32	6.43
50%	32.82	28.53	27.44	39.78	25.20	24.03	19.81	23.28	21.50	19.18	13.35
75%	48.40	49.79	43.36	56.94	46.21	39.62	34.92	41.01	37.98	32.28	25.26
90%	71.63	58.62	60.08	71.13	61.74	50.75	45.84	58.90	48.81	45.42	34.67
Max	77.37	97.42	79.51	88.70	85.41	84.87	87.89	78.68	94.65	72.29	67.10
Count	10	27	73	62	104	129	176	175	167	158	68
					Combined Funds						
Mean	5.07	6.92	8.55	7.61	8.78	7.56	7.77	9.35	10.57	8.42	11.24
SD	9.86	12.10	14.53	14.44	13.59	12.39	11.41	13.01	12.26	9.90	11.10
Min	0.01	0.01	0.00	0.00	0.00	0.00	0.00	0.00	0.00	0.00	0.00
10%	0.14	0.20	0.22	0.20	0.38	0.22	0.39	0.53	0.77	0.43	0.93
25%	0.45	0.55	0.62	0.62	1.10	0.91	1.20	1.62	2.28	1.60	2.72
50%	1.23	1.72	1.84	1.88	3.34	2.63	3.35	4.49	6.31	4.97	7.69
75%	4.89	7.67	8.96	6.25	9.81	7.92	9.03	11.28	13.94	11.74	16.46
90%	14.96	20.53	27.36	22.94	25.11	21.39	20.97	24.21	25.98	21.48	26.97
Max	77.37	97.42	79.51	90.06	85.41	87.06	87.89	92.36	94.65	92.44	79.96
Count	367	510	702	835	1,028	1,212	1,383	1,492	1,647	1,753	1,966

Table 7.3.
(continued)

Model 5

Statistic	1994	1995	1996	1997	1998	1999	2000	2001	2002	2003	2004
Live Funds											
Mean	1.06	2.22	4.30	3.43	4.70	4.05	3.80	3.40	4.07	4.45	1.76
SD	3.28	6.01	10.97	8.70	9.51	8.87	7.72	6.76	6.58	6.33	2.70
Min	0.00	0.00	0.00	0.00	0.00	0.00	0.00	0.00	0.00	0.00	0.00
10%	0.00	0.01	0.02	0.02	0.06	0.04	0.07	0.07	0.09	0.07	0.03
25%	0.02	0.04	0.09	0.10	0.27	0.23	0.33	0.33	0.44	0.43	0.15
50%	0.07	0.16	0.36	0.45	1.03	0.96	1.18	1.26	1.74	2.04	0.72
75%	0.52	1.25	2.61	2.26	4.03	3.22	3.49	3.63	4.75	6.01	2.31
90%	2.61	5.85	11.24	9.12	14.21	10.09	9.88	8.10	10.52	12.03	4.71
Max	35.62	42.56	76.54	86.91	77.72	80.45	75.95	91.82	73.06	81.10	29.28
Count	357	483	629	773	924	1,083	1,207	1,317	1,480	1,595	1,898
Graveyard Funds											
Mean	24.23	23.50	34.07	42.30	36.17	31.46	32.55	22.82	20.68	20.18	4.60
SD	24.12	20.12	25.19	26.95	25.12	21.96	22.47	19.84	18.94	16.27	6.20
Min	1.00	4.92	1.88	1.49	0.11	0.11	0.00	0.51	0.03	0.03	0.04
10%	5.31	5.53	5.25	8.61	4.49	2.12	3.95	2.00	2.61	3.02	0.13
25%	11.79	7.99	11.28	21.29	15.56	12.66	15.91	6.43	5.29	6.42	0.97
50%	18.02	17.66	33.94	37.54	28.92	30.16	27.57	19.11	14.32	14.03	3.16
75%	26.24	32.58	54.36	64.53	60.14	46.31	48.38	33.10	33.19	30.61	5.51
90%	48.95	51.10	68.87	80.97	69.54	64.68	61.91	55.75	46.84	43.06	10.17
Max	64.10	69.64	82.29	93.17	87.67	89.00	90.90	76.34	90.02	67.86	33.31
Count	5	14	41	46	68	64	68	58	76	89	35
Combined Funds											
Mean	1.38	2.82	6.12	5.62	6.85	5.58	5.33	4.22	4.88	5.29	1.81
SD	4.94	7.62	14.21	13.84	13.79	11.85	11.17	8.68	8.44	8.01	2.82
Min	0.00	0.00	0.00	0.00	0.00	0.00	0.00	0.00	0.00	0.00	0.00
10%	0.00	0.01	0.02	0.03	0.06	0.05	0.07	0.07	0.09	0.08	0.03
25%	0.02	0.04	0.10	0.11	0.30	0.24	0.35	0.35	0.48	0.49	0.15
50%	0.08	0.19	0.43	0.54	1.24	1.06	1.32	1.42	1.93	2.28	0.73
75%	0.56	1.38	3.58	3.02	5.57	4.27	4.40	4.15	5.36	6.63	2.36
90%	3.06	7.02	19.05	16.84	22.27	17.07	15.37	9.65	12.50	13.79	4.85
Max	64.10	69.64	82.29	93.17	87.67	89.00	90.90	91.82	90.02	81.10	33.31
Count	362	497	670	819	992	1,147	1,275	1,375	1,556	1,684	1,933

* Based on annual observations of the liquidation status of individual hedge funds in the Lipper TASS database for the sample period from January 1994 to August 2004.

the estimated liquidation probabilities by their liquidation status—Live funds in the top panel, Graveyard funds in the middle panel, and the Combined sample of funds in the bottom panel.[6]

For both Models 1 and 5, the mean and median liquidation probabilities are higher for Graveyard funds than for Live funds, a reassuring sign that the explanatory variables indeed provide explanatory power for the liquidation process. For Model 1, the Combined sample shows an increase in the mean and median liquidation probabilities in 1998 as expected, and another increase in 2001, presumably due to bursting of the technology bubble in U.S. equity markets. Most troubling from the perspective of systemic risk, however, is the fact that the mean and median liquidation probabilities for 2004 (which includes data only up to August) are 11.24% and 7.69%, respectively, the highest levels in our entire sample. This may be a symptom of the enormous growth that the hedge fund industry has enjoyed in recent years, which increases both the number of funds entering and exiting the industry but may also indicate more challenging market conditions for hedge funds in the coming months. Note that the mean and median liquidation probabilities for Model 5 do not show the same increase in 2004—this is another manifestation of the time lag with which the Graveyard database is updated (recall that Model 5 includes only funds with status code 1, but a large number of funds that eventually receive this classification have not yet reached their 8- to 10-month limit by August 2004). Therefore, Model 1's estimated liquidation probabilities are likely to be more accurate for the current year.[7]

The logit estimates and implied probabilities suggest that a number of factors influence the likelihood of a hedge fund's liquidation, including past performance, assets under management, fund flows, and age. Given these factors, our estimates imply that the average liquidation probability for funds in 2004 is greater than 11%, which is higher than the historical unconditional attrition rate of 8.8%. To the extent that a series of correlated liquidations stresses the capital reserves of financial counterparties, this is yet another indirect measure of an increase in systemic risk from the hedge fund industry.

7.3 Regime-Switching Models

Our final hedge fund–based measure of systemic risk is motivated by the phase-locking example of Lo (1999) where the return-generating process exhibits

---

[6] Note that usage of the term "Graveyard funds" in this context is somewhat different, involving a time dimension as well as liquidation status. For example, in this context the set of Graveyard funds in 1999 refers to only those funds that liquidated in 1999 and does not include liquidations before or after 1999.

[7] The Lipper TASS reporting delay affects Model 1 as well, suggesting that its estimated liquidation probabilities for 2004 are biased downward as well.

apparent changes in expected returns and volatility that are discrete and sudden, e.g., the Mexican peso crisis of 1994–1995, the Asian crisis of 1997, and the global flight to quality precipitated by the default of Russian GKO debt in August 1998. Linear models are generally incapable of capturing such discrete shifts; hence more sophisticated methods are required. In particular, we propose to model such shifts by a *regime-switching process* in which two states of the world are hypothesized and the data are allowed to determine the parameters of these states and the likelihood of transitioning from one to the other. Regime-switching models have been used in a number of contexts, ranging from Hamilton's (1989) model of the business cycle to Ang and Bekaert's (2004) regime-switching asset-allocation model, and we propose to apply it to the CS/Tremont indexes to obtain another measure of systemic risk, namely, the possibility of switching from a normal to a distressed regime.

Denote by R_t the return of a hedge fund index in period t and suppose R_t satisfies the following:

$$R_t = I_t \cdot R_{1t} + (1 - I_t) \cdot R_{2t}, \tag{7.7a}$$

$$R_{it} \sim \mathcal{N}(\mu_i, \sigma_i^2), \tag{7.7b}$$

$$I_t = \begin{cases} 1 & \text{with probability } p_{11} \text{ if } I_{t-1} = 1, \\ 1 & \text{with probability } p_{21} \text{ if } I_{t-1} = 0, \\ 0 & \text{with probability } p_{12} \text{ if } I_{t-1} = 1, \\ 0 & \text{with probability } p_{22} \text{ if } I_{t-1} = 0. \end{cases} \tag{7.7c}$$

This is the simplest specification for a two-state regime-switching process where I_t is an indicator that determines whether R_t is in state 1 or state 2 and R_{it} is the return in state i. Each state has its own mean and variance, and the regime-switching process I_t has two probabilities; hence there are a total of six parameters to be estimated. Despite the fact that state I_t is unobservable, it can be estimated statistically (see, for example, Hamilton, 1989, 1990) along with the parameters via maximum likelihood.

This specification is similar to the well-known *mixture of distributions model*. However, unlike standard mixture models, the regime-switching model is not independently distributed over time unless $p_{11} = p_{21}$. Once estimated, forecasts of changes in regime can be readily obtained, as well as forecasts of R_t itself. In particular, because the k-step transition matrix of a Markov chain is simply given by $\mathbf{P}^k$, the conditional probability of the regime I_{t+k} given date-t data $\mathcal{R}_t \equiv (R_t, R_{t-1}, \ldots, R_1)$ takes on a particularly simple form:

$$\text{Prob}(I_{t+k} = 1 | \mathcal{R}_t) = \pi_1 + (p_{11} - p_{21})^k [\text{Prob}(I_t = 1 | \mathcal{R}_t) - \pi_1], \tag{7.8a}$$

$$\pi_1 \equiv \frac{p_{21}}{p_{12} + p_{21}}, \tag{7.8b}$$

where Prob $(I_t = 1|\mathcal{R}_t)$ is the probability that the date-t regime is 1 given the historical data up to and including date t (this is a by-product of the maximum-likelihood estimation procedure). With similar recursions of the Markov chain, the conditional expectation of R_{t+k} can be readily derived as

$$E[R_{t+k}|\mathcal{R}_t] = \mathbf{a}_t' \mathbf{P}^k \boldsymbol{\mu}, \tag{7.9a}$$

$$\mathbf{a}_t = [\text{Prob}(I_t = 1|\mathcal{R}_t) \ \text{Prob}(I_t = 2|\mathcal{R}_t)]', \tag{7.9b}$$

$$\boldsymbol{\mu} \equiv [\mu_1 \ \mu_2]'. \tag{7.9c}$$

Table 7.4 reports the maximum-likelihood estimates of the means and standard deviations in each of two states for the 14 CS/Tremont hedge fund indexes, as well as the transition probabilities for the two states. Note that three rows in Table 7.4 are shaded—Dedicated Short Bias, Risk Arbitrage, and Managed Futures—because the maximum-likelihood estimation procedure did not converge properly for these three categories, implying that the regime-switching process may not be a good model of their returns. The remaining 12 series yielded well-defined parameter estimates, and by convention we denote by state 1 the lower-volatility state.

Consider the second row, corresponding to the Convertible Arbitrage index. The parameter estimates indicate that in state 1 this index has an expected return of 15.3% with a volatility of 1.9%, but in state 2 the expected return is −2.0% with a volatility of 5.8%. The latter state is clearly a crisis state for Convertible Arbitrage, while the former is a more normal state. The other hedge fund indexes have similar parameter estimates—the low-volatility state is typically paired with higher means, and the high-volatility state is paired with lower means. While such pairings may seem natural for hedge funds, there are three exceptions to this rule; for Equity Market Neutral, Global Macro, and Long/Short Equity, the higher-volatility state has higher expected returns. This suggests that for these strategies, volatility may be a necessary ingredient for their expected returns.

From these parameter estimates, it is possible to estimate the probability of being in state 1 or state 2 at each point in time for each hedge fund index. For example, in Plate 8 we plot the estimated probabilities of being in state 2, the high-volatility state, for the Fixed Income Arbitrage index for each month from January 1994 to October 2007. We see that this probability begins to increase in the months leading up to August 1998 and reaches 100% in August and several months thereafter. However, this is not an isolated event but occurs on several occasions both before and after August 1998.

To develop an aggregate measure of systemic risk based on this regime-switching model, we propose summing the state-2 probabilities across all hedge fund indexes every month to yield a time series that captures the likelihood of being in low-mean periods. Of course, the summed probabilities—even if

Table 7.4.

Maximum-Likelihood Parameter Estimates of a Two-State Regime-Switching Model for CS/Tremont Hedge Fund Indexes (January 1994 to October 2007)*

Index	p_{11}	p_{21}	p_{12}	p_{22}	Annualized Mean		Annualized SD		Log(L)
					State 1	State 2	State 1	State 2	
CSFB/Tremont Hedge Fund Index	100.0%	1.2%	0.0%	98.8%	9.4%	12.5%	3.7%	9.9%	433.0
Convertible Arbitrage	89.7%	17.9%	10.3%	82.1%	15.3%	−2.0%	1.9%	5.8%	524.7
Dedicated Short Bias	23.9%	9.6%	76.1%	90.4%	−75.7%	8.1%	2.5%	15.7%	275.8
Emerging Markets	100.0%	1.2%	0.0%	98.8%	15.9%	6.4%	7.8%	20.2%	309.2
Equity Market Neutral	100.0%	1.2%	0.0%	98.8%	7.7%	11.4%	1.9%	3.4%	576.5
Event Driven	98.4%	46.1%	1.6%	53.9%	13.6%	−45.7%	3.9%	13.9%	492.7
Distressed	98.4%	57.5%	1.6%	42.5%	14.9%	−56.3%	4.5%	15.5%	469.3
E.D. Multi-Strategy	98.9%	41.3%	1.1%	58.7%	12.8%	−55.1%	4.6%	15.0%	469.0
Risk Arbitrage	0.0%	1.2%	100.0%	98.8%	6.8%	7.9%	0.0%	4.2%	599.4
Fixed Income Arb	94.0%	35.6%	6.0%	64.4%	9.4%	−10.8%	2.0%	5.9%	568.7
Global Macro	100.0%	1.2%	0.0%	98.8%	13.3%	13.9%	3.6%	14.2%	403.0
Long/Short Equity	99.0%	2.4%	1.0%	97.6%	9.1%	20.6%	6.3%	15.3%	383.0
Managed Futures	13.4%	1.8%	86.6%	98.2%	2.0%	7.3%	0.0%	12.1%	328.5
Multi-Strategy	98.9%	23.1%	1.1%	76.9%	11.0%	−7.3%	3.4%	9.2%	504.8

* For the highlighted rows the algorithm did not converge.

renormalized to lie in the unit interval—cannot be interpreted formally as a probability because the regime-switching process was specified individually for each index, not jointly across all indexes. Therefore, the interpretation of the low-mean state for Convertible Arbitrage may be quite different from the interpretation of the low-mean state for Equity Market Neutral. Nevertheless, as an aggregate measure of the state of the hedge fund industry, the summed probabilities may contain useful information about systemic risk exposures. Plate 9 contains this indicator. The low-mean indicator has local maxima in 1994 and 1998 as expected, but there is a stronger peak around 2002, largely due to Equity Market Neutral, Global Macro, and Long/Short Equity. This corresponds remarkably well to the common wisdom that over the past 2 years these three strategy classes have underperformed for a variety of reasons.[8] The implications of Plate 9 for systemic risk are clear: The probability of being in low-mean regimes has increased for a number of hedge fund indexes, which may foreshadow increased leverage for funds in these categories as well as fund outflows in the coming months, both of which would place additional stress on the industry, leading to an increase in systemic risk.

7.4 The Current Outlook

A definitive assessment of the systemic risks posed by hedge funds requires certain data that are currently unavailable and are unlikely to become available in the near future, namely, counterparty credit exposures, the net degree of leverage of hedge fund managers and investors, the gross amount of structured products involving hedge funds, and so on. Therefore, we cannot determine the magnitude of current systemic risk exposures with any degree of accuracy. However, based on the analytics developed in this study, there are a few tentative inferences that we can draw.

1. The hedge fund industry has grown tremendously over the last few years, fueled by the demand for higher returns in the face of stock market declines and mounting pension fund liabilities. These massive fund inflows have had a material impact on hedge fund returns and risks in recent years, as evidenced by changes in correlations, reduced performance, and increased illiquidity as measured by the weighted autocorrelation ρ_t^*.

2. Mean and median liquidation probabilities for hedge funds increased in 2004, based on logit estimates that link several factors to the liquidation probability of a given hedge fund, including past performance, assets under

---

[8] Large fund flows into these strategies and changes in equity markets such as decimalization, the rise of ECNs, automated trading, and Regulation FD are often cited as reasons for the decreased profitability of these strategies.

management, fund flows, and age. In particular, our estimates imply that the average liquidation probability for funds in 2004 is greater than 11%, which is higher than the historical unconditional attrition rate of 8.8%. A higher attrition rate is not surprising for a rapidly growing industry, but it may foreshadow potential instabilities that can be triggered by seemingly innocuous market events.

3. The banking sector is exposed to hedge fund risks, especially smaller institutions, but the largest banks are also exposed through proprietary trading activities, credit arrangements and structured products, and prime brokerage services.

4. The risks facing hedge funds are nonlinear and more complex than those facing traditional asset classes. Because of the dynamic nature of hedge fund investment strategies and the impact of fund flows on leverage and performance, hedge fund risk models require more sophisticated analytics and more sophisticated users.

5. The sum of our regime-switching models' low-mean state probabilities is one proxy for the aggregate level of distress in the hedge fund sector. Recent measurements suggest that we may be entering a challenging period. This, coupled with the recent uptrend in the weighted autocorrelation ρ_t^* and the increased mean and median liquidation probabilities for hedge funds in 2004 from our logit model, implies that systemic risk is increasing.

We hasten to qualify our tentative conclusions by emphasizing the speculative nature of these inferences and hope that our analysis spurs additional research and data collection to refine both the analytics and the empirical measurement of systemic risk in the hedge fund industry. As with all risk management challenges, we should hope for the best and prepare for the worst. The question is how? One possibility has been put forward by Getmansky, Lo, and Mei (2004), which is to create an independent organization along the lines of the National Transportation Safety Board to sift through the wreckage of all major hedge fund collapses, ultimately producing a publicly available report that documents the specific causes of the collapse along with recommendations on how to avoid similar disasters in the future. Although there may be common themes in the demise of many hedge funds—too much leverage, too concentrated a portfolio, operational failures, securities fraud, or insufficient assets under management—each liquidation has its own unique circumstances and is an opportunity for hedge fund managers and investors to learn and improve. Section 9.4 provides a more detailed discussion of this proposal.

8
An Integrated Hedge Fund Investment Process

Despite the growing number of studies proposing quantitative approaches to alternative investments,[1] hedge fund investors have yet to embrace any single analytic framework for formulating their investment policies. There are several reasons for this state of affairs. One reason may lie in the cultural history of the hedge fund investor community, which was forged by high-net-worth individuals, family offices, foundations, and endowments. These early patrons of hedge funds, CTAs, and private equity placed more emphasis on the specific characteristics of individual managers and entrepreneurs than on detailed portfolio construction algorithms. It was in this milieu that the financial "gunslinger" was born, an iconoclast with often cryptic and occasionally brilliant market insights, a healthy appetite for risk, and little regard for convention and constraints. As a result, the legal, tax, and operational aspects of individual managers became the centerpiece of the typical investment process. Having gone through generations of refinements and trial-and-error improvements, the *due diligence process*, as this process is now known, has come to be an indispensable part of any serious hedge fund investor's deliberations. Because of the complexity and multifaceted nature of this process,[2] many seasoned professionals have concluded that investing in hedge funds is best done through qualitative judgment and is simply not amenable to quantitative analysis.

A second reason for the current state of hedge fund investment processes is the acknowledged limitations of traditional portfolio management tools for

---

[1] See, for example, Amenc and Martinelli (2002), Amin and Kat (2003c), Terhaar, Staub, and Singer (2003), and Cremers, Kritzman, and Page (2004).

[2] To develop a deeper appreciation for the intricacies of the hedge fund due diligence process, review any hedge fund due diligence questionnaire from an experienced investor. The document is typically 20 pages or longer and covers a remarkably broad spectrum of issues ranging from back-office systems to investment strategies to personnel employment contracts to the manager's personal history.

most alternative investments.[3] Experienced investors no doubt understand that diversification is important—indeed, this was the primary motivation for creation of the very first hedge fund—but apart from acknowledging this simple truth, it is unclear how best to proceed. The capital-allocation problem for a multimanager fund or a fund of funds differs in several respects from a standard portfolio construction problem. Issues such as lockup periods, incentive fees and high-water marks, clawback agreements, illiquidity and mark-to-market policies, leverage and credit exposure, dynamic shifts in trading strategies and objectives, enormous heterogeneity among managers, and an overall lack of transparency render the usual mean-variance portfolio optimization techniques less than compelling for alternative investments.

A third reason is simply the lack of data and research that is directly relevant for hedge funds. Until recently, there were no commercially available hedge fund databases, hence the barriers to entry for investors were quite high. Large family offices and endowments were among the few organizations with a long history of investing in hedge funds and enjoyed a significant competitive advantage because of the private collection of manager track records they possessed. The lack of data naturally also placed a constraint on the quantity and quality of published research on alternative investments.

However, the hedge fund industry has progressed dramatically in the last decade. There are now many vendors of hedge fund data, resulting in a thriving academic and practitioner literature on alternative investments[4] and a number of trade publications and professional organizations for hedge fund managers and investors.[5] Therefore, this is an opportune time to revisit the application of quantitative methods to the hedge fund investment process.

In this section, we propose an analytical framework for constructing a portfolio of hedge funds, namely, a risk-based approach to making capital allocations among multiple strategies or managers in an alternative investments context. However, contrary to the common belief that an investment process is either qualitative or quantitative but not both, we argue that it is possible—and essential—to combine the two approaches in a consistent fashion and within a single investment paradigm.

---

[3] See, in particular, Cremers, Kritzman, and Page (2004).

[4] See, for example, the *Journal of Alternative Investments*, and the related website of the Center for International Securities and Derivatives Markets at the University of Massachusetts at Amherst (http://www.cisdm.org), one of the pioneers in sponsored research on hedge funds.

[5] In addition to the CFA Institute, which has a considerably broader focus than just alternative investments, the nonprofit Alternative Investment Management Association was founded in 1990 and now boasts members in 42 countries. In 2002, AIMA and CISDM (see previous footnote) established the Chartered Alternative Investment Analyst Association with its own certification process for training analysts in the area of alternative investments.

To achieve this integration, we propose a two-stage investment process where capital allocations are made quantitatively across broad asset classes, and then within each asset class, capital is allocated to each manager according to a well-defined heuristic that integrates qualitative judgments in a quantitative framework.[6] The following is a summary of the design principles that underlie the approach described below.

- The target expected return for each strategy should be commensurate with the risks of that strategy—higher-risk strategies should have higher-target expected returns.

- The uses of funds should determine the target expected return, not the sources of funds.

- In evaluating the risk/reward ratio for each strategy, serial correlation and illiquidity exposure should be taken into account explicitly. In particular, the Sharpe ratios of strategies with large positively serially correlated returns should be deflated (for details see Lo, 2002; Getmansky, Lo, and Makarov, 2004; Chapter 3).

- Qualitative judgments about managers, strategies, and market conditions are valuable inputs into the capital allocation process that no quantitative models can replace, but those judgments should be integrated with traditional quantitative methods in a systematic and consistent fashion.

- Risk and performance attribution should be performed on a regular basis for and by each manager, as well as for the entire portfolio.

- Risk limits and related guidelines for each manager should be consistent across time and across managers and should be communicated clearly to all managers on a regular basis.

These design principles, coupled with insights from traditional portfolio management theory and practice, suggest a mean-variance optimization problem in which required or target expected returns and variances are determined in advance by investor mandates and market conditions, covariances are estimated via econometric methods, and then asset-class allocations are determined by minimizing variance subject to an expected-return constraint. Within each asset class, allocations are determined by incorporating qualitative information into the investment process through a scoring process. The seven components of such a capital allocation algorithm are as follows.

1. Define asset classes by strategy.
2. Set target portfolio expected return μ_o and desired volatility σ_o.

---

[6] A two-stage investment process is generally suboptimal relative to a single-stage optimization, but there are compelling reasons for adopting the former approach for alternative investments. See Section 8.10 for further discussion.

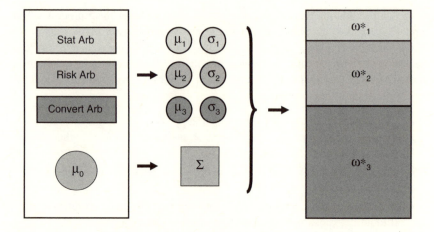

Figure 8.1. *Phase 1: Capital allocation over asset classes. First stage of a quantitative capital-allocation algorithm for alternative investments, in which asset classes are defined and optimal asset-class weights are determined as a function of target expected returns and risk levels, and an estimated covariance matrix.*

3. Set target expected returns and risks for asset classes.
4. Determine correlations via econometric analysis.
5. Compute minimum-variance asset-class allocations subject to μ_o constraint.
6. Allocate capital to managers within each asset class.
7. Monitor performance and risk budgets and reoptimize as needed.

Each of these components is described in more detail in Sections 8.1–8.7, and the general design of the two-stage process is outlined in Figures 8.1 and 8.2. All mathematical details are relegated to Appendix A.5. The final specifications for the entire framework are summarized in Section 8.8, and in Section 8.9 we describe a method for communicating risk limits to individual managers based on the overall portfolio's risk capital.

Before proceeding with the exposition of this capital-allocation algorithm, it is important to emphasize the disclaimer that the following discussion is not meant to be a detailed recipe for a specific hedge fund investment process. It is, instead, meant to serve as a prototype and framework for developing such a process within the context of each investor's particular objectives, constraints, and organizational infrastructure. Certain components will be appropriate for some investors but not for others, and all components require some degree of customization to render them applicable to a given investor and a given set of funds.

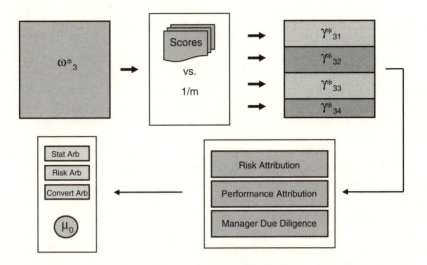

Figure 8.2. *Phase 2: Capital allocation within asset classes. Second stage of a quantitative capital allocation algorithm for alternative investments in which capital is allocated to managers within an asset class according to a scoring procedure that incorporates qualitative as well as quantitative information.*

8.1 Define Asset Classes by Strategy

The first step involves subdividing the universe of strategies into a small number n of relatively homogeneous managers or asset classes. Within each asset class, the strategies should have similar characteristics—expected returns, risks, legal and operational infrastructure, and so on—and should be highly correlated. Examples of asset classes include

- Equity market neutral
- Risk arbitrage
- Convertible arbitrage
- Fixed income relative value
- Global macro
- Emerging-market debt
- Short-sellers

and Appendix A.1 contains a more complete list of categories in the Lipper TASS hedge fund database.

8.2 Set Portfolio Target Expected Returns

Given client mandates and market conditions, a target expected return μ_o for the entire portfolio must be determined. For example, in the current economic environment, a portfolio of U.S. equity market neutral strategies may call for an expected return of 8%. In 1997, such a portfolio might have had a target of 15%. This parameter is typically set by a fund of funds' investment committee or chief investment officer.

A desired level of risk σ_o should also be specified. Note that σ_o is *not* called a target risk level because it is not generally possible to specify both the expected return and risk of a portfolio when the set of asset classes and managers is fixed. For a given set of assets, we can always construct a portfolio with expected return μ_o that is minimum-variance, or a portfolio with risk σ_o that has maximum expected return (as long as σ_o is greater than the risk of the global minimum-variance portfolio), but not both (Appendix A.5). Therefore, the portfolio construction process is necessarily an iterative one that requires some qualitative judgment as well as quantitative analysis.

8.3 Set Asset-Class Target Expected Returns and Risks

For each asset class i defined in Section 8.1, a target expected return μ_i and risk σ_i must be specified. This is a critical step in the capital-allocation process because it is here that the trade-off between risk and expected return is incorporated into the investment process. Managers undertaking more risky strategies should have a higher required rate of return regardless of the financing costs associated with the capital—the uses of capital should determine the target expected return, not the sources of capital.

A useful starting point for making this risk/reward trade-off is a linear factor model such as the Capital Asset Pricing Model or Arbitrage Pricing Theory, which typically implies a linear relation between an investment's expected return and its risk exposures. A modified version of such a relation for hedge fund applications is given by

$$\mu_i = R_f + \beta_{i1}\pi_1 + \beta_{i2}\pi_2 + \cdots + \beta_{ip}\pi_p + \alpha_i, \tag{8.1}$$

where β_{ij} is the risk exposure of asset class i to factor j, π_j is the risk premium associated with factor j, and α_i is the combined alpha of the managers in asset class i. The interpretation of (8.1) is that the expected return of asset class i above the cash return R_f is proportional to the risk exposures of the asset class, plus the value-added that active management provides. Factors that are most relevant for hedge fund strategies include

- Price factors
- Sectors
- Investment style
- Volatilities
- Credit
- Liquidity
- Macroeconomic factors
- Sentiment
- Nonlinear interactions

However, the examples in Chapter 1 provide compelling motivation for developing nonlinear extensions of these linear factor models so as to account for some of the more complex dynamics of hedge fund strategies.

Once a factor model is specified, risk exposures can be readily estimated from historical data, but in some cases it may be necessary to adjust these estimates to reflect changes in current market conditions, the specific managers or strategies in each asset class, and other factors. For example, the 10-year historical average return and volatility of fixed income arbitrage strategies are likely to be quite different from their post-1998 expected return and risk. Therefore, the target expected returns and risk levels should be set by the fund of funds' risk committee, perhaps using historical estimates as initial values that are modified periodically through qualitative evaluation as well as quantitative analysis.

8.4 Estimate Asset-Class Covariance Matrix

Using both back-test and historical performance data, the correlations of the returns of the n asset classes must be estimated. Ideally, the estimation method should incorporate nonlinearities that often characterize hedged strategies, as well as changes in regime as in the pre-1998 versus post-1998 periods (see the examples in Chapter 1). Once the correlations ρ_{ij} have been estimated, the covariance matrix of the n asset classes can be constructed using the definition of a covariance σ_{ij}:

$$\sigma_{ij} = \rho_{ij} \times \sigma_i \times \sigma_j, \tag{8.2}$$

where σ_i and σ_j have been specified in Section 8.3.

Note that we propose to estimate the *correlation matrix*, not the covariance matrix. There are at least three reasons for such an approach. First, there is some empirical evidence to suggest that correlations are more stable over time than covariances. This is not altogether surprising given the substantial literature documenting time-varying volatilities in financial asset returns (see, for example, Andersen, Bollerslev, and Diebold, 2004). If second moments vary through time in a similar manner, the ratios of these moments, such as correlation coefficients, are likely to be more stable. Second, time-varying correlation matrices can be modeled more parsimoniously than time-varying covariance matrices as Engle (2002) illustrates, which is particularly relevant for portfolios with a large number of funds. Third, recall that the variances of the asset classes are prespecified (Section 8.3) and not necessarily estimated from historical data. If such pre-specified values are inserted into an estimated covariance matrix, the result need not be positive-definite, which can yield anomalous results such as spurious arbitrage opportunities and unstable portfolio weights. By reconstructing the covariance matrix from the estimated correlation matrix using (8.2), we are guaranteed a well-behaved covariance matrix estimator.

8.5 Compute Minimum-Variance Asset Allocations

From Sections 8.1–8.4, we now have the following parameters:

μ_o = target expected return,

$\boldsymbol{\mu} = [\mu_1 \; \cdots \; \mu_n]'$ = target asset-class expected returns,

$\boldsymbol{\Sigma}$ = asset-class covariance matrix.

Given these parameters, we can now construct a portfolio of n managers to minimize the variance of the portfolio subject to a constraint that the expected return is at least μ_o:[7]

$$\min_{\boldsymbol{\omega}} \tfrac{1}{2} \boldsymbol{\omega}' \boldsymbol{\Sigma} \boldsymbol{\omega} \text{ subject to } \boldsymbol{\omega}' \boldsymbol{\mu} \geq \mu_o \text{ and } \boldsymbol{\omega}' \boldsymbol{\iota} = 1. \tag{8.3}$$

---

[7] For most fund-of-funds and multimanager applications, it is also necessary to impose nonnegativity constraints on the portfolio weights since it is typically impossible to establish a "short" position in a manager. However, as long as the target expected returns are realistic and the covariance matrix is well-behaved, (8.4) should yield nonnegative portfolio weights. If not, this may be a sign of model misspecification that can serve as a useful diagnostic for identifying potential problems with the portfolio construction process. Alternatively, recent innovations in structured products do allow the synthetic shorting of certain hedge fund strategies, in which case more efficient fund-of-funds portfolios may be possible. However, given the complexities of OTC derivatives on hedge funds and the significant risks they can generate, shorting hedge funds should be contemplated only by the most sophisticated and well capitalized of investors.

The solution to (8.3) is given by (Appendix A.5)

$$\boldsymbol{\omega}^* = \lambda \boldsymbol{\Sigma}^{-1} \boldsymbol{\mu} + \xi \boldsymbol{\Sigma}^{-1} \boldsymbol{\iota}, \tag{8.4}$$

where λ and ξ are defined in Appendix A.5. As a consistency check, it is useful to compute the volatility σ of the entire portfolio implied by $\boldsymbol{\omega}^*$:

$$\sigma = \sqrt{\boldsymbol{\omega}^{*\prime} \boldsymbol{\Sigma} \boldsymbol{\omega}^*} . \tag{8.5}$$

If σ is higher than σ_o, this implies an inconsistency with the following set of objectives:

- target expected return μ_o,
- desired risk level σ_o,
- target expected returns and risks of asset classes (μ_i, σ_i),

and at least one of these three objectives must be modified to restore consistency.

If the total investment capital is K, the optimal dollar allocation to each asset class is simply K_i^*, where

$$K_i^* = \omega_i^* K. \tag{8.6}$$

8.6 Determine Manager Allocations within Each Asset Class

For each asset class i, the optimal dollar allocation K_i^* must be distributed among m_i managers. Although these suballocations may also be determined quantitatively along the same lines as in Section 8.5, this is likely to be less than ideal because of the qualitative nature of manager selection and development, particularly for new managers who do not possess extensive track records from which parameter estimates can be estimated. Therefore, consider the following heuristic method. Let γ_{ik} denote the fraction of K_i^* allocated to manager k in asset class i; hence $\sum_k \gamma_{ik} = 1$. The starting point for the allocations is $\gamma_{ik} = 1/m_i$, i.e., identical allocations across all m_i managers. Now for each manager, construct a score S_{ik} by evaluating the manager against the following criteria, perhaps using a numerical score from 1 to 5 for each criterion:

- Anticipated alpha
- Anticipated risk
- Anticipated capacity

- Anticipated correlation with other managers and asset classes
- Trading experience and past performance
- Back-test performance attribution
- Tracking error
- Risk controls
- Risk transparency
- Alpha transparency
- Operational risks
- Other qualitative due diligence issues

For example, a manager with a high anticipated alpha (as determined through the largely qualitative manager-selection and due diligence processes) would receive a score of 5, and a manager with a low anticipated alpha would receive a score of 1. Similarly, a high-risk manager (relative to the asset-class volatility σ_i) would receive a score of 1, and a moderate-risk manager would receive a score of 3. The sum of each of these ratings yields the manager's score S_{ik}. Then define the relative score s_{ik} as

$$s_{ik} = \frac{S_{ik}}{S_{i1} + \cdots + S_{im_i}}. \tag{8.7}$$

Then the manager's allocation can be defined as

$$\gamma_{ik} = (1 - \delta) \times \frac{1}{m_i} + \delta \times s_{ik}, \tag{8.8}$$

where δ is a parameter that determines the weight placed on the relative scores versus equality.

For a given set of manager allocations $\boldsymbol{\gamma}_i \equiv [\gamma_{i1} \quad \cdots \quad \gamma_{im_i}]'$ in asset class i, the implied expected return and volatility of the asset class are given by

$$\tilde{\mu}_i = \boldsymbol{\gamma}_i' \boldsymbol{\nu}_i, \qquad \tilde{\sigma}_i = \sqrt{\boldsymbol{\gamma}_i' \boldsymbol{\Sigma}_i \boldsymbol{\gamma}_i}, \tag{8.9}$$

where $\boldsymbol{\nu}_i$ is the vector of expected returns of each manager in asset class i (as determined either by back-tests or historical performance) and $\boldsymbol{\Sigma}_i$ is the covariance matrix of the managers in asset class i. Before implementing the allocation $\boldsymbol{\gamma}_i$, it is important to check whether the implied expected return and risk of $\boldsymbol{\gamma}_i$ given in (8.9) are consistent with the target expected return and risk μ_i and σ_i for sector i. If not, then the allocations in $\boldsymbol{\gamma}_i$ may need to be adjusted or the target expected return and risk must be adjusted to reduce the discrepancy.

Given an allocation $\boldsymbol{\gamma}_i$, each manager's dollar allocation is then

$$K_{ik}^* = K_i^* \times \gamma_{ik}. \tag{8.10}$$

These scores should be recomputed at least quarterly, and possibly more frequently as changes in market conditions might dictate. Each manager should be given his or her score so that the manager is aware of the link between performance (as determined by the many dimensions of the score) and capital allocation. Moreover, such scores can be used as a hurdle for evaluating new managers so that the process of manager selection is less arbitrary over time and across individual fund analysts.

8.7 Monitor Performance and Risk Budgets

The performance of each manager should be monitored regularly to ensure that risk budgets and investment mandates are not being violated. In particular, if the target risk of asset class i is σ_i, then the realized volatility $\hat{\sigma}_i$ of the asset class can be compared to σ_i to determine any discrepancies that require further investigation, where

$$\hat{\sigma}_i \equiv \sqrt{\boldsymbol{\gamma}_i' \boldsymbol{\Sigma}_i \boldsymbol{\gamma}_i} \tag{8.11}$$

and $\boldsymbol{\Sigma}_i$ is the estimated covariance matrix of the m_i managers in asset class i. Those managers that contribute more than proportionally to the asset-class volatility $\hat{\sigma}_i$ may be required to accept lower capital allocations, and vice versa, other things being equal.

As performance varies and as parameters change, the allocations across asset classes and across managers will require periodic updating. Allocations should be recomputed monthly, although no action is needed unless the updated allocations are significantly different from the current allocations.

8.8 The Final Specification

The final specification of the proposed optimal capital allocation algorithm is given by the input parameters and the outputs listed below. A sample screenshot of an Excel-based implementation appears in Table 8.1.

Table 8.1.

Sample Screenshot of the AlphaSimplex Multimanager Capital Allocation Calculator

Total Capital ($MM)	Target Portfolio Return	Asset Class	Target Expected Return	Target Std. Dev.	Correlation and Covariance Matrices			ω^*	$\omega^\sim$	K^*	$K^\sim$
					Risk Arb	Convert Arb	Stat Arb				
1,000	10.00%	Risk Arb	7.50%	4.00%	100.00%	40.00%	−5.00%	12.66%	12.66%	127	127
		Convert Arb	12.00%	5.00%	40.00%	100.00%	30.00%	51.58%	51.58%	516	516
		Stat Arb	8.00%	3.50%	−5.00%	30.00%	100.00%	35.76%	35.76%	358	358

Stat Arb Allocations

Total	357.59		
δ	50%		
	Score	γ^*	K^*_{ik}
Manager 1	12	11.26%	40
Manager 2	13	11.50%	41
Manager 3	40	18.09%	65
Manager 4	81	28.09%	100
Manager 5	13	11.50%	41
Manager 6	46	19.55%	70

Legend

⇒ input
⇒ output

ω^* ⇒ optimal asset-class weights
$\omega^\sim$ ⇒ nonnegative asset-class weights
K^* ⇒ optimal asset-class dollar allocation
$K^\sim$ ⇒ nonnegative asset-class dollar allocation
γ^* ⇒ optimal manager weights
K^*_{ik} ⇒ optimal manager dollar allocation

Inputs

The following are input parameters:

$$\mu_o = \text{target expected return of the portfolio,} \qquad (8.12\text{a})$$

$$\mu = [\mu_1 \cdots \mu_n]' = \text{target asset-class expected returns,} \qquad (8.12\text{b})$$

$$\Sigma = \text{asset-class covariance matrix,} \qquad (8.12\text{c})$$

$$\Sigma_i = \text{covariance matrix of managers in asset class } i, \qquad (8.12\text{d})$$

$$S_{ik} = \text{manager scores,} \qquad (8.12\text{e})$$

$$\delta = \text{weighting parameter for manager scores,} \qquad (8.12\text{f})$$

$$K = \text{total capital of the fund.} \qquad (8.12\text{g})$$

Outputs

The three outputs of the optimal capital allocation process are

$$K_i^* = \text{optimal capital allocation for asset class } i, \qquad (8.13\text{a})$$

$$K_{ik}^* = \text{optimal capital allocation for manager } k, \qquad (8.13\text{b})$$

$$V_{ik}^* = K_{ik}^* \times \mu_i = \text{expected dollar revenue for manager } k. \qquad (8.13\text{c})$$

8.9 Risk Limits and Risk Capital

Given a target expected return μ_i and a target risk level σ_i for the managers in asset class i, we have the following expression for manager k's $100 \times (1 - \theta)\%$ unconditional Value at Risk (UVaR):

$$\theta = \text{Prob} \left(R_{ik} K_{ik}^* \leq \text{UVaR} \right) \qquad (8.14\text{a})$$

$$= \text{Prob} \left(\frac{R_{ik} - \mu_i}{\sigma_i} \leq \frac{(\text{UVaR}/K_{ik}^*) - \mu_i}{\sigma_i} \right) \qquad (8.14\text{b})$$

$$= \text{Prob} \left(Z \leq \frac{(\text{UVaR}/K_{ik}^*) - \mu_i}{\sigma_i} \right) \qquad (8.14\text{c})$$

$$F_z^{-1}(\theta) = \frac{(\text{UVaR}/K_{ik}^*) - \mu_i}{\sigma_i}, \qquad (8.14\text{d})$$

$$\text{UVaR} = K_{ik}^* \times (\mu_i + \sigma_i F_z^{-1}(\theta)), \qquad (8.14\text{e})$$

where R_{ik} is the manager's annual return and $F_z(\cdot)$ is the cumulative distribution function of the standardized return Z. If Z is assumed to be normally distributed and we set $\theta = 0.01$ or 1%, then $F_z^{-1}(0.01) = -2.326$. For a manager with \$100 million of capital, a target expected return of 15%, and an annual standard deviation of 7.5%, the annual 1% UVaR is

$$\$100 \text{ million} \times (0.15 - 0.075 \times 2.326) = -\$2.445 \text{ million.}$$

A more realistic distribution for Stat Arb returns is the t distribution with four degrees of freedom or less; in the case of four degrees of freedom, $F_z^{-1}(0.01) = 3.747$, yielding a 1% UVaR of

$$\$100 \text{ million} \times (0.15 - 0.075 \times 3.747) = -\$13.103 \text{ million.}$$

Of course, the proper aggregation UVaR across managers is a complex issue that involves correlated and highly nonlinear risk/reward functions. Moreover, the dynamic risk exposures of one manager can be very different from those of another—a Stat Arb manager has a very different dynamic risk profile than an equity derivatives manager—hence UVaR may not be the ideal quantity on which to base a risk limit for a heterogeneous group of managers and strategies. See Lo (2001) for further discussion.

Now denote by UVaR_p the monthly Value at Risk of the entire portfolio, which is defined as

$$\text{UVaR}_p \equiv K r_p(\theta), \tag{8.15}$$

where K is the total investment capital of the portfolio and $r_p(\theta)$ is the θ-percentile of the return distribution of the portfolio. For example, if the portfolio return is normally distributed with mean μ_p and standard deviation σ_p, then

$$r_p(\theta) = \mu_p + \sigma_p \, \Phi^{-1}(\theta), \tag{8.16}$$

where $\Phi^{-1}(\cdot)$ is the inverse of the normal cumulative distribution function. Now define the *risk capital* of the portfolio as the minimum level of funds X_p for which a loss of UVaR_p is no more than a fraction ξ_p of X_p:

$$X_p \equiv -\frac{\text{UVaR}_p}{\xi_p} = -\frac{K r_p(\theta)}{\xi_p}. \tag{8.17}$$

In other words, a minimum of X_p must be set aside to ensure that in the event of a loss of UVaR_p, the return on risk capital will be $-\xi_p$. The quantity ξ_p is called the *loss limit* of the portfolio.

To see how X_p is related to the required risk capital for each manager in the portfolio, define the following quantities for each manager k:

$$K_k \equiv \text{manager } k\text{'s total investment capital,} \tag{8.18a}$$

$$\omega_k \equiv K_k/K = \text{fraction of portfolio invested with manager } k, \tag{8.18b}$$

$$\text{UVaR}_k \equiv K_k\, r_k(\theta) = \text{manager } k\text{'s UVaR}, \tag{8.18c}$$

$$\mu_k \equiv \text{manager } k\text{'s expected return,} \tag{8.18d}$$

$$\sigma_k \equiv \text{manager } k\text{'s return standard deviation,} \tag{8.18e}$$

$$\xi_k \equiv \text{manager } k\text{'s monthly loss limit,} \tag{8.18f}$$

$$X_k \equiv -\,\text{UVaR}_k/\xi_k = \text{manager } k\text{'s risk capital.} \tag{8.18g}$$

Now from the definition of X_p, we have

$$X_p = \sum_{i=1}^{m} X_k = -\sum_{i=1}^{m} \frac{K_k r_k(\theta)}{\xi_k}, \tag{8.19}$$

and substituting (8.17) into (8.19) yields the following equality:

$$\sum_{i=1}^{m} K_k \frac{r_p(\theta)}{\xi_p} = \sum_{i=1}^{m} K_k \frac{r_k(\theta)}{\xi_k}. \tag{8.20}$$

For (8.20) to be satisfied for *all* capital allocations $\{K_k\}$, it must be the case that

$$\xi_k = \frac{r_k(\theta)}{r_p(\theta)}\, \xi_p. \tag{8.21}$$

This is the fundamental relationship between the portfolio loss limit ξ_p and the corresponding loss limits for each of the individual managers; (8.21) shows that the loss limit required for each manager need not be equal to the loss limit of the portfolio and that loss limits can and should differ from one manager to the next. In particular, the degree to which ξ_k differs from ξ_p is related to how much diversification the portfolio exhibits—the more diversification, the smaller $r_p(\theta)$ relative to the typical $r_k(\theta)$ and the greater the loss limit for manager k. A more readily interpretable version of (8.21) can be obtained by converting return percentiles to UVaR quantities:

$$\xi_k = \frac{r_k(\theta)}{r_p(\theta)}\, \xi_p = \frac{K_k r_k(\theta)}{K r_p(\theta)} \frac{K}{K_k}\, \xi_p = \frac{1}{\omega_k} \frac{\text{UVaR}_k}{\text{UVaR}_p}\, \xi_p. \tag{8.22}$$

Hence the loss limit for manager k is simply the loss limit of the portfolio multiplied by the reciprocal of his weight in the portfolio times the ratio of his UVaR to the portfolio UVaR.

Recall that X_k is defined as the risk capital of manager k, which is the ratio of his $UVaR_k$ to ξ_k. Using the setting of ξ_k in (8.22) yields

$$X_k = \frac{UVaR_k}{\xi_k} = \frac{\omega_k UVaR_k}{UVaR_k} \frac{UVaR_p}{\xi_p} = \omega_k \, X_p \qquad (8.23)$$

$$\Rightarrow \frac{X_k}{X_p} = \omega_k, \qquad (8.24)$$

which shows that the fraction of risk capital allocated to manager k under the loss-limit rule (8.22) is identical to the portfolio weight ω_k defined by the fraction of total investment capital K_k/K allocated to manager k.

These formulas for risk capital and loss limits can be made more explicit for more specific Value-at-Risk measures. For example, if we are willing to make parametric assumptions for the return distributions of individual managers and the portfolio as in Section 8.9, then $UVaR_k$ may be written as

$$UVaR_k = K_k \, (\mu_k + \sigma_k \, F_z^{-1}(\theta)), \qquad (8.25)$$

where $F^{-1}(\cdot)$ is the inverse of the cumulative distribution function for the standardized return of manager k (standardized to zero mean and unit variance). In many cases, risk management applications set $\mu_k = 0$, which yields a particularly convenient expression for an individual manager's loss limit:[8]

$$\xi_k = \frac{\sigma_k}{\sigma_p} \, \xi_p, \qquad (8.26)$$

where σ_p is the return standard deviation of the portfolio.

---

[8] Setting the expected return of a portfolio equal to zero for purposes of risk management is often motivated by a desire to be conservative. Most portfolios tend to have positive expected return; hence setting μ equal to zero generally yields larger values for VaR. However, for actively managed portfolios that contain both long and short positions, the practice of setting expected returns equal to zero need not be conservative, but in some cases can yield severely downward-biased estimates of VaR. This is particularly relevant for strategies designed to exploit mean reversion, such as fixed income relative and equity market neutral strategies. For such strategies, which involve buying "losers" and selling "winners," the unconditional mean is typically negative (since, by definition, losers include securities with lower expected returns than the winners), hence a zero expected return is, in fact, a more aggressive assumption from the risk management perspective.

For concreteness, observe that

$$\sigma_p = \sqrt{\omega' \Sigma \omega}, \tag{8.27}$$

where Σ is the covariance matrix of the m managers' returns, and consider the following three special cases.

Perfect Correlation. Suppose the returns of all m managers are perfectly correlated. In that case,

$$\sigma_p = \sqrt{\omega' \sigma \sigma' \omega} = \sum_{i=1} \omega_k \sigma_k = \overline{\sigma}, \tag{8.28}$$

where $\sigma \equiv [\sigma_1 \cdots \sigma_m]'$. This is simply the weighted average of the standard deviations of the m managers, and it implies that

$$\xi_k = \frac{\sigma_k}{\overline{\sigma}} \xi_p, \tag{8.29}$$

so that managers with higher-than-average standard deviations should be allowed larger loss limits (of course, they should also be required to yield higher expected returns because of their higher risks). Only in the special case where all managers have identical standard deviations does $\xi_k = \xi_p$.

No Correlation. If the returns of the m managers are all mutually uncorrelated, then

$$\sigma_p = \sqrt{\sum_{i=1}^{m} \omega_k^2 \sigma_k^2}, \tag{8.30}$$

and in the special case where all managers have identical return standard deviation σ and the portfolio is divided equally among them, we have

$$\xi_k = \sqrt{m} \, \xi_p. \tag{8.31}$$

For a group of $m = 25$ managers, the loss limit ξ_k for an individual manager is a factor of 5.00 times the portfolio loss limit ξ_p.

Equal Correlation. For a collection of managers with identical return standard deviation σ, identical portfolio weights $\omega_k = 1/m$, and equally correlated returns with correlation coefficient ρ, we have

$$\mathbf{\Sigma} = \sigma^2 [\rho u u' + (1-\rho)\mathbf{I}], \tag{8.32}$$

$$\sigma_p = \sqrt{\omega' \mathbf{\Sigma} \omega} = \sigma \sqrt{\rho + (1-\rho)/m}, \tag{8.33}$$

which implies

$$\xi_k = \frac{\sigma}{\sigma_p} \xi_p = \frac{1}{\sqrt{\rho + (1-\rho)/m}} \xi_p. \tag{8.34}$$

Values for the factor σ/σ_p in (8.34) are reported in Table 8.2, which shows that for $m = 25$ and $\rho = 30\%$, the loss limit for an individual manager is 1.75 times the portfolio loss limit ξ_p. Specifically, given a portfolio loss limit of 3% per month,

Table 8.2.
Portfolio Loss-Limit Multipliers σ/σ_p*

σ/σ_p				m			
	5	10	15	20	23	25	30
$\rho(\%)$							
0	2.24	3.16	3.87	4.47	4.80	5.00	5.48
5	2.04	2.63	2.97	3.20	3.31	3.37	3.50
10	1.89	2.29	2.50	2.63	2.68	2.71	2.77
15	1.77	2.06	2.20	2.28	2.31	2.33	2.37
20	1.67	1.89	1.99	2.04	2.06	2.08	2.10
25	1.58	1.75	1.83	1.87	1.88	1.89	1.91
30	1.51	1.64	1.70	1.73	1.74	1.75	1.76
35	1.44	1.55	1.59	1.62	1.63	1.63	1.64
40	1.39	1.47	1.51	1.52	1.53	1.54	1.54
45	1.34	1.41	1.43	1.45	1.45	1.46	1.46
50	1.29	1.35	1.37	1.38	1.38	1.39	1.39
55	1.25	1.30	1.31	1.32	1.33	1.33	1.33
60	1.21	1.25	1.26	1.27	1.27	1.27	1.28
65	1.18	1.21	1.22	1.22	1.23	1.23	1.23
70	1.15	1.17	1.18	1.18	1.18	1.19	1.19
75	1.12	1.14	1.14	1.15	1.15	1.15	1.15
80	1.09	1.10	1.11	1.11	1.11	1.11	1.11
85	1.07	1.08	1.08	1.08	1.08	1.08	1.08
90	1.04	1.05	1.05	1.05	1.05	1.05	1.05
95	1.02	1.02	1.02	1.02	1.02	1.02	1.03
100	1.00	1.00	1.00	1.00	1.00	1.00	1.00

*These factors, when multiplied by the monthly portfolio loss limit, yield the allowable monthly loss limits for individual managers with identical return standard deviations and mutual correlation coefficients of ρ.

each manager can be allowed a loss limit of 5.25% per month if the managers' returns are equally correlated with a 30% correlation.

8.10 Summary and Extensions

The framework outlined in Sections 8.1–8.9 is by no means a complete specification of a fund of fund's investment process but merely one possible blueprint for developing such a process. Unlike traditional investments that have well-circumscribed risk and performance parameters, hedge fund investments are heterogeneous, highly dynamic and adaptive, and risky in many different dimensions. Therefore, a purely quantitative approach to managing a portfolio of hedge funds is neither possible nor desirable at this stage of the industry's life cycle. Instead, we propose an integrated approach that blends qualitative judgments with quantitative rigor in a consistent manner.

But there are costs to such integration, one of which is the two-stage optimization process which, by definition, is suboptimal when compared to a single-stage optimization of all managers; hence this issue deserves further discussion. First, because of the time variation in correlations among individual hedge funds—due to estimation errors, data errors, and outliers, as well as shifts in the true correlations—mean-variance optimization of individual hedge funds yields highly unstable weights, fluctuating wildly from month to month and across managers. Mean-variance optimization of asset-class weights, however, is likely to be more stable. Second, quantitative information regarding aggregate trends, correlations, and volatilities of hedge fund investment styles is generally more reliable than similar information about individual funds, and it is easier to incorporate and track the value-added of such aggregate quantitative information in a two-stage process. And finally, the key differences between managers within a single hedge fund style category are easier to identify through qualitative judgment than quantitative analysis, especially given the lack of position transparency for most hedge funds. Therefore, a two-stage process where quantitative analysis is applied to the asset-allocation decision, where quantitative methods yield the highest value-added, and qualitative judgments are applied to manager selection, where quantitative methods are at a disadvantage, best exploits the best of both processes.

However, the two-stage process is clearly a compromise between the theoretical tenets of mean-variance portfolio optimization and the practical exigencies of hedge fund investing. As hedge funds provide more transparency and as the qualitative due diligence process for identifying operational risks becomes more quantitative, we can move closer to a single-stage optimization process and its corresponding performance benefits.

There are a number of additional directions for continuing research. Perhaps the most pressing is the need for further data, analysis, and quantification of operational risks such as potential conflicts of interest, weak corporate governance structures, improper accounting procedures, insufficient operational resources, and fraud. In a study of more than 100 liquidated hedge funds over the past two decades, Feffer and Kundro (2003) conclude that "half of all failures could be attributed to operational risk alone," of which fraud is just one example. In fact, they observe that "The most common operational issues related to hedge fund losses have been misrepresentation of fund investments, misappropriation of investor funds, unauthorized trading, and inadequate resources" (Feffer and Kundro, 2003, p. 5). The last of these issues is, of course, not related to fraud, but Feffer and Kundro (2003, Figure 2) report that only 6% of their sample involved inadequate resources, whereas 41% involved misrepresentation of investments, 30% misappropriation of funds, and 14% unauthorized trading. These results suggest that operational issues are a significant risk factor and deserve considerable attention from investors and managers alike.

Modeling correlations and nonlinear statistical relations among hedge fund categories and managers also requires further study. For example, Chan et al. (2004) propose several methods for constructing risk models for hedge funds, including statistical regime-switching models that seem especially promising for capturing sudden shifts in correlations among hedge funds. To capture optionlike risk exposures of certain hedge fund strategies, the synthetic option-replication approach of Haugh and Lo (2001) may be useful.

The asset-allocation decision among hedge fund categories is another area in which considerable progress can be made. Unlike traditional asset-class returns which have minimal levels of predictability, certain hedge fund returns are quite persistent, as the empirical analysis in Sections 8.2 and 8.3 confirm. Such levels of predictability imply that significant benefits may accrue to a truly dynamic portfolio optimization process, along the lines of Samuelson (1969).

Finally, perhaps the most pressing issue facing fund-of-funds managers beyond the basic investment process is how to avoid hedge fund failures. While operational due diligence reviews can spot certain warning signs, these reviews occur too infrequently to be of significant value in managing a fund-of-funds portfolio on a monthly and quarterly basis. Chan et al. (2004) tackle this issue explicitly by modeling hedge fund liquidations in the Lipper TASS Graveyard database using a logit regression model in which the probability of liquidation is parametrized as a function of a variety of explanatory variables including age, past performance, volatility, investment style, and assets under management. Although still at an early stage of research and development, this approach seems quite promising, as Chan et al. (2004) have shown that liquidation probabilities vary considerably across hedge fund styles and characteristics in intuitively sensible ways.

9

Practical Considerations

In addition to the new analytics proposed in this monograph, there are several practical considerations that should be kept in mind when evaluating alternative investments. The first is that despite the emphasis on alpha among hedge fund managers and investors, risk management can be a significant source of alpha in and of itself, as we illustrate through a simple example in Section 9.1. Of course, the ultimate determination of how much risk is appropriate for a hedge fund involves risk preferences—of both investors and managers—and this is discussed in Section 9.2. And finally, one of the most controversial issues surrounding alternative investments are the implications of the Efficient Markets Hypothesis (EMH) for the industry. If markets are efficient, then alternative investments do not offer any advantages over traditional investments because any excess expected returns must be the result of additional risk exposures. In Section 9.3, we review this debate and offer a resolution based on an alternative to market efficiency, the Adaptive Markets Hypothesis (AMH), and provide some preliminary empirical evidence to support this new theory. And in Section 9.4, we consider the need for regulatory reform in the hedge fund industry and propose a novel approach patterned after the National Transportation Safety Board's oversight of the airline industry.

9.1 Risk Management as a Source of Alpha

In contrast to traditional investment vehicles such as stocks, bonds, and mutual funds, hedge funds have rather different risk/return objectives. Most hedge fund investors expect high returns in exchange for the corresponding risks that they are expected to bear. Perhaps because it is taken for granted that hedge funds are riskier, few hedge fund investors and even fewer hedge fund managers seem to devote much attention to active risk management. Hedge fund investors and managers often dismiss risk management as a secondary objective, with alpha or performance as the main objective.

However, if there is one lasting insight that modern finance has given us, it is the inexorable trade-off between risk and expected return; hence one cannot be considered without reference to the other. Moreover, it is often overlooked that proper risk management can, by itself, be a source of alpha. This is summarized neatly in the old Street wisdom that "one of the best ways to make money is not to lose it." More formally, consider the case of a manager with a fund that has an annual expected return $E[R]$ of 10% and an annual volatility $SD[R]$ of 75%, a rather mediocre fund that few hedge fund investors would consider seriously. Now suppose that such a manager layered a risk management process on top of his investment strategy that eliminates the possibility of returns lower than -20%; i.e., his return after implementing this risk management protocol is R^*, where

$$R^* = \max[R, \ -20\%]. \tag{9.1}$$

Under the assumption of lognormally distributed returns, it can be shown that the expected value $E[R^*]$ of R^* is 20.9%—by truncating the left tail of the distribution of R below -20%, the expected value of the strategy is doubled! In this case, risk management has become a significant source of alpha, indeed. Moreover, the volatility $SD[R^*]$ of R^* is 66.8%, lower than the volatility of R; hence risk management can simultaneously increase alpha and decrease risk. Table 9.1 reports $E[R^*]$ and $SD[R^*]$ for various values of $E[R]$, $SD[R]$, and truncation levels and illustrates the potent and direct impact that risk management can have on performance.

Of course, risk management rarely takes the simple form of a guaranteed floor for returns. Indeed, such "portfolio insurance" is often quite costly—if it can be obtained at all—and is equivalent to the premium of a put option on the value of the portfolio. For example, the Black–Scholes premium for the put option implicit in (9.1) is equal to 15.4% of the value of the portfolio to be insured.[1] But this only highlights the relevance and economic value of risk management—according to the Black–Scholes formula, the ability to manage risks in such a way as to create a floor of -20% for annual performance is worth 15.4% of assets under management! The more effective a manager's risk management process is, the more it contributes to alpha.

---

[1] Assuming a 1-year term for the put, with a strike that is 20% out of the money, and annual volatility and risk-free rates of 75% and 5%, respectively.

9.2 Risk Preferences

Risk preferences play a major role in any investment process involving hedge funds, from both manager and investor perspectives. Hedge fund managers are typically compensated with both fixed and incentive fees, and this nonlinear payoff scheme can induce excess risk-taking behavior if it is not properly managed. Imposing hurdle rates, high-water marks, and other nonlinearities on the manager's compensation creates additional complexities that may have a material impact on the manager's investment decisions, particularly in extreme circumstances such as after large losses. Moreover, given the large swings that often characterize hedge fund performance, the financial and psychological pressures faced by managers each day are not trivial and take their toll.

At the same time, the risk preferences of investors are equally relevant for risk management for hedge funds since the behavior of investors greatly influences the behavior of managers. If the stereotype that hedge fund investors are "hot money" is true, this will affect the types of risks that hedge fund managers can bear. Lockup periods and redemption fees are typical methods of dealing with skittish investors, but these can sometimes exacerbate the all-too-human tendency to panic in the face of crisis. Ironically, despite all of the many tools offered to individual investors—risk-tolerance surveys, "what-if" scenario simulators, and lifetime financial planning software—there is virtually nothing comparable for helping institutional investors determine their collective risk preferences. Perhaps the magnitude of this challenge is too daunting for any single manager or consultant, but without a clear understanding of an investor's risk preferences, it is impossible to manage risks properly or to formulate an appropriate investment policy.

The fact that institutional investors are almost always represented by a small group of individuals makes risk preferences even more difficult to quantify, which is all the more reason to take up this challenge. Consider the case of a pension fund that enjoyed a surplus of 5% just a few years ago but finds itself underfunded by 3% today. When facing a surplus, the fund's investment committee was conservative, lowering its equity allocation so as to preserve its gain; faced with a 3% deficit, the investment committee has become more aggressive, hoping to make up the shortfall by overweighting higher-yielding assets, including its first foray into alternative investments. This pension fund's risk preferences have changed significantly as a result of a change in its funding status, and while academics can debate the rationality of such preference reversals, they are a reality that must be addressed explicitly. By developing a better understanding of the dynamics of group decision-making processes and the risk preferences that they represent, institutional investors will be better prepared to deal with the inevitable swings in market conditions.

Any complete investment process involving alternative investments must take into account the risk preferences of both investors and managers in determining

Table 9.1.

The Value of Risk Management*

Left panel:

		E[R]					
	SD[R]	−5%	0%	5%	10%	15%	20%
κ = −50%							
	5%	−5.0%	0.0%	5.0%	10.0%	15.0%	20.0%
		5.0%	5.0%	5.0%	5.0%	5.0%	5.0%
	10%	−5.0%	0.0%	5.0%	10.0%	15.0%	20.0%
		10.0%	10.0%	10.0%	10.0%	10.0%	10.0%
	25%	−5.0%	0.0%	5.0%	10.0%	15.0%	20.0%
		24.9%	25.0%	25.0%	25.0%	25.0%	25.0%
	50%	−3.5%	1.0%	5.7%	10.4%	15.3%	20.2%
		48.3%	48.8%	49.2%	49.4%	49.6%	49.8%
	75%	−0.5%	3.5%	7.8%	12.1%	16.6%	21.2%
		71.4%	72.0%	72.5%	73.0%	73.4%	73.7%
	100%	2.5%	6.3%	10.3%	14.4%	18.7%	23.0%
		95.2%	95.7%	96.2%	96.7%	97.1%	97.5%
κ = −40%							
	5%	−5.0%	0.0%	5.0%	10.0%	15.0%	20.0%
		5.0%	5.0%	5.0%	5.0%	5.0%	5.0%
	10%	−5.0%	0.0%	5.0%	10.0%	15.0%	20.0%
		10.0%	10.0%	10.0%	10.0%	10.0%	10.0%
	25%	−4.7%	0.1%	5.1%	10.0%	15.0%	20.0%
		24.5%	24.8%	24.9%	25.0%	25.0%	25.0%

Right panel:

		E[R]					
	SD[R]	−5%	0%	5%	10%	15%	20%
κ = −20%							
	5%	−5.0%	0.0%	5.0%	10.0%	15.0%	20.0%
		5.0%	5.0%	5.0%	5.0%	5.0%	5.0%
	10%	−4.8%	0.0%	5.0%	10.0%	15.0%	20.0%
		9.6%	9.9%	10.0%	10.0%	10.0%	10.0%
	25%	−1.6%	2.2%	6.3%	10.7%	15.4%	20.2%
		21.2%	22.3%	23.2%	23.9%	24.4%	24.7%
	50%	5.6%	8.6%	11.9%	15.4%	19.2%	23.1%
		41.6%	42.7%	43.8%	44.8%	45.7%	46.5%
	75%	12.0%	14.8%	17.8%	20.9%	24.3%	27.8%
		64.2%	65.0%	65.9%	66.8%	67.6%	68.5%
	100%	17.3%	20.0%	22.9%	25.9%	29.1%	32.4%
		88.2%	88.8%	89.4%	90.0%	90.7%	91.4%
κ = −10%							
	5%	−4.6%	0.0%	5.0%	10.0%	15.0%	20.0%
		4.4%	4.9%	5.0%	5.0%	5.0%	5.0%
	10%	−3.1%	0.7%	5.2%	10.0%	15.0%	20.0%
		7.8%	8.9%	9.6%	9.9%	10.0%	10.0%
	25%	2.2%	5.1%	8.5%	12.3%	16.4%	20.8%
		18.3%	19.8%	21.1%	22.2%	23.1%	23.8%

50%	−1.5%	2.6%	6.8%	11.3%	15.9%	20.6%	10.7%	13.2%	15.9%	18.9%	22.2%	25.7%
	46.6%	47.3%	47.9%	48.5%	48.9%	49.2%	38.7%	39.9%	41.0%	42.2%	43.3%	44.4%
75%	2.8%	6.4%	10.2%	14.2%	18.3%	22.6%	17.7%	20.2%	22.7%	25.5%	28.4%	31.5%
	69.3%	70.0%	70.7%	71.3%	71.9%	72.4%	61.5%	62.3%	63.2%	64.1%	65.0%	66.0%
100%	6.7%	10.2%	13.8%	17.5%	21.4%	25.4%	23.5%	25.9%	28.5%	31.2%	34.0%	37.0%
	93.0%	93.6%	94.2%	94.7%	95.3%	95.8%	85.7%	86.2%	86.8%	87.5%	88.2%	88.9%
			$\kappa = -30\%$						$\kappa = -5\%$			
5%	−5.0%	0.0%	5.0%	10.0%	15.0%	20.0%	−3.0%	0.4%	5.0%	10.0%	15.0%	20.0%
	5.0%	5.0%	5.0%	5.0%	5.0%	5.0%	3.0%	4.4%	4.9%	5.0%	5.0%	5.0%
10%	−5.0%	0.0%	5.0%	10.0%	15.0%	20.0%	−1.0%	1.9%	5.7%	10.2%	15.0%	20.0%
	10.0%	10.0%	10.0%	10.0%	10.0%	10.0%	6.2%	7.8%	8.9%	9.6%	9.9%	10.0%
25%	−3.8%	0.7%	5.3%	10.2%	15.1%	20.0%	4.8%	7.3%	10.2%	13.5%	17.3%	21.4%
	23.4%	24.0%	24.4%	24.7%	24.9%	24.9%	16.8%	18.3%	19.7%	21.0%	22.1%	23.0%
50%	1.5%	5.1%	8.9%	12.9%	17.1%	21.5%	13.6%	15.8%	18.3%	21.1%	24.1%	27.3%
	44.3%	45.2%	46.1%	46.9%	47.6%	48.2%	37.2%	38.4%	39.6%	40.8%	41.9%	43.1%
75%	7.0%	10.2%	13.6%	17.1%	20.9%	24.8%	20.9%	23.1%	25.5%	28.0%	30.8%	33.7%
	66.8%	67.6%	68.4%	69.2%	69.9%	70.7%	60.1%	60.9%	61.8%	62.7%	63.7%	64.6%
100%	11.7%	14.7%	18.0%	21.4%	24.9%	28.5%	26.7%	29.0%	31.4%	34.0%	36.7%	39.5%
	90.7%	91.2%	91.9%	92.5%	93.1%	93.8%	84.4%	84.9%	85.5%	86.2%	86.9%	87.6%

*Expected values $E[R^*]$ (first rows) and standard deviations $SD[R^*]$ (second rows) of $R^* \equiv \max[R, \kappa]$ for lognormally distributed return R with expectation $E[R]$, standard deviation $SD[R]$, and truncation point κ.

the appropriate risk exposures of a hedge fund. Given the magnitudes and many variations of risk that affect a typical hedge fund, it is even more important to integrate the "three P's of total risk management"—prices, probabilities, and preferences—in this context.[2] For example, Lo, Repin, and Steenbarger (2005) describe a series of questionnaires designed to elicit risk preferences and personality traits, which were administered to a group of day traders over a period of several weeks while the participants were actively trading in an attempt to relate risk and personality profiles to trading performance.[3] Similar profiling methods may be developed for hedge fund managers and investors and, eventually, included in discussions between manager and investor so as to reduce the likelihood of misaligned expectations.

The importance of risk preferences underscores the human element in hedge funds, which is part of a broader set of issues often categorized as *operational risks*. These include organizational aspects such as the reliability of back-office operations, legal infrastructure, accounting and trade reconciliation, personnel issues, and the day-to-day management of the business. Many of these aspects are not subject to quantitative analysis, but they are bona fide risks that cannot be ignored and, in some cases, can quickly overshadow market risks in determining fund performance. Organizations such as the Alternative Investment Management Association (AIMA, http://www.aima.org) provide sample due diligence question- naires that provide excellent starting points for operational risk reviews.

9.3 Hedge Funds and the Efficient Markets Hypothesis

One of the most influential ideas in modern economics and finance is the Efficient Markets Hypothesis, the idea that market prices incorporate all information rationally and instantaneously. Like so many of the ideas of modern economics, the origins of the EMH can be traced back to Paul Samuelson (1965), whose contribution is neatly summarized by the title of his article "Proof That Properly Anticipated Prices Fluctuate Randomly." In an informationally efficient market, price changes must be unforecastable if they are properly anticipated, i.e., if they fully incorporate the information and expectations of all market participants. Roberts (1967) and Fama (1970) operationalized this hypothesis—summarized in Fama's well-known epithet "Prices fully reflect all available information"—by placing structure on various information sets available to market participants.

This concept of market efficiency has a wonderfully counterintuitive and seemingly contradictory flavor to it: The more efficient the market, the more

---

[2] See Lo (1999) for further details.

[3] Lo and Repin provide related risk surveys and personality profiling tools at http://www.risk- psychology.net. See also MacCrimmon and Wehrung (1986).

random the sequence of price changes generated by such a market must be, and the most efficient market of all is one in which price changes are completely random and unpredictable. This, of course, is not an accident of nature but is the direct outcome of many active participants attempting to profit from their information. Legions of greedy investors aggressively pounce on even the smallest informational advantages at their disposal, and in doing so they incorporate their information into market prices and quickly eliminate the profit opportunities that gave rise to their actions. If this occurs instantaneously, which it must in an idealized world of "frictionless" markets and costless trading, then prices must always fully reflect all available information and no profits can be garnered from information-based trading (because such profits have already been captured).

The EMH is particularly relevant for the hedge fund industry because the primary attraction of hedge funds is their higher expected returns and, in many cases, lower risk as measured by correlation to broad-based market indexes such as the S&P 500. If the EMH is true, then it should not be possible to generate higher expected returns after adjusting for risk. For example, according to the Capital Asset Pricing Model the risk-adjusted expected return of any investment P is determined by the market beta of that investment:

$$E[R_p] = R_f + \beta\,(E[R_m] - R_f), \tag{9.2}$$

where R_f is the return on a riskless asset such as U.S. Treasury bills and $E[R_m]$ is the expected return of the market portfolio, often approximated by the S&P 500. But consider the example of Fund XYZ, a pseudonym for a live hedge fund drawn from the Altvest database with an annual mean return of 12.54% and an annual return standard deviation of 5.50% from January 1985 to December 2002 (Figure 9.1). Assuming a riskless rate of 2.5% and a market risk premium of 8% during this period, the CAPM implies that XYZ should have a beta of

$$\beta = \frac{E[R_{\text{XYZ}}] - R_f}{E[R_m] - R_f} = \frac{12.54\% - 2.5\%}{8\%} = 1.26.$$

However, a simple regression of XYZ's returns on the returns of the S&P 500 yields an estimated beta of -0.028 with an R^2 of 0.66%. In other words, Fund XYZ is an asset with virtually no market risk exposure and yet has had comparable returns over an 18-year period with considerably lower volatility. How can this be consistent with the EMH?

Proponents of market efficiency would respond by arguing that the CAPM is not synonymous with the EMH and that the higher expected returns of hedge fund investments may be fair compensation for other systematic risk factors contained in their returns, e.g., liquidity, volatility, and tail risk (see, in particular, the examples in Sections 1.1 and 1.2). However, even when such factors are taken

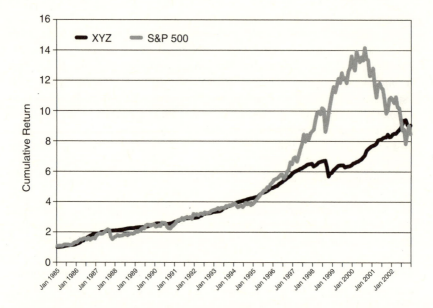

Figure 9.1. *Cumulative total return of Fund XYZ and the S&P 500 (January 1985 to January 2003). Data source: Altvest.*

into account, a number of funds still exhibit excess expected returns, implying either that the models are wrong or that markets are inefficient.

Others have argued that funds like XYZ are simply statistical flukes, products of sample selection and survivorship bias. In other words, if a fair coin is flipped enough times, eventually a sequence of 20 heads in a row will be realized (Lo and MacKinlay, 1990b; Lo, 1994). The difficulty with this argument is the existence of more than a few outliers in the hedge fund industry, e.g., Renaissance Technologies, D.E. Shaw, Soros Fund Group, Tudor Investments, Caxton, Highbridge, and Moore, implying either that they have been unusually lucky in this lifetime or that certain hedge fund managers do have genuine skill in producing excess risk-adjusted expected returns.

A more satisfying resolution to this apparent contradiction may be found in the Adaptive Markets Hypothesis, an alternative to the EMH proposed by Lo (2004) in which evolutionary principles are applied to financial markets along the lines of Bernstein (1998), Farmer and Lo (1999), and Farmer (2002). Prices reflect as much information as dictated by the combination of environmental conditions and the number and nature of "species" in the economy or, to use the appropriate biological term, the *ecology*. By species, we mean distinct groups of market participants each behaving in a common manner. For example, pension funds may be considered one species; retail investors, another; market makers, a third; and hedge fund managers, a fourth. If multiple species (or the members of a single highly populous species) are competing for rather scarce resources within a single market, that market is likely to be highly efficient, e.g., the market for 10-year U.S. Treasury notes, which reflects most relevant information very quickly indeed. If, on the other hand, a small number of species are competing for rather abundant resources in a given market, that market will be less efficient, e.g., the market for oil paintings from the Italian Renaissance. Market efficiency cannot be evaluated in a vacuum but is highly context-dependent and dynamic, just as insect populations advance and decline as a function of the seasons, the number of predators and prey they face, and their abilities to adapt to an ever-changing environment.

The profit opportunities in any given market are akin to the amount of food and water in a particular local ecology—the more resources present, the less fierce the competition. As competition increases, either because of dwindling food supplies or an increase in the animal population, resources are depleted, which in turn eventually causes a population decline, decreasing the level of competition and starting the cycle again. In some cases cycles converge to corner solutions; i.e., certain species become extinct, food sources are permanently exhausted, or environmental conditions shift dramatically. By viewing economic profits as the ultimate food source on which market participants depend for their survival, the dynamics of market interactions and financial innovation can be readily derived.

Under the AMH, behavioral biases abound. The origins of such biases are heuristics that are adapted to nonfinancial contexts, and their impact is determined by the size of the population with such biases versus the size of competing populations with more effective heuristics. During the fall of 1998, the desire for liquidity and safety of a certain population of investors overwhelmed the population of hedge funds attempting to arbitrage such preferences, causing those arbitrage relations to break down. However, in the years prior to August 1998, fixed income relative-value traders profited handsomely from these activities, presumably at the expense of individuals with seemingly "irrational" preferences (in fact, such preferences were shaped by a certain set of evolutionary forces and might be quite rational in other contexts). Therefore, under the AMH, investment strategies undergo cycles of profitability and loss in response to changing business conditions, the number of competitors entering and exiting the industry, and the type and magnitude of profit opportunities available. As opportunities shift, so too do the affected populations. For example, after 1998, the number of fixed income relative-value hedge funds declined dramatically—because of outright failures, investor redemptions, and fewer startups in this sector—but many have reappeared in recent years as performance for this type of investment strategy has improved.

A concrete example of these "population dynamics" can be found by considering the birth and death of funds in various style categories in the Lipper TASS database. Table 9.2 reports the number of entries and exits of funds in the unfiltered

Table 9.2.

Annual Entries and Exits within Three Style Categories in the Lipper TASS Hedge Fund Database (1994 to 2007)

Year	Existing Funds	New Entries	New Exits	Intrayear Entry/Exit	Total Funds	Attrition Rate (%)	Index Return (%)
				Global Macro			
1994	56	12	3	0	65	5.4	−5.7
1995	65	21	6	0	80	9.2	30.7
1996	80	14	16	4	78	20.0	25.6
1997	78	20	7	1	91	9.0	37.1
1998	91	20	8	2	103	8.8	−3.6
1999	103	15	15	1	103	14.6	5.8
2000	103	18	32	0	89	31.1	11.7
2001	89	18	13	0	94	14.6	18.4
2002	94	38	7	0	125	7.4	14.7
2003	125	41	10	1	156	8.0	18.0
2004	156	37	10	0	183	6.4	8.5
2005	183	43	29	1	197	15.8	9.2
2006	197	22	39	0	180	19.8	13.5
2007	180	7	13	0	174	7.2	9.0
				Long/Short Equity Hedge			
1994	198	58	3	0	253	1.5	−8.1
1995	253	80	9	0	324	3.6	23.0
1996	324	121	21	0	424	6.5	17.1
1997	424	130	22	3	532	5.2	21.5
1998	532	132	31	2	633	5.8	17.2
1999	633	178	47	3	764	7.4	47.2
2000	764	224	56	4	932	7.3	2.1
2001	932	225	99	2	1058	10.6	−3.7
2002	1,058	179	118	4	1119	11.2	−1.6
2003	1,119	212	110	3	1221	9.8	17.3
2004	1,221	252	136	4	1337	11.1	11.6
2005	1,337	221	166	4	1392	12.4	9.7
2006	1,392	143	207	3	1328	14.9	14.4
2007	1,328	24	119	0	1233	9.0	9.0
				Fixed Income Arbitrage			
1994	23	16	0	0	39	0.0	0.3
1995	39	12	5	0	46	12.8	12.5
1996	46	16	4	0	58	8.7	15.9
1997	58	16	3	1	71	5.2	9.3
1998	71	15	14	0	72	19.7	−8.2
1999	72	13	8	0	77	11.1	12.1
2000	77	14	11	0	80	14.3	6.3
2001	80	23	6	0	97	7.5	8.0
2002	97	29	7	0	119	7.2	5.8
2003	119	57	6	0	170	5.0	8.0
2004	170	53	10	0	213	5.9	6.9
2005	213	31	29	1	215	13.6	0.6
2006	215	22	41	0	196	19.1	8.7
2007	196	7	10	0	193	5.1	1.7

Lipper TASS database within each of the three style categories Global Macro, Long/Short Equity, and Fixed Income Arbitrage. As in Table 2.5, the entry-and-exit dynamics begin only in 1994 when Lipper TASS began maintaining their Graveyard database. The last column of Table 9.2 reports the annual compound return of the CS/Tremont style index corresponding to each of the three categories. By comparing the index returns with yearly attrition rates, it is apparent that performance has implications for future entries and exits, and vice versa. For example, 1995–1997 were exceptionally good years for Global Macro, with index returns of 30.7%, 25.6%, and 37.1%, respectively. Therefore, it is not surprising that the number of Global Macro funds increased from 65 at the end of 1994 to 103 at the end of 1998 with an attrition of 8.8% in 1998 that was considerably lower than the 20.0% attrition rate in 1996. However, from 1998 to 2000, the Global Macro index yielded considerably lower returns of −3.6%, 5.8%, and 11.7%, respectively, and during this period the attrition rate for Global Macro funds increased from 8.8% in 1998 to 31.1% in 2000. As returns improved from 2000 to 2002, new funds entered, fewer funds exited, and attrition rates declined once again. The Long/Short Equity and Fixed Income Arbitrage categories also exhibit the same kind of patterns.

This relation between attrition rates and performance is no accident but is a manifestation of the simple business dynamics of the hedge fund industry. Superior performance leads to greater demand for a particular style category, which spurs the launching of new funds in that category. The increased number of funds in the category, or increased capital among existing funds in the category, implies that for a given set of profit opportunities in that sector, returns will eventually decline. Such a decline will inevitably lead to a withdrawal of capital, which in turn implies that the weakest funds—those with the poorest performance, the lowest profit margins, and the least viable business entities—will be eliminated from the population.

The AMH has a number of concrete implications for the hedge fund industry in particular. The first implication is that contrary to the classical EMH, arbitrage opportunities do exist from time to time in the AMH. As Grossman and Stiglitz (1980) observed, without such opportunities, there would be no incentive to gather information, and the price discovery aspect of financial markets would collapse. From an evolutionary perspective, the existence of active liquid financial markets implies that profit opportunities must be present. As they are exploited, they disappear. But new opportunities are also continually being created as certain species die out, as others are born, and as institutions and business conditions change. Rather than the inexorable trend toward higher efficiency predicted by the EMH, the AMH implies considerably more complex market dynamics, with cycles as well as trends, panics, manias, bubbles, crashes, and other phenomena routinely witnessed in natural market ecologies. These dynamics provide the motivation for active management as Bernstein (1998) suggests, also giving rise to Niederhoffer's (1997) "carnivores" and "decomposers."

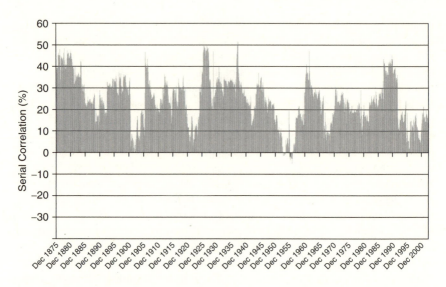

Figure 9.2. *First-order autocorrelation coefficients for monthly returns of the S&P composite index using 5-year rolling windows (January 1871 to April 2003).*

A second implication—highlighted by the entry-and-exit dynamics in Table 9.2—is that investment strategies also wax and wane, performing well in certain environments and performing poorly in other environments. Contrary to the classical EMH in which arbitrage opportunities are competed away, eventually eliminating the profitability of the strategy designed to exploit the arbitrage, the AMH implies that such strategies may decline for a time and then return to profitability when environmental conditions become more conducive to such trades. An obvious example is risk arbitrage, which has been unprofitable for several years because of the decline in investment banking activity since 2001. However, as merger and acquisition (M&A) activity begins to pick up again, risk arbitrage will start to regain its popularity among both investors and portfolio managers, as it has just this year. A more striking example can be found by computing the rolling first-order autocorrelation $\hat{\rho}_1$ of monthly returns of the S&P Composite Index from January 1871 to April 2003 (Figure 9.2). As a measure of market efficiency (recall that the Random Walk Hypothesis implies that returns are serially uncorrelated, hence ρ_1 should be 0 in theory), $\hat{\rho}_1$ might be expected to take on larger values during the early part of the sample and become progressively smaller during recent years as the U.S. equity market becomes more efficient. However, it is apparent from Figure 9.2 that the degree of efficiency—as measured by the first-order autocorrelation—varies through time in a cyclical fashion, and there are periods in the 1950s where the market was more efficient than in the early 1990s!

Such cycles are not ruled out by the EMH in theory, but in practice none of its existing empirical implementations have incorporated these dynamics, assuming instead a stationary world in which markets are perpetually in equilibrium. This widening gulf between the stationary EMH and obvious shifts in market conditions no doubt contributed to Bernstein's (2003) critique of the policy portfolio in strategic asset-allocation models and his controversial proposal to reconsider the case for tactical asset allocation.

A third implication is that innovation is the key to survival. The classical EMH suggests that certain levels of expected returns can be achieved simply by bearing a sufficient degree of risk. The AMH implies that the risk/reward relation varies through time and that a better way of achieving a consistent level of expected returns is to adapt to changing market conditions. By evolving a multiplicity of capabilities suited to a variety of environmental conditions, investment managers are less likely to become extinct as a result of rapid changes in business conditions. Consider the current theory of the demise of the dinosaurs (Alvarez, 1997) and ask where the next financial asteroid might come from.

Finally, the AMH has a clear implication for all financial market participants: Survival is the *only* objective that matters. While profit maximization, utility maximization, and general equilibrium are certainly relevant aspects of market ecology, the organizing principle in determining the evolution of markets and financial technology is simply survival.

These evolutionary underpinnings are more than simple speculation in the context of the hedge fund industry. The extraordinary degree of competitiveness of global financial markets, the outsize rewards that accrue to the "fittest" managers, and the low barriers to entry and minimal fixed costs of setup suggest that Darwinian selection—"survival of the richest," to be precise—is at work in determining the typical profile of a successful hedge fund. After all, unsuccessful managers are eventually eliminated from the population after suffering a certain level of losses.

The new paradigm of the AMH is still under development and certainly requires a great deal more research to render it "operationally meaningful" in Samuelson's sense. However, even at this early stage, it is clear that an evolutionary framework is able to reconcile many of the apparent contradictions between efficient markets and the hedge fund industry. The former may be viewed as the steady-state limit of a population with constant environmental conditions, and the latter involves specific adaptations of certain groups that may or may not persist, depending on the particular evolutionary paths that the economy experiences. More specific implications may be derived through a combination of deductive and inductive inference—e.g., theoretical analysis of evolutionary dynamics, empirical analysis of evolutionary forces in financial markets, and experimental analysis of decision making at the individual and group levels—and are currently under investigation (see Lo, 2004, for further discussion).

9.4 Regulating Hedge Funds

Despite the wealth of statistical information that the Lipper TASS database provides, it is silent on a great many issues surrounding the liquidation of hedge funds. For example, unlike the hand-collected sample of funds in Feffer and Kundro's (2003) study, we do not know the details of each Graveyard fund's liquidation, hence we cannot tell whether macroeconomic events are more important than operational risks in determining a hedge fund's fate. The historical lack of transparency of the hedge fund industry, coupled with the fact that it is still largely unregulated, suggests that a comprehensive analysis of hedge fund liquidations would be difficult to complete in the near term. The great heterogeneity of the hedge fund industry, even within a particular style category, makes it all the more challenging to draw specific inferences from existing data sources.

However, there is reason to be cautiously optimistic. The recent influx of assets from institutional investors—who require greater transparency to carry out their fiduciary obligations—is inducing hedge funds to be more forthcoming. Also, the regulatory environment is shifting rapidly. In particular, despite the fact that the initial attempt by the U.S. Securities and Exchange Commission to require hedge funds to register as investment advisers under the Investment Advisers Act of 1940 (Rule 203(b)(3)-2) was thwarted in June 2006 by the Washington, D.C. Circuit Court of Appeals, in May 2007 the Hedge Fund Registration Act was introduced and may very well become law in the near future. Registration under the 1940 act has generated considerable controversy, with compelling arguments on both sides of the debate. While registration might provide an additional layer of protection for investors, the costs of registration are substantial—both for the SEC and for many smaller hedge funds—which may stifle the growth of this vibrant industry.

Moreover, registering hedge funds may not be sufficient, especially if the goal is to protect the general public and promote the long-run health of the financial services industry. Registration requires filing certain information with the SEC on a regular basis and being subject to periodic on-site examinations, but the kind of information required does not necessarily address the main concern that these funds pose for the financial system: Are hedge funds engaged in activities that can destabilize financial markets and cause widespread dislocation throughout the industry? This concern was first brought to public awareness in August 1998 when the default of Russian government debt triggered a global flight to quality that caught many hedge funds by surprise. One of the most significant players in this market, LTCM, lost most of its multi-billion-dollar capital base in a matter of weeks. Ultimately, LTCM was bailed out by a consortium organized by the Federal Reserve Bank of New York because its collapse might have set off a chain reaction of failures of other major financial institutions.

The possibility of a domino effect in the hedge fund industry is one of the most important revelations to have come out of the LTCM debacle.

Prior to August 1998, vulnerabilities in the global financial system involved stock market crashes, bank runs, and hyperinflation—otherwise known as systemic risk—were largely the province of central bankers and finance ministers. Such events were rare but generally well understood, as in the case of the Asian crisis of 1997 in which overleveraged financial institutions and weak corporate governance led to a series of currency devaluations, stock market crashes, and defaults in Korea, Thailand, Indonesia, and other Asian countries. However, with the collapse of LTCM, a new source of systemic risk was born: the hedge fund. Given how little is known about these unregulated entities, a natural reaction to August 1998 is to regulate them. However, the specific information about LTCM's activities that might have helped regulators and investors to avoid the stunning losses of 1998—the fund's leverage, the number of credit lines available to the fund, the vulnerability of those credit lines during extreme market conditions, and the degree to which other funds had similar positions—is currently not required of registered investment advisers.

Apart from the costs and benefits of requiring hedge funds to register, it is clear that a different approach is needed to address the larger issue of systemic risk posed by these funds. We propose two specific innovations: a database of more detailed information about hedge funds and associated financial institutions to be collected and maintained by the SEC, and a separate unit within the SEC charged with the responsibility of conducting forensic examinations and providing publicly available summary reports in the wake of unintentional hedge fund liquidations.

Without data, it is virtually impossible for regulators to engage in any meaningful oversight of the hedge fund industry. An example of the importance of data for regulatory oversight is event analysis—one of the most powerful tools for detecting insider trading—in which the statistical properties of stock price movements are compared before, during, and after the release of material information regarding the stock. Unusual price movements prior to the release of material information sometimes signal an information leak, which can then be verified or refuted by a more detailed investigation. Without historical price data, the SEC's Division of Enforcement would lose its ability to monitor thousands of publicly traded securities simultaneously and in a timely fashion, making it virtually impossible for the SEC to enforce insider-trading laws broadly given the current size of its staff.

Regulators should have access to the following information from all hedge funds: monthly returns, leverage, assets under management, fees, instruments traded, and all brokerage, financing, and credit relationships. In addition, regulators should collect similar information from prime brokers, banks, and other hedge fund counterparties, as well as information about the capital adequacy of these financial institutions, as they are likely to be among the first casualties in any systemic event involving hedge funds. This information should be archived so that over time a complete historical database is developed and the dynamics of each entity and the industry can be tracked and measured.

There is, of course, a privacy issue regarding such highly confidential data that must be properly addressed. Unlike publicly traded companies such as mutual funds, which are required to disclose a great deal of information because they are selling their securities to the general public, hedge funds are private partnerships that can solicit only a limited clientele: investors who are deemed to be sophisticated and able to tolerate significant financial risks. As a result, managers willing to provide greater disclosure may choose a public offering such as a mutual fund, and those preferring opacity may choose instead to form a hedge fund. This menu of choices has great social benefits in providing a wider range of alternatives to suit different preferences and markets and should not be limited. However, it is possible to collect and analyze hedge fund data while protecting the confidentiality of all parties concerned, as illustrated by the relationship between U.S. banks and the Office of the Comptroller of the Currency.

In addition to serving as a repository for hedge fund data, the SEC can play an even more valuable role in reducing systemic risk by investigating and producing public reports of hedge fund liquidations. Although there may be common themes in the demise of many hedge funds—too much leverage, too concentrated a portfolio, operational failures, securities fraud, or insufficient assets under management—each liquidation has its own unique circumstances and is an opportunity for the hedge fund industry to learn and improve. We need look no further than the National Transportation Safety Board for an excellent and practical role model of an investigative unit specifically designed to provide greater transparency and improve public safety.

In the event of an airplane crash, the NTSB assembles a team of engineers and flight safety experts who are immediately dispatched to the crash site to conduct a thorough investigation, including interviewing witnesses, poring over historical flight logs and maintenance records, sifting through the wreckage to recover the flight recorder or "black box," and, if necessary, reassembling the aircraft from its parts so as to determine the ultimate cause of the crash. Once its work is completed, the NTSB publishes a report summarizing the team's investigation, concluding with specific recommendations for avoiding future occurrences of this type of accident. The report is entered into a searchable database that is available to the general public (http://www.ntsb.gov/ntsb/query.asp), and this has been one of the major factors underlying the remarkable safety record of commercial air travel.

For example, it is now current practice to spray airplanes with de-icing fluid just prior to take-off when the temperature is near freezing and it is raining or snowing. This procedure was instituted in the aftermath of the crash of USAir Flight 405 on March 22, 1992. Flight 405 stalled just after becoming airborne because of ice on its wings, despite the fact that de-icing fluid had been applied before it left the gate. Apparently, Flight 405's take-off was delayed because of air traffic, and ice re-accumulated on its wings while it waited for a departure slot on the runway in the freezing rain. The NTSB Aircraft Accident Report—published February 17, 1993, and available at several internet sites—contains a sobering summary of the NTSB's findings (Report AAR-93/02, p. vi):

> The National Transportation Safety Board determines that the probable cause of this accident was the failure of the airline industry and the Federal Aviation Administration to provide flightcrews with procedures, requirements, and criteria compatible with departure delays in conditions conducive to airframe icing and the decision by the flightcrew to take off without positive assurance that the airplane's wings were free of ice accumulation after 35 minutes of exposure to precipitation following de-icing. The ice contamination on the wings resulted in an aerodynamic stall and loss of control after liftoff. Contributing to the cause of the accident were the inappropriate procedures used by, and inadequate coordination between, the flightcrew that led to a takeoff rotation at a lower than prescribed air speed.
>
> The safety issues in this report focused on the weather affecting the flight, USAir's de-icing procedures, industry airframe de-icing practices, air traffic control aspects affecting the flight, USAir's takeoff and preflight procedures, and flightcrew qualifications and training. The dynamics of the airplane's impact with the ground, postaccident survivability, and crash/fire/rescue activities were also analyzed.

Current de-icing procedures have no doubt saved many lives thanks to NTSB Report AAR-93/02, but this particular innovation was paid for by the lives of the 27 individuals who did not survive the crash of Flight 405. Imagine the waste if the NTSB had not investigated this tragedy and produced concrete recommendations to prevent this from happening again.

Hedge fund liquidations are, of course, considerably less dire, generally involving no loss of life. However, as more pension funds make allocations to hedge funds, and as the "retailization" of hedge funds continues, losses in the hedge fund industry may have more significant implications for individual investors, in some cases threatening retirement wealth and basic living standards. Moreover, the spillover effects of an industrywide shock to hedge funds should not be underestimated, as the events surrounding LTCM in the fall of 1998 illustrated. For these reasons, an SEC-sponsored organization dedicated to investigating, reporting, and archiving the "accidents" of the hedge fund industry—and the financial services sector more generally—may yield significant social benefits in much the same way that the NTSB has improved transportation safety enormously for all air travelers. By maintaining teams of experienced professionals—forensic accountants, financial engineers from industry and academia, and securities and tax attorneys—who work together on a regular basis to investigate a number of hedge fund liquidations, the SEC would be able to determine quickly and accurately how each liquidation came about, and the resulting reports would be an invaluable source of ideas for improving financial markets and avoiding future liquidations of a similar nature.[4]

The establishment of an NTSB-like organization within the SEC will not be inexpensive. Currently, the SEC is understaffed and overburdened, and this is likely to worsen if all hedge funds are required to register under the Investment Advisers Act of 1940. In addition, the lure of the private sector makes it challenging for government agencies to attract and retain individuals with expertise in these highly employable fields. Individuals trained in forensic accounting, financial engineering, and securities law now command substantial premiums on Wall Street over government pay scales. Although a typical SEC employee is likely to be motivated more by civic duty than by financial gain, it would be unrealistic to build an organization on altruism alone.

The cost of an SEC-based Capital Markets Safety Board is more than justified by the valuable lessons that would be garnered from a systematic analysis of financial incidents and the public dissemination of recommendations by seasoned professionals who review multiple cases each year. The benefits would accrue not only to the wealthy—which is currently how the hedge fund industry is tilted—but would also flow to retail investors in the form of more stable financial markets, greater liquidity, reduced borrowing and lending costs as a result of decreased systemic risk exposures, and a wider variety of investment choices available to a larger segment of the population because of increased transparency, oversight, and, ultimately, financial security. It is unrealistic to expect that market crashes, panics, collapses, and fraud will ever be completely eliminated from our capital markets, but we should avoid compounding our mistakes by failing to learn from them.

---

[4] Formal government investigations of major financial events do occur from time to time, as in the April 1999 Hedge Funds, Leverage, and the Lessons of Long-Term Capital Management: Report of the President's Working Group in Financial Markets. However, this interagency report was put together on an ad hoc basis with committee members that had not worked together previously and regularly on forensic investigations of this kind. With multiple agencies involved, and none in charge of the investigation, the administrative overhead becomes more significant. Although any thorough investigation of the financial services sector is likely to involve the SEC, the CFTC, the U.S. Treasury, and the Federal Reserve—and interagency cooperation should be promoted—there are important operational advantages in tasking a single office with the responsibility for coordinating all such investigations and serving as a repository for the expertise in conducting forensic examinations of financial incidents.

10

What Happened to the Quants in August 2007?

The months leading up to August 2007 were a tumultuous period for global financial markets, with events in the U.S. subprime mortgage market casting long shadows over many parts of the financial industry. The blow-up of two Bear Stearns credit strategies funds in June, the sale of Sowood Capital Management's portfolio to Citadel after losses exceeding 50% in July, and mounting problems at Countrywide Financial—the nation's largest home lender—throughout the second and third quarters of 2007 set the stage for further turmoil in fixed income and credit markets during the month of August.

But during the week of August 6, something remarkable occurred. Several prominent hedge funds experienced unprecedented losses that week; however, unlike the Bear Stearns and Sowood funds, these hedge funds were invested primarily in exchange-traded equities, not in subprime mortgages or credit-related instruments. In fact, most of the hardest hit funds were employing long/short equity market neutral strategies—sometimes called *statistical arbitrage strategies*—that, by construction, did not have significant beta exposure, and which were supposed to be immune to most market gyrations. But the most remarkable aspect of these hedge fund losses was the fact that they were confined almost exclusively to funds using quantitative strategies. With laserlike precision, model-driven long/short equity funds were hit hard on Tuesday, August 7, and Wednesday, August 8, despite relatively little movement in fixed income and equity markets during those two days and no major losses reported in any other hedge fund sectors. Then, on Thursday, August 9, when the S&P 500 lost nearly 3%, most of these market neutral funds continued their losses, calling into question their market neutral status.

By Friday, August 10, the combination of movements in equity prices that caused the losses earlier in the week had reversed themselves, rebounding significantly but not completely. However, faced with mounting losses on August 7, 8, and 9 that exceeded all the standard statistical thresholds for extreme returns, many of the affected funds had cut their risk exposures along the way, which only served to exacerbate their losses while causing them to miss out on a portion of the reversals on August 10. And just as quickly as it had descended upon the quants, the perfect financial storm was over. At least for the moment.

The following week, the financial press surveyed the casualties and reported month-to-date losses ranging from −5% to −30% for some of the most consis-. tently profitable quant funds in the history of the industry.[1] David Viniar, chief financial officer of Goldman Sachs, argued that "We were seeing things that were 25-standard deviation moves, several days in a row.... There have been issues in some of the other quantitative spaces. But nothing like what we saw last week" (Thal Larsen, 2007).

What happened to the quants in August 2007?

In this chapter, we attempt to shed some light on this question by examining some indirect evidence about the profitability of long/short equity strategies over the past decade and during August 2007. We simulate the performance of a specific long/short equity strategy to see if we can capture the performance swings during the week of August 6, 2007, and then use this strategy to compare and contrast the events of August 2007 with those of August 1998. We then turn to individual and aggregate hedge fund data from the Lipper TASS database and the Credit Suisse/Tremont hedge fund indexes to develop a broader understanding of the evolution of long/short equity strategies over the past decade.

From these empirical results, we have developed the following tentative hypotheses about August 2007:

1. The losses to quant funds during the second week of August 2007 were initiated by the temporary price impact resulting from a large and rapid "unwinding" of one or more quantitative equity market neutral portfolios. The speed and magnitude of the price impact suggest that the unwind was likely the result of a sudden liquidation of a multi-strategy fund or proprietary trading desk, perhaps in response to margin calls from a deteriorating credit portfolio,

---

[1] For example, the *Wall Street Journal* reported on August 10, 2007, that

> After the close of trading, Renaissance Technologies Corp., a hedge fund company with one of the best records in recent years, told investors that a key fund has lost 8.7% so far in August and is down 7.4% in 2007. Another big fund company, Highbridge Capital Management, told investors its Highbridge Statistical Opportunities Fund was down 18% as of the 8th of the month, and was down 16% for the year. The $1.8 billion publicly traded Highbridge Statistical Market Neutral Fund was down 5.2% for the month as of Wednesday.... Tykhe Capital, LLC—a New York-based quantitative, or computer-driven, hedge fund firm that manages about $1.8 billion— has suffered losses of about 20% in its largest hedge fund so far this month ..." (see Zuckerman, Hagerty, and Gauthier-Villars, 2007)

and on August 14, the *Wall Street Journal* reported that the Goldman Sachs Global Equity Opportunities Fund "...lost more than 30% of its value last week ..." (Sender, Kelly, and Zuckerman, 2007).

a decision to cut risk in light of current market conditions, or a discrete change in business lines.

2. The price impact of the unwind on August 7–8 caused a number of other types of equity funds—long/short, 130/30, and long-only—to cut their risk exposures or "de-leverage," exacerbating the losses of many of these funds on August 8 and 9.

3. The majority of the unwind and de-leveraging occurred on August 7–9, after which the losses stopped and a significant—but not complete—reversal occurred on August 10.

4. This price-impact pattern suggests that the losses were the short-term side effects of a sudden (and probably forced) liquidation on August 7–8, not a fundamental or permanent breakdown in the underlying economic drivers of long/short equity strategies. However, the coordinated losses do imply a growing common component in this hedge fund sector.

5. Likely factors contributing to the magnitude of the losses of this apparent unwind were (a) the enormous growth in assets devoted to long/short equity strategies over the past decade and, more recently, to various 130/30 and other active-extension strategies; (b) the systematic decline in the profitability of quantitative equity market neutral strategies, due to increasing competition, technological advances, and institutional and environmental changes such as decimalization, the decline in retail order flow, and the decline in equity market volatility; (c) the increased leverage needed to maintain the levels of expected returns required by hedge fund investors in the face of lower profitability; (d) the historical liquidity of U.S. equity markets and the general lack of awareness (at least prior to August 6, 2007) of just how crowded the long/short equity category had become; and (e) the unknown size and timing of new subprime mortgage–related problems in credit markets, which created a climate of fear and panic, heightening the risk sensitivities of managers and investors across all markets and style categories.

6. The fact that quantitative funds were singled out during the week of August 6, 2007, had less to do with a breakdown of any specific quantitative algorithms than with the apparent sudden liquidation of one or more large quantitative equity market neutral portfolios. Because such portfolios consist primarily of exchanged-traded instruments, the price impact of the rapid unwind was quickly transmitted to other funds, with the most severe losses experienced by portfolios with the largest overlap with the portfolio that initiated the unwind. Not surprisingly, the portfolios with the largest overlap were those constructed using similar methods, i.e., quantitative equity market neutral methods. But the fact that these portfolios are typically highly diversified—involving several hundred positions on any given day—suggests that the impact of the unwind could be much broader, affecting many other types of portfolios.

7. The differences between the behavior of our test strategy in August 2007 and August 1998, the increase in the number of funds and the average assets under management per fund in the Lipper TASS hedge fund database, the increase in average absolute correlations among the CS/Tremont hedge fund indexes, and the growth of credit-related strategies among hedge funds and proprietary trading desks suggest that systemic risk in the hedge fund industry may have increased in recent years.

8. The ongoing problems in the subprime mortgage and credit sectors may trigger additional liquidity shocks in the more liquid hedge fund style categories such as long/short equity, global macro, and managed futures. However, the severity of the impact on long/short equity strategies is likely to be muted in the near future given that market participants now have more information regarding the size of this sector and the potential price impact of another fire-sale liquidation of a long/short equity portfolio.

We wish to emphasize at the outset that these hypotheses are tentative, based solely on indirect evidence, and without the benefit of very much hindsight given the recency of these events. For these reasons, this chapter should be interpreted more as an evolving case study, not formal academic research. We are focusing on a rather timely topic, which does not afford the luxury of multiple rounds of critical review and revision through which more enduring research findings are typically forged.

However, we wish to highlight another distinction between academic research and this chapter. Original research typically offers novel answers to questions that have yet to be resolved. There is little point, and no credit given, to answering questions for which the answers are already known. But the answer to the question of what happened to the quants in August 2007 is indeed known, at least to a number of industry professionals who were directly involved in these markets and strategies in August 2007.

Therefore, it is an odd task that we have undertaken—to attempt to explain something that, at least to a subset of potential readers, needs no explanation. And as a case study, our endeavor may seem even more misguided because we do not have ready access to any of the primary sources: the hedge funds, proprietary trading desks, and their prime brokers and major credit counterparties. For obvious reasons, such sources are not at liberty to disclose any information about their strategies—indeed, any disclosure of proprietary information is clearly not in the best interests of their investors or shareholders. Therefore, it is unlikely we will ever obtain the necessary information to conduct a *conclusive* study of the events of August 2007.

It is precisely this well-known lack of transparency of hedge funds, coupled with genuine intellectual curiosity and public policy concerns regarding systemic risks in this dynamic industry, that led us to undertake this effort. Because the relevant hedge fund managers and investors are not able to disclose their views on what happened in August 2007, we propose to construct a simple simulacrum of a quantitative equity market neutral strategy and study its performance, as well as to use other publicly available hedge fund data to round out our understanding of the long/short equity sector during this challenging period. However, we recognize that it is difficult for outsiders to truly understand such complex issues and do not intend to be self-appointed spokesmen for the quants.

Accordingly, we acknowledge in advance that we may be far off the mark given the limited data we have to work with, and caution readers to be appropriately skeptical of our analysis, as we are. While some academics may have warned that systemic risk in the hedge fund industry has been on the rise (see, for example, Carey and Stulz, 2007), none of the academic literature has produced any timely forecasts of when or how such shocks might occur. Indeed, by definition, a true "shock" is unforecastable. Nevertheless, it is our hope that the tentative hypotheses suggested by our empirical results, and the simple tools that we use to derive them, will stimulate additional investigations—especially by those who do have access to the data—that may lead to a deeper understanding of financial market dynamics under stress.

We begin in Section 10.1 with a brief discussion of terminology, and in Section 10.2 we describe the specific quantitative test strategy that we plan to use as our "microscope" to study the effects of August 6–10, 2007, on long/short equity strategies. We show in Section 10.3 that this test strategy does indeed capture the losses that affected so many quants during that week. By comparing August 2007 to August 1998, in Section 10.4 we observe that, despite the many similarities between the two periods, there is one significant difference that may be cause for great concern regarding the current level of systemic risk in the hedge fund industry—our microscope revealed not a single sign of stress in August 1998 but has shown systematic deterioration year by year since then until the outsized losses in August 2007. We attempt to trace the origins of this striking difference to various sources. In particular, in Section 10.5, we consider the near-exponential growth of assets and funds in the long/short equity category, the secular decline in the expected rate of return of our test strategy over the years, and the increases in leverage that these two facts imply. With the appropriate leverage assumptions in hand, we are able to produce a more realistic simulation of the test strategy's performance in August 2007, and in Section 10.6 we lay out our *unwind hypothesis*. This hypothesis relies on the assumption that long/short equity strategies are less liquid than market participants anticipated, and in Section 10.7 we estimate the illiquidity exposure of long/short equity funds in the Lipper TASS database. We find evidence that over the past 2 years, even this highly liquid sector of the hedge fund industry has become less liquid. And in Section 10.8, we investigate the changes in simple correlations across broad-based hedge fund indexes over time and find that the hedge fund industry is a more highly "connected" network now than ever before. We conclude by discussing the broader issue of whether quant failed in August 2007 (Section 10.9), some of the limitations of our analysis and possible extensions (Section 10.10), and our current outlook for systemic risk in the hedge fund industry (Section 10.11).

10.1 Terminology

Among experienced hedge fund investors and managers, there is a clear distinction among the terms "statistical arbitrage," "quantitative equity market neutral," and "long/short equity" in reference to strategies. The first category refers to highly technical short-term mean-reversion strategies involving large numbers of securities (hundreds to thousands, depending on the amount of risk capital), very short holding periods (measured in days to seconds), and substantial computational, trading, and information technology (IT) infrastructure. The second category is more general, involving broader types of quantitative models, some with lower turnover, fewer securities, and inputs other than past prices such as accounting variables, earnings forecasts, and economic indicators. The third category is the broadest, including any equity portfolios that engage in short-selling, that may or may not be market neutral (many long/short equity funds are long-biased), that may or may not be quantitative (fundamental stock pickers sometimes engage in short positions to hedge their market exposure as well as to bet on poorly performing stocks), and where technology need not play an important role. In most hedge fund databases, this is by far the largest single category, both in terms of assets and number of funds.

More recently, a fourth category has emerged, the 130/30 or active-extension strategies, in which a fund or, more commonly, a managed account of, say $100 million, maintains $130 million of long positions in one set of securities and $30 million of short positions in another set of securities. Such a strategy is a natural extension of a long-only fund where the long-only constraint is relaxed to a limited extent. It is currently one of the fastest growing areas in the institutional money management business, and because the portfolio construction process is rather technical by design, the managers of such products are primarily quantitative.

For the purposes of this chapter, we sometimes refer to all of these strategies as long/short equity for several reasons. First, these seemingly disparate approaches are beginning to overlap. A number of statistical arbitrage funds are now pursuing lower-turnover substrategies to increase their funds' capacities, while many long/short equity funds have turned to higher-turnover substrategies as they develop more trading infrastructure and seek more consistent returns. This natural business progression has blurred the distinction between the long/short equity sub-specialties. Second, as long/short equity managers have grown in size, technology has naturally begun to play a more important role, even among fundamental stock pickers who find that they cannot expand their businesses unless they make more efficient use of their time and skills. Such managers have begun to rely on stock-screening software and portfolio-construction tools that allow them to leverage their qualitative stock-selection skills, and automated trading platforms that allow them to execute their stock picks more cost-effectively. These new tools have made quants out of many fundamental stock pickers. Indeed, even among the long-only equity managers, 130/30 strategies are transforming the multi-trillion-dollar equity enhanced-index business into a quantitative endeavor. We argue that all four investment categories were impacted by the events of August 6–10, 2007, largely because their growth has pushed them into each other's domains. Accordingly, in the event of a rapid unwind of any equity portfolio, all four types of strategies are likely to be affected in one way or another.

Therefore, throughout the remainder of this chapter, we shall use the broader term "long/short equity" to refer generically to all of these distinct activities, making finer distinctions when appropriate.

10.2 Anatomy of a Long/Short Equity Strategy

To gauge the impact of the events of August 6–10, 2007, on long/short equity portfolios, we consider a specific strategy—first proposed by Lehmann (1990) and Lo and MacKinlay (1990c)—that we can analyze directly using individual U.S. equities returns. Given a collection of N securities, consider a long/short market neutral equity strategy consisting of an equal dollar amount of long and short positions, where at each rebalancing interval, the long positions consist of *losers* (underperforming stocks, relative to some market average) and the short positions consist of *winners* (outperforming stocks, relative to the same market average). Specifically, if ω_{it} is the portfolio weight of security i at date t, then

$$\omega_{it} = -\frac{1}{N}(R_{it-k} - R_{mt-k}), \qquad R_{mt-k} \equiv \frac{1}{N}\sum_{i=1}^{N} R_{it-k}, \qquad (10.1)$$

for some $k > 0$.

Note that the portfolio weights are the negative of the degree of outperformance k periods ago, so each value of k yields a somewhat different strategy. For our purposes, we set $k = 1$ day. By buying yesterday's losers and selling yesterday's winners at each date, such a strategy actively bets on mean reversion across all N stocks, profiting from reversals that occur within the rebalancing interval. For this reason, (10.1) has been called a *contrarian trading strategy* that benefits from market overreaction, i.e., when underperformance is followed by positive returns, and vice versa for outperformance (see Appendix A.6 for further details).

However, another source of profitability of contrarian trading strategies is the fact that they provide liquidity to the marketplace. By definition, losers are stocks that have underperformed relative to some market average, implying a supply/demand imbalance, i.e., an excess supply that caused the prices of those securities to drop, and vice versa for winners. By buying losers and selling winners, contrarians are adding to the demand for losers and increasing the supply of winners, thereby stabilizing supply/demand imbalances. Traditionally, designated market makers such as NYSE/AMEX specialists and NASDAQ dealers have played this role, for which they are compensated through the bid/offer spread. But over the last decade, hedge funds and proprietary trading desks have begun to compete with traditional market makers, adding enormous amounts of liquidity to U.S. stock markets and earning attractive returns for themselves and their investors in the process.

In providing liquidity to the market, contrarian trading strategies also have the effect of reducing market volatility because they attenuate the movement of prices by selling stocks for which there is excess demand and buying stocks for which there is excess supply. Therefore, an increasing amount of capital dedicated to market-making strategies is one potential explanation for the secular decline in U.S. equity market volatility during the past 10 years. Once this market-making capital is withdrawn from the marketplace, volatility should pick up, as it has over the past several months.

If mean reversion implies that contrarian trading strategies will be profitable, then momentum implies the reverse. In the presence of return persistence, i.e., positively autocorrelated returns, Lo and MacKinlay (1990c) show that the contrarian trading strategy (10.1) will exhibit negative profits. Like other market-making strategies, the contrarian strategy loses when prices exhibit trends, either because of private information, which the market microstructure literature calls "adverse selection," or a sustained liquidation in which the market maker bears the losses by taking the other side and losing value as prices move in response to the liquidation. Therefore, whether or not (10.1) is an interesting strategy in its own right, it can serve as a valuable indicator of broad-based strategy liquidations of long and/or short positions, and we will return to this interpretation in Section 10.6.

Note that the weights (10.1) have the property that they sum to 0, hence (10.1) is an example of an "arbitrage" or "market neutral" portfolio where the long positions are exactly offset by the short positions.[2] As a result, the portfolio "return" cannot be computed in the standard way because there is no net investment. In practice, however, the return of such a strategy over any finite interval is easily calculated as the profit-and-loss of that strategy's positions over the interval divided by the initial capital required to support those positions. For example, suppose that a portfolio consisting of $100 million of long positions and $100 million of short positions generated profits of $2 million over a 1-day interval. The return of this strategy is simply $2 million divided by the

[2] Such a strategy is more accurately described as a "dollar-neutral" portfolio since dollar-neutral does not necessarily imply that a strategy is also market neutral. For example, if a portfolio is long $100 million of high-beta stocks and short $100 million of low-beta stocks, it will be dollar-neutral but will have positive market-beta exposure. In practice, most dollar-neutral equity portfolios are also constructed to be market neutral, hence the two terms are used almost interchangeably, which is sloppy terminology but usually correct.

required amount of capital to support the $100 million long/short positions. Under Regulation T (RegT) the minimum amount of capital required is $100 million (often stated as 2:1 leverage, or a 50% margin requirement), hence the return to the strategy is 2%. If, however, the portfolio manager is a broker-dealer, then Regulation T does not apply (other regulations govern the capital adequacy of broker-dealers), and higher levels of leverage may be employed. For example, under certain conditions, it is possible to support a $100 million long/short portfolio with only $25 million of capital—leverage ratio of 8:1—which implies a portfolio return of $2/$25 = 8%.[3] Accordingly, the gross dollar investment I_t of the portfolio (10.1) and its unleveraged (Reg T) portfolio return R_{pt} are given by

$$I_t \equiv \frac{1}{2} \sum_{i=1}^{N} |\omega_{it}|, \quad R_{pt} \equiv \frac{\sum_{i=1}^{N} \omega_{it} R_{it}}{I_t}. \tag{10.2}$$

To construct leveraged portfolio returns $L_{pt}(\theta)$ using a regulatory leverage factor of $\theta : 1$, we simply multiply (10.2) by $\theta/2$:[4]

$$L_{pt}(\theta) \equiv \frac{(\theta/2) \sum_{i=1}^{N} \omega_{it} R_{it}}{I_t}. \tag{10.3}$$

Lo and MacKinlay (1990c) provide a detailed analysis of the unleveraged returns (10.2) of the contrarian trading strategy, tracing its profitability to mean reversion in individual stock returns as well as positive lead/lag effects and cross-autocorrelations across stocks and across time. However, for our purposes, such decompositions are of less relevance than simply using (10.1) as an instrument to study the impact of market events on long/short equity strategies during the second week of August 2007. To that end, we apply this strategy to the daily returns of all stocks in the University of Chicago's CRSP Database and to stocks within 10 market-cap deciles, from January 3, 1995, to August 31, 2007.[5]

Before turning to the performance of the contrarian strategy in August 2007, we summarize the strategy's historical performance to develop some intuition for

---

[3] The technical definition of leverage—and the one used by the U.S. Federal Reserve, which is responsible for setting leverage constraints for broker-dealers—is given by the sum of the absolute values of the long and short positions divided by the capital, so

$$\frac{|\$100| + |-\$100|}{\$25} = 8.$$

[4] Note that Reg-T leverage is, in fact, considered 2:1, which is exactly (10.2), hence θ:1 leverage is equivalent to a multiple of $\theta/2$.

[5] Specifically, we use only U.S. common stocks (CRSP share codes 10 and 11), which eliminates REITs, ADRs, and other types of securities, and we drop stocks with share prices below $5 and above $2,000. To reduce unnecessary turnover in our market-cap deciles, we form these deciles only twice a year (the first trading days of January and July). Since the CRSP data are available only through December 29, 2006, decile memberships for 2007 were based on market capitalizations as of

its properties. Table 10.1 provides year-by-year average market capitalizations and share prices of stocks in each decile from 1995 to 2007,[6] and Table 10.2 reports the year-by-year average daily return of (10.1) when applied to stocks within market-cap deciles, as well as for all stocks in our sample. The results are impressive. In the first year of our sample, 1995, the strategy produced an average daily return of 1.38% per day, or 345% per year assuming a 250-day year! Of course, this return is unrealistic because it ignores a number of market frictions such as transactions costs, price impact, short sales constraints, and other institutional limitations. In particular, a daily rebalancing interval would imply extraordinarily high turnover across the set of 4,781 individual stocks, which was simply not feasible in 1995. However, we intend to use this strategy to gauge the impact of market movements in August 2007 relative to its typical performance, hence we are not as concerned about whether the results are achievable in practice.

The high turnover and the large number of stocks involved also highlight the importance that technology plays in strategies like (10.1) and why funds that employ such strategies are predominantly quantitative. It is nearly impossible for human portfolio managers and traders to implement a strategy involving so many securities and trading so frequently without making substantial use of quantitative methods and technological tools such as automated trading platforms, electronic communications networks, and mathematical optimization algorithms. Indeed, part of the liquidity that such strategies seem to enjoy—the short holding periods, the rapid-fire implementation of trading signals, and the diversification of profitability across such a large number of instruments—is directly related to technological advances in trading, portfolio construction, and risk management. It is no wonder that the most successful funds in this discipline have been founded by computer scientists, mathematicians, and engineers, not by economists or fundamental stock pickers.

Table 10.2 confirms a pattern long recognized by long/short equity managers—the relation between profitability and market capitalization. Smaller-cap stocks

---

December 29, 2006. For 2007, we constructed daily close-to-close returns for the stocks in our CRSP universe as of December 29, 2006, using adjusted closing prices from finance.yahoo.com. We were unable to find prices for 135 stocks in our CRSP universe, potentially because of ticker symbol changes or mismatches between CRSP and Yahoo. To avoid any conflict, we also dropped 34 other securities that were mapped to more than one CRSP PERMNO identifier as of December, 29, 2006. The remaining 3,724 stocks were then placed in deciles and used for the analysis in 2007. Also, Yahoo's adjusted prices do not incorporate dividends, hence our 2007 daily returns are price returns, not *total returns*. This difference is unlikely to have much impact on our analysis.

[6] The market capitalizations reported in Table 10.1 for the year 2007 are based on shares outstanding as of December, 29, 2006, and should be interpreted as estimates for the average market cap in these deciles. The "All Count" column is the daily average number of stocks in our universe in each year. As stocks go bankrupt, delist, change from CRSP share code 10 or 11 to any other share code (prior to 2007), or fall outside of the $5–$2,000 price range, they are taken out of our universe.

Table 10.1.

Year-by-Year Average Market Capitalizations and Share Prices of All U.S. Common Stocks (CRSP Share Codes 10 and 11) with Share Prices above $5 and below $2,000 within Market-Capitalization Deciles (January 3, 1995, to August 31, 2007)

	Smallest	Decile 2	Decile 3	Decile 4	Decile 5	Decile 6	Decile 7	Decile 8	Decile 9	Largest	All	All Count
					Deciles by Market Capitalization							
					Panel A: Average Market Capitalization ($ million)							
1995	17	34	57	86	127	190	305	556	1,269	8,250	1,121	4,781
1996	18	38	61	92	140	210	334	591	1,349	9,599	1,293	5,273
1997	22	47	74	109	164	248	407	708	1,539	12,401	1,628	5,393
1998	24	49	78	115	172	274	444	773	1,735	16,011	2,088	5,195
1999	23	50	83	126	200	310	507	905	2,086	22,002	2,764	4,736
2000	22	53	92	148	249	398	647	1,145	2,545	26,050	3,361	4,566
2001	25	60	106	181	288	440	723	1,268	2,863	26,007	3,348	3,782
2002	27	64	111	188	289	450	711	1,235	2,696	23,463	3,082	3,486
2003	31	73	130	213	327	498	795	1,371	2,951	24,185	3,146	3,376
2004	37	86	149	244	363	569	875	1,554	3,268	26,093	3,425	3,741
2005	40	97	171	266	408	651	1,026	1,772	3,811	28,164	3,741	3,721
2006	44	105	187	298	452	717	1,145	1,907	4,073	30,154	3,988	3,764
2007	47	109	195	313	472	739	1,188	2,120	4,387	33,152	4,363	3,623
					Panel B: Average Price ($)							
1995	11.07	11.55	13.37	14.84	16.96	18.90	22.54	26.49	32.45	45.14	21.55	4,781
1996	11.30	11.92	13.06	14.36	17.11	20.12	23.47	28.29	33.02	47.95	22.40	5,273
1997	12.39	13.33	14.42	15.88	18.52	22.21	26.20	31.07	36.52	52.16	24.56	5,393
1998	11.37	13.15	14.34	15.55	17.94	21.76	25.40	29.97	36.55	54.06	24.53	5,195
1999	10.31	11.79	12.87	14.14	16.58	21.01	24.13	31.62	36.99	54.04	23.80	4,736
2000	9.74	11.59	12.31	13.85	17.86	21.85	25.89	34.03	40.49	60.25	25.39	4,566
2001	11.34	13.10	13.56	15.47	18.47	20.70	25.37	31.47	34.96	42.71	23.04	3,782
2002	12.15	14.20	15.02	16.16	18.88	21.38	25.35	28.43	33.18	39.52	22.73	3,486
2003	13.65	15.56	16.55	17.15	19.89	21.25	26.12	28.53	33.86	41.83	23.61	3,376
2004	13.81	16.33	16.88	17.84	20.33	24.37	28.21	32.54	38.68	46.92	25.84	3,741
2005	13.48	16.40	16.34	18.01	20.84	25.01	29.25	38.51	42.50	51.14	27.42	3,721
2006	13.06	16.08	16.28	19.33	21.56	25.95	30.44	40.08	45.42	51.94	28.24	3,764
2007	12.61	15.18	16.75	18.30	22.32	27.32	30.30	38.70	48.70	56.56	28.94	3,623

Table 10.2.

Year-by-Year Average Daily Returns, Standard Deviations of Daily Returns, and Annualized Sharpe Ratios of Lo and MacKinlay's (1990c) Contrarian Trading Strategy Applied to All U.S. Common Stocks (CRSP Share Codes 10 and 11) with Share Prices above $5 and below $2,000, and Market-Capitalization Deciles (January 3, 1995, to August 31, 2007)*

	Smallest	Decile 2	Decile 3	Decile 4	Decile 5	Decile 6	Decile 7	Decile 8	Decile 9	Largest	All
					Market-Capitalization Deciles						
					Average Daily Returns						
1995	3.57%	2.75%	1.94%	1.62%	1.07%	0.61%	0.21%	−0.01%	−0.02%	0.04%	1.38%
1996	3.58%	2.47%	1.82%	1.34%	0.84%	0.52%	0.19%	−0.11%	−0.04%	0.02%	1.17%
1997	2.83%	1.94%	1.34%	1.02%	0.62%	0.28%	0.04%	−0.12%	0.06%	0.14%	0.88%
1998	2.38%	1.45%	1.11%	0.62%	0.29%	0.03%	−0.04%	−0.12%	0.03%	0.10%	0.57%
1999	2.56%	1.41%	0.82%	0.38%	−0.01%	−0.11%	−0.21%	−0.35%	−0.01%	0.06%	0.44%
2000	2.58%	1.59%	0.92%	0.14%	0.03%	−0.02%	−0.14%	0.16%	0.00%	0.03%	0.44%
2001	2.15%	1.25%	0.57%	0.24%	−0.01%	0.06%	0.13%	−0.10%	−0.11%	−0.11%	0.31%
2002	1.67%	0.85%	0.53%	0.29%	0.28%	0.26%	0.28%	0.20%	0.11%	0.09%	0.45%
2003	1.00%	0.26%	−0.07%	0.04%	0.11%	0.20%	0.18%	0.15%	0.04%	0.05%	0.21%
2004	1.17%	0.48%	0.31%	0.38%	0.25%	0.29%	0.22%	0.15%	0.05%	−0.01%	0.37%
2005	1.05%	0.39%	0.13%	0.11%	0.09%	0.11%	0.05%	0.08%	0.01%	0.02%	0.26%
2006	0.86%	0.26%	0.11%	0.06%	0.05%	−0.02%	−0.02%	0.05%	0.06%	0.00%	0.15%
2007	0.57%	0.09%	0.08%	0.18%	0.16%	−0.08%	0.04%	−0.04%	0.00%	−0.04%	0.13%
					Standard Deviation of Daily Returns						
1995	0.92%	0.88%	0.81%	0.82%	0.78%	0.77%	0.73%	0.67%	0.63%	0.65%	0.40%
1996	1.07%	1.00%	0.79%	0.81%	0.88%	0.84%	0.90%	0.90%	0.83%	0.73%	0.48%
1997	1.04%	0.98%	0.96%	0.96%	1.12%	1.00%	0.91%	0.99%	0.98%	0.77%	0.68%
1998	1.59%	1.67%	1.23%	1.22%	1.57%	1.25%	1.29%	1.43%	1.08%	1.00%	0.84%

1999	1.66%	1.82%	1.44%	1.44%	1.79%	1.57%	1.71%	1.70%	1.57%	1.07%	1.02%
2000	1.57%	1.69%	2.06%	1.89%	1.76%	2.15%	2.18%	2.29%	2.44%	2.56%	1.68%
2001	1.33%	1.26%	1.46%	1.62%	1.65%	1.64%	1.83%	1.91%	2.28%	2.29%	1.43%
2002	1.17%	0.89%	1.14%	1.07%	1.25%	1.11%	1.30%	1.42%	1.50%	1.50%	0.98%
2003	1.11%	0.81%	0.95%	0.89%	0.86%	0.81%	0.77%	0.76%	0.75%	0.56%	0.54%
2004	1.35%	1.01%	0.87%	0.76%	0.76%	0.78%	0.80%	0.74%	0.69%	0.57%	0.53%
2005	1.35%	0.80%	0.89%	0.70%	0.77%	0.77%	0.65%	0.73%	0.57%	0.56%	0.46%
2006	1.07%	0.90%	0.83%	0.84%	0.70%	1.07%	0.68%	0.68%	0.64%	0.61%	0.52%
2007	0.96%	1.02%	1.00%	0.99%	1.06%	1.44%	1.00%	0.87%	0.67%	0.56%	0.72%

Annualized Sharpe Ratio (0% Risk-free Rate)*

1995	61.27	49.20	37.79	31.26	21.49	12.68	4.62	-0.22	-0.54	0.87	53.87
1996	53.08	39.12	36.27	26.10	15.17	9.85	3.38	-1.89	-0.69	0.36	38.26
1997	43.15	31.19	22.00	16.66	8.67	4.45	0.74	-1.88	0.95	2.79	20.46
1998	23.61	13.78	14.22	8.09	2.92	0.39	-0.54	-1.32	0.43	1.58	10.62
1999	24.32	12.25	9.05	4.22	-0.11	-1.08	-1.93	-3.23	-0.09	0.82	6.81
2000	25.96	14.91	7.04	1.18	0.31	-0.18	-1.04	1.14	0.01	0.21	4.17
2001	25.56	15.68	6.15	2.30	-0.05	0.57	1.09	-0.79	-0.79	-0.73	3.46
2002	22.54	15.10	7.30	4.28	3.57	3.68	3.38	2.24	1.13	0.98	7.25
2003	14.32	5.19	-1.11	0.63	1.94	3.91	3.64	3.09	0.89	1.33	5.96
2004	13.76	7.55	5.60	7.96	5.11	5.90	4.27	3.20	1.12	-0.33	11.07
2005	12.33	7.72	2.26	2.42	1.95	2.29	1.31	1.74	0.36	0.62	8.85
2006	12.72	4.49	2.08	1.18	1.14	-0.26	-0.56	1.08	1.60	-0.03	4.47
2007	9.40	1.45	1.33	2.93	2.40	-0.84	0.69	-0.74	-0.05	-1.03	2.79

* Sharpe ratio = $\sqrt{250} \times$ (average daily return/Standard deviation).

generally exhibit more significant inefficiencies, hence the profitability of the contrarian strategy in the smaller deciles is considerably higher than in the larger-cap portfolios. For example, the average daily return of the strategy in the smallest decile in 1995 is 3.57%, in contrast to 0.04% for the largest decile. Of course, smaller-cap stocks typically have much higher transactions costs and price impacts, hence they may not be as attractive as the data might suggest. The trade-off between apparent profitability and transactions costs implies that the intermediate deciles may be the most opportune from a practical perspective, a conjecture that we shall revisit below.

Table 10.2 also exhibits a strong secular trend of declining average daily returns, a feature that many long/short equity managers and investors have observed. In 1995 the average daily return of the contrarian strategy for all stocks in our sample is 1.38%, but by 2000 the average daily return drops to 0.44%, and the year-to-date figure for 2007 (up to August 31) is 0.13%. Plate 10 illustrates the near-monotonic decline of the expected returns of this strategy, no doubt a reflection of increased competition, changes in market structure, improvements in trading technology and electronic connectivity, the growth in assets devoted to this type of strategy, and the corresponding decline in U.S. equity market volatility over the last decade.[7] This secular decline in profitability has significant implications for the use of leverage, which we will explore in Section 10.5.

The third panel of Table 10.2 reports the annualized ratio of the contrarian strategy's daily mean return to its daily standard deviation, where the annualization is performed by multiplying the ratio by $\sqrt{250}$. This is the Sharpe ratio relative to a 0% risk-free rate and is one simple measure of the strategy's expected return per unit risk. Although a Sharpe ratio of 53.87 in 1995 may seem absurdly high, it should be kept in mind that in 1995, this strategy calls for the daily rebalancing of a portfolio with 4,781 stocks on average (see Table 10.1). The transaction costs involved in such rebalancing would have been formidable, but if one had the ability or technology to engage in such broad-based market making, extraordinary Sharpe ratios may not be so unrealistic.[8] Indeed, we expect the Sharpe ratios of more formal market-making activities such as specialist profits on the New York Stock Exchange to be quite high given the economics of price discovery. Therefore, the Sharpe ratios in Table 10.2 may be somewhat inflated because we have not incorporated transactions costs, but they are probably not off by an order of magnitude, and their attractive levels provide one explanation for the popularity of statistical arbitrage strategies among investors and hedge fund managers.

---

[7] Equity market-making profits are usually positively correlated with the level of volatility, and most quantitative equity market neutral strategies have a significant market-making component to their returns, especially at higher trading frequencies.

[8] In particular, in 1995 the minimum price variation on most stock exchanges was 12.5 cents per share, and while this may seem like a very high hurdle for any high-turnover strategy to overcome, recall that the contrarian strategy tends to be a *supplier* of liquidity, hence it will be earning the spread on average, not paying it.

10.3 What Happened in August 2007?

Table 10.3 presents the unleveraged daily returns of the contrarian strategy over the 5-week period from Monday, July 30, to Friday, August 31, 2007, applied to our entire universe of stocks and to market-cap deciles. The 3 days in the second week—August 7, 8, and 9—are the outliers, with losses of -1.16%, -2.83%, and -2.86%, respectively, yielding a cumulative 3-day loss of -6.85%.[9] Although this 3-day return may not seem that significant—especially in the hedge fund world where volatility is a fact of life—note from Table 10.2 that the contrarian strategy's 2006 daily standard deviation is 0.52%, so a -6.85% cumulative return represents a loss of 7.6 standard deviations assuming independently and identically distributed daily returns![10] Moreover, many long/short equity managers were employing leverage (see Section 10.5 for further discussion), hence their realized returns were magnified severalfold.

Curiously, a significant fraction of the losses was reversed on Friday, August 10, when the contrarian strategy yielded a return of 5.92%, which was another extreme outlier of 11.4 standard deviations. In fact, the strategy's cumulative return for the entire week of August 6 was -0.43%, not an unusual weekly return in any respect. This reversal is a tell-tale sign of a liquidity trade. In fact, the plot in Figure 10.1 of the cumulative return of the contrarian strategy from January 3 to August 31, 2007, shows a reasonably steady positive trend interrupted by a prominent dip during the second week of August, after which the trend seems to continue. The elevated levels of NYSE share volume during the latter part of July and the first half of August, along with a mini dip in July in the contrarian cumulative return series, suggest the possibility that liquidations may have started several weeks prior to the August 7–10 event. We shall return to this interpretation in Section 10.6.

The decile returns in Table 10.3 show that the losses on August 7–9 were even more pronounced in some of the intermediate deciles, with cumulative 3-day returns of -8.09% in decile 3, -9.33% in decile 4, -8.95% in decile 5, and -8.81% in decile 8. But as in the main strategy, these decile portfolios experienced sharp increases on Friday, August 10, in most cases recouping a significant fraction of the losses. We shall return to this empirical fact in Section 10.6 when we consider various interpretations for the pattern of losses on August 7–9.

[9] For simplicity, we use arithmetic compounding to arrive at the 3-day cumulative return, which is a reasonable approximation to geometrically compounded returns when the return values are relatively small in magnitude, and is also consistent with the typical way that long/short equity market neutral portfolios are implemented in practice.

[10] We use the strategy's standard deviation in 2006 instead of 2007 as the unit of comparison to provide a cleaner comparison between 2007 and previous years. In particular, if 2007 is viewed as unusual because of the phenomena we are studying in this chapter, it is presumably unusual relative to some benchmark other than its 2007 performance.

Table 10.3.

Daily Returns of Lo and MacKinlay's (1990c) Contrarian Trading Strategy Applied to All U.S. Common Stocks (CRSP Share Codes 10 and 11) with Share Prices above $5 and below $2,000, and Market-Capitalization Deciles (Monday, July 30, 2007, to Friday August 31, 2007)

	Deciles by Market Capitalization										
	Smallest	Decile 2	Decile 3	Decile 4	Decile 5	Decile 6	Decile 7	Decile 8	Decile 9	Largest	All
30 Jul 2007	-0.07%	0.02%	1.96%	-0.36%	0.07%	0.23%	0.26%	0.38%	0.51%	0.18%	0.44%
31 Jul 2007	0.19%	1.10%	0.28%	0.55%	-0.63%	0.02%	-0.80%	0.49%	-0.31%	0.06%	0.36%
1 Aug 2007	1.53%	0.45%	-1.39%	0.35%	0.95%	-0.88%	-0.71%	-0.63%	-2.02%	-0.22%	0.11%
2 Aug 2007	0.88%	-0.76%	-0.12%	-0.67%	-0.94%	-2.70%	2.16%	1.53%	-0.74%	-0.19%	-0.30%
3 Aug 2007	-0.95%	-0.62%	-0.78%	0.06%	0.88%	0.01%	-0.62%	-1.09%	-0.57%	-0.68%	-0.02%
6 Aug 2007	-0.83%	-1.77%	-0.39%	-1.03%	1.37%	-1.37%	-1.19%	-0.72%	0.27%	0.77%	0.50%
7 Aug 2007	0.75%	0.26%	-1.64%	-2.91%	-1.50%	-0.70%	0.36%	-1.02%	-1.72%	-0.67%	-1.16%
8 Aug 2007	0.88%	-1.33%	-2.59%	-3.65%	-4.27%	-2.16%	-2.23%	-3.46%	-1.26%	-1.48%	-2.83%
9 Aug 2007	0.91%	-1.86%	-3.87%	-2.77%	-3.18%	-3.95%	-3.27%	-4.33%	-2.58%	-1.31%	-2.86%
10 Aug 2007	-0.33%	3.65%	6.08%	7.90%	8.77%	7.67%	7.52%	6.70%	4.68%	2.39%	5.92%
13 Aug 2007	1.36%	-0.31%	-0.63%	-1.07%	-1.55%	-0.22%	-1.29%	-2.01%	-2.14%	-1.25%	-0.76%
14 Aug 2007	1.16%	0.91%	-0.26%	0.34%	0.56%	-0.28%	0.69%	-0.29%	0.16%	0.17%	0.08%
15 Aug 2007	0.88%	1.19%	-0.61%	-0.58%	-0.17%	-0.97%	-0.24%	-1.34%	-0.57%	-1.18%	-0.38%
16 Aug 2007	-1.26%	-0.54%	0.15%	-0.59%	-0.60%	-0.99%	-1.73%	-1.27%	0.27%	-1.83%	-0.81%
17 Aug 2007	3.57%	2.49%	0.10%	1.26%	1.33%	-0.52%	0.12%	-0.39%	0.31%	0.11%	0.38%
20 Aug 2007	3.75%	1.75%	0.35%	1.35%	0.51%	0.44%	1.22%	0.56%	0.39%	1.17%	1.14%
21 Aug 2007	1.24%	0.11%	0.01%	-0.45%	0.02%	-0.63%	-0.08%	-0.05%	0.19%	0.11%	0.06%
22 Aug 2007	-0.85%	-0.31%	-0.52%	-0.51%	-0.17%	-0.83%	-0.18%	-0.56%	0.39%	0.09%	-0.38%
23 Aug 2007	-0.03%	0.70%	0.70%	-0.16%	0.38%	1.04%	0.26%	-0.33%	0.32%	0.31%	0.33%
24 Aug 2007	0.62%	-0.28%	-0.07%	0.23%	0.92%	-0.06%	-0.07%	0.09%	-0.35%	0.61%	0.43%
27 Aug 2007	1.10%	0.70%	0.11%	0.20%	1.25%	-0.16%	0.39%	0.71%	0.71%	0.03%	0.75%
28 Aug 2007	0.41%	0.32%	0.08%	-0.61%	-0.64%	-0.50%	-0.33%	-0.44%	-0.47%	0.25%	-0.76%
29 Aug 2007	1.45%	0.08%	1.27%	2.08%	1.94%	-0.53%	1.42%	1.60%	0.91%	0.98%	1.76%
30 Aug 2007	1.07%	0.04%	0.62%	0.40%	0.89%	0.10%	-0.03%	-0.04%	0.12%	-0.05%	0.50%
31 Aug 2007	1.69%	0.97%	0.95%	-0.55%	0.05%	0.52%	-0.08%	-0.67%	0.01%	0.14%	0.36%

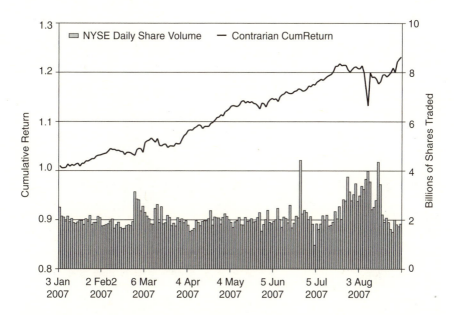

Figure 10.1. *Cumulative return of the contrarian trading strategy and the NYSE daily share volume (January 3 to August 31, 2007).*

What makes this pattern of loss and gain so puzzling is the fact that there were virtually no signs of market turmoil outside the world of quantitative equity market neutral funds on August 7 and 8. For example, Table 10.4 reports the daily returns of nine major market indexes spanning a broad array of asset classes (stocks, bonds, currencies, commodities, and volatility) from July 30 to August 31, 2007, and nothing remarkable occurred on August 7 and 8 when the contrarian strategy first began to suffer extreme losses. On August 9, the S&P 500 did lose 2.95% and the VIX jumped by 5.03, significant 1-day moves for both indexes. But these changes cannot explain the losses earlier in the week, nor can they explain the outsized losses of many genuinely market neutral equity hedge funds, i.e., funds that had virtually no beta exposure to the S&P 500 and positive exposure to volatility.

The one remaining explanation for these extraordinary return patterns is that they were the result of broad-based momentum due to a large-scale strategy liquidation, as discussed in Section 10.2, and when the liquidation had run its course, the liquidation-driven momentum turned into a strong burst of mean reversion that caused Friday's reversal. We shall return to this explanation in Section 10.6, after we explore the differences between August 1998 and August 2007 and the implications for expected returns and leverage.

Table 10.4.

Daily Returns of Various Market Indexes (Monday, July 30, 2007, to Friday, August 31, 2007)*

	S&P 500	S&P Small Cap 600	MSCI Emerging Markets	MSCI World Excluding U.S.	Lehman Aggregate U.S. Gov. Index	Lehman U.S. Universal Corp. High-Yield Index	Goldman Sachs Commodity Index	Trade Weighted USD Index	CBOE Volatility Index (VIX) Change
30 Jul 2007	1.03%	0.94%	0.87%	0.14%	−0.04%	0.18%	0.11%	−0.12%	−3.30
31 Jul 2007	−1.26%	−0.88%	1.67%	1.36%	0.17%	0.61%	1.18%	−0.10%	2.65
1 Aug 2007	0.73%	0.19%	−3.42%	−1.70%	0.04%	−0.15%	−1.34%	0.13%	0.15
2 Aug 2007	0.46%	0.98%	0.61%	0.62%	0.04%	0.53%	0.00%	−0.20%	−2.45
3 Aug 2007	−2.65%	−3.48%	−0.05%	−0.37%	0.29%	0.08%	−1.10%	−0.66%	3.94
6 Aug 2007	2.42%	1.35%	−1.99%	−0.57%	−0.14%	−0.29%	−2.76%	0.10%	−2.56
7 Aug 2007	0.62%	0.71%	0.45%	0.56%	−0.04%	0.38%	0.34%	0.28%	−1.04
8 Aug 2007	1.44%	1.52%	2.83%	1.88%	−0.48%	0.84%	−0.20%	−0.17%	−0.11
9 Aug 2007	−2.95%	−1.38%	−1.28%	−1.52%	0.31%	−0.07%	−0.37%	0.54%	5.03
10 Aug 2007	0.04%	1.01%	−3.30%	−2.85%	0.07%	−0.29%	−0.03%	−0.12%	1.82
13 Aug 2007	−0.03%	−0.84%	1.01%	1.08%	0.04%	0.34%	0.27%	0.46%	−1.73
14 Aug 2007	−1.81%	−1.87%	−1.42%	−1.10%	0.23%	−0.10%	0.35%	0.54%	1.11
15 Aug 2007	−1.36%	−1.45%	−2.39%	−1.52%	0.15%	−0.56%	0.80%	0.41%	2.99
16 Aug 2007	0.33%	1.70%	−5.63%	−2.91%	0.58%	−0.59%	−3.01%	−0.11%	0.16
17 Aug 2007	2.46%	2.30%	0.12%	0.96%	−0.28%	0.24%	1.49%	−0.37%	−0.84
20 Aug 2007	−0.03%	0.30%	3.78%	1.23%	0.23%	0.24%	−1.65%	−0.03%	−3.66
21 Aug 2007	0.11%	0.21%	−0.18%	0.61%	0.24%	0.19%	−1.14%	0.11%	−1.08
22 Aug 2007	1.18%	1.19%	2.58%	1.27%	−0.16%	0.37%	0.04%	−0.30%	−2.36
23 Aug 2007	−0.11%	−1.16%	1.76%	1.16%	−0.01%	0.22%	0.96%	−0.13%	−0.27
24 Aug 2007	1.16%	1.44%	0.44%	0.51%	−0.10%	0.04%	1.10%	−0.59%	−1.90
27 Aug 2007	−0.85%	−1.07%	1.90%	0.29%	0.23%	0.17%	0.28%	0.09%	2.00
28 Aug 2007	−2.34%	−2.70%	−0.85%	−1.26%	0.34%	−0.07%	−0.17%	0.02%	3.58
29 Aug 2007	2.22%	2.28%	−0.23%	0.04%	−0.09%	−0.06%	1.40%	−0.07%	−2.49
30 Aug 2007	−0.41%	−0.38%	1.31%	0.80%	0.29%	0.06%	0.15%	0.12%	1.25
31 Aug 2007	1.12%	1.28%	2.39%	1.58%	−0.16%	0.01%	0.48%	0.00%	−1.68

* With the exception of the Goldman Sachs Commodities Index and the Trade Weighted U.S. Dollar Index, which are obtained from the Global Financial Database, all other data series are obtained from Datastream. In all cases the total returns index is used, which captures the effects of any coupons and/or dividends that would accrue to an investor in the underlying assets of these indexes.

10.4 Comparing August 2007 with August 1998

The behavior of the contrarian strategy during the second week of August 2007 becomes even more significant when compared to the performance of the same strategy during August 1998, around the time of the Long Term Capital Management debacle. On August 17, 1998, Russia defaulted on its GKO government bonds, causing a global flight to quality that widened credit spreads which, in turn, generated extreme losses in the days that followed for LTCM and other fixed income arbitrage hedge funds and proprietary trading desks. The specific mechanism that caused these losses—widening credit spreads that generated margin calls, which caused the unwinding of illiquid portfolios, generating further losses and additional margin calls, leading ultimately to a fund's collapse—is virtually identical to the subprime mortgage problems that affected Bear Stearns and other credit-related hedge funds in 2007.

However, there is one significant difference between August 1998 and August 2007. Table 10.5 reports the daily returns of the contrarian strategy (10.1) during the months of August and September 1998, which show that the turmoil in fixed income markets had little or no effect on the profitability of our long/short equity strategy. In contrast to August 2007, where an apparent demand for liquidity caused a fire-sale liquidation that is easily observed in the contrarian strategy's daily returns, the well-documented demand for liquidity in the fixed income arbitrage space of August 1998 had no discernible impact on the very same strategy. This is a significant difference that signals a greater degree of financial market integration in 2007 than in 1998. While this may be viewed positively as a sign of progress in financial markets and technology, along with the many benefits of integration is the cost that a financial crisis in one sector can have dramatic repercussions in several others, i.e., contagion.

There are several possible explanations for the difference between August 1998 and August 2007. One interpretation is that in 1998, there were fewer multi-strategy funds and proprietary trading desks engaged in both fixed income arbitrage and long/short equity, so the demand for liquidity caused by deteriorating fixed income arbitrage strategies did not spill over as readily to long/short equity portfolios. Another possible explanation is that the amount of capital engaged in long/short equity strategies, particularly market neutral statistical arbitrage strategies, was not large enough to cause any significant dislocation even if such strategies were unwound quickly in August 1998. A third possibility is that in 1998, long/short equity funds did not employ as much leverage as they were apparently using in 2007.

We argue in the remaining sections that all three of these interpretations may be correct to some degree.

Table 10.5.

Daily Returns of Lo and MacKinlay's (1990c) Contrarian Trading Strategy Applied to All U.S. Common Stocks (CRSP Share Codes 10 and 11) with Share Prices above $5 and below $2,000, and Market-Capitalization Deciles (Monday, August 3, 1998, to Friday, September 30, 1998)*

	Smallest	Decile 2	Decile 3	Decile 4	Decile 5	Decile 6	Decile 7	Decile 8	Decile 9	Largest	All
					Deciles by Market Capitalization						
3 Aug 1998	3.35%	1.75%	1.68%	0.15%	3.25%	-0.33%	0.40%	0.06%	0.62%	0.16%	1.01%
4 Aug 1998	-0.29%	2.16%	1.64%	-1.35%	-1.18%	-0.51%	-0.82%	-0.07%	-1.22%	-0.16%	-0.18%
5 Aug 1998	2.75%	1.93%	0.68%	2.60%	2.04%	0.93%	-0.57%	0.38%	-0.59%	2.56%	1.27%
6 Aug 1998	2.25%	1.68%	2.01%	0.36%	0.17%	-0.33%	-1.35%	0.15%	0.85%	1.34%	0.66%
7 Aug 1998	3.05%	2.99%	0.79%	0.26%	-0.23%	0.03%	0.12%	0.39%	2.93%	-0.10%	0.67%
10 Aug 1998	3.48%	1.69%	1.53%	0.91%	0.48%	2.23%	1.03%	-0.23%	0.68%	0.27%	1.27%
11 Aug 1998	2.34%	1.72%	0.81%	-0.24%	0.60%	1.18%	-0.36%	0.79%	-0.29%	-0.14%	0.59%
12 Aug 1998	4.83%	2.88%	2.71%	1.31%	0.96%	0.58%	2.01%	0.93%	1.00%	0.68%	2.04%
13 Aug 1998	3.74%	2.24%	0.88%	2.72%	0.37%	0.39%	1.03%	0.48%	-0.11%	0.04%	1.33%
14 Aug 1998	2.25%	1.64%	3.57%	1.42%	-0.46%	-0.05%	0.66%	-0.07%	0.77%	-0.42%	0.94%
17 Aug 1998	2.46%	2.48%	1.81%	0.11%	-0.32%	1.66%	-0.01%	-0.80%	0.11%	0.49%	0.96%
18 Aug 1998	4.31%	1.85%	1.75%	3.86%	0.35%	-0.16%	-2.12%	0.03%	0.29%	0.12%	0.87%
19 Aug 1998	2.60%	2.15%	1.16%	0.45%	-0.65%	-0.36%	0.34%	-0.80%	0.06%	-0.13%	0.63%
20 Aug 1998	1.60%	3.04%	1.49%	0.42%	-0.64%	0.55%	0.87%	-0.61%	-0.55%	-1.47%	0.46%
21 Aug 1998	2.26%	4.06%	2.18%	1.79%	1.03%	-0.06%	-0.28%	-0.51%	0.06%	-0.36%	1.04%
24 Aug 1998	5.35%	1.84%	4.13%	0.63%	-0.83%	0.13%	-1.57%	-1.02%	-0.68%	0.73%	0.90%
25 Aug 1998	2.05%	2.19%	1.76%	0.85%	-0.45%	-0.34%	0.91%	-1.46%	-0.48%	-0.56%	0.36%
26 Aug 1998	4.02%	1.39%	1.78%	0.81%	-0.31%	0.06%	-0.43%	1.03%	-0.65%	-0.26%	0.61%
27 Aug 1998	1.69%	1.15%	0.24%	-1.16%	-2.02%	-0.47%	-1.54%	-1.91%	-0.63%	-2.20%	0.78%
28 Aug 1998	2.52%	2.29%	1.33%	1.35%	0.11%	1.12%	-1.29%	-1.32%	-1.18%	-0.36%	0.39%
31 Aug 1998	3.31%	1.79%	0.51%	-0.36%	-3.44%	-1.97%	-3.08%	-4.47%	-2.73%	-2.82%	-1.62%
1 Sep 1998	4.96%	4.42%	6.04%	4.67%	9.06%	6.68%	6.71%	6.67%	4.90%	6.10%	6.59%
2 Sep 1998	4.43%	2.74%	1.90%	0.82%	-1.33%	0.25%	0.86%	-0.39%	0.45%	0.33%	0.63%

3 Sep 1998	3.89%	3.78%	2.08%	2.09%	0.23%	-0.03%	0.79%	0.15%	0.51%	0.76%	1.41%
4 Sep 1998	5.10%	3.95%	2.09%	0.75%	-0.33%	-0.84%	-1.33%	-1.61%	-1.15%	-3.68%	0.26%
8 Sep 1998	3.53%	3.40%	3.82%	0.57%	0.60%	0.82%	1.35%	1.05%	0.97%	3.73%	2.08%
9 Sep 1998	1.99%	3.62%	1.38%	1.15%	1.12%	1.66%	1.70%	2.10%	2.32%	2.92%	2.42%
10 Sep 1998	4.26%	2.68%	0.08%	2.05%	0.96%	-0.27%	0.64%	-0.86%	-0.67%	-2.16%	0.29%
11 Sep 1998	3.34%	3.17%	2.15%	0.77%	0.20%	0.50%	-0.95%	1.28%	-0.18%	0.15%	1.24%
14 Sep 1998	3.53%	3.58%	1.54%	0.83%	-0.20%	-0.42%	-0.47%	-0.50%	0.02%	-0.23%	0.33%
15 Sep 1998	3.62%	2.36%	1.34%	0.77%	-0.17%	-0.98%	-0.52%	-1.15%	-0.95%	-0.63%	0.14%
16 Sep 1998	2.71%	3.33%	0.89%	1.48%	0.58%	0.83%	0.00%	0.05%	1.53%	-0.04%	1.01%
17 Sep 1998	3.70%	2.24%	1.54%	1.56%	-0.95%	0.23%	1.10%	-0.40%	-0.86%	0.38%	0.79%
18 Sep 1998	4.01%	3.94%	2.67%	1.27%	2.55%	1.20%	-1.17%	-1.41%	-0.51%	-0.45%	1.07%
21 Sep 1998	3.22%	1.28%	1.86%	-0.61%	-0.87%	-0.09%	-2.22%	1.08%	-0.47%	-0.32%	0.19%
22 Sep 1998	3.26%	2.15%	1.68%	1.76%	-0.21%	-0.16%	-0.62%	-2.06%	-1.46%	0.16%	0.42%
23 Sep 1998	4.24%	2.16%	0.78%	-1.66%	-0.34%	-2.33%	-3.08%	-3.27%	-0.60%	-0.42%	-0.71%
24 Sep 1998	2.54%	1.47%	3.13%	1.60%	0.63%	-0.38%	-0.06%	-0.27%	0.59%	1.63%	1.21%
25 Sep 1998	2.28%	3.27%	0.16%	0.86%	0.28%	-0.90%	-0.66%	0.67%	1.16%	0.36%	0.61%
28 Sep 1998	4.24%	1.24%	1.81%	2.64%	0.52%	-1.30%	0.47%	-1.58%	-0.59%	0.16%	0.60%
29 Sep 1998	2.75%	1.48%	-0.07%	0.81%	-0.83%	-1.61%	-1.58%	-0.83%	-1.19%	-0.83%	-0.29%
30 Sep 1998	2.98%	0.41%	0.33%	-0.96%	0.01%	-1.00%	-1.78%	-0.41%	-0.10%	-0.74%	-0.33%

* Highlighted dates are August 17 (default of Russian GKO bonds), August 21 (LTCM loses $550 million in 1 day), September 3 (first LTCM letter to investors regarding their losses), and September 24 (news about the bailout by the consortium).

10.5 Total Assets, Expected Returns, and Leverage

To see how crowded the long/short equity category has become in recent years, we consider the growth in the number of funds and assets under management in the Long/Short Equity Hedge and Equity Market Neutral categories of the Lipper TASS hedge fund database.[11] The Lipper TASS database is divided into two parts: Live and Graveyard funds. Hedge funds are recorded in the Live database if they are considered active as of the date of the snapshot. Once a hedge fund decides not to report its performance, liquidates, closes to new investment, restructures, or merges with other hedge funds, the fund is transferred into the Graveyard database. A hedge fund can be listed in the Graveyard database only after having been listed in the Live database.[12]

Plate 11 shows that the Long/Short Equity Hedge funds are the most numerous, with more than 600 funds in the Live database during the most recent months.[13] However, the number of Equity Market Neutral funds has clearly grown rapidly over the last 2 years, with slightly more than 100 live funds in the most recent months. Combining these two categories and dividing the total assets under management by the total number of funds in both Live and Graveyard databases, we see from Plate 11 that the average assets per fund has increased exponentially since 1994, starting out at $62 million in January 1994 and ending at $229 million in July 2007.

These assets do not reflect the inflows to active extension-strategies such as 130/30 funds, which is one of the fastest growing products in the institutional asset management industry. A recently published research report estimates that $75 billion is currently devoted to such strategies, and in 5 years this could grow to $1 trillion (see Merrill Lynch, 2007). Although such strategies are net long by construction, the fact that they hold short positions of up to 30% of their sizable asset base has significant implications for long/short equity hedge funds. For example, because of the increase in short-selling due to 130/30 strategies, shorting "hard-to-borrow" securities has become harder, more securities now fall into the hard-to-borrow category, short positions are less liquid, and "short squeezes" are more likely.

Of course, it is possible that the securities shorted by 130/30 strategies are held long by other long/short equity hedge funds, and vice versa, which

[11] We use the August 20, 2007, snapshot of the Lipper TASS database and consider only those funds reporting their AUM in U.S. dollars.

[12] The voluntary nature of reporting to the Lipper TASS and other commercially available hedge fund databases obviously imparts a selection bias, so our results should be interpreted with this bias in mind. See the review papers by Agarwal and Naik (2005) and Fung and Hsieh (2006) for comprehensive discussions of the impact of this and other biases in hedge fund databases.

[13] The fact that the number of funds drops in the most recent month is a common feature of the Lipper TASS data that is typically caused by reporting lags, not necessarily a genuine decline in the number of funds in the category, hence the most recent month or two of data should be discounted.

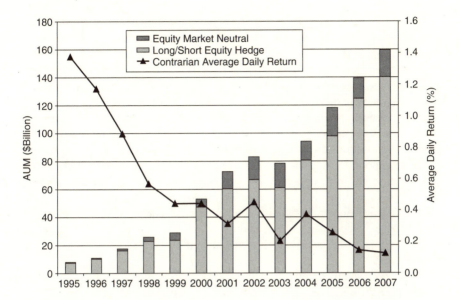

Figure 10.2. *Beginning-of-year assets under management for Lipper TASS Long/Short Equity Hedge and Equity Market Neutral funds, and year-by-year average daily returns of the contrarian trading strategy (January 3, 1995, to August 31, 2007). The contrarian trading strategy is applied to all U.S. common stocks (CRSP share codes 10 and 11) with share prices above $5 and below than $2,000.*

would enhance liquidity. But the factors causing 130/30 strategies to short a security (e.g., financial ratios, price patterns, bad news) are likely to be the same factors causing hedge funds to short that security. Moreover, the naturally quantitative nature of 130/30 strategies creates an unavoidable commonality between them and quantitative equity market neutral strategies. For example, the use of commercially available factor-based portfolio optimizers such as those of MSCI/BARRA, Northfield Information Systems, and APT by both 130/30 managers and equity market neutral managers can create common factor exposures between 130/30 and market neutral portfolios.

The simultaneous increase in the number of long/short equity funds, the aver-age assets per fund, and the growth of related strategies like 130/30, implies greater competition and, inevitably, reduced profitability of the strategies employed by such funds. This implication is confirmed in the case of the contrarian trading strategy (10.1), as Figure 10.2 illustrates. As the total assets in the Long/Short Equity Hedge and Equity Market Neutral categories grow, the average daily return of the contrarian strategy declines, reaching a low of 0.13% in 2007, and where the total assets in these two categories are at an all-time high of more than $160 billion at the beginning of 2007.

It may seem counterintuitive that assets would flow into hedge fund strategies with declining expected returns. However, recall that the average daily returns reported in Table 10.2 and plotted in Figure 10.2 are based on *unleveraged* returns. As these strategies begin to decay, hedge fund managers have typically employed more leverage so as to maintain the level of expected returns that investors have come to expect, particularly when the volatilities of the underlying instruments have experienced the kind of secular decline in volatility that U.S. equities have during this time period.[14] And because many hedge funds rely on leverage, the sizes of the positions are often considerably larger than the amount of collateral posted to support those positions. Leverage has the effect of a magnifying glass, expanding small profit opportunities into larger ones but also expanding small losses into larger losses. And when adverse changes in market prices reduce the market value of collateral, credit is withdrawn quickly, and the subsequent sudden liquidation of large positions over short periods of time can lead to widespread financial panic, as in the aftermath of the default of Russian government debt in August 1998.

To see how significant an effect this might be in the long/short equity sector, we compute the necessary amount of leverage required in each year after 1998 to yield an expected return for the contrarian strategy that is equal to the 1998 level. In other words, we seek values θ^* for the leverage ratio such that

$$\mathrm{E}[L_{pt}] \equiv \frac{\theta^*}{2}\,\mathrm{E}[R_{pt}] = \mathrm{E}[R_{p,1998}], \tag{10.4a}$$

$$\theta^* = \frac{2\,\mathrm{E}[R_{p,1998}]}{\mathrm{E}[R_{pt}]}, \quad t = 1999,\dots,2007, \tag{10.4b}$$

where (10.4) follows from the definition of leveraged returns (10.3) and the factor of 2 follows from the definition of leverage as the sum of the gross long and short positions (which are equal in the case of market neutral portfolios) divided by the investment capital. Table 10.6 shows that there has been significant 'alpha decay' of the contrarian strategy between 1998 and 2007, so much so that a leverage ratio of almost 9:1 was needed in 2007 to yield an expected return comparable to 1998 levels!

We can now simulate a more realistic version of the contrarian strategy in August 2007 using the 2006 leverage ratio of approximately 8:1 as suggested by Table 10.6, simply by multiplying the entries in Table 10.3 by $8/2 = 4$, which we do in Table 10.7 and Plate 12.[15] These returns illustrate the potential losses

---

[14] In fact, one can argue that the growth of quantitative equity market neutral strategies played a role in the downward trend in U.S. equity market volatility because most of these strategies are mean-reversion-based, hence they tend to attenuate market fluctuations rather than accentuate them as momentum strategies might.

[15] We use the leverage ratio of 8:1 instead of the 2007 level to capture the expectations of investors at the end of 2006 which, in turn, is taken into account by the portfolio managers. In particular, the

Table 10.6.

Year-by-Year Average Daily Returns of Lo and MacKinlay's (1990c) Contrarian Trading Strategy Applied to All U.S. Common Stocks (CRSP Share Codes 10 and 11) with Share Prices above $5 and below $2,000, from 1998 to 2007, and the Return Multipliers and Leverage Factors Needed to Yield the Same Average Return as in 1998

Year	Average Daily Return (%)	Return Multiplier	Required Leverage Ratio
1998	0.57	1.00	2.00
1999	0.44	1.28	2.57
2000	0.44	1.28	2.56
2001	0.31	1.81	3.63
2002	0.45	1.26	2.52
2003	0.21	2.77	5.53
2004	0.37	1.52	3.04
2005	0.26	2.20	4.40
2006	0.15	3.88	7.76
2007	0.13	4.48	8.96

that affected long/short equity managers during the week of August 6. A naive statistical arbitrage strategy like (10.1), with a leverage ratio of 8:1, would have lost −4.64% on August 7, followed by daily returns of −11.33% and −11.43%, respectively, on August 8 and 9. By the close of business on August 9, the leveraged contrarian strategy would have lost a little more than a quarter of the assets it started with 3 days before.

The fact that the strategy recovered sharply on August 10 with a leveraged return of 23.67% is small comfort for managers and investors who cut their risks on Wednesday and Thursday in response to the unusual size and speed of the losses over those 2 days. For those with the fortitude (and the credit lines) to maintain their positions throughout the week, they would have experienced an arithmetically compounded weekly return of −1.72%, which is not an unusual return in any respect.[16] However, with cumulative losses of −25% between August 6 and 9, many managers capitulated and were forced to de-leverage prior to Friday's reversal.

---

average daily return of the strategy in 2007 was not known to either the investors or the managers at the start of 2007.

[16] The corresponding geometrically compounded weekly return is −5.52% for the week, which is so different from the arithmetic case because of the magnitude of returns on August 8–10. This is certainly a bad return but not a terrible one under the circumstances. Whether geometric or arithmetic compounding is appropriate depends on how the strategy is implemented—some portfolio managers rebalance their positions each day to a fixed notional long/short exposure within the month, irrespective of daily profits and losses, in which case arithmetic compounding is the more appropriate method for aggregating daily returns.

Table 10.7.

Leveraged Daily Returns of Lo and MacKinlay's (1990c) Contrarian Trading Strategy Applied to All U.S. Common Stocks (CRSP Share Codes 10 and 11) with Share Prices above $5 and below $2,000, and Market-Capitalization Deciles (Monday, July 30, 2007, to Friday, August 31, 2007), with 8:1 Leverage or a Return Multiplier of 4

					Deciles by Market Capitalization						
	Smallest	Decile 2	Decile 3	Decile 4	Decile 5	Decile 6	Decile 7	Decile 8	Decile 9	Largest	All
30 Jul 2007	−0.28%	0.08%	7.85%	−1.43%	0.29%	0.91%	1.04%	1.51%	2.05%	0.71%	1.77%
31 Jul 2007	0.77%	4.41%	1.12%	2.20%	−2.53%	0.09%	−3.19%	1.94%	−1.23%	0.22%	1.46%
1 Aug 2007	6.10%	1.78%	−5.55%	1.39%	3.79%	−3.52%	−2.83%	−2.52%	−8.06%	−0.90%	0.43%
2 Aug 2007	3.54%	−3.04%	−0.46%	−2.68%	−3.77%	−10.79%	8.63%	6.12%	−2.97%	−0.77%	−1.22%
3 Aug 2007	−3.79%	−2.49%	−3.12%	0.24%	3.52%	0.05%	−2.49%	−4.35%	−2.29%	−2.74%	−0.10%
6 Aug 2007	−3.33%	−7.06%	−1.57%	−4.12%	5.47%	−5.47%	−4.75%	−2.86%	1.06%	3.08%	2.01%
7 Aug 2007	3.00%	1.03%	−6.55%	−11.65%	−6.01%	−2.79%	1.42%	−4.08%	−6.86%	−2.67%	−4.64%
8 Aug 2007	3.52%	−5.30%	−10.36%	−14.58%	−17.07%	−8.65%	−8.94%	−13.85%	−5.06%	−5.91%	−11.33%
9 Aug 2007	3.66%	−7.42%	−15.46%	−11.08%	−12.72%	−15.78%	−13.06%	−17.33%	−10.32%	−5.22%	−11.43%
10 Aug 2007	−1.32%	14.62%	24.32%	31.58%	35.08%	30.67%	30.07%	26.79%	18.73%	9.55%	23.67%
13 Aug 2007	5.42%	−1.24%	−2.53%	−4.26%	−6.20%	−0.88%	−5.15%	−8.04%	−8.58%	−4.99%	−3.05%
14 Aug 2007	4.65%	3.64%	−1.02%	1.35%	2.23%	−1.12%	2.74%	−1.16%	0.66%	0.67%	0.33%
15 Aug 2007	3.52%	4.74%	−2.42%	−2.33%	−0.69%	−3.89%	−0.97%	−5.36%	−2.29%	−4.73%	−1.53%
16 Aug 2007	−5.03%	−2.16%	0.59%	−2.36%	−2.39%	−3.95%	−6.94%	−5.08%	1.08%	−7.31%	−3.24%
17 Aug 2007	14.30%	9.94%	0.41%	5.04%	5.32%	−2.07%	0.47%	−1.56%	1.24%	0.44%	1.53%
20 Aug 2007	15.02%	7.02%	1.42%	5.40%	2.03%	1.74%	4.88%	2.22%	1.57%	4.67%	4.58%
21 Aug 2007	4.98%	0.43%	0.02%	−1.80%	0.09%	−2.54%	−0.33%	−0.20%	0.74%	0.43%	0.24%
22 Aug 2007	−3.39%	−1.23%	−2.07%	−2.05%	−0.67%	−3.31%	−0.74%	−2.26%	1.57%	0.37%	−1.51%
23 Aug 2007	−0.14%	2.79%	2.79%	−0.64%	1.51%	4.15%	1.04%	−1.33%	1.28%	1.23%	1.31%
24 Aug 2007	2.47%	−1.13%	−0.26%	0.92%	3.70%	−0.23%	−0.29%	0.37%	−1.42%	2.43%	1.73%
27 Aug 2007	4.38%	2.80%	0.46%	0.78%	5.01%	−0.63%	1.58%	2.85%	2.84%	0.10%	2.99%
28 Aug 2007	1.64%	1.26%	0.34%	−2.45%	−2.56%	−1.99%	−1.33%	−1.77%	−1.88%	0.99%	−3.04%
29 Aug 2007	5.79%	0.31%	5.07%	8.32%	7.75%	−2.14%	5.67%	6.39%	3.63%	3.94%	7.06%
30 Aug 2007	4.27%	0.16%	2.46%	1.61%	3.55%	0.41%	−0.11%	−0.16%	0.47%	−0.19%	2.01%
31 Aug 2007	6.75%	3.86%	3.80%	−2.21%	0.21%	2.08%	−0.32%	−2.68%	0.02%	0.58%	1.46%

10.6 The Unwind Hypothesis

With the empirically more plausible results of Table 10.7 in hand, we are now in a position to develop some additional hypotheses about the events of August 2007, which we shall refer to collectively as the *unwind hypothesis*.

The fact that the leveraged contrarian strategy lost −4.64% on Tuesday, August 7, and continued to lose another −11.33% on August 8, suggests a sudden liquidation of one or more sizable market neutral equity portfolios. Only a sudden liquidation would cause the strategy to lose close to −5% in the absence of any other significant market developments. And the logic behind the inference that market neutral funds were being liquidated is the fact that both the S&P 500 and MSCI-ex-U.S. indexes showed gains on August 7 and 8, hence it is unlikely that sizable long-biased funds were unwound on these 2 days.

The timing of these losses—shortly after month-end of a very challenging month for many hedge fund strategies—is also suggestive. The formal process of marking portfolios to market typically takes several business days after month-end, and August 7–9 may well be the first time managers and investors were forced to confront the extraordinary credit-related losses they suffered in July, which may have triggered the initial unwind of their more liquid investments, e.g., their equity portfolios, during this period.

The large losses on Tuesday and Wednesday—amounting to −15.98% for our leveraged contrarian strategy—would almost surely have spilled over to long/short equity funds as well as to certain quantitative long-only funds. In particular, if our hypothesis is correct that the losses on August 7 and 8 were caused by the unwinding of large equity market neutral portfolios, then any explicit factors used to construct that portfolio would have generated a loss for other portfolios with the same factor exposures. For example, if the portfolios that were unwound happened to be long low-P/E stocks and short low-dividend-yield stocks, the impact of the unwind would cause low-P/E stocks to decline and low-dividend-yield stocks to rise (albeit temporarily, until the unwind was complete). All other portfolios with these same factor exposures would suffer losses during the unwind process as well.

How likely is it that other funds will have the same factor exposures? If they use similar quantitative portfolio construction techniques, then more often than not, they will make the same kind of bets because these techniques are based on the same historical data, which will point to the same empirical anomalies to be exploited, e.g., the value premium, the size premium, the January effect, 6-month momentum, 1-month mean reversion, and earnings surprise. Moreover, the widespread use of standardized factor risk models such as those from MSCI/BARRA, Northfield Information Systems, and APT by many quantitative managers will almost certainly create common exposures among those managers to the risk factors contained in such platforms.

But even more significant is the fact that many of these empirical regularities have been incorporated into nonquantitative equity investment processes, including fundamental "bottom-up" valuation approaches like value/growth characteristics, earnings quality, and financial ratio analysis. Therefore, a sudden liquidation of a quantitative equity market neutral portfolio could have far broader repercussions, depending on that portfolio's specific factor exposures.

Table 10.7 contains another interesting pattern that is consistent with a statistical arbitrage unwind—the fact that the losses on August 7 and 8 were most severe for some of the intermediate-decile portfolios (deciles 3–5 and 8 each experienced cumulative losses greater than those of the other deciles and the entire universe of securities). Given the pattern of average daily returns of the contrarian strategy in decile portfolios (see Table 10.2), it is the intermediate-decile portfolios that should be most attractive to statistical arbitrage funds. Securities in the larger deciles do not exhibit sufficient profitability, and securities in the smaller deciles are too illiquid to trade in large volume, hence they will not be of interest to the larger funds.

In the face of the large losses of August 7–8, most of the affected funds—which includes market neutral, long/short equity, 130/30, and certain long-only funds—would likely have cut their risks prior to Thursday's open by reducing their exposures or de-leveraging, either voluntarily or because they exceeded borrowing and risk limits set by their prime brokers and other creditors. This was both prudent and, unfortunately, disastrous. The unintentionally coordinated efforts of so many equity managers to cut their risks simultaneously led to additional losses on Thursday, August 9, -11.43% in the case of our leveraged contrarian strategy. But this time, the S&P 500 was no longer immune and dropped by -2.95% by Thursday's close, presumably partly a reflection of the risk reduction by long-biased and long-only managers.[17]

By Thursday's close, the economic forces behind the unwind were apparently balanced by countervailing forces—either because the unwind and risk reductions were complete or because other market participants identified significant mispricings due to the rapid liquidations earlier in the week—and the losses stopped. Friday's massive reversal, which generated a 1-day return of 23.67% for the leveraged contrarian strategy, is the final piece of evidence that the losses of the previous 3 days were due to a sudden liquidation and not caused by any fundamental change in the equilibrium returns of long/short equity strategies, which would presumably have had a more permanent impact on price levels.

This pattern of short-term temporary price impact for purely liquidity-motivated trades is a classic consequence of market equilibrium with information

---

[17] On Friday August 10, the *Wall Street Journal* also cited growing concern about the subprime mortgage market, the move by BNP Paribas to suspend redemptions to three of its mortgage-related investment funds, and the injection of cash into money markets by the European and U.S. central banks as major factors in Thursday's market decline. See Zuckerman, Hagerty, and Gauthier-Villars (2007).

asymmetries between buyers and sellers. When large blocks of securities are executed quickly, equilibrium prices exhibit greater moves to induce the contra-parties to consummate the trades and bear the risk that they are less informed about the securities' true values.[18] If it is subsequently revealed that the trades were not based on information but merely liquidity trades, prices move back to their pre-block-trade equilibrium levels. And if there is lingering uncertainty as to whether the trades were motivated by information or liquidity, prices may only partially revert back to their pre-block-trade levels. This partial-adjustment property of the price discovery process is one compelling reason for "sunshine" trades, the practice of pre-announcing a large trade so as to identify oneself as a liquidity trader with no proprietary information, so as to reduce the price impact of the trade (see Admati and Pfleiderer, 1991, and Gennotte and Leland, 1990).

The particular dynamics of the bounce-back on August 10 may have taken several forms. One possibility is that the unwind and subsequent risk reductions were largely achieved by August 9, and the resulting cumulative price impact of the previous 3 days would have created even stronger trading signals for those long/short equity strategies that experienced the most significant losses.[19] In the absence of further unwind-motivated price momentum, the natural mean-reverting tendencies of equities that yield positive expected returns for long/short equity strategies during normal times would return. Moreover, the price impact of the previous days' unwind and risk-reduction trades would naturally revert to some degree as the fraction of market participants attributing such price movements to liquidity trades increases. However, only a partial reversal should be expected because not everyone would come to the same conclusion, and also because the de-leveraging of August 7–9 leaves a lower amount of capital to be deployed by long/short equity strategies on August 10.

Another possibility is that the price impact of August 7–9 was so severe that it drew the attention of new investors who (1) recognized that the closing prices

[18] See, for example, Kyle (1985), Easley and O'Hara (1987), O'Hara (1995, Chapter 6), and Gennotte and Leland (1990) for theories of equilibrium price dynamics with asymmetric information, and Barclay and Litzenberger (1988), Barclay and Warner (1993), Chan and Lakonishok (1993, 1995), and Holthausen, Leftwich, and Mayers (1987, 1990) for empirical evidence regarding the price impact of large trades. Ironically, Gennotte and Leland (1990) show that portfolio insurance and related hedging behavior—which includes mean-reversion trades like our contrarian strategy—can increase the likelihood of market crashes.

[19] For example, in the case of the contrarian strategy (10.1), consider the contribution of security i to the profits at date t, $\omega_{it} R_{it} = -R_{it}(R_{it-1} - R_{mt-1})/N$. Suppose this is an unusually large losing position for a given portfolio weight ω_{it}, which implies either that R_{it-1} is larger than R_{mt-1} and R_{it} is large and positive, or R_{it-1} is less than R_{mt-1} and R_{it} is large and negative. In either case, the loss is due to persistence or momentum in security i's price—the bigger the loss, the more significant the momentum. This, in turn, implies a much bigger position of the same sign for security i at date $t+1$ on average since $\omega_{it+1} = -(R_{it} - R_{mt})/N$ and R_{mt} has much lower volatility than R_{it}. Therefore, large losses will, on average, yield bigger bets for the contrarian strategy (10.1).

on August 9 were temporarily out of equilibrium purely because of a liquidity crunch, and (2) had access to significant sources of capital to seize the opportunity to buy (sell) securities at artificially deflated (inflated) prices. This injection of new capital—deployed in the opposite direction of the unwind—could have turned the tide, supporting the strong reversal on August 10.

These two possibilities are not mutually exclusive, but they both suggest that long/short equity strategies are not as liquid as we thought. Alternatively, the common factors driving these strategies have now become a significant source of risk, and the "phase-locking" behavior described in Lo (2001) apparently can cause as much dislocation in long/short equity strategies as in other parts of the hedge fund industry. To verify this possibility, we turn next to specific measures of illiquidity in long/short equity hedge funds in the Lipper TASS database.

10.7 Illiquidity Exposure

The rapid growth in the number of long/short equity funds and assets per fund, coupled with the likely increase in the amount of leverage each fund now employs (Section 10.5), suggest a significant decrease in liquidity of long/short equity strategies over the last decade. To explore this possibility, we propose to measure the illiquidity exposure of funds in the Long/Short Equity Hedge and Equity Market Neutral categories of the Lipper TASS database using the first-order autocorrelation coefficient of their monthly returns as suggested by Lo (1999) and Getmansky, Lo, and Makarov (2004). Specifically, using the monthly returns of each fund in the Lipper TASS database, we compute

$$\hat{\rho}_{1i} \equiv \frac{(T-2)^{-1} \sum_{t=2}^{T} (R_{it} - \hat{\mu}_i)(R_{it-1} - \hat{\mu}_i)}{(T-1)^{-1} \sum_{t=1}^{T} (R_{it} - \hat{\mu}_i)^2}, \ \hat{\mu}_i \equiv T^{-1} \sum_{t=1}^{T} R_{it}, \quad (10.5)$$

which is simply the correlation between fund i's return and its lagged return from the previous month. Getmansky, Lo, and Makarov (2004) show that funds with large positive values for $\hat{\rho}_{1i}$ tend to be less liquid,[20] and using a rolling window to

---

[20] They provide several arguments, both theoretical and empirical, but the basic intuition is straightforward: large positive autocorrelation in asset returns is usually a sign of informational inefficiencies in frictionless markets, but given how efficient hedge fund strategies tend to be, the only remaining explanation for such autocorrelation is significant market frictions, i.e., illiquidity. For example, it is well known that the historical returns of residential real estate investments are considerably more highly autocorrelated than, say, the returns of the S&P 500 index during the same sample period. Similarly, the returns of S&P 500 futures contracts exhibit less autocorrelation than those of the index itself. In both examples, the more liquid instrument exhibits less autocorrelation than the less liquid, and the economic rationale is a modified version of Samuelson's (1965) argument—predictability in asset returns will be exploited and eliminated only to the extent allowed by market frictions. Despite the fact

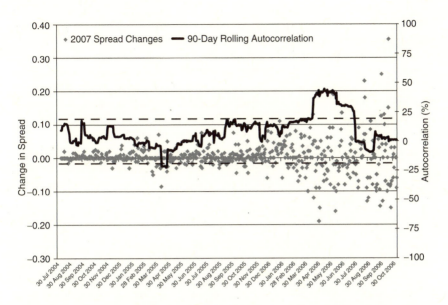

Figure 10.3. *First differences of March/April 2007 natural-gas futures spreads, and their 90-day rolling-window first-order autocorrelations $\hat{\rho}_1$ (August 9, 2004, to November 9, 2006). Dotted lines indicate the two-standard-deviation confidence band for the rolling-window autocorrelations under the null hypothesis of zero autocorrelation.*

estimate these autocorrelation coefficients for various asset return series allows us to capture changes in estimated illiquidity risk for those assets.

A striking example of the autocorrelation coefficient as a proxy for illiquidity is given in Figure 10.3, which plots the 90-day rolling-window autocorrelations of the first differences of daily spreads between the March and April 2007 natural-gas futures contracts from August 9, 2004, through November 9, 2006. The time series of first differences of the March/April 2007 spreads is a proxy for the daily returns of one of the largest strategies that Amaranth Advisors was allegedly engaged in and in which they were alleged to have built up a large and illiquid position prior to their demise in September 2006. Figure 10.3 shows that the rolling autocorrelations began climbing throughout 2005, nearly breached the 95% confidence interval in September and October 2005, and did breach this threshold on April 18, 2006, staying well above this level until August 2006 when Amaranth

---

that the returns to residential real estate are highly predictable, it is impossible to take full advantage of such predictability because of the costs associated with real estate transactions, the inability to short-sell real properties, and other market realities. These frictions have, in turn, led to the creation of real estate investment trusts, and the returns to these securities—which are considerably more liquid than the underlying assets on which they are based—exhibit much less autocorrelation.

and other similarly positioned hedge funds were presumably forced to unwind this spread trade.

Using $\hat{\rho}_{1i}$ as a measure of the illiquidity of each fund i, we can construct three aggregate measures of the illiquidity exposure of long/short equity funds along the lines of Chan et al. (2006, 2007), i.e., by computing the mean and median of rolling-window $\hat{\rho}_{1i}$'s over all funds i in the Lipper TASS Long/Short Equity Hedge and Equity Market Neutral categories month by month:

$$\hat{\rho}_{at} \equiv \frac{1}{n} \sum_{i=1}^{n} \hat{\rho}_{1it} \text{ (equal-weighted mean)}, \tag{10.6a}$$

$$\hat{\rho}_{bt} \equiv \sum_{i=1}^{n} \frac{\text{AUM}_{it}}{\sum_j \text{AUM}_{jt}} \hat{\rho}_{1it} \text{ (asset-weighted mean)}, \tag{10.6b}$$

$$\hat{\rho}_{ct} \equiv \text{median}(\hat{\rho}_{11t}, \ldots, \hat{\rho}_{1nt}). \tag{10.6c}$$

In Plate 13, the equal-weighted and asset-weighted means and the median of 60-month rolling-window autocorrelations of individual hedge fund returns are plotted from December 1994 to June 2007 using all funds in the two equity categories in both Live and Graveyard databases that report assets under management in U.S. dollars, and with at least 60 months of nonmissing returns.[21] These three series tell the same story: except for a brief decline in late 2004, the aggregate autocorrelation of Long/Short Equity Hedge and Equity Market Neutral funds has been on the rise since 2000, implying a significant decline in the liquidity of this sector over the past six years.[22]

Of course, the absolute level of illiquidity exposure in these two categories is still considerably lower than in many other categories, e.g., Convertible Arbitrage and Emerging Markets (see Getmansky, Lo, and, Makarov, 2004, and Chan et al., 2006, 2007, for further details). But the fact that the autocorrelations have increased at all in the most populous and, traditionally, among the most liquid of all sectors in the hedge fund industry, is certainly noteworthy. This is another indication that systemic risk in the hedge fund industry has increased recently.

10.8 A Network View of the Hedge Fund Industry

A common theme surrounding the unwind phenomenon in the hedge fund industry is credit and liquidity. Although they are separate sources of risk exposures for

[21] If a fund's AUM is missing in any given month, we use the fund's most recent nonmissing AUM instead.

[22] In particular, the approximate standard error for the equal-weighted mean of 400 60-month rolling autocorrelations is 0.65% under the assumption of cross-sectionally independently and identically distributed autocorrelations. Therefore, the statistical significance of the recent levels of autocorrelation in Plate 13 is quite high. See Appendix A.7 for details.

hedge funds and their investors—one type of risk can exist without the other—nevertheless, credit and liquidity have been inextricably intertwined in the minds of most investors because of the problems encountered by LTCM and many other fixed income relative-value hedge funds in August 1998. Much progress has been made in the recent literature in modeling credit and illiquidity risk,[23] but the complex network of creditor/obligor relationships, revolving credit agreements, and other financial interconnections is still largely unmapped. Perhaps some of the newly developed techniques in the mathematical theory of networks will allow us to construct systemic measures for liquidity and credit exposures and the robustness of the global financial system to idiosyncratic shocks. The "small-world" networks considered by Watts and Strogatz (1998) and Watts (1999) seem to be particularly promising starting points. However, given the lack of transparency in the hedge fund industry, we have no direct way of gathering the data required to estimate the "network topology" that is the starting point of these techniques.

One indirect and crude measure of the change in the "degree of connectedness" in the hedge fund industry is to calculate the changes in the absolute values of correlations between hedge fund indexes over time.[24] Using 13 indexes from April 1994 to June 2007 constructed by CS/Tremont,[25] we compare their estimated pairwise correlations between the first and second halves of our total sample period: April 1994 to December 2000 versus January 2001 to June 2007. If, for example, the absolute correlation between Multi-Strategy and Emerging Markets was 7% over the first half of the sample and 52% over the second half, as it was, this might be a symptom of increased connectedness between those two categories.

Figure 10.4 provides a graphical depiction of this network for the two subsamples, where we have used thick lines to represent absolute correlations greater than 50%, thinner lines to represent absolute correlations between 25% and 50%, and no lines for absolute correlations below 25%. For the earlier subsample, we estimate correlations with and without August 1998, and the difference is striking. Omitting August 1998 decreases the correlations noticeably, which is no

---

[23] See, for example, Bookstaber (1999, 2000, 2007), Getmansky, Lo, and Makarov (2004), Lo (1999, 2001, 2002), Kao (2002), and their citations.

[24] Because most hedge fund strategies involve short-selling of one type or another, the correlations between the returns of various hedge funds can be positive or negative and are less constrained than, for example, those of long-only vehicles such as mutual funds. And because in our context, connectedness can mean either large positive or large negative correlation, we focus on the absolute values of correlations in this analysis.

[25] Specifically, we use CS/Tremont's Convertible Arbitrage, Dedicated Short Bias, Emerging Markets, Equity Market Neutral, Event Driven, Fixed Income Arbitrage, Global Macro, Long/Short Equity, Managed Futures, Event Driven Multi-Strategy, Distressed Index, Risk Arbitrage, and Multi-Strategy indexes. See Appendix A.2 for the definitions of these categories, and www.hedgeindex.com for more detailed information about their construction. All indexes start in January 1994 except Multi-Strategy, which starts in April 1994.

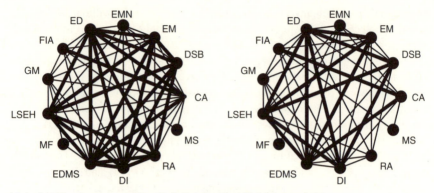

(a) April 1994 to December 2000, with (left) and without (right) August 1998

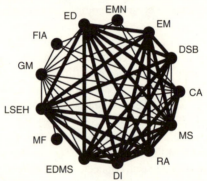

(b) January 2001 to June 2007

Figure 10.4. *Network diagrams of correlations among 13 CS/Tremont hedge fund indexes over two subperiods (April 1994 to December 2000 and January 2001 to June 2007). Thicker lines represent absolute correlations greater than 50%, thinner lines represent absolute correlations between 25% and 50%, and no connecting lines correspond to correlations less than 25%. CA = Convertible Arbitrage; DSB = Dedicated Short Bias; EM = Emerging Markets; EMN = Equity Market Neutral; ED = Event Driven; FIA = Fixed Income Arbitrage; GM = Global Macro; LSEH = Long/Short Equity Hedge; MF = Managed Futures; EDMS = Event Driven Multi-Strategy; DI = Distressed Index; RA = Risk Arbitrage, and MS = Multi-Strategy.*

surprise given the ubiquity and magnitude of the LTCM event. But a comparison of the two subperiods shows a significant increase in the absolute correlations in the more recent sample. The hedge fund industry has clearly become more closely connected.

Perhaps the most significant indicator of increased connectedness is the fact that the Multi-Strategy category is now more highly correlated with almost every other index, a symptom of the large influx of assets into the hedge fund industry.

This increased correlation is also consistent with the hypothesis that forces outside the long/short equity sector may have caused an unwind of statistical arbitrage strategies in August 2007. In August 1998, multi-strategy funds were certainly impacted by their deteriorating fixed income arbitrage positions, and no doubt many of them liquidated their statistical arbitrage portfolios to meet fixed income margin calls. But because multi-strategy funds were not as significant a market force in 1998 as they evidently are now, their correlations to other strategies were not as large as they are today.

Table 10.8 contains a more detailed comparison of the two correlation matrices. The absolute correlation matrix from the earlier sample is subtracted from that of the more recent sample, hence a positive entry represents an increase in the absolute correlation in the more recent period and is highlighted in boldface if it exceeds 20%. Table 10.4 confirms the patterns of Figure 10.4: absolute correlations among the various different hedge fund categories have indeed increased in the more recent sample.

To capture the dynamics of these changes in correlation structure among the CS/Tremont indexes, in Figure 10.5 we plot the means and medians of the absolute values of 36-month rolling-window correlations between the indexes, with and without the month of August 1998.[26] These graphs show that the mean and median absolute correlations among the indexes have been steadily increasing in recent years, especially after 2004. The inordinate amount of influence that August 1998 has on these correlations underscores the potential for systemwide shocks in the hedge fund industry.

The increase in correlations among hedge fund returns can be attributed to at least two potential sources: increased exposure of hedge funds to standard factors such as the S&P 500, the U.S. 10-year Treasury bond, and the U.S. Dollar Index, and increased linkages due to more complex channels such as liquidity and credit relationships through multi-strategy funds and proprietary trading desks. Unfortunately, without more detailed data from hedge funds and their creditors and obligors, we have no way of distinguishing between these two sources of commonality.

One subtlety in interpreting the time variation in correlations is the possibility that the changes are due to volatility shifts, not to changes in the covariances of returns. This distinction may not be particularly relevant from the perspective of systemic risk exposures because an increased correlation between variables X and Y does imply higher comovement of two variables per unit of $\sigma_x \sigma_y$, irrespective of whether that increase has come about from an increase in the numerator or a decrease in the denominator. For example, suppose that the volatility in X declines suddenly but the covariance between X and Y remains unchanged, yielding an increase in the absolute value of the correlation between X and Y. This increased

---

[26] We use a shorter rolling window in this case because the index returns are less noisy than the individual fund returns used to estimate the rolling autocorrelations in Plate 13.

Table 10.8.

The Difference of the Absolute Correlation Matrices of CS/Tremont Hedge Fund Indexes Using Recent Data (January 2001 to June 2007) and Earlier Data (April 1994 to December 2000)*

	Convertible Arbitrage	Dedicated Short Bias	Emerging Markets	Equity Market Neutral	Event Driven	Fixed Income Arbitrage	Global Macro	Long/Short Equity	Managed Futures	Event Driven Multi-Strategy	Distressed	Risk Arbitrage	Multi-Strategy
With August 1998 Included													
Convertible Arbitrage													
Dedicated Short Bias	−1%												
Emerging Markets	−24%	3%											
Equity Market Neutral	−4%	−35%	−6%										
Event Driven	−7%	−6%	−10%	−33%									
Fixed Income Arbitrage	−38%	2%	−25%	32%	−18%								
Global Macro	11%	4%	−2%	6%	−6%	1%							
Long/Short Equity	6%	−12%	11%	−15%	4%	−5%	−14%						
Managed Futures	−18%	−15%	−9%	−18%	−16%	−1%	15%	20%					
Event Driven Multi-Strategy	−14%	0%	−11%	−25%	3%	−25%	−13%	10%	−16%				
Distressed	1%	−11%	−10%	−40%	−3%	−9%	−2%	−7%	−12%	1%			
Risk Arbitrage	−3%	−5%	6%	−7%	0%	−5%	12%	12%	−23%	−2%	3%		
Multi-Strategy	31%	46%	45%	16%	69%	−3%	34%	69%	19%	67%	57%	53%	
Excluding August 1998													
Convertible Arbitrage													
Dedicated Short Bias	17%												
Emerging Markets	−9%	14%											
Equity Market Neutral	2%	−31%	1%										
Event Driven	5%	7%	0%	−33%									
Fixed Income Arbitrage	−37%	3%	−20%	34%	−19%								
Global Macro	15%	11%	1%	9%	−8%	3%							
Long/Short Equity	21%	−7%	20%	−10%	10%	2%	−11%						
Managed Futures	−8%	−2%	−3%	−27%	3%	4%	8%	15%					
Event Driven Multi-Strategy	−2%	19%	0%	−21%	10%	−26%	−14%	19%	3%				
Distressed	20%	3%	5%	−39%	4%	−4%	2%	3%	−13%	25%			
Risk Arbitrage	15%	11%	25%	1%	23%	5%	21%	27%	−6%	20%	32%		
Multi-Strategy	27%	47%	46%	15%	63%	−4%	34%	67%	18%	60%	54%	53%	

* The earlier correlation matrix is estimated with and without August 1998.

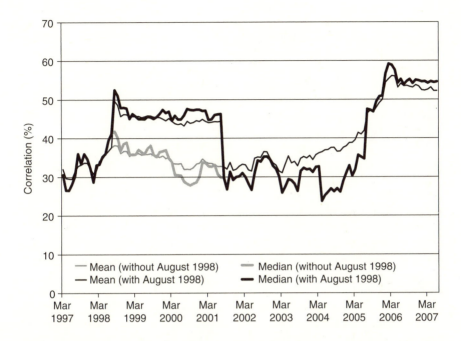

Figure 10.5. *Mean and median absolute 36-month rolling-window correlations among CS/Tremont hedge fund indexes (March 1997 to June 2007).*

absolute correlation is not spurious but is the direct result of the volatility of X declining while the covariance between X and Y remains unchanged, and this combination of facts does imply a more "significant" relation between X and Y, where significance is measured in units of $\sigma_x \sigma_y$.[27] Nevertheless, from the portfolio-construction perspective, increases in correlation need not imply increased portfolio risk, simply because the portfolio variance is the weighted sum of all the pairwise covariances of the constituent assets. Specifically, a decrease in the volatilities of all assets while covariances are held constant implies a lower portfolio volatility, despite the fact that all pairwise correlations have increased in absolute value because of the lower asset-volatility levels.

Plate 14 plots the 36-month rolling-window pairwise covariances between the CS/Tremont Multi-Strategy index and other CS/Tremont sector indexes from

---

[27] In particular, recall that the numerator of the correlation coefficient, the covariance, is given by the expectation of the cross product $(X_t - \mu_x)(Y_t - \mu_y)$. If σ_x were to decrease merely through a change in units (e.g., raw return instead of percentage return), then $(X_t - \mu_x)$ would undergo the same decrease, thereby leaving the correlation coefficient unchanged. Therefore, if σ_x were to decrease without a corresponding change in $(X_t - \mu_x)$, then it could be argued that there has been a genuine change in the relationship between X and Y.

December 1996 to June 2007, where the rolling covariances to the Long/Short Equity and Equity Market Neutral indexes are highlighted using thicker lines. The 36-month window following August 1998 is also marked with dotted lines to highlight the impact this period has on our rolling estimates. These plots show that in the 1990s, pairwise covariances between Multi-Strategy and other sectors were quite heterogeneous and noisy, but in the last 7 years, the covariances have clustered together, with the exception of Dedicated Short Bias (as expected), and exhibit upward trends.

The fact that Multi-Strategy did not have a reliably negative covariance with Dedicated Short Bias in the 1990s is notable, particularly in light of the strong negative covariance in the last half of the sample. One interpretation of this shift is that Multi-Strategy did not have a significant equity component in the 1990s, but this has changed over the past seven years and is consistent with the increased covariance between Multi-Strategy and the two equity indexes since 1999.

Of course, volatility in U.S. equity markets has declined over the past seven years, so a significant portion of the increased correlations between Multi-Strategy and the two equity indexes is due to smaller denominators, not just increased numerators. But both shifts have important implications for the systemic risk of the hedge fund industry, and neither should be ignored or dismissed.

Of course, pairwise correlations of indexes are very crude measures of the connectedness of the hedge fund industry. Moreover, the network map of the global financial system is considerably more complex, involving many different types of organizations (banks, hedge funds, prime brokers, investors, regulators, etc.) and different types of relationships between these organizations. Although a number of recent papers have applied the mathematical theory of networks to financial markets,[28] there is virtually no data with which to calibrate such models. In an industry that protects its intellectual property primarily through trade secrets, it may be impossible to collect the necessary information to map the network topology without additional regulatory oversight.

10.9 Did Quant Fail?

In light of the unwind hypothesis, in Section 10.6, what can we conclude about whether or not quantitative equity market neutral strategies failed en masse in August 2007? We have a specific definition of failure in mind: Do the losses of August 2007 signal a breakdown in the basic economic relationships that yield attractive risk/reward profiles for such strategies, or is August 2007 an unavoidable and integral aspect of those risk/reward profiles?

---

[28] See, for example, Allen and Gale (2000), Freixas, Parigi, and Rochet (2000), Furfine (2003), Boss et al. (2004), Degryse and Nguyen (2004), Upper and Worms (2004), and Leitner (2005).

An instructive thought experiment is to consider a market neutral portfolio strategy in which U.S. equities with odd-numbered CUSIP identifiers are held long and those with even-number CUSIPs are held short. Suppose such a portfolio strategy is quite popular, and a number of large hedge funds have implemented it. Now imagine that one of these large hedge funds decides to liquidate its holdings because of some liquidity shock. Regardless of this portfolio's typical expected return during normal times, in the midst of a rapid and large unwind, all such portfolios will experience losses, with the magnitudes of those losses directly proportional to the size and speed of the unwind. Moreover, it is easy to see how such an unwind can generate losses for other types of portfolios, e.g., long-only portfolios of securities with prime-number CUSIPs, and dedicated short-sellers that short only those securities with CUSIPs divisible by 10. If a portfolio is of sufficient size, and it is based on a sufficiently popular strategy that is broadly implemented, then unwinding even a small fraction of it can cascade into a major market dislocation.

Therefore, it is tempting to conclude that the events of August 2007 are not particularly relevant to the efficacy of quantitative investing. The losses were more likely the result of a fire-sale liquidation of quantitatively constructed portfolios rather than the specific shortcomings of quantitative methods. In this respect, the dislocation experienced by quantitative equity market neutral managers in August 2007 resembles the dislocation experienced by U.S. equityholders in October 1987, fixed income arbitrage managers in August 1998, subprime mortgage–related managers in 2007, Japanese real estate investors in the 1990s, internet stockholders in March 2000, and Dutch tulip bulb investors in February 1637.[29] What played out in August 2007 was not new at all but may be an age-old dynamic of risk-taking opportunism punctuated by occasional flights to safety and liquidity.

However, a successful investment strategy should include an assessment of the risk of ruin, and that risk should be managed appropriately. Moreover, the magnitude of tail risk should, in principle, be related to a strategy's expected return given the inevitable trade-off between risk and reward. Therefore, it is disingenuous to assert that "a strategy is successful except in the face of 25-standard-deviation events." Given the improbability of such events, we can only conclude that either the actual distribution of returns is extraordinarily leptokurtic or the standard deviation is time-varying and exhibits occasional spikes.

In particular, as Montier (2007) observed, risk has become "endogenous" in certain markets—particularly those that have recently become flush with large inflows of assets—which is one of the reasons that the largest players can no longer assume that historical estimates of volatility and price impact are accurate

---

[29] The differences in recovery times for these dislocations seem to be related to the liquidity of the underlying instruments and the breadth of participation in the specific strategies involved. This intriguing pattern bears further investigation and is one of the directions of our ongoing research.

measures of current risk exposures. Endogeneity is, in fact, an old economic concept illustrated by the well-known theory of imperfect competition—if an economic entity, or group of coordinated entities, is so large that it can unilaterally affect prices by its own actions, then the standard predictions of microeconomics under perfect competition no longer hold. Similarly, if a certain portfolio strategy is so popular that its liquidation can unilaterally affect the risks that it faces, then the standard tools of basic risk models such as Value-at-Risk and normal distributions no longer hold. In this respect, quantitative models may have failed in August 2007 by not adequately capturing the endogeneity of their risk exposures. Given the size and interconnectedness of the hedge fund industry, we may require more sophisticated analytics to model the feedback implicit in current market dynamics.

For example, from a purely statistical perspective, the mere threat of forced liquidation of a given strategy should increase the theoretical volatility of the entire class of such strategies, and the more illiquid the underlying assets and the larger the potential liquidation, the larger the increase in volatility. But theoretical volatilities are not observable and must be estimated, which is the crux of the problem: if the historical record contains no realizations of an extreme event, statistical estimators based on that record alone cannot reflect the possibility of such events. Moreover, by definition tail events are rare, hence any statistical estimator of such events will be based on very small samples and subject to large estimation error.

Therefore, August 2007 offers a number of insights for improving the quantitative methods for measuring and managing risks. One of the most important lessons is the need for measures of illiquidity risk, and that volatility is an inadequate measure of risk, especially for relative-value strategies like quantitative equity market neutral where the market-making characteristics of the strategy tend to attenuate market fluctuations, yielding lower volatility estimates that are used to justify higher amounts of leverage. In the case of August 2007, traditional risk measures could have been augmented with estimates of factor and illiquidity exposures in the Long/Short Equity and Equity Market Neutral categories of the Lipper TASS database to yield a broader assessment of the risks facing managers in this sector. To the extent that we can develop a better framework and a set of analytics for measuring illiquidity and other risk exposures in financial markets—perhaps along the lines of Gennotte and Leland (1990), Lo (1999, 2001, 2002), Getmansky, Lo, and Makarov (2004), Getmansky, Lo, and Mei (2004), and Chan et al. (2006, 2007)—we may be able to reduce the impact of future liquidity events (see Chapter 11 for a particular approach to risk reduction in the face of gates and other liquidity shocks).

Another important issue is the role that investment horizon played in the market reaction to August 2007. Short-term investors that reduced their risks intramonthly suffered the most, while many long-term investors enjoyed positive returns for the month, and this difference bears further study. A related issue is the differences between strategies employing exchange-traded securities that are marked to market continuously, versus strategies with OTC contracts or highly illiquid securities whose valuations are not observed as frequently. This distinction may well explain why the aftermath of August 2007 was so different from that of August 1998. One possible explanation is that the infrequent valuation of illiquid assets yields a certain degree of flexibility for portfolio managers that exchange-traded instruments do not allow. This flexibility comes from the fact that credit lines provided by prime brokers and other creditors are often contingent on the valuation of the corresponding collateral, and any material change in that valuation can trigger margin calls and, ultimately, a reduction or withdrawal of credit. For portfolios of continuously marked-to-market securities, margin calls can occur more frequently by definition than for portfolios with hard-to-value securities.[30] We conjecture that a major reason for the quick reversal of quantitative portfolios on August 10 is the fact that the securities involved were mostly exchange-traded equities, for which the price discovery mechanism allowed market participants to better understand the dynamics of the losses during August 7–9. Had the alleged unwind of August 2007 involved illiquid OTC contracts, we suspect that the losses would have been considerably larger and any reversal would have taken much longer to materialize.

While market participants will no doubt learn from August 2007 and improve their strategies and risk management protocols, it is unlikely that the possibility of future dislocations can be completely eliminated by such improvements. Events like August 2007 may simply be unavoidable features of quantitative equity market neutral strategies. In fact, the profit-and-loss patterns of these strategies in August 2007 are consistent with those of a broader set of market-making and relative-value strategies: small but steady positive returns most of the time, coupled with occasional short-lived bursts of significant loss. Such risk/reward profiles are quite attractive to a certain set of investors—those that understand the nature of tail risk and can withstand the inevitable rare event. For example, which of the following two gambles is best?

$$G_1 = \begin{cases} \$75,000 & \text{with probability 50\%} \\ \$25,000 & \text{with probability 50\%} \end{cases}$$

$$G_2 = \begin{cases} \$100,000 & \text{with probability 98\%} \\ -\$1,000,000 & \text{with probability 2\%} \end{cases}$$

The first gamble entails less risk of loss (the worst case is a gain of \$25,000) but has an expected return of \$50,000, which is lower than the expected return

---

[30] For example, suppose a margin call is triggered by a decline of 20% or more in the value of a given portfolio. If this portfolio contains exchange-traded instruments that are continuously marked to market, the first instance of a 20% decline will trigger a loss of credit even if the portfolio's value improves dramatically immediately after reaching this critical level. If, on the other hand, the portfolio contains OTC contracts that are valued only once a month, margin calls will occur less frequently.

of \$78,000 for the second gamble. The second gamble is almost sure to yield a higher payoff than the first but has a small probability of a very significant loss. There is no correct answer to which is best—the optimal choice depends entirely on an individual's risk preferences (see Lo, 1999).

A less contrived example is the catastrophe-insurance industry, in which insurers routinely bet against tail events, and most of the time, they enjoy steady cash flows from their policyholders. However, on occasion, they suffer great losses when disaster strikes, but they are adequately capitalized so that such events typically do not cause widespread dislocation in that industry. The one circumstance in which problems can arise in the catastrophe-insurance industry is when there is too much capital, causing so much downward pressure on insurance premiums that a number of insurers cannot cover their costs; i.e., they become undercapitalized and cannot survive a tail event. In such cases, the demand for catastrophe insurance cannot support the excess supply, and the occurrence of a tail event causes an industry shake-out where only the most well-capitalized insurers survive. In the aftermath of such a shake-out, premiums rise, creating great profit opportunities for the remaining players which, in turn, attracts new insurers to the industry, and the cycle begins again. The correspondence of this insurance cycle to the quantitative equity market neutral business is no accident.[31]

There is also a competitive and strategic element to whether a given manager or prime broker should reduce leverage given the actions of other managers and brokers. If we all agree to reduce leverage so as to decrease the likelihood of a major market dislocation due to forced liquidation, then each manager and prime broker has an incentive to deviate from this agreement and reap the benefits of increasing leverage while everyone else cuts back. Without a mechanism for enforcing cooperation, such agreements are not stable and are unlikely to arise in practice.[32] In fact, because of the lack of transparency and coordination within the hedge fund industry, and the strong relationship between performance and business viability, competitive pressures will lead managers and prime brokers to *increase* leverage in an "arms race" for generating better returns.

This perspective provides further support for the Adaptive Markets Hypothesis of Farmer and Lo (1999) and Lo (2004, 2005), in which financial markets are not always and everywhere efficient but where competition, mutation, adaptation, and

---

[31] However, an important difference is that the risks of the catastrophe-insurance business are exogenously determined, hence the primary source of variability in that business is the amount of risk capital available. In the case of hedge fund strategies, both the risks and the risk capital are endogenous and jointly determined, which significantly increases the complexity of the dynamics.

[32] More formally, they are not Nash equilibria and suffer from the "Prisoner's Dilemma." See Luce and Raiffa (1957). Moreover, the possibility of Brunnermeier and Pedersen's (2005) "predatory trading" becomes more likely in periods of financial distress, as in August 1998 and 2007, and in these cases, risks become endogenous in the sense of Montier (2007).

natural selection jointly determine the dynamics of market prices and quantities. The growth in hedge fund assets, the growth in the number of new hedge funds, the apparent increase in leverage, and the proliferation of hedge fund products and services are the most recent manifestations of the relentless search for investment performance and economic gain, i.e., the survival instinct. As a particular type of strategy becomes "crowded"—meaning too much capital deployed relative to the returns generated per unit risk—capital leaves this sector to seek out more attractive risk/reward profiles, thereby improving the risk/reward profile for the remaining population, which then attracts new capital and restarts the cycle.

Such cycles are commonplace in ecological models of population dynamics, and the Adaptive Markets Hypothesis is an application of this framework to the population of investors, managers, and creditors. If August 2007 is to be viewed as a failure, it was a failure to recognize the ineluctable cycle of profit and loss that all types of investment strategies seem to exhibit over time. But to expect individual market participants to identify and avoid such cycles is not only unrealistic but also flies in the face of basic economics. In the absence of any reason for coordination, market participants will seek to maximize their own welfare, and doing so implies that each will push the limits of his investments to the point at which the risk-adjusted expected returns are equalized across all investment opportunities. With limited information regarding the nature and extent of other market participants' investments, each participant must estimate the risk/reward profile of each strategy and determine the appropriate level of capital to deploy. Since such estimates are subject to error, the natural feedback of losses and gains, i.e., action is spurred by losses and complacency is induced by gains, implies the waxing and waning of strategies and the cyclical flow of capital described above.

A remaining open question is whether investors truly understood and preferred the particular risks of quantitative equity market neutral strategies in recent years. While only "qualified investors" are meant to have access to hedge funds, the ubiquity of delegated financial management suggests that the dislocation of August 2007 may well have spilled over to less sophisticated investors' pension funds and other retirement assets. Whether this type of spillover effect is appropriate touches upon a series of complex policy issues surrounding the implicit paternalism of pension fund management by fiduciaries. Can a pension plan sponsor make investment decisions that are in the "best interests" of all of the plan participants, even when those participants have widely varying risk preferences and financial objectives? Unfortunately, we have little to add to this controversy, other than to acknowledge its relevance for the question of whether quantitative equity market neutral managers should or should not have reduced their risk levels prior to August 2007. If all three sets of stakeholders—managers, investors, and creditors—were aware of the risks and willing to bear them, then August 2007 was merely the cost of doing business. If not, then August 2007 signalled another kind of failure in this industry.

10.10 Qualifications and Extensions

Although the unwind hypothesis in Section 10.6 seems to be consistent with our empirical results, we emphasize that all of our inferences are indirect, tentative, and without the benefit of much hindsight given the recency of these events. We have no inside information about the workings of the many hedge funds that were affected in August 2007, nor do we have any proprietary access to prime brokerage records, trading histories, or industry leverage data. Therefore, our academic perspective of the events during the week of August 6–10 should be interpreted with some caution and a healthy dose of skepticism.

In particular, our empirical findings are based on only one very simple strategy applied to U.S. stocks, which may be representative of certain short-term market neutral mean-reversion strategies but is not likely to be as good a proxy for the broader set of quantitative long/short equity products that involve both U.S. and international equities, and other securities. For example, we apply our naive strategy indiscriminately to an undistinguished universe of U.S. securities, using no other factors besides past returns, and with no consideration of execution costs or risk-adjusted return contributions. This test strategy is clearly missing many other features of long/short equity funds. To continue the microscope analogy, we have used just one lens of rather limited magnification to look at August 2007. A more refined analysis using multiple lenses with different resolutions will no doubt yield a more complex and accurate picture of the very same events. For example, the contrarian strategy does not contain any factor-based selection algorithms, hence its performance may not reflect as clearly the unwind of factor-based portfolios.

More importantly, even if our hypothesis is correct that an unwind initiated the losses on August 7, we cannot say much about the ultimate causes of such an unwind. It is tempting to conclude that a multi-strategy proprietary trading desk's increased exposure to subprime mortgage portfolios caused it to reduce leverage by liquidating a portion of its most liquid positions, e.g., a statistical arbitrage portfolio, thereby initiating the losses on August 7 that cascaded into the subsequent rout. However, another possible scenario is that several quantitative equity market neutral managers decided at the beginning of August that it would be prudent to reduce leverage in the wake of so many problems facing credit-related portfolios. They de-leveraged accordingly, not realizing that this strategy was so crowded and that the price impact of their liquidation would be so severe. Once this price impact had been realized, other funds employing similar strategies may have decided to cut their risks in response to their losses, which then led to the kind of "death spiral" that we witnessed in August 1998 as managers attempted to unwind their fixed income arbitrage positions to meet margin calls.

Whether or not the initial losses on August 7 were caused by a forced liquidation or a voluntary reduction in risk is impossible to determine from our

Table 10.9.

CS/Tremont Hedge Fund Index Returns for the Month of August 2007

Index/ Substrategies	*August 2007 (%)*
Credit Suisse/Tremont Hedge Fund Index	−1.53
Convertible Arbitrage	−1.08
Dedicated Short Bias	−1.14
Emerging Markets	−2.37
Equity Market Neutral	−0.39
Event Driven	−1.88
Distressed	−1.73
Multi-Strategy	−2.03
Risk Arbitrage	−0.65
Fixed Income Arbitrage	−0.87
Global Macro	−0.62
Long/Short Equity	−1.38
Managed Futures	−4.61
Multi-Strategy	−1.40

Source: www.hedgeindex.com.

outsider's perspective. But the fact that an entire category of strategies as liquid as Long/Short Equity could suffer such significant losses in the absence of any real market news suggests that the current level of liquidity is less than we thought. Alternatively, we learned in August 2007 that there is more commonality among long/short equity strategies than we anticipated. This commonality may be even broader, as suggested by the fact that all the CS/Tremont hedge fund indexes yielded losses in August 2007 (see Table 10.9).

Our use of the Lipper TASS hedge fund database also requires some qualification. The Lipper TASS database consists entirely of funds that have voluntarily agreed to be included, with no legal obligations to report either regularly or accurately. In fact, many of the high-profile managers that made headlines in August 2007 are not included in the Lipper TASS database, and while we hope that this database contains an unbiased cross section of funds in the industry, we have no way to ensure that it is representative.[33] And all of our inferences are indirect since we are unable to obtain direct information from hedge funds or their prime brokers. Accordingly, we cannot be any more definitive in our conclusions than to say that, for the moment, the empirical facts seem to be consistent with our hypotheses.

Finally, we conjecture that liquidations of various strategies and asset classes may have started earlier. For example, Figure 10.2 shows that the contrarian strategy exhibited a smaller dip during the second half of July, with NYSE

---

[33] See Agarwal and Naik (2005) and Fung and Hsieh (2006) for excellent overviews of the hedge fund industry and some of the pitfalls with various hedge fund databases.

daily volume at elevated levels during this period and into the first half of August. Other liquid investment categories such as global macro, managed futures, and currency strategies may have experienced similar unwinds during July and August as problems in the subprime mortgage markets became more prominent in the minds of managers and investors. For example, the "carry trade" among currencies was supposedly unwound to some extent in July and August 2007, generating losses for a number of global macro and currency-trading funds. Obviously, our long/short equity microscope is incapable of detecting dislocation among currency strategies, but a simple carry trade simulation—similar to our simulation of the contrarian trading strategy—could shed considerable light on the dynamics of the foreign exchange markets in recent months. Indeed, a collection of simulated strategies across all of the hedge fund categories can serve as a kind of multiresolution microscope, one with many lenses and magnifications, with which to examine the full range of financial market activity. We plan to explore such extensions in future research.

10.11 The Current Outlook

In this chapter, we have argued through indirect means that the events of August 6–10, 2007, may have been the result of a rapid unwinding of one or more large long/short equity portfolios, most likely initially a quantitative equity market neutral portfolio. This unwind created a cascade effect that ultimately spread more broadly to long/short equity portfolios, 130/30, and other active-extension strategies, and certain long-only portfolios (those based primarily on quantitative stock-selection and systematic portfolio-construction methods). By August 9, this unwind and de-leveraging process was over, and the affected portfolios and strategies experienced a significant but not complete rebound on August 10.

With the caveats of Section 10.10 in mind, we draw three broad conclusions from our indirect inferences.

The first is that the contrast between August 1998 and August 2007 has important ramifications for the connectedness of the global financial system. In August 1998, default of Russian government debt caused a flight to quality that ultimately resulted in the demise of LTCM and many other fixed income arbitrage funds. This series of events caught even the most experienced traders by surprise because of the unrelated nature of Russian government debt and the broadly diversified portfolios of some of the most successful fixed income arbitrage funds. Similarly, the events of August 2007 caught some of the most experienced quantitative equity market neutral managers by surprise. But August 2007 may be far more significant because it provides the first piece of evidence that problems in one corner of the financial system—possibly the subprime mortgage sector and related credit markets—can spill over so directly to a completely unrelated corner: long/short equity strategies. This is precisely the kind of "short-cut" described in the theory of mathematical networks that generates the "small-world phenomenon" of Watts (1999) in which a small random shock in one part of the network can rapidly propagate throughout the entire network.

The second implication of August 2007 is that the notion of "hedge fund beta" described in Hasanhodzic and Lo (2007) is now a reality. The fact that the entire class of long/short equity strategies moved together so tightly during August 2007 implies the existence of certain common factors within that class. Although more research is needed to identify those factors (e.g., liquidity, volatility, value/growth), there should be little doubt now about their existence. This is reminiscent of the evolution of the long-only index fund industry, which emerged organically through the realization by most institutional investors that they were invested in very similar portfolios and that a significant fraction of the expected returns of such portfolios could be achieved passively and, consequently, more cheaply. Of course, hedge fund beta replication technology is still in its infancy and largely untested, but the intellectual framework is well-developed and a few prominent broker-dealers and asset management firms are now offering the first generation of these products. To the extent that the demand for long/short equity strategies continues to grow, the increasing amounts of assets devoted to such endeavors will create its own common factors that can be measured, benchmarked, managed, and, ultimately, passively replicated.

Finally, the events of August 2007 have some implications for regulatory reform in the hedge fund sector. Recent debates among regulators and legislators have centered around the registration of hedge funds under the Investment Advisers Act of 1940. While there may be compelling arguments for registering hedge funds, these arguments are generally focused on investor protection which is, indeed, the main impetus behind the 1940 act. But investor protection is not directly related to systemic risk, and the best ways to deal with the former may not be optimal for the latter. In particular, registration does not address the systemic risks that hedge funds pose to the global financial system and currently, no regulatory body has a mandate to monitor, much less manage, such risks in the hedge fund sector.[34] Given the role that hedge funds have begun to play in financial markets—namely, significant providers of liquidity and credit—they now impose externalities on the economy that are no longer negligible.

In this respect, hedge funds are becoming more like banks. The fact that the banking industry is so highly regulated is due to the enormous social externalities

---

[34] A number of organizations have been actively involved in addressing systemic risk in the hedge fund industry including the Federal Reserve System (especially the New York Fed and the Board of Governors), the Office of the Comptroller of the Currency, the International Monetary Fund, the SEC, the Treasury Department, and the President's Working Group. However, none of these organizations have any regulatory authority over the largely unregulated hedge fund industry and cannot even obtain the necessary data from hedge funds or their credit counterparties to compute direct measures of systemic risk. Even the very influential New York Fed exercises its influence primarily through moral suasion.

banks generate when they succeed and when they fail. But unlike banks, hedge funds can decide to withdraw liquidity at a moment's notice, and while this may be benign if it occurs rarely and randomly, a coordinated withdrawal of liquidity among an entire sector of hedge funds could have disastrous consequences for the viability of the financial system if it occurs at the wrong time and in the wrong sector.

This observation should not be taken as a criticism of the hedge fund industry. On the contrary, hedge funds have created tremendous economic and social benefits by supplying liquidity, engaging in price discovery, improving risk transfer, and uncovering nontraditional sources of expected return. If hedge funds have increased systemic risk, the relevant questions are "By how much?" and "Do the benefits outweigh the risks?" No one would argue that the optimal level of systemic risk for the global financial system is zero. But then what is optimal, or acceptable?

The first step to addressing this issue is to develop a better understanding of the likelihood and proximate causes of systemic risk; one cannot manage that which one cannot measure. The proposal by Getmansky, Lo, and Mei (2004) to establish an organization similar to the National Transportation Safety Board for capital markets is one possible starting point. By establishing a dedicated and experienced team of forensic accountants, lawyers, and financial engineers to monitor various aspects of systemic risk in the financial sector, and by studying every financial blow-up and developing guidelines for improving our methods and models, a "Capital Markets Safety Board" may be a more direct way to deal with the systemic risks of the hedge fund industry than registration.

In the aftermath of World War II, a group of socially minded physicists joined to form the *Bulletin of Atomic Scientists* to raise public awareness of the potential for nuclear holocaust. To illustrate their current assessment of the appropriate state of alarm, they published a "Doomsday Clock" indicating how close we are to "midnight," i.e., nuclear annihilation.[35] Originally set at 7 minutes to midnight in 1947, the clock has changed from time to time as we have moved closer to (2 minutes to midnight in 1953) or farther from (17 minutes to midnight in 1993) the brink of nuclear disaster. If we were to develop a Doomsday Clock for the hedge fund industry's impact on the global financial system, calibrated to 5 minutes to midnight in August 1998, and 15 minutes to midnight in January 1999, then our current outlook for the state of systemic risk in the hedge fund industry is about 11:51 p.m.

For the moment, markets seem to have stabilized, but the clock is ticking.

---

[35] Specifically, "The Bulletin of the Atomic Scientists Doomsday Clock conveys how close humanity is to catastrophic destruction—the figurative midnight—and monitors the means humankind could use to obliterate itself. First and foremost, these include nuclear weapons, but they also encompass climate-changing technologies and new developments in the life sciences and nanotechnology that could inflict irrevocable harm." See www.thebulletin.org for further information.

11
Jumping the Gates

The financial crisis of 2007–2008 has created enormous stress in the hedge fund industry, with wholesale liquidations at firesale prices causing hedge fund managers to impose gates on investor redemptions. In many cases, such measures may well be justified because the unwinding of illiquid positions under duress can lead to extreme losses for both exiting and remaining investors. By instituting a gate, managers can unwind positions in a more orderly manner, preserving value for all investors. However, if unwinding positions in a more orderly manner takes months or, in some extreme cases, years, gated investors may be forced to bear certain risks that are no longer appropriate or "suitable."

In this chapter, we argue that such circumstances can be remedied to some degree by implementing a futures-overlay strategy in which the most significant factor risks of an investor's gated assets are hedged out or shaped to satisfy specific constraints from the moment an investor submits his redemption notice to the day when his assets are fully paid out. In this way, a manager can engage in the orderly liquidation of an investor's stake while, at the same time, a futures overlay can be implemented by either the manager or the investor to ensure that during a lengthy liquidation process, the investor's net exposures are more in line with original investment objectives.

The factors that we propose to use for hedging purposes are the most liquid exchange-traded futures contracts on stock indexes, bonds, interest rates, and commodities, and currency forward contracts on the major currencies. The reason for using liquid futures is simple: introducing illiquidity into the hedging vehicle would contradict the primary objective of the overlay, which is to reduce the main risk exposures of an illiquid hedge fund investment. The reason for using currency forwards is the fact that they are even more liquid than currency futures, although the popularity of the latter has grown significantly in recent years and may eventually surpass the liquidity of forwards.

Of course, any hedging program that uses liquid instruments to hedge an illiquid portfolio will exhibit a certain degree of tracking error arising from at least two distinct sources: common but illiquid factors, and manager-specific factors. The former is unavoidable, and the latter may actually be desirable (if the investor still believes the manager has unique alpha) or at least tolerable (if the investor is well diversified across multiple managers). The key issue in determining the efficacy of the hedging program is the relative contribution of the hedgeable factors to the overall risk of the investor's assets, i.e., the R^2 of the risk model or "hedging equation." If the R^2 is close to 100%, then a hedging-overlay strategy can neutralize nearly all of the risk of the investment; if the R^2 is close to 0%, the hedging strategy is nearly useless.

In between 0% and 100%—which is where most risk models fall—an investor can reduce part of the overall risk of his investment. We argue that this part—the risks due to the most liquid factor exposures—should be the highest priority for an investor to hedge for several reasons. First, it is the easiest set of risks to hedge by definition, since there exist liquid futures contracts with which to implement the hedge. Second, it is likely to account for a significant amount of risk (otherwise, the corresponding futures would not be as liquid as they are), especially during periods of market dislocation when gates are triggered. Third, if the investor's assets are gated for an extended period of time, the risk profile of those assets can change significantly as market conditions change, and the investor may not be equipped to monitor those changes continuously during this period. Fourth, the typical investor is likely to have significant exposure to these same common-factor risks in other parts of his portfolio, particularly among traditional investment vehicles, hence a hedging program can enhance diversification. And finally, the investor selected the manager presumably because of the manager's unique sources of alpha, not the manager's betas, hence neutralizing those betas should have little impact on the manager's value-added.

Apart from hedging, futures-overlay strategies can also be used to reposition an investor's overall portfolio to address broader liquidity constraints. For example, a pension fund that has experienced a significant market decline in its equity investments will be underweight stocks and overweight bonds, implying a significant rebalancing need to return to its strategic asset allocation. However, bond market illiquidity may make such a rebalancing unusually costly. A futures-overlay strategy that is long stock-index futures and short bond futures can alleviate this temporary imbalance, and as liquidity is restored to the bond markets, the overlay can be gradually reduced until it is no longer needed. Moreover, the liquidity, credit quality, and built-in leverage of exchange-traded futures allows such beta repositioning overlays to be implemented cheaply, safely, and with relatively small amounts of capital.[1] In such applications, some betas are temporarily enhanced

---

[1] In fact, some futures brokers will accept securities as collateral, albeit with some "haircut," but this should pose little concern for the pension fund, since a large fraction of their assets are intended to be buy-and-hold.

and others reduced, with the overall objective of maintaining a level set of exposures through changing market conditions.

In Section 11.1, we begin with a review of the basic definition of a linear risk model for alternative investments, and then describe the basic mechanics of beta hedging and beta repositioning in Section 11.2. We apply this framework in Section 11.3 to the universe of long/short equity hedge funds in the Lipper TASS database, and summarize the performance of the overlay during the past few years. In Section 11.4, we propose a dynamic implementation of beta-overlay strategies in which overlays are applied selectively over time as a function of market conditions. By hedging only during periods of clear market dislocation, the overall performance drag of beta overlays can be reduced significantly at the expense of more frequent trading. We conclude in Section 11.5.

11.1 Linear Risk Models

The first step in constructing a beta-hedging overlay strategy, and perhaps the most important step, is to determine the relationship between the portfolio to be hedged and the hedging factors. Most hedging programs begin with a linear relationship, although more sophisticated programs can be constructed using nonlinear relationships at greater expense and complexity. In this chapter, we shall focus only on linear hedging programs.

Denote by R_{it} the return of hedge fund i at date t, and let R_{it} satisfy the following linear relationship:

$$R_{it} = \alpha_i + \beta_{i1} \text{RiskFactor}_{1t} + \cdots + \beta_{iK} \text{RiskFactor}_{Kt} + \epsilon_{it}, \qquad (11.1)$$

where RiskFactor_{kt} denotes the date-t return of risk factor k, $k = 1, \ldots, K$,. This linear risk model may seem familiar to students of modern financial analysis, which is based on linear multifactor models such as the Capital Asset Pricing Model (CAPM) and the Arbitrage Pricing Theory (APT). However, (11.1) differs in a few important ways.

First, the relationship we hypothesize is primarily a statistical one that is unfettered by any particular economic theory or philosophy. In particular, we place no restrictions on α_i, whereas the CAPM and APT assume that managers add no value above and beyond the risk premia associated with the risk factors.[2]

Second, we define "risk factor" differently from the usual academic context— our notion of a risk factor is an economic variable that satisfies three criteria:

1. Definability. It is a well-defined and measurable economic variable, i.e., there is a commonly accepted definition of the concept and an explicit way to measure it accurately.

---

[2] This hypothesis, which seems to hold for mutual funds but has been soundly rejected for hedge funds, implies that $\alpha_i = (1 - \sum_k \beta_{ik})R_f$, where R_f is the return on the riskless asset.

2. Commonality. The variable is statistically significantly related to a broad set of hedge funds or other investment vehicles.

3. Tradability. There exist liquid futures or forward contracts that capture the full economic effects of the variable.

The motivation for the first two conditions is obvious, but the third requires some explanation. Although economists have derived a number of linear factor models with a variety of factors, not all of them are based on marketable securities.[3] However, from a practical perspective, if you cannot trade the factor, there is no actionable consequence that can be derived from the risk model, since it is impossible to alter the exposure to that factor. Therefore, our definition of a "risk factor" requires tradability so that any exposure identified in (11.1) can be actively managed.

Some examples and counterexamples may help to clarify these criteria. Examples of economic variables that satisfy our definition of risk factors are the S&P 500, Japanese 10-year government bonds, the U.S. dollar index, oil, and gold. In each case, the variable (1) has a precise definition that is widely agreed upon and which can be measured accurately; (2) is clearly related to many hedge funds and traditional investments; and (3) can be traded via futures or forward contracts.

On the other hand, the following counterexamples are not risk factors according to our criteria: fear, greed, illiquidity, and animal spirits. Despite the fact that all of these factors are quite relevant for hedge funds, none of them has a widely accepted definition that yields measurable quantities, nor can any of them be easily traded. Therefore, while such factors may have substantial economic justification, for the purposes of hedging beta exposures, we do not consider them risk factors.

Based on (11.1), we have the following characterization of the fund's expected return and variance:

$$E[R_{it}] = \alpha_i + \beta_{i1}E[\text{RiskFactor}_{1t}] + \cdots + \beta_{iK}E[\text{RiskFactor}_{Kt}] \quad (11.2)$$

$$\text{Var}[R_{it}] = \beta_{i1}^2 \text{Var}[\text{RiskFactor}_{1t}] + \cdots + \beta_{iK}^2 \text{Var}[\text{RiskFactor}_{Kt}]$$

$$+ \text{Covariances} + \text{Var}[\epsilon_{it}], \quad (11.3)$$

where "Covariances" is the sum of all pairwise covariances between RiskFactor_{pt} and RiskFactor_{qt} weighted by the product of their respective beta coefficients $\beta_{ip}\beta_{iq}$.

This characterization implies that there are two distinct sources of a hedge fund's expected return: beta exposures β_{ik} multiplied by the risk premia associated with those exposures $E[\text{RiskFactor}_{kt}]$, and manager-specific alpha α_i. By "manager-specific," we do not mean to imply that a hedge fund's unique source

[3] For example, Breeden's (1979) consumption-based CAPM (CCAPM) relates the expected return of an asset to its beta with respect to aggregate consumption, which currently has no tradable market instrument associated with it.

of alpha is without risk—we are simply distinguishing this source of expected return from those that have clearly identifiable risk factors associated with them. In particular, it may well be the case that α_i arises from factors other than the K risk factors identified in (11.1), and a more-refined version—one that better reflects the particular investment style of a given manager—may yield a better-performing risk model.

From (11.3) we see that a hedge fund's variance has three distinct sources: the variances of the risk factors multiplied by the squared beta coefficients, the variance of the residual ϵ_{it}—which may be related to the specific economic sources of α_i—and the weighted covariances among the factors. This decomposition highlights the fact that a hedge fund can have several sources of risk, each of which should yield some risk premium, otherwise investors would not be willing to bear such risk. By taking on exposure to multiple risk factors, a hedge fund can generate attractive expected returns from the investor's perspective (see, for example, Lo, 2001).

Litterman (2005) calls such risk exposures "exotic betas" and argues that "[t]he adjective 'exotic' distinguishes it from market beta, the only beta which deserves to get paid a risk premium." We disagree—there are several well-established economic models that illustrate the possibility of multiple sources of systematic risk, each of which commands a positive risk premium, e.g., Merton (1973) and Ross (1976). We believe that hedge funds are practical illustrations of these multifactor models of expected returns, and on average, have net long exposures to such risk factors. For example, long/short equity managers are typically net long the S&P 500, hence they benefit to some degree from the normally positive equity risk premium. Equity market–neutral managers are typically long volatility, CTAs are typically long commodities, and global macro managers are typically long bonds. Therefore, hedging away the beta exposures of these managers will, on average, require short positions in risk factors that normally yield positive expected returns.

Accordingly, by hedging away certain risk factors, an investor will be forgoing the normally positive risk premia associated with such factors. Therefore, one or more of the following conditions must hold for a rational investor to implement a beta-hedging overlay strategy:

(A1) The investor believes that the expected returns of the risk factors to be hedged are temporarily negative during the hedging period.

(A2) The investor believes that the risk reduction from hedging the risk factors is worth the price of forgoing the normally positive expected returns of the risk factors to be hedged during the hedging period.

(A3) The investor already has significant exposure to the risk factors to be hedged, and therefore does not wish to have any additional exposure.

(A4) The risk factors to be hedged are incidental to the expected return of the manager, but they contribute more than proportionally to the manager's volatility.

Of course, any successful hedging program also requires the following condition:

   (B) The risk factors in the linear risk model (11.1) account for a significant fraction of the variability in the manager's returns.

If (B) is not satisfied, there is no point to hedging, since the risk factors are unable to capture much of the manager's risks. In such cases, implementing a beta-hedging overlay can actually *increase* the overall risk to the investor while simultaneously reducing the expected return because of transaction costs and forgone potential risk premia. One measure of a risk model's effectiveness is its R^2, which is simply the estimated fraction of the total variance attributable to the risk model, i.e.,

$$R^2 \equiv \frac{\text{Var}[\sum_k \beta_{ik} \text{RiskFactor}_{kt}]}{\text{Var}[R_{it}]}. \tag{11.4}$$

For the majority of hedge funds in the Lipper TASS database, the R^2's range from 25% to 75% for a three-factor risk model, and where a hedge fund falls in this range depends on several characteristics: the hedge fund's investment style, the set of risk factors, and the time period. A very rough guideline for the minimum R^2 needed to implement an effective hedging-overlay strategy is 25%—any value lower than this threshold raises the possibility that the hedge will do more harm than good.

11.2 Beta Overlays

Assuming that one or more of conditions (A1)–(A4) and (B) hold, we now proceed to construct a beta-hedging overlay program or "beta blocker" for the investor's stake in manager i.[4] Denote by R_{ht} the return of a hedging portfolio consisting of futures or forward contracts corresponding to the K risk factors in (11.1). To hedge out all of the factor risks of manager i, we simply take countervailing positions in each of the factors, so that the sum of R_{ht} and R_{it} contains no factor exposures:

$$R_{ht} + R_{it} = \alpha_i + \epsilon_{it}$$

$$R_{ht} = -\sum_{k=1}^{K} \beta_{ik} \text{RiskFactor}_{kt}, \tag{11.5}$$

---

[4] We have borrowed the term "beta blocker" from the pharmaceutical industry where it refers to a class of drugs used to treat hypertension and heart-attack patients by blocking so-called beta receptors in the heart and kidneys. Given recent market conditions, blocking financial betas may yield similar salutary effects.

Table 11.1.

Percentage Volatility Reduction from Linear Beta Blockers for Various Levels of R^2.

R^2	δ
5%	3%
10%	5%
20%	11%
30%	16%
40%	23%
50%	29%
60%	37%
70%	45%
80%	55%
90%	68%
95%	78%

and this is always achievable given our definition of risk factors. Appendix A.8 provides a more detailed discussion of the mechanics of this process for a given dollar investment in manager i and specific notional values for futures contracts corresponding to the K risk factors.

With this beta blocker in place, the risk reduction of the post-hedge portfolio can be quantified as

$$\frac{\text{Var}[R_{ht} + R_{it}]}{\text{Var}[R_{it}]} = 1 - R^2, \tag{11.6}$$

where R^2 is defined in (11.4). Therefore, the percentage reduction in volatility δ due to the beta blocker is simply

$$\delta \equiv 100 \times (1 - \sqrt{1 - R^2}), \tag{11.7}$$

which is tabulated in Table 11.1 for various levels of R^2. These figures show that for a hedge fund with an R^2 of 50%, a beta blocker will reduce the volatility by about 29%.

Of course, the values in Table 11.1 and the beta blocker (11.5) are all based on *estimates*, not the true theoretical values of β_{ik} and R^2, which are unobservable. Therefore, the realized performance of the beta blocker may differ from the estimated performance. Moreover, as the parameters β_{ik} and R^2 change—which they are likely to do for the typical hedge fund—performance differences may arise. These and other practicalities create "tracking error" in the beta blocker, and a number of techniques can be employed to mitigate its effects, including time-varying parameter regression, regime-switching models, and robust estimation. Appendix A.9 contains a more detailed discussion of tracking error.

Given the generality of the beta-blocking framework (11.5) that we have proposed, it is clear that this approach can be applied more generally to any collection of managers, both alternative and traditional, and can be used to hedge only a portion of the beta exposures if desired. The only prerequisite is condition (B): we must be able to construct a risk model for *each manager* that adequately captures that manager's risk exposures. Unlike the case of traditional assets, where a single risk model, e.g., the MSCI/BARRA Global Equity Model or the Northfield Global Risk Model, can cover the risk profiles of an entire class of managers, alternative assets are considerably more heterogeneous. However, constructing individual risk models for each alternatives manager allows the investor to integrate his traditional and alternatives portfolios in a relatively seamless manner. We argue that such an integration is not only desirable, but indispensable in determining the overall risk/reward profile of an investor's portfolio.[5]

In some cases, an investor may be less interested in neutralizing certain betas than in gaining exposures to them in a cost-effective manner. In these cases, similar overlay strategies can be used to "reposition" the investor's betas, reducing those that the investor is not willing to bet on and accentuating those that the investor is. Since the mechanics are so similar to those of the beta blocker, we relegate the details of such beta-repositioning strategies to Appendix A.8.

11.3 Hedging Long/Short Equity Managers

To illustrate the empirical relevance of the beta-blocker program, we apply this hedge to the universe of Long/Short Equity funds from the Lipper TASS hedge fund database during the period from January 2000 through October 2008. We find that, on average, the beta-blocker program reduces the volatility, maximum drawdowns, and autocorrelations, and increases the Sharpe ratios of the funds with a modest reduction in average monthly return. We also find that the beta-blocker program is more effective for funds with higher average regression R^2 values, as suggested by (11.7) in Section 11.2.

For this analysis, we selected all Long/Short Equity funds from the Lipper TASS Live database (as of December 1, 2008) that report (1) returns on a monthly basis and value their assets under management in U.S. dollars; (2) assets under management of at least $500 million at some point during 2008; and (3) monthly returns for every month between January 2004 and October 2008. There are forty-seven funds that meet all of these criteria.

---

[5] See Chapter 8 for a more detailed discussion of this integrated investment framework.

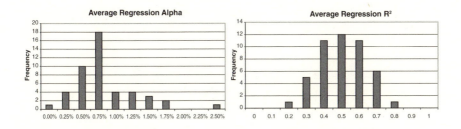

Figure 11.1. *Distribution of average regression alphas and R^2's for 24-month rolling-window regressions of the returns of forty-seven Long/Short Equity funds in the Lipper TASS Live database from January 2000 to October 2008 using two factors per regression chosen statistically from a universe of fifteen factors.*

To estimate the risk models of Section 11.1, we use the following fifteen factors:

- Six equity factors: S&P 500 Futures, S&P/TSE 60 Futures, FTSE 100 Futures, DAX Futures, CAC 40 Futures, TOPIX Futures
- Five 10-year government bond factors: U.S. 10-Year Futures, Canadian 10-Year Futures, Euro-Bund Futures, Long Gilt Futures, Japanese 10-Year Futures
- Four foreign exchange factors: EUR Forwards, CAD Forwards, GBP Forwards, JPY Forwards

To estimate the betas of each fund, we use a 24-month trailing window and a statistical factor-selection algorithm to select two of the fifteen factors and estimate the regression coefficients using ordinary least-squares regression on these two factors. In implementing the overlay strategy for month t, we employ the betas estimated using data through month $t - 2$, and scale the magnitude of the hedge based on the net-asset value at the end of month $t - 2$.[6] Our simulations do not include transaction costs; however, since the overlay positions change only on a monthly basis and involve only highly liquid instruments, the associated costs are likely to be negligible.

Figure 11.1 reports the distribution of average regression α's and average R^2's among the risk models for the forty-seven funds in our sample. The median R^2 is 0.49 and the distribution of average α has mean 0.83% and median 0.76%, suggesting that the selected risk factors do, in fact, account for a significant fraction of volatility, even in the presence of substantial manager-specific alpha. Indeed, the mean and median fund returns are 0.94% and 0.77% per month,

---

[6] This 2-month lag reflects the fact that fund returns for month t are not typically available in time to implement the hedge for month $t + 1$ because of reporting delays. Of course, if the returns are available before the end of month $t + 1$, then the hedge can and should be implemented earlier.

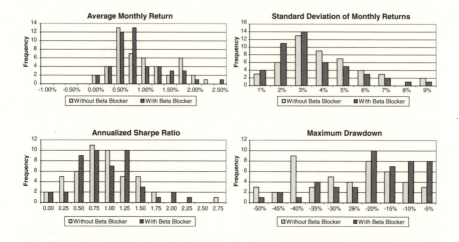

Figure 11.2. *Distribution of return statistics for forty-seven Long/Short Equity funds in the Lipper TASS Live database from January 2000 to October 2008 with and without beta-blocker overlays constructed from 24-month rolling-window regressions using two factors per regression chosen statistically from a universe of fifteen factors.*

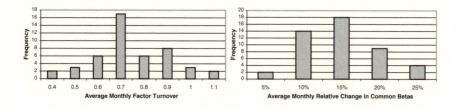

Figure 11.3. *The distribution of (i) monthly factor turnover and (ii) monthly changes in betas for the forty-seven Long/Short Equity funds in the Lipper TASS Live database from January 2000 to October 2008.*

respectively. Figure 11.2 shows the distribution of annual returns, standard deviation, Sharpe ratio,[7] and maximum drawdown for all funds and for all funds with the beta-blocker overlay.

To develop some intuition for the amount of monthly turnover generated by a beta-hedging program based on these estimates, note that there are two potential reasons for changing positions each month: (*i*) a change in the selected factors due to our factor-rotation algorithm; and (*ii*) a change in the estimated betas for those factors that persist from the previous month. The left half of Figure 11.3 shows the distribution of the average number of factors that change on a monthly basis; since

---

[7] All Sharpe ratios reported in this chapter are computed with respect to a 0% risk-free rate.

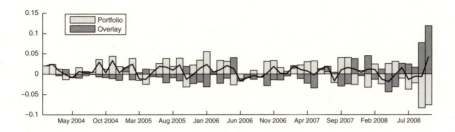

Figure 11.4. *The monthly returns of an equal-weighted portfolio of the forty-seven Long/Short Equity funds from the Lipper TASS Live database (light grey), the beta-blocker monthly overlay (dark grey), and the resulting performance of the hedged portfolio (line).*

we are selecting two factors each month, a value of 2 would represent a complete monthly turnover. To put these values into perspective, Plates 15a and 15b show the evolution of the betas of the funds with the maximum turnover (1.14) and median turnover (0.727), respectively. The right half of Figure 11.3 shows the distribution of the average turnover of the betas of factors that are selected in consecutive months.[8]

Plate 15c shows the average betas across the forty-seven Long/Short Equity funds in the Lipper TASS Live database. These are the betas that would be estimated for a portfolio consisting of an equal-weighted allocation to each of the forty-seven funds. The monthly performance of such a portfolio, together with the monthly performance of the overlay, is illustrated in Figure 11.4.

The left-hand panel of Table 11.2 summarizes the impact of the beta-blocker overlay on the forty-seven funds. On average, the overlay reduces the annual return by 0.61% while reducing volatility by 11.6% and maximum drawdowns by 20.4%. Equation (11.7) suggests that the degree of volatility reduction improves as the regression R^2 increases, and we confirm this empirically in the right-hand panel of Table 11.2, where we summarize the impact of the beta-blocker overlay for the subset of twenty-one funds with average R^2 greater than 0.5. We also note that the correlation between the percentage of volatility reduction and the empirical values of $1 - \sqrt{1 - R^2}$ is 75%, again demonstrating the relevance of the analysis of Section 11.2.

Another common consequence of the beta-blocker overlay is a reduction in the autocorrelation of returns. As shown in Lo (2001, 2002) and Getmansky, Lo, and Makarov (2004), autocorrelation in hedge fund returns is a proxy for illiquidity exposure, and Figure 11.5 implies that a number of long/short equity funds contain illiquid investments, e.g., the median first-order autocorrelation is 20.6%. Not surprisingly, Figure 11.5 shows that the combined returns of these funds and the overlay strategies have considerably lower autocorrelation and greater liquidity,

---

[8] For a given factor, the turnover is defined as $\|\beta_t - \beta_{t-1}\| / \|\beta_{t-1}\|$.

Table 11.2.

Impact of Beta-Blocker Overlay for Forty-Seven Long/Short Equity Funds in the Lipper TASS Live Database (January 2000 to October 2008).

	All 47 Funds				21 Funds with Average $R^2 > 0.5$			
	Change in Annual Return	% Change in Volatility	% Change in Sharpe Ratio	% Change in Max Drawdown	Change in Annual Return	% Change in Volatility	% Change in Sharpe Ratio	% Change in Max Drawdown
Mean	−0.61%	−11.6%	2.8%	−20.4%	0.38%	−25.1%	12.5%	−38.9%
25th Percentile	−1.86%	−26.7%	−15.3%	−48.0%	−0.93%	−36.0%	−7.2%	−61.8%
Median	−0.40%	−9.2%	3.1%	−32.7%	−0.36%	−31.4%	44.0%	−42.5%
75th Percentile	1.27%	3.0%	42.8%	−5.3%	1.76%	−16.1%	77.8%	−27.4%

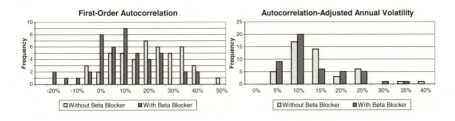

Figure 11.5. *Distributions of autocorrelations and autocorrelation-adjusted annual volatility of forty-seven Long/Short Equity funds in the Lipper TASS Live database from January 2000 to October 2008 constructed from 24-month rolling-window regressions using two factors chosen statistically from a universe of fifteen factors.*

with the distribution of autocorrelations shifted left by the beta blocker and a median autocorrelation of 9.2%.

Table 11.3 reports the percentage change in autocorrelation resulting from the beta blocker, as well as the percentage change in annual standard deviation (taking into account the first-order autocorrelation) and the annual Sharpe ratio (again, accounting for first-order autocorrelation; see Lo, 2002). As with Table 11.2, the beta-blocker overlay is, on average, more effective for the subset of funds with average R^2 in excess of 0.5. Table 11.3 shows that another advantage of the reduced autocorrelation is a reduction in longer-horizon (e.g., annual) volatility, even for fixed levels of monthly volatility, due to the fact that the annual variance is the sum of monthly variances plus all the pairwise covariances of the twelve individual monthly returns (which are directly related to the autocorrelations).

As noted in Section 11.1, the beta-blocker overlay is not without cost—we see in Table 11.2 that the overlay reduces annual returns by an average of 0.61% over the entire sample period. Moreover, the cost will tend to be greater during "normal" and/or favorable market conditions. Indeed, since funds tend to have long exposures to various risk factors, the overlay will often be short risk factors that, during normal market conditions, offer positive risk premia. Thus, the criteria set forth in Section 11.1 must be taken into consideration in deciding which factors to hedge and to what degree.

To help put these considerations in perspective, we tabulate in Plate 16 the annual returns, volatilities, and their ratios of the fifteen risk factors used in this analysis. These results show that during the last few years (other than 2008), U.S. and foreign equities have been the most costly factors to hedge, with annual returns that range from 1.4% to 44.9% during the 2003–2006 subperiod. Of course, equities are also the most volatile asset class, with annual volatilities during this same period ranging from 9.7% to 31.3%. While such high levels of volatility seem to go hand-in-hand with large risk premia, during periods of market dislocation such as 2000–2002 and 2008, equities can also yield double-digit losses. Therefore, hedging out equity-beta exposure may or may not cause

Table 11.3.

Impact of Beta-Blocker Overlay on First-Order Autocorrelations, Autocorrelation-Adjusted Annual Volatility, and Autocorrelation-Adjusted Annual Sharpe Ratios for Forty-Seven Long/Short Equity Funds in the Lipper TASS Live Database (January 2000 to October 2008).

	All 47 Funds			21 Funds with Average $R^2 > 0.5$		
	% Change in First-Order Autocorrelation	*% Change in AC-Adjusted Volatility*	*% Change in AC-Adjusted Sharpe Ratio*	*% Change in First-Order Autocorrelation*	*% Change in AC-Adjusted Volatility*	*% Change in AC-Adjusted Sharpe Ratio*
Mean	−52.6%	−14.5%	6.8%	−88.3%	−27.5%	16.4%
25th Percentile	−108.7%	−33.5%	−15.7%	−126.9%	−40.6%	−9.4%
Median	−37.2%	−14.2%	12.2%	−44.6%	−35.9%	50.2%
75th Percentile	−16.1%	4.7%	49.5%	−23.2%	−15.6%	86.0%

a performance drag, depending on market conditions, but it will definitely reduce portfolio risk.

The potential performance gaps between periods of calm and periods of dislocation are highlighted in Table 11.4, which summarizes the impact of the beta-blocker overlay during a period of relative calm (2005–2006) and a more turbulent period (2007–2008). While the goal of reducing volatility is achieved on average during both periods, it is clear that the costs of hedging are much greater on average during 2005–2006, underscoring the importance of the hedging conditions set out in Section 11.1, and opening the door for the possibility of hedging selectively as a function of market conditions. We turn to this possibility in the next section.

11.4 Dynamic Implementations of Beta Overlays

For those investors who have committed to a long-term hedging program, it may be possible to avoid some of the performance drag of a full beta-blocker overlay by formalizing conditions under which the overlay should be fully engaged and when it should be inactive. For example, one might choose to hedge portfolio betas—either completely or partially—only during periods where the volatility of the beta exposures exceeds a certain threshold, or based on an external condition, e.g., only when the VIX Index exceeds 50, or as part of other risk-management protocols. Hedging only during those periods when the portfolio is deemed to be at "high risk" and forgoing the overlay during other periods may seem like market timing, but in fact is closer to volatility timing, a considerably less daunting challenge. In fact, there is mounting evidence that volatility is both time-varying and persistent, and most investors do respond dynamically to sharp changes in risk, which is consistent with a dynamic implementation of beta-overlay strategies.

To maximize the effectiveness of such dynamic implementations, such beta-overlay strategies should be updated on a *daily* basis, despite the fact that the betas are updated only monthly. While the monthly estimated betas must (by definition) remain static until new return data is available—presumably at least a month later—selective hedging can occur on a daily basis as the volatilities of the hedging factors change from day to day.

To illustrate the flexibility of daily hedging using the beta-blocker framework, we implement dynamic hedging overlays for the forty-seven Long/Short Equity funds in the Lipper TASS Live database from January 2000 through October 2008 using the following simple algorithm: whenever the trailing 2-week (daily) volatility of the beta exposures exceeds the trailing 2-year (daily) volatility estimate of the beta exposures, we hedge the betas to bring them back in line with the 2-year volatility estimate. Thus if the 2-week volatility of the betas is 3.0% and

Table 11.4.

Impact of Beta-Blocker Overlay for Forty-Seven Long/Short Equity Funds in the Lipper TASS Live Database (January 2005 through December 2006 and January 2007 through October 2008).

	2005–2006				2007–2008			
	Change in Annual Return	% Change in Volatility	% Change in Sharpe Ratio	% Change in Max Drawdown	Change in Annual Return	% Change in Volatility	% Change in Sharpe Ratio	% Change in Max Drawdown
Mean	−8.87%	−21.5%	−47.2%	8.3%	8.63%	−14.8%	−87.0%	−27.7%
25th Percentile	−11.32%	−31.3%	−73.0%	−22.4%	3.26%	−42.9%	−157.6%	−60.5%
Median	−8.58%	−22.8%	−43.4%	3.5%	8.27%	−16.2%	−46.4%	−45.7%
75th Percentile	−4.81%	−11.3%	−17.2%	20.5%	14.63%	8.2%	16.4%	−20.7%

the 2-year volatility of the betas is 2.0%, then we put on a partial hedge equal to one-third of the beta exposure to bring the short-term volatility to the same level as the long-term volatility.

Table 11.5 reports the results of a daily simulation (not including transaction costs) of the hedge described above. Comparing the results with those from Table 11.4, we note that the overlay costs much less during the calm period from 2005–2006 (0.45% per year, on average, vs. 8.87%), while still providing a significant positive average annual return of 4.54% during the more turbulent period of 2007–2008. Not surprisingly, the return and volatility reduction of the dynamic hedge is not as great as the full beta-blocker overlay—indeed, the hedge is only active part of the time and when it is active it is only hedging a portion of the beta exposure. However, such a hedge is just one example of a dynamic hedging program, and the appropriate trade-offs of performance drag and volatility reduction for a given portfolio will vary depending on the investor's objectives and risk preferences.

11.5 Conclusion

The current credit crisis has upended the investment processes of many investors and managers, and the ubiquity of "unwind risk" has been used to justify a number of extraordinary measures, including the raising of gates, the creation of illiquidity side-pockets, and complete suspensions of all withdrawals. Originally motivated by the desire to protect a fund's remaining investors from the panicked unwinding of illiquid assets during periods of market dislocation, some managers of even relatively liquid assets such as exchange-traded equities are now using gates to retain investment capital, not necessarily to protect investor wealth.

In this chapter, we have argued that investors need not stand idly by during these periods, but can manage their risk exposures proactively by using beta blockers and beta-repositioning strategies to adjust their portfolios in the face of liquidity constraints. Although such strategies cannot generate liquidity from gated assets, the built-in leverage of exchange-traded futures allows investors great flexibility for reshaping their portfolio exposures in a capital-efficient manner. Moreover, because most broker-dealers accept securities as collateral for futures positions, even if an investor cannot liquidate his assets, he can often pledge them as collateral to support a futures-overlay program. Although illiquid assets will undoubtedly suffer significant "haircuts" in terms of their collateral value, the magnitude of the typical institutional investor's portfolio is likely to be many multiples greater than the margin needed to support a futures overlay for that portfolio.

Although we have focused on only two uses of overlay strategies in this chapter, there are clearly many other applications of our framework, including hedge-fund beta replication (Hasanhodzic and Lo, 2006, 2007), global tactical asset allocation,

Table 11.5.

Impact of a Daily Hedging Overlay for Forty-Seven Long/Short Equity Funds in the Lipper TASS Live Database (January 2000 to October 2008).

	2005–2006				2007–2008			
	Change in Annual Return	% Change in Volatility	% Change in Sharpe Ratio	% Change in Max Drawdown	Change in Annual Return	% Change in Volatility	% Change in Sharpe Ratio	% Change in Max Drawdown
Mean	−0.45%	−2.5%	−0.8%	−3.7%	4.54%	−8.1%	−8.0%	−16.6%
25th Percentile	−0.77%	−4.3%	−4.0%	−12.8%	1.85%	−18.5%	−56.0%	−23.2%
Median	−0.34%	−2.2%	0.3%	−1.1%	3.61%	−9.3%	−8.7%	−17.9%
75th Percentile	−0.10%	−0.3%	4.3%	2.6%	5.81%	0.2%	18.3%	−8.9%

transition management for alternatives (Chafkin and Lo, 2008), and dynamic risk management (Lo, 2001, 2008). Moreover, we have used linear factor models to highlight the potential value of beta hedging even with relatively simple risk models, but more sophisticated models that incorporate time-varying volatilities and nonlinear relations among the factors may yield even better performance. As investors become more familiar with the risks of alternatives, we expect all of these applications to grow in importance and sophistication.

Appendix

This appendix contains the Lipper TASS and CS/Tremont category definitions used throughout the volume (Sections A.1 and A.2), Matlab sourcecode for the Loeb price-impact function of Chapter 4 (Section A.3), a derivation of the GMM estimators used in the AP decomposition of Chapter 6 (Section A.4), some of the more technical aspects of the integrated hedge fund investment process in Chapter 8 (Section A.5), a more detailed exposition of the contrarian trading strategy of Lehmann (1990) and Lo and MacKinlay (1990) from Chapter 10 (Section A.6), and a derivation of the asymptotic standard errors of the aggregate autocorrelations of Section 10.7 (Section A.7).

A.1 LIPPER TASS CATEGORY DEFINITIONS

The following is a list of category descriptions, taken directly from Lipper TASS documentation, that define the criteria used by Lipper TASS in assigning funds in their database to one of 17 possible categories.

Equity Hedge

This directional strategy involves equity-oriented investing on both the long and short sides of the market. The objective is not to be market neutral. Managers have the ability to shift from value to growth, from small to medium to large capitalization stocks, and from a net long position to a net short position. Managers may use futures and options to hedge. The focus may be regional, such as long/short US or European equity, or sector specific, such as long and short technology or healthcare stocks. Long/short equity funds tend to build and hold portfolios that are substantially more concentrated than those of traditional stock funds. US equity hedge, European equity hedge, Asian equity hedge and global equity hedge are the regional focuses.

Dedicated Short Bias

Short biased managers take short positions in mostly equities and derivatives. The short bias of a manager's portfolio must be constantly greater than zero to be classified in this category.

Fixed Income Directional

This directional strategy involves investing in fixed income markets only on a directional basis.

Convertible Arbitrage

This strategy is identified by hedge investing in the convertible securities of a company. A typical investment is to be long the convertible bond and short the common stock of the same company. Positions are designed to generate profits from the fixed income security as well as the short sale of stock, while protecting principal from market moves.

Event Driven

This strategy is defined as 'special situations' investing designed to capture price movement generated by a significant pending corporate event such as a merger, corporate restructuring, liquidation, bankruptcy or reorganization. There are three popular sub-categories in event-driven strategies: risk (merger) arbitrage, distressed/high yield securities, and Regulation D.

Non Directional/Relative Value

This investment strategy is designed to exploit equity and/or fixed income market inefficiencies and usually involves being simultaneously long and short matched market portfolios of the same size within a country. Market neutral portfolios are designed to be either beta or currency neutral, or both.

Global Macro

Global macro managers carry long and short positions in any of the world's major capital or derivative markets. These positions reflect their views on overall market direction as influenced by major economic trends and/or events. The portfolios of these funds can include stocks, bonds, currencies, and commodities in the form of cash or derivatives instruments. Most funds invest globally in both developed and emerging markets.

Natural Resources

This trading strategy has a focus for the natural resources around the world.

Leveraged Currency

This strategy invests in currency markets around the world.

Managed Futures

This strategy invests in listed financial and commodity futures markets and currency markets around the world. The managers are usually referred to as commodity trading advisors, or CTAs. Trading disciplines are generally systematic or discretionary. Systematic traders tend to use price and market-specific information (often technical) to make trading decisions, while discretionary managers use a judgmental approach.

Emerging Markets

This strategy involves equity or fixed income investing in emerging markets around the world.

Property

The main focus of the investments is property.

Fund of Funds

A "multi manager" fund will employ the services of two or more trading advisors or hedge funds who will be allocated cash by the trading manager to trade on behalf of the fund.

A.2 CS/TREMONT CATEGORY DEFINITIONS

The following is a list of descriptions of the categories for which CS/Tremont constructs indexes taken directly from the CS/Tremont website (www.hedgeindex.com):

Convertible Arbitrage

This strategy is identified by investment in the convertible securities of a company. A typical investment is to be long the convertible bond and short the common stock of the same company. Positions are designed to generate profits from the fixed income security as well as the short sale of stock, while protecting principal from market moves.

Dedicated Short Bias

This strategy is to maintain net short as opposed to pure short exposure. Short biased managers take short positions in mostly equities and derivatives. The short bias of a manager's portfolio must be constantly greater than zero to be classified in this category.

Emerging Markets

This strategy involves equity or fixed income investing in emerging markets around the world. Because many emerging markets do not allow short selling, nor offer viable futures or other derivative products with which to hedge, emerging market investing often employs a long-only strategy.

Equity Market Neutral

This investment strategy is designed to exploit equity market inefficiencies and usually involves being simultaneously long and short matched equity portfolios of the same size within a country. Market neutral portfolios are designed to be either beta or currency neutral, or both. Well-designed portfolios typically control for industry, sector, market capitalization, and other exposures. Leverage is often applied to enhance returns.

Event Driven

This strategy is defined as "special situations" investing designed to capture price movement generated by a significant pending corporate event such as a merger, corporate restructuring, liquidation, bankruptcy or reorganization. There are three popular sub-categories in event-driven strategies: risk arbitrage, distressed securities, and multi-strategy.

Risk Arbitrage

Specialists invest simultaneously in long and short positions in both companies involved in a merger or acquisition. Risk arbitrageurs are typically long the stock of the company being acquired and short the stock of the acquiring company. The principal risk is deal risk, should the deal fail to close.

Distressed

Hedge fund managers invest in the debt, equity or trade claims of companies in financial distress and general bankruptcy. The securities of companies in need of legal action or restructuring to revive financial stability typically trade at substantial discounts to par value and thereby attract investments when managers perceive a turn-around will materialize. Managers may also take arbitrage positions within a company's capital structure, typically by purchasing a senior debt tier and short-selling common stock, in the hopes of realizing returns from shifts in the spread between the two tiers.

Multi-Strategy

This subset refers to hedge funds that draw upon multiple themes, including risk arbitrage, distressed securities, and occasionally others such as investments in micro and small capitalization public companies that are raising money in private capital markets. Hedge fund managers often shift assets between strategies in response to market opportunities.

Fixed Income Arbitrage

The fixed income arbitrageur aims to profit from price anomalies between related interest rate securities. Most managers trade globally with a goal of generating steady returns with low volatility. This category includes interest rate swap arbitrage, US and non-US government bond arbitrage, forward yield curve arbitrage, and mortgage-backed securities arbitrage. The mortgage-backed market is primarily US-based, over-the-counter and particularly complex.

Global Macro

Global macro managers carry long and short positions in any of the world's major capital or derivative markets. These positions reflect their views on overall market direction as influenced by major economic trends and or events. The portfolios of these hedge funds can include stocks, bonds, currencies, and commodities in the form of cash or derivatives instruments. Most hedge funds invest globally in both developed and emerging markets.

Long/Short Equity

This directional strategy involves equity-oriented investing on both the long and short sides of the market. The objective is not to be market neutral. Managers have the ability to shift from value to growth, from small to medium to large capitalization stocks, and from a net long position to a net short position. Managers may use futures and options to hedge. The focus may be regional, such as long/short US or European equity, or sector specific, such as long and short technology or healthcare stocks. Long/short equity hedge funds tend to build and hold portfolios that are substantially more concentrated than those of traditional stock hedge funds.

Managed Futures

This strategy invests in listed financial and commodity futures markets and currency markets around the world. The managers are usually referred to as commodity trading advisors, or CTAs. Trading disciplines are generally systematic or discretionary. Systematic traders tend to use price and market specific information (often technical) to make trading decisions, while discretionary managers use a judgmental approach.

Multi-Strategy

Multi-strategy hedge funds are characterized by their ability to dynamically allocate capital among strategies falling within several traditional hedge fund disciplines. The use of many strategies, and the ability to reallocate capital between strategies in response to market opportunities, means that such hedge funds are not easily assigned to any traditional category. The multi-strategy category also includes hedge funds employing unique strategies that do not fall under any of the other descriptions.

A.3 MATLAB LOEB FUNCTION tloeb

```
function tloeb

% the default value for the Loeb (1983) spread/price cost
b = 50;

% cap range
xi = [ 0.01 10 25 50 75 100 500 1000 1500 3000 ];

% block size range, in $1,000's
yi = [ 0.01 5 25 250 500 1000 2500 5000 10000 20000 ];


% original Loeb (1983) measure of liquidity (Table II)
zi = [

          17.3 17.3 27.3 43.8  NaN  NaN  NaN  NaN  NaN  NaN  ;
           8.9  8.9 12.0 23.8 33.4  NaN  NaN  NaN  NaN  NaN  ;
           5.0  5.0  7.6 18.8 25.9 30.0  NaN  NaN  NaN  NaN  ;
           4.3  4.3  5.8  9.6 16.9 25.4 31.5  NaN  NaN  NaN  ;
           2.8  2.8  3.9  5.9  8.1 11.5 15.7 25.7  NaN  NaN  ;
           1.8  1.8  2.1  3.2  4.4  5.6  7.9 11.0 16.2  NaN  ;
           1.9  1.9  2.0  3.1  4.0  5.6  7.7 10.4 14.3 20.0  ;
           1.9  1.9  1.9  2.7  3.3  4.6  6.2  8.9 13.6 18.1  ;
           1.1  1.1  1.2  1.3  1.7  2.1  2.8  4.1  5.9  8.0  ;
           1.1  1.1  1.2  1.3  1.7  2.1  2.8  4.1  5.9  8.0 ];


nx = size(xi,2); ny = size(yi,2);

% array of indices of last non-NaN points in zi matrix along
mcap dimension nonnan = [ 4 4 5 6 7 8 9 ];


% deal with NaN's in zi matrix

% loop over rows
for i = 1:size(xi,2)-3

    % last non-nan point
    f = nonnan(i);
```

```
    for j = f+1:1:ny

        % Loeb cost based on simple linear extrapolation
        % starting from the end points
        zi(i,j) = zi(i,f) + (zi(i,f)-zi(f-1))*(yi(j)-yi(f))/
                   (yi(f)-yi(f-1));

        % cap the cost zi by b = 50% if cost > 50%;
        if zi(i,j) > 50; zi(i,j) = b; end;

        % If trade size > 20% of market cap (not T. Loeb's
        % original 5%), zi is still NaN
        if (yi(j)/1000) > 0.2*xi(i); zi(i,j) = NaN; end;

    end

end

zi

% produce arrays acceptable by MATLAB for 3D graphics
for i=1:ny
    for j=1:nx
        x(i,j) = (xi(j));
        y(i,j) = (yi(i));
        z(i,j) = zi(j,i);
    end
end

% determine max-min for interpolation
maxx=max(xi); minx=min(xi); maxy=max(yi); miny=min(yi);

% the number of nodes in each direction
N=40; dx = (maxx - minx)/ N; dy = (maxy - miny)/ N;

% interpolated arrays

for i=1:N
    for j=1:N
        x1(i,j)=xi(1)+dx*j;
        y1(i,j)=yi(1)+dy*i;
    end
end
```

```
% plot extended Loeb function
mesh ( (x1), (y1), interp2(x, y, z, x1, y1, 'linear') )
view(30,50); colormap(jet); grid on; xlabel('Cap[$1,000,000]',
'FontSize', 8); ylabel('Block [$1000] ', 'FontSize', 8)
zlabel('Spread/Price Cost [%] ');
%title(' Loeb (1983) Total  Spread/Price  Cost');

print -depsc p:\\msl\\tloeb.eps
```

A.4 GMM ESTIMATORS FOR THE AP DECOMPOSITION

Denote by $\mathbf{X}_t$ the vector of period-t portfolio weights and returns $[\omega_{1t} \cdots \omega_{nt} \ R_{1t} \cdots R_{nt}]'$ and let $\{\mathbf{X}_t\}$ be a stochastic process that satisfies the following conditions:

(H1) $\{\mathbf{X}_t : t \in (-\infty, \infty)\}$ is stationary and ergodic.

(H2) $\boldsymbol{\gamma}_o \in \Gamma$ is an open subset of $\Re^k$.

(H3) $\forall \boldsymbol{\gamma} \in \Gamma$, $\boldsymbol{\varphi}(\cdot, \boldsymbol{\gamma})$ and $\boldsymbol{\varphi}_{\boldsymbol{\gamma}}(\cdot, \boldsymbol{\gamma})$ are Borel-measurable, and $\varphi_{\boldsymbol{\gamma}}(\mathbf{X}, \cdot)$ is continuous on Γ for all $\mathbf{X}$.

(H4) $\boldsymbol{\varphi}_{\boldsymbol{\gamma}}$ is first-moment continuous at $\boldsymbol{\gamma}_o$; $\mathrm{E}[\boldsymbol{\varphi}_{\boldsymbol{\gamma}}(\mathbf{X}, \cdot)]$ exists, is finite, and is of full rank.

(H5) Let $\boldsymbol{\varphi}_t \equiv \boldsymbol{\varphi}(\mathbf{X}_t, \boldsymbol{\gamma}_o)$ and

$$\mathbf{v}_j \equiv E[\boldsymbol{\varphi}_0|\boldsymbol{\varphi}_{-1}, \boldsymbol{\varphi}_{-2}, \ldots] - E[\boldsymbol{\varphi}_0|\boldsymbol{\varphi}_{-j-1}, \boldsymbol{\varphi}_{-j-2}, \ldots]$$

and assume:

(i) $\mathrm{E}[\boldsymbol{\varphi}_0\boldsymbol{\varphi}_0']$ exists and is finite,
(ii) $\mathbf{v}_j$ converges in mean square to 0,
(iii) $\sum_{j=0}^{\infty} \mathrm{E}[\mathbf{v}_j'\mathbf{v}_j]^{1/2}$ is finite,

which implies $\mathrm{E}[\boldsymbol{\varphi}(\mathbf{X}_t, \boldsymbol{\gamma}_o)] = 0$.

(H6) Let $\hat{\boldsymbol{\gamma}}$ solve $\frac{1}{T} \sum_{t=1}^{T} \boldsymbol{\varphi}(\mathbf{X}_t, \boldsymbol{\gamma}) = 0$.

Then Hansen (1982) shows that

$$\sqrt{T}(\hat{\boldsymbol{\gamma}} - \boldsymbol{\gamma}_o) \overset{a}{\sim} \mathcal{N}(0, \mathbf{V}_{\gamma}), \quad \mathbf{V}_{\gamma} \equiv \mathbf{H}^{-1}\boldsymbol{\Sigma}\mathbf{H}^{-1'}, \tag{A.1}$$

where

$$\mathbf{H} \equiv \lim_{T \to \infty} \mathrm{E}\left[\frac{1}{T} \sum_{t=1}^{T} \varphi_{\gamma}(\mathbf{X}_t, \boldsymbol{\gamma}_o)\right], \tag{A.2}$$

$$\boldsymbol{\Sigma} \equiv \lim_{T \to \infty} \mathrm{E} \left[\frac{1}{T} \sum_{t=1}^{T} \sum_{s=1}^{T} \boldsymbol{\varphi}(\mathbf{X}_t, \boldsymbol{\gamma}_o) \boldsymbol{\varphi}(\mathbf{X}_s, \boldsymbol{\gamma}_o)' \right] \tag{A.3}$$

and $\boldsymbol{\varphi}_{\boldsymbol{\gamma}}(R_t, \boldsymbol{\gamma})$ denotes the derivative of $\boldsymbol{\varphi}(R_t, \boldsymbol{\gamma})$ with respect to $\boldsymbol{\gamma}$.[1] Specifically, let $\boldsymbol{\varphi}(R_t, \boldsymbol{\gamma})$ denote the following vector function:

$$\boldsymbol{\varphi}(\boldsymbol{\omega}_t, \mathbf{R}_t, \boldsymbol{\gamma}) \equiv [\omega_{1t} - \mu_{\omega_1} \cdots \omega_{nt} - \mu_{\omega_n} \ R_{1t} - \mu_1 \cdots R_{nt} - \mu_n]', \tag{A.4}$$

where $\boldsymbol{\gamma} \equiv [\mu_{\omega_1} \cdots \mu_{\omega_n} \ \mu_1 \cdots \mu_n]'$. The GMM estimator of $\boldsymbol{\gamma}$, denoted by $\hat{\boldsymbol{\gamma}}$, is given implicitly by the solution to

$$\frac{1}{T} \sum_{t=1}^{T} \boldsymbol{\varphi}(\boldsymbol{\omega}_t, \mathbf{R}_t, \boldsymbol{\gamma}) = 0, \tag{A.5}$$

which yields the standard estimators $\overline{\omega}_i$ and $\overline{R}_i$ given in (6.30). For the moment conditions in (A.4), $\mathbf{H}$ is given by

$$\mathbf{H} = -\mathbf{I}, \tag{A.6}$$

where $\mathbf{I}$ is a $(2n \times 2n)$ identity matrix. Therefore, $\mathbf{V}_{\boldsymbol{\gamma}} = \boldsymbol{\Sigma}$ and the asymptotic distribution of the active ratio estimator $\hat{\theta}$ follows from the delta method:

$$\sqrt{T}(\hat{\theta} - \theta) \overset{a}{\sim} \mathcal{N}(0, V_{\mathrm{GMM}}), \qquad V_{\mathrm{GMM}} = \frac{\partial g}{\partial \boldsymbol{\gamma}} \boldsymbol{\Sigma} \frac{\partial g}{\partial \boldsymbol{\gamma}'}, \tag{A.7}$$

where $\partial g / \partial \boldsymbol{\gamma}$ is given by

$$\frac{\partial g}{\partial \boldsymbol{\gamma}} = [\mu_1 \cdots \mu_n \ \mu_{\omega_1} \cdots \mu_{\omega_n}]. \tag{A.8}$$

An estimator for $\partial g / \partial \boldsymbol{\gamma}$ may be obtained by substituting $\hat{\boldsymbol{\gamma}}$ into (A.8), and an estimator for $\boldsymbol{\Sigma}$ may be obtained using Newey and West's (1987) procedure:

$$\widehat{\boldsymbol{\Sigma}} = \widehat{\boldsymbol{\Omega}}_0 + \sum_{j=1}^{m} \omega(j, m)(\widehat{\boldsymbol{\Omega}}_j + \widehat{\boldsymbol{\Omega}}_j'), \qquad m \ll T, \tag{A.9}$$

---

[1] See Magnus and Neudecker (1988) for the specific definitions and conventions of vector and matrix derivatives of vector functions.

$$\widehat{\boldsymbol{\Omega}}_j \equiv \frac{1}{T} \sum_{t=j+1}^{T} \boldsymbol{\varphi}(R_t, \hat{\boldsymbol{\gamma}}) \boldsymbol{\varphi}(R_{t-j}, \hat{\boldsymbol{\gamma}})', \tag{A.10}$$

$$\omega(j, m) \equiv 1 - \frac{j}{m+1}, \tag{A.11}$$

and m is the truncation lag, which must satisfy the condition $m/T \to \infty$ as T increases without bound to ensure consistency. An estimator for V_{GMM} can then be constructed as

$$\widehat{V}_{\text{GMM}} = \frac{\partial g(\hat{\boldsymbol{\gamma}})}{\partial \boldsymbol{\gamma}} \widehat{\boldsymbol{\Sigma}} \frac{\partial g(\hat{\boldsymbol{\gamma}})}{\partial \boldsymbol{\gamma}'}. \tag{A.12}$$

A.5 Constrained Optimization

To solve the following optimization problem

$$\text{Min}_{\{\boldsymbol{\omega}\}} \ \tfrac{1}{2}\boldsymbol{\omega}'\boldsymbol{\Sigma}\boldsymbol{\omega} \tag{A.13}$$

$$\text{subject to} \qquad \boldsymbol{\omega}'\boldsymbol{\mu} \geq \mu_o, \tag{A.14}$$

$$\boldsymbol{\omega}'\boldsymbol{\iota} = 1, \tag{A.15}$$

we define the Lagrangian

$$\mathcal{L} = \tfrac{1}{2}\boldsymbol{\omega}'\boldsymbol{\Sigma}\boldsymbol{\omega} + \lambda(\mu_o - \boldsymbol{\omega}'\boldsymbol{\mu}) + \xi(1 - \boldsymbol{\omega}'\boldsymbol{\iota}), \tag{A.16}$$

which yields the following first-order conditions:

$$\frac{\partial \mathcal{L}}{\partial \boldsymbol{\omega}} = 0 = \boldsymbol{\Sigma}\boldsymbol{\omega} - \lambda\boldsymbol{\mu} - \xi\boldsymbol{\iota}, \tag{A.17}$$

$$\frac{\partial \mathcal{L}}{\partial \gamma} = 0 = \mu_o - \boldsymbol{\omega}'\boldsymbol{\mu}, \tag{A.18}$$

$$\frac{\partial \mathcal{L}}{\partial \lambda} = 0 = 1 - \boldsymbol{\omega}'\boldsymbol{\iota}. \tag{A.19}$$

Solving (A.17) for $\boldsymbol{\omega}$ yields the minimum-variance portfolio as a function of the two Lagrange multipliers:

$$\boldsymbol{\omega}^* = \lambda\boldsymbol{\Sigma}^{-1}\boldsymbol{\mu} + \xi\boldsymbol{\Sigma}^{-1}\boldsymbol{\iota}, \tag{A.20}$$

and applying (A.18) and (A.19) to (A.20) allows us to solve for the Lagrange multipliers explicitly as

$$\lambda = \frac{\mu_o A - B}{D}, \qquad \xi = -\frac{\mu_o B - C}{D}, \qquad (A.21)$$

where

$$A \equiv \iota' \Sigma^{-1} \iota > 0, \qquad (A.22)$$

$$B \equiv \iota' \Sigma^{-1} \mu, \qquad (A.23)$$

$$C \equiv \mu' \Sigma^{-1} \mu > 0, \qquad (A.24)$$

$$D \equiv AC - B^2 > 0. \qquad (A.25)$$

A.6 A CONTRARIAN TRADING STRATEGY

Consider a collection of N securities and denote by $\mathbf{R}_t$ the $N \times 1$-vector of their period t returns $[R_{1t} \cdots R_{Nt}]'$. For convenience, we maintain the following assumption:

(A1) $\mathbf{R}_t$ is a jointly covariance-stationary stochastic process with expectation $E[\mathbf{R}_t] = \mu \equiv [\mu_1 \ \mu_2 \ \cdots \ \mu_N]'$ and autocovariance matrices $E[(\mathbf{R}_{t-k} - \mu)(\mathbf{R}_t - \mu)'] = \Gamma_k$ where, with no loss of generality, we take $k \geq 0$ since $\Gamma_k = \Gamma'_{-k}$.[2]

In the spirit of virtually all contrarian strategies, consider buying at time t stocks that were losers at time $t-k$, and selling at time t stocks that were winners at time $t-k$, where winning and losing is determined with respect to the equal-weighted return on the market. More formally, if $\omega_{it}(k)$ denotes the fraction of the portfolio devoted to security i at time t, let

$$\omega_{it}(k) = -\frac{1}{N}(R_{it-k} - R_{mt-k}), \qquad i = 1, \ldots, N, \qquad (A.26)$$

where $R_{mt-k} \equiv \sum_{i=1}^{N} R_{it-k}/N$ is the equally weighted market index. By construction, $\omega_t(k) \equiv [\omega_{1t}(k) \ \omega_{2t}(k) \cdots \omega_{Nt}(k)]'$ is a "dollar-neutral" or "arbitrage" portfolio since the weights sum to zero. Accordingly, the weights have no natural scale since any multiple of the weights will also sum to zero. Therefore, it is most

---

[2] Assumption (A1) is made for notational simplicity since joint covariance-stationarity allows us to eliminate time indexes from population moments such as μ and Γ_k; the qualitative features of our results will not change under the weaker assumptions of weakly dependent heterogeneously distributed vectors $\mathbf{R}_t$. This would merely require replacing expectations with corresponding probability limits of suitably defined time averages. See Lo and MacKinlay (1990c) for further discussion.

convenient to define the weights to be the actual dollar positions in each security, in which case the total dollar investment long (or short) at time t is given by $I_t(k)$, where

$$I_t(k) \equiv \frac{1}{2} \sum_{i=1}^{N} |\omega_{it}(k)|. \tag{A.27}$$

Since the portfolio weights are proportional to the differences between the market index and the returns, securities that deviate more positively from the market at time $t-k$ will have greater negative weight in the time t portfolio, and vice versa. Such a strategy is designed to take advantage of stock market overreaction, but Lo and MacKinlay (1990c) show that this need not be the only reason that contrarian investment strategies are profitable. In particular, if returns are positively cross-autocorrelated, they show that a return-reversal strategy will yield positive profits on average, even if individual security returns are *serially independent*! The presence of stock market overreaction, i.e., negatively autocorrelated individual returns, enhances the profitability of the return-reversal strategy but is not required for such a strategy to earn positive expected returns.

Because of the linear nature of the strategy, its statistical properties are particularly easy to derive. For example, Lo and MacKinlay (1990c) show that the strategy's profit-and-loss at date t is given by

$$\pi_t(k) = \boldsymbol{\omega}_t'(k)\mathbf{R}_t, \tag{A.28}$$

and rearranging (A.28) and taking expectations yield the following:

$$E[\pi_t(k)] = \frac{\iota'\boldsymbol{\Gamma}_k\iota}{N^2} - \frac{1}{N}\text{trace}(\boldsymbol{\Gamma}_k) - \frac{1}{N}\sum_{i=1}^{N}(\mu_i - \mu_m)^2, \tag{A.29}$$

which shows that the contrarian strategy's expected profits are an explicit function of the means, variances, and autocovariances of returns. See Lo and MacKinlay (1990, 1999) for further details of this strategy's statistical properties and an empirical analysis of its historical returns.

A.7 STATISTICAL SIGNIFICANCE OF AGGREGATE AUTOCORRELATIONS

To gauge the statistical significance of the aggregate autocorrelations in Section 10.7, recall that under the null hypothesis of no autocorrelation, the autocorrelation coefficient $\hat{\rho}_{1i}$ is asymptotically normal with zero mean and variance $\sigma_\rho^2 \equiv 1/T$. Therefore, we can derive the asymptotic variance of the mean autocorrelation $\hat{\rho}$ in the usual manner:

$$\text{Var}\left[n^{-1}\sum_{i=1}^{n}\hat{\rho}_{1i}\right] = n^{-2}\iota'\boldsymbol{\Omega}\iota, \tag{A.30}$$

where $\boldsymbol{\Omega}$ is the covariance matrix of the vector of n first-order autocorrelation coefficients $[\hat{\rho}_{11} \cdots \hat{\rho}_{1n}]'$. If we assume that the $\hat{\rho}_{1i}$'s are uncorrelated, then $\boldsymbol{\Omega}$ is a diagonal matrix with $1/T$'s on the diagonal. Therefore, the asymptotic variance and standard error of $\hat{\rho}$ is given by

$$\mathrm{Var}[\hat{\rho}] \approx \frac{1}{nT}, \quad \mathrm{SE}[\hat{\rho}] \approx \frac{1}{\sqrt{nT}} . \tag{A.31}$$

For $n = 400$ and $T = 60$, the standard error for $\hat{\rho}$ is 0.65%, hence a two-standard-deviation confidence interval around the null hypothesis of zero correlation is the range $[-1.3\%, +1.3\%]$, which is clearly breached by the graphs in Figure 5.4 for most of the sample.

A.8 BETA-BLOCKER AND BETA-REPOSITIONING STRATEGIES

Consider a portfolio consisting of Strategy A plus a futures-overlay program involving K types of futures contracts, where N_{kt} contracts of contract k are held at date t, $k=1,\ldots,K$. Denote by PL_t the profit/loss of the portfolio at date t which is given by

$$\mathrm{PL}_t = V_{t-1} R_{at} + \sum_{k=1}^{K} N_{kt-1} m_k (F_{kt} - F_{kt-1}), \tag{A.32}$$

where F_{kt} denotes the date-t futures price of type k. Consider a linear regression of R_{at} on the K futures-contract returns:

$$R_{at} = \alpha + \sum_{k=1}^{K} \beta_k R_{kt} + \epsilon_t, \quad R^2 = 1 - \mathrm{Var}[\epsilon_t]/\mathrm{Var}[R_{at}], \tag{A.33}$$

where $\mathrm{E}[\epsilon_t|\{R_{kt}\}] = 0$ by construction, and assume that $\{\epsilon_t\}$ is white noise (which should be tested). Then (A.32) can be re-expressed as

$$\mathrm{PL}_t = V_{t-1}\alpha + \sum_{k=1}^{K} (V_{t-1}\beta_k + N_{kt-1} F_{kt-1} m_k) R_{kt} + V_{t-1}\epsilon_t \tag{A.34a}$$

$$R_{pt} = \frac{\mathrm{PL}_t}{V_{t-1}} = \alpha + \sum_{k=1}^{K} \gamma_{kt-1} R_{kt} + \epsilon_t \tag{A.34b}$$

$$\gamma_{kt-1} \equiv \beta_k + \frac{N_{kt-1} F_{kt-1} m_k}{V_{t-1}} . \tag{A.34c}$$

To minimize Strategy A's exposure to movements in the K futures prices, the number of futures contracts $\{N_{kt}\}$ held in the portfolio should be adjusted so as to minimize the net exposures $\{\gamma_{kt}\}$. Specifically,

$$\gamma_{kt}^* = \beta_k + \frac{N_{kt}^* F_{kt} m_k}{V_t} = 0 \qquad (A.35a)$$

$$\Rightarrow \quad N_{kt}^* = -\frac{V_t \beta_k}{F_{kt} m_k}. \qquad (A.35b)$$

With such a futures overlay in place, the return of the portfolio becomes[3]

$$\mathrm{PL}_t^* = V_{t-1}(\alpha + \epsilon_t) \qquad (A.36a)$$

$$R_{pt}^* = \frac{\mathrm{PL}_t^*}{V_{t-1}} = \alpha + \epsilon_t \qquad (A.36b)$$

$$\frac{\mathrm{Var}[R_{pt}^*]}{\mathrm{Var}[R_{at}]} = 1 - R^2, \qquad (A.36c)$$

so the reduction in the volatility of the portfolio due to the futures overlay is simply $1 - \sqrt{1-R^2}$, where R^2 is the coefficient of multiple determination of the linear projection (A.33).

Like beta blockers, beta-repositioning overlays make use of futures and forward contracts to alter the betas of an investor's portfolio. But in contrast to beta blockers, repositioning overlays are meant to *generate* beta exposures, not neutralize them. Denote by R_{pt} the date-t return of an investor's entire portfolio, and consider the risk model (11.1) applied to this portfolio:

$$R_{pt} = \alpha_p + \beta_{p1}\mathrm{RiskFactor}_{1t} + \cdots + \beta_{pK}\mathrm{RiskFactor}_{Kt} + \epsilon_{pt}. \qquad (A.37)$$

In this context, β_{pk} is the beta exposure of an investor's entire portfolio to risk factor $k, k = 1, \ldots, K$, which is of course a weighted average of the betas of each manager to factor k, weighted by the fraction of assets allocated to that manager. Denote by R_t^* the target portfolio of the investor, which is determined by the investor's strategic asset-allocation, and apply the same risk factors from (A.37) to this portfolio to obtain the target betas $\{\beta_k^*\}$:

$$R_t^* = \alpha^* + \beta_1^*\mathrm{RiskFactor}_{1t} + \cdots + \beta_K^*\mathrm{RiskFactor}_{Kt} + \epsilon_t^*. \qquad (A.38)$$

---

[3] Note that for practical purposes, N_{kt}^* must be rounded to an integer, hence the equalities (A.36a)–(A.36c) hold only approximately subject to rounding errors in $\{N_{kt}^*\}$.

Then the beta-repositioning portfolio return R_{ht} is given by the difference between (A.38) and (A.37):

$$
\begin{aligned}
R_{ht} &\equiv R_t^* - R_{pt} \\
&= \alpha_h + (\beta_1^* - \beta_{p1})\,\text{RiskFactor}_{1t} + \cdots + (\beta_K^* - \beta_{pK})\,\text{RiskFactor}_{Kt} + \epsilon_{ht} \\
&= \alpha_h + \beta_{h1}\,\text{RiskFactor}_{1t} + \cdots + \beta_{hK}\,\text{RiskFactor}_{Kt} + \epsilon_{ht}, \tag{A.39}
\end{aligned}
$$

where $\beta_{hk} \equiv \beta_k^* - \beta_{pk}$.

The beta-repositioning portfolio return R_{ht} can be achieved in the identical manner to the beta blocker using futures and forward contracts.

For purposes of repositioning a portfolio's aggregate exposures, it is often easier to formulate the hedging objective in terms of target portfolio weights or notional exposures rather than the target betas of (A.38). To that end, consider a portfolio with weights $\boldsymbol{\omega}_t \equiv [\omega_{1t} \cdots \omega_{nt}]'$ and suppose the target weights (perhaps from an investor's strategic asset-allocation process) are given by $\boldsymbol{\omega}_t^*$. Then the notional exposures $\mathbf{X}_t \equiv [X_{1t} \cdots X_{nt}]'$ required to restore the portfolio $\boldsymbol{\omega}_t$ to its desired weights $\boldsymbol{\omega}_t^*$ are given by

$$
X_{it} \equiv V_t\,(\omega_{it}^* - \omega_{it}), \tag{A.40}
$$

where V_t is the total assets in the portfolio. If E_i is the notional exposure of a futures contract for asset i, then the number of such contracts N_{it} required in a repositioning overlay is given by

$$
N_{it} \equiv \text{round}(X_{it}/E_i), \tag{A.41}
$$

where round$(\cdot)$ is the function that rounds its argument to the nearest integer.

Table A.1 presents an example of a \$1 billion passive portfolio that is initially 60% invested in the S&P 500 Index and 40% invested in the Lehman U.S. Aggregate Index at the start of 2008. By the end of November 2008, price movements alone have changed the asset allocation to 52.6% in the Lehman Index and 47.4% in the S&P 500. Table A.1 shows that by using S&P 500 and Lehman Index futures that trade on the Chicago Mercantile Exchange, it is simple to construct a beta-repositioning strategy. Morever, the last column of Table A.1 shows how capital-efficient such an overlay strategy is, with a maximum margin requirement of approximately \$15 million to reposition a \$1 billion portfolio.[4]

---

[4] These values are computed under the assumption that the initial margin requirements for the CME Lehman Index and S&P 500 futures contracts are currently \$1,620 and \$30,938, respectively, per contract, which are "speculative" margins (our hedging-overlay strategy may be eligible for the lower "hedging" margin levels). Also, these figures are initial margin requirements; maintenance margin levels may be lower. The maximum total margin is simply the sum of these two margin requirements, i.e., no crossnetting is assumed.

Table A.1.

Sample beta-repositioning overlay for a $1 billion portfolio initially invested 40% in the Lehman U.S. Aggregate Index and 60% in the S&P 500 on December 31, 2007, where the overlay consists of Lehman Aggregate and S&P 500 futures with notional exposures set to maintain a 40/60 asset allocation for the overall portfolio.

Date	Lehman U.S. Aggregate Index Total Return	S&P 500 Index Return*	Lehman U.S. Aggregate Index Level	S&P 500 Index Level	Bond AUM ($MM)	Stock AUM ($MM)	Bond Wgt	Stock Wgt	Target Notional Bond Exposure ($MM)	Target Notional Stock Exposure ($MM)	Target Number of Lehman Contracts	Target Number of S&P 500 Contracts	Bond Margin ($MM)	Stock Margin ($MM)	Max Total Margin ($MM)
Initial			1,281.70	1468.36	$ 400.00	$ 600.00	40.0%	60.0%	$ -	$ -	0	0			
200801	1.68%	−6.12%	1,304.91	1378.55	$ 406.72	$ 563.30	41.9%	58.1%	$ (18.71)	$ 18.71	−143	54	$ 0.2	$ 1.7	$ 1.9
200802	0.14%	−3.48%	1,306.86	1330.63	$ 407.28	$ 543.72	42.8%	57.2%	$ (26.88)	$ 26.88	−206	81	$ 0.3	$ 2.5	$ 2.8
200803	0.34%	−0.60%	1,311.66	1322.70	$ 408.67	$ 540.48	43.1%	56.9%	$ (29.01)	$ 29.01	−221	88	$ 0.4	$ 2.7	$ 3.1
200804	−0.21%	4.75%	1,308.71	1385.59	$ 407.82	$ 566.18	41.9%	58.1%	$ (18.22)	$ 18.22	−139	53	$ 0.2	$ 1.6	$ 1.9
200805	−0.73%	1.07%	1,298.38	1400.38	$ 404.83	$ 572.22	41.4%	58.6%	$ (14.01)	$ 14.01	−108	40	$ 0.2	$ 1.2	$ 1.4
200806	−0.08%	−8.60%	1,297.25	1280.00	$ 404.50	$ 523.03	43.6%	56.4%	$ (33.49)	$ 33.49	−258	105	$ 0.4	$ 3.2	$ 3.7
200807	−0.08%	−0.99%	1,296.11	1267.38	$ 404.17	$ 517.88	43.8%	56.2%	$ (35.35)	$ 35.35	−273	112	$ 0.4	$ 3.5	$ 3.9
200808	0.95%	1.22%	1,309.36	1282.83	$ 408.01	$ 524.19	43.8%	56.2%	$ (35.13)	$ 35.13	−268	110	$ 0.4	$ 3.4	$ 3.8
200809	−1.34%	−9.08%	1,290.43	1164.74	$ 402.53	$ 476.60	45.8%	54.2%	$ (50.88)	$ 50.88	−394	175	$ 0.6	$ 5.4	$ 6.1
200810	−2.36%	−16.94%	1,257.61	968.75	$ 393.03	$ 395.85	49.8%	50.2%	$ (77.48)	$ 77.48	−616	320	$ 1.0	$ 9.9	$ 10.9
200811	3.25%	−7.48%	1,301.80	896.24	$ 405.82	$ 366.22	52.6%	47.4%	$ (97.00)	$ 97.00	−745	433	$ 1.2	$ 13.4	$ 14.6

*S&P 500 Index Return does not include dividends.

As with beta blockers, beta-repositioning overlay strategies will be only as effective as the underlying risk models allow. However, because we are now applying the risk model (11.1) to an investor's entire portfolio containing both traditional and alternative assets, the R^2 is likely to be considerably higher. Moreover, the objective is no longer risk reduction, but rather changing the factor exposures of the portfolio, and the ability to achieve this latter objective does not depend on the risk model's R^2. In addition, the natural leverage incorporated into exchange-traded futures contracts, the standardization of those contracts, the existence of a clearing corporation that intermediates all transactions, and the fact that futures are marked-to-market daily make beta-repositioning strategies ideal for institutional investors.

A.9 TRACKING ERROR

If the optimal hedging strategy $\{N_{kt}^*\}$ is not implemented continuously—either because of transaction costs or other implementation frictions—tracking errors will arise due to the fact that the optimal net exposures $\{\gamma_{kt}^*\}$ will fluctuate as futures prices, capital, and betas fluctuate. To quantify the impact of such fluctuations, suppose that a futures overlay is implemented on date t_0 and left unchanged through date $t > t_0$. Denote by $\tilde{\gamma}_{kt}$ the resulting net exposure on date t, which is obviously not optimal in the sense of (A.35):

$$\tilde{\gamma}_{kt} = \beta_k + \frac{N_{kt_0}^* F_{kt} m_k}{V_{t-1}} = \left(1 - \frac{F_{kt}/F_{kt_0}}{V_{t-1}/V_{t_0}}\right)\beta_k. \tag{A.42}$$

This shows that the magnitude of the net exposure is inversely related to the absolute value of the ratio of the growth of the futures price to the growth of capital between t_0 and t. The larger the difference in growth between the k-th futures price and capital, the larger the absolute value of the net exposure $\tilde{\gamma}_{kt}$.

Another implication of (A.42) is that the sign of the net exposure is opposite to the relative growth of the futures price and capital, i.e., if the futures price grows faster than the capital, the net exposure $\tilde{\gamma}_{kt}$ to the futures price F_{kt} will be of the opposite sign of β_k, and if the capital grows faster than the futures price, the net exposure will be of the same sign as β_k.

Two special cases are worth noting. When capital is being injected into the strategy, V_t will be increasing much faster than F_{kt}, in which case $\tilde{\gamma}_{kt}$ is likely to be of the same sign as β_k. Therefore, it may be necessary to increase the frequency of rebalancings for those futures contracts k for which β_k is largest in absolute value.

The second special case involves the steady state in which the level of capital is fixed over time, say at V, hence $V_t/V_{t_0}=1$. In this case

$$\tilde{\gamma}_{kt} = \left(1 - \frac{F_{kt}}{F_{kt_0}}\right)\beta_k = -R_k(t_0, t)\beta_k, \tag{A.43}$$

where $R_k(t_0, t)$ is the compounded net return of the k-th futures contract between t_0 and t. For most index futures contracts, the expected return over any finite interval is positive (because of the risk premium implicit in the index), hence the net exposure $\tilde{\gamma}_{kt}$ will tend to be of the opposite sign of β_k. Moreover, assuming that the one-period futures return R_{kt} is independently and identically distributed with mean μ_k and variance σ_k^2, we have

$$\mathrm{E}_{t_0}[\tilde{\gamma}_{kt}] = -\mathrm{E}_{t_0}[R_k(t_0, t)]\beta_k = \left(1 - (1 + \mu_k)^{t-t_0-1}\right)\beta_k \qquad \text{(A.44a)}$$

$$\mathrm{Var}_{t_0}[\tilde{\gamma}_{kt}] = \mathrm{Var}_{t_0}[R_k(t_0, t)]\beta_k^2 = \left[\left(\sigma_k^2 - (1 + \mu_k)^2\right)^{t-t_0-1}\right.$$

$$\left. -(1 + \mu_k)^{2(t-t_0-1)}\right]\beta_k^2. \qquad \text{(A.44b)}$$

These expressions can be used to select the most important betas to hedge, as well as to quantify the remaining exposures of the hedged portfolio.

References

Acharya, V., and L. Pedersen, 2002, "Asset Pricing with Liquidity Risk," unpublished working paper, London Business School.

Ackermann, C., McEnally, R., and D. Ravenscraft, 1999, "The Performance of Hedge Funds: Risk, Return, and Incentives," *Journal of Finance* 54, 833–874.

Admati, A., and P. Pfleiderer, 1991, "Sunshine Trading and Financial Market Equilibrium," *Review of Financial Studies* 4, 443–481.

Agarwal, A., Daniel, N., and N. Naik, 2004, "Flows, Performance and Managerial Incentives in Hedge Funds," Georgia State University Working Paper.

Agarwal, V., and N. Naik, 2000a, "Performance Evaluation of Hedge Funds with Buy-and-Hold and Option-Based Strategies," Hedge Fund Centre Working Paper No. HF–003, London Business School.

Agarwal, V., and N. Naik, 2000b, "On Taking the 'Alternative' Route: The Risks, Rewards, and Performance Persistence of Hedge Funds," *Journal of Alternative Investments* 2, 6–23.

Agarwal, V., and N. Naik, 2000c, "Multi-Period Performance Persistence Analysis of Hedge Funds Source," *Journal of Financial and Quantitative Analysis* 35, 327–342.

Agarwal, V., and N. Naik, 2000d, "Generalized Style Analysis of Hedge Funds," *Journal of Asset Management* 1, 93–109.

Agarwal, V., and N. Naik, 2004, "Risks and Portfolio Decisions Involving Hedge Funds," *Review of Financial Studies* 17, 63–98.

Agarwal, V., and N. Naik, 2005, "Hedge Funds," *Foundations and Trends in Finance*, 1.

Aiyagari, R., and M. Gertler, 1991, "Asset Returns with Transaction Costs and Uninsured Individual Risk," *Journal of Monetary Economics* 27, 311–331.

Allen, F., and D. Gale, 2000, "Financial Contagion," *Journal of Political Economy* 108, 1–33.

Alvarez, W., 1997, *T. Rex and the Crater of Doom*. Princeton, NJ: Princeton University Press.

Amenc, N., El Bied, S., and L. Martinelli, 2003, "Predictability in Hedge Fund Returns," *Financial Analysts Journal* 59, 32–46.

Amenc, N., and L. Martinelli, 2002, "Portfolio Optimization and Hedge Fund Style Allocation Decisions," *Journal of Alternative Investments* 5, 7–20.

Amihud, Y., and H. Mendelson, 1986a, "Asset Pricing and the Bid-Ask Spread," *Journal of Financial Economics* 17, 223–249.

Amihud, Y., and H. Mendelson, 1986b, "Liquidity and Stock Returns," *Financial Analysts Journal* 42, 43–48.

Amin, G., and H. Kat, 2003a, "Hedge Fund Performance 1990–2000: Do the Money Machines Really Add Value?" *Journal of Financial and Quantitative Analysis* 38, 251–274.

Amin, G., and H. Kat, 2003b, "Welcome to the Dark Side: Hedge Fund Attrition and Survivorship Bias over the Period 1994–2001," *Journal of Alternative Investments* 6, 57–73.

Amin, G., and H. Kat, 2003c, "Stocks, Bonds, and Hedge Funds," *Journal of Portfolio Management* 29, 113–119.

Andersen, T., Bollerslev, T., and F. Diebold, 2004, "Parametric and Nonparametric Volatility Measurement," in L. Hansen and Y. Aït-Sahalia, eds., *Handbook of Financial Econometrics*. Amsterdam: North-Holland.

Ang, A., and G. Bekaert, 2004, "How Regimes Affect Asset Allocation," *Financial Analysts Journal* 60, 86–99.

Armistead, L., 2004, "Dalman Stakes His Own Cash on Hedge Fund," *UK Sunday Times*, Business Section, October 10.

Arnott, R., and W. Wagner, 1990, "The Measurement and Control of Trading Costs," *Financial Analysts Journal* 46, 73–80.

Arnott, R., Hsu, J., and P. Moore, 2005 "Fundamental Indexation," *Financial Analysts Journal* 61, 83–99.

Asness, C., Krail, R., and J. Liew, 2001, "Do Hedge Funds Hedge?" *The Journal of Portfolio Management* 28, 6–19.

Atchison, M., K. Butler, and R. Simonds, 1987, "Nonsynchronous Security Trading and Market Index Autocorrelation," *Journal of Finance* 42, 111–118.

Atkins, T., and S. Hays, 2004, "Worries Rise About Indebted Funds of Hedge Funds," *Reuters*, October 15.

Atkinson, C., and P. Wilmott, 1995, "Portfolio Management with Transaction Costs: An Asymptotic Analysis of the Morton and Pliska Model," *Mathematical Finance*, 357–367.

Bagehot, W. (a.k.a. Jack Treynor), 1971, "The Only Game in Town," *Financial Analysts Journal* 22, 12–14.

Baquero, G., Horst, J., and M. Verbeek, 2005, "Survival, Look-Ahead Bias and Persistence in Hedge Fund Performance," *Journal of Financial and Quantitative Analysis* 40, 493–517.

Barclay, M., and J. Warner, 1993, "Stealth Trading and Volatility: Which Trades Move Prices?" *Journal of Financial Economics* 34, 281–306.

Barclay, M., and R. Litzenberger, 1988, "Announcement Effects of New Equity Issues and the Use of Intraday Price Data," *Journal of Financial Economics* 21, 71–100.

Bares, P., Gibson, R., and S. Gyger, 2001, "Style Consistency and Survival Probability in the Hedge Funds' Industry," unpublished working paper.

Bares, P., Gibson, R., and S. Gyger, 2003, "Style Consistency and Survival Probability in the Hedge Funds Industry," University of Zurich Working Paper.

Beneish, M., 2001, "Earnings Management: A Perspective," *Managerial Finance* 27, 3–17.

Berk, J., and R. Green, 2002, "Mutual Fund Flows and Performance in Rational Markets," unpublished working paper.

Bernstein, P., 1998, "Why The Efficient Market Offers Hope To Active Management," in *Economics and Portfolio Strategy*, October 1. New York: Peter Bernstein.

Bertsimas, D., Hummel, P., and A. Lo, 2000, "Optimal Control of Execution Costs for Portfolios," *Computing in Science & Engineering* 1, 40–53.

Bertsimas, D., and A. Lo, 1998, "Optimal Control of Execution Costs," *Journal of Financial Markets* 1, 1–50.

Bhargava, R., Bose, A., and D. Dubofsky, 1998, "Exploiting International Stock Market Correlations with Open-End International Mutual Funds," *Journal of Business, Finance, and Accounting* 25, 765–773.

Bhattacharya, S., and P. Pfleiderer, 1985, "Delegated Portfolio Management," *Journal of Economic Theory* 36, 1–25.

Bickel, P., and K. Doksum, 1977, *Mathematical Statistics: Basic Ideas and Selected Topics*. San Francisco: Holden-Day.

Billingsley, P., 1968, *Convergence of Probability Measures*. New York: John Wiley & Sons.

Black, F., 1986, "Noise," *Journal of Finance* 41, 529–544.

Bodurtha, S., and T. Quinn, 1990, "Does Patient Program Trading Really Pay?" *Financial Analysts Journal* 46, 35–42.

Bookstaber, R., 1999, "A Framework for Understanding Market Crisis," in *Risk Management: Principles and Practices*. Charlottesville, VA: Association for Investment Management and Research.

Bookstaber, R., 2000, "Understanding and Monitoring the Liquidity Crisis Cycle," *Financial Analysts Journal*, 17–22.

Bookstaber, R., 2007, *A Demon of Our Own Design: Markets, Hedge Funds, and the Perils of Financial Innovation*. Hoboken, NJ: John Wiley & Sons.

Boss, M., Elsinger, H., Summer, M., and S. Thurner, 2004, "Network Topology of the Interbank Market," *Quantitative Finance* 4, 677–684.

Boudoukh, J., Richardson, M., Subrahmanyam, M., and R. Whitelaw, 2002, "Stale Prices and Strategies for Trading Mutual Funds," *Financial Analysts Journal* 58, 53–71.

Boyson, N., 2002, "How Are Hedge Fund Manager Characteristics Related to Performance, Volatility and Survival?" Ohio State University Working Paper.

Breeden, D., 1979, "An Intertemporal Asset Pricing Model with Stochastic Consumption and Investment Opportunities," *Journal of Financial Economics* 7, 265–296.

Brinson, G., Hood, R., and G. Beebower, 1986, "Determinants of Portfolio Performance," *Financial Analysts Journal* 42, 39–44.

Brinson, G., Singer, B., and G. Beebower, 1991, "Determinants of Portfolio Performance II: An Update," *Financial Analysts Journal* 47, 40–48.

Brockwell, P., and R. Davis, 1991, *Time Series: Theory and Methods*, Second Edition. New York: Springer-Verlag.

Brooks, C., and H. Kat, 2002, "The Statistical Properties of Hedge Fund Index Returns and Their Implications for Investors," *Journal of Alternative Investments* 5(2), 25–44.

Brown, S., and W. Goetzmann, 2003, "Hedge Funds With Style," *Journal of Portfolio Management* 29, 101–112.

Brown, S., Goetzmann, W., and R. Ibbotson, 1999, "Offshore Hedge Funds: Survival and Performance 1989–1995," *Journal of Business* 72, 91–118.

Brown, S., Goetzmann, W., Ibbotson, R., and S. Ross, 1992, "Survivorship Bias in Performance Studies," *Review of Financial Studies* 5, 553–580.

Brown, S., Goetzmann, W., and B. Liang, 2002, "Fees on Fees in Funds of Funds," Yale ICF Working Paper No. 02–33.

Brown, S., Goetzmann, W., and J. Park, 2000, "Hedge Funds and the Asian Currency Crisis," *Journal of Portfolio Management* 26, 95–101.

Brown, S., Goetzmann, W., and J. Park, 2001a, "Conditions for Survival: Changing Risk and the Performance of Hedge Fund Managers and CTAs," Yale School of Management Working Paper No. F–59.

Brown, S., Goetzmann, W., and J. Park, 2001b, "Careers and Survival: Competition and Risks in the Hedge Fund and CTA Industry," *Journal of Finance* 56, 1869–1886.

Brunnermeier, M., and L. Pedersen, 2005, "Predatory Trading," *Journal of Finance* 60, 1825–1863.

Campbell, J., Lo, A., and C. MacKinlay, 1997, *The Econometrics of Financial Markets*. Princeton, NJ: Princeton University Press.

Carey, M., and R. Stulz, eds., 2007, *The Risks of Financial Institutions*. Chicago, IL: University of Chicago Press.

Carpenter, J., 2000, "Does Option Compensation Increase Managerial Risk Appetite?" *Journal of Finance* 55, 2311–2331.

Carpenter, J., Dybvig, P., and H. Farnsworth, 2001, "Portfolio Performance and Agency," unpublished working paper, Stern School of Business, New York University.

Carpenter, J., and A. Lynch, 1999, "Survivorship Bias and Attrition Effects in Measures of Performance Persistence," *Journal of Financial Economics* 54, 337–374.

Cecchetti, S., and N. Mark, 1990, "Evaluating Empirical Tests of Asset Pricing Models," *American Economic Review* 80, 48–51.

Chafkin, J., and A. Lo, 2008, "The Promise of Hedge Fund Beta Replication," *Global Investor* June, 56–57.

Chalmers, J., Edelen, R., and G. Kadlec, 2001, "On the Perils of Security Pricing by Financial Intermediaries: The Wildcard Option in Transacting Mutual-Fund Shares," *Journal of Finance* 56, 2209–2236.

Chan, L., and J. Lakonishok, 1993, "Institutional Trades and Intra-Day Stock Price Behavior," *Journal of Financial Economics* 33, 173–199.

Chan, L., and J. Lakonishok, 1995, "The Behavior of Stock Prices Around Institutional Trades," *Journal of Finance* 50, 1147–1174.

Chan, N., Getmansky, M., Haas, S., and A. Lo, 2006, "Do Hedge Funds Increase Systemic Risk?" *Federal Reserve Bank of Atlanta Economic Review* Q4, 49–80.

Chan, N., Getmansky, M., Haas, S., and A. Lo, 2007, "Systemic Risk and Hedge Funds," in M. Carey and R. Stulz, eds., *The Risks of Financial Institutions and the Financial Sector*. Chicago: University of Chicago Press.

Chandar, N., and R. Bricker, 2002, "Incentives, Discretion, and Asset Valuation in Closed-End Mutual Funds," *Journal of Accounting Research* 40, 1037–1070.

Chevalier, J., and G. Ellison, 1997, "Risk Taking by Mutual Funds as a Response to Incentives," *Journal of Political Economy* 105, 1167–1200.

Chordia, T., Roll, R., and A. Subrahmanyam, 2000, "Commonality in Liquidity," *Journal of Financial Economics* 56, 3–28.

Chordia, T., Roll, R., and A. Subrahmanyam, 2001, "Market Liquidity and Trading Activity Source," *Journal of Finance* 56, 501–530.

Chordia, T., Roll, R., and A. Subrahmanyam, 2002, "Order Imbalance, Liquidity, and Market Returns," *Journal of Financial Economics* 65, 111–130.

Chordia, T., Subrahmanyam, A., and V. Anshuman, 2001, "Trading Activity and Expected Stock Returns," *Journal of Financial Economics* 59, 3–32.

Cohen, K., Hawawini, G., Maier, S., Schwartz, R., and D. Whitcomb, 1983a, "Estimating and Adjusting for the Intervalling-Effect Bias in Beta," *Management Science* 29, 135–148.

Cohen, K., Hawawini, G., Maier, S., Schwartz, R., and D. Whitcomb, 1983b, "Friction in the Trading Process and the Estimation of Systematic Risk," *Journal of Financial Economics* 12, 263–278.

Cohen, K., Maier, S., Schwartz, R., and D. Whitcomb, 1979, "On the Existence of Serial Correlation in an Efficient Securities Market," *TIMS Studies in the Management Sciences* 11, 151–168.

Cohen, K., Maier, S., Schwartz, R., and D. Whitcomb, 1981, "Transaction Costs, Order Placement Strategy and Existence of the Bid-Ask Spread," *Journal of Political Economy* 89, 287–305.

Cohen, K., Maier, S., Schwartz, R., and D. Whitcomb, 1978, "The Returns Generation Process, Returns Variance, and the Effect of Thinness in Securities Markets," *Journal of Finance* 33, 149–167.

Cohen, K., Maier, S., Schwartz, R., and D. Whitcomb, 1986, *The Microstructure of Securities Markets*. Englewood Cliffs, NJ: Prentice Hall.

Collins, B., and F. Fabozzi, 1991, "A Methodology for Measuring Transaction Costs," *Financial Analysts Journal* 47, 27–36.

Constantinides, G., 1986, "Capital Market Equilibrium with Transaction Costs," *Journal of Political Economy* 94(4), 842–862.

Copeland, T., and D. Mayers, 1982, "The Value Line Enigma (1965–1978): A Case Study of Performance Evaluation Issues," *Journal of Financial Economics* 10, 289–321.

Cornell, B., 1979, "Asymmetric Information and Portfolio Performance Measurement," *Journal of Financial Economics* 7, 381–390.

Cox, D., and E. Snell, 1989, *The Analysis of Binary Data*, Second Edition. London: Chapman and Hall.

Cremers, J., Kritzman, M., and S. Page, 2004, "Optimal Hedge Fund Allocations: Do Higher Moments Matter?" Revere Street Working Paper Series, Financial Economics 272–13.

Cuneo, L., and W. Wagner, 1975, "Reducing the Cost of Stock Trading," *Financial Analysts Journal* 26, 35–44.

Davis, M., and A. Norman, 1990, "Portfolio Selection with Transactions Costs," *Mathematics of Operations Research* 15, 676–713.

Degryse, H., and G. Nguyen, 2004, "Interbank Exposures: An Empirical Examination of Systemic Risk in the Belgian Banking System," Working Paper, Belgian National Bank No. 2004–04.

Demsetz, H., 1968, "The Cost of Transacting," *Quarterly Journal of Economics* 82, 35–53.

Dimson, E., 1979, "Risk Measurement When Shares Are Subject to Infrequent Trading," *Journal of Financial Economics* 7, 197–226.

Dumas, B., and E. Luciano, 1991, "An Exact Solution to a Dynamic Portfolio Choice Problem under Transactions Costs," *Journal of Finance* 46(2), 577–595.

Easley, D., and M. O'Hara, 1987, "Price, Trade Size, and Information in Securities Markets," *Journal of Financial Economics* 19, 69–90.

Edwards, F., and M. Caglayan, 2001, "Hedge Fund and Commodity Fund Investments in Bull and Bear Markets," *The Journal of Portfolio Management* 27, 97–108.

Elton et al. 2003, "Incentive Fees and Mutual Funds," *Journal of Finance* 58, 779–804.

Engle, R., 2002, "Dynamic Conditional Correlation—A Simple Class of Multivariate GARCH Models," *Journal of Business and Economic Statistics* 20, 339–350.

Epps, T., 1976, "The Demand for Brokers' Services: The Relation Between Security Trading Volume and Transaction Cost," *Bell Journal of Economics* 7, 163–196.

Fama, E., 1970, "Efficient Capital Markets: A Review of Theory and Empirical Work," *Journal of Finance* 25, 383–417.

Farmer, D., and A. Lo, 1999, "Frontiers of Finance: Evolution and Efficient Markets," *Proceedings of the National Academy of Sciences* 96, 9991–9992.

Farmer, D., 2002, "Market Force, Ecology and Evolution," *Industrial and Corporate Change* 11, 895–953.

Feffer, S., and C. Kundro, 2003, "Understanding and Mitigating Operational Risk in Hedge Fund Investments," Working Paper, The Capital Markets Company Ltd.

Fisher, J., Gatzlaff, D., Geltner, D., and D. Haurin, 2003, "Controlling for the Impact of Variable Liquidity in Commercial Real Estate Price Indices," *Real Estate Economics* 31, 269–303.

Fisher, J., Geltner, D., and R. Webb, 1994, "Value Indices of Commercial Real Estate: A Comparison of Index Construction Methods," *Journal of Real Estate Finance and Economics* 9, 137–164.

Fisher, L., 1966, "Some New Stock Market Indexes," *Journal of Business* 39, 191–225.

Freixas, X., Parigi, B., and J. Rochet, 2000, "Systemic Risk, Interbank Relations and Liquidity Provision by the Central Bank," *Journal of Money, Credit and Banking* 32, 611–638.

Fung, W., and D. Hsieh, 1997a, "Empirical Characteristics of Dynamic Trading Strategies: The Case of Hedge Funds," *Review of Financial Studies* 10, 275–302.

Fung, W., and D. Hsieh, 1997b, "Investment Style and Survivorship Bias in the Returns of CTAs: The Information Content of Track Records," *Journal of Portfolio Management* 24, 30–41.

Fung, W., and D. Hsieh, 1999, "A Primer on Hedge Funds," *Journal of Empirical Finance* 6, 309–31.

Fung, W., and D. Hsieh, 2000, "Performance Characteristics of Hedge Funds and Commodity Funds: Natural Versus Spurious Biases," *Journal of Financial and Quantitative Analysis* 35, 291–307.

Fung, W., and D. Hsieh, 2001, "The Risk in Hedge Fund Strategies: Theory and Evidence from Trend Followers," *Review of Financial Studies* 14, 313–341.

Fung, W., and D. Hsieh, 2002a, "Asset-Based Style Factors for Hedge Funds," *Financial Analysts Journal* 58, 16–27.

Fung, W., and D. Hsieh, 2002b, "Benchmarks of Hedge Fund Performance: Information Content and Measurement Biases," *Journal of Alternative Investments* 58, 22–34.

Fung, W., and D. Hsieh, 2006, "Hedge Funds: An Industry in Its Adolescence," *Federal Reserve Bank of Atlanta Economic Review* Q4, 1–34.

Furfine, C., 2003, "Interbank Exposures: Quantifying the Risk of Contagion," *Journal of Money, Credit and Banking* 35, 111–128.

Gammill, J., and A. Pérold, 1989, "The Changing Character of Stock Market Liquidity," *Journal of Portfolio Management* 15, 13–18.

Garman, M., and J. Ohlson, 1981, "Valuation of Risky Assets in Arbitrage-Free Economies with Transactions Costs," *Journal of Financial Economics* 9, 271–280.

Gennotte, G., and H. Leland, 1990, "Market Liquidity, Hedging, and Crashes," *American Economic Review* 80, 999–1021.

Getmansky, M., 2004, "The Life Cycle of Hedge Funds: Fund Flows, Size and Performance," unpublished working paper, MIT Laboratory for Financial Engineering.

Getmansky, M., and A. Lo, 2003, "A System Dynamics Model of the Hedge Fund Industry," unpublished working paper, MIT Laboratory for Financial Engineering.

Getmansky, M., Lo, A., and I. Makarov, 2004, "An Econometric Analysis of Serial Correlation and Illiquidity in Hedge-Fund Returns," *Journal of Financial Economics* 74, 529–609.

Getmansky, M., Lo, A., and S. Mei, 2004, "Sifting Through the Wreckage: Lessons from Recent Hedge-Fund Liquidations," *Journal of Investment Management* 2, 6–38.

Glosten, L., and L. Harris, 1988, "Estimating the Components of the Bid/Ask Spread," *Journal of Financial Economics* 21, 123–142.

Glosten, L., and P. Milgrom, 1985, "Bid, Ask, and Transaction Prices in a Specialist Market with Heterogeneously Informed Traders," *Journal of Financial Economics* 13, 71–100.

Goetzmann, W., Ingersoll, J., and S. Ross, 2003, "High-Water Marks and Hedge Fund Management Contracts," *Journal of Finance* 58, 1685–1718.

Goetzmann, W., Ingersoll, J., Spiegel, M., and I. Welch, 2002, "Sharpening Sharpe Ratios," National Bureau of Economic Research Working Paper No. W9116.

Goetzmann, W., Ivkovic, Z., and G. Rouwenhorst, 1999, "Day Trading International Mutual Funds: Evidence and Policy Solutions," *Journal of Financial and Quantitative Analysis* 36, 287–309.

Goetzmann, W., and N. Peles, 1997, "Cognitive Dissonance and Mutual Fund Investors," *Journal of Financial Research* 20, 145–158.

Goodwin, T., 1993, "Business-Cycle Analysis with a Markov-Switching Model," *Journal of Business and Economic Statistics* 11, 331–339.

Graham, J., and C. Harvey, 1997, "Grading the Performance of Market Timing Newsletters," *Financial Analysts Journal* 53, 54–66.

Granger, C., 1980, "Long Memory Relations and the Aggregation of Dynamic Models," *Journal of Econometrics* 14, 227–238.

Granger, C., 1988, "Aggregation of Time Series Variables—A Survey," Federal Reserve Bank of Minneapolis Institute for Empirical Macroeconomics, Discussion Paper 1.

Greene, J., and C. Hodges, 2002, "The Dilution Impact of Daily Fund Flows on Open-End Mutual Funds," *Journal of Financial Economics* 65, 131–158.

Greenspan, A., 1998. "Statement Before the Committee on Banking and Financial Services, U.S. House of Representatives," *Federal Reserve Bulletin* 84, 1046–1050.

Gregoriou, G., 2002, "Hedge Fund Survival Lifetimes," *Journal of Asset Management* 3, 237–252.

Grinblatt, M., and S. Titman, 1989, "Portfolio Performance Evaluation: Old Issues and New Insights," *Review of Financial Studies* 2, 393–421.

Grinblatt, M., and S. Titman, 1993, "Performance Measurement without Benchmarks: An Examination of Mutual Fund Returns," *Journal of Business* 66, 47–68.

Grinold, R., and R. Kahn, 2000, *Active Portfolio Management: A Quantitative Approach for Producing Superior Returns and Controlling Risk.* New York: McGraw-Hill.

Gromb, D., and D. Vayanos, 2002, "Equilibrium and Welfare in Markets with Financially Constrained Arbitrageurs," *Journal of Financial Economics* 66, 361–407.

Grossman, S., 1976, "On the Efficiency of Competitive Stock Markets Where Trades Have Diverse Information," *Journal of Finance* 31, 573–585.

Grossman, S.J., and G. Laroque, 1990, "Asset Pricing and Optimal Portfolio Choice in the Presence of Illiquid Durable Consumption Goods," *Econometrica* 58, 25–52.

Grossman, S., and J. Stiglitz, 1980, "On the Impossibility of Informationally Efficient Markets," *American Economic Review* 70, 393–408.

Gruber M., 1996, "Another Puzzle: The Growth in Actively Managed Mutual Funds," *The Journal of Finance* 51, 783–810.

Gyourko, J., and D. Keim, 1992, "What Does the Stock Market Tell Us About Real Estate Returns?" *AREUEA Journal* 20, 457–486.

Hamilton, J., 1989, "A New Approach to the Economic Analysis of Nonstationary Time Series and the Business Cycle," *Econometrica* 57, 357–384.

Hamilton, J., 1990, "Analysis of Time Series Subject to Changes in Regime," *Journal of Econometrics* 45, 39–70.

Hamilton, J., 1996, "Specification Testing in Markov-Switching Time Series Models," *Journal of Econometrics* 70, 127–157.

Hansen, L., 1982, "Large Sample Properties of Generalized Method of Moments Estimators," *Econometrica* 50, 1029–1054.

Harvey, A., 1981, *Time Series Models*. New York: John Wiley & Sons.

Hasanhodzic, J., and A. Lo, 2006, "Attack of the Clones," *Alpha* June, 54–63.

Hasanhodzic, J., and A. Lo, 2007, "Can Hedge-Fund Returns Be Replicated?: The Linear Case," *Journal of Investment Management* 5, 5–45.

Hasbrouck, J., and R. Schwartz, 1988, "Liquidity and Execution Costs in Equity Markets," *Journal of Portfolio Management* 14, 10–16.

Haugh, M., and A. Lo, 2001, "Asset Allocation and Derivatives," *Quantitative Finance* 1, 45–72.

Hausman, J., Lo, A., and C. MacKinlay, 1992, "An Ordered Probit Analysis of Transaction Stock Prices," *Journal of Financial Economics* 31, 319–379.

Healy, A., and A. Lo, 2009, "Jumping the Gates: Using Beta-Overlay Strategies to Hedge Liquidity Constraints," *Journal of Investment Management* 7, 1–20.

Healy, P., and J. Wahlen, 1999, "A Review of the Earnings Management Literature and Its Implications for Standard Setting," *Accounting Horizons* 14, 365–383.

Heaton, J., and D. Lucas, 1996, "Evaluating the Effects of Incomplete Markets on Risk Sharing and Asset Pricing," *Journal of Political Economy* 104, 443–487.

Hendricks, D., Patel, J., and R. Zeckhauser, 1997, "The J-Shape of Performance Persistence Given Survivorship Bias," *Review of Economics and Statistics* 79, 161–170.

Henriksson, R., 1984, "Market Timing and Mutual Fund Performance: An Empirical Investigation," *Journal of Business* 57, 73–96.

Henriksson, R., and R. Merton, 1981, "On Market Timing and Investment Performance II: Statistical Procedures for Evaluating Forecast Skills," *Journal of Business* 54, 513–533.

Herrndorf, N., 1984, "A Functional Central Limit Theorem for Weakly Dependent Sequences of Random Variables," *Annals of Probability* 12, 141–153.

Holmstrom, B., and J. Tirole, 2001, "LAPM: A Liquidity-Based Asset Pricing Model," *Journal of Finance* 57, 1837–1867.

Holthausen, R., Leftwich, R., and D. Mayers, 1987, "The Effect of Large Block Transactions on Security Prices: A Cross-Sectional Analysis," *Journal of Financial Economics* 19, 237–267.

Holthausen, R., Leftwich, R., and D. Mayers, 1990, "Large Block Transactions, the Speed of Response, and Temporary and Permanent Stock-Price Effects," *Journal of Financial Economics* 26, 71–95.

Horst, J., Nijman, T., and M. Verbeek, 2001, "Eliminating Look-Ahead Bias in Evaluating Persistence in Mutual Fund Performance," *Journal of Empirical Finance* 8, 345–373.

Howell, M.J., 2001, "Fund Age and Performance," *Journal of Alternative Investments*, 4(2), 57–60.

Huang, M., 2003, "Liquidity Shocks and Equilibrium Liquidity Premia," *Journal of Economic Theory* 109, 104–129.

Ibbotson Associates, 2004, *Stocks, Bonds, Bills, and Inflation 2004 Yearbook*. Chicago: Ibbotson Associates.

Ineichen, A., 2001, "The Myth of Hedge Funds: Are Hedge Funds the Fireflies Ahead of the Storm?" *Journal of Global Financial Markets*, 2(4), 34–46.

Ingersoll, J., 1987, *Theory of Financial Decision Making*. Totowa, NJ: Rowman & Littlefield.

Ippolito R., 1992, "Consumer Reaction to Measures of Poor Quality: Evidence from the Mutual Fund Industry," *Journal of Law and Economics* 35, 45–70.

Jen, P., Heasman, C., and K. Boyatt, 2001, "Alternative Asset Strategies: Early Performance in Hedge Fund Managers," Internal Document, Lazard Asset Management, London (http://www.aima.org).

Jensen, M., 1968, "The Performance of Mutual Funds in the Period 1945–1964," *Journal of Finance* 23, 389–416.

Jensen, M., 1969, "Risk, the Pricing of Capital Assets, and the Evaluation of Investment Performance," *Journal of Business* 42, 167–247.

Jobson, J., and R. Korkie, 1980, "Estimation for Markowitz Efficient Portfolios," *Journal of the American Statistical Association* 75, 544–554.

Jobson, J., and R. Korkie, 1981, "Performance Hypothesis Testing with the Sharpe and Treynor Measures," *Journal of Finance* 36, 889–908.

Kadlec, G., and D. Patterson, 1999, "A Transactions Data Analysis of Nonsynchronous Trading," *Review of Financial Studies* 12, 609–630.

Kaminski, K., and A. Lo, 2007, "When Do Stop-Loss Rules Stop Losses?" unpublished working paper, MIT Laboratory for Financial Engineering.

Kandel, S., and R. Stambaugh, 1991, "Asset Returns and Intertemporal Preferences," *Journal of Monetary Economics* 27, 39–71.

Kao, D., 2000, "Estimating and Pricing Credit Risk: An Overview," *Financial Analysts Journal* 56, 50–66.

Kao, D., 2002, "Battle for Alphas: Hedge Funds Versus Long-Only Portfolios," *Financial Analysts Journal* 58, 16–36.

Kaplan, S., and A. Schoar, 2003, "Private Equity Performance: Returns, Persistence and Capital Flows," MIT Sloan School of Management Working Paper.

Keim, D., and A. Madhavan, 1997, "Transactions Costs and Investment Style: An Inter-Exchange Analysis of Institutional Equity Trades," *Journal of Financial Economics* 46, 265–292.

Klein, R., and V. Bawa, 1976, "The Effect of Estimation Risk on Optimal Portfolio Choice," *Journal of Financial Economics* 3, 215–231.

Klein, R., and V. Bawa, 1977, "The Effect of Limited Information and Estimation Risk on Optimal Portfolio Diversification," *Journal of Financial Economics* 5, 89–111.

Kramer, D., 2001, "Hedge Fund Disasters: Avoiding the Next Catastrophe," *Alternative Investment Quarterly* 1, 5.

Kraus, A., and H. Stoll, 1972, "Price Impacts of Block Trading on the New York Stock Exchange," *Journal of Finance* 27, 569–588.

Kyle, A., 1985, "Continuous Auctions and Insider Trading," *Econometrica* 53, 1315–1336.

Leamer, E., 1978, *Specification Searches*. New York: John Wiley & Sons.

Leibowitz, M., 2005a, "Allocation Betas," *Financial Analysts Journal* 61, 70–82.

Leibowitz, M., 2005b, "Alpha Hunters and Beta Grazers," *Financial Analysts Journal* 61, 32–39.

Leibowitz, M., and A. Bova, 2007, "Gathering Implicit Alphas in a Beta World," *Journal of Portfolio Management* 33, 10–21.

Leibowitz, M., and B. Hammond, 2004, "The β-Plus Measure in Asset Allocation," *Journal of Portfolio Management* 30, 26–36.

Leinweber, D., 1993, "Using Information from Trading in Trading and Portfolio Management," in K. Sherrerd, ed., *Execution Techniques, True Trading Costs, and the Microstructure of Markets*. Charlottesville, VA: Association for Investment Management and Research.

Leinweber, D., 1994, "Careful Structuring Reins in Transaction Costs," *Pensions and Investments* July 25, 19.

Leitner, Y., 2005, "Financial Networks: Contagion, Commitment, and Private Sector Bailouts," *Journal of Finance* 60, 2925–2953.

Leroy, S., 1973, "Risk Aversion and the Martingale Property of Stock Returns," *International Economic Review* 14, 436–446.

Liang, B., 1999, "On the Performance of Hedge Funds," *Financial Analysts Journal* 55, 72–85.

Liang, B., 2000, "Hedge Funds: The Living and the Dead," *Journal of Financial and Quantitative Analysis* 35, 309–326.

Liang, B., 2001, "Hedge Fund Performance: 1990–1999," *Financial Analysts Journal* 57, 11–18.

Liang, B., 2003, "The Accuracy of Hedge Fund Returns," *Journal of Portfolio Management* 29, 111–122.

Lillo, F., Farmer, D., and R. Mantegna, 2003, "Master Curve for Price-Impact Function," *Nature* 421, 129–130.

Lintner, J., 1965, "The Valuation of Risky Assets and the Selection of Risky Investments in Stock Portfolios and Capital Budgets," *Review of Economics and Statistics* 47, 13–37.

Litterman, R., 2005, "Beyond Active Alpha," Goldman Sachs Asset Management.

Liu, J., and F. Longstaff, 2000, "Losing Money on Arbitrages: Optimal Dynamic Portfolio Choice in Markets with Arbitrage Opportunities," unpublished working paper, Anderson Graduate School of Management, UCLA.

Lo, A., 1994, "Data-Snooping Biases in Financial Analysis," in H. Russell Fogler, ed., *Blending Quantitative and Traditional Equity Analysis*. Charlottesville, VA: Association for Investment Management and Research.

Lo, A., ed., 1997, *Market Efficiency: Stock Market Behavior in Theory and Practice*, Volumes I and II. Cheltenham, UK: Edward Elgar Publishing.

Lo, A., 1999, "The Three P's of Total Risk Management," *Financial Analysts Journal* 55, 87–129.

Lo, A., 2001, "Risk Management for Hedge Funds: Introduction and Overview," *Financial Analysts Journal* 57, 16–33.

Lo, A., 2002, "The Statistics of Sharpe Ratios," *Financial Analysts Journal* 58, 36–50.

Lo, A., 2004, "The Adaptive Markets Hypothesis: Market Efficiency from an Evolutionary Perspective," *Journal of Portfolio Management* 30, 15–29.

Lo, A., and C. MacKinlay, 1988, "Stock Market Prices Do Not Follow Random Walks: Evidence from a Simple Specification Test," *Review of Financial Studies* 1, 41–66.

Lo, A., 2005, "Reconciling Efficient Markets with Behavioral Finance: The Adaptive Markets Hypothesis," *Journal of Investment Consulting* 7, 21–44.

Lo, A., and C. MacKinlay, 1990a, "An Econometric Analysis of Nonsynchronous Trading," *Journal of Econometrics* 45, 181–212.

Lo, A., and C. MacKinlay, 1990b, "Data Snooping Biases in Tests of Financial Asset Pricing Models," *Review of Financial Studies* 3, 431–468.

Lo, A., and C. MacKinlay, 1990c, "When Are Contrarian Profits Due to Stock Market Overreaction?" *Review of Financial Studies* 3, 175–206.

Lo, A., and C. MacKinlay, 1999, *A Non-Random Walk Down Wall Street*. Princeton, NJ: Princeton University Press.

Lo, A., H. Mamaysky, and J. Wang, 2004, "Asset Prices and Trading Volume Under Fixed Transactions Costs," *Journal of Political Economy* 112, 1054–1090.

Lo, A., Petrov, C., and M. Wierzbicki, 2003, "It's 11 PM—Do You Know Where Your Liquidity Is? The Mean-Variance-Liquidity Frontier," *Journal of Investment Management* 1, 55–93.

Lo, A., Repin, D., and B. Steenbarger, 2005, "Fear and Greed in Financial Markets: An Online Study," *American Economic Review* 95, 352–359.

Lo, A., and J. Wang, 2000, "Trading Volume: Definitions, Data Analysis, and Implications of Portfolio Theory," *Review of Financial Studies* 13, 257–300.

Lo, A., and J. Wang, 2006, "Trading Volume: Implications of an Intertemporal Capital Asset Pricing Model," *Journal of Finance* 61, 2805–2840.

Lochoff, R., 2002, "Hedge Funds and Hope," *The Journal of Portfolio Management* 28, 92–99.

Loeb, T., 1983, "Trading Cost: The Critical Link Between Investment Information and Results," *Financial Analysts Journal* 39, 39–44.

Lucas, R., 1978, "Asset Prices in an Exchange Economy," *Econometrica* 46, 1429–1446.

Luce, R., and H. Raiffa, 1957, *Games and Decisions: Introduction and Critical Survey*. New York: John Wiley & Sons.

MacCrimmon, K., and D. Wehrung, 1986, *Taking Risks*. New York: Free Press.

MacKenzie, D., 2003, "Long-Term Capital Management and the Sociology of Arbitrage," *Economy and Society* 32, 349–380.

Maddala, G., 1983, *Limited-Dependent and Qualitative Variables in Econometrics*. Cambridge, UK: Cambridge University Press.

Magnus, J., and H. Neudecker, 1988, *Matrix Differential Calculus: With Applications in Statistics and Economics*. New York: John Wiley & Sons.

Markowitz, H., 1952, "Portfolio Selection," *Journal of Finance* 7, 77–91.

McDonough, W., 1998, "Statement Before the Committe on Banking and Financial Services, U.S. House of Representatives," *Federal Reserve Bulletin* 84, 1050–1054.

Merrill Lynch, 2007, "Building the Organization to Support 130/30," Global Markets and Investment Banking, fourth quarter.

Merton, R., 1973, "An Intertemporal Capital Asset Pricing Model," *Econometrica* 41, 867–887.

Merton, R., 1981, "On Market Timing and Investment Performance I: An Equilibrium Theory of Value for Market Forecasts," *Journal of Business* 54, 363–406.

Metzger, L., and the IAFE Investor Risk Committee, 2004, "Valuation Concepts for Investment Companies and Financial Institutions and Their Stakeholders," Investor Risk Committee White Paper, International Association of Financial Engineers.

Michaud, R., 1989, "The Markowitz Optimization Enigma: Is 'Optimized' Optimal?" *Financial Analysts Journal* 45,31–42.

Michaud, R., 1998, *Efficient Asset Management: A Practical Guide to Stock Portfolio Optimization and Asset Allocation*. Boston: Harvard Business School Press.

Modigliani, F., and L. Modigliani, 1997, "Risk-Adjusted Performance," *Journal of Portfolio Management* Winter, 45–54.

Montier, J., 2007, "The Myth of Exogenous Risk and the Recent Quant Problems," `http://behaviouralinvesting.blogspot.com/2007/09/myth-of-exogenous-risk-and-recent-quant.html`.

Morton, A.J., and S.R. Pliska, 1995, "Optimal Portfolio Management with Fixed Transaction Costs," *Mathematical Finance* 5, 337–356.

Nagelkerke, N., 1991, "A Note on a General Definition of the Coefficient of Determination," *Biometrika* 78, 691–692.

Newey, W., and K. West, 1987, "A Simple Positive Definite Heteroskedasticity and Autocorrelation Consistent Covariance Matrix," *Econometrica* 55, 703–705.

Niederhoffer, V., 1998, *The Education of a Speculator*. New York: John Wiley & Sons.

O'Hara, M., 1995, *Market Microstructure Theory*. Cambridge, MA: Blackwell Publishers, Inc.

Pastor, L., and R. Stambaugh, 2003, "Liquidity Risk and Expected Stock Returns," *Journal of Political Economy* 111, 642–685.

Pérold, A., 1988, "The Implementation Shortfall: Paper Versus Reality," *Journal of Portfolio Management* 14, 4–9.

Pérold, A., 1999, "Long-Term Capital Management, L.P. (A-D)," Harvard Case Study. Boston: Harvard Business School Press.

Pérold, A., and R. Salomon, 1994, "The Right Amount of Assets Under Management," *Financial Analysts Journal* May–June, 31–39.

President's Working Group on Financial Markets, 1999, *Hedge Funds, Leverage, and the Lessons of Long-Term Capital Management*: Report of the President's Working Group on Financial Markets (April 28).

Richardson, M., and J. Stock, 1989, "Drawing Inferences from Statistics Based on Multiyear Asset Returns," *Journal of Financial Economics* 25, 323–348.

Roberts, H., 1967, "Statistical Versus Clinical Prediction of the Stock Market," unpublished manuscript, Center for Research in Security Prices, University of Chicago, May.

Ross, S., 1976, "The Arbitrage Theory of Capital Asset Pricing," *Journal of Economic Theory* 13, 341–360.

Ross, S., and R. Zisler, 1991, "Risk and Return in Real Estate," *Journal of Real Estate Finance and Economics* 4, 175–190.

Rubinstein, M., 1976, "The Valuation of Uncertain Income Streams and the Pricing of Options," *Bell Journal of Economics* 7, 407–425.

Sadka, R., 2003, "Momentum, Liquidity Risk, and Limits to Arbitrage," unpublished working paper, Kellogg Graduate School of Management, Northwestern University.

Samuelson, P., 1938, "A Note on the Pure Theory of Consumers Behavior," *Economica* 5, 61–71.

Samuelson, P., 1941, "Conditions That the Roots of a Polynomial Be Less than Unity in Absolute Value," *Annals of Mathematical Statistics* 45, 689–693.

Samuelson, P., 1948, "Consumption Theory in Terms of Revealed Preference," *Economica* 15, 243–253.

Samuelson, P., 1965, "Proof That Properly Anticipated Prices Fluctuate Randomly," *Industrial Management Review* 6, 41–49.

Samuelson, P., 1969, "Lifetime Portfolio Selection by Dynamic Stochastic Programming," *Review of Economics and Statistics* 51, 239–246.

Schneeweis, T., and R. Spurgin, 1996, "Survivor Bias in Commodity Trading Advisor Performance," *Journal of Futures Markets* 16, 757–772.

Scholes, M., and J. Williams, 1977, "Estimating Betas from Nonsynchronous Data," *Journal of Financial Economics* 5, 309–328.

Schwartz, R., and D. Whitcomb, 1988, *Transaction Costs and Institutional Investor Trading Strategies*. Monograph Series in Finance and Economics 1988–2/3, New York: Salomon Brothers Center for the Study of Financial Institutions, New York University.

Schwert, G., 1977, "Stock Exchange Seats as Capital Assets," *Journal of Financial Economics* 4, 51–78.

Sender, H., Kelly, K., and G. Zuckerman, 2007, "Goldman Wagers on Cash Infusion to Show Resolve," *Wall Street Journal* (Eastern edition), August 14, p. A.1.

Shanken, J., 1987, "Nonsynchronous Data and the Covariance-Factor Structure of Returns," *Journal of Finance* 42, 221–232.

Sharpe, W., 1964, "Capital Asset Prices: A Theory of Market Equilibrium under Conditions of Risk," *Journal of Finance* 19, 425–442.

Sharpe, W., 1966, "Mutual Fund Performance," *Journal of Business* 39, 119–138.

Sharpe, W., 1991, "The Arithmetic of Active Management," *Financial Analysts Journal* 47, 7–9.

Sharpe, W., 1992, "Asset Allocation: Management Style and Performance Measurement," *Journal of Portfolio Management* 18, 7–19.

Sharpe, W., 1994, "The Sharpe Ratio," *Journal of Portfolio Management* 21, 49–58.

Sherrerd, K., ed., 1993, *Execution Techniques, True Trading Costs, and the Microstructure of Markets*. Charlottesville, VA: Association for Investment Management and Research.

Shleifer, A., and R. Vishny, 1997, "The Limits of Arbitrage," *Journal of Finance* 52, 35–55.

Sirri, E., and P. Tufano, 1998, "Costly Search and Mutual Fund Flows," *The Journal of Finance* 53, 1589–1622.

Spurgin, R., 2001, "How to Game Your Sharpe Ratio," *The Journal of Alternative Investments* 4, 38–46.

Stoll, H., 1993, *Equity Trading Costs*. Charlottesville, VA: Association for Investment Management and Research.

Terhaar, K., Staub, R., and B. Singer, 2003, "Appropriate Policy Allocation for Alternative Investments," *Journal of Portfolio Management* 29, 101–110.

Thal Larsen, P., 2007, "Goldman Pays the Price of Being Big," *Financial Times*, August 13.

Tiniç, S., 1972, "The Economics of Liquidity Services," *Quarterly Journal of Economics* 86, 79–93.

Treynor, J., 1965, "How to Rate Management of Investment Funds," *Harvard Business Review* 43, 63–75.

Treynor, J., 2005, "Why Market-Valuation-Indifferent Indexing Works," *Financial Analysts Journal* 61, 65–69.

Treynor, J., and F. Black, 1973, "How to Use Security Analysis to Improve Portfolio Selection," *Journal of Business* 46, 66–86.

Treynor, J., and K. Mazuy, 1966, "Can Mutual Funds Outguess the Market?" *Harvard Business Review* 44, 131–163.

Tuckman, B., and J. Vila, 1992, "Arbitrage with Holding Costs: A Utility-Based Approach," *Journal of Finance* 47, 1283–1302.

Turner, C., Startz, R., and C. Nelson, 1989, "A Markov Model of Heteroskedasticity, Risk, and Learning in the Stock Market," *Journal of Financial Economics* 25, 3–22.

Upper, C., and A. Worms, 2004, "Estimating Bilateral Exposures in the German Interbank Market: Is There a Danger of Contagion?" *European Economic Review* 48, 827–849.

Varian, H., 2006, "Revealed Preference," in M. Szenberg, L. Ramrattan, and A. Gottesman, eds., *Samuelsonian Economics and the Twenty-First Century*. Oxford, UK: Oxford University Press.

Vayanos, D., 1998, "Transaction Costs and Asset Prices: A Dynamic Equilibrium Model," *Review of Financial Studies* 11, 1–58.

Vayanos, D., and J.L. Vila, 1999, "Equilibrium Interest Rate and Liquidity Premium with Transaction Costs," *Economic Theory* 13, 509–539.

Wagner, W., 1993, "Defining and Measuring Trading Costs," in K. Sherrerd, ed.: *Execution Techniques, True Trading Costs, and the Microstructure of Markets*. Charlottesville, VA: Association for Investment Management and Research.

Wagner, W., and M. Banks, 1992, "Increasing Portfolio Effectiveness via Transaction Cost Management," *Journal of Portfolio Management* 19, 6–11.

Wagner, W., and M. Edwards, 1993, "Best Execution," *Financial Analyst Journal* 49, 65–71.

Watts, D., 1999, *Small Worlds: The Dynamics of Networks Between Order and Randomness*. Princeton, NJ: Princeton University Press.

Watts, D., and S. Strogatz, 1998, "Collective Dynamics of 'Small-World' Networks," *Nature* 393, 440–442.

Weisman, A., 2002, "Informationless Investing and Hedge Fund Performance Measurement Bias," *The Journal of Portfolio Management* 28, 80–91.

White, H., 1984, *Asymptotic Theory for Econometricians*. New York: Academic Press.

Willard, G., and P. Dybvig, 1999, "Empty Promises and Arbitrage," *Review of Financial Studies* 12, 807–834.

Working, H., 1960, "Note on the Correlation of First Differences of Averages in a Random Chain," *Econometrica* 28, 916–918.

Zuckerman, G., Hagerty, J., and D. Gauthier-Villars, 2007, "Impact of Mortgage Crisis Spreads; Dow Tumbles 2.8% As Fallout Intensifies; Moves by Central Banks," *Wall Street Journal* (Eastern edition), August 10, p. A.1.

Index

The locators for figures and tables are in italic type; those for plates are in bold type. For key works discussed in the text, see under *publications cited*.

active-extension strategies, 257, 260, 300
active/passive (AP) decomposition, 168–69, 172–73
 alpha versus beta, 177–80
 components of expected returns and, 197
 general result of, 173–76
 GMM estimators and, 189, 330–32
 insights from, 169–70
 management activity and, 197
 management measurement issues and, 179–80
 market neutral strategies and, 193–96
 mean reversion and momentum strategies and, 181–85
 NASDAQ size deciles and, 193–95
 numerical example of, 181, *182–84*
 passive investing and, 176–77
 population versus sample moments and, 187–89
 sampling interval and, 189–93, *192*
 stop-loss policy and, 185–86
 transparency of, daily versus monthly, *196*, 195–96
active ratio, 176, 181, 187–89, 195, *196*
 sampling interval and, 195–96
Adaptive Markets Hypothesis (AMH), 244–49, 296–97
 arbitrage opportunities and, 247–49
 attrition rates and, 245–47
 behavioral biases and, 245
 innovation and, 249
 survival and, 249

alpha, hedge fund
 beta and, 173, 177–80, 197
 contrarian strategy and, 278
 manager-specific, 122–23, 137–38, 166, 226, 237
 risk management and, 237–38, *240–41*
 See also beta, hedge fund
Alternative Investment Management Association (AIMA), 218n5
alternative investments, 1
 data on, 34–63
 integrated investment process for, 217–36
 literature concerning, 30–33
 performance measures of, 168
 See also specific issues and concepts
American Express Extra Income Fund, 89
Arbitrage Pricing Theory, 222
asset classes, 1, 221, 323–27
 covariance matrices and, 223–24
 factor models and, 123
 See also under Credit Suisse/Tremont (CS/Tremont) database; Lipper TASS database
asymptotic distribution, 80–83
attrition of funds, 40, 43–63, *43–44*
August 2007, 299
 August 1998 and, 273, *274–75*, 300–1
 contrarian trading strategies and, **12**
 current outlook and, 300–2
 financial markets and, 255–56, 269–72
 hedge fund beta and, 301
 hypotheses concerning, 256–58
 investment horizons and, 294–95
 investor sophistication and, 297
 leverage and, 257, 259, 278–79, *280*, 298